Word Frequencies in Written and Spoken

Word Frequencies in Written and Spoken English

based on the British National Corpus

GEOFFREY LEECH
PAUL RAYSON
ANDREW WILSON

Longman

An imprint of **Pearson Education**

Harlow, England · London · New York · Reading, Massachusetts · San Francisco
Toronto · Don Mills, Ontario · Sydney · Tokyo · Singapore · Hong Kong · Seoul
Taipei · Cape Town · Madrid · Mexico City · Amsterdam · Munich · Paris · Milan

PEARSON EDUCATION LIMITED

Edinburgh Gate
Harlow CM20 2JE
Tel: +44 (0)1279 623623
Fax: +44 (0)1279 431059
www.pearsoned.co.uk

First published in Great Britain in 2001

© Pearson Education Limited 2001

The right of Geoffrey Leech, Paul Rayson and Andrew Wilson to be identified
as Authors of this Work has been asserted by them in accordance
with the Copyright, Designs and Patents Act 1988.

ISBN-10: 0-582-32007-0
ISBN-13: 978-0-582-32007-9

British Library Cataloguing in Publication Data
A CIP catalogue record for this book can be obtained from the British Library

Library of Congress Catologing in Publication Data
Applied for

Transferred to digital print on demand, 2007
Printed and bound by CPI Antony Rowe, Eastbourne

The Publishers' policy is to use paper manufactured from sustainable forests.

Contents

Symbols and abbreviations

_   indicates that the underscored numerical value is an estimate

*   indicates that the preceding word requires some explanation, which is given in the list on pages xiv–xv

~   preceding or following a word indicates that the word is actually part of a larger 'orthographic word unit', and ~ marks where it is attached to the preceding or following word: e.g. *wo*~ is the first part, and ~*n't* the second part, of *won't*.

BNC   British National Corpus

Abbreviations for parts of speech

Adj	adjective
Adv	adverb
ClO	clause opener
Conj	conjunction
Det	determiner
DetP	determiner/pronoun
Ex	existential *there*
Fore	foreign word
Gen	genitive marker
Inf	infinitive marker
Int	interjection or discourse marker
Lett	letter of the alphabet
NoC	common noun
NoP	proper noun
NoP–	word which is normally part of a proper noun
Num	(cardinal) number
Ord	ordinal
Prep	preposition
Pron	pronoun
Uncl	unclassified word
Verb	verb (general)
VMod	modal auxiliary verb

Abbreviations in column headers

Disp	dispersion (Juilland's D)
DiCo	dispersion in conversation
DiIm	dispersion in imaginative writing
DiIn	dispersion in informative writing
DiSp	dispersion in speech
DiTO	dispersion in task-oriented speech
DiWr	dispersion in writing
Freq	frequency (per million words)
FrCo	frequency in conversation
FrIm	frequency in imaginative writing
FrIn	frequency in informative writing
FrSp	frequency in speech
FrTO	frequency in task-oriented speech
FrWr	frequency in writing
LL	log likelihood
PoS	part of speech (word class)
Ra	range

List of interest boxes

Foreword

A glance through the pages of this book will show that it is an unusual type of publication. It consists largely of lists of words and of numbers, and looks like a cross between a dictionary and a telephone directory. These two analogies are not too wide of the mark, since this is a reference book: a book to refer to and to browse through, not a book to read through.

To be more precise: this is a **word frequency book**, a book which lists words of the English language and gives information about their frequency in actual use. Although quite a number of word frequency books have been published before (see below), a likely reaction of the present-day reader will be to ask: Why do we need to know about word frequency? What is the point of such a book?

There are a number of purposes for which knowledge about word frequency is needed, and probably the most important of these are educational.

(a) Educational needs

For the teaching of languages, whether as a mother tongue or as a foreign or second language, information about the frequencies of words is important for vocabulary grading and selection. Here frequency has applications to language learning in such areas as: syllabus design, materials writing, grading and simplification of readers, language testing and perhaps even at the 'chalkface' of classroom teaching.

Historically, the pioneering impetus[1] for frequency listings (for example, E. L. Thorndike's *Teacher's Wordbook*) in the early decades of the twentieth century was decidedly educational—see Thorndike (1921), (1932), Thorndike and Lorge (1944), Lorge (1949). It focused on the counting of word occurrences in texts used in the education of American children. Later counts were based also on magazines and general reading matter. A more modern and systematic project to obtain frequency counts from children's reading materials resulted in the *American Heritage Word Frequency Book* (Carroll *et al.* 1971). An improved kind of count (taking account of meaning but with a smaller wordlist), primarily for foreign learners of English, led to the publication of the *General Service List of English Words* by Michael West (1953—based on work begun in the 1930s).

Although these books, old as they are, have still not been entirely superseded, the lists of texts on which the frequency counts were founded strike the modern reader as decidedly dated. In fact, even when the first counts were made, they incorporated frequencies derived from books written many years before the twentieth century. These included such nineteenth century classics as Lamb's *Tales from Shakespeare*, Austen's *Pride and*

---

[1] Our concern here is with the English language. Word frequency lists have also been produced for other languages, such as Dutch, Italian, Japanese, Latin, Russian and Spanish (see Kennedy 1998: 16). For German, Kaeding's monumental work, which is claimed to have employed over 5,000 assistants, dates from the 1890s (*ibid*). For Spanish and French, the work of Juilland is particularly significant (see Juilland and Chang-Rodriguez 1964, Juilland et al 1970).

Prejudice, Hawthorne's *Tanglewood Tales,* and even older texts such as the United States *Declaration of Independence,* Gibbon's *Decline and Fall of the Roman Empire* and Defoe's *Robinson Crusoe* (see Thorndike and Lorge 1944: 249–55). Such works, however excellent for an education in English literature, cannot be said to represent the frequency of vocabulary in the present-day English language in any sense. Consequently, there has been a growing need for adequate frequency lists derived from more up-to-date sources.

(b) Other needs

Apart from educational applications, word frequency information can be used for **natural language processing by computer** (also known as **language technology**). In building modern language-processing software, from speech recognizers to machine-aided translation packages, it can be important to be able to determine which word, from a range of competing items, is more *likely* to occur. Yet other applications are to linguistic research—for example, in the study of style and register—and to psychological research, where frequency of vocabulary use is valuable evidence for understanding the human processing of language, whether in speaking, listening, writing or reading.

Finally, word frequency information can appeal to the curiosity of the general reader. Why, for example, in the British National Corpus on which this book is based, is *man* more than twice as common as *woman,* while the plural *women* is more common than *men*? Such observed facts of usage are worth pondering over, and may even spark off a small research project. In this book, we break up the monotony of wordlists by inserting 'interest boxes' focusing on the relative frequencies of a group of related words, such as colour words or words dealing with human kinship.

The advantages of a computer corpus

Since the early days of Thorndike and Lorge, a big transformation has taken place through the development of computers and modern computer technology. Nowadays, a very large collection of texts (normally called a **corpus**) can be stored and searched on a computer, and the frequencies of words in that corpus can be determined and listed by a fairly trivial computer program. The first to take advantage of this change were Francis and Kučera (1967), the compilers of the so-called Brown Corpus, consisting of 500 texts of varied kinds of written American English, and amounting in all to about a million words. A matching corpus of British English (the Lancaster-Oslo/Bergen Corpus) was compiled a few years later, and an equivalent frequency list for that corpus was produced by Hofland and Johansson (1982). This book also contained a comparison of the differences in frequency between the corresponding American and British corpora, thus introducing the idea that frequency lists could be **comparative**. Although these corpora were restricted to written English and were (by present standards) relatively small, they showed how a computer corpus could bring the advantages of accurate, automatic production of frequency lists, as well as providing additional statistical information on the dispersion of vocabulary through a corpus, and the distinctiveness of the vocabularies of two corpora or text collections.

A further important step forward was achieved when the Brown and Lancaster–Oslo/Bergen corpora were grammatically tagged: that is, each word in each text in each corpus was labelled with a grammatical tag (e.g. as a noun, an adverb or a preposition). After this had been done, it became possible to produce word frequency lists recognizing the **grammatical** identity of words, not merely their **orthographic** status as written sequences of letters. For example, in the Hofland and Johansson book just mentioned, the string *bear* has just one entry in each frequency list—there is no means of distinguishing between the verb *bear* (= 'carry, endure') and the noun *bear* (= 'thick-furred plantigrade quadruped'). Similarly, there is just one indiscriminate entry for *like*, a word which may be a verb, a preposition, an adjective, a noun or a conjunction, with a range of different meanings. By using a tagged corpus and these part-of-speech distinctions, later word frequency books based on these two corpora (for example, Johansson and Hofland 1989) were able to use the grammatical notion of 'word' which is found in a dictionary, and which is the basis for describing meaning.

Other frequency lists have been compiled for particular varieties of English: for example, James *et al.* (1994) is a frequency book for the vocabulary of computer science; Dahl (1979) is a frequency book for the English of psychiatric interviews. The latter is one of two existing frequency lists for spoken English (the other being an early list based on a limited corpus of 135,000 words, and published by Jones and Sinclair 1974). Although useful and interesting in their different ways, these publications cannot be said to fulfil the need for adequate and up-to-date frequency listings for the present-day English language.

The advantages and disadvantages of this book

In this book, we have aimed to satisfy the above-mentioned need, by making use of a grammatically tagged corpus—the British National Corpus—which is both large (100 times larger than the Brown Corpus) and representative of many varieties of both written and spoken English. Our claim is that this word frequency book goes far beyond any previously published word frequency book in

(*a*) using a corpus which is large enough and varied enough (100 million words) to represent an adequate cross-section of written and spoken language
(*b*) using a corpus which is far more up-to-date (dating mainly from the period 1985–94) than that used in any other comparable project
(*c*) providing frequency lists for spoken as well as written English
(*d*) providing frequency comparisons between different varieties of both spoken and written English.

This last provision is particularly important: for the various uses of frequency information mentioned earlier, particularly in the educational arena, we need to reckon on different frequency profiles for different varieties of the language. The idea that one monolithic frequency list for the whole language can satisfy all needs is, of course, unrealistic. As one small illustration of this, it is worth noting that of the top 50 words of the written part of the British National Corpus, there is an overlapping subset of only 33 words shared with the top 50 words of the spoken part of the corpus.

Having mentioned the advantages of this book over previous ones, we should end by admitting two significant drawbacks. Firstly, for reasons explained in Section 4.2.3 of the Introduction (page 14), there is a built-in element of approximation in the frequency data. On average, the margin of error is estimated to be 1.21 per cent—an amount too small to affect the interpretation of the majority of frequency figures in this book, given that they are normed to frequency per million words, but capable of affecting the figures for the most frequent words. Second, the book is far from exhaustive. For each list, we have had to recognize a frequency threshold below which a word does not qualify for listing. In all lists, this is 10 occurrences per million words or higher. If the book had been expanded to make each list complete, the result would have been a book of many thousands of pages. However, it is possible for the reader to consult exhaustive versions of each list, by visiting the Pearson Educational website—see www.booksites.net/leech—or the Lancaster (UCREL) website—www.comp.lancs.ac.uk/ucrel/bncfreq/—where such complete lists can be consulted and searched on-line.

Acknowledgements

As authors of this book, we owe a debt of gratitude to research staff and students of UCREL, who helped to develop the software, 'textware' and documentation which made this a feasible project. Roger Garside's contribution, as director of UCREL, has been indispensable. We are especially grateful to Nick Smith for his help on the grammatical tagging of the British National Corpus (BNC) and on the use of the BNC Sampler Corpus. We are also very grateful to David Lee, for hunting down errors of text classification and compiling a text information database of the existing version of the BNC: this enabled our lists to be more accurate in their reflection of text varieties. Peter Kahrel deserves our heartfelt thanks, too, for his care and expertise in the design and preparation of the book.

The British National Corpus is a collaborative initiative carried out by Oxford University Press, Longman, Chambers Harrap, Oxford University Computing Services, Lancaster University's UCREL, and the British Library. The project received funding from the UK Department of Trade and Industry and the Science and Engineering Research Council (1991–94) and was supported by additional research grants from the British Academy and the British Library. Later, in 1995–96, an additional grant from the Engineering and Physical Sciences Research Council (Research Grant GR/F99847) enabled the BNC to be retagged to a greater degree of accuracy.

Geoffrey Leech
Paul Rayson
Andrew Wilson
UCREL, Lancaster University, November, 2000

References

Carroll J B, Davies P and Richman B 1971 *The American Heritage word frequency book*. Boston, Houghton Mifflin.

Kučera H and Francis W N 1967 *Computational analysis of present-day American English*. Providence, RI, Brown University Press.

Dahl H 1979 *Word frequencies of spoken American English*. Michigan, Verbatim.

Hofland K and Johansson S 1982 *Word frequencies in British and American English*. Bergen, The Norwegian Computing Centre for the Humanities.

James G, Davison R, Cheung A H Y and Deerwester S (eds) 1994 *English in computer science: A corpus-based lexical analysis*. Hong Kong, Longman, for the Language Centre, Hong Kong University of Science and Technology.

Johansson S and Hofland K 1989 *Frequency analysis of English vocabulary and grammar*. 2 vols. Oxford, Clarendon Press.

Jones S and Sinclair J McH 1974 English lexical collocations: A study in computational linguistics. *Cahiers de Lexicologie* 24: 15–61.

Juilland A and Chang-Rodriguez E 1964 *Frequency dictionary of Spanish words*. The Hague, Mouton.

Juilland A, Brodin D and Davidovitch C 1970 *Frequency dictionary of French words*. Paris, Mouton.

Kennedy, G 1998 *An introduction to corpus linguistics*. London, Longman.

Lorge I 1949 *Semantic count of the 570 commonest English words*. New York, Columbia University Press.

Thorndike E L 1921 *Teacher's word book*. New York, Columbia Teachers College.

Thorndike E L 1932 *A teacher's word book of 20,000 words*. New York, Columbia Teachers College.

Thorndike E L and Lorge I 1944 *The teacher's word book of 30,000 words*. New York, Columbia University Press.

West M 1953 *A general service list of English words*. London, Longman.

Explanatory notes on words
marked * in the frequency lists

ai~   This is the initial part of *ain't*. It has not been assigned to a lemma, because of its ambiguity: in different contexts, it can be regarded as a reduced form of *am, is, are, has, have*, etc.

all right, alright   These variant spellings have been listed and counted separately.

be   The count for the lemma *be* is slightly underrepresented, because of the omission of *ain't* and *in~* (see *ai~* above and *in~* below).

because   is listed separately from the shortened spoken forms *cos* and *'cos* (q.v.).

bit   Note that the count for *bit* as a noun excludes tokens of *a bit* as a multiword adverb.

conservative(s), labour, liberal(s)   Whether as adjectives or nouns, these counts include references to political parties (usually spelt with a capital), as well as more general senses. These words are not capitalized in the lists.

cos, 'cos   These shortened forms of *because* are given separate entries in the lists.

course   (Adv), as a shortened form of *of course*, is given a separate entry.

data/datum   It is no longer realistic to treat *data* as the plural of *datum*, because most people these days treat *data* as a singular (uncountable) noun. Hence, the lemma is given the combined label *data/datum*.

de   When *de* is part of a foreign name (e.g. *de Gaulle*), it is counted as a NoP-. Elsewhere, e.g. in French quotations, it is counted as a foreign word (Fore).

du~   This is the first part of *dunno* (= *do* + *not* + *know*), and is lemmatized with *do*.

elite   The counts of *elite* (NoC) do not include tokens with the acute accent (*élite* NoC), of which there are about 3 per million words in the whole corpus.

fig   This word is ambiguous between *fig* (a fruit) and *fig* (also spelt *fig.*) as the abbreviation for *figure*. The two usages are not distinguished here; *fig* ('fruit') is the rarer usage, but is more widely scattered through the whole corpus.

further   (Adj): As an adjective, *further* is lemmatized as a comparative form of *far*. However, in meaning and function, *further* is not always comparative: it often means 'additional' and 'extra'.

goin', going   as forms of the verb *go*, exclude the semi-auxiliary verb *be going to* (see below).

going (to)   This shows the frequency of the semi-auxiliary verb *be going to*, which is given a separate count, rather than being included as a form of *go*.

good   (NoC): This is here treated as the lemma to which the plural form *goods* belongs. Note, however, that *goods* (in the sense of 'freight') has no corresponding singular form.

have   The count for the lemma *have* is slightly underrepresented, because of the omission of the form *ain't* (see *ai~* above).

her   (Det): As a possessive determiner (as in *her friends*), *her* is treated as a separate lemma from *her* as a personal pronoun (in the objective case).

his   (Pron): As a possessive pronoun (as in *This is his*), *his* is treated as a separate lemma from *his* as a possessive determiner (as in *It was his fault*).

in~   (Verb): The first part of the vernacular British tag question *innit*. Like *ai~*, it is difficult to assign this verb to *be, have* or any other verb, because it is commonly used across a range of functions.

Jan   (NoP): This entry is ambiguous between an abbreviation for *January* (also written *Jan.*) and a person's given name.

labour   see *conservative(s)* above.

lead   (NoC): Notice that this headword is ambiguous, according to whether it is pronounced as /liːd/ or as /lɛd/. Both pronunciations are included in the count for *lead*.

Les   (NoP): Counted as a proper noun, *Les* can be either a given name (= *Leslie*) or a part of a French name, as in *Les Routiers*.

liberal(s)   see *conservative(s)* above.

lot   (NoC): Note that the count for *lot* as a noun excludes tokens of *a lot* as an adverb.

me   (Det): As a possessive determiner, *my* sometimes occurs in the non-standard form *me* (as in *I'll ask me dad*). Notice that this form is distinct from *me* as an objective pronoun (e.g. *Don't ask me*).

miss   (NoC): This lemma is ambiguous, and includes both *Miss/miss* as a title of address for an unmarried woman, and *miss* in the sense of 'a near miss'.

more than   (Adv): *More than* is considered to be a multiword adverb of degree when it is followed by a numerical expression, as in *It costs more than £100* (= 'over').

~n~   A variant of the negative *not*: the middle part of *dunno* (= *do + not + know*).

need   (VMod): This count includes only the tokens of *need* as a modal auxiliary: e.g. where *need* is followed by a negative and/or a bare infinitive: *need not go, needn't leave, I doubt if you need say anything*. This is counted separately from *need* (main verb).

~na   This is a rendering of the infinitive marker *to*, when run together with the preceding verb in *gonna* and *wanna*.

~no   The final part of *dunno* (= *do + not + know*), lemmatized with *know*.

no one, no-one   The two variant spellings of this pronoun appear in separate entries.

of   (Prep): Note that the count for *of* as a preposition excludes the many cases of multi-word prepositions or adverbs including *of*: e.g. *of course, in spite of*.

of   (Verb): In the transcriptions of speech for the BNC, a weakened pronunciation of *have* was sometimes written as *of* (as in *could of done it*).

okay, OK   Note that *okay*, classified as an adverb or an adjective, also has a variant spelling *OK*, with a separate entry.

~ta   This is an informal spelling of the infinitive marker *to*, especially in the combination *gotta* (= *got + to*).

Introduction

In this introduction, we aim to provide the user with the necessary background information for understanding the frequency listings presented in the main part of the book. In Section 1, we discuss the content and structure of the text sample (or corpus) on which the lists are based. In Section 2, we then discuss the format of the book and the lists themselves. Section 3 gives a chapter-by-chapter summary of the book. Section 4 outlines some of the procedures and decisions made in processing the data of corpus texts and also explains the significance and dispersion statistics used in the lists. Finally, in Sections 5 and 6, we provide some notes of caution which users should observe in interpreting the frequency information presented, and explain our presentation of some findings in 'interest boxes'.

1. The British National Corpus (BNC)

This book is based on the British National Corpus (hereafter the BNC), a sample of some 100 million words of present-day spoken and written British English. It is made up of 4,124 different text files, each containing either a complete text, or a number of short related texts, or a substantial sample of a long text (see Burnard 1995, Aston and Burnard 1998). By 'present-day' we mean that:

- all imaginative texts are dated no earlier than 1960 (and 80% of them are no earlier than 1975)
- all informative texts are dated no earlier than 1975
- all spoken data are dated no earlier than 1991
- a large majority of BNC texts (over 93%) date from the period 1985–94.

In terms of size and currency, the BNC is only surpassed by the Bank of English based at Birmingham (see http://www.cobuild.collins.co.uk/boe_info.html). However, the BNC has one characteristic not shared by the Bank of English, and it is the one that has made this book feasible: the BNC is a finite, balanced, sampled corpus. It is possible to extrapolate from corpus frequencies to inferences about the language as a whole, because the compilers have taken pains to sample different kinds of speech and writing (e.g. conversation, novels, news reporting) broadly in accordance with their representation in everyday language use.

The BNC contains approximately 90 per cent written data and 10 per cent spoken data. Although spoken language, as the primary channel of communication, should by rights be given more prominence than this, in practice this has not been possible, since it is a skilled and very time-consuming task to transcribe speech into the computer-readable orthographic text that can be processed to extract linguistic information. In view of this problem, these proportions were chosen as realistic targets which, given the size of the BNC, are also sufficiently large to be broadly representative.

1.1. Written component

The written component of the BNC contains two broadly-defined kinds of text: **imaginative** (i.e., mostly fiction, but including some other literary texts such as poetry) and **informative** (i.e., non-fictional expository writing). Of these, imaginative texts account for about 20 per cent of the written component and informative texts for about 80 per cent. The sampling of texts attempted to follow broadly the pattern of book publishing in the UK. The imaginative files are not explicitly subdivided into text categories. However, they can be assigned easily enough to the different genres of poetry, prose, and drama. On the other hand, the informative data are additionally subdivided into eight general domains, whose proportional contribution is again intended to reflect the proportions of books published in these areas:

Percentages of the written corpus (measured in W-units)[1] in each domain*

Arts	8.08%	Natural science	4.18%
Belief and thought	3.40%	Applied science	8.21%
Commerce	7.93%	Social science	14.80%
Leisure	11.13%	World affairs	18.39%

*A further 1.93% of all W-units are unclassified.

58.58% of informative samples are taken from books and 31.08% from periodicals. The remainder includes other miscellaneous published and unpublished material (e.g. reports, leaflets, letters) as well as written-to-be-spoken texts (e.g. TV scripts).

Further details of the composition of the corpus can be found in the *Users Reference Guide to the British National Corpus* (Burnard 1995).

1.2. Spoken component

The spoken component of the BNC is divided into two parts: a **conversational** part and a **task-oriented** part.[2]

The conversational part is largely made up of 'fly on the wall' recordings of everyday spontaneous interactions engaged in by some 127 adults aged 15 and over. The volunteers, known as 'respondents', were selected according to demographic criteria of age, social class, and gender, with the aim of obtaining approximately equal numbers in each age band, socio-economic class, and gender.[3] Location was also taken into account,

---

[1] A W-unit is broadly equivalent to a word token. However, in the BNC, certain multiword units—for example, the conjunction *so that*—are considered to be single W-units (see 4.b.ii. below). The figures are percentages of the whole corpus, as stated in the *Users Reference Guide to the British National Corpus* (Burnard 1995: 11). However, these figures are being slightly revised for the second new release of the BNC, in which some erroneously classified texts are being corrected.

[2] Here and in the lists in Chapter 3, we prefer to use the terms **conversational** and **task-oriented** respectively, rather than the terms **demographic** and **context-governed** used in the *Users Reference Guide to the British National Corpus*, as in practice the latter terms are more difficult to interpret.

[3] In practice, the figures (shown below) are somewhat less than equal, because the sampling related only to the volunteers and not to their interlocutors.

although region of origin was not a primary sampling criterion. Some additional recordings of under 15s were included from the COLT (Corpus of London Teenager Language) project at Bergen (Haslerud and Stenström 1995, Andersen and Stenström 1996). All volunteers were asked to carry a walkman cassette recorder for two to seven days and to record all their spoken interactions, making notes on the conversational details of interlocutors. They were allowed to fail to record or to delete recordings if an interlocutor did not agree to the recording. Altogether, well over a thousand speakers (respondents and their interlocutors) are included in the conversational dialogue.

The task-oriented part of the spoken corpus material was intended to represent those types of task-oriented spoken activity that were unlikely to be recorded by the conversational volunteers during a typical day in their lives—e.g. lectures, consultations, sermons, TV/radio broadcasting, etc. Such (largely) public activities are socially important, even though only a small minority of language users regularly engage in them.

The conversational part makes up just over 40% of the spoken corpus (over 4 million words). Age, class, and sex are represented in the following proportions (using words, in the sense of W-units):

Subdivisions of the conversational spoken part of the corpus

Age	%	Social Group	%	Sex	%
Under 15	6.3	A, B	32.54	Male	41.14
15–24	15.88	C1	26.02	Female	58.47
25–34	20.11	C2	25.64	Unclassified	0.38
35–44	19.92	D, E	14.88		
45–59	22.71	Unclassified	0.89		
Over 60	15.05				

The task-oriented part makes up about 60% of the spoken corpus and contains the following activity types:

Educational and informative

Lectures, talks, educational demonstrations
News commentaries
Classroom interaction

Business

Company talks and interviews
Trade union talks
Sales demonstrations
Business meetings
Consultations

Public/Institutional

Political speeches
Sermons
Public/government talks
Council meetings
Religious meetings
Parliamentary proceedings
Legal proceedings

Leisure

Speeches
Sports commentaries
Talks to clubs
Broadcast chat shows and phone-ins
Club meetings

The regional distribution across the UK for the entire spoken component is as follows:

South	45.61	North	25.43
Midland	23.33	Unclassified	5.61

Further details of the spoken corpus sampling can be found in the *Users Reference Guide to the British National Corpus* and in Crowdy (1994, 1995).

1.3. Versions of the British National Corpus

The BNC has now been produced in two versions. The original release (Version 1.0) was distributed from 1995. The new BNC (Version 2.0), at the time of going to press, is expected to be released in the winter of 2000/1. The new release, unlike the old one, is to be available (under licence) worldwide. It has certain advantages over the old version, notably (*a*) improved accuracy of grammatical tagging (undertaken at Lancaster in 1995–96), and (*b*) correction of details of text classification,[4] which has resulted in the transfer of about a million words from the 'imaginative' category of written texts to the 'informative' category. However, it has also been necessary to reduce the size of the BNC in the worldwide release by 69 texts, owing to the difficulty or impossibility of obtaining world rights for the distribution of those texts.

For the purposes of this book, we are using the complete BNC of Version 1.0, and at the same time are making use of the improvements of Version 2.0—including improved grammatical tagging and text category corrections. This ensures that we base our frequency lists on the best and fullest information available.

2. Guidelines used for making the lists

Any discussion of word frequency presupposes a distinction between two senses of 'word': word (=type) and word (=token). When we speak of word **types**, we mean words as they occur in a vocabulary list, or a dictionary. When we speak of word **tokens**, we mean words as they occur in a text. For example, the word *she* will only occur once in a dictionary; but many examples (tokens) of the word *she* may occur in a single text. In speaking of word frequency, we are concerned with the number of tokens of a given type.

This book contains three kinds of listing: listings in **alphabetical** word order, listings in **descending frequency** (or *rank*) order, and listings sorted according to a statistical measure of **distinctiveness**, or the 'differentness' of a word's frequency in different parts of the corpus.

2.1. Alphabetic and other lists

By far the longest frequency list in the book is the General Alphabetic List (Chapter 1, List 1.1) which follows this introduction, and fills pages 21–115. We will illustrate some general points by referring primarily to this list. In alphabetical lists and some other lists (Chapter 5, Lists 5.1–5.3), words are listed by **lemma**. That is, the **headword** of an entry

---

[4] We are grateful to David Y. W. Lee for undertaking this work. The lists of BNC texts and their categories are available on the UCREL website (www.comp.lancs.ac.uk/ucrel/bncfreq/).

represents the word as you would look it up in a dictionary, and the **inflectional variants** of the headword are listed underneath it. For example, here is part of the entry for the verb *like* in List 1.1 (omitting the dispersion scores—see Section 4.5):

		Freq
like	Verb	424
like		*344*
liked		*56*
likes		*21*
liking		*3*

Like as a verb has four variants (or word forms): *like, liked, likes* and *liking*. At the top of the entry, the frequency of the whole lemma—that is, *like* as a verb—is given as a normalized frequency score of **occurrences** (tokens) **per million words**. (Since the whole corpus is about 100 million words (tokens), the actual raw frequency count for the verb *like* is 42,403.) It will be noted that the frequency scores of the individual variants, 344+56+21+3, add up to the figure for the whole lemma. This is as it should be, since the frequency of the lemma is simply the sum of the frequencies of its variants. However, it will also be noted, in the lists, that this addition is not always precise, because of rounding up or down to the nearest whole number. This will be illustrated from the entries in List 1.1 for the noun *score*, which like most nouns has two variants, the singular and the plural forms, and the adjective *old*, which like many adjectives has positive, comparative and superlative variants (NoC=common noun):

score	NoC	45
score		*27*
scores		*17*
old	Adj	648
old		*544*
older		*90*
oldest		*15*

The main parts of speech which have inflectional variants in English are nouns, verbs, adjectives and personal pronouns.[5] These are the word classes which are lemmatized in our alphabetical lists, in contrast to prepositions and conjunctions, for example, which are invariant. Even with the variant word classes, however, some words have no inflectional variants, e.g. nouns like *aluminium*, verbs like *must* and adjectives like *personal*. In cases where a word type (=lemma) is invariant, we give it a separate entry on a single line of the alphabetical list, and do not make any distinction between lemma and variant.

Apart from the lists of nouns, verbs and adjectives in Lists 5.1–5.3, the entries in the **rank order** and **distinctiveness order** listings are individual word forms only, and are not lemmatized like the alphabetical listings. (Also there is a frequency threshold below which the words are not included in the list—see Section 2.4.) Note that, in the rank

---

[5] A small number of adverbs and determiners/pronouns, such as *well, late, soon* and *many/ much*, also have inflectional variants: e.g. *better, best, sooner, soonest, more, most*. These forms, however, are not lemmatized in the lists, but are treated as their own headwords.

order lists, items are still sorted by *actual* frequency, even when the rounded frequency *per million* works out the same.

2.2. Distinctions made or not made in the lists

2.2.1. *Homographs: different words spelt alike*

In all listings, in general, words spelt the same (homographs) are distinguished only at the level of major parts of speech—for example, *like* as a verb is distinct from *like* as a preposition or *like* as an adverb; *score* as a noun is distinct from *score* as a verb. As the distinction between common nouns and proper nouns is normally marked in orthography by the initial capital or lower-case letter, this is retained as a special case, so that there are separate entries, for example, for *brown* (the colour noun) and *Brown* (name). Otherwise word-form frequencies are not sub-divided according to finer-grained grammatical functions: for instance, *liked* (past participle) and *liked* (simple past tense) are not distinguished.

Some entries remain ambiguous even after parts of speech have been distinguished. This is routinely the case where a word type has two or more different senses: for example, the noun *chest* can refer to a piece of furniture or to a part of the human anatomy. This book makes no claim to deal with frequencies of different meanings such as these. Because of the limitations of automatic counting by computer, this is true also for cases where two meanings are associated with different orthographic practices or pronunciations. For example, the frequency count for the string *polish* as a noun represents both *polish* (cleaning substance) and *Polish* (language). Without human inspection of the word in its context, it is not possible to distinguish these: for example, *Polish* with an initial capital may turn out to be the word *polish* occurring at the beginning of a sentence. In cases such as these, to show that the word can be canonically spelt either with or without an initial capital, the entry is presented as follows: *P/polish*.

2.2.2. *Abbreviations or acronyms*

Another rather similar set of cases is that of abbreviations or acronyms. In the corpus, the same abbreviatory sequence may be spelled in different ways, such as *P.C., PC, p.c., pc*. Although such forms may reflect different origins (*Police Constable, postcard, personal computer*) it is not part of our plan to distinguish these different interpretations—a laborious task that could be done only by hand.[6] Hence we treat the different orthographic renderings as variants of the same lemma, and use the most common orthographic form in spelling the lemma.[7]

---

[6] This policy is difficult to avoid in the automatic analysis of a corpus, because of uncertainty about the status of capitals (both at the beginning of a word and throughout it) and the status of full stops. Capitals can indicate the beginning of a sentence, or the beginning of a word of certain classes, such as a proper noun. Capitals throughout a word may be a highlighting device, but their effect may also be to neutralize the distinction between a word normally spelt with an initial capital and one normally spelt without it: for example, POLISH may be a token of *Polish* or of *polish*. A full stop at the end of a word, as in *Ed.*, may signal the end of a sentence or the end of an abbreviation.

[7] Another problem of different orthographic renderings occurs where the same spelling is used for an abbreviation as well as for an ordinary word of the same part of speech: for example, the nouns *VAT*

2.2.3. *Cases of ambiguous lemmatization*

Lemmatization is made possible by the grammatical tagging of the BNC (see Section 4.2), which distinguishes different grammatical functions within the same general part of speech, so that, for example, *found* (tagged VVD or VVN as the past tense or past participle of the verb *find*) is clearly distinguishable from *found* as the base form of a different verb (tagged VVO or VVI). One of these is lemmatized with the set of variants *find, finding, finds, found*, while the other is lemmatized with the set of variants *found, founded, founding, founds*. There is generally no problem in the compilation of lemmatized lists on this basis; however, there are also a few forms of exactly the same word class that could belong to two different lemmas. For instance, the noun *bases* can be the plural of either *base* or *basis*. In these cases, tokens of the same string have to be split into two sets and assigned to the different lemmas. This cannot be done automatically, and so we have to give an estimate of the two normalized frequencies (derived from a hand count of a random sample of instances). There also has to be an estimate of the dispersion values of the two variants (see Section 4.5). It is rare that frequency and dispersion figures have to be estimated in this way, and the fact that such figures are based on estimates is signalled by underscoring.[8]

2.2.4. *Spelling variants*

On the whole, vocabulary items that exhibit variations in spelling—e.g. *organise* and *organize*—have not been standardized to a single lemma, since the information about the frequencies of different spelling variants may be of interest to the user. However, where the spelling variation affects only certain variants of a lemma, but not the headword—e.g. *labeled* or *labelled* as a spelling of the past forms of *label*—they are lemmatized together. Also, as already noted, spelling variants of abbreviations have been merged into a single lemma, under a headword representing the common or conventional spelling which predominates. For example, *C*(.) (proper noun) may be an abbreviated name of a person (*C. Smith*) or the name of a programming language *C*, or some other name. Although the different spellings *C* and *C.* are preserved in the list, these are treated as variants of a single lemma.

2.2.5. *Capitalization in headwords and variants*

As a rule, the use of capitals in the representation of words follows 'canonical' practice for those words. Thus, as proper nouns in English are conventionally spelt with an initial capital, they appear in that form in the lists: *Tokyo, Mary*, etc. Words of other word classes generally do not begin with a capital (although there are exceptional circumstances, such as at the beginning of the sentence, where they do), and so are represented in lower case in the lists: *book, well*, etc.

(= valued added tax) and *vat* (= a vessel). Here again, spelling may not be decisive (for example, VAT could be the noun *vat* occurring in a headline), so we merge the two forms into a single lemma, which is spelt as follows: VAT / vat.

[8] Underscoring is also used for a few estimates which were undertaken because of minor defects in the lemmatization rules: for example, the verbs *focus* and *travel* have variants with and without doubling of the consonant: *focuses, focusses; traveled, travelled*. The single-consonant variants had to be found by use of a concordance search.

However, English orthography has exceptions to this generalization: for example, nouns and adjectives which are derived from proper names are spelt with an initial capital: *Arabic, Australian, Christian, Scotsman*, and this is again reflected in the lists. Similarly, the lists reflect the tendency to use capitals throughout in abbreviations and acronyms (e.g. *IBM, UNO, AIDS*), although variants are also shown.

Where there is a genuine ambiguity within a word class, reflected in the use of capitalization, this is shown (as we have already seen) by the use of an oblique: *P/polish* (noun); *VAT / vat* (noun). Also, Roman numerals and letters of the alphabet (when used, for example, as mathematical symbols or enumerators) are shown with both variants: *IV / iv, A / a, B / b*, etc.[9]

There are certain classes of nouns (especially titular and locative nouns) which commonly occur with an initial capital, particularly when they are part of a naming expression: for example: *queen* in *Queen Elizabeth, president* in *President Reagan, square* in *Leicester Square*, and *hill* in *Bunker Hill*. In spite of the frequency of capitalization, these words are regarded as canonically spelt in lower case, and are so represented in the lists. Thus the headword *square* (common noun) will subsume both the lower case and capitalized instances. This applies also to names of political parties, such as *Conservative, Labour* and *Republican* (lemmatized as *conservative, labour* and *republican*), as well as to words such as *Catholic* (in the sense of Roman Catholic, lemmatized as *catholic*).

2.3. Multiword units

Multiword units are items which are treated as a single word token, even though they are spelt as a sequence of orthographic words. Because they function grammatically as single words (e.g. the conjunction *so that*, the preposition *in spite of*, *at least* as an adverb), they are treated as entries in their own right. This, however, does not apply to proper names spelt as two or more words, such as *New York* or *San Francisco*.[10] It also does not apply to idiomatic sequences such as phrasal verbs: for example, the phrasal verb *sum up* (meaning 'summarize') is analysed as two words—a verb followed by a particle adverb—not as a single multiword item. The reason for this is that, although such expressions are semantically a single unit, there is no reason not to regard them as existing grammatically as two words. For example, the first word of *sum up* can be independently varied (*summed up, summing up*, etc.) and the second word can be separated from it by other words (as in *to sum it all up*).

2.4. Size of vocabulary, and cut-off points used in the lists

The size of the vocabulary employed in the British National Corpus is enormous: according to our count, 757,087 different word forms occur in the whole corpus. But the vast majority of these occur only a few times, as the following list shows very clearly:

---

[9] One exceptional case is the word *and/or*, where the oblique / does not signal different spellings of the same word, but is rather, for our purposes, an intrinsic part of the spelling of a single conjunction.

[10] However, the part-of-speech label NoP- is used (alongside NoP for a proper noun) to signal a word which is typically or invariably a **part** of a name, rather than a **whole** name. This label applies, for instance, to *New* as in *New York* or *New Orleans*, and to both halves of *Hong Kong*. But *York* is capable of standing alone as a name, and is thus labelled not NoP- but NoP.

Word forms occurring 10 or more times in the BNC:	124,002
Word forms occurring 5–9 times in the BNC:	62,041
Word forms occurring 4 times in the BNC:	28,770
Word forms occurring 3 times in the BNC:	46,459
Word forms occurring twice in the BNC:	98,774
Word forms occurring only once in the BNC:	397,041

In fact, over half the word forms in the corpus (52.44%) occur only once. This book shows only the tip of the iceberg: to keep it within a manageable size, only headwords with an overall frequency of **10 per million words** or more are included in the lists. Some of the lists have an even higher cut-off: List 1.2 has a cut-off of 100 mentions per million words; List 2.1 has a cut-off of 160 mentions per million words (for the entire lemma in either speech or writing); List 2.2 has a cut-off of 10 mentions per million words (in the spoken corpus); List 2.3 has a cut-off of 20 mentions per million words (in the written corpus); List 2.4 has a cut-off of a log-likelihood (distinctiveness) index of 1000; List 3.1 has a cut-off of 120 mentions per million words (for the entire lemma, in either part of the spoken corpus); List 3.2 has a cut-off of a log-likelihood (distinctiveness) index of 300; List 4.1 has a cut-off of 185 mentions per million words (for the entire lemma); List 4.2 has a cut- off of a log-likelihood (distinctiveness) index of 2811. (Other lists have a cut-off of 10 per million.) In all the lists, frequency figures are given as occurrences per million words.

It is important to note, here, that if there are two (or more) homographs in the language, there is no necessary expectation that they will both occur in the lists. For example, English very commonly has a noun and a verb spelt in the same way, but it may sometimes happen that only one of these words is frequent enough to be in the list. For example, in List 1.1, the verb *roar* is found, but not the noun *roar*. On the other hand, in the same list, the noun *rifle* is found, but not the verb *rifle*. Such cases can mislead the casual reader: the lists in this book, in particular List 1.1, do not reliably give information on the frequency of a particular 'orthographic word' (such as *roar*) defined simply as a string of letters. We can infer, from the presence of the verb *roar* in the list, and the non-occurrence of the noun *roar*, that the noun is (*a*) less frequent than 10 per million, and (*b*) less frequent than the verb. However, the precise frequency of the noun usage cannot be recovered, except by referring to the lists on the Lancaster UCREL website (www.comp.lancs.ac.uk/ucrel/bncfreq/).

In the alphabetical lemmatized lists (Lists 1.1, 2.1, 3.1, and 4.1), a much lower threshold is used for including inflectional and orthographic variants of a headword: if a variant occurs **10 times or more in the whole corpus** (or in one of the relevant **subcorpora**), it will be included in the list.[11] This means that a large number of variants are recorded with a frequency of '0', as in these examples:

---

[11] This low threshold of 10 is set so as to make sure that all reasonably acceptable variants of a lemma will occur in the list, whereas accidental misspellings, non-standard forms, anomalous usages, etc. will tend to be excluded.

(a)	alcohol	NoC	31	(b)	rough	Adj	35
	alcohol		30		rough		34
	alcohols		0		rougher		1
					roughest		0

Entry (a) tells us that the plural *alcohols* is a rare variant—a rounding down to zero per million words means that this form occurs less than 50 times in the whole 100-million-word corpus. However, the fact that it occurs in the list at all indicates that it occurs at least 10 times in the corpus. (Actually there are 34 tokens of *alcohols* in the BNC.) The same is true of the superlative form *roughest*, in entry (b).

An even lower frequency of variants is implied by the following examples:

(c)	knitting	NoC	10	(d)	dead	Adj	114
	knitting		10		dead		114

The entry for the singular noun *knitting* tells us that there *is* a plural variant (*knittings*), but that it is so rare that it does not even qualify for listing: i.e. it occurs less than 10 times in the whole corpus. A similar inference can be made for the missing variants for *dead*: viz. *deader* and *deadest*. The reason why these inferences can be made is that if the unlisted variants did not occur *at all* in the corpus, the lemma would occur on a single line, and no variants (not even the variant representing the base form) would be listed.[12] Hence examples (c) and (d) may be contrasted with entries (e) and (f):

(e)	smoking	NoC	12	(f)	rival	Adj	14

These entries indicate that, from the evidence of the corpus, these are invariable words: there are no occurrences of a plural form *smokings*, and there are no occurrences of comparative or superlative forms *rivaler*, *rivalest*. The three sets of examples (a)–(f) above therefore signal inflectional variants with 10–49 occurrences (in a, b), 1–9 occurrences (in c, d), and zero occurrences (in e, f).

3. The plan of the book

The lists are organized as follows. Chapter 1 gives the frequencies of words in the BNC as a whole, i.e., without any distinction between speech and writing or between genres. The data are presented in two tables: one in alphabetical order (List 1.1), the other in descending frequency (or **rank**) order (List 1.2). Indices of **range** and **dispersion** are shown for each headword or variant, indicating how well that word is distributed throughout the corpus (see Section 4.5 for details).

Chapter 2 gives the frequencies of words in the BNC **across speech and writing**. The frequency information is presented in four tables: an alphabetical table (List 2.1), two rank order tables, one for speech (List 2.2) and one for writing (List 2.3), and a distinctiveness-ordered table (List 2.4). In List 2.1, range and dispersion indices are given for each headword and variant for each of the two channels. In all lists, each headword or variant is also associated with an index of distinctiveness, showing how

---

[12] Note that some of these rare variants will reflect usage errors or one-off coinages in the corpus texts.

significantly different—that is, higher or lower—its frequency is in speech as contrasted with writing (see Section 4.4 for further details).

Chapter 3 is concerned only with the **spoken** part of the BNC, and compares demographically-sampled **conversation** (i.e. informal dialogue) with the **task-oriented** corpus samples (largely more formal or public speech). The data are presented in alphabetical order (List 3.1) and distinctiveness order (List 3.2), and in addition to frequency, we show dispersion measures (in List 3.1) and distinctiveness measures (in both lists).

Chapter 4 is concerned only with the **written** data in the corpus, and compares **imaginative** and **informative** writing. Lists 4.1 and 4.2 present the data in the same way as Lists 3.1 and 3.2 in Chapter 3.

Chapter 5 differs considerably from the preceding chapters. It presents tables of the most frequent words within each **major grammatical word class**. The tables are given in rank frequency order only. In Lists 5.1–5.3 (nouns, verbs, adjectives), the frequencies are for whole lemmas, not for variant word forms, but in the other lists, Lists 5.4–5.10, it is the individual word forms that are listed. The lists include only the overall frequencies of words in the corpus: further information on dispersion and on differences between channels and text types can be extracted from the main tables in Chapters 1–4.

Finally, Chapter 6 presents the frequencies of the grammatical word classes themselves, that is, as categories without their individual lexical contents. The word classes are based upon the detailed subdivisions identified in the part-of-speech tagged BNC—that is, they distinguish, for example, between past participles and simple past tense forms. This chapter is based upon the two-million-word Sampler Corpus of the BNC, rather than the whole 100 million words. This smaller corpus (see info.ox.ac.uk/bnc/getting/sampler.html) extracted from the BNC has been chosen for Chapter 6 for two reasons: (*a*) word classes (as opposed to individual words) are of sufficient frequency not to require the larger corpus, and (*b*) the Sampler Corpus has been manually checked for accuracy of part-of-speech tagging (see Section 4.2). The Sampler Corpus, unlike the whole BNC Corpus, is subdivided more or less equally between spoken and written texts: it contains approximately a million words of speech and a million words of writing. In Chapter 6, frequencies are presented in tables corresponding to those in Chapters 1–4: Lists 6.1.1–2 (for the whole Sampler Corpus); Lists 6.2.1–6.2.4 (speech and writing); Lists 6.3.1–6.3.2 (conversational and task-oriented speech); and Lists 6.4.1–6.4.2 (imaginative and informative writing). Dispersion indices and distinctiveness statistics are included.

4. Processing the data of the BNC

Section 4 explains how, starting with the BNC material, we arrived at the data presented in this book. This explanation will hopefully help the reader to a better appreciation of what can be learned (or cannot be learned) from the lists.

4.1. Transcription of speech

The spoken material in the BNC is not used in its original audio format but has been transcribed into the written medium. The material was transcribed according to standard orthographic practices. The transcribers aimed to be as consistent as possible, but some inconsistencies and anomalies do exist in the transcription—for example, between the use of digital and spelt-out numbers—and this should be borne in mind when interpreting the spoken frequencies.

One linguistic feature that is (almost) confined to speech is that of **word fragments**. These occur when a speaker has begun to say a word but then breaks off before completing it. For example, the speaker may be intending to say the word *convict* but only utters the first syllable, *con*. As a hesitation phenomenon, this is in fact quite widespread in spontaneous speech. The Claws tagger (the software discussed in Section 4.2) is able to identify cases where word fragments occur and mark them with a tag as 'unclassified', i.e., as non-words, which could not be found even in a detailed dictionary of English. As these fragments do not constitute complete words, and can be highly ambiguous out of context, they have been excluded from the lists in this book, even though (in their orthographic form) they may otherwise meet the frequency threshold for inclusion.[13]

Another feature of spoken language is that speakers often fill pauses in their flow of speech with pause fillers such as *erm* or *er*. Since these are technically non-verbal sounds, there is no dictionary standard for their spelling. For the BNC, therefore, a standardized spelling of forms for such fillers was agreed and followed by the transcribers. These hesitation fillers, like interjections (*oh*, *ah*, for instance) and discourse markers (such as *yeah*, *bye*), are included in the lists.

4.2. Parts of speech

Parts of speech (word classes such as noun, verb, adjective) were identified automatically by the Claws automatic tagging software (Garside and Smith 1997) and by the Template Tagger (Fligelstone, Rayson and Smith 1996), using a set of 134 detailed part-of-speech distinctions.[14] Tags, representing these word classes, were attached to the words in the corpus. These are listed in Appendix A (see p. 20). These categories are relatively fine-grained in so far as they distinguish, for example, 22 subclasses of nouns and 31 subclasses of verbs. Such distinctions may be useful for retrieving data from a large text base and for other research purposes, but they are somewhat superfluous in a book of word frequencies. As noted above, therefore, for the purposes of this book, only 23 major parts of speech (rather than subcategories) have been used to disambiguate ambiguous word forms: thus we distinguish *spent* as an adjective from *spent* as a verb, but not *spent* as a finite past-tense verb from *spent* as a past participle verb. The major parts of speech and their abbreviations are listed below. In Chapter 6,

---

[13] Although word fragments are excluded from the frequency lists, they are tagged as separate words in the automatically tagged form of the BNC. This means that they are included as tokens in calculating the number of words in the BNC, and hence the overall frequency per million word tokens of word types in the printed lists. This has the effect of slightly understating the frequency of words, especially in the spoken part of the corpus. But this effect is minor, and is consistently applied in all relevant lists, so that no misleading result is to be feared.

[14] The set of 134 word-class tags used in connection with the tagging software is called the C6 tagset. Note that in the published form of the BNC (available on-line or on CD-Roms), a smaller and less fine-grained tagset known as C5 has been used. C5 contains only 61 tags (see Garside *et al.* 1997: 256–60).

however, distributions of all the detailed part-of-speech categories are shown, using the BNC Sampler Corpus.[15]

List of part of speech categories used in Chapters 1–5

Adj	adjective (e.g. *good, old, fine, early, regional*)
Adv	adverb (e.g. *now, well, suddenly, early, further*)
ClO	clause opener (*in order* [*that*/ *to*], *so as* [*to*])[16]
Conj	conjunction (e.g. *and, but, if, because, so that*)
Det	determiner (e.g. *a, an, every, no, the*)
DetP	determiner/pronoun (e.g. *this, these, those, some, all*)[17]
Ex	existential particle (*there* in *there is, there are*, etc.)
Fore	foreign word (e.g. *de, du, la*)
Form	formula (e.g. *2x+z*)
Gen	genitive (*'s, '*)[18]
Inf	infinitive marker (*to*)
Int	interjection or discourse marker (e.g. *oh, aha, oops, yep, no*)
Lett	letter of the alphabet, treated as a word (e.g. *p, P, Q, r, z*)
Neg	negative marker (*not, ~n't*)
NoC	common noun (e.g. *wealth, walls, child, times, mission*)
NoP	proper noun (e.g. *Malaysia, Paris, Susan, Roberts, Tuesday*)
NoP-	word which is normally part of a proper noun (e.g. *San* in *San Diego*)
Num	(cardinal) number (e.g. *one, four, forty, viii, 8, 55, 1969*)
Ord	ordinal (e.g. *first, 1st, 9th, twenty-first, next, last*)
Prep	preposition (e.g. *of, in, without, up to, in charge of*)
Pron	pronoun (e.g. *I, you, she, him, theirs, none, something*)
Verb	verb—excluding modal auxiliaries (e.g. *tell, find, increase, realize*)
VMod	modal auxiliary verb (e.g. *can, will, would, could, may, must, should*)

4.2.1. *Tokenization*

One major task of the Claws tagger, important for this book, is **tokenization**: that is, the segmentation of texts into individual word units (or word tokens). By and large, a word token is considered to be a string of uninterrupted non-punctuation characters with

---

[15] Details of how part-of-speech categories are distinguished can be consulted at www.comp.lancs.ac.uk/ucrel/bnc2/bnc2guide.htm.

[16] The clause opener is not a widely-recognized part-of-speech category, but is needed to account for multiword sequences like *in order* and *so as* preceding a conjunction or infinitive marker. The possibility that a negative particle may occur between the clause-initial operator and the infinitive marker (as in *in order not to, so as not to*) necessitates the recognition of *in order* or *so as* as a token.

[17] Demonstratives (*this, that, these, those*) and quantifiers (*all, both, some, each*, etc.) are the main members of this category. A common classification is to treat all such words as ambiguous between a determiner function (as in *This book is mine*) and a pronoun function (as in *This is my book*). However, in the BNC tagging scheme these two functions are merged into a single determiner-pronoun category.

[18] Note that the genitive ending (spelt *'s* or *'*) counts as an enclitic particle—as a separate word token—for the purposes of this book.

white space or punctuation at each end. Hence a sequence such as the following consists of 18 word tokens, each of which is separately underlined:[19]

> <u>This</u> <u>chapter</u> <u>is</u> <u>based</u> <u>upon</u> <u>the</u> <u>two-million-word</u> <u>Sampler</u> <u>Corpus</u> <u>of</u> <u>the</u>
> <u>BNC</u>, <u>rather</u> <u>than</u> <u>the</u> <u>whole</u> <u>100</u> <u>million</u> <u>words</u>.

One exception to this, however, is the case of reduced forms—e.g. *isn't, gonna, dunno*. These informal spellings are separated into their constituent words, so that *isn't* is separated into *is* and the reduced form of *not* (*n't*), *gonna* into the notional constituent words *gon-* (a reduced form of *going*) and *-na* (a variant form of *to*), and *dunno* into *du-* (variant form of *do*), *-n-* (reduced form of *not*) and *-no* (variant form of *know*). Counts are thus given for the constituent words (e.g. *is* and *n't*) and not for the fused strings (*isn't*, for instance). To show that the reduced forms do not occur in isolation, a swung dash ~ has been used in the lists, to show that these are clitic forms linked to other words: for example, *gon~*; *~na*.

In the lemmatized lists, these reduced forms are regarded as variants of their full forms: hence *~n't* is counted as a variant of the negative particle *not*, *~na* is counted as a variant of the infinitive marker *to*.

4.2.2. *Multiword units*

Multiword units are another exception to the principle of segmenting word tokens according to the occurrence of white space.

As noted earlier, some 'words' will, in fact, be made up of several word strings. This is because certain groups of words may be interpreted more sensibly in grammatical terms if they are treated as single words: although they may be several word strings in length, they *function* as individual words. For example, *so that* is made up of two word strings but functions in the same way as a one-word conjunction: it simply does not make sense to analyse it (say) as an adverb preceding a conjunction. We call these groups of functionally inseparable words *multiword units* and treat them as single words for the purpose of part-of-speech assignment. Thus, some sequences of orthographic words, such as *a bit, instead of,* will be found in the frequency lists.

4.2.3. *Accuracy*

Unfortunately, no automatic tagger, however well crafted, achieves complete accuracy in assigning grammatical labels to word tokens. Claws identifies the detailed parts of speech with an accuracy in the region of 96.5%. Many of the remaining errors are within-category errors—for example, with a verb form like *told*, there can be confusion between past participle and finite past-tense form, or with a verb form like *tell*, confusion between plural present tense and infinitive. Because we are only using the major parts of speech and not the detailed sub-categories, such errors are irrelevant for us and, in fact, do not exist for the purposes of our lists. Nevertheless, a further program—the

---

[19] This sentence has one example of a multiword expression (see 4.2.2), *rather than*, which is considered to act as a single preposition. Also, notice that words containing hyphens (like *two-million-word*) are counted as a single token, rather than split up into two or more separate words.

Template Tagger—was used to correct these and many other common errors in Claws-tagged text. The resulting tagged texts, after correction by the Template Tagger, are 98% accurate. Furthermore, a subset of the corpus, the Sampler Corpus (two million words), was manually corrected to achieve notionally complete accuracy, although, in practice, this falls *slightly* short of the mark (see Baker 1997). The word frequencies given in this book may thus, overall, be assumed to achieve considerably more than 98% accuracy (actually 98.36%). Moreover, in practice, a still greater degree of accuracy (98.79%) can be expected, because errors in opposite directions frequently cancel one another out.[20]

4.3. Headword identification: the process of lemmatization

The identification of the lemma to which a word token belongs means, in practice, assigning the token to a particular headword: for example, the verb form *liked* tagged as a past tense verb will be assigned to the headword *like* (Verb). This task can be done automatically by a lemmatization program that operates on part-of-speech tagged output. The program which performed this task for the BNC made use of a set of lemmatization rules devised by Beale (1987) as further developed and implemented by Beale (1989), Fligelstone (1994) and Rayson (1996–2000). Some of these rules are very general: for example, to find the headword for a plural noun ending in -*s*, one generally simply deletes the -*s*, as with *computers* > *computer*, sometimes making consequential changes such as the change from *ie* to *y*: *abilities* > *ability*. However, there is also a somewhat large set of special rules which apply to only a few words or perhaps only one: for example, the rules for irregular plurals such as *teeth* > *tooth*. Using the C6 tagset employed for tagging the BNC, we find interestingly very few ambiguities in the lemmatization rules; i.e., each rule, applied to a particular word form, has a unique solution. But there are one or two exceptions to this: for example, there are two differ-ent verb lemmas containing the word *lying*: (*a*) *lie, lied, lies, lying*, meaning 'to tell an untruth' and (*b*) *lie, lay, lain, lies, lying* meaning 'to adopt a recumbent posture'. These two have to be treated as having different headwords with the same spelling (let us call

---

[20] To calculate the percentage of error remaining in the tagging of the BNC, for the purposes of this book, we refer to a manual analysis of tagging errors in 50,000 words (twenty-five 2,000-word samples), taken from a cross-section of spoken and written BNC text files. This error analysis, undertaken by Geoffrey Leech and Nicholas Smith, can be consulted on the UCREL website (URL: www.comp.lancs.ac.uk/ucrel/bnc2/bnc2postag_manual.htm). The percentage of error found in this study was very slightly less than 2 per cent. However, in applying this to the present book, two compensatory factors have to be taken into account:

(*a*) Many of the tagging errors in the Leech and Smith study do not count as errors for the purposes of this book, as they are mistakes of tag assignment within the same major part of speech (e.g. *seek* as infinitive v. present tense of the verb; *sought* as past tense v. past participle of the verb). This enables us to discount a further 0.36% out of the 2% errors—ignoring common/proper noun errors, which must count as real errors for the purposes of our lists.

(*b*) The error analysis shows that typically errors in one direction (e.g. adverb in place of adjective) are offset by errors in the opposite direction (e.g. adjective in place of adverb). If we allow that these errors, for each pair of tags, cancel one another out, a further 0.43% of error is discounted.

Taking account of these factors, and estimating on the basis of the Leech and Smith 50,000 word sample, we find that the error rate in the tagging of the corpus, for the present book, is reduced to 1.21%. For most purposes, this can be disregarded, given frequency scores no more precise than occurrences per million words are under consideration. However, we have to allow that the proportion of errors is likely to vary with particular words and particular word classes.

them *lie*[1] and *lie*[2]), because they have different past tense and past participle forms. Hence, the verb forms *lie*, *lies* and *lying* have ambiguous lemmatization. Another example of lemma ambiguity has already been mentioned: the plural noun *bases* has two possible headwords: *base* or *basis*. Such exceptional ambiguities have to be resolved by hand-sorting examples, and estimating frequency on the basis of a random sample.[21]

4.4. Significance statistics: distinctiveness

Chapters 2–4 of this book present comparisons between various channels and text-types: between speech and writing; between conversation and task-orientated speech; and between imaginative and informative writing. However, differences between raw frequency counts cannot be assumed to tell us something important about word frequency in general usage. This is for two reasons:

1. The samples are of different sizes (e.g. speech accounts for only 10% of the corpus and writing for 90%), hence raw frequencies cannot be compared directly.
2. Even when, as is the case in this book, proportional or normalized frequencies are given (occurrences per million word tokens), direct comparison is still uninformative. This is because we cannot tell just by looking at a difference between two proportional frequencies whether it is due to chance or to a substantive divergence between two language varieties.

We have therefore provided in the comparative lists a statistic to show how high or low is the probability that the difference observed is due to chance. This statistic can be considered to demonstrate how significantly **characteristic** or **distinctive** of a given variety of language a word is, when its usage in that variety is compared with its usage in another. For this statistic, we have employed the log-likelihood ratio or G^2 (Dunning 1993), (rather than, for instance, the more familiar Pearson's chi-square value). We have selected this statistic for three main reasons:

1. We need a statistic that does not require the data to be distributed in a particular pattern. Many statistical tests assume that data are in a so-called 'normal distribution'. With linguistic data such as word frequencies in texts this is often simply not the case and invalidates the use of such measures.
2. We need a statistic that does not over- or under-estimate the significance of a difference between two samples. The Pearson chi-squared test, one of the most commonly-used measures, has been shown to over-estimate the importance of rare events; the G^2 has been proved better in this regard.
3. We need a statistic that is insensitive to differences of size between two samples. Again, Pearson's chi-square test has been shown to be poor in this respect, whereas G^2 performs better.

G^2 is calculated by constructing a contingency table as follows:

---

[21] Such estimates are signalled by underscoring in the lists.

	SubCorpus 1	SubCorpus 2	Total
Frequency of word	a	b	a+b
Frequency of other words	c−a	d−b	c+d−a−b
Total	c	d	c+d

Note that the value 'c' corresponds to the number of words in subcorpus one, and 'd' corresponds to the number of words in subcorpus two (N values). The values 'a' and 'b' are called the observed values (O), whereas we need to calculate the expected values (E) according to the following formula:

$$E_i = \frac{N_i \sum_i O_i}{\sum_i N_i}$$

In our case $N1=c$, and $N2=d$. So, for this word, $E1=c \times (a+b)/(c+d)$ and $E2=d \times (a+b)/(c+d)$. The calculation for the expected values takes account of the size of the two subcorpora, so we do not need to normalize the figures before applying the formula. We can then calculate the log-likelihood value according to this formula:

$$-2\ln \lambda = 2\sum_i O_i \ln \left(\frac{O_i}{E_i} \right)$$

This equates to calculating log-likelihood G^2 as follows:

$$G^2 = 2 \times ((a \times \ln (a/E1)) + (b \times \ln (b/E2)))$$

The higher the G^2 value, the more significant is the difference between two frequency scores. For our lists, a G^2 of 3.8 or higher is significant at the level of $p < 0.05$ and a G^2 of 6.6 or higher is significant at $p < 0.01$. In practice, in the distinctiveness lists in Chapters 2 and 4, which show only the top end of the distinctiveness scales, the differences between the subcorpora (e.g. between speech and writing) show up as massively significant. For example, for the hesitation filler *er* at the top of List 2.4, the G^2 score for speech and writing reaches the level of 390869.9.

4.5. Dispersion statistics

Even in a large and varied corpus such as the BNC, simple word-frequency counts can be misleading. If a word has a high frequency count, the user may infer, because the compilers have attempted to build a large, maximally representative corpus, that the word has a similarly high currency of usage in the English language as a whole. However, this may be a false inference. It is possible that the word has a high frequency not because it is widely used in the language as a whole but because it is 'overused' in a much smaller number of texts, or parts of texts, within the corpus. Moreover, this 'overuse' may be due to some factor which was not controlled during the selection of samples for the corpus: for example, the selection of a leisure book about fly-fishing rather than hang-gliding.

To keep track of such distorting effects, we have also provided dispersion statistics. These show how widely spread the use of a word is: whether it is frequent because it occurs in a lot of text samples in the corpus or whether it is frequent because of a very high usage in only a few samples. Frequent words with high dispersion values may be considered to have high currency in the language as a whole; high frequencies associated with low dispersion values should, in contrast, be treated with caution.

We provide two dispersion indices, which are referred to simply as Ra and Disp in the lists:

1. **Ra: [Range]** a simple count of how many text sectors (out of the total number of 100 equalized sectors in the corpus) include the word in question. Each of these 100 sectors contains about 1 million word tokens across whole text files, although sometimes text files have been split across two sectors. The text files have been sorted so as to give a single text type (spoken, written, imaginative, informative, etc.) in each sector.[22]
2. **Disp: [Dispersion]** a statistical coefficient (Juilland's D) of how evenly distributed a word is across successive million-word sectors of the corpus. This is useful, because many sectors and texts are made up of a number of smaller, relatively independent units—for example, sections and stories in newspapers. It may be that, even *within* a text, certain vocabulary items are restricted mainly to a given part—for example, the football-reporting section of a newspaper. Juilland's D is more sensitive to this degree of variation. It is calculated as follows:

$$D = 100 \times \left(1 - \frac{V}{\sqrt{n-1}} \right)$$

where n is the number of sectors in the corpus. The variation coefficient V is given by:

$$V = \frac{S}{X}$$

where x is the mean sub-frequency of the word in the corpus (that is, its frequency in each million-word sector averaged) and s is the standard deviation of these sub-frequencies. We have selected Juilland's D as it has been shown to be the most reliable of the various dispersion coefficients that are available (Lyne 1985).[23]

Let us take an example to show how these statistics may be of use. The lemmas *HIV*, *keeper* and *lively* have quite similar frequencies overall in the BNC (approx. 16 occurrences each per million words). We might therefore be tempted to infer that

---

[22] Notice that Ra is interpreted differently in different lists, because of the varying number of one-million-word sectors in various subcorpora. For the whole corpus, the maximum Ra is 100. In Chapter 2, the maximum Ra for speech is 10, and for writing 90. In Chapter 3, the maximum Ra for conversation is 4 and for task-oriented speech 6. In Chapter 4, the maximum Ra for imaginative writing is 19 and for informative writing 71. However, in Chapter 6, where the 2-million-word BNC Sampler Corpus is used, the corpus is subdivided into 100 sectors of 20,000 words each. Here, as in Chapters 1–4, the number of sectors varies according to the size of subcorpora. For example, as the quantities of spoken and written material in the Sampler Corpus are equivalent, List 6.2.1 has a maximum Ra of 50 for both speech and writing.

[23] We have multiplied Juilland's D by 100 so that it varies between 0 and 100 rather than 0 and 1.

they all have a similar currency of usage in the English language. However, when we look at how many corpus sectors they occur in, we find that *lively* occurs in 97 as compared with *HIV*'s 62. (*Keeper* occurs in 97.) Up to a point, this already confirms what we know: *HIV* appears to be a rather specialized term, used in a restricted number of sectors, whereas *lively* is a much more widespread word. But even these figures do not tell the whole story. If we look at Juilland's D for each word, *lively* has a value of 92, *keeper* a value of 87 and *HIV* a value of 56. What does this difference between *lively* (92) and *keeper* (87) tell us? Remember that there was a much smaller difference in terms of how many corpus sectors they occurred in. The dispersion values, in contrast, suggest that, across corpus sectors, *lively* is more evenly distributed whereas *keeper* occurs more in bursts or clumps. Thus, by taking these dispersion values, we are able to avoid the false conclusion that these three words have roughly equivalent currency: in fact, only one is of widespread and general occurrence, with the others much more restricted to particular domains of discourse.

5. Dangers of over-interpretation

In what has gone before, we have already sounded some notes of caution for the user. Whilst we believe that word frequency lists constitute a very valuable resource, we must also warn the user about what can, and cannot, be inferred from them. We should, therefore, list here some potential pitfalls in interpreting the data:

1. As explained in the previous section, users should take account of dispersion values as well as frequencies.
2. Users should be aware that certain orthographic distinctions are maintained in lemmatization—for instance, between *organize* and *organise*. A reader interested in comparing this verb with other verbs will normally want to add the two frequencies for *organise* (56 per million) and *organize* (34 per million) together.
3. A word's frequency in this book is not tied to its context. For example, *York* is a frequent place name—but our lists do not say how many of these references are to *New York* and how many to *York* (England) or even the *Duchess of York*.
4. These are word frequencies, not sense frequencies. We cannot say how many of the tokens under *hard* (Adj) mean 'difficult' and how many mean 'the opposite of soft'. Similarly, we cannot say how many of the references to *heart* are to a body part and how many are metaphorical.
5. If a given form, or combination of form plus part of speech, does not occur in the lists, this does not mean that it does not occur in the BNC at all. For inclusion in the alphabetical List 1.1, for example, there is a minimum frequency of 10 per million for all lemmas. (Hence, for example, *resort* as a noun occurs in the list, but *resort* as a verb does not.) However, this threshold does not apply to individual variants, which are included under a lemma if they occur at least 10 times *in the whole corpus* (that is, 1 in 10 million).
6. It should be recalled that there is some inconsistency in the transcription of speech—for example, in spelling and in the use of numbers.

6. Interest boxes

This book is most likely to be of value as a reference work. However, for convenience and interest, we have also extracted information on groups of words which, we believe, says something useful about how the English language is used in the BNC. As in the lists in general, these frequency findings may be related to the English language in general, or only to British English or indeed to British culture. The reader will find this information in 'interest boxes' placed here and there throughout the main chapters of the book.

Appendix A. The UCREL C6 Tagset

APPGE	possessive pronoun, pre-nominal (e.g. *my, your, our*)
AT	article (e.g. *the, no*)
AT1	singular article (e.g. *a, an, every*)
BCL	before-clause marker (e.g. *in order* (*that*), *in order* (*to*))
CC	coordinating conjunction (e.g. *and, or*)
CCB	adversative coordinating conjunction (*but*)
CS	subordinating conjunction (e.g. *if, because, unless, so, for*)
CSA	*as* (as conjunction)
CSN	*than* (as conjunction)
CST	*that* (as conjunction)
CSW	*whether* (as conjunction)
DA	after-determiner or post-determiner capable of pronominal function (e.g. *such, former, same*)
DA1	singular after-determiner (e.g. *little, much*)
DA2	plural after-determiner (e.g. *few, several, many*)
DAR	comparative after-determiner (e.g. *more, less, fewer*)
DAT	superlative after-determiner (e.g. *most, least, fewest*)
DB	before determiner or pre-determiner capable of pronominal function (*all, half*)
DB2	plural before-determiner (*both*)
DD	determiner (capable of pronominal function) (e.g. *any, some*)
DD1	singular determiner (e.g. *this, that, another*)
DD2	plural determiner (*these, those*)
DDQ	wh-determiner (*which, what*)
DDQGE	wh-determiner, genitive (*whose*)
DDQV	wh-ever determiner, (*whichever, whatever*)
EX	existential *there*
FO	formula
FU	unclassified word
FW	foreign word
GE	Germanic genitive marker - (' or '*s*)
IF	*for* (as preposition)
II	general preposition

IO	*of* (as preposition)
IW	*with, without* (as prepositions)
JJ	general adjective
JJR	general comparative adjective (e.g. *older, better, stronger*)
JJT	general superlative adjective (e.g. *oldest, best, strongest*)
JK	catenative adjective (*able* in *be able to, willing* in *be willing to*)
MC	cardinal number, neutral for number (*two, three, . . .*)
MC1	singular cardinal number (*one*)
MC2	plural cardinal number (e.g. *sixes, sevens*)
MCGE	genitive cardinal number, neutral for number (*two's*, 100's)
MCMC	hyphenated number (40–50, 1770–1827)
MD	ordinal number (e.g. *first, second, next, last*)
MF	fraction, neutral for number (e.g. *quarters, two-thirds*)
ND1	singular noun of direction (e.g. *north, southeast*)
NN	common noun, neutral for number (e.g. *sheep, cod, headquarters*)
NN1	singular common noun (e.g. *book, girl*)
NN2	plural common noun (e.g. *books, girls*)
NNA	following noun of title (e.g. *M.A.*)
NNB	preceding noun of title (e.g. *Mr., Prof.*)
NNL1	singular locative noun (e.g. *Island, Street*)
NNL2	plural locative noun (e.g. *Islands, Streets*)
NNO	numeral noun, neutral for number (e.g. *dozen, hundred*)
NNO2	numeral noun, plural (e.g. *hundreds, thousands*)
NNT1	temporal noun, singular (e.g. *day, week, year*)
NNT2	temporal noun, plural (e.g. *days, weeks, years*)
NNU	unit of measurement, neutral for number (e.g. *in, cc*)
NNU1	singular unit of measurement (e.g. *inch, centimetre*)
NNU2	plural unit of measurement (e.g. *ins., feet*)
NP	proper noun, neutral for number (e.g. *IBM, Andes*)
NP1	singular proper noun (e.g. *London, Jane, Frederick*)
NP2	plural proper noun (e.g. *Browns, Reagans, Koreas*)
NPD1	singular weekday noun (e.g. *Sunday*)
NPD2	plural weekday noun (e.g. *Sundays*)
NPM1	singular month noun (e.g. *October*)
NPM2	plural month noun (e.g. *Octobers*)
PN	indefinite pronoun, neutral for number (*none*)
PN1	indefinite pronoun, singular (e.g. *anyone, everything, nobody, one*)
PNQO	objective wh-pronoun (*whom*)
PNQS	subjective wh-pronoun (*who*)
PNQV	wh-ever pronoun (*whoever*)
PNX1	reflexive indefinite pronoun (*oneself*)
PPGE	nominal possessive personal pronoun (e.g. *mine, yours*)
PPH1	3rd person sing. neuter personal pronoun (*it*)
PPHO1	3rd person sing. objective personal pronoun (*him, her*)

PPHO2	3rd person plural objective personal pronoun (*them*)
PPHS1	3rd person sing. subjective personal pronoun (*he, she*)
PPHS2	3rd person plural subjective personal pronoun (*they*)
PPIO1	1st person sing. objective personal pronoun (*me*)
PPIO2	1st person plural objective personal pronoun (*us*)
PPIS1	1st person sing. subjective personal pronoun (*I*)
PPIS2	1st person plural subjective personal pronoun (*we*)
PPX1	singular reflexive personal pronoun (e.g. *yourself, itself*)
PPX2	plural reflexive personal pronoun (e.g. *yourselves, themselves*)
PPY	2nd person personal pronoun (*you*)
RA	adverb, after nominal head (e.g. *else, galore*)
REX	adverb introducing appositional constructions (*namely, e.g.*)
RG	degree adverb (*very, so, too*)
RGQ	*wh-* degree adverb (*how*)
RGQV	*wh-*ever degree adverb (*however*)
RGR	comparative degree adverb (*more, less*)
RGT	superlative degree adverb (*most, least*)
RL	locative adverb (e.g. *alongside, forward*)
RP	prep. adverb, particle (e.g *about, in*)
RPK	prep. adv., catenative (*about* in *be about to*)
RR	general adverb
RRQ	*wh-* general adverb (*where, when, why, how*)
RRQV	*wh-*ever general adverb (*wherever, whenever*)
RRR	comparative general adverb (e.g. *better, longer*)
RRT	superlative general adverb (e.g. *best, longest*)
RT	quasi-nominal adverb of time (e.g. *now, tomorrow*)
TO	infinitive marker (*to*)
UH	interjection (e.g. *oh, yes, um*)
VB0	*be*, base form (finite i.e. imperative, subjunctive)
VBDR	*were*
VBDZ	*was*
VBG	*being*
VBI	*be*, infinitive (*To be or not . . . It will be . . .*)
VBM	*am*
VBN	*been*
VBR	*are*
VBZ	*is*
VD0	*do*, base form (finite)
VDD	*did*
VDG	*doing*
VDI	*do*, infinitive (*I may do . . . To do . . .*)
VDN	*done*
VDZ	*does*
VH0	*have*, base form (finite)

MERTHYR LOANS

MAXIMUM RENEWAL PERIODS

1 WEEK LOAN 10 WEEKS

4 WEEK LOAN 16 WEEKS

HIGH DEMAND 1 WEEK

PLEASE MONITOR YOUR

EMAILS CAREFULLY FOR

ANY RECALLS ON YOUR

BOOKS, FINES WILL BE

CHARGED FOR LATE RETURNS.

VHD	*had* (past tense)
VHG	*having*
VHI	*have,* infinitive
VHN	*had* (past participle)
VHZ	*has*
VM	modal auxiliary (*can, will, would,* etc.)
VMK	modal catenative (*ought, used*)
VV0	base form of lexical verb (e.g. *give, work*)
VVD	past tense of lexical verb (e.g. *gave, worked*)
VVG	-*ing* participle of lexical verb (e.g. *giving, working*)
VVGK	-*ing* participle catenative (*going* in *be going to*)
VVI	infinitive (e.g. *to give . . . It will work . . .*)
VVN	past participle of lexical verb (e.g. *given, worked*)
VVNK	past participle catenative (e.g. *bound* in *be bound to*)
VVZ	-*s* form of lexical verb (e.g. *gives, works*)
XX	*not, n't*
YEX	punctuation tag—exclamation mark
YQUO	punctuation tag—quotes
YBL	punctuation tag—left bracket
YBR	punctuation tag—right bracket
YCOM	punctuation tag—comma
YDSH	punctuation tag—dash
YSTP	punctuation tag—full-stop
YLIP	punctuation tag—ellipsis
YCOL	punctuation tag—colon
YSCOL	punctuation tag—semicolon
YQUE	punctuation tag—question mark
ZZ1	singular letter of the alphabet (e.g. *A, b*)
ZZ2	plural letter of the alphabet (e.g. *A's, b's*)

References

Andersen G and Stenström A-B 1996 COLT: a progress report. *ICAME Journal* **20**: 133–36.

Aston G and Burnard L 1998 *The BNC Handbook. Exploring the British National Corpus with SARA*. Edinburgh, Edinburgh University Press.

Baker J P 1997 Consistency and accuracy in correcting automatically tagged data. In Garside R, Leech G and McEnery A (eds), pp. 243–50.

Beale A 1987 Towards a distributional lexicon. In Garside R, Leech G, and Sampson G. (eds), *The computational analysis of English: A corpus-based approach*. London, Longman, pp. 149–62.

Beale A 1989 *The development of a distributional lexicon: a contribution to computational lexicography*. Unpublished PhD thesis, Lancaster University.

Berlin B and Kay P 1969 *Basic color terms*. Berkeley, University of California Press.

Burnard L (ed) 1995 *Users reference guide to the British National Corpus. Version 1.0*. Oxford, Oxford University Computing Services.

Crowdy S 1994 Spoken corpus transcription. *Literary and Linguistic Computing* 9(1): 25–8.

Crowdy S 1995 The BNC spoken corpus. In Leech G, Myers G and Thomas J (eds), pp. 224–35.

Dunning T 1993 Accurate methods for the statistics of surprise and coincidence. *Computational Linguistics* 19(1): 61–74.

Fligelstone S 1994 *Jaws: using lemmatization rules and contextual disambiguation rules to enhance Claws output*. Lancaster Database of Linguistic Corpora: Project Report, Linguistics Department, Lancaster University.

Fligelstone S, Rayson P and Smith N 1996 Template analysis: bridging the gap between grammar and the lexicon. In Thomas and Short (eds), pp 181–207.

Garside R and Smith N 1997 A hybrid grammatical tagger: Claws 4. In Garside, Leech and McEnery (eds), pp. 102–21.

Garside R, Leech G and McEnery A (eds) 1997 *Corpus annotation: Linguistic information from computer text corpora*. London, Longman.

Haslerud V and Stenström A-B 1995 The Bergen Corpus of London Teenager Language (COLT). In Leech, Myers and Thomas (eds), pp. 235–42.

Leech G, Myers G and Thomas J (eds), *Spoken English on computer: Transcription, mark-up and application*. London, Longman.

Lyne A 1985 *The vocabulary of French business correspondence*. Geneva, Slatkine.

Rayson P 1996–2000 Lemmings software. Computing Department, Lancaster University.

Thomas J and Short M (eds) 1996 *Using corpora for language research: Studies in the honour of Geoffrey Leech*. Longman, London.

Zipf G 1935 *The psycho-biology of language*. New York, Houghton Mifflin.

Zipf G 1949 *Human behavior and the principle of least effort*. Reading, Addison-Wesley.

List 1.1. Alphabetical frequency list for the whole corpus (lemmatized)

Word = Word type (headword followed by any variant forms)—see pp. 4–5
PoS = Part of speech (grammatical word class)—see pp. 12–13
Freq = Rounded frequency per million word tokens (down to a minimum of 10 occurrences of a lemma per million)—see p. 5
Ra = Range: number of sectors of the corpus (out of a maximum of 100) in which the word occurs
Di = Dispersion value (Juilland's D) from a minimum of 0 to a maximum of 100.

Word	PoS	Freq	Ra	Di	Word	PoS	Freq	Ra	Di	Word	PoS	Freq	Ra	Di
&	Conj	136	97	91	14		80	91	89	33	Num	17	79	91
×	Prep	16	63	75	14		80	91	89	33		17	79	91
'	Gen	479	100	95	14s		0	10	65	34	Num	15	81	91
's	Gen	4599	100	97	15	Num	110	88	90	34		15	81	91
*	Uncl	15	71	77	15		109	88	90	35	Num	25	85	91
0	Num	26	88	85	15s		0	21	73	35		25	85	91
0		26	88	85	16	Num	81	90	90	35s		0	12	70
0s		0	9	61	16		81	90	90	36	Num	17	83	91
000	Num	15	64	74	16s		1	23	62	36		17	83	91
000	.	15	63	74	17	Num	63	91	87	37	Num	14	84	90
01	Num	11	34	12	17		63	91	87	37		14	84	90
1	Num	385	96	90	18	Num	81	92	89	38	Num	15	80	91
1		385	96	90	18		81	91	89	38		15	80	91
1s		1	28	66	18s		0	18	76	39	Num	13	81	90
1st	Ord	13	86	89	18th	Ord	10	79	89	40	Num	58	89	92
2	Num	345	95	90	19	Num	53	90	86	40		57	89	92
2		344	95	90	19		53	90	86	40s		1	47	86
2s		1	27	66	19th	Ord	12	82	89	41	Num	12	79	91
3	Num	251	95	91	20	Num	133	90	91	41		12	79	91
3		250	95	91	20		131	90	91	42	Num	14	85	91
3s		0	20	71	20s		1	46	84	42		14	84	91
4	Num	202	93	92	20%	NoC	11	65	82	42s		0	4	19
4		201	93	92	21	Num	56	89	86	43	Num	12	82	90
4s		0	24	75	21		56	89	86	44	Num	12	82	91
5	Num	176	93	92	21s		0	8	60	44		12	82	91
5		176	93	92	22	Num	53	91	87	45	Num	22	83	91
5s		1	23	67	22		53	91	87	45		22	83	92
6	Num	135	94	92	23	Num	48	88	86	45s		0	11	64
6		134	94	92	23		48	88	86	46	Num	11	80	91
6s		0	16	70	23s		0	8	62	47	Num	11	81	89
7	Num	107	94	91	24	Num	65	85	88	47		11	81	89
7		107	94	91	24		65	85	88	48	Num	15	82	90
7s		0	17	49	25	Num	77	85	89	50	Num	68	87	92
8	Num	97	93	91	25		77	85	89	50		67	87	92
8		97	93	91	25s		0	14	72	50s		1	51	87
8s		0	12	64	26	Num	44	86	84	50%	NoC	11	69	84
9	Num	80	93	90	26		44	86	84	52	Num	10	79	88
9		80	93	90	27	Num	43	88	84	52		10	79	88
9s		0	8	47	27		43	88	84	55	Num	12	80	91
10	Num	187	93	91	28	Num	50	88	85	55		12	80	91
10		186	93	91	28		50	88	85	60	Num	43	85	92
10s		1	35	70	28s		0	7	57	60		41	84	92
10%	NoC	13	69	83	29	Num	40	85	83	60s		2	63	87
11	Num	93	91	89	29		40	85	83	65	Num	17	80	87
11		92	91	89	30	Num	116	88	89	65		17	80	87
11s		0	12	71	30		114	88	89	70	Num	29	83	91
12	Num	121	91	90	30s		1	50	85	70		26	83	91
12		121	91	90	31	Num	51	87	79	70s		2	60	87
12s		0	12	54	31		51	87	79	75	Num	17	82	91
13	Num	76	90	89	32	Num	20	89	89	75		17	82	91
13		76	90	89	32		20	89	89	75s		0	9	60
13s		0	12	69	32s		0	6	43	80	Num	28	85	92

1.1

Word	PoS	Freq	Ra	Di
80		26	85	92
80s		2	48	85
90	Num	25	79	92
90		23	79	92
90s		1	46	83
93	Num	13	76	55
100	Num	69	88	92
100		69	88	92
120	Num	10	78	92
120		10	78	92
150	Num	18	82	92
150		18	82	92
200	Num	35	84	92
200		35	84	92
250	Num	12	82	91
250		12	82	91
300	Num	24	79	91
300		24	79	91
400	Num	17	81	91
400		17	81	91
500	Num	24	85	92
500		23	85	92
500s		0	5	44
600	Num	11	80	91
600		11	80	91
1,000	Num	19	78	90
1914	Num	11	83	82
1920	Num	20	87	89
1920		8	80	86
1920s		11	79	88
1930	Num	25	89	89
1930		8	81	86
1930s		17	83	88
1936	Num	10	80	87
1939	Num	13	86	87
1940	Num	19	89	90
1940		12	86	89
1940s		7	77	89
1944	Num	11	85	89
1945	Num	18	86	89
1946	Num	10	80	89
1947	Num	12	82	88
1948	Num	13	83	88
1949	Num	10	76	86
1950	Num	33	87	90
1950		13	81	89
1950s		20	85	89
1951	Num	10	79	89
1953	Num	10	77	88
1954	Num	10	83	87
1956	Num	11	80	90
1957	Num	12	79	89
1958	Num	11	78	90
1959	Num	12	82	90
1960	Num	45	91	90
1960		15	85	90
1960s		30	87	89
1961	Num	14	81	90
1962	Num	14	81	90
1963	Num	14	79	90
1964	Num	18	86	91
1965	Num	16	83	90
1966	Num	17	83	90
1967	Num	21	83	89
1968	Num	24	82	89
1969	Num	20	85	90
1970	Num	60	86	91
1970		26	84	90
1970s		34	77	90
1971	Num	26	81	89
1972	Num	27	79	89
1973	Num	29	83	90
1974	Num	33	82	91
1975	Num	34	82	90
1976	Num	36	82	89
1977	Num	37	82	90
1978	Num	37	83	90
1979	Num	54	82	90
1980	Num	90	90	91
1980		52	86	91
1980s		38	82	89
1981	Num	56	81	90
1981		56	81	90
1982	Num	52	81	90
1983	Num	57	85	91
1984	Num	58	87	90
1984		58	87	90
1985	Num	74	82	88
1986	Num	79	83	88
1987	Num	85	86	88
1988	Num	103	84	83
1988		103	84	83
1989	Num	134	82	70
1990	Num	160	87	73
1990		150	84	72
1990s		10	78	89
1991	Num	128	75	79
1991		128	75	79
1992	Num	102	79	86
1992		102	79	86
1993	Num	57	73	82
1994	Num	16	63	81
2000	Num	16	78	87
2000		16	78	87
2,000	Num	13	75	89
10,000	Num	12	84	90
£1	NoC	14	77	88
£1.00	NoC	1	22	76
£10	NoC	11	78	89
£100	NoC	13	79	90
£100		13	79	90
£1,000	NoC	10	75	86
£1,000		10	75	86
a	Det	21626	100	99
a		21626	100	99
A / a	Lett	268	100	93
A	NoP	38	91	85
A		10	76	62
A.		28	87	86
a bit	Adv	119	99	87
a great deal	Adv	14	96	95
a little	Adv	104	100	92
a lot	Adv	40	99	93
abandon	Verb	44	99	96
abandon		12	98	94
abandoned		26	97	96
abandoning		5	90	93
abandons		1	47	87
abbey	NoC	20	95	90
abbey		19	95	90
abbeys		1	34	75
Aberdeen	NoP	14	88	80
Aberdeen		14	88	80
ability	NoC	105	100	94
abilities		13	96	91
ability		91	100	94
able	Adj	304	100	97
abolish	Verb	19	92	89
abolish		6	85	88
abolished		11	87	89
abolishes		0	17	68
abolishing		2	67	85
abolition	NoC	12	86	88
abortion	NoC	15	97	86
abortion		12	94	86
abortions		3	58	83
about	Adv	447	100	97
about	Prep	1524	100	96
above	Adj	27	96	89
above	Adv	94	100	93
above	Prep	137	100	96
abroad	Adv	39	100	94
abruptly	Adv	12	88	83
absence	NoC	59	100	93
absence		58	100	93
absences		2	69	88
absent	Adj	15	98	94
absolute	Adj	35	100	95
absolute		35	100	95
absolutely	Adv	58	100	91
absorb	Verb	27	99	94
absorb		8	98	93
absorbed		15	98	93
absorbing		2	78	91
absorbs		2	61	85
abstract	Adj	19	93	86
abuse	NoC	37	98	90
abuse		34	98	90
abuses		3	72	86
abuse	Verb	12	97	92
abuse		2	82	91
abused		7	94	90
abuses		1	35	71
abusing		2	72	90
ac	NoC	16	72	51
a.c.		8	26	12
ac		7	69	68
academic	Adj	47	98	88
academy	NoC	15	95	89
academies		1	37	82
academy		14	95	89
accelerate	Verb	11	95	92
accelerate		4	84	89
accelerated		4	88	92
accelerates		1	40	80
accelerating		1	64	86
accent	NoC	19	96	93
accent		14	95	92
accents		4	89	89
accept	Verb	202	100	96
accept		98	100	94
accepted		79	100	96
accepting		17	98	95
accepts		8	90	92
acceptable	Adj	36	99	94
acceptance	NoC	27	97	92
acceptance		27	97	92
acceptances		1	19	64

Word	PoS	Freq	Ra	Di
accepted	Adj	10	97	93
access	NoC	100	100	92
access		100	100	92
accesses		0	7	25
access	Verb	15	93	78
access		9	88	79
accessed		4	59	72
accesses		0	21	72
accessing		2	45	81
accessible	Adj	16	96	88
accident	NoC	84	100	92
accident		64	100	91
accidents		20	99	89
accommodate	Verb	21	98	94
accommodate		14	97	94
accommodated		5	82	91
accommodates		1	41	84
accommodating		2	78	91
accommodation	NoC	44	100	92
accommodation		44	100	92
accommodations		0	26	75
accompany	Verb	48	98	96
accompanied		33	96	95
accompanies		2	71	89
accompany		9	95	94
accompanying		4	91	93
accord	Verb	10	96	91
accord		3	76	89
accorded		5	84	90
according		1	52	88
accords		2	63	88
according to	Prep	157	100	92
accordingly	Adv	23	100	86
account	NoC	200	100	93
account		135	100	93
accounts		65	100	88
account	Verb	58	100	91
account		24	99	92
accounted		14	97	91
accounting		12	78	79
accounts		8	93	91
accountability	NoC	12	77	84
accountabilities		0	9	61
accountability		12	77	84
accountant	NoC	22	100	82
accountant		10	98	87
accountants		12	89	77
accounting	NoC	25	92	75
accumulate	Verb	12	97	92
accumulate		4	86	90
accumulated		5	93	91
accumulates		1	38	81
accumulating		2	67	90
accuracy	NoC	17	98	92
accuracy		17	98	92
accurate	Adj	29	100	95
accurately	Adv	14	99	93
accusation	NoC	12	96	91
accusation		4	88	91
accusations		7	96	88
accuse	Verb	48	100	87
accuse		4	89	92
accused		38	99	86
accuses		1	55	85
accusing		5	90	87
accused	Adj	11	82	49
ace	NoC	13	77	69
ace		11	72	65
aces		1	43	82
achieve	Verb	169	100	94
achieve		68	99	94
achieved		79	100	94
achieves		3	74	91
achieving		18	97	93
achievement	NoC	46	98	93
achievement		31	98	92
achievements		15	96	93
acid	NoC	59	100	71
acid		49	100	70
acids		10	68	72
acknowledge	Verb	43	98	95
acknowledge		15	97	94
acknowledged		19	97	94
acknowledges		5	82	91
acknowledging		4	91	93
acquire	Verb	68	99	92
acquire		20	95	91
acquired		37	99	93
acquires		2	63	85
acquiring		8	93	89
acquisition	NoC	33	95	86
acquisition		26	93	85
acquisitions		7	82	86
acre	NoC	22	99	92
acre		6	88	90
acres		16	98	91
across	Adv	35	99	90
across	Prep	217	100	95
act	NoC	248	100	88
act		215	100	91
acts		32	100	92
act	Verb	137	100	94
act		59	100	94
acted		23	99	94
acting		41	100	93
acts		14	98	92
action	NoC	269	100	94
action		221	100	94
actions		48	100	93
activate	Verb	14	97	72
activate		3	65	74
activated		6	90	80
activates		1	42	82
activating		4	40	29
active	Adj	73	100	91
actively	Adv	15	96	93
activist	NoC	13	89	87
activist		3	77	88
activists		10	79	86
activity	NoC	231	100	92
activities		116	99	93
activity		115	100	90
actor	NoC	36	99	91
actor		20	98	90
actors		16	95	90
actress	NoC	13	91	88
actress		11	86	87
actresses		2	66	86
actual	Adj	68	100	93
actually	Adv	260	100	86
acute	Adj	23	95	84
acute		23	95	84
AD	Adv	11	84	85
A.D.		3	29	57
AD		9	83	85
AD.		0	7	53
ad	NoC	15	98	85
ad		9	96	87
ads		6	79	81
Adam	NoP	35	100	78
adapt	Verb	28	100	93
adapt		10	99	93
adapted		14	94	92
adapting		3	78	91
adapts		1	40	85
adaptation	NoC	11	87	88
adaptation		8	85	88
adaptations		4	68	83
add	Verb	275	100	96
add		82	100	93
added		139	100	94
adding		32	100	94
adds		22	97	91
added	Adj	15	98	94
addition	NoC	28	98	91
addition		21	98	92
additions		7	87	82
additional	Adj	74	98	93
address	NoC	60	100	94
address		51	100	94
addresses		9	97	91
address	Verb	62	100	95
address		20	98	93
addressed		27	99	95
addresses		4	82	91
addressing		11	99	93
adequate	Adj	36	98	93
adequately	Adv	11	97	93
adjacent	Adj	11	91	91
adjective	NoC	10	82	46
adjective		5	65	39
adjectives		5	67	52
adjust	Verb	28	100	94
adjust		11	100	93
adjusted		11	98	93
adjusting		5	93	93
adjusts		1	42	84
adjustment	NoC	21	97	91
adjustment		14	94	89
adjustments		7	90	91
administer	Verb	19	96	93
administer		5	94	92
administered		10	94	91
administering		3	85	91
administers		1	42	86
administration	NoC	69	99	89
administration		66	99	89
administrations		2	65	86
administrative	Adj	35	98	90
administrator	NoC	15	95	91
administrator		7	88	89
administrators		8	87	89
admire	Verb	22	99	93
admire		8	93	93
admired		11	98	92
admires		1	52	86
admiring		2	54	85
admission	NoC	29	99	90

1.1

Word	PoS	Freq	Ra	Di	Word	PoS	Freq	Ra	Di	Word	PoS	Freq	Ra	Di
admission		23	97	90	*affecting*		17	99	93	ai~*	Verb	36	88	71
admissions		6	82	85	*affects*		14	92	93	aid	NoC	91	100	90
admit	Verb	112	100	94	affection	NoC	16	99	93	*aid*		78	100	89
admit		38	100	94	*affection*		14	99	93	*aids*		13	91	89
admits		13	94	89	*affections*		2	75	90	aid	Verb	16	97	94
admitted		56	100	91	afford	Verb	54	100	96	*aid*		8	95	93
admitting		5	96	93	*afford*		45	100	95	*aided*		6	90	93
adopt	Verb	87	100	93	*afforded*		6	96	93	*aiding*		2	67	90
adopt		25	99	93	*affording*		1	53	86	*aids*		0	33	83
adopted		51	99	91	*affords*		2	64	87	AIDS	NoC	19	87	80
adopting		8	95	92	afraid	Adj	60	100	88	*AIDS*		19	87	80
adopts		3	75	89	Africa	NoP	78	100	88	aim	NoC	75	100	92
adoption	NoC	16	90	88	*Africa*		78	100	88	*aim*		50	100	92
adoption		16	90	88	African	Adj	43	99	88	*aims*		25	91	91
adoptions		0	10	61	after	Conj	233	100	96	aim	Verb	77	100	92
adult	NoC	79	100	93	after	Prep	927	100	96	*aim*		14	100	94
adult		45	100	91	afternoon	NoC	89	100	93	*aimed*		36	99	92
adults		33	99	93	*afternoon*		84	100	93	*aiming*		10	99	94
advance	NoC	48	100	93	*afternoons*		5	87	91	*aims*		17	82	80
advance		36	100	91	afterwards	Adv	46	100	96	air	NoC	191	100	95
advances		12	95	92	again	Adv	561	100	94	*air*		189	100	95
advance	Verb	30	100	94	against	Prep	562	100	96	*airs*		1	50	82
advance		8	97	93	age	NoC	252	100	94	aircraft	NoC	62	99	84
advanced		17	98	94	*age*		216	100	94	*aircraft*		62	99	84
advances		2	76	90	*ages*		36	99	94	airline	NoC	20	97	87
advancing		3	80	91	age	Verb	21	99	90	*airline*		11	92	86
advanced	Adj	33	98	88	*age*		3	83	90	*airlines*		9	84	85
advantage	NoC	103	100	95	*aged*		14	99	89	airport	NoC	33	99	93
advantage		73	100	95	*ageing*		3	64	80	*airport*		29	99	92
advantages		29	98	93	*ages*		1	38	79	*airports*		4	77	90
adventure	NoC	20	96	90	*aging*		0	9	60	Al	NoP	10	95	82
adventure		15	95	89	aged	Prep	27	99	87	*Al*		10	94	82
adventures		5	89	92	agency	NoC	96	100	91	Alan	NoP	52	98	89
adverse	Adj	12	89	90	*agencies*		37	96	90	*Alan*		52	98	89
advertise	Verb	16	100	94	*agency*		59	100	90	*Alans*		0	4	18
advertise		5	98	92	agenda	NoC	25	99	92	alarm	NoC	25	100	94
advertised		7	97	94	*agenda*		24	99	91	*alarm*		21	100	94
advertises		0	31	83	*agendas*		2	54	86	*alarms*		4	86	87
advertising		3	87	91	agent	NoC	81	100	95	albeit	Conj	14	93	94
advertisement	NoC	22	100	89	*agent*		43	100	94	Albert	NoP	22	96	88
advertisement		12	97	88	*agents*		37	100	94	*Albert*		22	96	88
advertisements		10	96	89	aggregate	Adj	11	70	63	album	NoC	26	93	79
advertising	NoC	41	99	88	aggression	NoC	13	95	86	*album*		22	92	78
advice	NoC	104	100	93	*aggression*		13	95	86	*albums*		5	68	80
advice		104	100	93	*aggressions*		0	11	71	alcohol	NoC	31	99	89
advise	Verb	54	100	95	aggressive	Adj	19	99	92	*alcohol*		30	99	89
advise		20	99	93	ago	Adv	198	100	94	*alcohols*		0	15	65
advised		25	100	96	agony	NoC	10	97	90	alert	Verb	12	98	93
advises		3	72	90	*agonies*		1	47	86	*alert*		6	95	92
advising		6	92	92	*agony*		10	95	89	*alerted*		5	93	91
adviser	NoC	33	98	90	agree	Verb	236	100	93	*alerting*		1	55	88
adviser		15	96	90	*agree*		82	100	88	*alerts*		0	22	78
advisers		18	94	88	*agreed*		136	100	91	Alex	NoP	19	88	85
advisory	Adj	16	88	90	*agreeing*		8	100	94	Alexander	NoP	26	98	88
advocate	Verb	17	92	91	*agrees*		9	98	88	*Alexander*		26	98	88
advocate		3	82	91	agreed	Adj	10	94	91	Alfred	NoP	12	90	85
advocated		9	79	89	agreement	NoC	160	100	85	*Alfred*		12	90	85
advocates		2	58	86	*agreement*		133	100	84	Ali	NoP	13	81	76
advocating		3	77	90	*agreements*		27	87	85	*Ali*		13	81	76
aesthetic	Adj	12	86	83	agricultural	Adj	41	97	89	Alice	NoP	25	97	73
affair	NoC	106	100	87	agriculture	NoC	39	93	85	*Alice*		25	97	73
affair		33	100	93	*agriculture*		39	93	85	alike	Adv	12	97	94
affairs		73	100	83	ah	Int	99	94	71	Alison	NoP	14	88	83
affect	Verb	133	100	95	aha	Int	26	51	65	*Alison*		14	88	83
affect		48	100	94	ahead	Adv	63	100	95	alive	Adj	43	100	93
affected		54	100	94	ahead of	Prep	26	100	94	all	Adv	193	100	96

Word	PoS	Freq	Ra	Di	Word	PoS	Freq	Ra	Di	Word	PoS	Freq	Ra	Di
all	DetP	2436	100	98	although	Conj	436	100	96	*analysis*		132	99	89
all right*	Adv	64	97	84	altogether	Adv	32	100	96	analyst	NoC	19	91	87
Allan	NoP	10	81	87	aluminium	NoC	10	97	88	*analyst*		8	82	84
allegation	NoC	21	92	83	always	Adv	462	100	96	*analysts*		11	82	86
allegation		4	76	85	am	Adv	21	90	92	ANC	NoP	10	36	63
allegations		18	90	82	*a.m*		3	67	87	*ANC*		10	36	63
allege	Verb	19	92	86	a.m.		7	85	90	ancestor	NoC	13	93	91
allege		1	51	84	*am*		10	88	89	*ancestor*		4	82	89
alleged		13	91	85	amateur	Adj	12	96	90	*ancestors*		9	92	91
alleges		2	46	83	amazing	Adj	19	98	93	ancient	Adj	50	99	93
alleging		3	67	83	ambassador	NoC	14	90	84	and	Conj	26817	100	99
alleged	Adj	18	93	85	*ambassador*		11	88	84	and/or	Conj	19	80	90
allegedly	Adv	10	85	86	*ambassadors*		3	70	80	and so on	Adv	49	99	92
Allen	NoP	18	90	83	ambiguity	NoC	11	90	88	Anderson	NoP	15	90	86
Allen		18	90	83	*ambiguities*		2	61	85	*Anderson*		15	90	86
alliance	NoC	37	98	87	*ambiguity*		9	87	87	Andrew	NoP	45	99	89
alliance		31	97	86	ambition	NoC	23	100	94	Andy	NoP	28	87	86
alliances		6	79	85	*ambition*		13	100	94	*Andy*		28	87	86
allied	Adj	14	92	84	*ambitions*		10	98	93	angel	NoC	22	99	88
allocate	Verb	25	98	91	ambitious	Adj	15	98	94	*angel*		14	95	82
allocate		5	81	90	ambulance	NoC	18	96	85	*angels*		8	93	91
allocated		17	97	90	*ambulance*		17	96	85	Angela	NoP	11	90	84
allocates		1	33	81	*ambulances*		1	55	85	Angeles	NoP-	11	91	88
allocating		3	73	90	amend	Verb	14	94	86	anger	NoC	34	99	89
allocation	NoC	23	87	89	*amend*		4	78	87	*anger*		33	99	89
allocation		18	86	89	*amended*		9	90	85	*angers*		0	20	74
allocations		5	63	84	*amending*		1	48	82	angle	NoC	37	99	91
allow	Verb	342	100	95	*amends*		0	15	73	*angle*		24	99	91
allow		115	100	96	amendment	NoC	28	87	82	*angles*		13	96	87
allowed		143	100	90	*amendment*		18	81	80	angrily	Adv	11	84	83
allowing		43	100	95	*amendments*		10	83	84	angry	Adj	43	100	89
allows		41	100	91	America	NoP	103	100	90	*angrier*		1	31	81
allowance	NoC	34	100	89	*America*		103	100	90	*angry*		42	100	89
allowance		22	100	90	*Americas*		0	7	56	animal	NoC	153	100	90
allowances		13	93	86	American	Adj	157	100	92	*animal*		67	100	91
ally	NoC	24	98	91	American	NoC	35	100	90	*animals*		86	100	89
allies		16	94	89	*American*		7	94	90	ankle	NoC	15	93	88
ally		8	94	92	*Americans*		28	100	89	*ankle*		10	88	85
almost	Adv	316	100	96	amid	Prep	11	92	89	*ankles*		5	83	88
alone	Adj	54	100	92	amnesty	NoC	11	62	68	Ann	NoP	20	94	81
alone		54	100	92	*amnesties*		0	8	57	*Ann*		19	94	81
alone	Adv	74	100	96	*amnesty*		11	60	68	*Anns*		0	4	36
along	Adv	70	100	94	among	Prep	229	100	95	Anna	NoP	28	90	77
along	Prep	123	100	95	amongst	Prep	45	100	94	*Anna*		28	90	77
along with	Prep	51	100	96	amount	NoC	171	100	88	Anne	NoP	44	99	81
alongside	Prep	29	100	95	*amount*		146	100	87	*Anne*		44	99	81
alpha	NoC	11	78	59	*amounts*		25	100	92	Annie	NoP	11	81	81
alpha		11	78	60	amount	Verb	27	99	91	anniversary	NoC	21	96	89
alphas		0	7	47	*amount*		8	92	89	*anniversaries*		1	45	84
already	Adv	343	100	98	*amounted*		10	94	87	*anniversary*		21	96	89
alright*	Adj	40	73	63	*amounting*		4	84	87	announce	Verb	127	100	82
alright*	Adv	43	48	65	*amounts*		6	89	90	*announce*		11	98	86
also	Adv	1248	100	95	amusement	NoC	11	94	85	*announced*		105	99	80
alter	Verb	42	100	95	*amusement*		10	92	85	*announces*		3	72	88
alter		19	100	94	*amusements*		1	38	83	*announcing*		8	94	89
altered		16	100	94	an	Det	3430	100	97	announcement	NoC	28	100	86
altering		5	93	94	analogy	NoC	11	91	89	*announcement*		24	99	85
alters		2	74	90	*analogies*		2	56	84	*announcements*		4	80	84
alteration	NoC	15	96	92	*analogy*		9	88	89	annual	Adj	81	100	93
alteration		7	88	88	analyse	Verb	42	96	89	annually	Adv	11	88	91
alterations		8	93	92	*analyse*		13	96	89	anonymous	Adj	12	99	86
alternative	Adj	51	99	93	*analysed*		18	89	86	another	DetP	581	100	98
alternative	NoC	53	100	95	*analyses*		2	64	87	answer	NoC	124	100	96
alternative		36	100	95	*analysing*		9	87	89	*answer*		92	100	95
alternatives		17	98	93	analysis	NoC	143	100	89	*answers*		32	99	94
alternatively	Adv	17	92	91	*analyses*		11	79	86	answer	Verb	103	100	93

Word	PoS	Freq	Ra	Di	Word	PoS	Freq	Ra	Di	Word	PoS	Freq	Ra	Di
answer		52	100	93	apparatus	NoC	11	96	88	appointed		61	100	87
answered		38	100	89	apparent	Adj	53	98	94	appointing		4	80	88
answering		8	100	94	apparently	Adv	78	100	96	appoints		2	45	65
answers		5	91	93	appeal	NoC	106	100	83	appointment	NoC	60	100	91
ant	NoC	10	82	81	*appeal*		91	100	82	*appointment*		45	100	91
ant		4	65	73	*appeals*		15	95	88	*appointments*		15	98	90
ants		6	72	81	appeal	Verb	40	100	91	appraisal	NoC	12	96	89
Anthony	NoP	24	98	90	*appeal*		19	100	89	*appraisal*		11	96	89
Anthony		24	98	90	*appealed*		14	94	89	*appraisals*		1	48	85
antibody	NoC	16	47	65	*appealing*		6	93	89	appreciate	Verb	45	100	96
antibodies		8	43	67	*appeals*		2	70	89	*appreciate*		26	100	95
antibody		8	28	62	appear	Verb	307	100	96	*appreciated*		15	100	94
anticipate	Verb	24	99	95	*appear*		109	100	95	*appreciates*		1	59	89
anticipate		7	95	93	*appeared*		107	100	95	*appreciating*		2	73	91
anticipated		11	99	94	*appearing*		14	99	95	appreciation	NoC	13	98	95
anticipates		1	56	84	*appears*		77	100	94	*appreciation*		13	98	95
anticipating		4	91	93	appearance	NoC	66	100	94	approach	NoC	171	100	92
anxiety	NoC	32	98	90	*appearance*		54	100	95	*approach*		145	100	93
anxieties		5	91	91	*appearances*		12	95	82	*approaches*		26	93	90
anxiety		27	98	89	appendix	NoC	19	90	82	approach	Verb	70	100	97
anxious	Adj	31	100	95	*appendices*		1	46	85	*approach*		17	100	96
any	Adv	20	100	93	*appendix*		18	90	82	*approached*		29	100	95
any	DetP	1220	100	96	appetite	NoC	11	95	93	*approaches*		6	90	92
anybody	Pron	50	100	85	*appetite*		9	95	92	*approaching*		17	100	96
anyone	Pron	150	100	85	*appetites*		2	69	89	appropriate	Adj	113	100	92
anything	Pron	288	100	93	apple	NoC	35	99	85	approval	NoC	40	98	87
anyway	Adv	122	100	86	*apple*		27	99	81	*approval*		39	98	87
anywhere	Adv	41	100	95	*apples*		9	94	89	*approvals*		1	46	73
apart	Adv	35	100	95	applicable	Adj	14	87	87	approve	Verb	53	100	84
apart from	Prep	65	100	97	applicant	NoC	24	91	80	*approve*		11	99	92
apartment	NoC	19	96	85	*applicant*		12	82	73	*approved*		39	100	81
apartment		13	94	87	*applicants*		12	87	83	*approves*		1	63	89
apartments		6	85	74	application	NoC	163	100	85	*approving*		2	72	86
apologise	Verb	11	96	89	*application*		100	100	88	approximately	Adv	28	96	91
apologise		6	89	87	*applications*		63	91	77	April	NoP	147	100	84
apologised		4	79	88	apply	Verb	193	100	92	*April*		147	100	84
apologises		0	29	81	*applied*		66	100	93	Arab	Adj	22	86	71
apologising		1	52	86	*applies*		28	97	87	arbitrary	Adj	11	94	89
apology	NoC	12	99	92	*apply*		79	100	90	arch	NoC	13	95	87
apologies		5	89	89	*applying*		20	100	93	*arch*		8	87	88
apology		7	96	90	appoint	Verb	76	100	88	*arches*		5	84	83
appalling	Adj	11	99	92	*appoint*		10	93	90	archbishop	NoC	17	92	83
										archbishop		16	91	83
										archbishops		1	42	73
										architect	NoC	27	99	86
										architect		16	98	87
										architects		11	92	83
										architectural	Adj	12	92	86
										architecture	NoC	30	98	81
										architecture		28	98	82
										architectures		2	19	41
										archive	NoC	13	92	82
										archive		6	81	80
										archives		7	86	81
										area	NoC	585	100	93
										area		351	100	92
										areas		234	100	93
										argue	Verb	149	100	93
										argue		43	99	94
										argued		65	98	92
										argues		23	86	89
										arguing		18	100	95
										argument	NoC	122	100	92
										argument		83	100	92
										arguments		38	100	93
										arise	Verb	96	99	91

A selection of antonyms

Adjectives are often paired with another adjective as antonyms. The most common combination of antonyms is *new* (1154 per million) and *old* (648 per million), but in this case there is also a third term, *young* (379 per million) which contrasts with *old* when referring to living beings. Other common pairs of antonyms are (frequencies per million words):

good	1276	*bad*	264	One member of the pair tends to have a
high	574	*low*	286	'positive' or 'favourable' meaning, and
large	471	*small*	518	this is the word which is normally the
early	353	*late*	302	more frequent (as *good* and *bad* show
long	392	*short*	177	very clearly). Where this rule is broken,
big	338	*little*	306	there is often a good reason: for example,
full	289	*empty*	54	*large* is less frequent than *small*, but this
public	285	*private*	173	may be because *small* also has a second
major	238	*minor*	47	antonym: *great* (635).
easy	198	*difficult*	220	
strong	197	*weak*	45	
true	183	*false*	36	
hot	94	*cold*	103	

Word	PoS	Freq	Ra	Di	Word	PoS	Freq	Ra	Di	Word	PoS	Freq	Ra	Di
arise		33	98	90	artificial	Adj	20	100	93	*assessing*		14	99	92
arisen		7	95	91	artist	NoC	81	100	84	assessment	NoC	78	100	90
arises		18	88	89	*artist*		41	99	84	*assessment*		67	100	89
arising		22	90	88	*artists*		40	99	84	*assessments*		11	83	87
arose		16	97	92	artistic	Adj	16	97	90	asset	NoC	64	98	87
arm	NoC	202	100	90	as	Adv	567	100	98	*asset*		20	97	87
arm		91	100	89	as	Conj	3006	100	98	*assets*		43	98	86
arms		110	100	91	as	Prep	1774	100	96	assign	Verb	18	93	88
arm	Verb	12	97	90	as for	Prep	25	100	95	*assign*		4	67	83
arm		0	37	84	as if	Conj	157	100	88	*assigned*		12	91	89
armed		11	96	89	as it were	Adv	10	94	82	*assigning*		2	56	86
arming		0	32	83	as long as	Conj	29	100	95	*assigns*		1	41	81
arms		0	9	64	as opposed to	Prep	17	97	93	assignment	NoC	18	99	84
armed	Adj	37	98	75	as soon as	Conj	45	100	93	*assignment*		12	97	81
army	NoC	124	100	90	as though	Conj	54	99	88	*assignments*		6	80	83
armies		10	92	85	as to	Prep	73	100	90	assist	Verb	41	100	93
army		114	100	90	as usual	Adv	13	100	92	*assist*		25	98	92
Arnold	NoP	10	94	89	as well	Adv	113	100	87	*assisted*		10	97	92
Arnold		10	94	89	*as well*		113	100	87	*assisting*		5	90	90
around	Adv	215	100	96	as well as	Prep	176	100	95	*assists*		2	63	88
around	Prep	237	100	96	as yet	Adv	14	100	95	assistance	NoC	43	99	91
arouse	Verb	14	96	94	ash	NoC	13	98	90	*assistance*		43	99	91
arouse		3	87	92	*ash*		8	98	87	assistant	Adj	18	97	91
aroused		9	95	94	*ashes*		5	88	91	assistant	NoC	27	100	92
arouses		1	36	84	ashamed	Adj	11	97	89	*assistant*		20	100	92
arousing		1	61	87	Ashley	NoP	11	80	54	*assistants*		7	96	89
arrange	Verb	72	100	96	*Ashley*		11	80	53	associate	NoC	12	98	92
arrange		23	100	95	*Ashleys*		1	3	04	*associate*		3	87	89
arranged		40	100	96	Asia	NoP	30	96	80	*associates*		8	97	91
arranges		1	56	87	Asian	Adj	19	94	87	associate	Verb	81	100	90
arranging		8	98	95	aside	Adv	36	100	93	*associate*		5	96	93
arrangement	NoC	91	100	94	ask	Verb	610	100	94	*associated*		73	98	90
arrangement		33	100	93	*ask*		194	100	93	*associates*		1	53	76
arrangements		58	100	93	*asked*		334	100	92	*associating*		1	58	87
array	NoC	13	95	89	*asking*		63	100	95	associated	Adj	19	87	89
array		11	95	90	*asks*		20	100	92	association	NoC	135	100	93
arrays		1	34	75	asleep	Adj	25	97	88	*association*		115	100	93
arrest	NoC	22	98	84	aspect	NoC	116	100	93	*associations*		20	91	90
arrest		16	96	84	*aspect*		43	99	94	assume	Verb	112	100	94
arrests		6	75	80	*aspects*		73	100	92	*assume*		41	100	94
arrest	Verb	42	99	87	aspiration	NoC	13	95	92	*assumed*		42	100	94
arrest		6	94	92	*aspiration*		3	74	83	*assumes*		10	87	91
arrested		35	99	85	*aspirations*		10	93	92	*assuming*		19	99	94
arresting		2	70	89	assault	NoC	26	98	89	assumption	NoC	56	97	91
arrests		0	12	71	*assault*		22	98	89	*assumption*		31	97	91
arrival	NoC	38	100	95	*assaults*		4	84	87	*assumptions*		25	93	90
arrival		34	99	95	assemble	Verb	17	99	94	assurance	NoC	24	97	89
arrivals		4	87	89	*assemble*		4	96	92	*assurance*		18	97	88
arrive	Verb	142	100	96	*assembled*		10	97	94	*assurances*		5	84	86
arrive		29	100	96	*assembles*		0	33	83	assure	Verb	31	100	93
arrived		88	100	94	*assembling*		2	83	92	*assure*		10	98	85
arrives		9	100	94	assembly	NoC	59	100	75	*assured*		18	98	93
arriving		16	100	95	*assemblies*		5	69	83	*assures*		1	62	90
arrow	NoC	16	98	90	*assembly*		54	100	73	*assuring*		1	72	90
arrow		10	97	88	assert	Verb	21	96	92	asylum	NoC	10	88	80
arrows		6	88	90	*assert*		7	89	91	*asylum*		9	83	78
Arsenal	NoP	12	54	73	*asserted*		7	89	90	*asylums*		1	36	68
art	NoC	206	100	86	*asserting*		3	78	90	at	Prep	4790	100	98
art		153	100	83	*asserts*		3	69	89	at all	Adv	148	100	94
arts		53	100	88	assertion	NoC	11	92	91	at first	Adv	41	99	94
Arthur	NoP	29	99	91	*assertion*		8	90	91	at last	Adv	44	100	89
Arthur		28	99	91	*assertions*		3	72	89	at least	Adv	257	100	98
Arthurs		0	5	47	assess	Verb	64	100	90	at once	Adv	36	100	90
article	NoC	97	100	91	*assess*		27	99	90	at present	Adv	29	98	93
article		68	100	90	*assessed*		22	97	86	Athens	NoP	11	78	71
articles		29	99	91	*assesses*		1	55	82	Atlantic	NoP	22	99	91

Word	PoS	Freq	Ra	Di
atmosphere	NoC	49	100	93
atmosphere		49	100	93
atmospheres		1	34	75
atom	NoC	16	86	79
atom		6	76	80
atoms		11	72	78
atomic	Adj	11	87	84
attach	Verb	49	100	95
attach		8	98	91
attached		36	100	96
attaches		2	66	88
attaching		3	79	87
attack	NoC	109	100	91
attack		77	100	92
attacks		31	98	88
attack	Verb	59	100	93
attack		18	99	92
attacked		29	98	92
attacking		10	98	93
attacks		3	77	89
attain	Verb	12	95	91
attain		5	86	90
attained		5	87	91
attaining		2	60	85
attains		1	32	83
attempt	NoC	135	100	94
attempt		89	100	94
attempts		47	100	94
attempt	Verb	82	100	95
attempt		26	99	94
attempted		27	99	94
attempting		24	97	95
attempts		5	86	92
attend	Verb	91	99	94
attend		36	99	95
attended		35	99	92
attending		18	98	94
attends		2	77	83
attendance	NoC	20	100	92
attendance		18	100	92
attendances		2	56	86
attention	NoC	140	100	96
attention		137	100	96
attentions		3	82	91
attitude	NoC	108	100	94
attitude		60	100	95
attitudes		48	98	90
attract	Verb	64	100	95
attract		25	99	94
attracted		28	99	95
attracting		6	93	93
attracts		5	93	91
attraction	NoC	24	99	94
attraction		15	99	94
attractions		9	95	91
attractive	Adj	52	100	95
attribute	NoC	13	92	83
attribute		4	69	77
attributes		9	88	85
attribute	Verb	23	95	92
attribute		4	78	89
attributed		16	92	91
attributes		2	67	88
attributing		1	55	87
auction	NoC	15	95	85
auction		13	93	85

Word	PoS	Freq	Ra	Di
auctions		2	60	86
audience	NoC	65	100	94
audience		55	100	94
audiences		10	90	90
audit	NoC	24	80	76
audit		22	79	76
audits		2	43	78
auditor	NoC	18	73	71
auditor		6	61	73
auditors		12	69	68
Aug	NoP	29	42	49
Aug		3	35	66
Aug.		26	15	43
August	NoP	79	100	90
aunt	NoC	33	94	81
aunt		31	91	80
aunts		2	71	86
Australia	NoP	50	100	92
Australia		50	100	92
Australian	Adj	24	98	90
Austria	NoP	13	93	86
author	NoC	69	99	92
author		43	99	92
authors		25	91	89
authority	NoC	313	100	92
authorities		130	100	91
authority		183	100	91
automatic	Adj	23	100	94
automatically	Adv	28	100	93
autonomous	Adj	11	75	85
autonomy	NoC	18	83	86
autonomy		18	83	86
autumn	NoC	39	99	94
autumn		39	99	94
availability	NoC	19	90	90
availability		19	90	90
available	Adj	272	100	93
avenue	NoC	19	100	89
avenue		16	99	87
avenues		3	86	92
average	Adj	62	100	93
average		62	100	93
average	NoC	39	98	93
average		36	97	93
averages		3	79	88
avoid	Verb	121	100	96
avoid		80	100	96
avoided		22	97	95
avoiding		14	98	95
avoids		4	79	90
await	Verb	21	99	95
await		5	92	94
awaited		5	90	93
awaiting		9	98	94
awaits		2	75	91
awake	Adj	13	94	87
award	NoC	170	99	37
award		148	98	28
awards		23	87	84
award	Verb	31	95	91
award		4	76	87
awarded		25	95	90
awarding		2	63	84
awards		1	41	83
aware	Adj	108	100	93
awareness	NoC	36	97	91

Word	PoS	Freq	Ra	Di
awareness		36	97	91
away	Adv	371	100	92
away from	Prep	120	100	94
awful	Adj	31	98	90
awkward	Adj	16	99	94
axis	NoC	14	87	86
axis		10	87	86
axes		4	79	85
aye	Int	52	64	67
B / b	Lett	179	100	91
B	NoP	26	90	88
B		7	72	77
B.		19	89	85
baby	NoC	115	100	93
babies		25	100	93
baby		91	100	92
back	Adj	19	98	92
back	Adv	793	100	93
back	NoC	212	100	93
back		200	100	93
backs		12	98	93
back	Verb	46	100	94
back		11	99	94
backed		25	100	94
backing		8	99	92
backs		3	76	88
background	NoC	69	100	95
background		62	100	95
backgrounds		8	92	91
backing	NoC	12	96	92
backing		12	96	92
backings		0	6	42
backwards	Adv	18	99	92
bacterium	NoC	14	80	82
bacteria		13	80	82
bacterium		1	31	73
bad	Adj	264	100	95
bad		153	100	94
worse		65	100	94
worst		46	100	95
badly	Adv	43	100	95
bag	NoC	75	99	91
bag		53	98	90
bags		22	98	93
Baker	NoP	20	93	86
balance	NoC	85	100	93
balance		81	100	93
balances		5	70	77
balance	Verb	23	100	96
balance		8	99	94
balanced		9	99	95
balances		2	62	85
balancing		4	97	94
balanced	Adj	11	94	93
balcony	NoC	11	91	80
balconies		2	53	74
balcony		10	87	79
ball	NoC	89	100	92
ball		74	99	91
balls		15	95	93
ballet	NoC	15	89	70
ballet		12	88	74
ballets		2	22	41
balloon	NoC	10	95	89
balloon		6	93	86
balloons		4	81	89

Word	PoS	Freq	Ra	Di	Word	PoS	Freq	Ra	Di	Word	PoS	Freq	Ra	Di
ballot	NoC	11	85	87	basic	Adj	109	100	93	bear	Verb	93	100	96
ballot		10	81	87	basically	Adv	31	100	86	*bear*		46	100	96
ballots		1	36	78	basin	NoC	15	96	84	*bearing*		22	100	96
ban	NoC	26	94	84	*basin*		12	95	85	*bears*		7	91	93
ban		24	93	84	*basins*		3	60	75	*bore*		7	96	92
bans		2	53	82	basis	NoC	148	100	93	*borne*		11	96	93
ban	Verb	28	100	87	*basis*		145	100	93	bearing	NoC	11	99	86
ban		7	87	87	*bases*		3	80	88	*bearing*		7	98	87
banned		16	99	87	basket	NoC	18	98	92	*bearings*		4	82	81
banning		3	77	85	*basket*		13	96	91	beast	NoC	14	98	90
bans		1	36	77	*baskets*		5	88	91	*beast*		9	95	88
band	NoC	88	100	87	bass	NoC	10	74	62	*beasts*		4	86	89
band		67	100	86	*bass*		9	73	62	beat	NoC	14	95	89
bands		20	100	86	*basses*		1	15	57	*beat*		11	90	87
bang	Verb	14	95	90	bastard	NoC	19	89	84	*beats*		3	64	83
bang		5	82	88	*bastard*		14	83	84	beat	Verb	82	100	90
banged		4	73	85	*bastards*		5	73	83	*beat*		45	100	90
banging		4	84	89	bat	NoC	13	96	85	*beaten*		19	98	89
bangs		0	30	81	*bat*		8	90	87	*beating*		15	98	91
bank	NoC	234	100	90	*bats*		4	79	79	*beats*		3	85	91
bank		168	100	91	bath	NoC	33	98	92	beautiful	Adj	87	99	93
banks		66	100	86	*bath*		26	96	91	beautifully	Adv	12	97	93
banker	NoC	15	97	90	*baths*		7	91	90	beauty	NoC	44	100	93
banker		6	91	87	Bath	NoP	12	91	86	*beauties*		2	74	89
bankers		9	86	88	bathroom	NoC	28	100	90	*beauty*		42	100	93
banking	NoC	21	95	87	*bathroom*		25	97	89	because*	Conj	852	100	94
banking		21	95	87	*bathrooms*		3	73	85	because of	Prep	178	100	97
bankruptcy	NoC	11	91	80	battery	NoC	21	99	89	become	Verb	675	100	96
bankruptcies		1	44	81	*batteries*		7	92	86	*became*		223	100	94
bankruptcy		10	88	79	*battery*		13	98	88	*become*		304	100	96
bar	NoC	101	100	92	battle	NoC	72	100	93	*becomes*		77	100	94
bar		77	100	92	*battle*		63	100	93	*becoming*		71	100	96
bars		24	100	90	*battles*		9	96	94	bed	NoC	180	100	90
Barbara	NoP	17	96	84	bay	NoC	37	100	93	*bed*		159	100	89
bare	Adj	23	100	90	*bay*		34	100	93	*beds*		21	98	94
bare		22	100	89	*bays*		3	75	87	bedroom	NoC	60	98	89
barest		1	35	83	BBC	NoP	43	91	88	*bedroom*		44	96	90
barely	Adv	23	100	91	*B.B.C.*		0	19	76	*bedrooms*		16	93	74
bargain	NoC	12	100	94	*BBC*		43	91	88	bee	NoC	13	95	88
bargain		9	100	94	BC	Adv	11	68	77	*bee*		5	86	89
bargains		3	81	89	*B.C.*		3	25	42	*bees*		7	84	85
bargaining	NoC	12	86	71	*BC*		8	64	79	beef	NoC	15	99	87
bargaining		12	86	71	be*	Verb	42277	100	98	*beef*		15	99	87
barn	NoC	16	93	86	*'m*		658	100	87	beer	NoC	38	100	86
barn		13	91	85	*'re*		835	100	85	*beer*		33	100	88
barns		3	65	80	*'s*		3190	100	85	*beers*		5	79	68
Barnes	NoP	13	83	80	*am*		250	100	92	before	Adv	143	100	94
baron	NoC	12	93	81	*are*		4707	100	96	*before*		143	100	94
baron		8	84	74	*be*		6644	100	98	before	Conj	305	100	96
barons		4	75	84	*been*		2686	100	98	before	Prep	434	100	97
barrel	NoC	14	100	92	*being*		862	100	98	beg	Verb	20	98	91
barrel		9	97	92	*is*		9982	100	96	*beg*		8	91	88
barrels		6	89	88	*was*		9236	100	96	*begged*		5	88	87
barrier	NoC	31	100	95	*were*		3227	100	98	*begging*		4	89	91
barrier		16	100	95	beach	NoC	48	99	87	*begs*		2	74	91
barriers		15	97	92	*beach*		38	99	87	begin	Verb	440	100	95
Barry	NoP	19	96	88	*beaches*		10	93	85	*began*		237	100	91
Barry		19	96	88	beam	NoC	17	99	89	*begin*		75	100	96
base	NoC	98	100	95	*beam*		11	97	88	*beginning*		53	100	95
base		86	100	95	*beams*		6	88	87	*begins*		33	100	94
bases		12	81	82	bean	NoC	18	100	89	*begun*		42	99	95
base	Verb	194	100	94	*bean*		5	85	84	beginning	NoC	78	100	96
base		5	91	93	*beans*		13	97	88	*beginning*		70	100	96
based		186	100	93	bear	NoC	18	99	92	*beginnings*		7	96	94
bases		1	46	86	*bear*		12	95	90	behalf	NoC	13	99	95
basing		2	70	90	*bears*		6	97	90	*behalf*		13	99	95

1.1

Word	PoS	Freq	Ra	Di	Word	PoS	Freq	Ra	Di	Word	PoS	Freq	Ra	Di
behave	Verb	34	100	95	best	Adv	81	100	96	birth		52	100	91
behave		17	99	95	bet	Verb	23	96	81	*births*		7	83	71
behaved		8	97	93	*bet*		21	93	79	birthday	NoC	34	99	90
behaves		2	77	90	*bets*		0	25	80	*birthday*		32	99	90
behaving		6	96	92	*betting*		2	72	88	*birthdays*		2	69	84
behaviour	NoC	128	100	90	better	Adv	143	100	95	biscuit	NoC	16	93	85
behaviour		123	100	90	Betty	NoP	14	90	62	*biscuit*		6	80	81
behaviours		5	53	73	*Betty*		13	90	62	*biscuits*		10	90	86
behind	Adv	34	100	94	between	Prep	903	100	95	bishop	NoC	40	98	88
behind	Prep	202	100	93	beyond	Adv	12	97	93	*bishop*		28	97	88
being	NoC	46	100	94	beyond	Prep	105	100	96	*bishops*		12	80	82
being		28	100	95	bias	NoC	14	90	88	Bishop	NoP	18	92	78
beings		18	97	90	bible	NoC	21	97	88	bit*	NoC	171	100	87
Belfast	NoP	36	95	71	*bible*		20	97	88	*bit*		137	100	86
Belgium	NoP	14	98	91	*bibles*		1	48	83	*bits*		34	99	89
belief	NoC	75	99	91	bicycle	NoC	11	96	91	bite	Verb	22	99	88
belief		51	99	92	*bicycle*		9	96	90	*bit*		11	88	84
beliefs		24	98	87	*bicycles*		3	78	90	*bite*		6	97	92
believe	Verb	347	100	97	bid	NoC	37	96	86	*bites*		1	43	86
believe		212	100	95	*bid*		31	95	85	*biting*		4	85	88
believed		82	100	96	*bids*		6	79	87	bitter	Adj	24	100	94
believes		40	100	91	bid	Verb	14	97	89	bitterly	Adv	11	95	89
believing		14	98	95	*bade*		1	56	85	bizarre	Adj	11	96	93
bell	NoC	28	99	92	*bid*		8	95	84	black	Adj	226	100	95
bell		18	95	90	*bidden*		0	27	80	*black*		225	100	95
bells		10	96	93	*bidding*		3	76	89	*blacker*		1	40	85
Bell	NoP	16	92	87	*bids*		1	53	87	*blackest*		1	36	84
belong	Verb	64	100	96	big	Adj	338	100	94	black	NoC	27	100	88
belong		21	100	95	*big*		255	100	93	*black*		13	98	93
belonged		16	100	94	*bigger*		36	100	93	*blacks*		14	91	79
belonging		14	98	93	*biggest*		46	99	90	Black	NoP	11	95	88
belongs		12	100	96	bike	NoC	23	96	88	bladder	NoC	11	78	52
below	Adv	88	100	94	*bike*		18	93	88	*bladder*		10	76	51
below	Prep	55	100	96	*bikes*		5	72	87	*bladders*		1	22	62
belt	NoC	27	100	94	bile	NoC	12	56	34	blade	NoC	17	96	90
belt		21	99	94	*bile*		12	56	34	*blade*		11	92	89
belts		5	94	91	*biles*		0	1	00	*blades*		5	88	90
Ben	NoP	32	96	84	bill	NoC	121	100	86	Blake	NoP	11	83	70
Ben		32	96	84	*bill*		90	100	83	*Blake*		11	83	70
bench	NoC	26	100	91	*bills*		30	100	89	blame	Verb	44	100	94
bench		20	100	91	Bill	NoP	47	100	92	*blame*		23	100	94
benches		6	92	87	billion	NoC	51	95	82	*blamed*		14	99	91
bend	Verb	35	99	90	*billion*		48	93	82	*blames*		2	70	84
bend		7	93	89	*billions*		3	77	86	*blaming*		4	90	92
bending		6	90	89	Billy	NoP	22	89	84	Blanche	NoP	11	35	40
bends		1	60	86	*Billy*		22	89	84	blank	Adj	15	98	91
bent		21	97	87	bin	NoC	11	93	89	*blank*		15	98	91
beneath	Prep	48	100	89	*bin*		8	90	87	blanket	NoC	17	99	91
beneficial	Adj	14	94	90	*bins*		3	76	88	*blanket*		11	98	91
benefit	NoC	152	100	92	bind	Verb	48	100	90	*blankets*		6	87	90
benefit		78	100	91	*bind*		7	88	83	blast	NoC	10	97	90
benefits		74	99	92	*binding*		10	90	80	*blast*		9	94	90
benefit	Verb	45	100	94	*binds*		3	70	78	*blasts*		1	53	82
benefit		30	99	94	*bound*		28	100	95	bless	Verb	11	97	92
benefited		8	89	92	binding	Adj	12	86	73	*bless*		6	83	88
benefiting		2	76	90	biography	NoC	10	94	87	*blessed*		4	91	92
benefits		4	79	91	*biographies*		2	69	84	*blesses*		0	14	72
benefitted		1	29	81	*biography*		8	89	87	*blessing*		1	43	84
benefitting		0	17	74	biological	Adj	20	93	87	blind	Adj	26	100	95
Benjamin	NoP	17	83	69	biology	NoC	11	92	86	*blind*		26	100	95
Benjamin		17	83	69	*biology*		11	92	86	*blinder*		0	24	79
Berlin	NoP	27	94	86	bird	NoC	93	100	90	block	NoC	57	100	95
Berlin		27	94	86	*bird*		36	100	90	*block*		36	100	95
Bernard	NoP	21	97	83	*birds*		57	99	89	*blocks*		21	100	93
beside	Prep	58	100	87	Birmingham	NoP	34	97	91	block	Verb	27	100	95
besides	Adv	18	97	90	birth	NoC	59	100	89	*block*		8	99	94

Word	PoS	Freq	Ra	Di	Word	PoS	Freq	Ra	Di	Word	PoS	Freq	Ra	Di
blocked		13	100	95	*bonds*		19	97	81	*bottle*		41	100	92
blocking		5	94	93	Bond	NoP	10	89	84	*bottles*		18	99	94
blocks		1	67	88	*bone*	NoC	47	100	88	bottom	Adj	18	99	94
bloke	NoC	16	82	78	*bone*		24	98	87	bottom	NoC	60	100	94
bloke		13	79	77	*bones*		23	99	88	*bottom*		57	100	94
blokes	•	3	62	81	*bonus*	NoC	18	100	90	*bottoms*		3	81	87
blood	NoC	102	100	93	*bonus*		14	100	90	bounce	Verb	13	94	92
blood		101	100	93	*bonuses*		4	67	84	*bounce*		3	85	90
bloods		0	21	74	book	NoC	374	100	95	*bounced*		5	86	90
bloody	Adj	53	100	78	*book*		243	100	95	*bounces*		1	48	87
bloodiest		0	27	80	*books*		131	100	94	*bouncing*		3	80	91
bloody		52	100	77	book	Verb	21	97	92	bound	Verb	23	100	96
bloody	Adv	20	90	77	*book*		5	83	88	*bound*		19	100	96
blow	NoC	24	99	93	*booked*		12	97	92	*bounded*		3	83	91
blow		20	99	93	*booking*		4	78	88	*bounding*		1	50	86
blows		4	92	92	*books*		0	25	81	*bounds*		0	22	78
blow	Verb	51	99	93	booking	NoC	14	93	87	boundary	NoC	44	100	91
blew		13	97	90	*booking*		8	83	85	*boundaries*		24	98	92
blow		13	98	91	*bookings*		6	80	89	*boundary*		20	97	88
blowed		0	13	67	booklet	NoC	12	86	90	bow	NoC	14	96	90
blowing		10	99	93	*booklet*		10	85	89	*bow*		10	93	90
blown		12	99	93	*booklets*		2	61	88	*bows*		4	78	86
blows		3	79	92	boom	NoC	17	100	90	bow	Verb	14	100	87
blue	Adj	92	100	93	*boom*		16	99	90	*bow*		3	83	89
blue	NoC	25	97	91	*booms*		1	44	84	*bowed*		8	81	83
blue		12	95	93	boost	NoC	10	94	86	*bowing*		2	64	85
blues		12	92	84	*boost*		10	94	86	*bows*		1	44	84
board	NoC	162	100	92	boost	Verb	17	93	89	bowel	NoC	15	84	52
board		134	100	92	*boost*		10	90	88	*bowel*		12	60	44
boards		28	100	89	*boosted*		4	80	87	*bowels*		2	71	89
boast	Verb	12	97	92	*boosting*		2	65	88	bowl	NoC	30	98	92
boast		3	92	92	*boosts*		1	52	87	*bowl*		23	94	91
boasted		3	82	91	boot	NoC	41	99	91	*bowls*		7	89	91
boasting		2	67	90	*boot*		15	97	91	bowler	NoC	10	82	79
boasts		4	73	86	*boots*		26	96	90	*bowler*		7	77	81
boat	NoC	74	100	93	border	NoC	52	100	88	*bowlers*		4	41	75
boat		54	100	92	*border*		40	100	87	box	NoC	114	100	95
boats		20	100	91	*borders*		12	98	90	*box*		88	100	94
Bob	NoP	40	99	87	bored	Adj	14	95	92	*boxes*		27	100	91
Bob		40	99	87	boring	Adj	16	98	91	boxing	NoC	12	91	85
body	NoC	325	100	96	*boring*		16	98	91	boy	NoC	213	100	93
bodies		70	100	95	born	Verb	82	100	90	*boy*		133	100	91
body		255	100	96	borough	NoC	24	94	86	*boys*		80	100	94
boil	Verb	12	99	93	*borough*		19	92	84	boyfriend	NoC	13	91	89
boil		5	85	90	*boroughs*		5	69	80	*boyfriend*		11	87	89
boiled		3	83	91	borrow	Verb	31	100	93	*boyfriends*		2	62	82
boiling		3	84	91	*borrow*		15	99	91	BR	NoP	13	57	78
boils		1	64	88	*borrowed*		10	100	95	*B.R.*		0	8	51
bold	Adj	14	99	95	*borrowing*		5	96	89	*BR*		13	54	77
bold		12	99	94	*borrows*		1	51	85	bracket	NoC	10	97	89
bolder		1	71	88	borrowing	NoC	13	86	88	*bracket*		4	89	90
boldest		0	27	82	*borrowing*		10	81	87	*brackets*		6	89	86
bolt	NoC	12	95	89	*borrowings*		3	56	82	Bradford	NoP	12	91	89
bolt		7	87	88	Bosnia	NoP	10	45	78	*Bradford*		12	91	89
bolts		5	86	88	*Bosnia*		10	45	78	*Bradfords*		0	2	12
bomb	NoC	39	98	90	boss	NoC	40	97	83	brain	NoC	57	100	93
bomb		27	97	89	*boss*		32	97	83	*brain*		47	100	92
bombs		12	95	90	*bosses*		8	89	80	*brains*		10	97	92
bomber	NoC	11	85	85	both	Adv	378	100	95	brake	NoC	11	97	90
bomber		6	73	84	both	DetP	310	100	98	*brake*		5	92	88
bombers		5	75	86	bother	Verb	42	99	89	*brakes*		6	93	90
bombing	NoC	11	88	86	*bother*		22	98	89	branch	NoC	85	100	92
bombing		9	88	86	*bothered*		15	96	88	*branch*		53	100	91
bombings		2	48	82	*bothering*		4	85	87	*branches*		32	100	93
bond	NoC	36	100	82	*bothers*		1	63	89	brand	NoC	21	100	89
bond		17	97	81	bottle	NoC	59	100	93	*brand*		13	99	91

Word	PoS	Freq	Ra	Di	Word	PoS	Freq	Ra	Di	Word	PoS	Freq	Ra	Di
brands		7	77	86	bridge	NoC	66	100	94	*brushes*		0	29	81
brass	NoC	16	98	92	*bridge*		58	100	93	*brushing*		5	74	86
brass		15	98	92	*bridges*		8	96	93	Brussels	NoP	15	93	89
brasses		1	27	76	brief	Adj	49	99	96	bucket	NoC	14	99	87
brave	Adj	18	99	92	*brief*		47	99	96	*bucket*		10	93	87
brave		17	99	92	*briefer*		0	36	84	*buckets*		4	87	82
braver		1	40	85	*briefest*		1	46	84	budget	NoC	94	98	87
bravest		1	36	84	*briefly*	Adv	33	100	94	*budget*		82	98	85
Brazil	NoP	17	88	86	brigade	NoC	13	94	87	*budgets*		13	81	90
Brazil		17	88	86	*brigade*		12	92	87	build	Verb	230	100	95
Brazils		0	5	41	*brigades*		1	41	84	*build*		68	100	95
breach	NoC	35	98	76	bright	Adj	62	100	93	*building*		28	100	95
breach		31	97	75	*bright*		54	100	92	*builds*		6	87	91
breaches		4	76	84	*brighter*		5	92	92	*built*		129	100	94
bread	NoC	38	100	92	*brightest*		2	80	74	builder	NoC	19	99	89
bread		38	100	92	Brighton	NoP	15	92	82	*builder*		9	97	85
breads		0	25	72	*Brighton*		15	92	82	*builders*		10	99	91
break	NoC	43	100	95	brilliant	Adj	35	100	93	building	NoC	229	100	94
break		36	100	95	bring	Verb	439	100	98	*building*		163	100	95
breaks		7	95	92	*bring*		154	100	97	*buildings*		66	99	92
break	Verb	193	100	97	*bringing*		49	100	98	bulb	NoC	10	92	88
break		58	100	97	*brings*		32	100	96	*bulb*		4	83	89
breaking		30	100	96	*brought*		204	100	97	*bulbs*		6	87	84
breaks		11	99	95	Bristol	NoP	29	96	88	bulk	NoC	21	100	95
broke		52	100	97	*Bristol*		29	96	88	*bulk*		20	100	95
broken		43	100	96	Britain	NoP	251	100	92	bull	NoC	12	97	85
breakdown	NoC	16	99	94	British	Adj	357	100	93	*bull*		8	95	88
breakdown		15	99	94	broad	Adj	65	100	94	*bulls*		3	72	70
breakdowns		1	63	88	*broad*		49	100	95	bullet	NoC	13	97	90
breakfast	NoC	45	99	90	*broader*		14	94	91	*bullet*		7	96	90
breakfast		44	99	90	*broadest*		2	69	89	*bullets*		6	86	90
breakfasts		1	56	86	broadcast	NoC	12	91	83	bunch	NoC	14	98	93
breast	NoC	29	95	90	*broadcast*		6	90	89	*bunch*		12	97	92
breast		17	94	91	*broadcasts*		6	75	68	*bunches*		2	64	89
breasts		13	86	85	broadcasting	NoC	16	89	84	burden	NoC	30	99	94
breath	NoC	53	99	85	*broadly*	Adv	16	93	93	*burden*		26	99	93
breath		51	99	85	brochure	NoC	13	96	84	*burdens*		4	84	91
breaths		2	53	86	*brochure*		9	90	82	bureau	NoC	19	99	79
breathe	Verb	35	100	89	*brochures*		4	87	85	*bureau*		14	99	83
breathe		11	98	91	broken	Adj	29	100	93	*bureaus*		1	12	30
breathed		9	83	83	broker	NoC	11	93	86	*bureaux*		4	61	55
breathes		1	49	87	*broker*		5	86	84	bureaucracy	NoC	15	89	75
breathing		14	95	90	*brokers*		6	73	86	*bureaucracies*		2	47	75
breed	NoC	19	95	65	bronze	NoC	17	93	87	*bureaucracy*		13	89	75
breed		12	94	66	*bronze*		15	93	89	burial	NoC	11	90	89
breeds		6	69	61	*bronzes*		2	36	71	*burial*		9	89	89
breed	Verb	17	100	89	brother	NoC	123	100	94	*burials*		1	43	77
bred		7	99	89	*brethren*		2	61	88	burn	Verb	53	100	94
breed		7	91	85	*brother*		85	100	93	*burn*		12	98	93
breeding		2	55	84	*brothers*		36	100	95	*burned*		14	100	91
breeds		1	50	84	brow	NoC	12	83	81	*burning*		13	99	92
breeding	NoC	19	97	84	*brow*		8	78	83	*burns*		3	87	92
breeze	NoC	15	91	70	*brows*		4	51	75	*burnt*		10	98	93
breeze		14	91	70	brown	Adj	45	99	91	burning	Adj	13	99	92
breezes		1	43	85	*brown*		45	99	91	burst	Verb	25	100	90
brewery	NoC	10	87	74	*browner*		0	12	45	*burst*		19	99	89
breweries		3	53	74	Brown	NoP	38	99	92	*bursting*		5	91	91
brewery		8	82	73	Bruce	NoP	17	93	87	*bursts*		1	53	88
Brian	NoP	45	98	89	*Bruce*		17	93	87	bury	Verb	31	99	92
Brian		45	98	89	*Bruces*		0	3	33	*buried*		24	99	91
brick	NoC	28	100	93	brush	NoC	17	98	90	*buries*		0	21	78
brick		18	99	91	*brush*		13	98	91	*bury*		5	89	91
bricks		10	99	92	*brushes*		4	83	83	*burying*		2	77	90
bride	NoC	12	91	87	brush	Verb	21	98	89	bus	NoC	68	100	92
bride		11	88	87	*brush*		6	96	90	*bus*		54	100	92
brides		2	61	83	*brushed*		9	92	86	*buses*		15	98	88

Word	PoS	Freq	Ra	Di	Word	PoS	Freq	Ra	Di	Word	PoS	Freq	Ra	Di
bush	NoC	17	98	91	cake	NoC	38	99	84	*cancelled*		12	100	92
bush		9	98	90	*cake*		28	99	82	*cancelling*		2	73	88
bushes		8	87	89	*cakes*		10	90	89	*cancels*		1	41	86
Bush	NoP	29	86	72	calcium	NoC	13	68	74	cancer	NoC	47	98	84
business	NoC	394	100	93	calculate	Verb	41	100	90	*cancer*		42	98	85
business		358	100	93	*calculate*		10	96	89	*cancers*		5	58	77
businesses		37	98	90	*calculated*		24	99	88	candidate	NoC	80	100	87
businessman	NoC	20	97	92	*calculates*		1	53	86	*candidate*		40	99	87
businessman		10	95	91	*calculating*		6	95	92	*candidates*		40	97	86
businessmen		10	97	90	calculation	NoC	23	99	91	candle	NoC	16	95	89
busy	Adj	53	100	94	*calculation*		11	96	90	*candle*		8	89	88
busier		1	58	88	*calculations*		12	96	91	*candles*		8	88	88
busiest		2	78	88	calendar	NoC	13	99	89	Canterbury	NoP	12	88	78
busy		50	100	94	*calendar*		11	99	91	canvas	NoC	14	97	88
but	Conj	4577	100	97	*calendars*		2	56	70	*canvas*		11	97	90
but	Prep	22	100	94	calf	NoC	11	89	88	*canvases*		2	54	74
Butler	NoP	11	84	88	*calf*		6	84	89	cap	NoC	26	99	94
Butler		10	84	88	*calves*		4	71	79	*cap*		20	99	94
butter	NoC	21	99	88	California	NoP	22	98	82	*caps*		7	93	90
butter		21	99	88	call	NoC	92	100	95	capability	NoC	18	98	87
butters		0	7	60	*call*		60	100	93	*capabilities*		9	95	83
butterfly	NoC	11	96	90	*calls*		31	100	94	*capability*		9	93	89
butterflies		5	78	88	call	Verb	535	100	97	capable	Adj	49	100	95
butterfly		6	91	90	*call*		135	100	94	capacity	NoC	63	100	94
button	NoC	26	97	90	*called*		329	100	97	*capacities*		4	78	88
button		16	96	88	*calling*		41	100	94	*capacity*		59	100	94
buttons		9	90	90	*calls*		30	100	95	capital	NoC	138	100	90
buy	Verb	262	100	94	calm	Adj	14	100	91	*capital*		133	100	89
bought		91	100	93	*calm*		12	99	91	*capitals*		5	88	80
buy		124	100	94	*calmer*		2	64	88	capitalism	NoC	19	86	83
buying		41	100	95	calm	Verb	13	97	90	*capitalism*		19	86	83
buys		6	94	90	*calm*		8	96	89	capitalist	Adj	21	89	80
buyer	NoC	44	100	77	*calmed*		3	71	88	captain	NoC	56	100	90
buyer		27	92	67	*calming*		2	61	80	*captain*		54	100	90
buyers		17	94	89	*calms*		0	23	80	*captains*		3	80	89
by	Adv	32	99	94	Cambridge	NoP	36	99	89	capture	Verb	31	98	94
by	Prep	5096	100	96	camera	NoC	39	100	93	*capture*		9	97	94
by means of	Prep	16	94	91	*camera*		27	97	92	*captured*		17	97	93
by no means	Adv	16	96	92	*cameras*		12	98	92	*captures*		2	70	89
by now	Adv	22	99	92	camp	NoC	43	100	93	*capturing*		3	83	91
by way of	Prep	14	97	87	*camp*		31	100	93	car	NoC	353	100	93
bye	Int	17	66	67	*camps*		11	93	88	*car*		278	100	93
C / c	Lett	147	100	88	campaign	NoC	105	99	90	*cars*		75	100	94
C		142	100	88	*campaign*		91	99	89	caravan	NoC	13	92	84
Cs		5	43	59	*campaigns*		14	93	92	*caravan*		10	89	82
C	NoP	41	93	89	campaign	Verb	14	94	91	*caravans*		3	71	87
C		19	85	81	*campaign*		4	80	90	carbon	NoC	25	95	81
C.		22	90	86	*campaigned*		4	74	87	*carbon*		25	94	81
Ca	NoP	15	60	64	*campaigning*		6	83	89	*carbons*		0	18	63
C.A.		6	10	26	*campaigns*		0	28	81	card	NoC	96	100	93
Ca		8	55	69	Campbell	NoP	16	87	87	*card*		57	100	92
cab	NoC	17	95	78	*Campbell*		16	86	87	*cards*		39	100	94
cab		15	95	77	*Campbells*		0	16	50	Cardiff	NoP	18	87	72
cabs		1	55	83	can	NoC	15	99	94	care	NoC	198	100	90
cabin	NoC	13	91	87	*can*		9	98	93	*care*		198	100	90
cabin		11	89	86	*cans*		6	89	91	*cares*		1	44	86
cabins		2	57	84	can	VMod	2672	100	96	care	Verb	81	100	94
cabinet	NoC	69	100	81	*ca~*		318	100	87	*care*		51	100	93
cabinet		65	100	80	*can*		2354	100	96	*cared*		13	99	92
cabinets		4	89	89	Canada	NoP	29	100	91	*cares*		6	94	93
cable	NoC	25	99	85	Canadian	Adj	14	96	91	*caring*		10	98	92
cable		18	97	84	canal	NoC	26	99	86	career	NoC	94	100	93
cables		6	87	87	*canal*		21	97	86	*career*		77	99	93
cage	NoC	13	95	78	*canals*		5	84	82	*careers*		17	97	90
cage		10	93	82	cancel	Verb	23	100	94	careful	Adj	52	100	96
cages		3	67	65	*cancel*		9	97	93	carefully	Adv	72	100	94

Word	PoS	Freq	Ra	Di	Word	PoS	Freq	Ra	Di	Word	PoS	Freq	Ra	Di
carer	NoC	17	66	82	catch		9	95	91	centre	NoC	282	100	93
carer		*5*	*50*	*78*	*catches*		*2*	*53*	*78*	*centre*		*230*	*100*	*93*
carers		*12*	*63*	*82*	catch	Verb	147	100	93	*centres*		*52*	*99*	*90*
cargo	NoC	10	93	90	*catch*		*43*	*100*	*94*	centre	Verb	16	97	92
cargo		*9*	*92*	*89*	*catches*		*5*	*92*	*93*	*centre*		*1*	*59*	*88*
cargoes		*2*	*63*	*85*	*catching*		*13*	*98*	*93*	*centred*		*13*	*97*	*92*
Carl	NoP	11	90	84	*caught*		*86*	*100*	*92*	*centres*		*2*	*62*	*88*
Carol	NoP	10	90	87	category	NoC	67	100	92	*centring*		*1*	*47*	*82*
Caroline	NoP	19	85	66	*categories*		*34*	*91*	*91*	century	NoC	233	100	92
Caroline		*19*	*85*	*66*	*category*		*33*	*98*	*92*	*centuries*		*36*	*98*	*92*
carpet	NoC	34	100	86	cater	Verb	18	99	90	*century*		*197*	*100*	*91*
carpet		*24*	*99*	*87*	*cater*		*6*	*93*	*92*	ceremony	NoC	22	97	93
carpets		*10*	*93*	*82*	*catered*		*3*	*84*	*90*	*ceremonies*		*4*	*90*	*91*
carriage	NoC	24	100	84	*catering*		*8*	*89*	*83*	*ceremony*		*18*	*97*	*92*
carriage		*20*	*99*	*82*	*caters*		*1*	*60*	*87*	certain	Adj	220	100	96
carriages		*4*	*81*	*87*	cathedral	NoC	27	98	86	certainly	Adv	186	100	95
Carrie	NoP	12	35	41	*cathedral*		*24*	*97*	*87*	certainty	NoC	15	99	94
carrier	NoC	19	100	87	*cathedrals*		*3*	*67*	*72*	*certainties*		*2*	*65*	*90*
carrier		*13*	*100*	*85*	Catherine	NoP	16	97	84	*certainty*		*14*	*99*	*93*
carriers		*6*	*91*	*87*	catholic	Adj	32	100	86	certificate	NoC	37	100	83
carry	Verb	313	100	97	catholic	NoC	15	98	89	*certificate*		*29*	*99*	*81*
carried		*138*	*100*	*96*	*catholic*		*7*	*94*	*86*	*certificates*		*9*	*92*	*88*
carries		*18*	*100*	*94*	*catholics*		*8*	*89*	*87*	ch	NoC	12	71	75
carry		*101*	*100*	*97*	cattle	NoC	26	98	82	*ch*		*4*	*49*	*63*
carrying		*56*	*100*	*96*	causal	Adj	12	64	72	*ch.*		*7*	*43*	*66*
cart	NoC	12	93	86	cause	NoC	99	100	94	chain	NoC	50	100	91
cart		*9*	*91*	*86*	*cause*		*72*	*100*	*95*	*chain*		*37*	*100*	*91*
carts		*3*	*69*	*86*	*causes*		*26*	*96*	*92*	*chains*		*13*	*98*	*89*
Carter	NoP	13	90	85	cause	Verb	206	100	95	chair	NoC	97	100	90
Carter		*13*	*89*	*85*	*cause*		*58*	*100*	*94*	*chair*		*77*	*100*	*90*
Carters		*0*	*9*	*56*	*caused*		*96*	*100*	*95*	*chairs*		*20*	*100*	*92*
carve	Verb	12	100	93	*causes*		*20*	*99*	*93*	chair	Verb	11	93	88
carve		*2*	*75*	*88*	*causing*		*33*	*100*	*95*	*chair*		*2*	*72*	*76*
carved		*8*	*96*	*92*	caution	NoC	13	97	94	*chaired*		*7*	*83*	*85*
carves		*0*	*14*	*74*	*caution*		*13*	*97*	*94*	*chairing*		*1*	*51*	*87*
carving		*2*	*78*	*87*	*cautions*		*1*	*31*	*76*	*chairs*		*1*	*30*	*81*
case	NoC	613	100	89	cautious	Adj	11	99	95	chairman	NoC	116	100	89
case		*431*	*100*	*93*	cave	NoC	16	96	88	*chairman*		*112*	*100*	*89*
cases		*183*	*100*	*91*	*cave*		*11*	*89*	*87*	*chairmen*		*5*	*75*	*79*
cash	NoC	82	100	91	*caves*		*5*	*82*	*88*	challenge	NoC	63	100	94
cash		*82*	*100*	*91*	CD	NoC	14	83	82	*challenge*		*52*	*100*	*93*
cassette	NoC	11	99	89	*CD*		*10*	*72*	*80*	*challenges*		*11*	*92*	*93*
cassette		*8*	*96*	*89*	*CDs*		*3*	*50*	*80*	challenge	Verb	40	98	95
cassettes		*3*	*78*	*87*	cease	Verb	30	100	95	*challenge*		*16*	*98*	*93*
cast	NoC	11	99	91	*cease*		*10*	*99*	*93*	*challenged*		*16*	*97*	*95*
cast		*10*	*99*	*90*	*ceased*		*15*	*98*	*94*	*challenges*		*2*	*73*	*90*
casts		*2*	*64*	*86*	*ceases*		*3*	*85*	*90*	*challenging*		*6*	*95*	*94*
cast	Verb	37	100	94	*ceasing*		*1*	*66*	*89*	chamber	NoC	36	100	91
cast		*30*	*99*	*94*	ceiling	NoC	27	100	92	*chamber*		*29*	*100*	*91*
casting		*6*	*91*	*90*	*ceiling*		*23*	*99*	*92*	*chambers*		*7*	*93*	*90*
casts		*2*	*71*	*90*	*ceilings*		*4*	*87*	*90*	champagne	NoC	20	97	80
castle	NoC	53	99	90	celebrate	Verb	35	99	92	*champagne*		*19*	*97*	*81*
castle		*47*	*99*	*90*	*celebrate*		*14*	*99*	*93*	*champagnes*		*0*	*11*	*37*
castles		*6*	*87*	*87*	*celebrated*		*10*	*95*	*92*	champion	NoC	47	99	84
casual	Adj	18	100	89	*celebrates*		*3*	*63*	*87*	*champion*		*32*	*96*	*84*
casual		*18*	*100*	*89*	*celebrating*		*8*	*96*	*89*	*champions*		*15*	*80*	*83*
casualty	NoC	17	99	89	celebration	NoC	21	100	93	championship	NoC	49	88	82
casualties		*10*	*93*	*86*	*celebration*		*12*	*100*	*94*	*championship*		*34*	*83*	*83*
casualty		*7*	*95*	*89*	*celebrations*		*9*	*91*	*91*	*championships*		*15*	*72*	*79*
cat	NoC	55	100	82	cell	NoC	131	100	78	chance	NoC	161	100	95
cat		*39*	*99*	*83*	*cell*		*55*	*100*	*80*	*chance*		*130*	*100*	*95*
cats		*16*	*98*	*78*	*cells*		*76*	*98*	*76*	*chances*		*30*	*100*	*93*
catalogue	NoC	30	98	86	census	NoC	12	80	84	chancellor	NoC	37	92	86
catalogue		*24*	*97*	*85*	*census*		*10*	*77*	*84*	*chancellor*		*37*	*92*	*86*
catalogues		*7*	*85*	*87*	*censuses*		*2*	*45*	*79*	*chancellors*		*1*	*34*	*80*
catch	NoC	11	95	89	central	Adj	193	100	93	change	NoC	384	100	93

Word	PoS	Freq	Ra	Di	Word	PoS	Freq	Ra	Di	Word	PoS	Freq	Ra	Di
change		201	100	94	*chase*	Verb	21	100	93	*chief*		38	99	89
changes		183	100	92	*chase*		5	95	92	*chiefs*		9	79	85
change	Verb	273	100	98	*chased*		6	94	92	child	NoC	710	100	94
change		119	100	97	*chases*		1	60	83	*child*		244	100	92
changed		109	100	97	*chasing*		9	98	92	*children*		466	100	95
changes		8	96	94	chat	Verb	13	97	92	childhood	NoC	29	100	93
changing		36	100	96	*chat*		4	90	92	*childhood*		28	100	93
changing	Adj	24	100	92	*chats*		0	28	82	*childhoods*		0	22	79
channel	NoC	58	100	92	*chatted*		3	74	89	chin	NoC	16	90	85
channel		40	100	92	*chatting*		6	92	90	*chin*		16	89	85
channels		18	99	89	cheap	Adj	68	100	95	*chins*		1	37	83
chaos	NoC	16	100	88	*cheap*		39	100	95	China	NoP	46	99	83
chap	NoC	20	96	88	*cheaper*		23	100	93	*China*		46	99	83
chap		16	94	87	*cheapest*		5	91	92	Chinese	Adj	40	99	88
chaps		4	78	88	check	NoC	27	100	94	chip	NoC	36	99	79
chapel	NoC	23	96	89	*check*		18	100	91	*chip*		18	93	72
chapel		20	95	89	*checks*		9	96	92	*chips*		18	99	85
chapels		3	71	80	check	Verb	100	100	95	chocolate	NoC	24	96	88
Chapman	NoP	11	72	60	*check*		54	100	95	*chocolate*		21	94	88
Chapman		11	72	60	*checked*		25	100	92	*chocolates*		3	76	85
Chapmans		0	11	66	*checking*		16	100	95	choice	NoC	138	100	95
chapter	NoC	169	100	91	*checks*		4	87	91	*choice*		120	100	95
chapter		149	100	91	cheek	NoC	35	97	84	*choices*		18	96	91
chapters		20	92	90	*cheek*		19	93	85	choir	NoC	12	92	85
character	NoC	125	100	92	*cheeks*		16	80	82	*choir*		10	91	86
character		86	100	94	cheer	Verb	12	93	92	*choirs*		2	49	67
characters		39	99	87	*cheer*		5	83	91	choose	Verb	168	100	96
characterise	Verb	14	84	90	*cheered*		5	82	90	*choose*		68	100	95
characterise		3	69	87	*cheering*		3	79	91	*chooses*		6	99	92
characterised		10	79	90	cheerful	Adj	12	95	91	*choosing*		17	100	94
characterises		1	60	88	cheese	NoC	30	97	85	*chose*		28	100	96
characterising		1	31	81	*cheese*		26	97	88	*chosen*		49	100	96
characteristic	Adj	17	91	90	*cheeses*		4	66	63	chop	Verb	10	93	87
characteristic	NoC	51	100	91	Chelsea	NoP	15	93	81	*chop*		3	73	84
characteristic		13	92	90	Cheltenham	NoP	14	76	62	*chopped*		5	85	81
characteristics		38	98	91	*Cheltenham*		14	76	62	*chopping*		2	67	89
characterize	Verb	13	76	86	chemical	Adj	33	97	87	*chops*		0	16	74
characterize		2	54	85	chemical	NoC	33	99	85	chord	NoC	10	87	67
characterized		9	71	86	*chemical*		11	92	84	*chord*		6	81	68
characterizes		1	42	85	*chemicals*		22	97	84	*chords*		5	59	63
characterizing		0	24	79	chemist	NoC	12	96	84	chorus	NoC	11	95	89
charge	NoC	149	100	92	*chemist*		7	93	85	*chorus*		10	94	88
charge		90	100	91	*chemists*		5	81	79	*choruses*		1	40	81
charges		60	100	89	chemistry	NoC	20	97	82	chosen	Adj	11	98	93
charge	Verb	69	100	94	cheque	NoC	29	100	91	Chris	NoP	45	97	88
charge		14	100	93	*cheque*		20	100	91	Christ	NoP	47	97	89
charged		46	100	91	*cheques*		9	99	88	*Christ*		47	97	89
charges		3	78	87	Cheshire	NoP	11	95	79	*Christs*		0	6	48
charging		6	97	93	*Cheshire*		11	95	80	Christian	Adj	62	100	91
charity	NoC	45	100	89	*Cheshires*		0	6	44	Christian	NoC	21	95	84
charities		9	92	86	chest	NoC	40	99	89	*Christian*		5	81	84
charity		35	100	88	*chest*		38	99	89	*Christians*		16	89	83
Charles	NoP	91	100	88	*chests*		2	66	87	Christianity	NoC	18	91	83
Charlie	NoP	28	93	79	Chester	NoP	11	83	77	Christie	NoP	12	84	76
Charlotte	NoP	16	89	77	chew	Verb	10	93	90	Christine	NoP	11	84	81
Charlotte		16	89	77	*chew*		3	76	89	Christmas	NoC	88	100	89
charm	NoC	15	96	92	*chewed*		3	67	85	Christopher	NoP	23	97	88
charm		13	95	91	*chewing*		4	76	89	*Christopher*		23	97	88
charms		3	66	89	*chews*		0	24	79	chronic	Adj	17	95	71
charming	Adj	14	96	91	Chicago	NoP	11	90	87	church	NoC	238	100	91
chart	NoC	26	99	90	chicken	NoC	25	99	90	*church*		203	100	92
chart		15	98	89	*chicken*		20	99	89	*churches*		35	97	86
charts		11	94	89	*chickens*		5	89	91	Churchill	NoP	14	94	88
charter	NoC	25	94	89	chief	Adj	75	100	93	*Churchill*		14	94	88
charter		22	92	88	*chief*		75	100	93	cigarette	NoC	36	99	89
charters		3	60	81	chief	NoC	47	99	89	*cigarette*		23	99	87

Word	PoS	Freq	Ra	Di	Word	PoS	Freq	Ra	Di	Word	PoS	Freq	Ra	Di
cigarettes		13	96	89	classic	NoC	16	96	90	*climbed*		24	96	88
cinema	NoC	22	97	87	*classic*		8	90	88	*climbing*		13	96	90
cinema		19	97	86	*classics*		7	90	89	*climbs*		3	68	82
cinemas		3	77	87	classical	Adj	33	97	88	cling	Verb	17	97	89
circle	NoC	50	100	95	classification	NoC	19	88	82	*cling*		4	89	92
circle		34	100	94	*classification*		17	86	81	*clinging*		6	83	88
circles		17	99	94	*classifications*		2	64	85	*clings*		1	49	86
circuit	NoC	33	100	86	classify	Verb	16	95	91	*clung*		7	83	85
circuit		26	99	85	*classified*		10	92	90	clinic	NoC	22	99	86
circuits		6	85	86	*classifies*		0	26	79	*clinic*		15	98	88
circular	Adj	13	98	91	*classify*		3	78	89	*clinics*		8	78	79
circulate	Verb	14	99	93	*classifying*		2	57	86	clinical	Adj	30	94	77
circulate		3	85	92	classroom	NoC	28	98	87	Clinton	NoP	20	58	75
circulated		6	92	91	*classroom*		23	98	86	*Clinton*		20	58	75
circulates		1	34	82	*classrooms*		5	79	86	*Clintons*		0	8	62
circulating		4	91	89	Claudia	NoP	11	39	40	Clive	NoP	10	88	84
circulation	NoC	15	99	91	clause	NoC	49	97	66	*Clive*		10	88	84
circulation		15	99	91	*clause*		36	94	65					
circulations		0	19	72	*clauses*		13	80	66					
circumstance	NoC	110	100	92	clay	NoC	17	98	90					
circumstance		6	94	70	*clay*		15	98	90					
circumstances		104	100	92	*clays*		2	40	81					
cite	Verb	26	89	88	clean	Adj	52	100	95					
cite		3	76	89	*clean*		48	100	95					
cited		14	83	84	*cleaner*		3	88	87					
cites		5	69	80	*cleanest*		1	37	83					
citing		3	73	86	clean	Verb	40	100	94					
citizen	NoC	47	100	92	*clean*		16	100	93					
citizen		14	100	92	*cleaned*		11	96	93					
citizens		33	98	91	*cleaning*		12	100	92					
city	NoC	275	100	95	*cleans*		1	54	86					
cities		44	100	91	cleaner	NoC	12	96	88					
city		231	100	94	*cleaner*		7	94	89					
civic	Adj	10	91	83	*cleaners*		4	87	84					
civil	Adj	87	100	92	cleaning	NoC	12	98	83					
civilian	Adj	12	95	84	*cleaning*		12	98	83					
claim	NoC	118	100	90	clear	Adj	239	100	96					
claim		66	100	89	*clear*		227	100	96					
claims		53	99	91	*clearer*		9	100	95					
claim	Verb	189	100	92	*clearest*		3	80	92					
claim		47	100	94	clear	Verb	59	100	95					
claimed		83	100	89	*clear*		24	100	96					
claiming		22	100	90	*cleared*		27	100	93					
claims		37	98	85	*clearing*		7	97	93					
Claire	NoP	11	81	82	*clears*		2	82	91					
Claire		11	81	82	clearly	Adv	153	100	95					
Clare	NoP	21	90	76	clergy	NoC	14	80	80					
Clare		21	90	76	clerk	NoC	26	99	92					
clarify	Verb	14	96	92	*clerk*		19	99	91					
clarified		3	80	92	*clerks*		6	85	88					
clarifies		1	36	83	Cleveland	NoP	17	75	31					
clarify		9	92	91	clever	Adj	25	99	92					
clarifying		2	61	88	*clever*		24	98	92					
clarity	NoC	11	93	93	*cleverer*		1	46	86					
clarity		11	93	93	*cleverest*		0	34	83					
Clark	NoP	17	92	88	client	NoC	110	100	86					
Clarke	NoP	21	90	85	*client*		61	100	83					
Clarke		20	88	85	*clients*		49	99	88					
Clarkes		0	8	44	cliff	NoC	20	97	90					
clash	NoC	18	94	86	*cliff*		11	93	89					
clash		11	93	86	*cliffs*		9	88	89					
clashes		7	80	74	climate	NoC	31	100	91					
class	NoC	241	100	92	*climate*		28	100	91					
class		181	100	92	*climates*		2	60	81					
classes		61	100	91	climb	Verb	57	100	91					
classic	Adj	26	98	93	*climb*		16	98	92					

Top 25 city names

There are two major sub-categories within this group: (1) world capitals and (2) UK cities and towns, with the latter predominating. Peculiarities of the BNC sampling account for the particularly high popularity of *Oxford, Middlesbrough,* and *Darlington* (frequencies in occurrences per million words):

1.	*London*	351
2.	*York*	99[a]
3.	*Oxford*	86
4.	*Paris*	61
5.	*Edinburgh*	60
6.	*Darlington*	56
7.	*Liverpool*	55
8.	*Manchester*	50
9.	*Leeds*	48
10.	*Glasgow*	42
11.	*Cambridge*	36
12.	*Belfast*	36
13.	*Middlesbrough*	36
14.	*Birmingham*	34
15.	*Rome*	34
16.	*Washington*	33[b]
17.	*Gloucester*	32
18.	*Moscow*	30
19.	*Bristol*	29
20.	*Hong Kong*	28
21.	*Berlin*	27
22.	*Newcastle*	27
23.	*Durham*	25
24.	*Dublin*	23
25.	*Westminster*	22

[a]To a large extent, the high frequency of *York* is due to its appearing in the name *New York*. Without this contribution, the frequency of *York* would be 45 per million.
[b]*Washington* has, of course, other uses than as the name of a city. Without these other uses, its frequency would be reduced to approximately 23 per million words.

Word	PoS	Freq	Ra	Di
clock	NoC	33	99	91
clock		29	99	90
clocks		5	89	89
close	Adj	154	100	97
close		126	100	97
closer		21	100	96
closest		8	99	94
close	Adv	42	99	95
close	NoC	11	99	89
close		11	99	89
closes		0	12	63
close	Verb	133	100	93
close		35	100	95
closed		79	100	91
closes		5	95	92
closing		14	100	93
closed	Adj	20	100	95
closely	Adv	55	99	95
closer	Adv	26	100	92
closure	NoC	25	89	90
closure		19	87	90
closures		6	75	87
cloth	NoC	22	98	91
cloth		20	98	91
cloths		2	66	85
clothes	NoC	73	100	91
clothing	NoC	21	100	94
clothing		21	100	94
cloud	NoC	37	100	92
cloud		21	100	92
clouds		16	96	91
club	NoC	202	100	88
club		164	100	88
clubs		38	100	90
clue	NoC	20	100	95
clue		11	98	93
clues		9	96	93
cluster	NoC	15	95	86
cluster		8	93	84
clusters		7	86	86
clutch	Verb	13	88	85
clutch		1	49	86
clutched		4	51	82
clutches		0	16	74
clutching		7	83	86
cm	NoC	22	63	75
cm		21	62	75
cm.		1	16	45
CO/Co	NoC	46	94	78
C.O.		0	8	60
CO/Co		40	93	75
Co.		6	69	68
co-operation	NoC	35	96	78
co-operation		35	96	78
co-ordinate	Verb	10	87	90
co-ordinate		5	78	88
co-ordinated		3	70	88
co-ordinates		1	39	83
co-ordinating		2	69	89
coach	NoC	37	99	89
coach		29	98	89
coaches		9	85	86
coal	NoC	53	100	88
coal		51	100	88
coals		3	65	69
coalition	NoC	26	77	72
coalition		24	76	70
coalitions		2	41	82
coast	NoC	49	100	93
coast		46	100	93
coasts		3	62	80
coastal	Adj	14	94	86
coat	NoC	42	98	90
coat		34	98	89
coats		8	93	93
code	NoC	65	100	89
code		52	100	87
codes		13	96	90
coffee	NoC	68	100	90
coffee		67	100	90
coffees		1	34	78
coffin	NoC	16	94	73
coffin		14	92	73
coffins		2	62	67
cognitive	Adj	12	63	81
coherent	Adj	11	97	90
coin	NoC	26	99	79
coin		12	98	85
coins		14	95	74
coincide	Verb	16	97	93
coincide		6	89	92
coincided		6	84	91
coincides		3	75	90
coinciding		1	59	84
cold	Adj	103	100	92
cold		99	100	92
colder		3	85	90
coldest		1	61	89
cold	NoC	25	99	91
cold		23	99	91
colds		1	49	82
Colin	NoP	25	94	87
Colin		25	94	87
colitis	NoC	10	14	35
colitis		10	14	35
collaboration	NoC	14	89	89
collaboration		13	89	89
collaborations		1	32	80
collapse	NoC	23	99	91
collapse		21	99	91
collapses		2	72	89
collapse	Verb	24	100	94
collapse		5	94	92
collapsed		16	100	93
collapses		1	38	85
collapsing		2	79	91
collar	NoC	16	92	91
collar		14	92	90
collars		2	71	89
colleague	NoC	72	99	94
colleague		17	98	95
colleagues		56	99	93
collect	Verb	80	100	96
collect		28	100	95
collected		33	100	94
collecting		15	100	95
collects		3	85	92
collection	NoC	96	100	89
collection		78	100	89
collections		18	90	86
collective	Adj	24	97	89
collector	NoC	19	98	81
collector		11	93	73
collectors		7	87	84
college	NoC	126	100	88
college		102	100	89
colleges		25	91	83
Collins	NoP	11	91	90
colonel	NoC	20	96	83
colonel		19	96	83
colonels		1	35	84
colonial	Adj	15	89	87
colony	NoC	21	96	85
colonies		10	92	79
colony		11	95	88
colour	NoC	156	99	93
colour		111	99	93
colours		45	99	92
colour	Verb	12	99	90
colour		4	89	79
coloured		6	98	93
colouring		2	72	89
colours		0	14	74
coloured	Adj	19	100	95
colourful	Adj	11	96	91
column	NoC	45	100	89
column		28	99	90
columns		16	98	87
combination	NoC	54	100	93
combination		44	100	94
combinations		10	90	89
combine	Verb	59	100	94
combine		16	97	93
combined		27	99	94
combines		6	80	91
combining		10	93	92
combined	Adj	17	97	93
come	Verb	1512	100	94
came		472	100	94
come		695	100	93
comes		160	100	95
cometh		0	20	79
comin'		1	29	77
coming		185	100	92
comedy	NoC	16	95	89
comedies		1	47	81
comedy		14	95	89
comfort	NoC	28	99	94
comfort		26	99	94
comforts		2	81	89
comfort	Verb	10	97	91
comfort		6	93	91
comforted		3	68	87
comforting		1	42	86
comforts		1	37	80
comfortable	Adj	40	100	94
coming	Adj	11	99	93
command	NoC	41	100	91
command		34	100	92
commands		7	85	86
command	Verb	19	99	95
command		7	96	93
commanded		8	94	92
commanding		1	56	88
commands		3	75	90
commander	NoC	24	97	88
commander		20	96	87
commanders		5	80	86

Word	PoS	Freq	Ra	Di	Word	PoS	Freq	Ra	Di	Word	PoS	Freq	Ra	Di
commence	Verb	15	98	89	compact	Adj	14	99	75	*completed*		55	99	94
commence		4	89	90	*compact*		14	99	75	*completes*		2	66	89
commenced		7	88	86	companion	NoC	25	99	92	*completing*		9	96	93
commences		1	56	86	*companion*		17	97	91	completely	Adv	86	100	97
commencing		3	74	88	*companions*		8	90	91	completion	NoC	25	97	82
comment	NoC	75	100	94	company	NoC	579	100	91	*completion*		25	97	82
comment		34	100	94	*companies*		178	100	90	*completions*		1	19	69
comments		41	100	92	*company*		401	100	91	complex	Adj	72	99	92
comment	Verb	47	100	95	comparable	Adj	19	91	90	complex	NoC	28	100	84
comment		19	100	91	comparative	Adj	14	94	85	*complex*		23	100	89
commented		20	97	94	comparatively	Adv	12	96	92	*complexes*		6	72	57
commenting		6	92	90	compare	Verb	130	100	93	complexity	NoC	22	95	91
comments		2	70	88	*compare*		24	100	93	*complexities*		5	89	91
commentary	NoC	10	96	91	*compared*		88	100	91	*complexity*		17	88	90
commentaries		2	61	87	*compares*		6	82	91	compliance	NoC	13	92	86
commentary		9	95	91	*comparing*		11	96	91	*compliance*		13	92	86
commentator	NoC	14	86	88	comparison	NoC	46	99	92	complicated	Adj	29	100	95
commentator		3	79	90	*comparison*		33	99	92	complication	NoC	12	98	81
commentators		10	80	86	*comparisons*		13	91	89	*complication*		4	83	83
commerce	NoC	16	94	87	compatible	Adj	12	88	85	*complications*		9	97	80
commercial	Adj	79	100	93	compel	Verb	12	98	93	comply	Verb	21	96	88
commission	NoC	111	100	90	*compel*		2	76	89	*complied*		4	82	86
commission		102	100	90	*compelled*		8	96	92	*complies*		1	43	83
commissions		8	89	89	*compelling*		2	68	90	*comply*		14	94	88
commission	Verb	17	96	92	*compels*		1	36	84	*complying*		2	58	86
commission		2	77	90	compensate	Verb	14	100	93	component	NoC	58	97	89
commissioned		14	95	91	*compensate*		9	96	93	*component*		26	92	89
commissioning		1	48	88	*compensated*		4	91	91	*components*		32	95	89
commissioner	NoC	24	98	88	*compensates*		1	35	83	compose	Verb	24	97	92
commissioner		15	92	84	*compensating*		1	63	89	*compose*		2	79	90
commissioners		9	84	87	compensation	NoC	32	98	91	*composed*		20	97	91
commit	Verb	68	100	94	*compensation*		31	98	91	*composes*		0	13	74
commit		14	100	94	*compensations*		1	48	85	*composing*		2	66	85
commits		2	63	84	compete	Verb	32	100	93	composer	NoC	15	82	79
committed		46	100	94	*compete*		19	97	93	*composer*		10	74	80
committing		6	97	94	*competed*		3	80	88	*composers*		5	60	75
commitment	NoC	70	100	93	*competes*		1	43	82	composition	NoC	27	93	90
commitment		57	100	92	*competing*		9	93	91	*composition*		23	92	90
commitments		13	98	92	competence	NoC	16	93	88	*compositions*		4	69	81
committee	NoC	217	100	92	*competence*		15	93	90	compound	NoC	20	91	86
committee		190	100	92	*competences*		1	23	63	*compound*		11	91	88
committees		27	93	90	competent	Adj	12	97	92	*compounds*		9	72	82
commodity	NoC	15	95	89	competition	NoC	101	100	92	comprehensive	Adj	35	99	92
commodities		6	83	88	*competition*		94	100	92	comprise	Verb	34	97	91
commodity		9	93	89	*competitions*		7	86	89	*comprise*		7	79	90
common	Adj	182	100	94	competitive	Adj	37	94	91	*comprised*		7	90	89
commonly	Adv	26	96	91	competitor	NoC	22	96	91	*comprises*		9	80	90
Commons	NoP	33	93	89	*competitor*		6	86	88	*comprising*		11	86	86
C/common-					*competitors*		16	94	91	compromise	NoC	19	97	91
wealth	NoC	18	89	84	compile	Verb	14	95	93	*compromise*		16	97	90
C/commonwealth		18	89	84	*compile*		2	79	91	*compromises*		3	74	90
communicate	Verb	25	100	93	*compiled*		9	90	92	compulsory	Adj	17	96	92
communicate		15	98	92	*compiles*		0	17	76	computer	NoC	174	100	85
communicated		5	92	92	*compiling*		3	84	92	*computer*		138	100	85
communicates		1	60	87	complain	Verb	44	100	97	*computers*		36	100	82
communicating		4	87	91	*complain*		14	100	96	computing	NoC	19	82	74
communication	NoC	96	100	88	*complained*		19	100	95	conceal	Verb	17	96	93
communication		61	100	85	*complaining*		9	99	96	*conceal*		7	94	93
communications		35	97	83	*complains*		2	73	90	*concealed*		7	91	92
communist	Adj	42	94	81	complaint	NoC	45	100	94	*concealing*		2	72	89
communist	NoC	13	86	82	*complaint*		18	100	93	*conceals*		1	57	87
communist		1	47	85	*complaints*		27	100	93	concede	Verb	18	95	93
communists		12	81	81	complete	Adj	94	100	95	*concede*		5	89	92
community	NoC	272	100	92	*complete*		94	100	95	*conceded*		10	94	92
communities		41	89	89	complete	Verb	100	100	94	*concedes*		2	60	87
community		231	100	92	*complete*		34	100	94	*conceding*		2	68	89

Word	PoS	Freq	Ra	Di	Word	PoS	Freq	Ra	Di	Word	PoS	Freq	Ra	Di
conceive	Verb	18	99	91	_conference_		101	100	88	_connections_		21	99	91
conceive		5	93	90	_conferences_		12	95	90	conscience	NoC	15	100	92
conceived		12	95	91	confess	Verb	16	99	93	_conscience_		14	100	92
conceives		1	35	81	_confess_		7	91	90	_consciences_		1	53	85
conceiving		1	34	81	_confessed_		7	90	91	conscious	Adj	31	100	94
concentrate	Verb	71	100	96	_confesses_		2	58	87	consciousness	NoC	26	96	87
concentrate		31	100	96	_confessing_		1	54	88	_consciousness_		26	96	87
concentrated		24	98	94	confidence	NoC	71	100	95	_consciousnesses_		0	9	61
concentrates		5	82	90	_confidence_		70	100	95	consensus	NoC	18	88	91
concentrating		12	100	96	_confidences_		1	43	84	consent	NoC	34	98	82
concentration	NoC	60	100	79	confident	Adj	32	100	94	_consent_		32	98	82
concentration		39	100	86	confidential	Adj	11	99	86	_consents_		2	35	61
concentrations		21	71	63	configuration	NoC	13	86	68	consequence	NoC	79	100	93
concept	NoC	91	98	91	_configuration_		10	78	62	_consequence_		34	98	92
concept		64	98	92	_configurations_		3	57	74	_consequences_		44	100	92
concepts		27	93	89	confine	Verb	27	97	93	consequently	Adv	25	99	92
conception	NoC	23	96	87	_confine_		3	87	91	conservation	Adj	14	76	81
conception		19	96	88	_confined_		22	97	93	conservation	NoC	25	88	67
conceptions		5	60	83	_confines_		0	31	81	_conservation_		25	88	67
conceptual	Adj	10	75	87	_confining_		1	58	89	conservative*	Adj	64	98	88
concern	NoC	121	100	95	confirm	Verb	87	100	93	conservative*	NoC	31	94	86
concern		96	100	95	_confirm_		26	100	88	_conservative_		7	89	90
concerns		25	98	93	_confirmed_		48	98	91	_conservatives_		23	85	85
concern	Verb	30	100	94	_confirming_		5	92	93	consider	Verb	289	100	94
concern		8	98	94	_confirms_		7	93	92	_consider_		117	100	93
concerned		5	92	93	confirmation	NoC	12	98	92	_considered_		134	100	94
concerning		3	85	91	_confirmation_		12	98	93	_considering_		26	99	93
concerns		13	96	93	_confirmations_		0	17	66	_considers_		12	94	92
concerned	Adj	158	100	95	conflict	NoC	70	99	92	considerable	Adj	96	99	93
concerning	Prep	31	98	92	_conflict_		56	99	92	considerably	Adv	29	100	94
concert	NoC	26	100	91	_conflicts_		15	87	90	consideration	NoC	78	100	90
concert		19	100	90	conform	Verb	13	93	92	_consideration_		54	100	89
concerts		8	94	90	_conform_		8	90	92	_considerations_		24	94	91
concession	NoC	18	98	91	_conformed_		1	61	88	consist	Verb	64	99	92
concession		7	93	90	_conforming_		1	61	87	_consist_		12	94	91
concessions		11	94	89	_conforms_		2	64	88	_consisted_		13	96	92
conclude	Verb	56	99	93	confront	Verb	24	99	95	_consisting_		13	91	91
conclude		15	97	92	_confront_		7	96	93	_consists_		26	91	91
concluded		31	97	92	_confronted_		12	99	95	consistent	Adj	31	96	91
concludes		8	84	91	_confronting_		4	88	93	consistently	Adv	16	94	94
concluding		3	78	89	_confronts_		1	59	88	conspiracy	NoC	12	93	89
conclusion	NoC	75	100	93	confrontation	NoC	12	97	91	_conspiracies_		0	36	85
conclusion		51	100	92	_confrontation_		10	97	92	_conspiracy_		11	93	89
conclusions		24	99	92	_confrontations_		2	69	87	constable	NoC	22	95	88
concrete	Adj	18	97	94	confuse	Verb	13	100	95	_constable_		18	93	88
condemn	Verb	23	98	91	_confuse_		5	96	94	_constables_		4	74	82
condemn		5	93	91	_confused_		6	98	93	Constance	NoP	12	50	40
condemned		14	98	90	_confuses_		1	51	87	constant	Adj	47	100	94
condemning		3	83	89	_confusing_		1	69	91	constantly	Adv	31	100	95
condemns		1	58	85	confused	Adj	19	100	96	constituency	NoC	27	91	79
condition	NoC	237	100	94	confusion	NoC	30	99	96	_constituencies_		8	75	82
condition		83	100	93	_confusion_		29	99	96	_constituency_		19	89	77
conditions		154	100	93	_confusions_		1	56	87	constituent	NoC	17	88	79
conduct	NoC	29	95	87	congregation	NoC	12	92	85	_constituent_		9	80	84
conduct		29	95	87	_congregation_		10	89	86	_constituents_		8	85	66
conduct	Verb	52	99	93	_congregations_		2	51	84	constitute	Verb	39	97	91
conduct		12	96	93	congress	NoC	56	94	76	_constitute_		16	89	90
conducted		30	97	93	_congress_		55	94	76	_constituted_		10	90	89
conducting		7	96	92	_congresses_		1	38	74	_constitutes_		10	85	90
conducts		2	61	88	connect	Verb	44	100	94	_constituting_		2	66	88
confer	Verb	13	95	88	_connect_		7	100	90	constitution	NoC	42	93	79
confer		4	87	88	_connected_		31	100	94	_constitution_		40	93	78
conferred		6	85	83	_connecting_		4	87	89	_constitutions_		2	50	73
conferring		1	60	87	_connects_		2	69	85	constitutional	Adj	31	86	80
confers		2	65	87	connection	NoC	56	100	93	constraint	NoC	26	95	90
conference	NoC	112	100	88	_connection_		35	100	94	_constraint_		7	86	86

Word	PoS	Freq	Ra	Di	Word	PoS	Freq	Ra	Di	Word	PoS	Freq	Ra	Di
constraints		19	87	90	*context*		86	99	90	*controversy*		19	90	91
construct	Verb	44	99	92	*contexts*		12	76	85	convenient	Adj	20	100	94
construct		13	93	91	continent	NoC	19	100	92	convention	NoC	47	97	86
constructed		25	98	92	*continent*		16	100	93	*convention*		35	96	84
constructing		5	90	92	*continents*		4	72	80	*conventions*		12	91	86
constructs		1	52	87	continental	Adj	17	95	86	conventional	Adj	39	99	93
construction	NoC	66	100	92	continually	Adv	13	99	94	conversation	NoC	65	100	92
construction		63	100	92	continue	Verb	283	100	96	*conversation*		55	100	92
constructions		3	69	85	*continue*		118	100	95	*conversations*		10	99	92
consult	Verb	28	99	95	*continued*		106	100	94	conversion	NoC	24	97	91
consult		12	99	93	*continues*		40	99	93	*conversion*		21	97	91
consulted		12	97	94	*continuing*		19	99	94	*conversions*		3	59	81
consulting		4	93	92	continued	Adj	21	97	92	convert	Verb	39	100	93
consults		0	24	79	continuing	Adj	34	98	92	*convert*		11	96	92
consultant	NoC	32	99	89	continuity	NoC	14	92	91	*converted*		20	98	93
consultant		16	97	90	*continuities*		1	33	80	*converting*		6	88	89
consultants		16	90	85	*continuity*		13	92	91	*converts*		2	60	86
consultation	NoC	29	95	90	continuous	Adj	26	100	93	convey	Verb	19	97	93
consultation		24	95	90	contract	NoC	159	100	83	*convey*		12	96	93
consultations		5	80	86	*contract*		114	100	82	*conveyed*		2	76	91
consume	Verb	19	100	92	*contracts*		44	100	83	*conveying*		3	83	90
consume		5	94	89	contract	Verb	16	99	93	*conveys*		3	75	89
consumed		8	97	91	*contract*		5	93	90	convict	Verb	13	90	87
consumes		1	41	81	*contracted*		7	97	93	*convict*		1	46	81
consuming		5	95	92	*contracting*		3	78	89	*convicted*		12	89	86
consumer	NoC	67	96	90	*contracts*		1	44	80	*convicting*		0	21	79
consumer		44	91	89	contractor	NoC	16	96	88	conviction	NoC	28	98	93
consumers		23	86	89	*contractor*		7	85	83	*conviction*		21	98	92
consumption	NoC	33	97	88	*contractors*		9	92	90	*convictions*		8	90	91
consumption		33	97	88	contradiction	NoC	15	96	90	convince	Verb	23	99	95
contact	NoC	83	100	95	*contradiction*		8	95	90	*convince*		12	99	95
contact		62	100	95	*contradictions*		7	87	87	*convinced*		8	99	94
contacts		21	99	92	contrary	NoC	13	95	93	*convinces*		1	38	85
contact	Verb	57	100	94	*contrary*		13	95	93	*convincing*		2	73	91
contact		42	100	90	contrary to	Prep	13	93	88	convinced	Adj	25	100	95
contacted		11	99	91	contrast	NoC	66	99	92	convincing	Adj	12	100	94
contacting		3	82	90	*contrast*		62	99	92	Cook	NoP	15	98	88
contacts		1	36	82	*contrasts*		4	76	87	cook	Verb	37	100	90
contain	Verb	181	99	93	contrast	Verb	15	96	92	*cook*		16	95	87
contain		45	99	92	*contrast*		4	77	91	*cooked*		9	93	90
contained		49	98	93	*contrasted*		5	86	91	*cooking*		11	99	92
containing		41	96	89	*contrasting*		2	77	90	*cooks*		1	46	86
contains		46	97	93	*contrasts*		4	69	89	cooking	NoC	16	97	91
container	NoC	16	98	90	contribute	Verb	64	100	93	cool	Adj	34	100	91
container		8	95	90	*contribute*		27	95	92	*cool*		31	100	90
containers		7	92	88	*contributed*		23	98	93	*cooler*		3	76	90
contemplate	Verb	17	98	95	*contributes*		5	80	91	*coolest*		0	30	83
contemplate		6	94	94	*contributing*		9	97	93	cool	Verb	14	98	92
contemplated		5	93	92	contribution	NoC	82	100	93	*cool*		6	91	90
contemplates		1	46	86	*contribution*		54	99	93	*cooled*		3	80	89
contemplating		5	97	94	*contributions*		28	98	91	*cooling*		4	86	89
contemporary	Adj	44	96	89	control	NoC	270	100	94	*cools*		1	42	81
contemporary	NoC	10	89	89	*control*		238	100	94	Cooper	NoP	12	91	89
contemporaries		9	89	88	*controls*		32	100	87	cooperation	NoC	12	89	89
contemporary		1	57	86	control	Verb	116	100	95	*cooperation*		12	89	89
contempt	NoC	13	96	88	*control*		53	100	95	cope	Verb	52	100	95
contempt		13	96	88	*controlled*		36	99	95	*cope*		40	100	95
contempts		0	5	52	*controlling*		17	97	93	*coped*		3	88	92
content	Adj	16	98	94	*controls*		11	93	92	*copes*		1	48	87
content	NoC	75	100	93	controlled	Adj	10	97	91	*coping*		8	98	92
content		45	100	92	controller	NoC	12	91	86	copper	NoC	19	99	89
contents		30	100	91	*controller*		9	85	84	*copper*		18	99	89
contest	NoC	17	100	90	*controllers*		3	66	84	*coppers*		1	42	82
contest		14	100	90	controversial	Adj	21	95	91	copy	NoC	85	100	93
contests		3	63	87	controversy	NoC	21	91	91	*copies*		35	100	92
context	NoC	98	99	90	*controversies*		2	61	88	*copy*		51	100	92

Word	PoS	Freq	Ra	Di	Word	PoS	Freq	Ra	Di	Word	PoS	Freq	Ra	Di
copy	Verb	21	100	91	core		34	100	92	cottages		9	89	90
copied		7	97	90	cores		2	46	78	cotton	NoC	23	98	92
copies		0	30	82	corn	NoC	12	99	87	cotton		22	98	92
copy		9	96	87	corn		12	99	87	cottons		0	22	77
copying		4	92	91	corns		0	19	77	could	VMod	1683	100	96
copyright	NoC	11	77	74	corner	NoC	90	100	93	council	NoC	348	100	89
copyright		10	76	73	corner		75	100	93	council		313	100	89
copyrights		1	21	73	corners		16	98	93	councils		35	94	89
coral	NoC	10	86	79	Cornwall	NoP	13	97	89	councillor	NoC	45	97	79
coral		7	82	83	Corp	NoC	53	47	37	councillor		25	89	71
corals		3	35	65	Corp		52	45	36	councillors		20	93	82
Corbett	NoP	16	52	39	Corp.		1	15	62	counselling	NoC	13	91	85
Corbett		15	48	38	corporate	Adj	46	95	88	count	NoC	32	100	89
Corbetts		0	11	48	corporation	NoC	45	97	89	count		21	100	90
core	NoC	36	100	92	corporation		35	95	88	counts		12	97	82
					corporations		10	82	83	count	Verb	50	100	97
					corps	NoC	12	85	81	count		21	100	95
					corpse	NoC	12	88	83	counted		13	100	95
					corpse		8	80	82	counting		9	100	95
					corpses		4	75	85	counts		7	100	94
					correct	Adj	59	100	94	counter	NoC	20	100	94
					correct	Verb	19	100	94	counter		17	99	93
					correct		9	98	93	counters		2	77	90
					corrected		7	99	93	counter	Verb	13	98	94
					correcting		2	83	90	counter		7	93	92
					corrects		0	28	81	countered		4	85	90
					correctly	Adv	19	100	93	countering		1	51	87
					correlation	NoC	18	78	81	counters		0	24	79
					correlation		14	75	80	counterpart	NoC	17	92	91
					correlations		4	61	77	counterpart		8	88	87
					correspond	Verb	23	97	88	counterparts		9	84	92
					correspond		8	86	88	country	NoC	486	100	93
					corresponded		2	68	90	countries		168	100	89
					corresponding		7	77	84	country		319	100	94
					corresponds		6	72	86	countryside	NoC	39	100	91
					correspondence	NoC	16	96	91	county	NoC	129	100	87
					correspondence		15	96	91	counties		16	94	89
					correspondences		0	27	79	county		113	100	86
					correspondent	NoC	23	93	82	coup	NoC	18	89	68
					correspondent		20	90	80	coup		17	88	67
					correspondents		3	73	90	coups		1	44	80
					corresponding	Adj	14	86	88	couple	NoC	138	100	94
					corridor	NoC	28	100	88	couple		123	100	94
					corridor		21	98	87	couples		16	100	90
					corridors		7	98	89	couple	Verb	14	100	94
					corruption	NoC	15	97	82	couple		2	67	90
					corruption		14	96	82	coupled		12	96	93
					corruptions		0	12	71	coupling		0	25	81
					cos/'cos*	Conj	163	53	64	courage	NoC	19	99	94
					cost	NoC	269	100	93	course	NoC	267	100	91
					cost		149	100	93	course		187	100	93
					costs		120	100	91	courses		80	99	84
					cost	Verb	100	100	94	court	NoC	344	100	86
					cost		57	100	94	court		285	100	85
					costed		1	46	79	courts		59	100	88
					costing		10	97	92	courtesy	NoC	11	98	93
					costs		32	99	91	courtesies		1	33	81
					costly	Adj	12	99	93	courtesy		11	98	93
					costlier		0	12	69	cousin	NoC	25	100	90
					costliest		0	17	71	cousin		18	97	88
					costly		11	99	93	cousins		7	95	90
					costume	NoC	12	92	92	covenant	NoC	14	72	58
					costume		7	89	91	covenant		9	66	63
					costumes		5	88	89	covenants		5	40	47
					cottage	NoC	40	97	91	Coventry	NoP	12	87	85
					cottage		32	96	90	cover	NoC	56	100	93

Countries and continents

(a) The British Isles

Britain	251
England	231
UK	177
Scotland	131
Ireland	96[a]
Wales	93
United Kingdom	44
Ulster	24

[a] Note: About 45% of the occurrences of Ireland are in the combination Northern Ireland

(b) The twenty most frequent country names (outside the British Isles)

US	162
France	123
Germany	106
United States	85
Japan	65
USA	51
Italy	52
Australia	50
India	47
China	46
Spain	45
Russia	43
Israel	32
Iraq	32
Canada	29
New Zealand	26
Egypt	22
Poland	21
Iran	20
Korea	19

(c) Continents

Europe	181
America	103
Africa	78
Asia	30
Antarctica	3
Australasia	1

Note: America is sometimes used to refer to the United States of America

Word	PoS	Freq	Ra	Di	Word	PoS	Freq	Ra	Di	Word	PoS	Freq	Ra	Di
cover		47	100	92	*creditor*		8	49	70	*cruder*		1	39	83
covers		9	97	93	*creditors*		12	76	83	*crudest*		0	32	82
cover	Verb	191	100	96	creep	Verb	16	96	89	cruel	Adj	14	100	91
cover		64	100	96	*creep*		4	88	91	*cruel*		14	100	91
covered		79	100	96	*creeping*		4	81	88	*crueller*		0	9	64
covering		29	100	95	*creeps*		1	42	85	*cruellest*		0	34	85
covers		19	100	93	*crept*		8	87	86	crush	Verb	12	98	93
coverage	NoC	22	95	90	crew	NoC	40	100	91	*crush*		3	74	91
coverage		22	95	90	*crew*		30	99	91	*crushed*		8	97	92
coverages		0	4	35	*crews*		11	91	86	*crushes*		0	21	80
cow	NoC	26	100	90	cricket	NoC	34	99	83	*crushing*		2	72	89
cow		14	100	91	*cricket*		33	99	83	cry	NoC	23	99	91
cows		12	97	85	*crickets*		1	33	78	*cries*		7	89	89
crack	NoC	19	97	89	crime	NoC	89	100	88	*cry*		16	97	91
crack		12	93	87	*crime*		72	100	88	cry	Verb	63	99	86
cracks		7	95	90	*crimes*		18	98	87	*cried*		30	90	81
crack	Verb	16	98	93	criminal	Adj	44	98	87	*cries*		2	77	84
crack		6	96	93	criminal	NoC	16	99	90	*cry*		17	97	89
cracked		7	92	91	*criminal*		7	93	89	*crying*		14	93	88
cracking		3	88	92	*criminals*		10	94	89	crystal	NoC	21	98	88
craft	NoC	25	99	92	crisis	NoC	65	100	90	*crystal*		15	98	89
craft		20	99	92	*crises*		6	86	89	*crystals*		6	82	81
crafts		5	80	89	*crisis*		59	100	90	cult	NoC	11	91	88
Craig	NoP	13	85	82	criterion	NoC	52	93	90	*cult*		9	88	88
Craig		13	85	82	*criteria*		39	90	90	*cults*		1	45	82
crash	NoC	23	100	88	*criterion*		13	80	86	cultural	Adj	65	95	88
crash		21	100	88	critic	NoC	39	97	90	culture	NoC	102	100	90
crashes		1	63	86	*critic*		12	90	82	*culture*		86	100	90
crash	Verb	22	100	89	*critics*		27	93	91	*cultures*		16	96	88
crash		4	81	90	critical	Adj	58	100	92	cup	NoC	134	100	90
crashed		13	93	87	criticise	Verb	21	96	91	*cup*		122	100	89
crashes		1	49	85	*criticise*		5	88	91	*cups*		12	95	91
crashing		4	86	90	*criticised*		13	87	89	cupboard	NoC	19	97	88
crawl	Verb	12	97	89	*criticises*		1	44	85	*cupboard*		14	89	87
crawl		3	82	90	*criticising*		2	83	91	*cupboards*		5	82	85
crawled		5	77	86	criticism	NoC	59	100	91	cure	NoC	11	98	93
crawling		3	76	88	*criticism*		48	100	91	*cure*		10	98	93
crawls		0	31	83	*criticisms*		12	90	91	*cures*		1	56	87
crazy	Adj	18	98	90	criticize	Verb	17	91	81	cure	Verb	11	99	94
crazier		0	17	76	*criticize*		3	78	89	*cure*		5	98	93
craziest		0	19	78	*criticized*		11	81	75	*cured*		5	87	92
crazy		18	98	90	*criticizes*		1	32	78	*cures*		0	32	83
cream	NoC	33	99	90	*criticizing*		2	72	86	*curing*		1	58	87
cream		31	99	90	crop	NoC	31	99	88	curiosity	NoC	12	94	91
creams		2	59	84	*crop*		15	98	88	*curiosities*		1	31	80
create	Verb	217	100	94	*crops*		16	99	86	*curiosity*		12	92	91
create		82	100	94	cross	NoC	46	100	94	curious	Adj	22	98	93
created		85	100	94	*cross*		43	100	94	*curious*		22	98	93
creates		14	96	92	*crosses*		3	89	90	*curiouser*		0	10	70
creating		35	100	94	cross	Verb	70	100	94	curl	Verb	12	88	86
creation	NoC	50	98	92	*cross*		23	100	94	*curl*		2	65	86
creation		47	98	92	*crossed*		31	100	91	*curled*		7	76	84
creations		2	78	91	*crosses*		4	87	90	*curling*		3	54	84
creative	Adj	25	99	90	*crossing*		14	99	94	*curls*		0	12	71
creature	NoC	39	98	89	crossing	NoC	12	100	91	currency	NoC	43	95	83
creature		19	96	88	*crossing*		10	100	91	*currencies*		7	62	78
creatures		21	97	87	*crossings*		2	67	87	*currency*		35	95	83
credit	NoC	77	100	84	crowd	NoC	56	99	93	current	Adj	133	100	93
credit		71	100	83	*crowd*		43	99	92	current	NoC	16	98	85
credits		6	87	87	*crowds*		13	95	93	*current*		9	96	83
credit	Verb	10	100	92	crown	NoC	53	100	89	*currents*		7	90	87
credit		3	88	88	*crown*		51	100	89	currently	Adv	70	100	91
credited		5	90	90	*crowns*		2	73	89	curriculum	NoC	56	96	82
crediting		0	21	79	crucial	Adj	45	99	93	*curricula*		3	48	80
credits		2	63	74	crude	Adj	14	98	93	*curriculum*		53	95	82
creditor	NoC	20	78	80	*crude*		13	98	93	*curriculums*		0	7	54

Word	PoS	Freq	Ra	Di	Word	PoS	Freq	Ra	Di	Word	PoS	Freq	Ra	Di
curtain	NoC	34	99	87	daddy	NoC	22	84	74	date		5	92	92
curtain		14	99	86	*daddies*		0	16	72	*dated*		13	98	84
curtains		20	94	86	*daddy*		22	84	74	*dates*		8	93	91
curve	NoC	34	97	86	daily	Adj	55	100	93	*dating*		9	97	90
curve		25	97	84	daily	Adv	14	99	92	daughter	NoC	115	100	86
curves		9	92	88	dairy	NoC	10	95	83	*daughter*		94	100	87
custody	NoC	15	92	87	*dairies*		1	37	79	*daughters*		21	100	78
custody		15	92	87	*dairy*		9	94	82	Dave	NoP	27	94	86
custom	NoC	37	99	93	damage	NoC	93	100	89	*Dave*		27	94	86
custom		15	99	90	*damage*		71	100	91	David	NoP	157	100	90
customs		23	97	91	*damages*		22	84	73	*David*		157	100	90
customer	NoC	114	100	89	damage	Verb	40	100	93	*Davids*		0	12	69
customer		47	100	87	*damage*		13	100	91	Davies	NoP	21	83	86
customers		68	100	89	*damaged*		20	100	92	Davis	NoP	14	94	89
cut	NoC	58	100	93	*damages*		1	38	80	dawn	NoC	15	94	91
cut		29	100	94	*damaging*		6	94	92	*dawn*		15	94	91
cuts		29	100	90	damp	Adj	18	97	91	*dawns*		0	14	73
cut	Verb	184	100	96	*damp*		18	96	91	Dawson	NoP	10	79	61
cut		145	100	96	*damper*		0	15	52	*Dawson*		10	79	61
cuts		12	100	96	dance	NoC	35	99	88	day	NoC	940	100	97
cutting		28	100	96	*dance*		30	99	88	*day*		610	100	97
cutting	NoC	16	100	92	*dances*		5	89	85	*days*		331	100	97
cutting		10	100	93	dance	Verb	37	99	91	Day	NoP	12	97	91
cuttings		5	84	83	*dance*		14	94	91	daylight	NoC	11	98	91
cycle	NoC	40	100	92	*danced*		8	88	87	*daylight*		10	97	91
cycle		32	100	92	*dances*		2	61	73	*daylights*		0	31	83
cycles		8	84	89	*dancing*		13	98	91	DC	NoP	18	81	49
cylinder	NoC	13	92	83	dancer	NoC	14	91	81	*D.C.*		2	30	51
cylinder		9	87	80	*dancer*		6	74	84	*DC*		15	76	42
cylinders		3	69	83	*dancers*		8	90	77	de	Fore	19	97	88
Czechoslovakia	NoP	11	90	80	dancing	NoC	12	96	91	de*	NoP-	107	100	90
D / d	Lett	72	100	93	danger	NoC	76	100	96	dead	Adj	114	100	92
D	NoP	27	87	82	*danger*		60	100	96	*dead*		114	100	92
D		12	74	65	*dangers*		16	96	94	deadline	NoC	11	97	88
D.		15	87	85	dangerous	Adj	58	100	96	*deadline*		9	96	87
dad	NoC	74	97	81	Daniel	NoP	15	94	88	*deadlines*		2	70	88
dad		73	96	81	dare	Verb	23	99	89	deaf	Adj	27	98	62
dads		1	49	84	*dare*		10	95	89	*deaf*		27	98	62
					dared		9	94	87	deal	NoC	100	100	94
					dares		1	55	86	*deal*		88	100	94
					daring		3	76	87	*deals*		12	96	91
					dare	VMod	12	95	89	deal	Verb	168	100	94
					dark	NoC	104	100	89	*deal*		67	100	94
					dark	Adj	113	100	89	*dealing*		53	100	93
					dark		104	100	89	*deals*		13	97	92
					darker		7	95	91	*dealt*		35	100	94
					darkest		2	76	90	dealer	NoC	35	98	78
					darkness	NoC	34	96	87	*dealer*		18	94	81
					darkness		34	96	87	*dealers*		18	94	74
					darling	NoC	23	87	82	dealing	NoC	14	98	86
					darling		23	83	82	*dealing*		5	75	72
					darlings		1	39	83	*dealings*		9	97	89
					Darlington	NoP	56	60	33	Dean	NoP	19	96	87
					Darlington		56	60	33	*Dean*		18	94	86
					Darwin	NoP	11	74	74	*Deans*		1	25	61
					Darwin		11	74	74	dear	Adj	41	100	90
					data/datum*	NoC	183	97	86	*dear*		36	99	90
					data		182	97	86	*dearer*		1	52	83
					datum		1	31	81	*dearest*		3	76	86
					database	NoC	44	77	75	dear	Int	37	95	81
					database		34	77	74	dear	NoC	16	93	84
					databases		10	62	76	*dear*		16	91	83
					date	NoC	177	100	78	*dears*		1	38	83
					date		158	100	75	death	NoC	230	100	95
					dates		19	100	93	*death*		205	100	95
					date	Verb	35	100	91	*deaths*		25	99	90

Frequency of names of days

Occurrences per million words (singular forms only)

The figures suggest a strong devotion to the (long) weekend. The most frequently mentioned days are *Sunday* (93) and *Saturday* (83), with *Friday* (55) and *Monday* (53) following well behind in third and fourth place. The mid-week days of *Tuesday* (36), *Wednesday* (44) and *Thursday* (37) are mentioned still less often, with a slight halfway 'peak' on *Wednesday*.

Word	PoS	Freq	Ra	Di	Word	PoS	Freq	Ra	Di	Word	PoS	Freq	Ra	Di
debate	NoC	82	98	89	decree	NoC	11	78	74	definitions		13	81	86
debate		70	98	88	decree		8	74	72	degree	NoC	131	100	91
debates		12	85	90	decrees		3	52	78	degree		100	100	91
debate	Verb	13	100	86	dedicate	Verb	13	100	94	degrees		31	100	89
debate		4	82	76	dedicate		1	54	85	delay	NoC	33	100	93
debated		7	93	90	dedicated		12	100	93	delay		23	100	93
debating		3	88	85	dedicates		0	12	73	delays		11	93	91
debt	NoC	73	100	87	dedicating		0	34	85	delay	Verb	27	99	94
debt		54	100	85	deed	NoC	13	97	83	delay		9	97	94
debts		19	100	90	deed		7	90	81	delayed		14	99	94
debtor	NoC	12	71	72	deeds		6	93	85	delaying		3	79	90
debtor		9	49	68	deem	Verb	16	96	87	delays		0	26	82
debtors		4	59	74	deem		1	58	86	delegate	NoC	19	93	84
debut	NoC	16	74	82	deemed		14	94	87	delegate		3	80	88
debut		16	73	83	deeming		0	12	69	delegates		16	89	82
debuts		1	24	54	deems		1	35	60	delegation	NoC	18	89	76
Dec.	NoP	44	61	56	deep	Adj	97	100	95	delegation		16	89	77
Dec		16	58	44	deep		79	100	94	delegations		3	47	64
Dec.		28	21	38	deeper		12	98	94	deliberate	Adj	13	98	95
decade	NoC	62	98	93	deepest		5	95	93	deliberately	Adv	28	100	95
decade		37	98	93	deep	Adv	27	100	92	delicate	Adj	18	100	93
decades		25	94	92	deeply	Adv	37	100	94	delicious	Adj	11	87	90
December	NoP	94	100	99	default	NoC	10	82	78	delight	NoC	21	99	93
decent	Adj	19	97	94	default		10	82	77	delight		18	99	93
decide	Verb	245	100	97	defaults		1	32	76	delights		3	81	91
decide		67	100	96	defeat	NoC	33	97	88	delighted	Adj	26	100	92
decided		151	100	89	defeat		30	97	88	delightful	Adj	11	96	91
decides		9	100	94	defeats		4	69	85	deliver	Verb	65	100	95
deciding		19	100	93	defeat	Verb	25	98	92	deliver		22	100	93
decision	NoC	243	100	93	defeat		7	92	93	delivered		31	100	95
decision		168	100	92	defeated		15	97	90	delivering		9	100	92
decisions		75	100	92	defeating		3	74	88	delivers		3	87	87
decision-making	NoC	14	76	88	defeats		1	38	84	delivery	NoC	41	100	89
decisive	Adj	12	98	92	defect	NoC	15	91	85	deliveries		5	86	86
deck	NoC	17	100	89	defect		7	76	82	delivery		36	100	89
deck		14	99	88	defects		9	84	86	demand	NoC	139	100	92
decks		2	74	89	defence	NoC	128	100	88	demand		89	100	89
declaration	NoC	23	98	82	defence		116	100	87	demands		51	98	93
declaration		20	98	82	defences		11	95	89	demand	Verb	84	100	95
declarations		3	69	83	defend	Verb	42	99	94	demand		21	99	95
declare	Verb	62	100	90	defend		21	99	95	demanded		37	97	91
declare		10	100	93	defended		10	97	93	demanding		18	100	93
declared		43	99	88	defending		10	95	88	demands		7	89	92
declares		4	82	90	defends		2	55	86	democracy	NoC	46	97	86
declaring		6	95	88	defendant	NoC	49	82	68	democracies		4	69	83
decline	NoC	41	96	91	defendant		33	76	67	democracy		42	97	85
decline		41	96	91	defendants		16	62	67	democrat	NoC	30	84	81
declines		0	20	76	defender	NoC	19	93	83	democrat		10	74	80
decline	Verb	34	97	93	defender		12	81	78	democrats		20	78	79
decline		6	93	92	defenders		7	81	87	democratic	Adj	59	93	76
declined		21	95	93	defensive	Adj	13	97	94	demolish	Verb	10	100	90
declines		3	70	89	deficiency	NoC	11	92	87	demolish		2	81	86
declining		4	85	91	deficiencies		4	78	90	demolished		7	94	89
decorate	Verb	17	98	92	deficiency		7	85	84	demolishes		0	10	70
decorate		4	81	85	deficit	NoC	27	87	81	demolishing		1	55	87
decorated		11	89	91	deficit		23	86	80	demonstrate	Verb	68	100	94
decorates		0	10	68	deficits		3	56	83	demonstrate		24	100	93
decorating		2	79	90	define	Verb	95	99	91	demonstrated		27	95	93
decoration	NoC	14	96	91	define		24	95	92	demonstrates		9	82	91
decoration		9	92	88	defined		54	97	90	demonstrating		8	97	93
decorations		4	88	90	defines		6	76	90	demonstration	NoC	33	99	85
decrease	Verb	16	88	87	defining		10	83	90	demonstration		19	97	90
decrease		5	81	89	definite	Adj	16	100	95	demonstrations		15	90	78
decreased		6	80	81	definitely	Adv	32	100	91	Denmark	NoP	13	93	90
decreases		3	58	85	definition	NoC	62	100	90	Dennis	NoP	15	90	83
decreasing		2	69	89	definition		48	100	91	Dennis		15	90	83

Word	PoS	Freq	Ra	Di
density	NoC	19	91	84
densities		3	54	83
density		16	89	84
deny	Verb	77	100	94
denied		37	99	90
denies		8	89	86
deny		23	100	95
denying		8	93	94
denys		2	36	57
depart	Verb	14	98	94
depart		4	93	91
departed		6	93	92
departing		3	82	91
departs		1	59	87
department	NoC	219	100	87
department		177	100	85
departments		42	97	89
departure	NoC	27	96	93
departure		23	96	94
departures		4	74	84
depend	Verb	101	100	94
depend		35	100	93
depended		12	98	93
depending		4	83	89
depends		50	100	94
dependence	NoC	13	88	89
dependence		13	88	89
dependent	Adj	37	97	91
depending on	Prep	23	99	94
depict	Verb	15	94	91
depict		2	67	87
depicted		7	89	90
depicting		4	80	88
depicts		2	61	87
deposit	NoC	36	100	85
deposit		17	99	87
deposits		19	85	79
deposit	Verb	12	97	92
deposit		3	80	89
deposited		8	93	91
depositing		1	55	89
deposits		0	30	81
depressed	Adj	15	100	94
depression	NoC	24	99	89
depression		23	98	89
depressions		1	51	83
deprive	Verb	14	99	91
deprive		3	84	84
deprived		7	96	92
deprives		1	41	86
depriving		2	79	87
depth	NoC	41	100	94
depth		30	100	93
depths		11	94	92
deputy	NoC	51	99	75
deputies		12	68	64
deputy		39	98	78
Derby	NoP	13	87	86
Derby		12	87	86
Derbys		0	10	57
Derek	NoP	20	93	88
derive	Verb	52	95	91
derive		9	82	90
derived		33	93	90
derives		6	80	89
deriving		3	70	89
Des	NoP	12	89	84
descend	Verb	17	97	93
descend		4	86	91
descended		8	93	92
descending		3	77	89
descends		2	54	84
descent	NoC	11	92	88
descent		11	92	88
descents		0	19	67
describe	Verb	237	100	94
describe		43	100	94
described		148	100	93
describes		26	92	92
describing		19	98	94
description	NoC	66	100	92
description		51	100	91
descriptions		15	95	91
desert	NoC	21	97	90
desert		18	95	90
deserts		3	74	81
desert	Verb	11	98	93
desert		3	84	91
deserted		7	96	91
deserting		1	53	87
deserts		0	23	78
deserve	Verb	31	100	95
deserve		13	100	94
deserved		9	97	92
deserves		9	99	93
design	NoC	148	100	91
design		119	100	91
designs		28	99	90
design	Verb	118	100	94
design		10	98	92
designed		100	100	94
designing		7	97	91
designate	Verb	11	91	91
designate		2	71	89
designated		9	91	90
designates		0	25	80
designating		1	35	84
designer	NoC	29	99	91
designer		19	98	91
designers		10	90	90
desirable	Adj	21	98	93
desire	NoC	58	98	93
desire		51	97	93
desires		7	90	90
desire	Verb	14	98	93
desire		4	87	90
desired		8	97	93
desires		2	64	88
desiring		1	44	86
desk	NoC	49	100	88
desk		45	100	87
desks		4	88	91
desktop	NoC	15	58	56
desktop		15	56	57
desktops		1	7	31
despair	NoC	13	96	91
despair		13	96	91
desperate	Adj	26	100	93
desperately	Adv	20	99	91
despite	Prep	146	100	95
destination	NoC	15	98	92
destination		11	97	91
destinations		4	78	87
destroy	Verb	62	100	95
destroy		20	100	95
destroyed		31	100	95
destroying		8	99	94
destroys		2	88	91
destruction	NoC	24	99	93
destruction		24	99	93
detail	NoC	178	100	94
detail		61	100	94
details		117	100	93
detailed	Adj	60	100	91
detect	Verb	34	98	88
detect		13	97	90
detected		16	97	83
detecting		4	78	86
detects		1	49	83
detective	NoC	27	95	85
detective		18	94	83
detectives		9	73	76
determination	NoC	29	96	91
determination		28	96	91
determinations		1	33	78
determine	Verb	119	100	93
determine		39	99	91
determined		61	99	94
determines		7	76	90
determining		13	84	89
determined	Adj	16	99	95
develop	Verb	237	100	93
develop		86	100	93
developed		109	100	92
developing		31	99	93
develops		10	86	92
developed	Adj	15	92	90
developer	NoC	19	92	75
developer		8	80	77
developers		12	86	72
developing	Adj	31	93	91
development	NoC	375	100	92
development		324	99	92
developments		51	99	92
device	NoC	51	99	91
device		29	97	91
devices		22	97	89
devil	NoC	20	98	89
devil		17	98	89
devils		3	70	82
devise	Verb	23	98	93
devise		6	88	91
devised		13	96	93
devises		0	22	78
devising		3	79	91
Devon	NoP	13	94	88
Devon		13	94	88
Devons		0	2	18
devote	Verb	21	98	93
devote		6	95	94
devoted		13	96	92
devotes		1	50	87
devoting		1	63	89
devoted	Adj	12	97	94
diagnose	Verb	10	91	83
diagnose		2	66	90
diagnosed		7	88	81
diagnoses		0	18	75

1.1

Word	PoS	Freq	Ra	Di	Word	PoS	Freq	Ra	Di	Word	PoS	Freq	Ra	Di
diagnosing		1	33	77	digital	Adj	20	90	71	disappear	Verb	56	100	95
diagnosis	NoC	19	92	75	dignity	NoC	13	96	93	*disappear*		14	99	95
diagnoses		2	37	61	*dignities*		0	11	70	*disappeared*		33	100	93
diagnosis		17	92	75	*dignity*		13	96	93	*disappearing*		5	96	93
diagram	NoC	18	96	89	dilemma	NoC	14	96	92	*disappears*		4	91	92
diagram		13	88	87	*dilemma*		11	96	92	disappointed	Adj	21	100	94
diagrams		5	84	90	*dilemmas*		3	67	85	disappointment	NoC	17	99	94
dialogue	NoC	19	99	90	dimension	NoC	30	99	91	*disappointment*		15	99	94
dialogue		17	99	90	*dimension*		16	98	91	*disappointments*		2	76	92
dialogues		2	55	81	*dimensions*		14	92	90	disaster	NoC	34	100	94
diameter	NoC	14	90	85	diminish	Verb	14	97	94	*disaster*		28	100	93
diameter		13	90	85	*diminish*		5	92	93	*disasters*		5	93	90
diameters		1	33	73	*diminished*		6	96	94	disastrous	Adj	11	98	94
diamond	NoC	17	99	90	*diminishes*		1	53	87	disc	NoC	24	97	85
diamond		11	99	89	*diminishing*		2	70	90	*disc*		16	97	84
diamonds		6	86	86	dining	NoC	16	99	89	*discs*		8	89	85
Diana	NoP	23	88	71	dinner	NoC	67	100	91	discharge	NoC	14	89	86
diary	NoC	26	100	93	*dinner*		63	100	91	*discharge*		11	88	87
diaries		5	88	88	*dinners*		4	84	90	*discharges*		3	55	75
diary		20	100	93	dioxide	NoC	14	77	74	discharge	Verb	15	98	90
Dick	NoP	14	98	91	*dioxide*		14	77	74	*discharge*		4	85	88
Dick		13	98	91	dip	Verb	12	97	94	*discharged*		9	96	90
Dicks		1	23	75	*dip*		4	89	92	*discharges*		1	35	76
dictate	Verb	13	100	95	*dipped*		6	88	90	*discharging*		2	68	88
dictate		5	97	93	*dipping*		2	84	92	disciplinary	Adj	11	84	84
dictated		6	94	93	*dips*		1	42	86	discipline	NoC	66	100	61
dictates		2	69	90	diplomatic	Adj	20	96	78	*discipline*		55	100	55
dictating		1	58	89	direct	Adj	104	100	94	*disciplines*		11	83	84
dictionary	NoC	22	96	83	direct	Verb	55	100	94	disclose	Verb	18	93	81
dictionaries		4	60	72	*direct*		13	100	93	*disclose*		7	85	75
dictionary		19	95	84	*directed*		34	96	94	*disclosed*		9	84	83
die	Verb	220	100	93	*directing*		6	97	93	*discloses*		1	32	79
die		53	100	94	*directs*		3	76	87	*disclosing*		1	55	81
died		140	100	91	direction	NoC	109	100	95	disclosure	NoC	12	86	75
dies		10	98	93	*direction*		87	100	96	*disclosure*		10	80	74
dying		17	100	93	*directions*		22	100	92	*disclosures*		2	51	76
diesel	NoC	14	88	73	directive	NoC	23	90	86	discount	NoC	24	96	87
diesel		13	88	74	*directive*		17	87	85	*discount*		19	95	85
diesels		1	31	56	*directives*		6	72	85	*discounts*		5	75	87
diet	NoC	46	100	84	directly	Adv	88	99	95	discourage	Verb	11	98	94
diet		41	100	84	director	NoC	165	100	92	*discourage*		5	93	93
diets		5	67	77	*director*		122	100	92	*discouraged*		5	93	93
differ	Verb	33	98	91	*directors*		43	98	89	*discourages*		1	45	87
differ		18	96	90	directory	NoC	19	98	67	*discouraging*		1	57	88
differed		5	87	90	*directories*		3	66	72	discourse	NoC	27	81	70
differing		2	56	84	*directory*		15	95	66	*discourse*		23	80	66
differs		8	80	88	dirt	NoC	10	96	90	*discourses*		4	43	68
difference	NoC	191	100	94	dirty	Adj	27	100	92	discover	Verb	107	100	95
difference		113	100	95	*dirtier*		0	26	80	*discover*		33	99	95
differences		78	99	90	*dirtiest*		0	25	67	*discovered*		64	100	95
different	Adj	484	100	95	*dirty*		26	100	92	*discovering*		7	92	94
differentiate	Verb	12	88	84	disability	NoC	22	97	85	*discovers*		3	79	90
differentiate		5	86	84	*disabilities*		7	79	87	discovery	NoC	35	97	92
differentiated		5	67	86	*disability*		15	97	82	*discoveries*		7	88	88
differentiates		1	44	84	disabled	Adj	31	96	84	*discovery*		28	96	92
differentiating		1	50	79	disadvantage	NoC	20	99	93	discretion	NoC	19	98	83
differently	Adv	15	100	95	*disadvantage*		12	98	93	*discretion*		19	98	83
difficult	Adj	220	100	96	*disadvantages*		9	90	91	*discretions*		0	11	69
difficulty	NoC	132	100	94	disagree	Verb	13	100	93	discrimination	NoC	20	92	87
difficulties		68	100	93	*disagree*		7	98	91	*discrimination*		20	91	87
difficulty		63	100	95	*disagreed*		3	93	92	*discriminations*		0	20	71
dig	Verb	28	100	94	*disagreeing*		1	49	85	discuss	Verb	150	100	95
dig		9	98	93	*disagrees*		1	59	89	*discuss*		56	100	95
digging		7	92	92	disagreement	NoC	12	95	90	*discussed*		70	100	92
digs		1	59	87	*disagreement*		8	95	92	*discusses*		4	73	88
dug		11	97	93	*disagreements*		4	80	85	*discussing*		20	99	96

Word	PoS	Freq	Ra	Di	Word	PoS	Freq	Ra	Di	Word	PoS	Freq	Ra	Di
discussion	NoC	116	100	94	distinguished	Adj	13	97	93	does		687	100	95
discussion		85	100	93	distress	NoC	15	99	93	doing		279	100	91
discussions		31	97	91	*distress*		15	99	93	done		354	100	94
disease	NoC	107	100	80	*distresses*		0	16	76	doth		1	53	86
disease		89	100	77	distribute	Verb	31	98	89	du~*		20	43	62
diseases		18	98	88	*distribute*		6	95	85	dock	NoC	20	99	88
dish	NoC	30	98	88	*distributed*		20	96	90	*dock*		12	95	86
dish		16	96	86	*distributes*		1	49	80	*docks*		8	92	87
dishes		14	97	88	*distributing*		4	91	89	doctor	NoC	150	100	93
disk	NoC	34	77	68	distribution	NoC	66	97	90	*doctor*		105	100	90
disk		26	72	70	*distribution*		63	97	90	*doctors*		45	100	91
disks		8	53	55	*distributions*		3	58	81	doctrine	NoC	20	84	87
dislike	Verb	12	99	92	district	NoC	93	100	90	*doctrine*		17	83	87
dislike		5	92	92	*district*		75	100	89	*doctrines*		3	60	84
disliked		6	89	90	*districts*		18	93	88	document	NoC	95	100	89
dislikes		1	56	89	disturb	Verb	22	100	93	*document*		51	99	90
disliking		1	34	82	*disturb*		6	96	92	*documents*		44	100	87
dismiss	Verb	43	99	90	*disturbed*		12	99	93	document	Verb	11	88	90
dismiss		8	98	92	*disturbing*		2	77	91	*document*		2	69	86
dismissed		30	97	89	*disturbs*		1	47	87	*documented*		7	81	89
dismisses		1	61	88	disturbance	NoC	15	99	90	*documenting*		1	45	85
dismissing		4	87	85	*disturbance*		9	97	88	*documents*		1	43	84
dismissal	NoC	17	97	82	*disturbances*		7	86	86	documentation	NoC	12	87	86
dismissal		15	97	81	disturbing	Adj	10	99	94	*documentation*		12	87	86
dismissals		1	47	80	dive	Verb	11	97	90	dog	NoC	124	100	89
disorder	NoC	25	95	87	*dive*		3	83	87	*dog*		80	100	88
disorder		16	95	86	*dived*		4	80	88	*dogs*		44	99	89
disorders		8	78	87	*dives*		1	32	80	doll	NoC	12	91	88
display	NoC	55	100	93	*diving*		3	85	88	*doll*		7	87	88
display		44	100	93	diverse	Adj	13	92	92	*dolls*		4	77	83
displays		11	93	90	diversity	NoC	14	83	90	dollar	NoC	37	100	87
display	Verb	56	100	86	*diversities*		0	16	73	*dollar*		20	97	79
display		19	99	82	*diversity*		14	81	90	*dollars*		17	98	92
displayed		25	98	85	divert	Verb	12	100	94	dolphin	NoC	16	89	48
displaying		6	92	94	*divert*		4	96	94	*dolphin*		8	70	54
displays		6	88	88	*diverted*		5	98	92	*dolphins*		8	64	43
disposal	NoC	23	99	91	*diverting*		2	80	91	domain	NoC	22	94	79
disposal		21	99	91	*diverts*		0	34	78	*domain*		17	94	80
disposals		2	46	82	divide	Verb	61	100	94	*domains*		5	57	74
dispose	Verb	16	99	93	*divide*		12	99	92	domestic	Adj	69	99	92
dispose		6	96	92	*divided*		40	100	94	dominance	NoC	11	88	89
disposed		6	94	93	*divides*		3	80	91	dominant	Adj	30	96	90
disposes		1	38	84	*dividing*		5	96	93	dominate	Verb	44	100	94
disposing		3	88	91	dividend	NoC	25	96	81	*dominate*		10	96	93
dispute	NoC	44	97	89	*dividend*		15	77	80	*dominated*		27	98	93
dispute		30	96	89	*dividends*		10	91	81	*dominates*		4	77	91
disputes		14	88	87	divine	Adj	13	97	88	*dominating*		3	86	93
dissolve	Verb	16	99	91	*divine*		13	97	88	Don	NoP	13	94	90
dissolve		4	91	90	division	NoC	112	99	92	Donald	NoP	16	93	82
dissolved		8	95	89	*division*		90	98	91	*Donald*		16	93	82
dissolves		1	64	87	*divisions*		22	96	91	donate	Verb	10	93	90
dissolving		1	65	90	divorce	NoC	18	96	90	*donate*		2	75	90
distance	NoC	75	100	96	*divorce*		17	95	90	*donated*		7	87	89
distance		66	100	96	*divorces*		1	37	82	*donates*		0	10	66
distances		9	96	92	divorce	Verb	11	100	92	*donating*		1	48	86
distant	Adj	29	100	93	*divorce*		4	90	90	donation	NoC	13	96	90
distinct	Adj	32	98	92	*divorced*		7	96	92	*donation*		6	92	89
distinction	NoC	49	98	90	*divorces*		0	14	73	*donations*		7	83	90
distinction		41	98	90	*divorcing*		0	32	83	donor	NoC	11	84	88
distinctions		7	85	87	DNA	NoC	34	70	61	*donor*		6	79	89
distinctive	Adj	22	99	91	*DNA*		33	70	62	*donors*		5	64	83
distinguish	Verb	39	98	90	*DNAs*		1	5	36	door	NoC	302	100	89
distinguish		20	98	90	do	Verb	5594	100	92	*door*		254	100	87
distinguished		12	85	88	*d'*		16	59	76	*doors*		48	100	93
distinguishes		4	74	88	*did*		1434	100	92	doorway	NoC	19	94	86
distinguishing		4	77	88	*do*		2802	100	90	*doorway*		17	87	85

1.1

Word	PoS	Freq	Ra	Di	Word	PoS	Freq	Ra	Di	Word	PoS	Freq	Ra	Di
doorways		2	73	87	draw	NoC	15	96	85	*driving*		38	100	93
Dorothy	NoP	12	87	80	*draw*		14	90	84	*drove*		37	99	90
Dorothy		12	87	80	*draws*		2	63	86	driver	NoC	80	100	91
dose	NoC	23	94	78	draw	Verb	224	100	97	*driver*		54	100	91
dose		16	92	77	*draw*		60	100	96	*drivers*		26	99	89
doses		7	75	79	*drawing*		31	100	96	driving	Adj	13	99	93
dot	NoC	16	98	69	*drawn*		75	100	97	driving	NoC	14	98	90
dot		11	93	57	*draws*		11	96	93	drop	NoC	29	100	95
dots		5	80	83	*drew*		46	100	90	*drop*		22	100	95
double	Adj	57	100	95	drawer	NoC	16	95	88	*drops*		7	90	88
double	NoC	13	99	90	*drawer*		10	87	87	drop	Verb	107	100	95
double		11	98	91	*drawers*		6	81	87	*drop*		31	100	94
doubles		3	63	81	drawing	NoC	48	100	87	*dropped*		57	100	93
double	Verb	25	100	94	*drawing*		25	100	92	*dropping*		13	99	94
double		7	99	93	*drawings*		23	100	79	*drops*		7	95	94
doubled		12	100	94	dreadful	Adj	14	95	90	drown	Verb	14	99	90
doubles		2	65	88	dream	NoC	63	100	90	*drown*		4	83	89
doubling		3	90	91	*dream*		38	100	91	*drowned*		7	94	90
doubt	NoC	84	100	94	*dreams*		25	99	88	*drowning*		3	70	88
doubt		64	100	93	dream	Verb	26	100	89	*drowns*		0	31	81
doubts		20	98	95	*dream*		8	94	91	drug	NoC	104	100	91
doubt	Verb	31	99	93	*dreamed*		8	91	89	*drug*		50	99	90
doubt		21	99	92	*dreaming*		7	89	78	*drugs*		53	100	92
doubted		7	90	91	*dreams*		1	37	83	drum	NoC	16	95	89
doubting		2	70	83	*dreamt*		3	78	90	*drum*		9	93	86
doubts		1	51	86	dress	NoC	48	100	90	*drums*		7	88	89
doubtful	Adj	13	100	95	*dress*		42	100	89	drunk	Adj	16	94	89
Douglas	NoP	24	95	88	*dresses*		7	89	90	*drunk*		16	94	89
down	Adv	845	100	94	dress	Verb	56	100	92	*drunker*		0	7	59
down	NoC	13	98	90	*dress*		10	96	92	dry	Adj	56	100	94
down		6	90	86	*dressed*		37	100	90	*drier*		1	65	86
downs		6	92	90	*dresses*		1	44	84	*driest*		0	24	77
down	Prep	98	100	92	dressing	NoC	11	93	91	*dry*		54	100	94
downstairs	Adv	17	88	87	*dressing*		10	90	91	dry	Verb	28	100	93
dozen	NoC	36	100	95	*dressings*		2	55	83	*dried*		10	98	92
dozen		27	100	95	drift	Verb	20	99	91	*dries*		2	67	89
dozens		9	99	91	*drift*		5	92	91	*dry*		12	96	90
Dr	NoC	124	98	86	*drifted*		9	91	88	*drying*		5	92	92
Dr		112	98	85	*drifting*		6	93	91	du	Fore	12	93	86
Dr.		12	77	80	*drifts*		0	34	84	dual	Adj	12	96	92
draft	NoC	28	99	86	drill	NoC	11	93	78	Dublin	NoP	23	94	84
draft		26	98	87	*drill*		7	87	84	duck	NoC	19	95	89
drafts		2	64	87	*drills*		3	60	59	*duck*		12	92	87
draft	Verb	15	94	87	drill	Verb	11	97	83	*ducks*		7	87	87
draft		4	85	83	*drill*		3	59	81	due	Adj	75	100	93
drafted		7	90	89	*drilled*		4	80	81	due to	Prep	78	100	94
drafting		3	74	79	*drilling*		4	78	80	duke	NoC	35	100	88
drafts		0	18	75	*drills*		0	10	70	*duke*		33	100	88
drag	Verb	33	100	90	drink	NoC	70	100	92	*dukes*		2	55	82
drag		8	97	91	*drink*		49	99	91	dull	Adj	18	99	92
dragged		17	98	89	*drinks*		21	98	93	*dull*		18	99	92
dragging		7	93	89	drink	Verb	75	100	92	*duller*		0	34	82
drags		1	51	88	*drank*		14	95	86	*dullest*		0	21	78
dragon	NoC	13	90	83	*drink*		32	99	92	dump	Verb	16	97	89
dragon		9	86	84	*drinking*		20	100	93	*dump*		3	76	89
dragons		4	67	80	*drinks*		2	73	88	*dumped*		9	92	89
drain	Verb	17	99	92	*drunk*		6	88	90	*dumping*		4	78	81
drain		5	90	88	drinking	NoC	15	100	90	*dumps*		0	28	78
drained		8	93	89	drive	NoC	54	100	92	Duncan	NoP	15	90	76
draining		3	83	90	*drive*		47	100	93	*Duncan*		15	90	76
drains		1	55	87	*drives*		7	87	80	*Duncans*		0	4	45
drama	NoC	38	99	84	drive	Verb	156	100	94	duration	NoC	19	97	84
drama		36	99	83	*drive*		44	100	95	*duration*		18	97	84
dramas		2	73	90	*driven*		30	100	95	*durations*		1	31	77
dramatic	Adj	39	100	94	*drives*		7	96	94	Durham	NoP	25	88	60
dramatically	Adv	15	99	95						*Durham*		25	88	60

Word	PoS	Freq	Ra	Di	Word	PoS	Freq	Ra	Di	Word	PoS	Freq	Ra	Di
during	Prep	440	100	95	eats		4	89	89	effects		0	35	85
dust	NoC	26	100	93	eating	NoC	13	96	90	effective	Adj	99	100	93
dust		26	100	93	*eating*		13	96	90	effectively	Adv	51	100	94
dusts		0	12	71	EC	NoP	67	77	81	effectiveness	NoC	21	86	89
Dutch	Adj	23	100	91	*EC*		67	76	81	efficiency	NoC	38	99	91
duty	NoC	119	100	92	echo	NoC	16	100	82	*efficiencies*		1	38	80
duties		39	100	93	*echo*		12	96	77	*efficiency*		37	99	91
duty		81	100	93	*echoes*		4	87	89	efficient	Adj	40	100	93
dwelling	NoC	14	93	85	echo	Verb	20	99	93	efficiently	Adv	11	94	93
dwelling		5	87	91	*echo*		4	91	81	effort	NoC	134	100	96
dwellings		8	86	78	*echoed*		10	93	91	*effort*		78	100	96
dying	Adj	11	98	92	*echoes*		2	75	90	*efforts*		56	99	94
dynamic	Adj	16	90	90	*echoing*		3	80	90	eg	Adv	71	80	88
E / e	Lett	69	100	87	*echos*		0	4	33	*e.g*		1	20	63
E	NoP	24	86	80	economic	Adj	236	99	88	*e.g.*		49	74	87
E		6	67	74	economically	Adv	10	90	91	*eg*		18	67	77
E.		18	86	76	economics	NoC	29	97	67	*eg.*		3	43	63
each	DetP	508	100	95	economist	NoC	16	89	88	egg	NoC	62	100	90
each other	Pron	108	100	95	*economist*		7	83	88	*egg*		25	99	90
eager	Adj	14	98	93	*economists*		9	79	86	*eggs*		37	99	89
eagle	NoC	18	97	79	economy	NoC	124	100	90	ego	NoC	10	90	76
eagle		13	93	81	*economies*		19	88	88	*ego*		10	88	74
eagles		5	78	73	*economy*		105	100	89	*egos*		1	43	85
ear	NoC	59	99	91	ed	NoC	10	69	62	Egypt	NoP	22	99	88
ear		29	98	91	*ed*		6	54	46	eh	Int	35	77	72
ears		30	99	91	*ed.*		2	28	55	eight	Num	174	100	90
earl	NoC	24	93	83	*eds*		3	37	65	*eight*		173	100	90
earl		23	92	82	Ed	NoP	11	81	73	*eights*		1	31	73
earls		2	42	77	Eddie	NoP	12	82	84	eighteen	Num	30	100	87
earlier	Adv	97	100	96	edge	NoC	92	100	94	*eighteen*		30	100	87
early	Adj	353	100	95	*edge*		75	100	94	eighteenth	Ord	20	96	88
earlier		70	100	94	*edges*		17	98	92	eighth	Ord	13	98	89
earliest		18	99	92	Edinburgh	NoP	60	99	84	eighty	Num	47	98	74
early		264	100	95	*Edinburgh*		60	99	84	*eighties*		8	87	86
early	Adv	76	100	97	edit	Verb	17	99	89	*eighty*		38	97	69
earn	Verb	54	100	95	*edit*		4	80	79	either	Adv	220	100	97
earn		20	100	95	*edited*		10	89	89	either	DetP	58	100	97
earned		19	100	94	*editing*		3	69	85	El	NoP-	12	89	83
earning		12	100	94	*edits*		0	21	78	elaborate	Adj	13	98	93
earns		3	79	89	edition	NoC	33	100	90	elbow	NoC	16	96	89
earnings	NoC	32	93	85	*edition*		25	100	90	*elbow*		11	95	89
earth	NoC	97	100	93	*editions*		7	83	86	*elbows*		5	76	86
earth		97	100	93	editor	NoC	47	97	90	elder	NoC	10	96	89
earths		0	22	72	*editor*		39	97	89	*elder*		5	91	88
ease	NoC	20	100	94	*editors*		8	86	86	*elders*		5	86	88
ease	Verb	24	100	94	educate	Verb	19	99	83	elderly	Adj	50	100	90
ease		11	100	95	*educate*		4	91	93	eldest	Adj	10	97	77
eased		9	99	91	*educated*		13	98	76	Eleanor	NoP	12	76	73
eases		1	57	87	*educates*		0	17	77	*Eleanor*		12	76	73
easing		4	88	93	*educating*		2	73	91	elect	Verb	52	99	77
easier	Adv	12	100	95	education	NoC	260	100	90	*elect*		4	84	88
easily	Adv	99	100	96	*education*		260	100	90	*elected*		45	99	76
east	NoC	128	100	93	*educations*		0	11	70	*electing*		1	54	84
East	NoP-	48	100	86	educational	Adj	59	98	89	*elects*		1	33	68
Easter	NoC	18	98	91	Edward	NoP	69	100	86	election	NoC	157	100	79
Easter		18	98	91	Edwards	NoP	13	82	86	*election*		98	100	83
eastern	Adj	59	100	90	EEC	NoP	13	72	76	*elections*		59	92	68
easy	Adj	198	100	96	*E.E.C.*		1	7	09	electoral	Adj	22	84	83
easier		47	100	96	*EEC*		12	71	75	electorate	NoC	11	83	86
easiest		8	98	93	effect	NoC	336	100	93	*electorate*		11	83	86
easy		143	100	96	*effect*		228	100	93	*electorates*		1	28	80
eat	Verb	144	100	92	*effects*		108	100	92	electric	Adj	34	100	93
ate		18	97	89	effect	Verb	13	97	89	electrical	Adj	23	100	92
eat		75	100	90	*effect*		5	92	92	electricity	NoC	38	100	90
eaten		17	96	93	*effected*		6	85	84	*electricity*		38	100	90
eating		30	98	92	*effecting*		1	60	88	electron	NoC	16	67	75

Word	PoS	Freq	Ra	Di	Word	PoS	Freq	Ra	Di	Word	PoS	Freq	Ra	Di
electron		9	61	75	emission	NoC	21	80	69	*encounters*		2	69	88
electrons		6	48	73	*emission*		6	62	73	encourage	Verb	113	100	94
electronic	Adj	34	99	85	*emissions*		15	67	62	*encourage*		51	100	94
electronics	NoC	15	92	83	Emma	NoP	15	86	79	*encouraged*		46	99	94
elegant	Adj	18	98	91	*Emma*		15	86	79	*encourages*		8	86	92
element	NoC	120	100	92	emotion	NoC	35	97	91	*encouraging*		8	99	93
element		56	100	92	*emotion*		15	95	91	encouragement	NoC	15	100	94
elements		64	98	92	*emotions*		19	96	90	*encouragement*		15	100	94
elephant	NoC	15	98	86	emotional	Adj	36	99	93	*encouragements*		0	14	74
elephant		9	94	89	emperor	NoC	24	90	83	encouraging	Adj	21	99	94
elephants		6	85	81	*emperor*		21	88	82	end	NoC	458	100	98
eleven	Num	38	100	88	*emperors*		2	60	77	*end*		429	100	98
eleven		38	100	88	emphasis	NoC	55	98	92	*ends*		29	100	94
elevens		0	8	56	emphasise	Verb	30	100	93	End	NoP-	12	95	91
eligible	Adj	13	93	90	*emphasise*		10	95	92	end	Verb	158	100	88
eliminate	Verb	24	99	93	*emphasised*		12	95	93	*end*		55	100	96
eliminate		11	92	93	*emphasises*		5	73	90	*ended*		73	100	75
eliminated		8	91	92	*emphasising*		4	90	92	*ending*		14	99	93
eliminates		1	54	88	emphasize	Verb	20	89	90	*ends*		15	100	94
eliminating		4	83	92	*emphasize*		7	85	90	ending	NoC	11	99	93
Eliot	NoP	19	71	64	*emphasized*		9	82	88	*ending*		9	99	93
Eliot		19	71	64	*emphasizes*		3	61	86	*endings*		2	60	87
Eliots		0	2	10	*emphasizing*		2	70	88	endless	Adj	16	99	94
elite*	NoC	16	91	74	empire	NoC	39	100	88	endorse	Verb	16	93	88
elite		12	91	78	*empire*		36	100	87	*endorse*		5	87	87
elites		4	42	59	*empires*		2	65	81	*endorsed*		9	83	85
Elizabeth	NoP	36	100	87	empirical	Adj	15	70	85	*endorses*		1	40	84
Elizabeth		36	100	87	employ	Verb	79	100	94	*endorsing*		1	57	86
Ellen	NoP	10	66	69	*employ*		17	100	94	endure	Verb	11	97	94
else	Adv	209	100	93	*employed*		49	100	93	*endure*		5	95	93
elsewhere	Adv	57	100	95	*employing*		8	93	92	*endured*		4	84	91
embark	Verb	14	98	94	*employs*		6	87	90	*endures*		1	42	85
embark		4	87	92	employee	NoC	89	99	89	*enduring*		1	65	90
embarked		6	94	93	*employee*		31	95	85	enemy	NoC	49	100	91
embarking		3	85	91	*employees*		58	99	89	*enemies*		15	97	93
embarks		0	22	78	employer	NoC	73	100	90	*enemy*		34	99	89
embarrassed	Adj	13	97	91	*employer*		30	99	86	energy	NoC	131	100	89
embarrassing	Adj	11	99	94	*employers*		42	94	89	*energies*		9	93	86
embarrassment	NoC	14	99	93	employment	NoC	107	99	90	*energy*		122	100	89
embarrassment		13	99	93	*employment*		107	99	90	enforce	Verb	20	94	88
embarrassments		0	32	84	*employments*		0	23	78	*enforce*		10	89	87
embassy	NoC	15	93	86	empty	Adj	54	100	91	*enforced*		7	89	88
embassies		2	51	76	*emptier*		0	10	68	*enforces*		0	29	82
embassy		13	91	86	*empty*		54	100	91	*enforcing*		3	75	87
embody	Verb	12	91	90	empty	Verb	11	97	92	enforcement	NoC	13	83	85
embodied		6	81	90	*emptied*		5	88	92	*enforcement*		13	83	85
embodies		2	69	89	*empties*		0	32	82	engage	Verb	44	100	95
embody		3	68	87	*empty*		4	86	92	*engage*		12	98	92
embodying		1	54	87	*emptying*		2	64	85	*engaged*		27	100	95
embrace	Verb	17	97	95	enable	Verb	101	100	92	*engages*		1	64	87
embrace		6	94	93	*enable*		48	100	92	*engaging*		4	84	91
embraced		6	91	93	*enabled*		18	98	94	engagement	NoC	17	99	80
embraces		2	67	89	*enables*		21	91	87	*engagement*		12	97	76
embracing		3	91	93	*enabling*		14	86	90	*engagements*		5	86	69
emerge	Verb	78	97	95	enclose	Verb	15	98	90	engine	NoC	69	100	91
emerge		21	97	94	*enclose*		4	82	86	*engine*		50	100	90
emerged		38	96	95	*enclosed*		8	92	89	*engines*		19	100	92
emerges		10	90	91	*encloses*		1	26	61	engineer	NoC	48	100	89
emerging		10	97	94	*enclosing*		3	76	90	*engineer*		22	100	89
emergence	NoC	12	84	90	encounter	NoC	15	95	93	*engineers*		25	99	88
emergence		12	84	90	*encounter*		10	93	93	engineering	NoC	51	100	90
emergency	NoC	43	100	89	*encounters*		5	84	91	*engineering*		51	100	90
emergencies		3	85	91	encounter	Verb	27	98	94	England	NoP	231	100	93
emergency		40	100	89	*encounter*		7	95	93	*England*		231	100	93
Emily	NoP	20	74	74	*encountered*		17	97	93	English	Adj	150	100	94
Emily		20	74	74	*encountering*		1	73	91	*English*		150	100	94
										English	NoC	81	100	90

Word	PoS	Freq	Ra	Di	Word	PoS	Freq	Ra	Di	Word	PoS	Freq	Ra	Di
English		81	100	90	*entitles*		1	51	84	*erect*	Verb	15	98	93
Englishman	NoC	11	96	90	*entitling*		1	32	80	*erect*		3	90	92
Englishman		8	93	88	entitled	Adj	26	100	85	*erected*		10	96	91
Englishmen		3	79	87	entity	NoC	18	94	76	*erecting*		1	69	89
enhance	Verb	31	96	93	*entities*		6	80	78	*erects*		0	16	74
enhance		14	93	93	*entity*		12	93	74	Eric	NoP	19	96	90
enhanced		11	93	91	entrance	NoC	34	100	94	erm	Uncl	627	45	68
enhances		3	73	89	*entrance*		31	100	93	erosion	NoC	13	80	74
enhancing		4	80	91	*entrances*		3	86	89	*erosion*		12	80	73
enjoy	Verb	146	100	96	entry	NoC	69	100	91	*erosions*		1	8	32
enjoy		66	100	96	*entries*		18	97	86	error	NoC	59	100	81
enjoyed		51	100	97	*entry*		52	100	91	*error*		38	100	78
enjoying		22	100	94	envelope	NoC	19	98	90	*errors*		21	94	86
enjoys		8	99	93	*envelope*		14	96	89	escape	NoC	21	99	94
enjoyment	NoC	10	98	92	*envelopes*		4	92	92	*escape*		19	99	94
enjoyment		10	98	92	environment	NoC	144	100	89	*escapes*		2	69	88
enjoyments		0	12	73	*environment*		130	100	89	escape	Verb	55	100	95
enormous	Adj	42	100	96	*environments*		14	80	78	*escape*		28	100	95
enough	Adv	244	100	95	environmental	Adj	84	93	80	*escaped*		19	100	92
enough	DetP	82	100	96	envisage	Verb	18	98	91	*escapes*		2	80	91
enquire	Verb	15	97	86	*envisage*		4	89	93	*escaping*		5	92	93
enquire		4	90	93	*envisaged*		12	94	89	especially	Adv	177	100	95
enquired		9	80	80	*envisages*		2	60	87	essay	NoC	24	95	83
enquires		0	23	82	*envisaging*		1	30	78	*essay*		16	92	80
enquiring		2	72	90	enzyme	NoC	12	62	71	*essays*		8	87	86
enquiry	NoC	34	100	92	*enzyme*		7	52	70	essence	NoC	20	98	91
enquiries		17	99	91	*enzymes*		5	51	73	*essence*		18	98	92
enquiry		18	100	91	episode	NoC	21	99	91	*essences*		1	28	54
ensure	Verb	142	99	92	*episode*		13	99	91	essential	Adj	87	100	93
ensure		103	99	92	*episodes*		8	87	86	essentially	Adv	36	98	92
ensured		10	94	93	equal	Adj	61	100	93	Essex	NoP	23	97	81
ensures		9	83	91	equal	Verb	10	95	88	establish	Verb	176	99	93
ensuring		19	96	93	*equal*		2	63	82	*establish*		53	98	93
entail	Verb	14	96	90	*equalled*		2	77	90	*established*		99	99	93
entail		4	86	90	*equalling*		0	29	81	*establishes*		3	73	89
entailed		4	87	90	*equals*		6	85	83	*establishing*		21	93	92
entailing		1	40	86	equality	NoC	16	93	91	established	Adj	20	95	91
entails		5	84	86	*equalities*		0	6	52	establishment	NoC	48	98	93
enter	Verb	143	100	94	*equality*		15	93	91	*establishment*		40	98	92
enter		53	100	93	equally	Adv	66	100	96	*establishments*		8	96	87
entered		59	100	92	equation	NoC	35	94	76	estate	NoC	74	100	93
entering		22	100	95	*equation*		25	92	74	*estate*		54	100	93
enters		8	99	92	*equations*		11	70	77	*estates*		20	96	90
enterprise	NoC	60	99	89	equilibrium	NoC	17	80	75	estimate	NoC	36	98	90
enterprise		42	99	90	equip	Verb	19	99	93	*estimate*		17	94	88
enterprises		17	85	84	*equip*		2	78	91	*estimates*		19	90	90
entertain	Verb	14	99	94	*equipped*		16	99	92	estimate	Verb	51	99	90
entertain		7	97	91	*equipping*		1	51	88	*estimate*		10	92	90
entertained		5	94	93	*equips*		0	14	72	*estimated*		32	99	87
entertaining		1	70	90	equipment	NoC	89	100	93	*estimates*		6	74	87
entertains		0	31	83	*equipment*		89	100	93	*estimating*		3	67	85
entertainment	NoC	23	100	93	*equipments*		0	11	54	estimated	Adj	17	84	82
entertainment		20	100	93	equity	NoC	22	87	84	et al	Adv	42	72	80
entertainments		2	74	87	*equities*		3	39	77	*et al*		30	71	74
enthusiasm	NoC	30	100	95	*equity*		20	86	84	*et al.*		12	45	80
enthusiasm		30	100	95	equivalent	Adj	25	96	91	etc	Adv	75	99	91
enthusiasms		1	48	84	equivalent	NoC	22	100	93	*etc*		50	98	90
enthusiast	NoC	10	91	88	*equivalent*		19	100	93	*etc.*		24	93	90
enthusiast		4	79	88	*equivalents*		3	74	89	ethical	Adj	11	84	84
enthusiasts		7	84	86	E.R.	NoP	14	36	39	ethnic	Adj	23	96	87
enthusiastic	Adj	14	100	95	*E.R.*		8	11	05	Europe	NoP	181	100	91
entire	Adj	48	100	97	*ER*		5	32	45	*Europe*		181	100	91
entirely	Adv	69	100	96	er	Uncl	896	78	67	European	Adj	195	100	90
entitle	Verb	27	99	90	era	NoC	22	97	93	European	NoC	15	96	89
entitle		2	53	77	*era*		21	97	93	*European*		8	88	84
entitled		23	99	91	*eras*		1	39	84	*Europeans*		7	88	88

Word	PoS	Freq	Ra	Di	Word	PoS	Freq	Ra	Di	Word	PoS	Freq	Ra	Di
evaluate	Verb	24	84	88	*example*		125	100	92	*executive*		78	100	91
evaluate		11	77	87	*examples*		71	97	91	*executives*		13	88	90
evaluated		7	73	84	exceed	Verb	30	96	91	exemption	NoC	13	80	80
evaluates		1	33	81	*exceed*		10	89	91	*exemption*		10	78	77
evaluating		5	74	88	*exceeded*		9	92	91	*exemptions*		3	60	85
evaluation	NoC	30	84	86	*exceeding*		5	80	89	exercise	NoC	79	100	93
evaluation		28	83	86	*exceeds*		6	74	88	*exercise*		63	100	93
evaluations		2	61	86	excellent	Adj	67	100	93	*exercises*		16	100	88
Evans	NoP	19	94	85	except	Conj	41	100	96	exercise	Verb	49	100	89
even	Adv	716	100	97	except	Prep	30	100	96	*exercise*		24	100	90
even if	Conj	87	100	97	except for	Prep	20	100	95	*exercised*		15	96	88
even so	Adv	15	100	94	except that	Conj	14	100	93	*exercises*		3	79	90
even though	Conj	59	100	96	exception	NoC	44	100	93	*exercising*		7	97	88
even when	Conj	24	100	96	*exception*		29	99	94	exert	Verb	12	94	92
evening	NoC	153	100	93	*exceptions*		15	97	91	*exert*		6	90	91
evening		138	100	93	exceptional	Adj	17	97	93	*exerted*		4	82	90
evenings		15	99	93	excess	Adj	11	92	89	*exerting*		1	66	89
event	NoC	208	100	94	excess	NoC	14	97	89	*exerts*		1	54	84
event		104	100	93	*excess*		9	95	86	exhaust	Verb	12	99	94
events		105	100	94	*excesses*		4	86	90	*exhaust*		2	70	89
eventual	Adj	10	97	92	excessive	Adj	17	98	94	*exhausted*		9	99	93
eventually	Adv	91	100	97	exchange	NoC	92	100	90	*exhausting*		1	53	87
ever	Adv	259	100	95	*exchange*		82	100	89	*exhausts*		0	23	80
every	Det	401	100	97	*exchanges*		11	95	88	exhibit	Verb	18	94	90
everybody	Pron	61	99	87	exchange	Verb	20	100	94	*exhibit*		6	84	89
everyday	Adj	21	100	92	*exchange*		6	97	93	*exhibited*		7	90	88
everyone	Pron	133	100	95	*exchanged*		10	98	93	*exhibiting*		3	74	85
everything	Pron	187	100	93	*exchanges*		0	29	83	*exhibits*		2	63	87
everywhere	Adv	32	100	95	*exchanging*		3	92	92	exhibition	NoC	67	100	82
evidence	NoC	215	100	93	excited	Adj	16	99	91	*exhibition*		54	100	82
evidence		215	100	93	excitement	NoC	27	98	91	*exhibitions*		13	82	80
evidences		0	21	73	*excitement*		26	98	91	exile	NoC	12	92	87
evident	Adj	26	97	93	*excitements*		1	38	84	*exile*		10	92	87
evidently	Adv	15	98	92	exciting	Adj	33	99	95	*exiles*		3	66	84
evil	Adj	15	99	91	exclaim	Verb	11	76	81	exist	Verb	114	100	94
evil	NoC	16	99	91	*exclaim*		1	42	86	*exist*		54	100	94
evil		13	99	91	*exclaimed*		10	68	79	*existed*		25	99	94
evils		3	80	91	*exclaiming*		1	32	80	*existing*		2	76	89
evoke	Verb	10	90	79	*exclaims*		0	24	79	*exists*		32	100	92
evoke		3	71	78	exclude	Verb	47	98	89	existence	NoC	66	98	93
evoked		4	77	85	*exclude*		13	95	85	*existence*		66	98	93
evokes		3	60	66	*excluded*		23	97	90	*existences*		0	22	80
evoking		1	41	79	*excludes*		4	74	88	existing	Adj	94	96	92
evolution	NoC	25	92	87	*excluding*		7	90	91	exit	NoC	12	100	94
evolution		25	92	87	exclusion	NoC	17	91	79	*exit*		10	100	94
evolutions		0	17	76	*exclusion*		15	90	78	*exits*		1	67	89
evolutionary	Adj	11	77	83	*exclusions*		2	47	73	exotic	Adj	11	96	93
evolve	Verb	21	95	90	exclusive	Adj	21	100	93	expand	Verb	42	100	94
evolve		5	83	88	exclusively	Adv	17	96	93	*expand*		18	98	93
evolved		12	89	90	excuse	NoC	23	100	94	*expanded*		14	100	93
evolves		1	42	84	*excuse*		17	99	94	*expanding*		8	97	93
evolving		3	77	90	*excuses*		6	94	91	*expands*		3	80	89
exact	Adj	22	100	95	excuse	Verb	17	100	88	expansion	NoC	37	95	92
exactly	Adv	107	100	95	*excuse*		14	94	86	*expansion*		36	95	92
exam	NoC	16	95	88	*excused*		3	84	90	*expansions*		1	34	81
exam		9	92	86	*excuses*		0	17	77	expect	Verb	288	100	96
exams		7	89	89	*excusing*		0	30	81	*expect*		106	100	97
examination	NoC	62	100	90	execute	Verb	19	96	90	*expected*		146	100	94
examination		48	100	91	*execute*		4	80	84	*expecting*		21	100	92
examinations		14	89	84	*executed*		13	95	90	*expects*		14	95	78
examine	Verb	95	100	91	*executes*		0	21	73	expectation	NoC	46	99	90
examine		37	99	89	*executing*		1	57	86	*expectation*		13	96	92
examined		36	99	93	execution	NoC	17	97	87	*expectations*		33	99	88
examines		7	74	78	*execution*		14	96	88	expected	Adj	21	99	88
examining		15	98	93	*executions*		2	57	76	expedition	NoC	15	95	91
example	NoC	196	100	92	executive	NoC	91	100	91	*expedition*		11	92	90

Word	PoS	Freq	Ra	Di	Word	PoS	Freq	Ra	Di	Word	PoS	Freq	Ra	Di
expeditions		4	78	89	expose	Verb	32	100	95	face	Verb	164	100	96
expenditure	NoC	57	96	88	*expose*		6	97	94	*face*		67	100	95
expenditure		55	96	88	*exposed*		20	98	94	*faced*		45	100	96
expenditures		2	51	83	*exposes*		1	60	88	*faces*		14	98	88
expense	NoC	47	100	93	*exposing*		4	94	93	*facing*		38	100	95
expense		27	100	95	exposure	NoC	24	96	89	facilitate	Verb	17	88	91
expenses		20	100	90	*exposure*		23	96	89	*facilitate*		10	86	91
expensive	Adj	59	100	96	*exposures*		1	47	80	*facilitated*		3	67	88
experience	NoC	223	100	94	express	NoC	11	96	91	*facilitates*		2	53	87
experience		189	100	94	*express*		11	96	91	*facilitating*		2	58	88
experiences		34	99	92	express	Verb	121	99	93	facility	NoC	98	100	92
experience	Verb	69	100	94	*express*		32	97	94	*facilities*		75	100	92
experience		25	100	93	*expressed*		69	97	92	*facility*		22	99	91
experienced		35	100	95	*expresses*		6	80	89	fact	NoC	426	100	96
experiences		1	44	83	*expressing*		14	97	92	*fact*		374	100	96
experiencing		8	96	93	expression	NoC	88	100	92	*facts*		53	99	91
experienced	Adj	21	100	94	*expression*		75	100	91	faction	NoC	14	89	74
experiment	NoC	57	100	89	*expressions*		13	98	91	*faction*		7	71	69
experiment		27	99	89	extend	Verb	97	100	95	*factions*		7	85	78
experiments		29	95	87	*extend*		31	100	94	factor	NoC	150	100	92
experimental	Adj	24	94	88	*extended*		40	100	95	*factor*		63	99	90
expert	NoC	72	100	84	*extending*		16	99	94	*factors*		87	94	91
expert		40	100	77	*extends*		10	91	92	factory	NoC	63	100	94
experts		32	98	90	extended	Adj	14	98	93	*factories*		17	99	90
expertise	NoC	26	96	92	extension	NoC	42	100	94	*factory*		46	100	94
expertise		26	96	92	*extension*		35	100	94	faculty	NoC	17	92	73
explain	Verb	193	100	97	*extensions*		7	93	85	*faculties*		4	84	80
explain		79	100	96	extensive	Adj	41	98	92	*faculty*		13	80	70
explained		71	100	96	extent	NoC	101	100	92	fade	Verb	20	100	91
explaining		18	99	96	*extent*		100	100	92	*fade*		5	93	93
explains		25	97	93	*extents*		0	20	77	*faded*		9	91	88
explanation	NoC	64	99	92	external	Adj	49	97	90	*fades*		1	66	89
explanation		47	99	93	extra	Adj	92	100	95	*fading*		4	83	91
explanations		17	97	87	extract	NoC	15	92	85	fail	Verb	161	100	96
explicit	Adj	19	94	89	*extract*		8	83	85	*fail*		33	100	95
explicitly	Adv	13	86	89	*extracts*		7	81	83	*failed*		89	100	95
explode	Verb	17	99	92	extract	Verb	18	99	94	*failing*		21	100	94
explode		4	92	93	*extract*		7	97	92	*fails*		19	96	92
exploded		10	95	90	*extracted*		7	98	91	failure	NoC	88	99	94
explodes		1	58	88	*extracting*		3	84	91	*failure*		78	99	94
exploding		2	71	89	*extracts*		0	37	85	*failures*		11	93	93
exploit	Verb	25	98	93	extraordinary	Adj	29	99	95	faint	Adj	19	97	86
exploit		12	97	92	extreme	Adj	33	100	94	*faint*		15	96	85
exploited		9	91	91	*extreme*		33	100	94	*fainter*		1	28	56
exploiting		4	81	91	extreme	NoC	10	97	93	*faintest*		3	62	84
exploitation	NoC	13	88	90	*extreme*		4	88	92	fair	Adj	87	100	96
exploitation		13	88	90	*extremes*		6	93	93	*fair*		84	100	96
exploration	NoC	17	96	86	extremely	Adv	68	100	95	*fairer*		3	85	90
exploration		15	96	85	eye	NoC	392	100	87	*fairest*		1	47	86
explorations		1	58	87	*eye*		95	100	95	fairly	Adv	67	100	94
explore	Verb	48	100	92	*eyes*		297	100	84	faith	NoC	54	100	88
explore		23	99	90	eyebrow	NoC	14	89	83	*faith*		52	100	88
explored		12	94	92	*eyebrow*		4	56	79	*faiths*		1	41	80
explores		3	71	86	*eyebrows*		9	84	84	faithful	Adj	10	98	94
exploring		10	95	93	F / f	Lett	39	99	86	fall	NoC	50	100	94
explosion	NoC	22	99	92	F	NoP	16	88	86	*fall*		41	100	93
explosion		17	99	92	*F*		4	66	71	*falls*		9	98	92
explosions		5	80	86	*F.*		11	86	84	fall	Verb	273	100	96
export	NoC	40	93	85	FA	NoP	15	51	75	*fall*		70	100	97
export		21	93	87	*FA*		15	50	74	*fallen*		36	100	95
exports		19	81	82	fabric	NoC	29	99	83	*falling*		44	100	96
export	Verb	18	94	88	*fabric*		21	98	83	*falls*		22	100	94
export		6	85	88	*fabrics*		7	79	82	*fell*		101	100	94
exported		5	80	85	face	NoC	315	100	88	false	Adj	36	100	95
exporting		3	74	89	*face*		282	100	88	fame	NoC	12	95	91
exports		4	62	75	*faces*		33	100	91	familiar	Adj	57	100	96

1.1

Word	PoS	Freq	Ra	Di	Word	PoS	Freq	Ra	Di	Word	PoS	Freq	Ra	Di
family	NoC	428	100	95	favour	Verb	29	97	93	*females*		20	94	84
families		83	100	93	*favour*		9	93	92	feminist	Adj	14	82	69
family		345	100	95	*favoured*		13	96	92	feminist	NoC	12	83	78
famous	Adj	65	100	94	*favouring*		3	84	90	*feminist*		3	66	84
fan	NoC	48	98	86	*favours*		4	81	91	*feminists*		9	66	74
fan		15	95	90	favourable	Adj	15	95	93	fence	NoC	22	98	91
fans		33	95	84	favourite	Adj	33	100	94	*fence*		17	97	91
fancy	Verb	18	96	88	favourite	NoC	24	99	91	*fences*		6	89	87
fancied		4	82	88	*favourite*		15	99	92	Ferguson	NoP	10	72	78
fancies		1	49	77	*favourites*		9	94	90	*Ferguson*		10	71	78
fancy		12	93	87	fax	NoC	10	84	77	ferry	NoC	14	93	90
fancying		0	21	77	*fax*		9	80	77	*ferries*		3	59	81
fantastic	Adj	12	99	93	*faxes*		1	36	66	*ferry*		11	90	90
fantasy	NoC	19	99	93	fear	NoC	93	100	91	fertility	NoC	12	85	75
fantasies		5	87	91	*fear*		65	100	94	festival	NoC	36	99	88
fantasy		13	99	93	*fears*		29	98	93	*festival*		31	99	87
far	Adj	288	100	96	fear	Verb	53	100	94	*festivals*		5	82	89
far		68	100	95	*fear*		25	99	94	fetch	Verb	19	97	90
farther		1	50	86	*feared*		19	97	94	*fetch*		12	93	89
farthest		1	39	84	*fearing*		4	86	93	*fetched*		5	84	88
further		216	100	94	*fears*		5	88	88	*fetches*		0	33	84
furthest		2	70	90	feather	NoC	13	93	89	*fetching*		1	60	88
far	Adv	310	100	98	*feather*		4	81	88	fever	NoC	11	95	88
far		310	100	98	*feathers*		8	89	88	*fever*		11	95	89
far from	Adv	11	94	94	feature	NoC	135	100	93	*fevers*		1	31	64
fare	NoC	14	99	93	*feature*		54	99	93	few	DetP	450	100	97
fare		8	97	93	*features*		81	100	93	fewer	DetP	31	98	94
fares		6	87	89	feature	Verb	38	97	90	fibre	NoC	23	99	84
farm	NoC	86	100	91	*feature*		9	83	90	*fibre*		15	97	80
farm		68	100	91	*featured*		13	93	91	*fibres*		8	89	83
farms		18	100	88	*features*		8	79	87	fiction	NoC	21	97	87
farmer	NoC	72	100	89	*featuring*		9	87	88	*fiction*		20	97	87
farmer		22	100	91	Feb.	NoP	29	56	49	*fictions*		1	46	78
farmers		50	100	87	*Feb*		3	52	80	field	NoC	201	100	93
farming	NoC	22	99	89	*Feb.*		27	26	44	*field*		143	100	93
fascinating	Adj	17	99	92	February	NoP	84	100	90	*fields*		58	100	93
fashion	NoC	49	100	94	federal	Adj	38	89	76	fierce	Adj	17	99	93
fashion		45	100	94	federation	NoC	23	88	86	*fierce*		16	99	93
fashions		4	87	90	*federation*		22	88	85	*fiercer*		1	42	85
fashionable	Adj	12	97	94	*federations*		1	37	79	*fiercest*		1	43	85
fast	Adj	50	100	94	fee	NoC	58	100	91	fifteen	Num	54	100	89
fast		31	100	95	*fee*		29	100	90	*fifteen*		54	100	89
faster		12	100	94	*fees*		29	98	90	fifth	Ord	35	100	95
fastest		7	91	88	feed	Verb	67	100	94	fifty	Num	96	100	80
fast	Adv	44	100	93	*fed*		22	99	94	*fifties*		10	95	87
faster	Adv	17	100	94	*feed*		24	100	93	*fifty*		86	100	79
fat	Adj	28	97	90	*feeding*		18	100	91	fig*	NoC	78	92	79
fat		28	97	90	*feeds*		3	86	90	*fig*		16	81	67
fatter		1	35	81	feedback	NoC	13	91	88	*fig.*		59	51	75
fattest		0	14	72	*feedback*		13	91	88	*figs*		3	65	81
fat	NoC	21	97	90	*feedbacks*		0	9	63	fight	NoC	34	100	92
fat		18	96	90	feel	Verb	624	100	94	*fight*		29	100	92
fats		3	57	82	*feel*		256	100	94	*fights*		5	85	90
fatal	Adj	14	100	93	*feeling*		58	100	90	fight	Verb	108	100	95
fate	NoC	23	100	95	*feels*		33	100	95	*fight*		40	100	94
fate		22	100	95	*felt*		278	100	94	*fighting*		36	100	94
fates		1	54	87	feeling	NoC	126	100	94	*fights*		2	71	87
father	NoC	252	100	92	*feeling*		73	100	94	*fought*		30	100	95
father		239	100	91	*feelings*		53	100	93	fighter	NoC	17	96	88
fathers		12	98	92	fellow	Adj	26	99	94	*fighter*		10	91	87
fault	NoC	43	100	96	fellow	NoC	26	99	91	*fighters*		7	93	86
fault		34	100	95	*fellow*		19	97	90	fighting	NoC	21	99	88
faults		9	100	92	*fellows*		7	96	91	*fighting*		21	99	88
favour	NoC	28	100	94	female	Adj	60	100	84	figure	NoC	282	100	94
favour		24	100	94	female	NoC	41	100	87	*figure*		170	100	93
favours		4	90	91	*female*		21	99	88	*figures*		112	100	94

Word	PoS	Freq	Ra	Di	Word	PoS	Freq	Ra	Di	Word	PoS	Freq	Ra	Di
figure	Verb	14	100	93	finished		79	100	93	flags		5	95	92
figure		6	99	94	*finishes*		3	84	90	flame	NoC	23	100	90
figured		4	95	91	*finishing*		9	96	93	*flame*		11	92	89
figures		2	82	80	fire	NoC	145	100	94	*flames*		13	95	89
figuring		1	37	79	*fire*		133	100	94	flash	NoC	11	96	91
file	NoC	86	100	81	*fires*		12	99	92	*flash*		9	94	90
file		56	100	78	fire	Verb	35	100	93	*flashes*		2	81	91
files		29	99	84	*fire*		8	98	90	flash	Verb	17	96	88
file	Verb	15	100	89	*fired*		20	99	93	*flash*		2	75	89
file		4	94	89	*fires*		1	59	88	*flashed*		8	83	84
filed		8	97	86	*firing*		6	93	91	*flashes*		1	47	86
files		0	10	69	firm	Adj	37	100	96	*flashing*		6	84	88
filing		2	78	88	*firm*		35	100	96	flat	Adj	38	99	95
fill	Verb	110	100	96	*firmer*		2	87	92	*flat*		37	99	95
fill		39	100	96	*firmest*		0	18	77	*flatter*		1	55	87
filled		52	100	94	firm	NoC	163	100	88	flat	NoC	66	100	88
filling		15	100	95	*firm*		88	100	87	*flat*		47	100	90
fills		5	94	93	*firms*		75	98	87	*flats*		19	100	72
film	NoC	136	100	90	firmly	Adv	40	99	94	flavour	NoC	17	98	86
film		101	100	92	first	Ord	1193	100	98	*flavour*		15	98	86
films		35	100	85	firstly	Adv	17	97	92	*flavours*		3	64	85
filter	NoC	20	95	72	fiscal	Adj	13	78	82	flee	Verb	21	98	92
filter		15	89	70	fish	NoC	105	100	84	*fled*		14	96	92
filters		5	70	76	*fish*		103	100	84	*flee*		5	91	89
final	Adj	129	100	95	*fishes*		2	66	86	*fleeing*		3	81	90
final	NoC	36	100	84	fish	Verb	11	89	84	*flees*		0	23	78
final		28	96	84	*fish*		5	86	83	fleet	NoC	21	98	89
finals		8	77	81	*fished*		3	67	81	*fleet*		19	98	89
finally	Adv	130	100	97	*fishes*		0	7	59	*fleets*		2	69	86
finance	NoC	63	100	88	*fishing*		2	60	83	flesh	NoC	25	98	89
finance		55	98	87	fisherman	NoC	11	97	90	*flesh*		25	98	88
finances		7	95	93	*fisherman*		4	85	88	flexibility	NoC	20	90	92
finance	Verb	34	99	90	*fishermen*		7	90	87	*flexibility*		20	90	92
finance		20	97	87	fishing	NoC	32	100	88	flexible	Adj	24	97	92
financed		9	85	90	*fishing*		32	100	88	flick	Verb	11	90	86
finances		0	33	82	fist	NoC	16	95	85	*flick*		2	61	88
financing		4	77	89	*fist*		10	91	86	*flicked*		6	63	82
financial	Adj	165	100	95	*fists*		6	67	83	*flicking*		3	71	86
find	Verb	990	100	98	fit	Adj	33	100	95	*flicks*		1	37	84
find		420	100	97	*fit*		30	100	95	flight	NoC	64	100	92
finding		55	100	97	*fitter*		2	68	89	*flight*		52	100	91
finds		29	100	94	*fittest*		1	58	85	*flights*		12	98	92
found		487	100	97	fit	NoC	11	98	93	fling	Verb·	14	95	84
finding	NoC	45	97	87	*fit*		8	97	93	*fling*		1	54	85
finding		12	93	83	*fits*		3	85	91	*flinging*		2	43	81
findings		33	94	88	fit	Verb	95	100	94	*flings*		0	23	77
fine	Adj	150	100	96	*fit*		45	100	94	*flung*		11	93	83
fine		127	100	96	*fits*		9	99	94	float	Verb	20	100	93
finer		5	92	91	*fitted*		33	100	92	*float*		6	93	90
finest		18	98	92	*fitting*		8	99	91	*floated*		6	90	90
fine	NoC	10	95	90	fitness	NoC	16	92	90	*floating*		7	97	91
fine		4	81	88	*fitness*		16	92	90	*floats*		1	65	88
fines		7	82	89	fitting	NoC	13	98	80	flock	NoC	11	95	88
fine	Verb	12	96	84	*fitting*		5	85	78	*flock*		6	88	91
fine		0	35	85	*fittings*		8	91	81	*flocks*		4	77	78
fined		11	91	83	five	Num	409	100	91	flood	NoC	16	99	93
fines		0	29	80	*five*		407	100	91	*flood*		12	99	93
fining		0	22	78	*fives*		2	46	78	*floods*		4	82	88
finger	NoC	90	99	88	fix	Verb	46	100	95	flood	Verb	13	100	94
finger		32	99	90	*fix*		12	99	94	*flood*		3	90	93
fingers		58	98	86	*fixed*		28	100	95	*flooded*		7	96	92
finish	NoC	18	99	89	*fixes*		1	53	85	*flooding*		3	80	91
finish		16	99	89	*fixing*		5	95	92	*floods*		1	36	84
finishes		3	68	85	fixed	Adj	36	100	92	floor	NoC	127	100	93
finish	Verb	120	100	93	flag	NoC	20	100	92	*floor*		115	100	92
finish		29	100	92	*flag*		15	100	91	*floors*		12	97	92

Word	PoS	Freq	Ra	Di	Word	PoS	Freq	Ra	Di	Word	PoS	Freq	Ra	Di
flour	NoC	11	94	88	*follower*		2	69	84	forgive	Verb	21	99	91
flour		10	94	88	*followers*		10	95	92	*forgave*		1	52	88
flours		0	11	64	following	Adj	134	100	92	*forgive*		14	97	88
flourish	Verb	10	98	93	following	Prep	12	95	86	*forgiven*		5	94	93
flourish		4	93	92	folly	NoC	11	91	55	*forgives*		0	19	74
flourished		4	86	92	*follies*		1	51	84	*forgiving*		0	17	77
flourishes		0	25	81	*folly*		10	88	50	fork	NoC	10	96	91
flourishing		1	62	89	fond	Adj	12	99	90·	*fork*		9	93	91
flow	NoC	53	100	89	*fond*		12	99	91	*forks*		2	65	88
flow		45	100	90	*fonder*		0	19	77	form	NoC	365	100	93
flows		9	83	81	*fondest*		0	14	73	*form*		266	100	94
flow	Verb	26	100	95	food	NoC	211	100	94	*forms*		98	100	91
flow		8	100	93	*food*		190	100	95	form	Verb	184	100	94
flowed		6	90	91	*foods*		21	96	81	*form*		79	100	94
flowing		7	100	94	fool	NoC	19	99	88	*formed*		70	100	93
flows		6	94	90	*fool*		15	94	86	*forming*		18	98	94
flower	NoC	76	100	91	*fools*		4	90	91	*forms*		18	95	93
flower		22	98	92	foolish	Adj	12	98	90	formal	Adj	64	100	93
flowers		54	100	90	foot	NoC	214	100	93	formally	Adv	22	97	88
fluid	NoC	19	98	85	*feet*		141	99	92	format	NoC	25	86	86
fluid		15	98	84	*foot*		73	100	94	*format*		21	86	86
fluids		4	72	82	football	NoC	67	100	88	*formats*		5	64	82
flush	Verb	11	90	84	*football*		67	100	87	formation	NoC	44	98	90
flush		2	67	88	*footballs*		0	26	81	*formation*		40	97	89
flushed		7	72	81	for	Conj	139	100	95	*formations*		4	73	83
flushes		0	13	73	for	Prep	8412	100	98	former	DetP	170	100	88
flushing		2	56	84	for ever	Adv	13	98	91	formerly	Adv	20	93	92
fly	NoC	16	98	92	for example	Adv	239	100	92	formidable	Adj	11	93	94
flies		8	93	91	for instance	Adv	74	100	93	formula	NoC	32	99	92
fly		9	95	90	forbid	Verb	13	100	94	*formula*		27	99	92
fly	Verb	90	100	92	*forbade*		2	70	91	*formulae*		4	71	84
flew		23	98	91	*forbid*		3	86	91	*formulas*		1	59	85
flies		4	89	91	*forbidden*		7	92	93	formulate	Verb	16	96	92
flown		11	98	88	*forbidding*		1	41	85	*formulate*		5	86	91
fly		29	98	92	*forbids*		1	50	86	*formulated*		8	89	91
flying		22	100	92	force	NoC	250	100	90	*formulates*		0	17	76
flying	Adj	19	99	90	*force*		136	100	94	*formulating*		3	71	91
focus	NoC	39	99	92	*forces*		114	99	84	formulation	NoC	11	84	90
foci		1	32	67	force	Verb	113	100	96	*formulation*		9	82	90
focus		38	99	92	*force*		22	100	96	*formulations*		2	61	84
focuses		0	12	69	*forced*		74	100	95	forth	Adv	13	99	93
focus	Verb	56	100	92	*forces*		3	83	91	forthcoming	Adj	16	98	93
focus		21	100	92	*forcing*		14	98	94	fortnight	NoC	15	99	91
focused		17	96	93	Ford	NoP	22	99	89	*fortnight*		14	99	91
focuses		6	77	86	*Ford*		22	99	89	fortunate	Adj	13	99	95
focusing		8	93	90	*Fords*		0	17	75	fortunately	Adv	16	100	95
focussed		2	66	87	forecast	NoC	17	97	90	fortune	NoC	31	100	95
focusses		0	20	74	*forecast*		9	96	90	*fortune*		21	99	94
focussing		1	46	83	*forecasts*		8	79	87	*fortunes*		10	99	93
fog	NoC	11	90	85	forehead	NoC	14	86	85	forty	Num	71	99	83
fog		10	89	85	*forehead*		13	84	85	*forties*		5	87	91
fogs		0	28	80	*foreheads*		0	35	85	*forty*		66	99	82
fold	Verb	17	97	91	foreign	Adj	161	100	83	forum	NoC	19	87	88
fold		5	89	90	foreigner	NoC	12	100	92	*fora*		0	14	69
folded		10	94	87	*foreigner*		3	87	89	*forum*		18	86	88
folding		2	59	87	*foreigners*		10	98	90	*forums*		1	45	86
folds		0	34	83	forest	NoC	90	100	82	forward	Adj	12	99	90
folk	NoC	26	99	92	*forest*		70	100	82	forward	Adv	137	100	95
folk		21	99	92	*forests*		20	94	73	*forwards*		13	97	82
folks		4	80	89	forever	Adv	18	99	92	fossil	NoC	14	85	73
follow	Verb	460	100	93	forget	Verb	124	100	92	*fossil*		9	76	73
follow		94	100	97	*forget*		62	100	93	*fossils*		5	60	70
followed		149	100	96	*forgets*		2	67	88	foster	Verb	10	95	91
following		116	100	93	*forgetting*		8	98	92	*foster*		5	83	91
follows		100	99	70	*forgot*		16	98	87	*fostered*		3	77	90
follower	NoC	12	96	93	*forgotten*		38	100	92	*fostering*		1	61	88

Word	PoS	Freq	Ra	Di	Word	PoS	Freq	Ra	Di	Word	PoS	Freq	Ra	Di
fosters		0	31	82	*freeze*		5	97	92	ft	NoC	13	68	77
found	Verb	32	98	92	*freezes*		1	42	86	*ft*		12	68	75
found		2	77	89	*freezing*		1	46	85	*ft.*		1	21	62
founded		27	97	92	*froze*		5	75	86	fuck	Verb	12	61	71
founding		2	71	89	*frozen*		9	99	92	*fuck*		9	56	70
founds		0	18	77	French	Adj	134	100	93	*fucked*		2	41	77
foundation	NoC	51	99	91	*French*		134	100	93	*fucking*		1	15	49
foundation		37	98	89	French	NoC	35	100	94	*fucks*		0	11	65
foundations		14	98	92	*French*		35	100	94	fucking	Adj	18	58	59
founder	NoC	16	92	90	frequency	NoC	36	95	84	fucking	Adv	12	52	47
founder		12	90	90	*frequencies*		8	77	80	fuel	NoC	47	100	88
founders		4	69	82	*frequency*		28	94	85	*fuel*		41	100	89
four	Num	465	100	93	frequent	Adj	24	99	93	*fuels*		6	73	81
four		461	100	93	frequently	Adv	58	99	93	fulfil	Verb	26	98	95
fours		4	79	87	fresh	Adj	69	100	95	*fulfil*		12	98	95
fourteen	Num	27	100	88	*fresh*		68	100	95	*fulfilled*		9	94	94
fourteen		27	100	88	*fresher*		1	55	87	*fulfilling*		4	90	92
fourteens		0	7	61	*freshest*		0	25	78	*fulfils*		2	72	91
fourth	Ord	61	100	94	Freud	NoP	16	80	64	full	Adj	289	100	98
fox	NoC	13	90	86	Friday	NoP	58	100	90	*full*		281	100	98
fox		9	88	84	*Friday*		55	100	90	*fuller*		5	94	92
foxes		4	72	85	*Fridays*		3	72	89	*fullest*		2	77	90
Fox	NoP	14	90	78	fridge	NoC	11	85	87	full-time	Adj	21	99	88
fraction	NoC	20	100	89	*fridge*		9	82	86	fully	Adv	89	100	95
fraction		15	99	91	*fridges*		1	52	83	fun	Adj	17	97	92
fractions		5	56	78	friend	NoC	315	100	88	fun	NoC	34	98	94
fragment	NoC	22	89	80	*friend*		164	100	79	function	NoC	129	100	91
fragment		9	76	72	*friends*		151	100	95	*function*		78	100	90
fragments		14	88	85	friendly	Adj	39	100	94	*functions*		51	98	91
frame	NoC	41	100	93	*friendlier*		1	38	85	function	Verb	17	97	93
frame		32	100	93	*friendliest*		0	23	76	*function*		9	94	92
frames		9	96	92	*friendly*		39	100	94	*functioned*		2	61	87
frame	Verb	11	100	95	friendship	NoC	24	100	94	*functioning*		4	91	92
frame		2	85	92	*friendship*		20	100	92	*functions*		2	63	89
framed		6	98	93	*friendships*		4	80	90	functional	Adj	20	96	88
frames		1	66	89	frighten	Verb	12	95	90	fund	NoC	118	100	91
framing		2	73	90	*frighten*		4	89	91	*fund*		55	100	90
framework	NoC	41	99	90	*frightened*		6	86	88	*funds*		62	100	91
framework		39	99	91	*frightening*		1	51	87	fund	Verb	25	94	92
frameworks		2	49	83	*frightens*		1	50	87	*fund*		9	87	91
France	NoP	123	100	92	frightened	Adj	21	99	90	*funded*		13	86	91
France		123	100	92	fringe	NoC	13	100	93	*funding*		3	74	89
Francis	NoP	25	97	86	*fringe*		10	100	92	*funds*		0	28	82
Frank	NoP	37	99	90	*fringes*		3	89	92	fundamental	Adj	45	94	92
Frank		37	99	90	from	Prep	4134	100	98	funding	NoC	40	91	90
Fraser	NoP	10	81	85	from time to time	Adv	17	98	94	*funding*		39	91	90
Fraser		10	81	85	front	Adj	69	100	94	funeral	NoC	25	100	90
fraud	NoC	19	99	88	front	NoC	84	100	93	*funeral*		21	99	90
fraud		18	99	88	*front*		81	100	93	*funerals*		3	72	83
frauds		1	45	83	*fronts*		4	93	92	funny	Adj	47	98	85
Fred	NoP	21	97	89	frontier	NoC	14	96	91	*funnier*		1	31	81
Fred		21	97	89	*frontier*		9	92	90	*funniest*		1	55	85
free	Adj	200	100	96	*frontiers*		5	86	90	*funny*		45	98	85
free		198	100	96	frown	Verb	19	85	80	fur	NoC	12	96	90
freer		2	71	88	*frown*		1	39	84	*fur*		10	93	90
freest		0	10	69	*frowned*		13	72	80	*furs*		2	63	83
free	Verb	23	99	95	*frowning*		4	51	79	furious	Adj	13	97	90
free		10	96	95	*frowns*		1	24	76	furnish	Verb	11	99	88
freed		9	98	91	frozen	Adj	11	99	92	*furnish*		2	77	88
freeing		3	80	90	fruit	NoC	51	100	92	*furnished*		7	93	84
frees		1	58	89	*fruit*		41	100	92	*furnishes*		0	25	77
freedom	NoC	64	100	94	*fruits*		10	98	86	*furnishing*		1	61	88
freedom		61	100	94	frustration	NoC	17	99	95	furniture	NoC	35	100	93
freedoms		4	64	85	*frustration*		14	99	95	*furniture*		35	100	93
freely	Adv	16	100	95	*frustrations*		3	82	92	further*	Adj	[see *far*]		
freeze	Verb	20	99	93						further	Adv	144	100	97

Word	PoS	Freq	Ra	Di	Word	PoS	Freq	Ra	Di	Word	PoS	Freq	Ra	Di
furthermore	Adv	29	92	90	*gates*		*19*	*100*	*93*	German	Adj	98	100	90
fury	NoC	12	88	87	gather	Verb	52	100	95	German	NoC	41	100	92
furies		*0*	*18*	*74*	*gather*		*16*	*100*	*95*	*German*		*16*	*99*	*93*
fury		*11*	*87*	*87*	*gathered*		*26*	*100*	*94*	*Germans*		*25*	*98*	*88*
fusion	NoC	12	86	61	*gathering*		*9*	*97*	*94*	Germany	NoP	107	100	89
fusion		*12*	*85*	*61*	*gathers*		*2*	*79*	*91*	*Germanies*		*0*	*12*	*63*
fusions		*0*	*12*	*56*	gathering	NoC	12	99	95	*Germany*		*106*	*100*	*89*
future	Adj	85	100	94	*gathering*		*10*	*99*	*95*	*Germanys*		*0*	*6*	*15*
future	NoC	156	100	94	*gatherings*		*2*	*74*	*90*	gesture	NoC	27	99	91
future		*142*	*100*	*95*	Gaulle	NoP	10	51	38	*gesture*		*20*	*99*	*90*
futures		*14*	*85*	*55*	gay	Adj	16	89	76	*gestures*		*6*	*94*	*90*
G / g	Lett	41	98	82	*gay*		*16*	*89*	*76*	get	Verb	2210	100	87
G	NoP	24	88	83	gaze	NoC	21	89	80	*get*		*995*	*100*	*90*
G		*9*	*69*	*66*	*gaze*		*21*	*88*	*80*	*gets*		*78*	*99*	*92*
G.		*15*	*86*	*83*	*gazes*		*0*	*15*	*72*	*gettin'*		*1*	*25*	*70*
Gabriel	NoP	13	68	58	gaze	Verb	23	90	83	*getting*		*203*	*100*	*93*
Gabriel		*13*	*68*	*58*	*gaze*		*2*	*56*	*86*	*got*		*932*	*100*	*82*
gain	NoC	36	94	89	*gazed*		*11*	*69*	*81*	*gotten*		*1*	*52*	*87*
gain		*15*	*94*	*89*	*gazes*		*1*	*33*	*72*	ghost	NoC	20	98	89
gains		*21*	*86*	*86*	*gazing*		*9*	*81*	*84*	*ghost*		*14*	*97*	*89*
gain	Verb	89	100	95	gear	NoC	21	99	93	*ghosts*		*6*	*82*	*86*
gain		*37*	*100*	*95*	*gear*		*19*	*99*	*93*	giant	Adj	18	99	93
gained		*37*	*100*	*94*	*gears*		*3*	*70*	*88*	giant	NoC	16	99	91
gaining		*12*	*98*	*94*	Gen.	NoC	15	41	58	*giant*		*10*	*95*	*91*
gains		*2*	*76*	*90*	*Gen*		*3*	*32*	*49*	*giants*		*7*	*90*	*88*
gall	NoC	10	66	31	*Gen.*		*11*	*10*	*43*	Gibson	NoP	10	79	74
gall		*10*	*63*	*28*	*Gens*		*1*	*7*	*21*	*Gibson*		*10*	*79*	*74*
galls		*0*	*7*	*44*	gender	NoC	20	84	80	*Gibsons*		*0*	*4*	*34*
gallery	NoC	55	100	95	*gender*		*20*	*83*	*80*	gift	NoC	47	100	94
galleries		*12*	*91*	*78*	*genders*		*0*	*22*	*77*	*gift*		*30*	*99*	*94*
gallery		*43*	*100*	*79*	gene	NoC	42	89	75	*gifts*		*17*	*100*	*94*
game	NoC	212	100	90	*gene*		*21*	*71*	*71*	Gilbert	NoP	11	89	78
game		*150*	*100*	*90*	*genes*		*21*	*82*	*77*	*Gilbert*		*11*	*89*	*78*
games		*62*	*100*	*90*	general	Adj	301	100	93	girl	NoC	254	100	92
gang	NoC	20	97	91	general	NoC	47	100	92	*girl*		*158*	*100*	*90*
gang		*15*	*97*	*91*	*general*		*43*	*100*	*92*	*girls*		*96*	*100*	*93*
gangs		*5*	*88*	*89*	*generals*		*4*	*82*	*86*	girlfriend	NoC	14	92	90
gap	NoC	45	100	96	generally	Adv	116	100	93	*girlfriend*		*12*	*90*	*89*
gap		*34*	*100*	*96*	generate	Verb	55	99	92	*girlfriends*		*2*	*69*	*89*
gaps		*11*	*99*	*94*	*generate*		*20*	*94*	*92*	give	Verb	1284	100	98
garage	NoC	24	99	89	*generated*		*25*	*98*	*92*	*gave*		*229*	*100*	*95*
garage		*21*	*99*	*89*	*generates*		*5*	*81*	*89*	*give*		*451*	*100*	*96*
garages		*3*	*81*	*88*	*generating*		*5*	*82*	*91*	*given*		*375*	*100*	*96*
garden	NoC	144	100	93	generation	NoC	71	100	94	*gives*		*104*	*100*	*95*
garden		*108*	*100*	*93*	*generation*		*49*	*100*	*93*	*giveth*		*0*	*10*	*69*
gardens		*37*	*100*	*91*	*generations*		*21*	*100*	*93*	*giving*		*125*	*100*	*98*
gardener	NoC	13	96	86	generous	Adj	23	100	95	given	Adj	31	99	89
gardener		*8*	*89*	*89*	genetic	Adj	18	88	85	given that	Conj	12	99	92
gardeners		*6*	*88*	*80*	Geneva	NoP	10	87	87	glad	Adj	41	98	90
garment	NoC	13	92	74	genius	NoC	12	97	91	*glad*		*41*	*98*	*90*
garment		*7*	*85*	*66*	*genius*		*11*	*97*	*91*	glance	NoC	26	97	84
garments		*6*	*85*	*82*	*geniuses*		*0*	*28*	*82*	*glance*		*23*	*96*	*84*
Gary	NoP	24	90	84	gentle	Adj	29	98	90	*glances*		*4*	*57*	*83*
Gary		*24*	*90*	*84*	gentleman	NoC	66	98	61	glance	Verb	41	89	80
gas	NoC	82	100	90	*gentleman*		*52*	*97*	*51*	*glance*		*4*	*73*	*83*
gas		*73*	*100*	*91*	*gentlemen*		*15*	*94*	*90*	*glanced*		*30*	*68*	*79*
gases		*9*	*80*	*82*	gently	Adv	40	98	88	*glances*		*1*	*40*	*80*
gasses		*0*	*8*	*58*	genuine	Adj	33	100	95	*glancing*		*7*	*61*	*81*
gasp	Verb	12	77	82	genuinely	Adv	14	100	96	glare	Verb	11	66	78
gasp		*1*	*37*	*81*	Geoff	NoP	12	76	81	*glare*		*1*	*30*	*73*
gasped		*8*	*48*	*79*	Geoffrey	NoP	17	97	85	*glared*		*8*	*41*	*78*
gasping		*3*	*59*	*85*	geographical	Adj	16	88	89	*glares*		*0*	*17*	*70*
gasps		*0*	*17*	*75*	geography	NoC	17	98	77	*glaring*		*2*	*48*	*80*
gastric	Adj	21	47	28	*geographies*		*0*	*13*	*68*	Glasgow	NoP	42	96	85
gate	NoC	55	100	92	*geography*		*16*	*98*	*77*	*Glasgow*		*42*	*96*	*85*
gate		*35*	*100*	*92*	George	NoP	111	100	93	glass	NoC	120	99	91

Word	PoS	Freq	Ra	Di	Word	PoS	Freq	Ra	Di	Word	PoS	Freq	Ra	Di
glass		95	99	91	Gould	NoP	12	69	56	*graph*		10	83	83
glasses		25	98	89	*Gould*		12	69	56	*graphs*		4	71	85
glimpse	NoC	11	94	92	govern	Verb	25	96	91	graphics	NoC	20	84	69
glimpse		9	91	91	*govern*		6	85	89	grasp	Verb	17	97	92
glimpses		2	75	90	*governed*		10	89	90	*grasp*		7	97	93
global	Adj	36	92	83	*governing*		7	82	90	*grasped*		7	89	89
glorious	Adj	11	97	93	*governs*		2	69	89	*grasping*		3	69	88
glory	NoC	18	99	92	governing	Adj	10	86	83	*grasps*		0	25	78
glories		2	64	87	government	NoC	670	100	88	grass	NoC	45	100	92
glory		17	99	92	*government*		622	100	87	*grass*		41	100	92
Gloucester	NoP	33	86	64	*governments*		47	95	90	*grasses*		3	70	88
Gloucester		32	86	64	governor	NoC	40	100	87	grateful	Adj	27	99	89
Gloucesters		0	5	43	*governor*		23	98	84	grave	NoC	19	100	91
Gloucestershire	NoP	15	79	47	*governors*		17	91	83	*grave*		13	99	91
Gloucestershire		15	79	47	gown	NoC	10	84	86	*graves*		6	91	85
glove	NoC	14	97	91	*gown*		8	81	86	gravel	NoC	13	93	86
glove		4	82	86	*gowns*		2	59	87	*gravel*		12	93	85
gloves		10	89	91	GP	NoC	17	83	84	*gravels*		0	19	75
go	NoC	21	98	83	*G.P.*		1	25	31	gravity	NoC	12	99	87
go		21	97	83	*GP*		10	80	83	*gravities*		0	6	46
goes		1	37	79	*GPs*		7	61	82	*gravity*		12	99	87
go	Verb	2078	100	91	grab	Verb	29	98	90	Gray	NoP	11	84	85
go		881	100	90	*grab*		8	95	92	*Gray*		11	82	85
goes		148	100	89	*grabbed*		15	92	87	*Grays*		0	23	78
goin'*		4	34	66	*grabbing*		4	79	90	great	Adj	635	100	97
going*		366	100	90	*grabs*		1	63	89	*great*		442	100	97
gone		195	100	92	grace	NoC	16	99	92	*greater*		141	100	94
went		483	100	92	*grace*		15	98	92	*greatest*		51	100	95
goal	NoC	107	100	88	*graces*		1	48	87	Great	NoP-	22	97	92
goal		59	100	87	grade	NoC	28	100	88	Greater	NoP-	13	81	64
goals		47	95	88	*grade*		19	100	86	greatly	Adv	33	100	94
goat	NoC	12	90	84	*grades*		8	86	89	Greece	NoP	17	98	87
goat		6	80	83	gradual	Adj	11	95	92	*Greece*		17	98	87
goats		6	81	82	gradually	Adv	37	100	95	Greek	Adj	29	100	85
god	NoC	49	98	87	graduate	NoC	19	97	87	Greek	NoC	16	94	81
god		36	95	85	*graduate*		8	94	89	*Greek*		7	86	88
gods		14	94	88	*graduates*		11	87	83	*Greeks*		9	84	74
God	NoP	202	100	90	Graham	NoP	42	100	86	green	Adj	101	100	95
going* (to)	Verb	417	100	85	*Graham*		42	99	86	*green*		99	100	95
going		292	100	90	grain	NoC	23	98	86	*greener*		1	61	87
gon~		125	68	66	*grain*		18	97	89	*greenest*		0	21	80
gold	NoC	75	100	94	*grains*		5	72	75	green	NoC	39	99	92
gold		74	100	94	grammar	NoC	26	97	85	*green*		30	99	91
golds		1	36	82	*grammar*		24	97	85	*greens*		9	96	88
golden	Adj	39	100	94	*grammars*		1	26	55	Green	NoP	17	100	88
golf	NoC	34	98	88	grand	Adj	49	100	94	greenhouse	NoC	11	86	83
golf		34	98	88	*grand*		46	100	94	*greenhouse*		10	85	82
golfs		0	8	64	*grander*		2	69	89	*greenhouses*		1	43	84
good	Adj	1276	100	97	*grandest*		1	45	84	greet	Verb	22	98	93
best		266	100	97	grandfather	NoC	16	94	90	*greet*		6	91	91
better		214	100	97	*grandfather*		15	94	89	*greeted*		14	97	93
good		795	100	95	*grandfathers*		1	37	78	*greeting*		1	56	87
good*	NoC	25	100	94	grandmother	NoC	15	97	89	*greets*		1	45	85
good		25	100	94	*grandmother*		14	94	89	Gregory	NoP	10	84	73
goods		101	100	84	*grandmothers*		1	50	79	*Gregory*		10	84	73
goodbye	Int	10	88	87	grant	NoC	58	97	88	grey	Adj	48	99	90
goodness	NoC	15	95	88	*grant*		39	96	83	*grey*		48	99	90
Gorbachev	NoP	17	66	66	*grants*		19	90	91	*greyer*		0	26	62
Gorbachev		17	66	65	Grant	NoP	23	93	71	grid	NoC	13	99	89
Gordon	NoP	26	97	90	*Grant*		23	93	71	*grid*		11	98	90
Gordon		26	97	89	grant	Verb	68	100	93	*grids*		2	51	80
Gordons		0	15	71	*grant*		13	99	90	grief	NoC	15	97	91
gospel	NoC	13	93	78	*granted*		46	100	93	*grief*		14	97	91
gospel		11	90	79	*granting*		4	79	87	*griefs*		0	18	73
gospels		3	45	69	*grants*		5	82	90	grim	Adj	11	94	91
gothic	Adj	12	88	78	graph	NoC	14	93	85	*grim*		11	94	90

Word	PoS	Freq	Ra	Di	Word	PoS	Freq	Ra	Di	Word	PoS	Freq	Ra	Di
grimmer		0	26	81	guessing		3	82	91	halt		6	91	87
grimmest		0	10	70	guest	NoC	57	100	90	halted		7	94	90
grin	NoC	12	84	83	guest		23	100	89	halting		1	46	84
grin		11	81	83	guests		34	99	89	halts		1	36	78
grins		1	43	85	guidance	NoC	32	99	91	Hamilton	NoP	15	90	90
grin	Verb	24	83	81	guide	NoC	57	100	91	Hamilton		15	90	90
grin		1	38	83	guide		47	100	91	Hamiltons		0	10	53
grinned		18	62	79	guides		10	97	90	hammer	NoC	12	99	88
grinning		5	57	82	guide	Verb	23	100	95	hammer		10	98	88
grins		1	30	78	guide		12	99	93	hammers		2	63	82
grip	NoC	21	100	93	guided		9	99	95	Hampshire	NoP	12	91	87
grip		17	98	91	guides		1	61	87	Hampshire		12	91	87
grips		4	90	92	guideline	NoC	26	86	91	hand	NoC	532	100	92
grip	Verb	13	91	86	guideline		2	62	80	hand		344	100	93
grip		2	68	89	guidelines		23	85	91	hands		188	100	91
gripped		7	80	85	guild	NoC	10	90	86	hand	Verb	54	100	94
gripping		3	48	82	guild		8	84	84	hand		9	100	94
grips		1	39	85	guilds		3	65	83	handed		36	100	92
gross	Adj	23	100	87	guilt	NoC	18	98	92	handing		8	99	93
gross		23	100	86	guilt		18	98	92	hands		1	51	84
grosser		0	12	71	guilts		0	5	41	handful	NoC	15	100	95
ground	NoC	215	100	96	guilty	Adj	42	100	92	handful		14	100	95
ground		154	100	96	guilty		42	100	92	handfuls		1	43	84
grounds		61	100	93	Guinness	NoP	13	84	68	handicap	NoC	15	92	79
group	NoC	607	100	94	Guinness		13	83	68	handicap		13	91	78
group		414	100	94	guitar	NoC	34	84	53	handicaps		2	63	84
groups		193	100	93	guitar		27	79	53	handicapped	Adj	10	86	71
grouping	NoC	12	84	87	guitars		7	54	52	handle	NoC	16	93	91
grouping		7	78	85	Gulf	NoP	24	89	73	handle		12	91	91
groupings		5	78	89	Gulf		24	89	73	handles		4	85	90
grow	Verb	191	100	96	gun	NoC	55	100	92	handle	Verb	59	100	96
grew		46	100	94	gun		35	100	90	handle		26	100	96
grow		55	100	95	guns		20	99	92	handled		16	100	95
growing		35	100	96	guy	NoC	36	92	90	handles		3	84	90
grown		43	100	95	guy		24	91	89	handling		14	99	94
grows		13	99	93	guys		12	85	90	handling	NoC	15	98	92
growing	Adj	59	100	94	Guy	NoP	18	89	68	handling		15	98	92
growth	NoC	131	99	92	H / h	Lett	45	100	74	handsome	Adj	17	92	90
growth		130	99	92	H		45	100	74	handsome		17	92	90
growths		1	39	81	Hs		0	22	61	handsomest		0	15	75
guarantee	NoC	22	100	92	H	NoP	24	90	84	hang	Verb	93	100	92
guarantee		16	100	92	H		7	73	76	hang		31	100	88
guarantees		6	92	88	H.		17	90	80	hanged		4	86	87
guarantee	Verb	33	100	94	ha	Int	30	87	67	hanging		23	98	92
guarantee		14	99	94	habit	NoC	39	100	94	hangs		5	93	93
guaranteed		13	100	94	habit		23	100	94	hung		29	99	88
guaranteeing		2	72	86	habits		17	98	92	happen	Verb	325	100	95
guarantees		4	80	92	habitat	NoC	14	91	81	happen		88	100	95
guard	NoC	39	100	92	habitat		10	87	80	happened		139	100	94
guard		25	100	92	habitats		5	64	79	happening		40	100	93
guards		15	98	91	hair	NoC	150	100	88	happens		58	100	94
guard	Verb	14	100	94	hair		144	100	88	happily	Adv	18	98	94
guard		6	98	94	hairs		6	81	87	happiness	NoC	17	97	90
guarded		5	91	91	half	Adv	16	100	92	happiness		17	97	90
guarding		3	83	92	half	DetP	209	100	95	happy	Adj	129	100	95
guards		1	49	88	half	NoC	76	100	94	happier		9	98	93
guardian	NoC	26	100	79	half		72	100	94	happiest		3	81	92
guardian		21	99	74	halfs		0	8	61	happy		117	100	95
guardians		5	84	80	halves		4	92	92	harbour	NoC	20	99	90
guerrilla	NoC	13	69	69	hall	NoC	126	100	93	harbour		18	99	90
guerrilla		6	62	71	hall		118	100	93	harbours		2	49	75
guerrillas		7	51	67	halls		8	93	92	hard	Adj	176	100	96
guess	Verb	40	98	90	halt	NoC	12	99	91	hard		157	100	96
guess		24	98	91	halt		12	99	91	harder		14	100	94
guessed		12	95	85	halts		0	9	64	hardest		4	90	93
guesses		1	42	85	halt	Verb	15	96	90	hard	Adv	71	100	93

Word	PoS	Freq	Ra	Di
hardly	Adv	88	100	94
hardware	NoC	21	97	75
hardware		21	97	75
harm	NoC	23	100	92
harm		23	100	92
harms		0	17	71
harm	Verb	10	100	95
harm		7	100	94
harmed		2	72	90
harming		1	64	89
harms		0	24	80
harmony	NoC	13	99	86
harmonies		1	42	77
harmony		12	99	86
Harold	NoP	12	94	88
Harold		12	94	88
Harriet	NoP	17	69	59
Harriet		17	69	59
Harris	NoP	19	95	89
Harrison	NoP	10	91	87
Harrison		10	91	87
Harrisons		0	5	39
Harry	NoP	46	99	81
Harries		0	17	62
Harry		46	99	81
harsh	Adj	17	99	93
harsh		15	99	93
harsher		1	66	88
harshest		0	31	82
harvest	NoC	11	99	91
harvest		10	97	91
harvests		1	52	86
Harvey	NoP	13	89	72
Harvey		12	89	71
Harveys		0	10	64
hat	NoC	40	99	91
hat		31	98	90
hats		8	94	91
hate	Verb	50	100	89
hate		27	97	87
hated		17	97	87
hates		4	78	89
hating		2	55	80
hatred	NoC	11	94	89
hatred		11	94	89
hatreds		0	19	77
haul	Verb	11	93	90
haul		2	74	89
hauled		6	86	89
hauling		2	65	87
hauls		0	19	73
have*	Verb	13655	100	97
'ave		2	19	61
'd		315	99	87
's		298	98	80
've		891	100	84
had		4452	100	94
has		2593	100	95
have		4735	100	97
having		353	100	98
*of**		17	28	57
hazard	NoC	15	98	88
hazard		8	92	89
hazards		7	90	84
he	Pron	8469	100	92
'e		6	27	52
'im		3	23	64
he		6810	100	93
him		1649	100	90
head	Adj	15	98	91
head	NoC	402	100	92
head		350	100	92
heads		52	100	95
head	Verb	61	100	94
head		13	99	94
headed		27	100	92
heading		18	100	93
heads		3	77	89
headache	NoC	12	97	88
headache		8	90	87
headaches		4	84	88
heading	NoC	19	99	86
heading		10	97	85
headings		9	84	82
headline	NoC	14	99	92
headline		6	93	90
headlines		8	96	91
headmaster	NoC	13	94	81
headmaster		12	94	80
headmasters		1	31	78
headquarters	NoC	28	100	92
health	NoC	246	100	91
health		246	100	91
healthy	Adj	40	100	92
healthier		4	82	89
healthiest		0	26	80
healthy		36	100	92
heap	NoC	10	96	90
heap		7	90	90
heaps		3	74	89
hear	Verb	367	100	93
hear		137	100	92
heard		202	100	92
hearing		23	100	94
hears		5	94	93
hearing	NoC	34	100	89
hearing		30	100	88
hearings		4	73	84
heart	NoC	152	100	93
heart		137	100	93
hearts		15	98	93
heat	NoC	55	100	94
heat		54	100	94
heats		1	42	77
heat	Verb	13	98	92
heat		6	92	89
heated		5	90	91
heating		1	67	88
heats		1	38	83
heating	NoC	20	100	91
heaven	NoC	31	99	92
heaven		24	98	92
heavens		6	90	88
heavily	Adv	41	100	96
heavy	Adj	105	100	96
heavier		8	100	94
heaviest		3	81	90
heavy		94	100	96
hedge	NoC	16	98	92
hedge		9	92	90
hedges		7	94	92
heel	NoC	20	98	91
heel		8	89	90
heels		12	96	90
height	NoC	47	100	94
height		38	100	93
heights		10	97	92
heir	NoC	14	91	88
heir		10	85	87
heirs		4	78	86
Helen	NoP	27	98	80
Helen		27	97	80
Helens		0	18	70
helicopter	NoC	16	96	88
helicopter		11	95	86
helicopters		4	77	88
hell	NoC	54	97	88
hell		54	97	88
hells		0	11	68
hello	Int	38	91	78
help	NoC	110	100	96
help		107	100	96
helps		3	79	91
help	Verb	416	100	97
help		272	100	97
helped		76	100	96
helping		39	100	96
helps		28	99	94
helpful	Adj	32	100	93
hemisphere	NoC	10	80	65
hemisphere		9	80	65
hemispheres		1	34	61
hence	Adv	48	98	91
Henry	NoP	74	100	86
Henry		74	100	86
her*	Det	2183	100	87
herb	NoC	12	91	76
herb		4	70	73
herbs		9	85	77
Herbert	NoP	12	93	87
Herbert		12	93	87
Herberts		0	9	66
herd	NoC	10	88	85
herd		6	82	85
herds		4	72	82
here	Adv	699	100	93
Hereford	NoP	11	70	53
Hereford		11	69	53
Herefords		0	7	44
heritage	NoC	20	95	89
heritage		20	95	89
hero	NoC	34	100	91
hero		23	98	91
heroes		11	96	92
heros		0	15	74
hers	Pron	25	91	81
herself	Pron	172	100	85
hesitate	Verb	22	100	85
hesitate		6	98	93
hesitated		15	77	81
hesitates		1	39	81
hesitating		1	42	83
Hewlett-Packard	NoP	10	23	38
hey	Int	18	87	82
hidden	Adj	13	97	94
hide	Verb	64	100	92
hid		7	89	87
hidden		21	100	93

Word	PoS	Freq	Ra	Di
hide		23	99	91
hides		2	76	90
hiding		12	99	91
hierarchy	NoC	20	92	88
hierarchies		3	58	81
hierarchy		17	91	88
high	Adj	574	100	96
high		370	100	97
higher		156	100	93
highest		47	100	93
high	Adv	11	99	95
highlight	Verb	28	95	92
highlight		8	83	91
highlighted		11	93	92
highlighting		3	81	91
highlights		5	75	91
highly	Adv	91	100	94
highway	NoC	14	100	91
highway		10	100	91
highways		5	82	83
hill	NoC	88	100	95
hill		57	100	94
hills		31	100	93
Hill	NoP	14	100	89
himself	Pron	311	100	93
hint	NoC	20	100	94
hint		14	98	92
hints		6	96	93
hip	NoC	19	97	91
hip		10	94	90
hips		8	81	87
hire	NoC	10	96	87
hire		10	96	87
hire	Verb	20	100	95
hire		7	98	94
hired		10	99	94
hires		0	24	81
hiring		3	89	92
his	Det	4287	100	94
'is		2	20	60
his		4285	100	94
his*	Pron	49	100	91
historian	NoC	30	95	86
historian		14	90	87
historians		16	87	84
historic	Adj	23	97	90
historical	Adj	56	99	90
history	NoC	201	100	92
histories		8	82	87
history		193	100	92
hit	NoC	17	95	88
hit		11	93	88
hits		6	79	84
hit	Verb	107	100	92
hit		88	100	92
hits		7	93	90
hitting		11	95	92
hitherto	Adv	16	94	83
Hitler	NoP	17	95	72
Hitler		17	95	72
HIV	NoC	16	62	56
HIV		16	62	56
hold	NoC	31	100	94
hold		30	100	94
holds		1	48	79
hold	Verb	481	100	96
held		276	100	93
hold		106	100	97
holding		72	100	94
holds		26	100	95
holder	NoC	41	100	56
holder		29	99	38
holders		12	98	91
holding	NoC	18	95	89
holding		6	90	84
holdings		12	86	88
hole	NoC	72	100	93
hole		46	100	92
holes		27	99	92
holiday	NoC	105	100	93
holiday		76	100	92
holidays		28	100	92
Holland	NoP	16	98	91
Holland		16	98	91
Hollands		0	9	66
holly	NoC	10	77	62
hollies		0	15	53
holly		10	76	61
Hollywood	NoP	16	92	85
holy	Adj	30	99	90
holier		0	15	75
holiest		0	19	76
holy		30	99	89
home	Adv	194	100	93
home	NoC	390	100	95
home		330	100	95
homes		61	100	91
homeless	Adj	11	98	88
hon	Adj	107	71	18
hon		1	48	80
hon.		105	53	17
honest	Adj	30	100	94
honest		30	100	94
honestly	Adv	14	98	89
honey	NoC	11	95	89
honey		11	95	89
Hong	NoP-	28	96	82
honour	NoC	36	100	90
honour		22	100	94
honours		14	92	76
honour	Verb	12	98	94
honour		5	96	93
honoured		5	97	92
honouring		1	51	86
honours		0	26	82
hook	NoC	15	97	89
hook		11	96	86
hooks		5	92	91
hope	NoC	80	100	95
hope		55	100	96
hopes		24	100	92
hope	Verb	219	100	95
hope		115	100	93
hoped		51	100	95
hopes		18	95	85
hoping		35	99	92
hopefully	Adv	19	99	91
horizon	NoC	18	98	91
horizon		14	98	91
horizons		5	90	89
horizontal	Adj	12	91	89
horn	NoC	16	100	89
horn		10	97	90
horns		7	94	85
horrible	Adj	17	92	85
horror	NoC	26	100	92
horror		21	100	91
horrors		4	88	93
horse	NoC	126	99	87
horse		77	99	86
horses		49	99	87
hospital	NoC	180	100	91
hospital		151	100	90
hospitals		29	98	88
host	NoC	33	99	92
host		27	99	93
hosts		6	89	87
host	Verb	11	87	89
host		5	76	88
hosted		4	70	87
hosting		2	66	88
hosts		1	46	83
hostage	NoC	11	90	82
hostage		5	80	84
hostages		7	75	78
hostile	Adj	16	96	94
hostility	NoC	17	96	92
hostilities		3	75	85
hostility		14	96	93
hot	Adj	94	100	94
hot		91	100	94
hotter		2	75	90
hottest		2	69	89
hotel	NoC	138	100	88
hotel		114	100	87
hotels		24	100	87
hour	NoC	302	100	96
hour		113	100	94
hours		189	100	96
house	NoC	598	100	95
house		501	100	95
houses		96	100	95
house	Verb	49	100	92
house		7	100	93
housed		9	97	92
houses		4	75	86
housing		28	97	89
household	NoC	57	100	91
household		39	100	93
households		18	88	86
housewife	NoC	10	90	68
housewife		6	87	64
housewives		4	72	74
housing	NoC	66	100	90
housing		66	100	90
housings		0	13	68
how	Adv	1016	100	95
Howard	NoP	27	97	81
Howard		27	97	80
Howards		1	26	76
however	Adv	605	100	94
HP	NoP	11	53	43
huge	Adj	79	100	95
huge		79	100	95
Hugh	NoP	21	94	89
Hughes	NoP	17	88	86
Hull	NoP	11	89	85
Hull		11	88	85

Word	PoS	Freq	Ra	Di	Word	PoS	Freq	Ra	Di	Word	PoS	Freq	Ra	Di
human	Adj	183	100	93	*idea*		*217*	*100*	*97*	imagine	Verb	83	100	93
human	NoC	33	100	89	*ideas*		*111*	*100*	*93*	*imagine*		*61*	*100*	*93*
human		*13*	*99*	*91*	ideal	Adj	47	100	93	*imagined*		*17*	*98*	*88*
humans		*20*	*100*	*86*	ideal	NoC	17	97	90	*imagines*		*1*	*67*	*89*
humanity	NoC	12	97	91	*ideal*		*9*	*90*	*88*	*imagining*		*4*	*89*	*89*
humour	NoC	23	98	93	*ideals*		*8*	*90*	*90*	IMF	NoP	11	42	64
humour		*22*	*98*	*93*	ideally	Adv	12	100	93	*IMF*		*11*	*42*	*64*
humours		*0*	*24*	*79*	identical	Adj	22	100	92	immediate	Adj	61	100	94
hundred	NoC	231	100	84	identification	NoC	23	97	92	immediately	Adv	102	100	97
hundred		*191*	*100*	*81*	*identification*		*22*	*97*	*92*	immense	Adj	14	96	94
hundreds		*40*	*100*	*93*	*identifications*		*1*	*35*	*82*	immigration	NoC	11	86	86
Hungary	NoP	15	90	82	identify	Verb	133	99	93	impact	NoC	77	99	92
hunger	NoC	11	98	92	*identified*		*62*	*99*	*92*	*impact*		*74*	*99*	*92*
hunger		*11*	*98*	*92*	*identifies*		*6*	*78*	*90*	*impacts*		*3*	*59*	*77*
hungry	Adj	19	97	91	*identify*		*50*	*99*	*92*	imperial	Adj	24	97	89
hungrier		*0*	*22*	*79*	*identifying*		*15*	*97*	*91*	implement	Verb	42	92	91
hungry		*19*	*97*	*91*	identity	NoC	44	98	93	*implement*		*15*	*83*	*90*
hunt	NoC	11	93	86	*identities*		*4*	*87*	*90*	*implemented*		*17*	*83*	*91*
hunt		*10*	*93*	*86*	*identity*		*40*	*98*	*93*	*implementing*		*9*	*80*	*89*
hunts		*1*	*40*	*79*	ideological	Adj	17	83	85	*implements*		*1*	*42*	*82*
Hunt	NoP	11	85	82	ideology	NoC	25	87	83	implementation	NoC	30	77	85
hunt	Verb	15	97	92	*ideologies*		*4*	*67*	*84*	*implementation*		*28*	*77*	*86*
hunt		*6*	*90*	*91*	*ideology*		*21*	*83*	*81*	*implementations*		*2*	*22*	*46*
hunted		*4*	*81*	*90*	ie	Adv	64	91	90	implication	NoC	58	99	92
hunting		*5*	*89*	*89*	*i.e*		*1*	*30*	*73*	*implication*		*13*	*95*	*92*
hunts		*1*	*38*	*84*	*i.e.*		*46*	*88*	*89*	*implications*		*45*	*98*	*91*
hunting	NoC	18	97	90	*ie*		*15*	*74*	*82*	implicit	Adj	12	92	86
hunting		*18*	*97*	*90*	*ie.*		*3*	*42*	*64*	imply	Verb	56	100	91
hurry	Verb	25	94	85	if	Conj	2369	100	96	*implied*		*16*	*97*	*88*
hurried		*12*	*75*	*82*	ignorance	NoC	11	98	94	*implies*		*20*	*92*	*90*
hurries		*0*	*24*	*79*	*ignorance*		*11*	*98*	*94*	*imply*		*15*	*94*	*91*
hurry		*9*	*85*	*87*	ignore	Verb	74	100	96	*implying*		*5*	*96*	*92*
hurrying		*4*	*69*	*84*	*ignore*		*25*	*100*	*96*	import	NoC	29	100	86
hurt	Verb	47	100	90	*ignored*		*32*	*100*	*96*	*import*		*9*	*96*	*88*
hurt		*38*	*100*	*89*	*ignores*		*5*	*87*	*90*	*imports*		*19*	*87*	*84*
hurting		*5*	*79*	*88*	*ignoring*		*12*	*100*	*93*	import	Verb	16	98	92
hurts		*5*	*84*	*86*	II / ii	Num	89	92	90	*import*		*5*	*91*	*90*
husband	NoC	123	100	94	*II*		*88*	*92*	*90*	*imported*		*8*	*91*	*89*
husband		*112*	*100*	*91*	*IIs*		*0*	*14*	*63*	*importing*		*3*	*78*	*90*
husbands		*10*	*99*	*91*	III / iii	Num	50	91	89	*imports*		*0*	*12*	*71*
hut	NoC	16	92	89	*III*		*50*	*91*	*89*	importance	NoC	97	100	93
hut		*12*	*87*	*88*	*IIIs*		*0*	*8*	*60*	*importance*		*97*	*100*	*93*
huts		*4*	*80*	*89*	ill	Adj	46	100	94	important	Adj	392	100	95
hydrogen	NoC	12	75	78	*ill*		*46*	*100*	*94*	importantly	Adv	13	98	94
hydrogen		*12*	*75*	*79*	illegal	Adj	24	100	88	impose	Verb	63	99	92
hypothesis	NoC	23	86	86	illness	NoC	38	100	93	*impose*		*19*	*98*	*92*
hypotheses		*6*	*64*	*79*	*illness*		*33*	*100*	*93*	*imposed*		*34*	*97*	*91*
hypothesis		*17*	*85*	*86*	*illnesses*		*5*	*84*	*89*	*imposes*		*4*	*72*	*86*
I / i	Lett	53	100	88	illusion	NoC	13	100	93	*imposing*		*6*	*90*	*92*
I	NoP	14	88	92	*illusion*		*9*	*96*	*93*	impossible	Adj	71	100	96
I		*3*	*59*	*77*	*illusions*		*3*	*89*	*91*	impress	Verb	16	100	95
I.		*11*	*88*	*92*	illustrate	Verb	56	100	91	*impress*		*6*	*99*	*95*
I / i	Num	86	94	91	*illustrate*		*16*	*94*	*91*	*impressed*		*8*	*99*	*95*
I	Pron	10241	100	90	*illustrated*		*26*	*93*	*90*	*impresses*		*1*	*38*	*84*
I		*8875*	*100*	*89*	*illustrates*		*11*	*79*	*91*	*impressing*		*1*	*50*	*84*
me		*1364*	*100*	*90*	*illustrating*		*3*	*81*	*90*	impressed	Adj	16	100	96
Ian	NoP	53	96	87	illustration	NoC	21	100	91	impression	NoC	49	100	96
Ian		*53*	*96*	*87*	*illustration*		*12*	*94*	*91*	*impression*		*42*	*100*	*96*
IBM	NoP	48	71	51	*illustrations*		*10*	*89*	*88*	*impressions*		*7*	*95*	*92*
IBM		*48*	*71*	*51*	image	NoC	110	100	93	impressive	Adj	30	100	94
ice	NoC	41	100	92	*image*		*75*	*100*	*93*	imprisonment	NoC	15	90	84
ice		*40*	*100*	*92*	*images*		*36*	*95*	*92*	*imprisonment*		*15*	*90*	*84*
ices		*0*	*22*	*75*	imagination	NoC	28	99	93	improve	Verb	110	100	94
ICI	NoP	14	61	60	*imagination*		*27*	*99*	*93*	*improve*		*62*	*100*	*94*
ICI		*14*	*61*	*60*	*imaginations*		*1*	*62*	*89*	*improved*		*27*	*100*	*95*
idea	NoC	328	100	96	imaginative	Adj	10	93	92	*improves*		*4*	*87*	*92*

Word	PoS	Freq	Ra	Di	Word	PoS	Freq	Ra	Di	Word	PoS	Freq	Ra	Di
improving		16	99	93	*including*		11	93	93	*inducing*		2	55	81
improved	Adj	21	89	92	including	Prep	230	100	93	indulge	Verb	10	98	94
improvement	NoC	66	100	92	inclusion	NoC	12	86	91	*indulge*		5	96	92
improvement		42	100	92	*inclusion*		12	86	91	*indulged*		2	84	91
improvements		24	96	92	*inclusions*		1	22	71	*indulges*		0	24	81
impulse	NoC	11	93	91	income	NoC	135	100	89	*indulging*		2	82	92
impulse		7	88	91	*income*		120	100	89	industrial	Adj	116	100	91
impulses		4	70	84	*incomes*		15	85	87	industry	NoC	242	100	91
in	Adv	573	100	98	incorporate	Verb	43	99	92	*industries*		43	92	90
in	Prep	18214	100	98	*incorporate*		11	91	91	*industry*		198	100	91
in		18214	100	98	*incorporated*		19	92	91	inequality	NoC	15	80	84
in~*	Verb	20	32	54	*incorporates*		6	71	88	*inequalities*		7	66	80
in accordance with	Prep	20	88	85	*incorporating*		8	85	91	*inequality*		8	76	82
in addition	Adv	45	92	92	increase	NoC	119	100	91	inevitable	Adj	28	98	95
in addition to	Prep	34	99	93	*increase*		96	100	91	inevitably	Adv	31	97	93
in case	Conj	22	99	92	*increases*		23	86	90	infant	NoC	26	100	87
in charge of	Prep	17	100	94	increase	Verb	192	100	93	*infant*		17	99	87
in conjunction with	Prep	13	86	92	*increase*		73	100	93	*infants*		9	90	83
in connection with	Prep	16	93	87	*increased*		73	100	92	infection	NoC	34	96	79
in favour of	Prep	36	98	93	*increases*		20	86	91	*infection*		27	94	79
in front of	Prep	66	100	92	*increasing*		26	99	94	*infections*		7	75	79
in general	Adv	42	100	92	increased	Adj	57	96	90	inflation	NoC	45	96	86
in line with	Prep	12	92	92	increasing	Adj	55	97	93	*inflation*		45	96	86
in order	ClO	131	100	94	increasingly	Adv	66	98	94	inflict	Verb	11	96	93
in part	Adv	21	93	92	incredible	Adj	12	99	94	*inflict*		3	86	91
in particular	Adv	67	100	94	incur	Verb	17	95	86	*inflicted*		5	93	92
in relation to	Prep	46	96	89	*incur*		3	80	85	*inflicting*		1	66	90
in respect of	Prep	29	85	79	*incurred*		12	91	83	*inflicts*		0	28	70
in response to	Prep	20	96	92	*incurring*		2	70	89	influence	NoC	94	99	92
in search of	Prep	10	96	94	*incurs*		1	37	81	*influence*		80	99	92
in short	Adv	13	92	87	indeed	Adv	188	100	95	*influences*		14	87	90
in spite of	Prep	28	99	94	independence	NoC	45	100	87	influence	Verb	59	100	92
in support of	Prep	11	90	88	independent	Adj	98	100	92	*influence*		25	99	92
in terms of	Prep	102	100	92	independently	Adv	14	95	92	*influenced*		26	100	92
in that	Conj	18	100	92	index	NoC	52	99	83	*influences*		2	65	88
in the light of	Prep	18	96	92	*index*		45	99	83	*influencing*		5	82	90
in touch with	Prep	13	99	95	*indexes*		3	53	73	influential	Adj	18	94	91
in view of	Prep	15	98	92	*indices*		4	62	78	inform	Verb	54	100	95
inability	NoC	11	95	91	India	NoP	47	100	91	*inform*		15	100	93
inability		11	95	93	*India*		47	100	91	*informed*		33	100	96
inadequate	Adj	23	98	93	Indian	Adj	38	100	91	*informing*		4	92	93
inappropriate	Adj	13	93	93	Indian	NoC	13	95	90	*informs*		2	75	89
Inc	Adj	59	73	39	*Indian*		2	64	85	informal	Adj	24	98	91
Inc		57	65	37	*Indians*		12	93	89	information	NoC	387	100	92
Inc.		2	47	78	indicate	Verb	124	100	92	*information*		386	100	92
incentive	NoC	23	93	91	*indicate*		41	99	90	*informations*		0	12	71
incentive		13	92	92	*indicated*		44	100	93	infrastructure	NoC	10	81	88
incentives		10	79	89	*indicates*		23	92	91	*infrastructure*		10	81	88
inch	NoC	41	100	94	*indicating*		15	99	91	*infrastructures*		0	18	76
inch		18	99	93	indication	NoC	31	98	94	ingredient	NoC	18	97	91
inches		23	97	93	*indication*		23	98	94	*ingredient*		6	88	91
incidence	NoC	18	85	80	*indications*		8	90	92	*ingredients*		13	95	90
incidence		17	85	80	indicator	NoC	20	95	88	inhabitant	NoC	16	95	92
incidences		0	26	74	*indicator*		8	90	91	*inhabitant*		1	53	87
incident	NoC	52	100	92	*indicators*		11	84	83	*inhabitants*		15	94	91
incident		37	99	92	indirect	Adj	16	88	88	inherent	Adj	13	88	91
incidents		15	97	90	indirectly	Adv	10	92	91	inherit	Verb	18	99	94
incidentally	Adv	11	99	93	individual	Adj	136	100	93	*inherit*		4	92	92
inclined	Adj	13	99	94	individual	NoC	135	100	92	*inherited*		13	99	93
include	Verb	353	100	94	*individual*		55	99	92	*inheriting*		1	54	88
include		152	100	93	*individuals*		80	100	91	*inherits*		1	41	85
included		123	100	92	individually	Adv	11	98	93	inheritance	NoC	13	95	89
includes		68	96	91	induce	Verb	22	97	81	*inheritance*		12	95	89
					induce		6	89	88	*inheritances*		0	17	69
					induced		12	95	75	inhibit	Verb	12	91	83
					induces		2	59	81	*inhibit*		5	75	82

Word	PoS	Freq	Ra	Di	Word	PoS	Freq	Ra	Di	Word	PoS	Freq	Ra	Di
inhibited		4	86	82	*insight*		14	98	93	*insure*	Verb	11	93	68
inhibiting		2	56	86	*insights*		8	83	90	*insure*		3	68	72
inhibits		2	54	79	insist	Verb	67	100	95	*insured*		7	86	61
initial	Adj	62	100	93	*insist*		16	100	94	*insures*		0	15	73
initially	Adv	38	100	93	*insisted*		34	99	93	*insuring*		1	31	82
initiate	Verb	21	97	92	*insisting*		7	97	94	intact	Adj	12	99	91
initiate		5	87	92	*insists*		10	94	90	intake	NoC	12	98	83
initiated		12	94	92	inspect	Verb	15	99	93	*intake*		12	97	82
initiates		1	47	85	*inspect*		7	98	92	*intakes*		1	42	84
initiating		3	70	87	*inspected*		5	91	91	integral	Adj	12	91	91
initiative	NoC	56	99	91	*inspecting*		3	76	90	integrate	Verb	22	89	85
initiative		36	99	91	*inspects*		0	30	80	*integrate*		8	78	82
initiatives		19	78	90	inspection	NoC	23	100	90	*integrated*		9	84	87
inject	Verb	10	97	89	*inspection*		20	100	91	*integrates*		1	42	74
inject		3	82	88	*inspections*		3	75	82	*integrating*		4	73	86
injected		4	92	88	inspector	NoC	39	98	90	integrated	Adj	17	83	86
injecting		3	66	80	*inspector*		29	98	89	integration	NoC	24	81	86
injects		0	20	76	*inspectors*		9	89	87	*integration*		24	81	86
injection	NoC	14	96	83	inspiration	NoC	14	98	93	integrity	NoC	15	95	90
injection		10	93	82	*inspiration*		14	98	93	*integrity*		15	95	90
injections		4	83	83	*inspirations*		0	35	83	Intel	NoP	12	29	41
injunction	NoC	10	88	77	inspire	Verb	23	99	93	*Intel*		12	29	41
injunction		8	81	75	*inspire*		4	92	92	intellectual	Adj	25	97	91
injunctions		2	54	75	*inspired*		16	97	93	intellectual	NoC	12	90	89
injure	Verb	25	99	88	*inspires*		1	62	88	*intellectual*		5	83	90
injure		2	68	82	*inspiring*		1	70	90	*intellectuals*		7	79	86
injured		21	99	87	install	Verb	32	99	90	intelligence	NoC	35	99	91
injures		0	25	82	*install*		8	96	87	*intelligence*		35	99	91
injuring		2	51	83	*installed*		20	97	91	*intelligences*		0	14	66
injured	Adj	11	95	89	*installing*		4	81	86	intelligent	Adj	19	100	94
injury	NoC	72	100	88	*installs*		0	27	79	intend	Verb	108	100	95
injuries		26	97	86	installation	NoC	19	90	88	*intend*		21	100	92
injury		46	100	88	*installation*		13	86	86	*intended*		70	99	95
inland	Adj	12	92	88	*installations*		6	78	87	*intending*		6	97	93
inn	NoC	18	96	90	instance	NoC	35	99	92	*intends*		11	95	87
inn		15	95	91	*instance*		18	98	92	intense	Adj	23	99	95
inns		3	68	75	*instances*		17	89	91	intensity	NoC	17	94	91
inner	Adj	45	99	92	instant	Adj	12	99	94	*intensities*		1	32	68
innocent	Adj	21	97	93	instantly	Adv	16	98	91	*intensity*		16	94	92
innovation	NoC	24	94	84	instead	Adv	75	100	96	intensive	Adj	18	98	92
innovation		17	92	83	instead of	Prep	72	100	97	intent	NoC	13	98	94
innovations		7	76	85	instinct	NoC	18	97	91	*intent*		12	97	93
innovative	Adj	10	82	91	*instinct*		11	97	92	*intents*		1	68	90
input	NoC	39	92	84	*instincts*		7	88	87	intention	NoC	62	100	94
input		32	91	83	institute	NoC	58	98	86	*intention*		47	100	93
inputs		7	68	84	*institute*		53	98	86	*intentions*		15	100	93
inquiry	NoC	44	96	89	*institutes*		5	73	83	interaction	NoC	34	82	87
inquiries		9	87	89	institution	NoC	114	98	82	*interaction*		23	81	87
inquiry		35	96	88	*institution*		49	98	64	*interactions*		11	67	84
insect	NoC	21	95	81	*institutions*		65	93	89	interest	NoC	376	100	94
insect		8	83	81	institutional	Adj	20	85	90	*interest*		272	100	94
insects		14	92	81	instruct	Verb	18	98	94	*interests*		104	100	92
insert	Verb	18	99	92	*instruct*		4	92	91	interested	Adj	88	100	97
insert		5	92	90	*instructed*		12	97	94	interesting	Adj	96	100	95
inserted		10	97	91	*instructing*		2	77	91	interface	NoC	23	76	62
inserting		2	80	90	*instructs*		1	38	82	*interface*		17	74	63
inserts		1	39	85	instruction	NoC	59	100	86	*interfaces*		5	50	57
inside	Adv	50	100	92	*instruction*		23	100	77	interfere	Verb	18	100	94
inside	NoC	13	98	93	*instructions*		36	100	90	*interfere*		11	98	93
inside		12	98	93	instrument	NoC	55	100	90	*interfered*		3	87	91
insides		2	65	88	*instrument*		26	100	89	*interferes*		1	66	88
inside	Prep	74	100	93	*instruments*		29	99	90	*interfering*		4	96	93
insider	NoC	11	78	60	insufficient	Adj	13	93	92	interference	NoC	14	98	90
insider		8	67	53	insurance	NoC	71	100	90	*interference*		14	98	90
insiders		3	65	78	*insurance*		71	100	90	*interferences*		0	12	72
insight	NoC	22	98	93	*insurances*		1	27	77	interim	Adj	17	85	82

Word	PoS	Freq	Ra	Di	Word	PoS	Freq	Ra	Di	Word	PoS	Freq	Ra	Di
interior	Adj	13	92	77	invest		16	100	92	isle	NoC	22	100	92
interior	NoC	22	98	88	invested		13	98	93	isle		14	99	91
interior		18	97	87	*investing*		7	95	91	*isles*		8	92	89
interiors		4	75	85	*invests*		1	58	87	isolate	Verb	18	98	91
intermediate	Adj	13	85	90	investigate	Verb	55	100	90	*isolate*		4	82	90
internal	Adj	67	100	92	*investigate*		24	100	88	*isolated*		12	97	90
international	Adj	221	100	90	*investigated*		15	98	89	*isolates*		1	36	65
interpret	Verb	43	99	92	*investigates*		2	56	66	*isolating*		1	55	87
interpret		13	98	92	*investigating*		14	100	90	isolated	Adj	16	99	91
interpreted		21	95	91	investigation	NoC	68	100	91	isolation	NoC	19	98	93
interpreting		7	83	87	*investigation*		51	98	90	*isolation*		19	98	93
interprets		1	53	86	*investigations*		17	99	91	Israel	NoP	32	94	78
interpretation	NoC	54	99	89	investigator	NoC	11	90	79	*Israel*		32	94	78
interpretation		43	99	89	*investigator*		4	77	77	Israeli	Adj	15	68	67
interpretations		11	88	88	*investigators*		7	73	78	issue	NoC	269	100	93
interrupt	Verb	21	100	90	investment	NoC	124	100	90	*issue*		148	100	93
interrupt		5	91	91	*investment*		109	100	90	*issues*		121	99	93
interrupted		14	99	88	*investments*		15	96	88	issue	Verb	79	100	91
interrupting		2	77	89	investor	NoC	35	83	84	*issue*		16	98	92
interrupts		1	47	87	*investor*		8	70	79	*issued*		56	99	89
interval	NoC	30	100	96	*investors*		27	82	85	*issues*		2	69	87
interval		14	97	88	invisible	Adj	13	96	93	*issuing*		5	91	92
intervals		16	98	91	invitation	NoC	23	100	95	IT	NoC	14	91	86
intervene	Verb	17	98	93	*invitation*		19	100	95	*IT*		14	89	86
intervene		10	97	92	*invitations*		4	90	91	it	Pron	10878	100	95
intervened		5	90	92	invite	Verb	63	100	97	*'t*		3	38	66
intervenes		1	49	85	*invite*		12	100	94	*it*		10875	100	95
intervening		1	56	87	*invited*		42	100	96	Italian	Adj	40	100	91
intervention	NoC	36	96	90	*invites*		3	84	91	Italian	NoC	15	100	93
intervention		32	96	90	*inviting*		5	98	94	*Italian*		9	98	92
interventions		4	64	83	invoke	Verb	10	90	90	*Italians*		6	93	91
interview	NoC	67	100	91	*invoke*		3	75	87	Italy	NoP	51	100	92
interview		43	100	91	*invoked*		5	78	89	*Italy*		51	100	92
interviews		24	99	84	*invokes*		1	39	82	item	NoC	105	100	92
interview	Verb	24	100	94	*invoking*		2	69	90	*item*		38	100	90
interview		4	95	92	involve	Verb	229	100	94	*items*		67	100	92
interviewed		15	100	94	*involve*		42	100	93	its	Det	1632	100	95
interviewing		5	91	89	*involved*		103	100	95	itself	Pron	237	100	96
intimate	Adj	11	98	93	*involves*		41	97	92	IV / iv	Num	28	89	88
into	Prep	1634	100	97	*involving*		43	99	93	*IV*		28	89	88
introduce	Verb	144	100	94	involved	Adj	96	100	95	J / j	Lett	15	89	83
introduce		35	100	94	involvement	NoC	42	97	92	J	NoP	63	89	80
introduced		86	100	94	*involvement*		42	97	92	*J*		22	74	67
introduces		6	83	92	*involvements*		0	32	80	*J.*		42	88	76
introducing		18	100	94	Ipswich	NoP	12	78	76	Jack	NoP	57	100	87
introduction	NoC	69	99	93	IRA	NoP	18	81	81	jacket	NoC	36	98	91
introduction		66	99	93	*IRA*		18	80	80	*jacket*		30	95	90
introductions		3	82	91	Iran	NoP	20	79	75	*jackets*		6	88	90
invade	Verb	10	97	94	*Iran*		20	79	75	Jackson	NoP	20	98	90
invade		3	76	91	Iraq	NoP	32	71	68	*Jackson*		20	98	90
invaded		6	96	94	Iraqi	Adj	17	60	59	*Jacksons*		0	16	73
invades		0	23	76	Ireland	NoP	96	100	86	jail	NoC	12	93	80
invading		1	68	91	*Ireland*		96	100	86	*jail*		11	91	80
invariably	Adv	16	99	93	Irish	Adj	59	100	88	*jails*		1	32	72
invasion	NoC	21	98	89	iron	NoC	48	100	94	jam	NoC	10	97	91
invasion		19	98	88	*iron*		45	100	94	*jam*		8	93	90
invasions		1	57	87	*irons*		3	77	89	*jams*		2	64	88
invent	Verb	19	99	94	irony	NoC	10	94	92	James	NoP	102	100	93
invent		4	92	91	*ironies*		1	40	84	Jan*	NoP	45	89	59
invented		12	98	94	*irony*		10	94	92	*Jan*		14	88	77
inventing		2	79	91	irrelevant	Adj	14	98	93	*Jan.*		31	22	42
invents		0	20	71	Isabel	NoP	13	51	24	Jane	NoP	42	99	86
invention	NoC	13	96	89	Islamic	Adj	13	69	73	*Jane*		42	99	86
invention		11	93	89	island	NoC	102	100	92	*Janes*		0	11	70
inventions		2	69	86	*island*		66	100	93	January	NoP	102	100	90
invest	Verb	37	100	93	*islands*		36	100	89	Japan	NoP	65	97	83

Word	PoS	Freq	Ra	Di	Word	PoS	Freq	Ra	Di	Word	PoS	Freq	Ra	Di
Japan		65	97	83	Jones	NoP	46	99	88	justice	NoC	75	100	88
Japanese	Adj	51	100	86	Jordan	NoP	15	89	80	*justice*		67	100	90
Japanese	NoC	11	94	86	*Jordan*		14	89	80	*justices*		7	67	55
jar	NoC	10	92	89	*Jordans*		0	10	66	justification	NoC	19	96	87
jar		6	87	88	Joseph	NoP	30	97	86	*justification*		18	96	88
jars		4	79	89	journal	NoC	34	98	88	*justifications*		2	59	76
Jason	NoP	11	69	84	*journal*		24	96	87	justify	Verb	46	100	92
Jason		11	69	84	*journals*		10	91	84	*justified*		20	96	91
jaw	NoC	17	96	90	journalist	NoC	32	98	92	*justifies*		2	73	90
jaw		11	92	89	*journalist*		14	98	93	*justify*		21	100	93
jaws		6	88	88	*journalists*		18	93	90	*justifying*		2	74	90
jazz	NoC	10	88	86	journey	NoC	56	100	95	K / k	Lett	27	96	82
Jean	NoP	30	99	81	*journey*		48	100	95	K	NoP	12	83	84
jeans	NoC	13	91	89	*journeys*		8	97	92	*K*		5	54	68
jean		0	11	70	joy	NoC	27	99	93	*K.*		7	78	84
jeans		13	88	89	*joy*		24	98	93	*Ks*		1	19	62
Jenny	NoP	18	92	79	*joys*		3	80	88	Karen	NoP	16	85	75
Jenny		18	92	79	Joyce	NoP	13	88	73	*Karen*		16	85	75
Jesus	NoP	55	99	82	*Joyce*		13	88	73	*Karens*		0	6	44
jet	NoC	18	97	90	*Joyces*		0	3	15	Kate	NoP	24	89	72
jet		13	97	89	judge	NoC	70	100	82	*Kate*		24	89	72
jets		5	82	88	*judge*		45	99	78	*Kates*		0	6	47
Jew	NoC	22	98	87	*judges*		25	96	86	Katherine	NoP	11	73	40
Jew		4	76	87	judge	Verb	48	100	96	*Katherine*		11	73	40
Jews		18	94	86	*judge*		20	100	95	*keen*	Adj	38	100	95
jewellery	NoC	13	95	92	*judged*		17	99	95	*keen*		37	100	95
Jewish	Adj	22	97	88	*judges*		3	73	88	*keener*		1	62	89
Jim	NoP	43	99	91	*judging*		9	99	95	*keenest*		1	34	81
Jim		43	99	91	judgement	NoC	34	99	93	keep	Verb	505	100	96
Jimmy	NoP	24	94	78	*judgement*		25	99	94	*keep*		276	100	95
Joan	NoP	19	98	79	*judgements*		9	89	89	*keeping*		60	100	96
Joan		19	97	79	judgment	NoC	38	94	69	*keeps*		26	100	94
job	NoC	326	100	95	*judgment*		33	92	67	*kept*		143	100	95
job		229	100	95	*judgments*		6	71	79	keeper	NoC	16	97	87
jobs		97	100	91	judicial	Adj	25	84	78	*keeper*		14	92	85
Joe	NoP	43	99	80	juice	NoC	19	94	87	*keepers*		3	73	89
Joe		43	99	80	*juice*		17	94	86	Keith	NoP	28	94	87
Joes		0	9	67	*juices*		3	67	88	*Keith*		28	94	87
John	NoP	328	100	93	Julia	NoP	15	84	65	Kelly	NoP	21	91	78
Johnny	NoP	16	88	76	*Julia*		15	84	65	*Kelly*		21	91	78
Johnnies		0	7	31	Julie	NoP	14	83	82	Ken	NoP	30	93	79
Johnny		15	86	76	Juliet	NoP	12	68	31	*Ken*		30	93	79
Johnson	NoP	32	98	80	July	NoP	119	100	81	Kennedy	NoP	14	96	89
Johnson		32	98	80	jump	Verb	52	100	92	*Kennedy*		13	96	89
Johnsons		0	5	47	*jump*		16	99	92	*Kennedys*		0	12	69
join	Verb	174	100	96	*jumped*		24	99	89	Kenneth	NoP	16	89	87
join		74	100	96	*jumping*		9	96	92	*Kenneth*		16	89	87
joined		72	100	95	*jumps*		3	82	89	Kent	NoP	26	100	88
joining		22	100	95	junction	NoC	24	98	80	*Kent*		26	100	88
joins		6	95	91	*junction*		18	98	84	Kenya	NoP	10	86	84
joint	Adj	64	100	89	*junctions*		6	64	62	Kevin	NoP	23	92	85
joint		64	100	89	June	NoP	146	100	83	*Kevin*		23	92	85
joint	NoC	14	98	89	jungle	NoC	11	96	88	key	Adj	76	100	93
joint		6	89	88	*jungle*		10	95	88	key	NoC	71	100	92
joints		9	93	89	*jungles*		1	51	86	*key*		49	100	93
jointly	Adv	11	90	91	junior	Adj	28	100	91	*keys*		23	100	89
joke	NoC	33	100	92	jurisdiction	NoC	21	87	71	keyboard	NoC	11	93	86
joke		21	100	91	*jurisdiction*		19	87	69	*keyboard*		10	91	84
jokes		11	96	93	*jurisdictions*		2	45	79	*keyboards*		2	62	87
joke	Verb	11	95	89	jury	NoC	25	96	87	Keynes	NoP	10	78	66
joke		1	56	88	*juries*		2	53	80	kick	NoC	17	90	82
joked		3	67	87	*jury*		23	95	87	*kick*		13	87	82
jokes		0	30	81	just	Adj	19	100	95	*kicks*		3	71	80
joking		7	86	86	*just*		19	100	95	kick	Verb	36	97	92
Jonathan	NoP	16	91	84	just	Adv	1277	100	92	*kick*		10	92	92
Jonathan		16	91	84	just about	Adv	14	97	93	*kicked*		16	96	90

Word	PoS	Freq	Ra	Di
kicking		9	91	92
kicks		2	70	88
kid	NoC	60	97	90
kid		16	91	90
kids		44	97	90
kill	Verb	157	100	93
kill		46	100	92
killed		86	100	91
killing		20	100	93
kills		5	93	91
killer	NoC	19	97	88
killer		14	93	87
killers		4	84	86
killing	NoC	16	96	85
killing		11	96	87
killings		6	71	79
kilometre	NoC	14	95	87
kilometre		2	74	87
kilometres		11	93	87
Kim	NoP	13	80	80
Kim		13	80	80
kind	Adj	16	98	90
kind		14	95	88
kinder		2	75	90
kindest		1	50	87
kind	NoC	271	100	96
kind		225	100	96
kinds		47	100	92
king	NoC	162	100	92
king		147	100	92
kings		15	95	89
King	NoP	16	100	87
King		16	100	87
kingdom	NoC	25	97	87
kingdom		22	97	86
kingdoms		3	61	83
Kingdom	NoP-	44	93	82
Kinnock	NoP	15	57	62
Kinnock		15	57	62
Kinnocks		0	7	55
kiss	NoC	19	87	84
kiss		15	86	84
kisses		4	58	81
kiss	Verb	36	93	83
kiss		12	83	85
kissed		18	77	81
kisses		1	34	76
kissing		6	73	84
kit	NoC	22	100	87
kit		18	98	87
kits		4	77	83
kitchen	NoC	89	100	89
kitchen		82	98	89
kitchens		6	91	89
km	NoC	15	59	78
km		14	58	77
km.		0	7	49
kms		1	17	58
knee	NoC	46	98	90
knee		20	95	91
knees		26	97	87
kneel	Verb	11	86	84
kneel		2	56	85
kneeled		0	15	65
kneeling		3	65	85
kneels		0	21	75
knelt		5	57	81
knife	NoC	34	100	92
knife		27	99	91
knives		7	93	88
knight	NoC	12	87	86
knight		6	82	86
knights		6	80	84
knit	Verb	22	93	50
knit		11	73	48
knits		1	18	51
knitted		4	57	51
knitting		6	66	51
knitting	NoC	10	78	52
knitting		10	78	52
knock	Verb	46	100	92
knock		12	96	90
knocked		23	99	91
knocking		9	92	91
knocks		1		
knot	NoC	12	94	90
knot		7	86	89
knots		6	87	86
know	Verb	1882	100	88
knew		261	100	88
know		1233	100	86
knowing		47	99	93
known		238	100	97
knows		84	100	94
*~no**		19	43	63
knowledge	NoC	146	100	92
knowledge		146	100	92
knowledges		0	11	56
known	Adj	20	99	90
Kong	NoP-	28	97	82
Kong		28	97	82
Korea	NoP	19	85	71
Korea		19	85	71
Koreas		0	12	65
korean	Adj	12	66	72
Kuwait	NoP	16	65	65
L / l	Lett	32	99	86
L	NoP	13	85	85
L		5	58	69
L.		9	80	84
la	Fore	19	97	88
La/LA	NoP-	24	94	92
L.A.		0	24	73
La/LA		24	94	92
lab	NoC	13	89	72
lab		7	83	82
labs		6	51	48
label	NoC	29	99	93
label		17	98	91
labels		12	98	92
label	Verb	18	99	92
label		3	85	91
labelled		12	98	92
labelling		2	67	87
labels		0	17	76
labeled		0	7	58
laboratory	NoC	38	96	88
laboratories		10	87	82
laboratory		27	96	89
labour*	Adj	131	100	84
labour*	NoC	139	100	91
labour		137	100	91
labours		3	77	90
lace	NoC	13	89	78
lace		12	89	76
laces		1	48	85
lack	NoC	90	100	95
lack	Verb	45	100	94
lack		10	95	93
lacked		12	96	94
lacking		15	98	94
lacks		8	91	92
lad	NoC	35	97	90
lad		20	94	89
lads		15	93	89
ladder	NoC	16	97	92
ladder		13	97	92
ladders		2	72	88
lady	NoC	130	100	91
ladies		33	98	92
lady		97	100	90
lake	NoC	51	100	91
lake		39	100	91
lakes		12	93	87
lamb	NoC	16	95	89
lamb		10	88	89

Frequency of kinship terms

In the **nuclear family**, frequency highlights the traditionally key roles of *wife* and *mother* (as compared with *husband* and *father*). But in other roles, males (*son, brother*) are mentioned more often than females (*daughter, sister*) (figures give frequency per million words):

mother	295	*father*	252	*sister*	95	*brother*	123
wife	190	*husband*	123	*daughter*	115	*son*	166

In the **extended family**, the most frequent terms are:

uncle 38, *aunt* 33; *cousin* 25; *grandfather* 16, *grandmother* 15.

In **conversation**, the picture is somewhat different, with a predominance of short and pet terms for senior members of the family (some non-pet terms are in brackets for comparison):

mum 951; *dad* 598; *mummy* 388; *daddy* 256; (*mother* 232; *father* 116;) *ma* 35; *aunty/auntie* 67; *grandma* 65; *granddad* 61; (*uncle* 37;) *granny* 20; *grandpa* 20; *nana* 17; (*grandmother* 7; *grandfather* 5)

Word	PoS	Freq	Ra	Di	Word	PoS	Freq	Ra	Di	Word	PoS	Freq	Ra	Di
lambs		6	77	83	laugh	Verb	98	97	86	*leaflet*		12	93	88
Lamont	NoP	12	55	74	*laugh*		21	96	89	*leaflets*		8	90	90
Lamont		12	55	74	*laughed*		49	93	82	league	NoC	85	100	84
lamp	NoC	22	95	89	*laughing*		24	91	87	*league*		83	100	84
lamp		14	93	88	*laughs*		4	76	87	*leagues*		2	63	85
lamps		8	87	89	laughter	NoC	22	97	87	lean	Verb	49	98	84
Lancashire	NoP	17	93	89	launch	NoC	20	93	88	*lean*		6	86	90
Lancaster	NoP	12	92	86	*launch*		19	92	89	*leaned*		23	75	81
Lancaster		12	92	86	*launches*		1	51	81	*leaning*		14	91	86
Lancasters		0	14	67	launch	Verb	67	98	91	*leans*		2	58	80
land	NoC	208	100	94	*launch*		13	97	90	*leant*		5	59	81
land		188	100	93	*launched*		45	98	90	leap	Verb	21	97	90
lands		21	99	90	*launches*		3	57	76	*leap*		5	93	92
Land	NoP-	13	94	78	*launching*		6	92	92	*leaped*		2	50	83
land	Verb	38	100	94	Laura	NoP	25	86	70	*leaping*		4	83	89
land		13	100	94	law	NoC	318	100	91	*leaps*		1	60	86
landed		18	100	93	*law*		270	100	90	*leapt*		9	86	87
landing		7	95	91	*laws*		48	100	93	learn	Verb	193	100	96
lands		1	32	83	lawn	NoC	14	93	90	*learn*		83	100	96
landing	NoC	20	98	90	*lawn*		11	91	90	*learned*		46	100	93
landing		18	98	90	*lawns*		3	71	89	*learning*		38	99	93
landings		2	61	82	Lawrence	NoP	22	96	84	*learns*		5	92	90
landlord	NoC	35	99	68	*Lawrence*		22	96	84	*learnt*		22	100	95
landlord		27	98	59	lawyer	NoC	46	100	90	learner	NoC	13	72	72
landlords		8	87	85	*lawyer*		22	100	90	*learner*		6	62	69
landowner	NoC	11	89	90	*lawyers*		24	99	89	*learners*		7	49	71
landowner		3	80	87	lay	Verb	104	100	97	learning	NoC	54	99	87
landowners		8	84	89	*laid*		59	100	96	*learning*		54	99	87
landscape	NoC	39	98	90	*lay*		28	100	95	lease	NoC	25	97	66
landscape		33	98	89	*laying*		13	100	95	*lease*		21	97	64
landscapes		7	86	88	*lays*		4	93	92	*leases*		5	62	73
lane	NoC	53	100	90	layer	NoC	39	100	91	least	Adv	45	99	96
lane		43	100	91	*layer*		25	100	88	leather	NoC	26	97	91
lanes		10	91	78	*layers*		14	97	92	*leather*		26	97	91
language	NoC	221	100	88	layout	NoC	14	96	86	*leathers*		1	33	78
language		188	100	87	*layout*		12	95	86	leave	NoC	22	100	89
languages		34	100	86	*layouts*		1	49	82	*leave*		22	100	89
lap	NoC	16	97	90	lb	NoC	10	72	68	leave	Verb	647	100	96
lap		13	96	89	*l.b.*		0	6	29	*leave*		185	100	95
laps		3	60	82	*lb*		7	60	56	*leaves*		29	99	96
large	Adj	471	100	95	*lb.*		1	19	56	*leaving*		96	100	96
large		337	100	95	*lbs*		2	43	79	*left*		336	100	95
larger		76	100	94	le	Fore	11	93	85	Lebanon	NoP	11	69	71
largest		58	99	92	Le	NoP-	16	96	89	lecture	NoC	32	100	91
large-scale	Adj	11	84	90	LEA/Lea	NoP	17	62	74	*lecture*		17	99	91
largely	Adv	73	97	92	*LEA/Lea*		10	61	73	*lectures*		15	96	89
laser	NoC	13	90	83	*LEAs/Leas*		7	35	69	lecturer	NoC	14	99	88
laser		10	87	84	lead*	NoC	58	100	93	*lecturer*		10	96	86
lasers		2	52	73	*lead*		55	100	92	*lecturers*		5	84	87
last	Ord	691	100	93	*leads*		3	87	89	Lee	NoP	37	99	82
last	Verb	52	100	97	lead	Verb	334	100	96	*Lee*		36	98	81
last		28	100	96	*lead*		91	100	96	*Lees*		1	40	81
lasted		14	100	96	*leading*		52	100	96	Leeds	NoP	48	98	77
lasting		5	93	92	*leads*		37	100	94	left	Adj	95	100	94
lasts		5	99	93	*led*		154	100	95	*left*		95	100	94
late	Adj	302	100	97	leader	NoC	165	100	86	left	NoC	34	100	94
late		159	100	97	*leader*		93	100	86	*left*		34	100	94
later		78	100	93	*leaders*		72	99	86	*lefts*		0	8	64
latest		65	100	92	leadership	NoC	49	96	88	leg	NoC	118	100	92
late	Adv	41	100	96	*leadership*		48	96	89	*leg*		53	100	90
later	Adv	317	100	97	*leaderships*		1	24	70	*legs*		65	99	90
Latin	Adj	22	97	82	leading	Adj	61	99	93	legacy	NoC	12	94	85
latter	DetP	78	98	93	leaf	NoC	51	99	91	*legacies*		2	46	56
laugh	NoC	19	94	87	*leaf*		15	99	90	*legacy*		11	94	89
laugh		17	93	86	*leaves*		36	98	90	legal	Adj	131	100	90
laughs		2	66	88	leaflet	NoC	20	95	90	legally	Adv	12	100	93

Word	PoS	Freq	Ra	Di	Word	PoS	Freq	Ra	Di	Word	PoS	Freq	Ra	Di
legend	NoC	17	93	92	liberation	NoC	18	93	78	*lights*		1	38	85
legend		12	92	92	*liberation*		18	92	78	*lit*		23	96	87
legends		4	83	90	liberty	NoC	19	100	91	lighting	NoC	17	100	89
legislation	NoC	70	89	90	*liberties*		5	89	91	lightly	Adv	20	99	89
legislation		70	89	90	*liberty*		14	99	90	like	Adj	16	99	94
legislative	Adj	19	76	75	librarian	NoC	14	82	74	like	Adv	88	87	66
legitimate	Adj	15	97	92	*librarian*		8	79	74	like	Conj	25	96	88
Leicester	NoP	19	97	86	*librarians*		6	45	69	like	Prep	1064	100	94
leisure	NoC	29	100	91	library	NoC	104	100	88	like	Verb	424	100	91
leisure		29	100	91	*libraries*		22	93	82	*like*		344	100	91
lemon	NoC	14	94	86	*library*		82	100	88	*liked*		56	99	90
lemon		12	91	85	licence	NoC	44	100	83	*likes*		21	99	91
lemons		1	51	82	*licence*		36	100	82	*liking*		3	79	89
lend	Verb	29	100	94	*licences*		8	83	85	likelihood	NoC	12	97	92
lend		13	100	94	lid	NoC	14	97	90	*likelihood*		12	97	92
lending		5	90	89	*lid*		11	94	90	likely	Adj	228	100	95
lends		3	82	92	*lids*		3	69	87	*likelier*		0	11	65
lent		8	99	94	lie	NoC	22	100	93	*likeliest*		0	28	78
length	NoC	85	100	95	*lie*		9	98	91	*likely*		227	100	95
length		72	100	95	*lies*		12	100	94	likewise	Adv	12	96	93
lengths		13	100	92	lie (/lay)	Verb	187	100	94	Lily	NoP	14	69	45
lengthy	Adj	12	97	94	*lain*		3	70	88	limb	NoC	17	97	90
lengthier		0	17	75	*lay*		64	100	90	*limb*		6	93	84
lengthy		12	97	94	*lie*		41	100	95	*limbs*		11	92	90
Leonard	NoP	10	79	66	*lies*		40	100	94	limit	NoC	64	100	94
Leonard		10	79	66	*lying*		39	100	91	*limit*		34	100	93
Leonards		0	4	44	lie (/lied)	Verb	15	75	85	*limits*		30	99	93
Les*	NoP	13	90	86	*lie*		2	62	83	limit	Verb	66	100	93
less	Adv	243	100	95	*lied*		6	76	84	*limit*		16	93	92
less	DetP	101	100	96	*lies*		0	20	70	*limited*		40	99	93
less than	Adv	40	100	94	*lying*		7	84	84	*limiting*		4	86	91
lesser	Adj	18	99	93	lieutenant	NoC	10	93	88	*limits*		6	86	91
lesson	NoC	46	100	95	*lieutenant*		9	91	87	limitation	NoC	27	97	89
lesson		23	99	94	*lieutenants*		1	49	82	*limitation*		9	85	81
lessons		23	100	94	life	NoC	645	100	96	*limitations*		18	94	89
let	Verb	284	100	93	*life*		566	100	96	limited	Adj	64	100	93
let		253	100	92	*lifes*		1	20	63	Linda	NoP	12	86	85
lets		9	96	91	*lives*		78	100	96	line	NoC	323	100	97
letting		22	100	92	lifespan	NoC	37	51	04	*line*		221	100	96
let's	Verb	84	98	85	*lifespan*		37	50	04	*lines*		102	100	96
let alone	Prep	13	99	95	*lifespans*		0	13	64	line	Verb	22	100	95
letter	NoC	215	100	96	lifestyle	NoC	14	98	92	*line*		5	91	92
letter		136	100	95	*lifestyle*		11	96	92	*lined*		12	99	93
letters		79	100	96	*lifestyles*		2	72	90	*lines*		0	30	81
level	Adj	25	100	93	lifetime	NoC	19	100	93	*lining*		4	91	91
level	NoC	360	100	94	*lifetime*		18	100	93	linear	Adj	13	80	84
level		239	100	94	*lifetimes*		1	47	81	linguistic	Adj	25	78	82
levels		121	100	92	lift	NoC	28	99	91	link	NoC	75	100	94
level	Verb	10	99	94	*lift*		24	99	90	*link*		40	100	94
level		4	92	91	*lifts*		4	84	89	*links*		35	99	93
levelled		5	92	94	lift	Verb	71	100	92	link	Verb	74	100	95
levelling		1	70	90	*lift*		19	100	93	*link*		13	97	93
levels		0	13	72	*lifted*		38	99	88	*linked*		40	99	95
Lewis	NoP	37	99	84	*lifting*		10	98	91	*linking*		12	96	93
lexical	Adj	11	36	67	*lifts*		3	86	91	*links*		8	94	92
liability	NoC	48	95	74	light	Adj	71	100	95	lion	NoC	21	99	90
liabilities		9	70	76	*light*		62	100	95	*lion*		12	99	92
liability		39	93	73	*lighter*		8	99	93	*lions*		9	87	84
liable	Adj	22	99	84	*lightest*		1	50	87	lip	NoC	66	99	83
liaison	NoC	11	96	92	light	NoC	191	100	93	*lip*		16	98	87
liaison		10	96	91	*light*		145	100	93	*lips*		50	96	81
liaisons		1	44	87	*lights*		46	98	92	liquid	Adj	13	95	89
liberal*	Adj	54	100	88	light	Verb	36	98	89	liquid	NoC	15	97	86
liberal*	NoC	11	88	86	*light*		9	98	93	*liquid*		12	97	89
liberal		1	59	87	*lighted*		1	45	83	*liquids*		3	66	73
liberals		10	81	85	*lighting*		3	75	88	Lisa	NoP	13	78	62

Word	PoS	Freq	Ra	Di	Word	PoS	Freq	Ra	Di	Word	PoS	Freq	Ra	Di
Lisa		13	77	62	local	NoC	27	100	92	*look*		433	100	92
list	NoC	140	100	95	*local*		18	99	89	*looked*		352	100	87
list		118	100	95	*locals*		8	94	91	*looking*		264	100	94
lists		22	100	92	locality	NoC	11	91	87	*looks*		102	100	93
list	Verb	45	100	93	*localities*		5	66	84	loop	NoC	13	96	87
list		9	92	84	*locality*		7	87	87	*loop*		9	91	86
listed		25	99	93	locally	Adv	18	99	92	*loops*		4	81	83
listing		4	94	90	locate	Verb	38	99	93	loose	Adj	26	100	95
lists		6	86	92	*locate*		9	98	92	lord	NoC	160	100	91
listen	Verb	118	100	92	*located*		25	98	93	*lord*		145	100	91
listen		57	100	91	*locates*		1	42	84	*lords*		15	96	84
listened		24	97	88	*locating*		3	80	89	Lord	NoP	20	98	90
listening		34	99	91	location	NoC	55	100	92	Lords	NoP	20	89	86
listens		2.	77	91	*location*		40	99	92	lordship	NoC	13	80	73
listener	NoC	11	94	90	*locations*		15	92	92	*lordship*		8	74	75
listener		5	89	89	loch	NoC	15	79	74					
listeners		6	85	89	*loch*		13	74	74					
listing	NoC	10	90	72	*lochs*		2	41	67					
listing		7	85	73	lock	NoC	24	98	91					
listings		3	66	68	*lock*		15	97	91					
literally	Adv	20	99	96	*locks*		9	94	88					
literary	Adj	34	95	85	lock	Verb	37	100	92					
literature	NoC	53	99	88	*lock*		7	91	91					
literature		52	99	88	*locked*		26	99	91					
literatures		0	22	74	*locking*		4	84	90					
little	Adj	306	100	91	*locks*		1	52	87					
little	Adv	45	98	95	locomotive	NoC	12	74	72					
little	DetP	183	100	96	*locomotive*		8	62	71					
live	Adj	29	100	91	*locomotives*		4	50	72					
live	Verb	329	100	96	lodge	NoC	11	96	90					
live		142	100	96	*lodge*		10	96	90					
lived		82	100	95	*lodges*		1	46	75					
lives		27	98	93	lodge	Verb	11	98	91					
living		78	100	96	*lodge*		2	73	85					
lively	Adj	16	97	92	*lodged*		7	94	90					
livelier		1	38	84	*lodging*		2	77	90					
liveliest		0	34	83	log	NoC	15	98	86					
lively		15	97	92	*log*		11	97	83					
liver	NoC	17	96	70	*logs*		4	81	89					
liver		17	96	69	logic	NoC	23	100	90					
livers		1	32	77	*logic*		23	100	91					
Liverpool	NoP	55	100	80	*logics*		0	13	61					
Liverpool		55	100	80	logical	Adj	23	100	92					
living	Adj	36	100	92	London	NoP	351	100	94					
living	NoC	46	100	96	*London*		351	100	94					
living		46	100	96	*Londons*		0	2	06					
livings		1	31	69	lonely	Adj	18	97	91					
Liz	NoP	17	85	72	*lonelier*		0	11	71					
Liz		17	85	72	*loneliest*		0	20	77					
Lloyd	NoP	23	95	88	*lonely*		18	97	91					
load	NoC	40	100	89	long	Adj	392	100	97					
load		26	99	90	*long*		345	100	97					
loads		15	98	84	*longer*		39	100	96					
load	Verb	22	100	94	*longest*		9	100	94					
laden		2	83	91	long	Adv	181	100	96					
load		6	92	88	long	Verb	13	96	88					
loaded		11	100	93	*long*		3	83	91					
loading		3	89	91	*longed*		6	72	84					
loads		0	21	80	*longing*		3	67	86					
loan	NoC	65	100	89	*longs*		1	44	85					
loan		38	100	88	long-term	Adj	41	98	92					
loans		27	95	87	longer	Adv	33	100	96					
lobby	NoC	11	96	93	look	NoC	124	100	92					
lobbies		1	52	86	*look*		110	100	91					
lobby		10	96	93	*looks*		13	96	91					
local	Adj	445	100	93	look	Verb	1151	100	92					

Living creatures
(frequencies = occurrences per million words)

Apart from *people* (1256) the most commonly mentioned animal is the *horse* (126), closely followed by the more domestic *dog* (124). In contrast, the *cat* is surprisingly neglected (just 55—less than half the number of references to dogs). Frequently mentioned creatures, in descending order, are:

horse	126
dog	124
cat	55
sheep	30
mouse	28
cow	26
cattle	26
pig	25
chicken	25
rabbit	25
rat	24
lion	21
duck	19
eagle	18
fly	16
dolphin	16
elephant	15
fox	13
whale	13
tiger	13
snake	12
wolf	12
bull	12

The broad picture is that domestic animals are most mentioned, then domesticated farm animals, then wild animals.
The following are the frequencies of general terms for living creatures:

animal	153
fish	105
bird	93
insect	21
mammal	12
reptile	4

1.1

Word	PoS	Freq	Ra	Di	Word	PoS	Freq	Ra	Di	Word	PoS	Freq	Ra	Di
lordships		5	44	47	*luckier*		1	37	82	*mainframes*		3	27	46
lorry	NoC	20	99	90	*luckiest*		0	22	77	mainland	NoC	11	92	90
lorries		7	92	90	*lucky*		41	98	93	*mainland*		11	92	90
lorry		13	98	89	Lucy	NoP	27	81	69	mainly	Adv	71	100	94
Los	NoP-	12	92	88	*Lucy*		27	81	69	maintain	Verb	123	100	94
lose	Verb	277	100	97	Luke	NoP	36	89	65	*maintain*		54	100	94
lose		65	100	96	*Luke*		35	88	65	*maintained*		39	99	94
loses		8	97	94	*Lukes*		0	13	67	*maintaining*		21	96	92
losing		35	100	95	lump	NoC	15	98	93	*maintains*		9	85	91
lost		169	100	96	*lump*		11	98	92	maintenance	NoC	40	100	92
loss	NoC	154	100	92	*lumps*		4	83	90	majesty	NoC	11	97	88
loss		116	100	93	lunch	NoC	58	100	92	*majesties*		0	11	68
losses		38	99	84	*lunch*		54	100	92	*majesty*		11	97	88
lost	Adj	25	100	95	*lunches*		4	77	82	major	Adj	238	100	94
lot*	NoC	246	100	88	lung	NoC	18	99	90	major	NoC	12	99	88
lot		246	100	88	*lung*		9	96	84	*major*		11	99	87
lots		0	11	69	*lungs*		9	94	90	*majors*		1	36	80
Lothian	NoP	12	59	64	luxury	NoC	11	100	94	Major	NoP	41	99	81
Lothian		11	57	64	*luxuries*		2	76	91	*Major*		41	99	81
Lothians		1	20	67	*luxury*		9	100	93	*Majors*		0	22	76
lots	Pron	45	99	91	M / m	Lett	47	99	81	majority	NoC	101	100	92
loud	Adj	23	99	91	m	NoC	45	88	81	*majorities*		2	47	83
loud		16	98	91	*m*		19	80	81	*majority*		100	100	92
louder		6	85	89	*m.*		26	85	71	make	Verb	2165	100	98
loudest		1	56	87	M	NoP	15	74	68	*made*		943	100	98
loudly	Adv	11	87	86	*M*		13	67	63	*make*		791	100	98
Louis	NoP	21	97	85	*M.*		2	49	66	*makes*		166	100	97
Louise	NoP	15	85	81	Maastricht	NoP	12	52	76	*maketh*		0	11	68
Louise		15	85	81	MacDonald	NoP	11	88	87	*making*		264	100	98
lounge	NoC	15	90	84	*MacDonald*		10	84	86	make-up	NoC	13	99	91
lounge		14	90	84	*MacDonalds*		1	27	72	*make-up*		13	99	91
lounges		1	37	71	machine	NoC	132	100	89	maker	NoC	24	100	91
love	NoC	150	99	92	*machine*		84	100	91	*maker*		10	95	90
love		148	99	92	*machines*		48	100	85	*makers*		14	91	90
loves		1	66	87	machinery	NoC	24	100	92	making	NoC	14	99	93
love	Verb	150	99	91	*machinery*		24	100	92	*making*		14	99	93
love		86	99	91	mad	Adj	32	100	90	*makings*		1	44	86
loved		46	99	91	*mad*		31	100	90	Malcolm	NoP	18	95	88
loves		12	95	92	*madder*		1	25	75	*Malcolm*		18	95	88
loving		5	85	88	madame	NoC	11	79	79	*Malcolms*		0	1	00
lovely	Adj	64	99	86	*madame*		11	79	78	male	Adj	89	100	72
lovelier		0	22	78	magazine	NoC	64	100	94	male	NoC	44	100	85
loveliest		1	44	83	*magazine*		47	100	93	*male*		22	99	87
lovely		63	99	86	*magazines*		17	99	93	*males*		22	96	82
lover	NoC	29	99	91	Maggie	NoP	27	81	59	mammal	NoC	12	68	80
lover		18	98	90	*Maggie*		27	81	59	*mammal*		3	46	60
lovers		12	95	92	magic	Adj	17	99	82	*mammals*		9	63	82
low	Adj	286	100	95	magic	NoC	15	97	89	man	NoC	1003	100	95
low		158	100	96	*magic*		15	97	89	*man*		614	100	93
lower		111	100	93	magistrate	NoC	28	98	85	*mans*		0	18	72
lowest		17	99	93	*magistrate*		7	87	85	*men*		389	100	95
lower	Verb	26	100	93	*magistrates*		21	93	81	manage	Verb	133	100	97
lower		8	99	93	magnetic	Adj	15	89	82	*manage*		41	100	96
lowered		13	97	89	magnificent	Adj	20	98	92	*managed*		75	100	96
lowering		4	94	92	magnitude	NoC	10	86	80	*manages*		6	95	93
lowers		1	54	86	*magnitude*		10	86	80	*managing*		11	99	95
loyal	Adj	14	100	94	*magnitudes*		1	22	70	management	NoC	219	100	90
loyalty	NoC	20	96	93	maid	NoC	12	85	86	*management*		218	100	90
loyalties		4	82	88	*maid*		9	84	86	*managements*		2	57	83
loyalty		17	96	93	*maids*		2	58	85	manager	NoC	197	100	90
ltd	Adj	64	89	74	mail	NoC	34	100	84	*manager*		138	100	89
ltd		51	88	71	*mail*		33	100	84	*managers*		58	99	91
ltd.		13	63	46	*mails*		0	18	61	managerial	Adj	13	84	87
luck	NoC	32	99	93	main	Adj	245	100	96	managing	Adj	22	95	90
luck		32	99	93	mainframe	NoC	11	53	51	Manchester	NoP	50	100	90
lucky	Adj	42	98	93	*mainframe*		8	48	52	*Manchester*		50	100	90

Word	PoS	Freq	Ra	Di	Word	PoS	Freq	Ra	Di	Word	PoS	Freq	Ra	Di
manipulate	Verb	13	99	93	marked	Adj	21	100	92	*matter*		168	100	95
manipulate		6	95	92	marker	NoC	12	97	83	*matters*		80	99	93
manipulated		5	90	91	*marker*		7	92	84	matter	Verb	52	99	93
manipulates		0	26	81	*markers*		6	72	80	*matter*		38	99	91
manipulating		3	86	92	market	NoC	346	100	92	*mattered*		7	90	90
manner	NoC	69	100	96	*market*		287	100	92	*matters*		8	98	95
manner		61	100	95	*markets*		59	97	89	Matthew	NoP	26	100	79
manners		8	93	91	market	Verb	16	98	83	mature	Adj	16	98	91
manor	NoC	15	91	87	*market*		11	96	80	*mature*		15	98	91
manor		13	91	88	*marketed*		4	79	88	*maturer*		0	11	70
manors		1	30	74	*markets*		0	22	64	maturity	NoC	15	98	80
manual	Adj	12	95	88	marketing	NoC	49	96	88	*maturities*		1	14	65
manual	NoC	15	94	86	*marketing*		49	96	88	*maturity*		14	98	80
manual		12	93	85	marriage	NoC	87	100	93	Maurice	NoP	10	85	74
manuals		3	72	86	*marriage*		79	100	92	Max	NoP	13	93	87
manufacture	NoC	14	97	91	*marriages*		8	98	92	*Max*		13	93	87
manufacture		13	96	90	married	Adj	54	99	94	maximum	Adj	35	100	93
manufactures		1	35	78	marry	Verb	81	100	89	maximum	NoC	17	96	90
manufacture	Verb	14	98	92	*married*		47	100	86	*maxima*		1	31	80
manufacture		4	86	89	*marries*		1	60	86	*maximum*		16	94	90
manufactured		6	93	92	*marry*		27	97	88	Maxwell	NoP	13	86	84
manufactures		2	65	87	*marrying*		6	88	89	*Maxwell*		13	85	84
manufacturing		2	70	89	Marshall	NoP	16	88	88	*Maxwells*		0	10	56
manufacturer	NoC	45	99	91	*Marshall*		15	88	88	May	NoP	150	100	84
manufacturer		18	93	89	*Marshalls*		1	22	68	*May*		150	100	84
manufacturers		28	93	91	Martin	NoP	53	100	92	*Mays*		0	15	70
manufacturing	NoC	42	97	87	*Martin*		53	100	92	may	VMod	1135	100	94
manuscript	NoC	14	93	86	*Martins*		0	21	76	maybe	Adv	105	99	90
manuscript		8	88	86	marvellous	Adj	18	98	94	mayor	NoC	23	99	84
manuscripts		6	74	82	Marx	NoP	19	84	74	*mayor*		21	99	84
many	DetP	902	100	96	Marxist	Adj	12	74	82	*mayors*		1	47	80
map	NoC	56	100	89	Mary	NoP	72	100	91	meal	NoC	67	100	93
map		40	100	88	*Maries*		0	8	64	*meal*		43	99	92
maps		17	100	88	*Mary*		71	100	91	*meals*		24	99	91
marble	NoC	16	93	89	*Marys*		0	16	74	mean	Adj	26	100	82
marble		14	91	89	mask	NoC	15	98	90	*mean*		25	100	81
marbles		2	66	86	*mask*		11	96	88	*meaner*		0	23	77
march	NoC	14	98	91	*masks*		4	89	91	*meanest*		1	37	84
march		11	97	91	mass	Adj	35	98	91	mean	Verb	677	100	90
marches		3	79	87	mass	NoC	49	100	92	*mean*		411	100	84
March	NoP	145	100	83	*mass*		36	100	91	*meaning*		15	100	95
march	Verb	19	99	92	*masses*		13	99	89	*means*		138	100	96
march		4	86	90	massive	Adj	44	100	95	*meant*		112	100	96
marched		10	97	91	master	NoC	80	100	93	meaning	NoC	80	100	89
marches		1	51	87	*master*		62	100	91	*meaning*		66	99	90
marching		4	87	90	*masters*		18	98	90	*meanings*		15	88	86
Marcus	NoP	11	83	71	match	NoC	91	100	88	meaningful	Adj	10	94	92
Margaret	NoP	38	100	92	*match*		69	100	88	means	NoC	96	100	94
Margaret		38	100	92	*matches*		23	98	89	meantime	NoC	14	100	95
margin	NoC	26	99	89	match	Verb	52	100	96	meanwhile	Adv	48	100	91
margin		15	98	89	*match*		27	100	96	measure	NoC	112	100	92
margins		12	89	87	*matched*		14	99	94	*measure*		47	100	94
marginal	Adj	22	82	76	*matches*		7	92	92	*measures*		65	99	89
Maria	NoP	21	97	77	*matching*		4	88	92	measure	Verb	65	100	90
Maria		21	97	77	mate	NoC	25	95	89	*measure*		18	100	93
Marie	NoP	18	89	59	*mate*		17	94	87	*measured*		30	100	85
marine	Adj	20	94	85	*mates*		8	93	91	*measures*		4	79	90
mark	NoC	62	100	93	material	NoC	199	100	93	*measuring*		14	99	91
mark		33	100	96	*material*		131	100	93	measurement	NoC	31	97	86
marks		28	100	87	*materials*		68	99	91	*measurement*		17	83	85
Mark	NoP	66	100	88	mathematical	Adj	13	93	85	*measurements*		14	94	84
mark	Verb	77	100	96	mathematics	NoC	20	92	78	meat	NoC	38	100	94
mark		25	100	95	matrix	NoC	17	80	63	*meat*		36	100	94
marked		37	100	95	*matrices*		2	30	41	*meats*		2	58	83
marking		8	99	93	*matrix*		14	76	67	mechanic	NoC	12	98	87
marks		7	93	93	matter	NoC	248	100	94	*mechanic*		3	83	90

Word	PoS	Freq	Ra	Di	Word	PoS	Freq	Ra	Di	Word	PoS	Freq	Ra	Di
mechanics		9	96	83	mention	NoC	16	100	96	*methodology*		10	72	80
mechanical	Adj	20	99	91	*mention*		16	100	96	metre	NoC	43	99	90
mechanism	NoC	49	97	90	*mentions*		1	43	86	*metre*		9	96	92
mechanism		29	97	91	mention	Verb	110	100	95	*metres*		34	98	88
mechanisms		20	84	88	*mention*		31	100	95	metropolitan	Adj	17	98	89
medal	NoC	16	92	85	*mentioned*		70	100	95	Mexico	NoP	16	95	86
medal		11	89	84	*mentioning*		5	97	94	mhm	Int	75	12	59
medals		5	81	86	*mentions*		4	88	91	Michael	NoP	95	100	91
medical	Adj	93	100	92	menu	NoC	20	97	87	*Michael*		95	100	91
medicine	NoC	34	100	91	*menu*		16	97	87	*Michaels*		0	14	62
medicine		28	100	91	*menus*		5	78	86	Mick	NoP	15	82	84
medicines		6	92	89	merchant	NoC	29	100	90	*Mick*		15	82	84
medieval	Adj	25	97	89	*merchant*		18	97	88	*Micks*		0	6	46
medium	NoC	105	100	89	*merchants*		10	96	90	Microsoft	NoP	20	33	48
media		80	99	88	mercy	NoC	12	97	93	*Microsoft*		20	33	48
medium		24	99	90	*mercies*		1	35	84	mid	Adj	15	96	92
mediums		1	29	78	*mercy*		11	96	93	*mid*		15	95	92
meet	Verb	339	100	97	mere	Adj	35	99	95	middle	Adj	70	100	91
meet		141	100	97	*mere*		34	99	95	middle	NoC	60	100	96
meeting		46	100	94	*merest*		1	54	86	*middle*		59	100	96
meets		14	100	94	merely	Adv	76	98	95	*middles*		0	19	71
met		138	100	95	merge	Verb	13	99	93	middle-class	Adj	13	86	87
meeting	NoC	215	100	92	*merge*		5	97	92	Middlesbrough	NoP	36	55	12
meeting		162	100	94	*merged*		5	93	92	Midland	NoP	26	96	87
meetings		54	100	93	*merges*		1	44	85	*Midland*		15	90	80
melt	Verb	14	97	92	*merging*		2	77	91	*Midlands*		11	86	90
melt		6	91	91	merger	NoC	21	87	85	midnight	NoC	19	100	88
melted		5	83	90	*merger*		14	82	85	*midnight*		19	100	88
melting		3	76	88	*mergers*		7	69	83	might	VMod	614	100	97
melts		1	49	83	merit	NoC	19	99	93	mighty	Adj	10	95	90
member	NoC	471	100	90	*merit*		9	97	93	*mightier*		0	20	75
member		175	100	85	*merits*		10	97	92	*mightiest*		0	28	78
members		297	100	91	Merseyside	NoP	11	72	68	*mighty*		10	94	91
membership	NoC	53	96	91	mess	NoC	21	96	92	migration	NoC	14	84	82
membership		53	96	91	*mess*		20	96	92	*migration*		13	82	81
memberships		1	39	85	*messes*		0	28	83	*migrations*		1	36	80
membrane	NoC	13	80	77	message	NoC	89	100	92	Mike	NoP	43	97	87
membrane		9	73	77	*message*		70	100	93	*Mike*		43	97	87
membranes		4	52	74	*messages*		20	100	89	mild	Adj	18	100	93
memorandum	NoC	11	85	77	metal	NoC	56	100	93	*mild*		16	100	93
memoranda		2	56	81	*metal*		46	100	94	*milder*		1	62	88
memorandum		9	78	75	*metals*		10	90	82	*mildest*		0	35	85
memorial	NoC	17	97	88	metaphor	NoC	12	89	82	mile	NoC	130	100	93
memorial		15	97	88	*metaphor*		9	85	81	*mile*		32	99	93
memorials		1	51	83	*metaphors*		3	67	82	*miles*		98	100	93
memory	NoC	102	100	93	method	NoC	180	100	92	military	Adj	108	100	84
memories		26	99	94	*method*		91	100	92	milk	NoC	48	100	92
memory		76	100	92	*methods*		89	100	91	*milk*		48	100	92
mental	Adj	58	100	90	methodology	NoC	11	73	81	*milks*		0	15	72
mentally	Adv	20	99	83	*methodologies*		1	41	82	mill	NoC	42	100	68
										mill		33	99	67
										mills		9	88	71
										Miller	NoP	20	94	81
										million	NoC	272	100	89
										million		245	100	88
										millions		27	100	93
										Milton	NoP	15	92	75
										Milton		15	92	75
										min	NoC	12	75	81
										min		7	64	74
										min.		0	16	68
										mins		5	43	76
										mind	NoC	241	100	94
										mind		213	100	94
										minds		28	100	95
										mind	Verb	78	99	87

Metals

Among metals, frequency of mention follows the same hierarchy that is used for sporting medals and the like.
That may indeed be one of the contributing factors to this rank order. Other commonly mentioned metals are below:

gold	75	iron	48	copper	18
silver	39	steel	38	brass	16
bronze	17	tin	20[a]	aluminium	10

[a]This is the frequency of the singular form only

Note, however, that words such as *iron*, *brass* and (especially) *tin* are ambiguous: they do not necessarily refer to the metals alone.

Word	PoS	Freq	Ra	Di
mind		72	99	86
minded		5	94	93
minding		1	62	89
minds		0	33	83
mine	NoC	31	100	89
mine		17	100	89
mines		14	96	87
mine	Pron	46	99	84
miner	NoC	22	95	89
miner		4	77	87
miners		18	93	88
mineral	NoC	23	99	86
mineral		12	94	87
minerals		11	82	84
minimal	Adj	14	96	93
minimum	Adj	30	97	92
minimum	NoC	21	99	94
minima		1	27	78
minimum		20	99	94
mining	NoC	15	94	84
minister	NoC	305	100	77
minister		237	100	76
ministers		68	96	80
ministerial	Adj	10	84	84
ministry	NoC	55	99	86
ministries		6	72	80
ministry		50	99	87
minor	Adj	47	100	94
minority	NoC	43	98	91
minorities		8	85	88
minority		34	94	91
minus	Prep	13	94	74
minute	NoC	266	100	94
minute		82	100	91
minutes		183	100	94
miracle	NoC	16	99	89
miracle		11	97	90
miracles		5	84	85
mirror	NoC	43	100	88
mirror		37	100	86
mirrors		5	92	91
miserable	Adj	12	96	92
misery	NoC	13	100	93
miseries		1	38	85
misery		13	100	93
misleading	Adj	13	94	92
miss*	NoC	92	99	85
miss		91	99	85
misses		1	58	86
miss	Verb	108	100	94
miss		35	99	93
missed		41	100	94
misses		3	91	92
missing		29	100	95
missile	NoC	19	90	80
missile		9	83	82
missiles		10	82	78
missing	Adj	15	100	95
mission	NoC	32	99	92
mission		27	99	92
missions		5	81	87
mist	NoC	13	94	87
mist		11	91	86
mists		2	67	88
mistake	NoC	53	100	96
mistake		37	100	95

Word	PoS	Freq	Ra	Di
mistakes		16	100	96
mistake	Verb	11	98	93
mistake		1	62	89
mistaken		8	97	93
mistakes		0	11	71
mistaking		1	56	86
mistook		1	47	87
mistress	NoC	13	93	87
mistress		12	89	86
mistresses		1	56	87
Mitchell	NoP	10	88	89
Mitchell		10	88	89
Mitchells		0	5	38
mix	NoC	16	100	92
mix		15	100	92
mixes		1	57	82
mix	Verb	41	100	95
mix		12	97	90
mixed		23	100	96
mixes		1	42	86
mixing		6	95	93
mixed	Adj	20	100	93
mixture	NoC	35	100	93
mixture		33	100	93
mixtures		3	66	84
ml	NoC	11	51	63
ml		11	48	62
mls		0	10	50
mm	Int	330	48	64
mm	NoC	18	76	70
mm		17	74	70
mobile	Adj	14	100	92
mobility	NoC	15	90	88
mobility		15	90	88
mode	NoC	40	98	89
mode		27	98	90
modes		12	79	85
model	NoC	183	100	91
model		130	100	91
models		53	100	90
model	Verb	11	98	91

Word	PoS	Freq	Ra	Di
model		3	78	88
modelled		5	91	91
modelling		3	80	88
models		0	18	75
moderate	Adj	14	95	92
modern	Adj	131	100	93
modest	Adj	23	100	95
modest		23	100	95
modification	NoC	19	88	87
modification		10	76	86
modifications		8	83	88
modify	Verb	23	96	91
modified		12	90	91
modifies		1	38	84
modify		7	89	91
modifying		3	64	88
module	NoC	59	76	41
module		32	66	30
modules		27	63	52
molecular	Adj	13	70	79
molecule	NoC	23	76	78
molecule		8	57	74
molecules		15	73	80
moment	NoC	254	100	92
moment		221	100	91
moments		32	98	92
monarch	NoC	10	89	88
monarch		8	87	87
monarchs		2	59	85
monarchy	NoC	10	82	85
monarchies		0	27	79
monarchy		10	80	85
Monday	NoP	56	100	90
Monday		53	100	90
Mondays		3	79	83
monetary	Adj	28	87	82
money	NoC	375	100	95
money		374	100	95
moneys		1	24	48
monitor	NoC	11	97	83
monitor		8	92	81

Modal verbs

The modal auxiliary verbs are a well-defined group in English, but they vary a great deal in frequency. The four 'top' modals, *will, would, can* and *could*, account for over 72% of all modals. Other, less frequent, modals (e.g. *may, must, shall*) are declining in frequency in current English. In the list below, the figures represent occurrences per million words.

	The whole corpus	Conversation
will	3,357	6,726
would	2,904	3,737
can	2,672	5,573
could	1,683	1,922
may	1,135	151
should	1,112	1,047
must	723	716
might	614	856
shall	208	392
used (to)	156	607
ought (to)	61	108
need	33	17
dare	12	17
Total	14,670	21,869

The figures on the right represent frequency in the conversation subcorpus. Modals in general are 50% more frequent in conversation, but the trend in the language as a whole is taken to extremes in conversation: the 'top' four modals represent well over 80% of all usage of modals.

Note: *need* and *dare* are modal verbs only when they occur with a following bare infinitive verb, with or without an intervening negative: *You needn't worry. I dare not object.*

Word	PoS	Freq	Ra	Di	Word	PoS	Freq	Ra	Di	Word	PoS	Freq	Ra	Di
monitors		3	69	86	morning	NoC	219	100	92	mount	Verb	32	99	95
monitor	Verb	35	100	92	*morning*		211	100	92	*mount*		6	98	94
monitor		14	91	92	*mornings*		8	93	92	*mounted*		17	99	94
monitored		9	95	91	Morris	NoP	18	99	90	*mounting*		8	95	93
monitoring		11	96	91	mortality	NoC	23	90	76	*mounts*		1	45	86
monitors		2	67	86	*mortalities*		0	12	70	mountain	NoC	68	100	91
monitoring	NoC	17	85	89	*mortality*		23	90	76	*mountain*		39	100	90
monitoring		17	85	89	mortgage	NoC	34	100	87	*mountains*		28	100	90
monk	NoC	13	92	86	*mortgage*		29	99	86	mouse	NoC	28	98	84
monk		5	82	80	*mortgages*		6	75	87	*mice*		10	90	77
monks		8	84	85	mosaic	NoC	12	69	29	*mouse*		18	95	83
monkey	NoC	11	90	89	*mosaic*		7	60	28	*mouses*		0	6	49
monkey		6	88	90	*mosaics*		5	40	30	mouth	NoC	99	98	87
monkeys		5	83	85	Moscow	NoP	30	94	86	*mouth*		93	98	86
monopoly	NoC	21	95	87	most	Adv	565	100	96	*mouths*		6	93	91
monopolies		5	68	85	most	DetP	422	100	96	move	NoC	84	100	93
monopoly		16	94	86	mostly	Adv	39	100	96	*move*		68	100	93
monster	NoC	17	97	88	mother	NoC	295	100	92	*moves*		16	100	91
monster		13	95	88	*mother*		262	100	91	move	Verb	391	100	96
monsters		4	80	81	*mothers*		33	100	89	*move*		136	100	95
month	NoC	398	100	95	motif	NoC	13	78	72	*moved*		146	100	94
month		150	100	93	*motif*		9	70	64	*moves*		20	100	95
months		248	100	95	*motifs*		4	59	78	*moving*		89	100	97
monthly	Adj	19	99	90	motion	NoC	53	99	87	movement	NoC	179	100	94
monument	NoC	13	97	89	*motion*		46	99	87	*movement*		135	100	93
monument		7	92	89	*motions*		7	93	87	*movements*		44	100	92
monuments		6	89	85	motivate	Verb	12	93	92	movie	NoC	28	93	86
mood	NoC	37	100	95	*motivate*		2	71	90	*movie*		18	92	85
mood		33	100	95	*motivated*		7	91	92	*movies*		10	87	84
moods		4	85	90	*motivates*		1	45	85	Mozart	NoP	12	80	65
moon	NoC	31	100	89	*motivating*		1	56	87	*Mozart*		12	80	65
moon		29	100	88	motivation	NoC	18	94	91	*Mozarts*		0	4	34
moons		2	55	85	*motivation*		15	93	91	MP	NoC	58	96	85
moor	NoC	15	93	86	*motivations*		2	66	86	*M.P.*		0	11	70
moor		9	86	84	motive	NoC	21	98	93	*MP*		32	93	84
moors		6	82	84	*motive*		10	98	92	*MPs*		26	80	85
Moore	NoP	19	94	88	*motives*		10	96	93	Mr	NoC	673	100	84
moral	Adj	52	100	89	motor	NoC	48	100	86	*Mr*		524	100	87
morale	NoC	10	94	92	*motor*		42	100	85	*Mr.*		148	93	40
morale		10	94	92	*motors*		6	90	85	Mrs	NoC	221	100	91
morales		0	15	67	motorway	NoC	14	96	89	*Mrs*		198	100	90
morality	NoC	13	97	86	*motorway*		12	96	88	*Mrs.*		23	74	75
moralities		0	11	68	*motorways*		3	79	89	Ms	NoC	18	97	87
morality		12	97	86	mould	NoC	10	95	87	*Ms*		17	95	86
more	Adv	1275	100	96	*mould*		8	93	85	*Ms.*		1	25	39
more	DetP	699	100	98	*moulds*		2	60	84	much	Adv	390	100	97
more than*	Adv	148	100	93	mount	NoC	12	98	91	much	DetP	531	100	97
moreover	Adv	43	96	91	*mount*		11	97	90	mucosa	NoC	11	15	35
Morgan	NoP	18	90	85	*mounts*		2	58	87	*mucosa*		10	14	35
										mucosae		0	3	31
										mud	NoC	20	99	91
										mud		19	98	91
										muds		0	20	71
										mug	NoC	10	87	87
										mug		8	79	86
										mugs		3	71	87
										multiple	Adj	22	99	88
										multiply	Verb	12	96	90
										multiplied		4	86	90
										multiplies		0	30	78
										multiply		5	89	86
										multiplying		2	65	86
										mum	NoC	90	95	77
										mum		86	95	76
										mums		4	67	75
										mummy	NoC	26	83	67

Frequency of month names

Frequency per million words. The figures include abbreviations such as *Jan* for *January*.

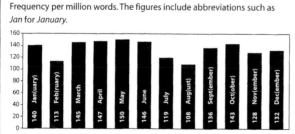

Word	PoS	Freq	Ra	Di	Word	PoS	Freq	Ra	Di	Word	PoS	Freq	Ra	Di
mummies		1	29	76	*named*		44	100	94	*necks*		4	90	85
mummy		26	82	67	*names*		1	55	86	need	NoC	273	100	95
murder	NoC	60	100	89	*naming*		3	91	92	*need*		169	100	96
murder		54	100	89	namely	Adv	22	93	90	*needs*		105	100	92
murders		7	88	89	narrative	NoC	12	85	85	need	Verb	627	100	97
murder	Verb	23	99	90	*narrative*		11	84	84	*need*		356	100	95
murder		6	92	89	*narratives*		2	44	84	*needed*		165	100	97
murdered		14	99	89	narrow	Adj	54	100	95	*needing*		10	100	95
murdering		4	72	81	*narrow*		49	100	95	*needs*		97	100	96
murders		0	10	69	*narrower*		4	89	91	need*	VMod	33	100	95
murderer	NoC	12	90	85	*narrowest*		1	41	85	needle	NoC	23	97	71
murderer		8	87	83	narrow	Verb	12	100	86	*needle*		13	96	77
murderers		3	71	88	*narrow*		1	61	89	*needles*		11	88	64
murmur	Verb	22	75	76	*narrowed*		8	90	81	negative	Adj	45	99	91
murmur		1	41	82	*narrowing*		2	66	85	neglect	Verb	14	99	94
murmured		19	51	75	*narrows*		1	57	88	*neglect*		3	90	92
murmuring		2	35	81	nasty	Adj	19	99	92	*neglected*		8	98	94
murmurs		0	23	71	*nastier*		1	36	83	*neglecting*		2	78	90
Murray	NoP	12	84	86	*nastiest*		0	23	72	*neglects*		1	43	82
Murray		12	84	86	*nasty*		18	98	92	negligence	NoC	13	90	69
Murrays		0	9	67	nation	NoC	85	100	92	*negligence*		13	90	69
muscle	NoC	38	98	91	*nation*		44	99	93	negotiate	Verb	32	100	92
muscle		18	97	88	*nations*		41	98	90	*negotiate*		13	99	92
muscles		20	95	89	national	Adj	376	100	91	*negotiated*		10	96	91
museum	NoC	82	99	80	nationalism	NoC	10	76	83	*negotiates*		1	36	83
museum		68	99	80	*nationalism*		10	76	84	*negotiating*		8	94	91
museums		14	89	75	*nationalisms*		0	12	53	negotiation	NoC	48	99	85
music	NoC	150	100	91	nationalist	NoC	10	74	84	*negotiation*		12	95	89
music		150	100	91	*nationalist*		4	65	81	*negotiations*		37	97	83
musics		0	13	58	*nationalists*		6	61	85	neighbour	NoC	49	100	95
musical	Adj	29	99	87	nationality	NoC	10	93	81	*neighbour*		18	99	95
musician	NoC	19	97	84	*nationalities*		3	72	79	*neighbours*		31	100	95
musician		6	89	89	*nationality*		7	84	77	neighbourhood	NoC	17	99	89
musicians		12	90	81	native	Adj	24	96	92	*neighbourhood*		15	99	89
must	VMod	723	100	97	NATO	NoP	15	77	75	*neighbourhoods*		2	59	83
mutter	Verb	21	82	81	*NATO*		15	77	75	neighbouring	Adj	14	96	92
mutter		1	49	85	natural	Adj	142	100	94	Neil	NoP	31	92	80
muttered		16	64	79	naturally	Adv	43	99	96	*Neil*		31	92	80
muttering		4	61	83	nature	NoC	182	100	94	neither	Adv	54	100	96
mutters		0	25	72	*nature*		181	100	94	neither	DetP	28	100	96
mutual	Adj	22	98	94	*natures*		1	46	75	Nelson	NoP	10	90	89
my	Det	1549	100	92	naval	Adj	15	94	89	*Nelson*		10	90	89
me		23	12	64	navy	NoC	21	100	93	nerve	NoC	25	100	93
mine		0	22	78	*navies*		1	24	70	*nerve*		13	99	92
my		1525	100	93	*navy*		20	100	93	*nerves*		12	98	92
myself	Pron	125	100	92	near	Adj	44	100	97	nervous	Adj	31	100	94
mysterious	Adj	13	95	93	*near*		18	100	96	nest	NoC	18	95	86
mystery	NoC	28	100	93	*nearer*		5	97	94	*nest*		13	94	86
mysteries		5	89	88	*nearest*		20	100	95	*nests*		5	77	85
mystery		22	100	93	near	Adv	16	100	93	net	Adj	41	97	76
myth	NoC	21	98	91	near	Prep	138	100	94	*net*		41	97	76
myth		15	94	90	nearby	Adj	22	96	92	net	NoC	31	100	82
myths		6	86	91	nearby	Adv	14	98	92	*net*		25	100	79
N / n	Lett	. 43	96	85	nearly	Adv	115	100	97	*nets*		7	92	82
N	NoP	11	79	84	neat	Adj	18	98	93	Netherlands	NoP	14	84	86
N		5	54	70	*neat*		17	98	93	network	NoC	91	98	82
N.		6	76	85	*neater*		1	42	84	*network*		72	98	82
nail	NoC	20	97	80	*neatest*		0	23	80	*networks*		19	87	81
nail		6	96	92	neatly	Adv	13	98	93	neutral	Adj	16	98	91
nails		13	90	72	necessarily	Adv	57	100	93	never	Adv	559	100	94
naked	Adj	20	100	90	necessary	Adj	181	100	94	nevertheless	Adv	72	99	94
name	NoC	326	100	96	necessity	NoC	21	100	93	new	Adj	1154	100	95
name		250	100	95	*necessities*		2	79	90	*new*		1145	100	95
names		76	100	96	*necessity*		18	100	93	*newer*		5	93	92
name	Verb	61	100	95	neck	NoC	60	98	89	*newest*		4	89	91
name		13	100	96	*neck*		56	98	89	New	NoP-	106	100	91

Word	PoS	Freq	Ra	Di	Word	PoS	Freq	Ra	Di	Word	PoS	Freq	Ra	Di
Newcastle	NoP	27	98	73	nineteenth	Ord	33	98	89	nonetheless	Adv	13	91	91
Newcastle		27	98	73	nineteenth-					nonsense	NoC	16	100	92
newcomer	NoC	11	96	88	century	Adj	10	78	86	*nonsense*		16	100	92
newcomer		5	92	93	ninety	Num	47	97	74	nor	Conj	124	100	95
newcomers		5	89	80	*nineties*		5	80	87	Norfolk	NoP	14	95	89
newly	Adv	27	100	94	*ninety*		42	94	71	*Norfolk*		14	95	89
Newman	NoP	10	81	73	no	Adv	17	100	94	norm	NoC	19	95	86
Newman		10	81	73	no	Det	1343	100	98	*norm*		10	95	90
news	NoC	145	100	94	no	Int	662	100	75	*norms*		9	72	80
newspaper	NoC	86	100	94	*no*		662	100	75	normal	Adj	124	100	92
newspaper		50	100	94	no	NoC	100	90	64	normally	Adv	83	100	95
newspapers		35	100	92	*no*		66	87	46	Norman	NoP	25	96	89
Newton	NoP	15	89	85	no.		33	86	84	*Norman*		23	95	89
Newton		15	89	84	*nos*		1	33	69	*Normans*		1	41	66
Newtons		0	7	57	no-one*	Pron	21	99	92	north	NoC	163	100	94
next	Ord	431	100	96	no doubt	Adv	37	99	95	North	NoP-	54	98	88
next to	Prep	30	100	93	no longer	Adv	88	100	97	*North*		54	98	88
NHS	NoP	25	76	83	no matter how	Adv	10	97	95	north-east	NoC	17	93	67
nice	Adj	134	100	83	no one*	Pron	81	100	92	north-west	NoC	10	89	87
nice		129	100	83	noble	Adj	13	93	85	northern	Adj	66	100	90
nicer		3	72	87	nobody	Pron	62	100	92	Northern	NoP-	43	97	80
nicest		2	63	86	nod	Verb	60	90	81	Norway	NoP	15	94	86
Nicholas	NoP	24	97	82	*nod*		2	60	85	*Norway*		15	94	86
Nicholson	NoP	11	72	70	*nodded*		51	79	80	Norwich	NoP	15	94	86
Nicholson		11	72	70	*nodding*		5	73	84	nose	NoC	48	100	90
Nick	NoP	29	93	85	*nods*		1	35	76	*nose*		43	98	90
Nick		28	93	85	node	NoC	13	65	74	*noses*		4	93	92
Nicks		0	7	53	*node*		8	49	73	not	Neg	7995	100	94
Nigel	NoP	34	94	82	*nodes*		5	54	74	*~n~**		42	50	59
Nigel		34	94	82	noise	NoC	56	100	93	*~n't*		3328	100	87
night	NoC	393	100	93	*noise*		47	99	93	*not*		4626	100	98
night		365	100	93	*noises*		9	96	91	notable	Adj	16	93	92
nights		28	99	93	noisy	Adj	11	99	93	notably	Adv	24	92	90
nightmare	NoC	18	99	92	*noisier*		0	25	81	note	NoC	117	100	95
nightmare		14	99	91	*noisiest*		0	20	79	*note*		60	100	95
nightmares		3	81	89	*noisy*		10	98	93	*notes*		57	100	93
nine	Num	137	100	88	nominate	Verb	10	92	89	note	Verb	126	100	93
nine		136	100	88	*nominate*		3	75	90	*note*		46	99	91
nines		1	24	62	*nominated*		7	89	87	*noted*		61	100	93
nineteen	Num	48	98	72	*nominates*		0	14	72	*notes*		9	92	91
nineteen		48	98	72	*nominating*		1	42	86	*noting*		10	94	93
nineteens		0	1	00	none	Pron	84	100	96	notebook	NoC	11	90	87
										notebook		8	83	86
										notebooks		3	70	80
										nothing	Pron	341	100	93
										notice	NoC	62	100	84
										notice		56	100	84
										notices		5	94	86
										notice	Verb	96	100	93
										notice		36	100	94
										noticed		53	99	91
										notices		2	87	89
										noticing		5	86	88
										notion	NoC	46	99	91
										notion		36	99	91
										notions		10	92	90
										Nottingham	NoP	21	93	87
										Nov	NoP	34	58	51
										Nov		5	51	40
										Nov.		29	21	43
										novel	Adj	11	91	91
										novel	NoC	43	97	86
										novel		31	97	86
										novels		13	88	85
										November	NoP	94	100	90
										now	Adv	1382	100	95

North–South–East–West

It appears that the British focus more on the 'vertical' compass points than on the 'horizontal' ones: references to *north* (163 per million words) and *south* (165) are commoner than those to *east* (128) and *west* (127) (frequencies per million words). This may partly reflect the often-mentioned 'north–south divide' in Great Britain, or may simply be a more general reflection of the primacy of the north–south axis (Notice that we say *north–west*, *south–east*, etc., not *west–north* or *east–south*.)

However, the adjectival forms *northern*, *southern*, *eastern* and *western* show a slightly different pattern: *western* (99) is far more common than *northern* (66), *eastern* (59), or *southern* (55). This could be a reflection partly of the contrast between *western* and *eastern* Europe and partly of the existence of the genre of western (i.e. cowboy) films and literature. Among compound terms, the *north–east* (17) is mentioned most, followed by the *south–east*, (13) *north–west* (10), and *south–west* (9).

NOTE: These figures do not include the use of *North*, *South*, etc. as part of a name, as in *North Sea* and *South Africa*. The figures for these proper name usages are *North* 54, *South* 67, *West* 88 and *East* 48.

Word	PoS	Freq	Ra	Di	Word	PoS	Freq	Ra	Di
now that	Conj	30	100	94	observer	NoC	31	100	89
nowadays	Adv	16	99	94	*observer*		17	99	91
nowhere	Adv	24	99	94	*observers*		14	.90	84
NT	NoP	14	28	36	obstacle	NoC	14	97	94
NT		14	26	36	*obstacle*		6	94	93
nuclear	Adj	81	99	83	*obstacles*		8	94	93
nuisance	NoC	11	97	77	obtain	Verb	127	100	90
nuisance		10	97	77	*obtain*		46	97	91
nuisances		1	33	75	*obtained*		63	97	89
number	NoC	606	100	95	*obtaining*		16	88	89
number		493	100	95	*obtains*		3	63	83
numbers		113	100	94	obvious	Adj	85	100	96
numerous	Adj	32	99	93	obviously	Adv	110	99	93
nurse	NoC	57	100	89	occasion	NoC	91	100	96
nurse		32	100	89	*occasion*		53	100	96
nurses		25	99	87	*occasions*		39	100	96
nursery	NoC	21	100	91	occasional	Adj	26	100	95
nurseries		3	71	87	occasionally	Adv	40	99	95
nursery		18	100	91	occupation	NoC	32	100	90
nursing	Adj	12	91	81	*occupation*		23	100	91
nursing	NoC	13	98	87	*occupations*		9	85	85
nut	NoC	15	100	90	occupational	Adj	17	92	86
nut		7	92	85	occupy	Verb	45	100	95
nuts		9	96	91	*occupied*		26	100	95
O / o	Lett	46	99	82	*occupies*		4	78	91
o'clock	Adv	47	98	87	*occupy*		11	99	93
oak	NoC	19	99	92	*occupying*		4	92	92
oak		16	99	93	occur	Verb	157	100	93
oaks		3	68	83	*occur*		56	100	91
obey	Verb	12	99	91	*occurred*		55	100	93
obey		7	97	90	*occurring*		13	88	91
obeyed		2	57	84	*occurs*		33	95	91
obeying		2	67	89	occurrence	NoC	14	96	88
obeys		0	28	80	*occurrence*		11	94	88
object	NoC	97	100	90	*occurrences*		3	66	82
object		53	99	89	ocean	NoC	25	100	89
objects		45	100	90	*ocean*		20	98	89
object	Verb	20	100	90	*oceans*		5	73	83
object		10	100	90	Oct	NoP	37	54	51
objected		7	99	94	*Oct*		5	48	50
objecting		1	59	87	*Oct.*		32	22	43
objects		1	60	88	October	NoP	106	100	89
objection	NoC	26	100	93	odd	Adj	45	100	93
objection		13	98	91	odds	NoC	15	100	94
objections		13	100	93	of*	Prep	29391	100	97
objective	Adj	17	93	89	of course	Adv	310	100	94
objective	NoC	73	98	90	*of course*		310	100	94
objective		29	96	92	off	Adv	486	100	94
objectives		43	88	89	off	Prep	214	100	95
obligation	NoC	41	99	83	offence	NoC	61	100	85
obligation		22	99	83	*offence*		37	99	83
obligations		19	94	82	*offences*		24	94	85
obliged	Adj	17	99	94	offender	NoC	19	88	80
obscure	Verb	10	97	93	*offender*		6	76	68
obscure		4	87	92	*offenders*		13	81	83
obscured		5	87	92	offer	NoC	73	100	90
obscures		1	53	87	*offer*		60	100	89
obscuring		1	56	87	*offers*		13	100	91
observation	NoC	50	99	89	offer	Verb	293	100	95
observation		29	99	87	*offer*		99	100	95
observations		22	94	89	*offered*		106	100	96
observe	Verb	75	99	93	*offering*		42	100	94
observe		17	98	92	*offers*		46	98	91
observed		46	97	92	offering	NoC	13	98	83
observes		4	71	87	*offering*		9	96	83
observing		8	99	93	*offerings*		5	82	83

Word	PoS	Freq	Ra	Di
office	NoC	300	100	96
office		257	100	96
offices		44	100	94
officer	NoC	181	100	94
officer		92	100	95
officers		89	100	92
official	Adj	77	100	91
official	NoC	83	98	87
official		21	98	86
officials		62	96	87
officially	Adv	18	100	91
offset	Verb	10	91	91
offset		9	88	91
offsets		0	29	80
offsetting		0	31	83
often	Adv	376	100	94
oh	Int	684	99	70
oil	NoC	110	100	90

Frequency of numbers
(frequencies per million)

• Cardinal numbers

The cardinal numbers from *one* to *nine* occur in their natural order in the descending rank frequency list—i.e. the number and its rank position are perfectly correlated. This pattern applies equally to spelt-out and digital numbers:

one	1,962	*1*	385
two	1,561	*2*	344
three	797	*3*	250
four	461	*4*	201
five	407	*5*	176
six	303	*6*	134
seven	173	*7*	107
eight	173	*8*	97
nine	136	*9*	80

The overall pattern, however, is not quite so neat, since both lists are liable to 'interruption' by higher numbers. In the spelt-out list, the round numbers *ten* (203) and *twenty* (156) have an inflated frequency. This is also true of the digital sequence (with *10* occurring 186 times per million words and *20* 156 times).

• Ordinal numbers

There is also a clear correlation between ordinal numbers and their positions in the descending rank order of frequency of use:

first 1193; *second* 358; *third* 211; *fourth* 61; *fifth* 35; *sixth* 25; *seventh* 15; *eighth* 13; *ninth* 9; *tenth* 11.

As with the cardinal numbers, however, a round number (in this case *tenth*) has higher frequency than the number preceding it.

Word	PoS	Freq	Ra	Di	Word	PoS	Freq	Ra	Di	Word	PoS	Freq	Ra	Di
oil		102	100	90	*operation*		100	100	93	*organises*		1	48	84
oils		8	86	74	*operations*		60	100	91	*organising*		10	96	92
OK*	Adj	12	95	88	operational	Adj	17	92	90	organiser	NoC	17	88	85
O.K.		1	30	74	operator	NoC	30	99	90	*organiser*		6	78	83
OK		11	95	88	*operator*		15	96	89	*organisers*		11	78	85
OK*	Adv	19	91	86	*operators*		15	93	89	organism	NoC	18	79	84
O.K.		1	29	71	opinion	NoC	93	100	94	*organism*		8	73	84
OK		18	89	85	*opinion*		75	100	94	*organisms*		10	71	82
okay*	Adj	17	75	76	*opinions*		18	99	94	organization	NoC	93	96	85
okay*	Adv	105	76	68	opponent	NoC	31	98	88	*organization*		63	94	85
old	Adj	648	100	95	*opponent*		15	95	78	*organizations*		30	83	85
old		544	100	95	*opponents*		16	91	91	organize	Verb	34	96	91
older		90	100	92	opportunity	NoC	161	100	94	*organize*		8	90	89
oldest		15	100	94	*opportunities*		58	100	92	*organized*		20	95	90
old-fashioned	Adj	12	98	92	*opportunity*		103	100	95	*organizes*		1	43	85
Oliver	NoP	23	97	76	oppose	Verb	33	97	90	*organizing*		6	84	90
Oliver		23	96	76	*oppose*		9	90	91	orientation	NoC	12	82	87
Olympic	Adj	13	81	81	*opposed*		19	94	88	*orientation*		11	81	86
omit	Verb	15	96	90	*opposes*		2	57	85	*orientations*		2	42	82
omit		2	69	90	*opposing*		4	81	90	origin	NoC	48	99	92
omits		1	41	84	opposite	Adj	32	100	96	*origin*		29	98	91
omitted		11	94	88	opposite	NoC	11	99	94	*origins*		18	94	91
omitting		1	59	88	*opposite*		9	99	95	original	Adj	108	100	94
on	Adv	756	100	93	*opposites*		2	62	82	originally	Adv	45	100	94
on	Prep	6475	100	97	opposite	Prep	12	97	92	originate	Verb	15	93	92
on behalf of	Prep	27	98	91	opposition	NoC	92	99	81	*originate*		2	73	90
on board	Adv	14	98	94	*opposition*		91	99	81	*originated*		7	87	91
on the part of	Prep	15	93	91	*oppositions*		1	37	77	*originates*		2	64	89
on to	Prep	92	100	94	opt	Verb	18	98	92	*originating*		3	68	86
on top of	Prep	26	100	95	*opt*		7	92	92	orthodox	Adj	12	95	90
once	Adv	183	100	96	*opted*		6	95	93	other	Adj	1336	100	97
once	Conj	90	100	97	*opting*		4	83	86	other	NoC	367	100	97
once again	Adv	37	100	96	*opts*		1	36	84	*other*		85	100	97
once more	Adv	24	100	96	optimistic	Adj	12	98	93	*others*		282	100	96
one	NoC	118	100	93	option	NoC	92	100	85	other than	Prep	43	100	94
one	Num	1962	100	97	*option*		54	100	78	otherwise	Adv	88	100	95
one	Pron	953	100	93	*options*		38	100	91	ought	VMod	61	100	93
one another	Pron	28	100	94	or	Conj	3707	100	96	our	Det	950	100	96
onion	NoC	12	91	85	oral	Adj	21	90	79	ours	Pron	17	99	88
onion		7	77	81	orange	Adj	14	97	92	ourselves	Pron	45	100	94
onions		6	75	87	orange	NoC	17	98	91	out	Adv	1542	100	96
only	Adj	231	100	98	*orange*		13	97	91	out of	Prep	491	100	95
only	Adv	1298	100	98	*oranges*		4	83	88	outbreak	NoC	12	94	90
onto	Prep	62	99	94	orchestra	NoC	17	93	82	*outbreak*		10	93	89
onwards	Adv	14	100	92	*orchestra*		15	93	82	*outbreaks*		2	68	85
ooh	Int	46	64	58	*orchestras*		2	46	79	outcome	NoC	46	100	92
open	Adj	219	100	95	order	NoC	250	100	91	*outcome*		37	100	93
open	Verb	235	100	95	*order*		197	100	90	*outcomes*		9	69	86
open		76	100	96	*orders*		52	100	94	outdoor	Adj	11	92	88
opened		115	100	93	order	Verb	76	100	94	outer	Adj	24	100	92
opening		26	100	94	*order*		18	100	90	outfit	NoC	11	92	91
opens		17	100	93	*ordered*		49	100	93	*outfit*		8	90	90
opening	NoC	54	100	94	*ordering*		7	100	92	*outfits*		3	74	89
opening		50	100	94	*orders*		2	73	88	outlet	NoC	14	98	91
openings		4	84	89	ordinary	Adj	68	100	95	*outlet*		6	95	89
openly	Adv	12	98	94	organ	NoC	24	100	91	*outlets*		8	92	91
opera	NoC	26	96	88	*organ*		13	98	91	outline	NoC	20	99	94
opera		23	95	88	*organs*		10	94	90	*outline*		14	98	94
operas		3	60	82	organic	Adj	21	92	88	*outlines*		6	91	93
operate	Verb	103	100	94	organisation	NoC	134	98	90	outline	Verb	28	98	94
operate		40	100	94	*organisation*		83	98	89	*outline*		5	89	91
operated		21	99	93	*organisations*		51	89	89	*outlined*		20	96	93
operates		15	89	92	organisational	Adj	10	75	80	*outlines*		1	30	79
operating		27	99	93	organise	Verb	56	100	92	*outlining*		4	87	92
operating	NoC	31	100	75	*organise*		13	98	93	outlook	NoC	12	95	92
operation	NoC	161	100	93	*organised*		32	100	91	*outlook*		12	95	92

Word	PoS	Freq	Ra	Di	Word	PoS	Freq	Ra	Di	Word	PoS	Freq	Ra	Di
outlooks		1	23	70	*ps*		0	6	45	*pans*		3	83	90
output	NoC	62	96	86	P	NoP	24	88	82	panel	NoC	49	100	91
output		58	96	86	*P*		10	69	61	*panel*		37	100	90
outputs		4	54	80	*P.*		14	87	86	*panels*		12	99	90
outside	Adj	37	100	96	pace	NoC	34	100	95	panic	NoC	18	100	92
outside	Adv	53	100	92	*pace*		31	100	95	*panic*		17	100	91
outside	Prep	116	100	97	*paces*		4	76	88	*panics*		0	31	80
outsider	NoC	13	98	93	Pacific	NoP	27	92	76	paper	NoC	237	100	96
outsider		6	94	91	*Pacific*		27	92	76	*paper*		173	100	96
outsiders		7	96	91	pack	NoC	32	100	92	*papers*		64	100	93
outstanding	Adj	30	97	93	*pack*		25	99	92	para	NoC	10	70	72
oven	NoC	16	94	88	*packs*		7	96	92	*para*		7	58	63
oven		13	88	87	pack	Verb	33	100	95	*para.*		2	31	63
ovens		2	70	83	*pack*		9	95	92	*paras*		1	37	74
over	Adv	584	100	89	*packed*		18	100	95	parade	NoC	12	98	91
over	Prep	735	100	98	*packing*		5	94	92	*parade*		10	98	91
over there	Adv	18	89	80	package	NoC	72	100	73	*parades*		1	56	84
overall	Adj	60	99	93	*package*		57	100	71	paragraph	NoC	34	99	83
overall	Adv	13	86	92	*packages*		15	94	80	*paragraph*		26	98	82
overcome	Verb	34	100	95	packet	NoC	18	99	91	*paragraphs*		8	89	84
overcame		3	86	91	*packet*		12	96	89	parallel	Adj	18	95	80
overcome		26	100	95	*packets*		6	93	92	parallel	NoC	14	92	91
overcomes		1	53	87	pact	NoC	12	88	80	*parallel*		11	91	90
overcoming		4	84	91	*pact*		11	88	79	*parallels*		3	74	90
overlook	Verb	21	99	93	*pacts*		1	35	76	parameter	NoC	17	81	79
overlook		4	91	91	pad	NoC	11	97	91	*parameter*		6	49	65
overlooked		8	95	95	*pad*		7	94	90	*parameters*		11	80	85
overlooking		8	95	90	*pads*		4	88	89	parcel	NoC	12	100	92
overlooks		2	62	85	page	NoC	151	100	93	*parcel*		7	98	92
overnight	Adv	12	99	94	*page*		106	100	93	*parcels*		5	88	88
overseas	Adj	26	93	90	*pages*		44	100	95	pardon	NoC	17	87	76
overseas	Adv	12	92	91	pain	NoC	84	100	93	*pardon*		17	87	75
overwhelming	Adj	14	97	95	*pain*		73	100	93	*pardons*		0	25	76
owe	Verb	37	100	95	*pains*		11	99	86	parent	NoC	201	100	93
owe		13	100	93	painful	Adj	19	99	94	*parent*		37	100	91
owed		16	99	92	paint	NoC	26	97	90	*parents*		163	100	93
owes		6	95	93	*paint*		22	96	91	parental	Adj	13	89	86
owing		2	75	90	*paints*		3	75	79	Paris	NoP	61	100	91
Owen	NoP	22	89	72	paint	Verb	44	100	94	parish	NoC	46	100	87
owl	NoC	16	81	66	*paint*		13	99	91	*parish*		39	100	86
owl		11	73	64	*painted*		24	99	93	*parishes*		6	70	84
owls		5	68	67	*painting*		5	91	92	park	NoC	118	100	90
own	DetP	695	100	97	*paints*		3	81	89	*park*		103	100	89
own	Verb	65	100	96	painter	NoC	20	94	85	*parks*		14	97	90
own		16	100	95	*painter*		12	92	86	park	Verb	19	95	90
owned		36	100	95	*painters*		7	80	81	*park*		5	81	86
owning		4	91	92	painting	NoC	71	100	83	*parked*		13	90	88
owns		10	99	93	*painting*		38	100	87	*parking*		1	54	88
owner	NoC	87	100	93	*paintings*		33	96	78	*parks*		0	30	82
owner		50	100	91	pair	NoC	81	100	95	Parker	NoP	11	93	87
owners		38	100	93	*pair*		60	100	95	*Parker*		11	93	87
ownership	NoC	31	95	90	*pairs*		21	98	91	parking	NoC	15	94	89
ownership		31	95	90	Pakistan	NoP	18	85	81	parliament	NoC	101	100	88
Oxford	NoP	86	100	77	palace	NoC	47	100	84	*parliament*		97	100	89
Oxford		86	100	77	*palace*		45	100	84	*parliaments*		4	62	82
Oxfords		0	7	59	*palaces*		3	69	86	parliamentary	Adj	43	92	87
Oxfordshire	NoP	16	85	60	pale	Adj	38	97	88	part	NoC	612	100	97
oxygen	NoC	19	95	85	*pale*		35	97	88	*part*		496	100	97
oxygen		19	95	85	*paler*		2	56	74	*parts*		116	100	95
oxygens		0	7	55	*palest*		0	25	79	part	Verb	13	99	90
ozone	NoC	13	74	62	Palestinian	Adj	10	49	67	*part*		3	92	92
ozone		13	74	62	palm	NoC	19	96	90	*parted*		8	93	87
P / p	Lett	79	93	83	*palm*		13	95	91	*parting*		2	69	88
p	NoC	148	79	67	*palms*		6	74	87	*parts*		0	15	76
p		3	52	84	pan	NoC	15	98	88	part-time	Adj	20	99	88
p.		145	67	66	*pan*		12	97	86	partial	Adj	18	99	91

Word	PoS	Freq	Ra	Di	Word	PoS	Freq	Ra	Di	Word	PoS	Freq	Ra	Di
partially	Adv	13	97	93	patient	Adj	14	97	88	*pen*		20	99	92
participant	NoC	28	91	89	patient	NoC	242	100	72	*pens*		5	93	92
participant		6	78	83	*patient*		69	100	81	penalty	NoC	38	100	88
participants		22	88	89	*patients*		173	100	66	*penalties*		11	92	90
participate	Verb	29	97	90	Patrick	NoP	30	98	80	*penalty*		27	99	87
participate		17	92	90	*Patrick*		30	98	80	pence	NoC	13	91	82
participated		5	79	87	patrol	NoC	11	87	87	pencil	NoC	14	97	93
participates		1	41	84	*patrol*		8	85	87	*pencil*		12	94	92
participating		6	89	90	*patrols*		3	67	85	*pencils*		3	82	89
participation	NoC	27	90	89	patron	NoC	12	94	91	penetrate	Verb	12	95	94
participation		27	90	89	*patron*		8	90	90	*penetrate*		6	93	92
particle	NoC	24	93	79	*patrons*		4	82	89	*penetrated*		4	85	93
particle		7	77	76	pattern	NoC	149	100	91	*penetrates*		1	47	86
particles		17	88	80	*pattern*		91	100	91	*penetrating*		2	72	91
particular	Adj	223	100	93	*patterns*		58	99	90	penny	NoC	15	98	92
particularly	Adv	220	100	95	Paul	NoP	114	100	91	*pennies*		3	76	85
partly	Adv	57	100	95	*Paul*		114	100	91	*penny*		12	96	92
partner	NoC	88	100	88	*Pauls*		0	10	57	pension	NoC	64	100	87
partner		49	100	89	Paula	NoP	11	70	72	*pension*		45	99	86
partners		39	100	85	pause	NoC	18	98	86	*pensions*		19	92	88
partnership	NoC	42	97	86	*pause*		16	96	84	pensioner	NoC	20	93	85
partnership		35	97	86	*pauses*		2	65	84	*pensioner*		6	73	84
partnerships		7	71	78	pause	Verb	33	96	84	*pensioners*		14	91	85
party	NoC	529	100	88	*pause*		4	88	92	people	NoC	1256	100	95
parties		127	100	86	*paused*		25	81	81	*people*		1241	100	95
party		403	100	88	*pauses*		1	43	84	*peoples*		15	97	88
pass	NoC	24	100	94	*pausing*		3	75	86	pepper	NoC	11	87	80
pass		18	100	93	pavement	NoC	18	96	84	*pepper*		9	83	79
passes		6	95	92	*pavement*		14	94	86	*peppers*		2	50	82
pass	Verb	204	100	97	*pavements*		5	87	73	per	Prep	135	100	91
pass		58	100	97	pay	NoC	45	100	92	per cent	NoC	384	100	88
passed		107	100	95	pay	Verb	381	100	95	*per cent*		382	100	88
passes		13	99	93	*paid*		144	100	95	perceive	Verb	29	98	92
passing		27	100	96	*pay*		175	100	94	*perceive*		9	94	90
passage	NoC	52	100	92	*payed*		0	18	72	*perceived*		17	95	92
passage		40	100	92	*paying*		46	100	94	*perceives*		1	63	88
passages		11	98	90	*pays*		15	99	94	*perceiving*		2	63	87
passenger	NoC	45	100	93	payable	Adj	17	87	81	percent	NoC	29	86	70
passenger		20	100	93	payment	NoC	99	100	89	*percent*		29	86	70
passengers		26	99	92	*payment*		54	100	87	percentage	NoC	32	98	91
passing	Adj	12	100	93	*payments*		45	97	90	*percentage*		28	98	91
passion	NoC	26	99	92	PC	NoC	37	87	76	*percentages*		4	76	87
passion		23	99	92	*p.c*		1	3	15	perception	NoC	33	99	90
passions		3	85	90	*P.C.*		8	19	34	*perception*		22	99	90
passive	Adj	14	98	90	*pc*		23	83	76	*perceptions*		12	90	85
passport	NoC	11	97	91	*pc.*		1	2	01	perfect	Adj	56	99	95
passport		8	94	91	*PCs*		4	48	71	perfectly	Adv	44	100	95
passports		3	70	86	peace	NoC	89	100	89	perform	Verb	88	100	92
past	Adj	89	100	93	*peace*		89	100	89	*perform*		32	100	93
past	Adv	21	99	93	peaceful	Adj	17	99	91	*performed*		39	98	86
past	NoC	86	100	97	peak	NoC	38	98	92	*performing*		13	98	94
past		86	100	97	*peak*		28	97	92	*performs*		4	82	91
pasts		0	25	82	*peaks*		10	93	89	performance	NoC	146	100	93
past	Prep	67	100	90	peasant	NoC	33	97	83	*performance*		130	100	93
Pat	NoP	18	92	90	*peasant*		16	95	84	*performances*		16	97	87
Pat		18	92	90	*peasants*		17	90	82	performer	NoC	11	93	89
patch	NoC	25	97	92	peculiar	Adj	14	99	94	*performer*		5	86	89
patch		16	95	91	peer	NoC	13	97	92	*performers*		6	82	87
patches		9	93	90	*peer*		5	86	89	perhaps	Adv	350	100	96
patent	NoC	13	91	80	*peers*		8	92	91	period	NoC	283	100	93
patent		9	90	79	peer	Verb	18	88	84	*period*		243	100	93
patents		4	57	79	*peer*		3	79	89	*periods*		40	100	92
path	NoC	76	100	93	*peered*		9	54	81	permanent	Adj	45	100	94
path		62	100	93	*peering*		6	73	84	permanently	Adv	12	100	94
paths		14	98	89	*peers*		0	9	66	permission	NoC	34	100	93
patience	NoC	12	100	93	pen	NoC	25	99	93	*permission*		32	100	93

Word	PoS	Freq	Ra	Di	Word	PoS	Freq	Ra	Di	Word	PoS	Freq	Ra	Di
permissions		2	32	60	*petitions*		3	77	84	piece	NoC	148	100	96
permit	Verb	45	98	92	petrol	NoC	24	100	91	*piece*		92	100	96
permit		14	96	92	*petrol*		24	100	91	*pieces*		56	100	95
permits		5	81	90	pH	NoC	16	60	68	pier	NoC	11	95	78
permitted		21	96	92	*p.H.*		0	9	64	*pier*		5	84	88
permitting		5	87	91	*pH*		15	60	68	*piers*		6	78	62
persist	Verb	18	99	94	phase	NoC	56	100	87	pig	NoC	25	100	89
persist		5	90	93	*phase*		46	100	87	*pig*		13	97	89
persisted		9	94	91	*phases*		10	89	86	*pigs*		12	95	88
persisting		1	51	84	phenomenon	NoC	36	99	90	pile	NoC	23	97	92
persists		3	74	90	*phenomena*		14	87	87	*pile*		17	95	91
persistent	Adj	13	98	93	*phenomenon*		22	97	91	*piles*		6	92	91
person	NoC	290	100	93	Phil	NoP	20	84	86	pile	Verb	11	98	92
person		250	100	93	*Phil*		20	84	86	*pile*		2	67	89
persons		40	99	87	Philip	NoP	40	99	78	*piled*		7	93	90
personal	Adj	176	100	94	Phillips	NoP	12	88	88	*piling*		2	77	91
personality	NoC	37	100	94	philosopher	NoC	13	93	89	pill	NoC	12	98	92
personalities		7	96	93	*philosopher*		6	86	89	*pill*		6	93	87
personality		29	100	94	*philosophers*		7	80	87	*pills*		6	89	91
personally	Adv	27	100	96	philosophical	Adj	13	94	90	pillar	NoC	10	97	93
personnel	NoC	33	98	88	philosophy	NoC	37	98	91	*pillar*		5	93	90
personnel		33	98	88	*philosophies*		2	65	88	*pillars*		5	95	92
perspective	NoC	38	99	91	*philosophy*		35	98	91	pillow	NoC	11	86	86
perspective		31	99	91	phone	NoC	71	100	91	*pillow*		7	78	86
perspectives		7	77	87	*phone*		67	100	90	*pillows*		4	59	83
persuade	Verb	52	100	96	*phones*		4	83	85	pilot	NoC	43	100	88
persuade		24	100	96	phone	Verb	31	96	86	*pilot*		31	100	89
persuaded		21	100	95	*phone*		14	91	86	*pilots*		11	82	82
persuades		1	33	82	*phoned*		13	88	84	pin	NoC	14	97	86
persuading		6	96	94	*phones*		1	35	80	*pin*		9	94	84
pet	NoC	19	97	90	*phoning*		3	75	85	*pins*		5	91	89
pet		13	95	90	photo	NoC	21	99	92	pin	Verb	13	100	92
pets		5	84	88	*photo*		12	98	91	*pin*		4	92	89
Pete	NoP	13	84	82	*photos*		8	93	91	*pinned*		7	96	90
Peter	NoP	124	100	92	photograph	NoC	58	100	95	*pinning*		2	63	88
petition	NoC	15	96	85	*photograph*		25	100	93	*pins*		0	14	73
petition		12	93	84	*photographs*		33	100	94	pine	NoC	12	92	91
					photographer	NoC	17	97	88	*pine*		10	87	90
					photographer		11	94	89	*pines*		2	57	85
					photographers		6	90	86	pink	Adj	30	99	91
					photography	NoC	11	92	85	*pink*		30	99	91
					phrase	NoC	43	100	92	*pinker*		0	13	72
					phrase		30	100	92	pint	NoC	17	97	90
					phrases		13	96	91	*pint*		12	95	90
					physical	Adj	95	100	93	*pints*		5	83	88
					physically	Adv	20	100	96	pipe	NoC	35	100	79
					physics	NoC	19	95	79	*pipe*		23	99	77
					piano	NoC	21	95	84	*pipes*		12	98	83
					piano		20	95	84	pit	NoC	27	99	92
					pianos		1	42	58	*pit*		17	98	92
					pick	Verb	150	100	93	*pits*		9	93	89
					pick		60	100	92	pitch	NoC	31	99	90
					picked		63	100	91	*pitch*		27	99	90
					picking		21	99	94	*pitches*		4	73	86
					picks		6	95	92	pity	NoC	18	99	91
					picture	NoC	159	100	95	*pity*		17	99	91
					picture		105	100	95	place	NoC	534	100	98
					pictures		54	100	93	*place*		443	100	98
					picture	Verb	12	94	91	*places*		91	100	97
					picture		4	86	90	place	Verb	150	100	96
					pictured		7	85	88	*place*		43	100	93
					pictures		1	45	85	*placed*		86	100	96
					picturing		1	32	81	*places*		7	92	92
					pie	NoC	16	94	89	*placing*		14	97	95
					pie		12	91	88	placement	NoC	11	80	79
					pies		5	80	88	*placement*		8	76	77

The top 12 personal names
(occurrences per million words)

These lists include only those names which are (more or less) unambiguous for gender. We have thus omitted from the lists *Chris* (45), *Jean* (30), and *Sam* (31) (*Jean* can be a male French name). *George* is sometimes be used as an abbreviated form of *Georgina*, but this is infrequent enough not to affect the position of *George* in the male list.

Male		Female	
John	328	Mary	71
David	157	Anne	44
Peter	124	Jane	42
Paul	114	Margaret	38
George	111	Elizabeth	36
James	102	Sarah	35
Richard	100	Ruth	30
Michael	95	Anna	28
Charles	91	Rose	28
William	84	Helen	27
Robert	79	Lucy	27
Henry	74	Maggie	27

Word	PoS	Freq	Ra	Di	Word	PoS	Freq	Ra	Di	Word	PoS	Freq	Ra	Di
placements		3	58	80	plead	Verb	18	100	91	pole/Pole	NoC	26	100	88
plain	Adj	29	99	94	*plead*		4	90	90	*pole/Pole*		13	100	91
plain		29	99	94	*pleaded*		10	92	89	*poles/Poles*		13	96	78
plainer		0	24	81	*pleading*		4	88	90	police	NoC	278	100	89
plainest		0	14	72	*pleads*		1	49	87	policeman	NoC	34	99	88
plain	NoC	16	99	92	pleasant	Adj	27	99	93	*policeman*		21	97	89
plain		11	99	92	*pleasant*		27	99	93	*policemen*		12	94	82
plains		5	78	87	*pleasanter*		0	31	83	policy	NoC	348	100	91
plaintiff	NoC	39	62	60	*pleasantest*		0	13	71	*policies*		88	97	91
plaintiff		30	51	60	please	Adv	133	99	91	*policy*		260	100	91
plaintiffs		9	43	53	please	Verb	17	99	92	Polish	Adj	15	97	74
plan	NoC	220	100	93	*please*		11	93	91	polite	Adj	12	98	90
plan		123	100	92	*pleased*		5	90	88	*polite*		12	98	90
plans		97	100	93	*pleases*		2	70	89	*politest*		0	14	75
plan	Verb	141	100	94	*pleasing*		0	29	83	political	Adj	306	100	90
plan		26	100	95	pleased	Adj	47	100	93	politically	Adv	17	95	92
planned		44	100	95	pleasure	NoC	58	100	93	politician	NoC	44	100	91
planning		50	100	94	*pleasure*		52	100	93	*politician*		11	97	88
plans		20	96	83	*pleasures*		6	87	91	*politicians*		33	100	91
plane	NoC	45	100	93	pledge	Verb	10	92	87	politics	NoC	75	100	91
plane		34	100	92	*pledge*		2	62	84	poll	NoC	39	97	85
planes		11	97	91	*pledged*		7	87	85	*poll*		28	97	84
planet	NoC	24	99	88	*pledges*		1	30	80	*polls*		11	78	79
planet		18	99	89	*pledging*		1	48	84	pollution	NoC	42	94	67
planets		6	77	82	plenty	Pron	46	98	95	*pollution*		41	94	67
planned	Adj	14	92	90	plot	NoC	24	100	93	*pollutions*		0	6	16
planner	NoC	12	89	89	*plot*		18	100	93	polymer	NoC	12	48	55
planner		3	70	84	*plots*		6	94	90	*polymer*		7	43	45
planners		9	85	88	plot	Verb	11	98	91	*polymers*		5	34	64
planning	NoC	96	100	90	*plot*		3	85	89	polytechnic	NoC	19	84	77
plant	NoC	146	100	90	*plots*		0	18	77	*polytechnic*		12	81	79
plant		74	100	90	*plotted*		4	84	86	*polytechnics*		6	55	69
plants		72	100	89	*plotting*		4	90	90	pond	NoC	22	94	80
plant	Verb	27	100	90	plunge	Verb	14	97	91	*pond*		17	92	78
plant		7	99	90	*plunge*		3	86	91	*ponds*		5	85	84
planted		14	99	90	*plunged*		8	94	90	pony	NoC	11	91	82
planting		6	93	86	*plunges*		1	42	84	*ponies*		4	69	78
plants		0	17	76	*plunging*		3	73	90	*pony*		7	82	82
plastic	NoC	45	100	93	plus	Prep	70	100	92	pool	NoC	56	100	90
plastic		41	100	93	pm	Adv	24	95	87	*pool*		45	100	89
plastics		5	67	82	*p.m*		7	75	67	*pools*		11	100	93
plate	NoC	64	99	91	*p.m.*		6	79	88	poor	Adj	166	100	96
plate		41	99	92	*pm*		11	81	87	*poor*		151	100	96
plates		23	96	86	pocket	NoC	52	100	91	*poorer*		9	93	92
platform	NoC	34	99	88	*pocket*		35	99	90	*poorest*		6	87	89
platform		26	99	92	*pockets*		16	98	91	pop	NoC	23	98	81
platforms		8	89	70	poem	NoC	41	99	86	*pop*		22	97	81
play	NoC	79	100	94	*poem*		25	96	87	*pops*		2	48	80
play		67	100	94	*poems*		16	93	85	pop	Verb	20	98	91
plays		12	97	89	poet	NoC	32	98	87	*pop*		10	94	89
play	Verb	386	100	94	*poet*		22	97	88	*popped*		6	84	89
play		149	100	94	*poets*		9	89	82	*popping*		3	84	90
played		112	100	94	poetry	NoC	29	99	85	*pops*		1	70	89
playing		101	100	93	*poetry*		29	99	85	pope	NoC	20	92	72
plays		24	99	93	point	NoC	484	100	95	*pope*		19	91	73
player	NoC	138	99	87	*point*		369	100	95	*popes*		2	29	58
player		57	98	88	*points*		115	100	94	popular	Adj	106	100	93
players		82	98	86	point	Verb	142	100	97	popularity	NoC	14	93	92
plc	NoC	18	73	71	*point*		33	99	95	population	NoC	147	100	91
p.l.c		0	1	00	*pointed*		58	100	95	*population*		132	100	91
plc		16	73	69	*pointing*		22	100	95	*populations*		15	81	88
plc.		1	7	08	*points*		30	97	93	port	NoC	41	100	91
plcs		0	14	67	poison	NoC	10	96	89	*port*		30	100	91
plea	NoC	15	95	90	*poison*		8	94	88	*ports*		11	95	88
plea		12	95	89	*poisons*		2	60	85	portfolio	NoC	19	93	79
pleas		4	89	89	Poland	NoP	21	94	82	*portfolio*		16	92	81

Word	PoS	Freq	Ra	Di	Word	PoS	Freq	Ra	Di	Word	PoS	Freq	Ra	Di
portfolios		4	56	67	*pours*		1	61	89	predict	Verb	38	100	93
portion	NoC	15	100	93	poverty	NoC	31	97	90	*predict*		14	98	92
portion		11	99	92	powder	NoC	15	100	92	*predicted*		16	99	91
portions		4	91	91	*powder*		13	99	92	*predicting*		4	84	91
portrait	NoC	25	96	87	*powders*		2	53	85	*predicts*		4	72	87
portrait		17	90	88	power	NoC	385	100	94	prediction	NoC	16	95	91
portraits		8	89	83	*power*		318	100	94	*prediction*		8	90	90
Portugal	NoP	11	94	88	*powers*		68	99	92	*predictions*		8	88	90
Portugal		11	94	88	powerful	Adj	72	100	95	predominantly	Adv	12	87	91
pose	Verb	29	100	94	pp	NoC	60	75	65	prefer	Verb	68	100	97
pose		8	95	93	*p.p.*		0	5	27	*prefer*		37	100	96
posed		13	97	94	*pp*		4	37	60	*preferred*		21	100	95
poses		5	82	91	*pp.*		55	63	63	*preferring*		5	89	93
posing		4	89	93	practical	Adj	77	100	93	*prefers*		5	95	91
position	NoC	268	100	95	practically	Adv	14	100	95	preference	NoC	31	100	91
position		228	100	95	practice	NoC	216	100	92	*preference*		22	100	91
positions		39	99	92	*practice*		171	100	92	*preferences*		10	87	87
position	Verb	13	95	92	*practices*		45	99	89	preferred	Adj	11	97	90
position		3	79	89	practise	Verb	29	100	93	pregnancy	NoC	18	99	88
positioned		7	92	91	*practise*		12	96	91	*pregnancies*		2	64	84
positioning		1	64	87	*practised*		10	98	93	*pregnancy*		16	99	88
positions		1	34	82	*practises*		1	50	86	pregnant	Adj	22	100	89
positive	Adj	83	100	92	*practising*		6	98	93	prejudice	NoC	16	99	88
positively	Adv	13	98	95	practitioner	NoC	31	90	81	*prejudice*		11	98	86
possess	Verb	42	99	94	*practitioner*		11	83	82	*prejudices*		4	84	90
possess		15	97	92	*practitioners*		20	79	80	preliminary	Adj	18	96	91
possessed		16	96	93	praise	NoC	13	98	93	premier	Adj	17	79	78
possesses		5	77	89	*praise*		12	97	93	premise	NoC	42	99	83
possessing		5	87	92	*praises*		1	53	88	*premise*		4	84	90
possession	NoC	37	100	90	praise	Verb	15	99	93	*premises*		39	99	82
possession		29	98	87	*praise*		5	91	90	premium	NoC	19	91	85
possessions		9	96	93	*praised*		8	96	92	*premium*		12	88	86
possibility	NoC	96	100	95	*praises*		1	42	82	*premiums*		7	76	82
possibilities		25	99	93	*praising*		2	77	91	preparation	NoC	43	99	93
possibility		71	100	95	pray	Verb	25	97	88	*preparation*		33	99	93
possible	Adj	342	100	95	*pray*		14	94	84	*preparations*		10	97	92
possibly	Adv	73	100	95	*prayed*		5	76	87	prepare	Verb	111	100	96
post	NoC	111	100	93	*praying*		5	87	90	*prepare*		30	100	95
post		88	100	93	*prays*		1	35	79	*prepared*		52	99	96
posts		22	99	90	prayer	NoC	31	100	89	*prepares*		4	76	90
post-war	Adj	16	88	88	*prayer*		21	100	88	*preparing*		26	100	95
poster	NoC	17	99	93	*prayers*		10	96	89	prepared	Adj	53	100	96
poster		8	95	92	preach	Verb	11	100	88	prescribe	Verb	13	97	88
posters		9	99	93	*preach*		3	82	87	*prescribe*		3	81	90
postpone	Verb	11	96	87	*preached*		3	78	86	*prescribed*		6	92	88
postpone		3	85	90	*preaches*		0	37	85	*prescribes*		1	38	83
postponed		7	95	84	*preaching*		4	80	86	*prescribing*		3	55	71
postpones		0	11	70	precede	Verb	15	97	92	prescription	NoC	10	96	90
pot	NoC	29	97	92	*precede*		2	77	90	*prescription*		7	92	90
pot		19	97	92	*preceded*		8	94	92	*prescriptions*		4	80	88
pots		10	92	89	*precedes*		2	60	88	presence	NoC	81	99	93
potato	NoC	25	100	89	*preceding*		3	76	87	*presence*		80	99	93
potato		9	95	90	precedent	NoC	12	92	70	*presences*		0	30	80
potatoes		16	98	88	*precedent*		9	91	71	present	Adj	148	100	94
potential	Adj	66	100	93	*precedents*		3	72	65	present	NoC	50	100	95
potential	NoC	48	100	93	precious	Adj	16	99	89	*present*		41	100	95
potential		46	100	93	precise	Adj	29	99	94	*presents*		9	92	89
potentials		1	36	80	precisely	Adv	35	100	94	present	Verb	143	100	94
potentially	Adv	24	97	94	precision	NoC	12	95	89	*present*		33	99	95
pound	NoC	184	100	80	*precision*		12	95	89	*presented*		80	100	93
pound		61	100	81	predator	NoC	13	87	72	*presenting*		14	97	93
pounds		123	99	77	*predator*		6	71	65	*presents*		16	93	93
pour	Verb	37	100	92	*predators*		8	71	76	presentation	NoC	38	98	91
pour		11	95	90	predecessor	NoC	16	94	92	*presentation*		32	98	92
poured		18	100	88	*predecessor*		9	94	91	*presentations*		6	80	86
pouring		7	91	91	*predecessors*		7	87	91	preservation	NoC	11	92	88

Word	PoS	Freq	Ra	Di	Word	PoS	Freq	Ra	Di	Word	PoS	Freq	Ra	Di
preservation		11	92	88	pride	NoC	27	99	94	probable	Adj	12	96	92
preserve	Verb	38	100	93	*pride*		27	99	94	probably	Adv	273	100	95
preserve		15	98	93	priest	NoC	33	100	92	probe	NoC	13	75	62
preserved		16	97	89	*priest*		21	98	91	*probe*		9	70	68
preserves		1	61	89	*priests*		12	95	91	*probes*		4	45	45
preserving		5	92	93	primarily	Adv	31	94	92	problem	NoC	565	100	95
presidency	NoC	12	72	73	primary	Adj	86	99	78	*problem*		290	100	96
presidencies		0	8	64	primary	NoC	10	85	90	*problems*		275	100	95
presidency		12	72	73	*primaries*		2	39	75	procedure	NoC	111	100	91
president	NoC	170	100	78	*primary*		9	84	90	*procedure*		58	100	89
president		164	99	77	prime	Adj	121	100	80	*procedures*		53	100	92
presidents		6	80	79	primitive	Adj	17	94	87	proceed	NoC	11	93	88
presidential	Adj	21	88	64	prince	NoC	65	100	91	*proceeds*		11	93	88
press	NoC	104	100	93	*prince*		59	99	91	proceed	Verb	43	99	94
press		102	100	93	*princes*		6	82	84	*proceed*		21	97	92
presses		2	70	82	princess	NoC	30	100	85	*proceeded*		11	96	93
press	Verb	73	100	94	*princess*		29	100	85	*proceeding*		7	96	92
press		29	100	92	*princesses*		1	37	78	*proceeds*		4	82	91
pressed		29	100	91	principal	Adj	40	97	89	proceeding	NoC	43	98	77
presses		1	51	86	principal	NoC	12	97	90	*proceeding*		0	18	69
pressing		14	100	93	*principal*		9	93	90	*proceedings*		43	98	77
pressure	NoC	146	100	94	*principals*		3	68	85	process	NoC	269	100	92
pressure		119	100	94	principle	NoC	139	100	92	*process*		215	100	93
pressures		27	96	92	*principle*		82	100	91	*processes*		54	94	89
Preston	NoP	13	85	60	*principles*		57	99	92	process	Verb	26	99	90
Preston		13	85	60	print	NoC	34	100	91	*process*		11	91	90
presumably	Adv	33	100	95	*print*		21	100	92	*processed*		7	94	88
presume	Verb	12	100	94	*prints*		12	95	85	*processes*		1	45	86
presume		6	95	90	print	Verb	35	100	91	*processing*		7	82	88
presumed		5	91	91	*print*		10	97	87	processing	NoC	30	88	84
presumes		1	45	86	*printed*		18	100	91	processor	NoC	22	91	71
presuming		1	45	87	*printing*		6	89	88	*processor*		15	89	73
pretend	Verb	27	99	90	*prints*		0	26	78	*processors*		7	67	63
pretend		12	98	91	printed	Adj	13	100	90	proclaim	Verb	13	97	92
pretended		5	82	85	printer	NoC	25	94	78	*proclaim*		2	69	90
pretending		8	96	89	*printer*		17	85	75	*proclaimed*		7	88	89
pretends		1	61	89	*printers*		8	87	80	*proclaiming*		2	82	92
pretty	Adj	30	96	90	printing	NoC	13	93	86	*proclaims*		1	62	88
prettier		1	44	86	*printing*		13	93	86	produce	Verb	304	100	94
prettiest		1	52	87	prior	Adj	12	95	90	*produce*		110	100	94
pretty		28	96	90	prior to	Prep	31	98	92	*produced*		129	100	94
pretty	Adv	52	100	92	priority	NoC	54	100	94	*produces*		25	95	92
prevail	Verb	12	96	93	*priorities*		20	99	92	*producing*		40	100	94
prevail		5	88	91	*priority*		34	100	94	producer	NoC	37	100	91
prevailed		5	91	93	prison	NoC	74	100	87	*producer*		18	95	92
prevails		2	65	88	*prison*		64	100	88	*producers*		18	90	89
prevent	Verb	106	100	95	*prisons*		9	89	76	product	NoC	217	100	89
prevent		68	100	94	prisoner	NoC	47	100	89	*product*		111	99	89
prevented		19	98	94	*prisoner*		17	99	90	*products*		106	99	89
preventing		12	98	93	*prisoners*		30	99	86	production	NoC	162	100	92
prevents		7	90	91	privacy	NoC	11	99	93	*production*		156	100	92
prevention	NoC	15	87	89	*privacy*		11	98	93	*productions*		6	84	89
prevention		15	87	89	private	Adj	173	100	94	productive	Adj	14	96	90
previous	Adj	123	100	94	privately	Adv	12	100	94	productivity	NoC	20	84	89
previously	Adv	69	99	92	privatisation	NoC	13	67	81	*productivity*		20	84	89
prey	NoC	16	95	80	*privatisation*		13	66	81	profession	NoC	40	99	90
prey		16	94	80	*privatisations*		1	25	75	*profession*		31	99	90
preys		0	10	69	privilege	NoC	25	100	81	*professions*		9	83	87
price	NoC	271	100	92	*privilege*		16	100	83	professional	Adj	105	100	93
price		170	100	92	*privileges*		9	91	76	professional	NoC	30	99	91
prices		101	100	91	prize	NoC	42	100	92	*professional*		7	94	89
price	Verb	18	97	84	*prize*		31	100	92	*professionals*		23	98	90
price		4	79	84	*prizes*		11	95	91	professor	NoC	55	100	86
priced		11	93	78	probability	NoC	19	95	86	*professor*		52	100	86
prices		0	12	72	*probabilities*		4	64	82	*professors*		3	74	89
pricing		3	65	82	*probability*		16	92	86	profile	NoC	28	100	93

Word	PoS	Freq	Ra	Di	Word	PoS	Freq	Ra	Di	Word	PoS	Freq	Ra	Di
profile		23	*99*	*94*	pronounce	Verb	12	*99*	*92*	*proud*	Adj	32	*100*	*94*
profiles		6	*84*	*86*	*pronounce*		3	*84*	*89*	*proud*		32	*100*	*94*
profit	NoC	113	*100*	*88*	*pronounced*		8	*96*	*91*	*prouder*		0	*11*	*70*
profit		56	*100*	*88*	*pronounces*		0	*19*	*76*	*proudest*		1	*38*	*85*
profits		58	*100*	*86*	*pronouncing*		1	*53*	*88*	prove	Verb	149	*100*	*96*
profitable	Adj	14	*99*	*92*	proof	NoC	29	*100*	*93*	*prove*		57	*100*	*96*
profound	Adj	15	*94*	*93*	*proof*		27	*100*	*94*	*proved*		69	*100*	*95*
profound		14	*94*	*93*	*proofs*		2	*69*	*86*	*proven*		3	*90*	*92*
profounder		0	*8*	*64*	propaganda	NoC	12	*93*	*90*	*proves*		8	*94*	*93*
profoundest		0	*14*	*74*	proper	Adj	65	*100*	*95*	*proving*		11	*98*	*93*
program	NoC	57	*88*	*79*	properly	Adv	57	*100*	*96*	provide	Verb	505	*100*	*94*
program		39	*86*	*77*	property	NoC	167	*100*	*90*	*provide*		223	*100*	*94*
programs		18	*77*	*81*	*properties*		41	*99*	*91*	*provided*		130	*100*	*94*
programme	NoC	255	*100*	*92*	*property*		125	*100*	*88*	*provides*		84	*96*	*91*
programme		190	*100*	*91*	proportion	NoC	78	*100*	*92*	*providing*		69	*100*	*94*
programmes		65	*100*	*92*	*proportion*		63	*100*	*91*	provided	Conj	30	*99*	*94*
programming	NoC	11	*80*	*78*	*proportions*		15	*99*	*91*	provided that	Conj	11	*84*	*86*
progress	NoC	76	*100*	*94*	proposal	NoC	111	*99*	*89*	provider	NoC	12	*86*	*85*
progress	Verb	19	*100*	*95*	*proposal*		42	*99*	*90*	*provider*		4	*82*	*86*
progress		6	*92*	*93*	*proposals*		68	*94*	*88*	*providers*		8	*68*	*84*
progressed		7	*98*	*94*	propose	Verb	74	*99*	*93*	province	NoC	33	*96*	*85*
progresses		3	*74*	*90*	*propose*		14	*99*	*91*	*province*		22	*94*	*84*
progressing		3	*87*	*92*	*proposed*		45	*99*	*91*	*provinces*		11	*85*	*83*
progressive	Adj	17	*95*	*91*	*proposes*		7	*83*	*88*	provincial	Adj	16	*94*	*89*
prohibit	Verb	10	*84*	*87*	*proposing*		8	*96*	*91*	provision	NoC	129	*100*	*88*
prohibit		2	*72*	*86*	proposed	Adj	39	*97*	*89*	*provision*		87	*96*	*90*
prohibited		5	*81*	*87*	proposition	NoC	20	*98*	*87*	*provisions*		41	*100*	*82*
prohibiting		2	*53*	*80*	*proposition*		14	*98*	*89*	provoke	Verb	20	*96*	*93*
prohibits		1	*47*	*81*	*propositions*		6	*73*	*79*	*provoke*		6	*95*	*93*
project	NoC	197	*100*	*89*	prosecute	Verb	11	*90*	*87*	*provoked*		11	*96*	*91*
project		141	*100*	*87*	*prosecute*		3	*81*	*90*	*provokes*		1	*60*	*89*
projects		55	*99*	*91*	*prosecuted*		4	*82*	*89*	*provoking*		2	*81*	*90*
project	Verb	14	*98*	*94*	*prosecuting*		4	*57*	*73*	psychiatric	Adj	11	*89*	*80*
project		5	*95*	*92*	prosecution	NoC	26	*94*	*83*	psychological	Adj	28	*99*	*85*
projected		5	*93*	*90*	*prosecution*		21	*93*	*84*	psychologist	NoC	14	*89*	*71*
projecting		2	*69*	*89*	*prosecutions*		5	*71*	*79*	*psychologist*		5	*82*	*86*
projects		2	*63*	*89*	prospect	NoC	54	*100*	*95*	*psychologists*		9	*74*	*59*
projection	NoC	11	*93*	*89*	*prospect*		32	*99*	*95*	psychology	NoC	26	*97*	*66*
projection		6	*87*	*87*	*prospects*		22	*99*	*92*	*psychologies*		0	*5*	*15*
projections		5	*83*	*87*	prospective	Adj	13	*95*	*90*	*psychology*		26	*97*	*66*
prominent	Adj	23	*98*	*92*	prosperity	NoC	11	*94*	*91*	pub	NoC	51	*100*	*88*
promise	NoC	35	*100*	*91*	*prosperity*		11	*94*	*91*	*pub*		38	*99*	*89*
promise		24	*100*	*90*	protect	Verb	87	*100*	*95*	*pubs*		13	*97*	*82*
promises		10	*100*	*91*	*protect*		51	*100*	*95*	public	Adj	285	*100*	*94*
promise	Verb	64	*100*	*94*	*protected*		20	*99*	*93*	public	NoC	96	*100*	*94*
promise		15	*99*	*90*	*protecting*		12	*98*	*93*	*public*		96	*100*	*94*
promised		39	*100*	*90*	*protects*		4	*89*	*91*	*publics*		0	*16*	*69*
promises		7	*92*	*89*	protection	NoC	81	*99*	*92*	publication	NoC	57	*96*	*91*
promising		3	*88*	*90*	*protection*		80	*99*	*92*	*publication*		37	*94*	*91*
promising	Adj	13	*100*	*94*	*protections*		1	*27*	*70*	*publications*		20	*90*	*89*
promote	Verb	66	*100*	*94*	protective	Adj	13	*100*	*94*	publicity	NoC	25	*100*	*94*
promote		32	*99*	*93*	protein	NoC	41	*83*	*74*	publicly	Adv	16	*97*	*93*
promoted		16	*98*	*93*	*protein*		28	*82*	*74*	publish	Verb	123	*100*	*92*
promotes		4	*74*	*90*	*proteins*		13	*65*	*71*	*publish*		13	*97*	*92*
promoting		15	*93*	*93*	protest	NoC	40	*96*	*87*	*published*		98	*99*	*92*
promoter	NoC	13	*77*	*60*	*protest*		28	*96*	*88*	*publishes*		2	*68*	*89*
promoter		8	*59*	*56*	*protests*		12	*94*	*81*	*publishing*		8	*87*	*90*
promoters		5	*68*	*64*	protest	Verb	25	*98*	*91*	publisher	NoC	30	*98*	*81*
promotion	NoC	37	*100*	*94*	*protest*		8	*95*	*91*	*publisher*		15	*91*	*70*
promotion		33	*100*	*91*	*protested*		12	*95*	*88*	*publishers*		15	*97*	*85*
promotions		4	*79*	*88*	*protesting*		4	*88*	*87*	publishing	NoC	22	*89*	*80*
prompt	Verb	23	*98*	*93*	*protests*		1	*37*	*85*	pudding	NoC	11	*92*	*86*
prompt		3	*85*	*92*	protestant	Adj	11	*86*	*78*	*pudding*		9	*91*	*86*
prompted		16	*98*	*92*	protocol	NoC	14	*90*	*81*	*puddings*		2	*58*	*82*
prompting		3	*79*	*87*	*protocol*		10	*88*	*81*	pull	Verb	140	*100*	*91*
prompts		1	*67*	*90*	*protocols*		4	*47*	*74*	*pull*		40	*99*	*93*

Word	PoS	Freq	Ra	Di	Word	PoS	Freq	Ra	Di	Word	PoS	Freq	Ra	Di
pulled		70	99	88	Q / q	Lett	18	86	85	*quotations*		5	83	89
pulling		24	100	92	qualification	NoC	36	99	87	quote	Verb	44	100	94
pulls		6	90	91	*qualification*		13	93	88	*quote*		10	99	91
pulse	NoC	15	94	87	*qualifications*		23	98	85	*quoted*		24	100	92
pulse		11	91	87	qualified	Adj	15	97	90	*quotes*		4	77	89
pulses		4	72	84	qualify	Verb	30	100	93	*quoting*		5	95	92
pump	NoC	15	98	89	*qualified*		13	100	93	qv	Uncl	30	16	25
pump		10	95	87	*qualifies*		2	63	86	*q.v*		7	6	25
pumps		5	94	88	*qualify*		13	99	92	*q.v.*		23	8	24
punch	NoC	11	96	81	*qualifying*		2	66	87	*qv*		0	7	40
punch		9	93	79	quality	NoC	188	100	93	R / r	Lett	53	99	84
punches		2	63	85	*qualities*		25	99	93	R	NoP	32	90	82
punish	Verb	13	99	93	*quality*		163	100	93	*R*		12	66	61
punish		5	93	91	quantity	NoC	43	100	91	*R.*		19	88	83
punished		7	95	93	*quantities*		19	100	91	rabbit	NoC	25	98	76
punishes		0	25	81	*quantity*		24	98	90	*rabbit*		14	97	82
punishing		2	67	88	quarry	NoC	13	93	85	*rabbits*		10	90	66
punishment	NoC	25	99	88	*quarries*		3	64	82	race	NoC	90	100	90
punishment		23	99	88	*quarry*		10	92	84	*race*		74	100	90
punishments		2	72	81	quarter	NoC	92	100	85	*races*		16	96	90
pupil	NoC	105	100	87	*quarter*		74	100	82	race	Verb	36	98	89
pupil		23	97	86	*quarters*		18	100	95	*race*		5	88	89
pupils		81	100	86	queen	NoC	80	100	93	*raced*		7	77	89
purchase	NoC	39	99	89	*queen*		77	100	93	*races*		1	39	83
purchase		31	99	88	*queens*		2	75	86	*racing*		23	94	88
purchases		8	94	91	query	NoC	11	97	90	Rachel	NoP	22	83	69
purchase	Verb	36	98	92	*queries*		7	92	89	racial	Adj	14	93	87
purchase		14	96	90	*query*		5	87	88	racism	NoC	11	84	70
purchased		16	96	91	question	NoC	390	100	91	*racism*		11	84	71
purchases		1	30	81	*question*		248	100	95	radiation	NoC	18	89	82
purchasing		5	84	91	*questions*		143	100	95	*radiation*		17	88	82
purchaser	NoC	24	89	61	question	Verb	41	99	95	*radiations*		1	22	70
purchaser		18	85	53	*question*		15	99	95	radical	Adj	37	95	91
purchasers		6	76	79	*questioned*		18	97	93	radio	NoC	91	100	93
pure	Adj	36	99	95	*questioning*		7	96	93	*radio*		87	100	93
pure		34	99	95	*questions*		1	69	89	*radios*		3	86	88
purer		1	43	86	questionnaire	NoC	17	89	87	RAF	NoP	20	86	77
purest		1	66	89	*questionnaire*		12	85	87	*R.A.F.*		1	21	71
purely	Adv	26	100	94	*questionnaires*		5	78	84	*RAF*		19	84	76
purple	Adj	11	95	92	queue	NoC	12	98	94	rage	NoC	13	90	87
purple		11	95	92	*queue*		9	96	93	*rage*		12	89	87
purpose	NoC	152	100	92	*queues*		4	84	91	*rages*		1	40	85
purpose		93	100	93	quick	Adj	66	100	95	raid	NoC	21	97	89
purposes		58	99	89	*quick*		58	100	95	*raid*		13	95	87
pursue	Verb	46	98	95	*quicker*		6	99	94	*raids*		8	90	89
pursue		20	98	94	*quickest*		2	81	91	rail	NoC	46	100	90
pursued		15	97	94	quickly	Adv	124	100	95	*rail*		40	100	89
pursues		1	59	88	quid	NoC	15	77	69	*rails*		7	95	91
pursuing		10	97	94	*quid*		14	77	69	railway	NoC	91	100	86
pursuit	NoC	16	100	94	*quids*		0	18	75	*railway*		73	100	85
pursuit		13	98	94	quiet	Adj	66	100	93	*railways*		19	93	86
pursuits		4	81	90	*quiet*		62	100	92	rain	NoC	64	100	86
push	Verb	107	100	93	*quieter*		4	90	92	*rain*		62	100	85
push		30	100	95	*quietest*		1	40	86	*rains*		2	76	88
pushed		50	100	89	quietly	Adv	41	100	86	rain	Verb	14	97	91
pushes		3	85	92	quit	Verb	11	97	85	*rain*		3	83	88
pushing		23	100	93	*quit*		9	95	85	*rained*		3	80	90
put (putt)	Verb	700	100	93	*quits*		1	40	82	*raining*		6	84	88
put		596	100	93	*quitted*		0	12	71	*rains*		2	76	89
puts		29	99	95	*quitting*		1	52	80	rainbow	NoC	10	92	64
putted		0	12	66	quite	Adv	412	100	93	*rainbow*		9	92	61
putting		76	100	95	quota	NoC	14	92	85	*rainbows*		1	38	74
puzzled	Adj	10	92	87	*quota*		8	88	86	raise	Verb	196	100	97
pylorus	NoC	11	6	19	*quotas*		6	71	81	*raise*		61	100	94
pylori		11	6	20	quotation	NoC	11	95	90	*raised*		95	100	96
pylorus		0	2	10	*quotation*		7	90	89	*raises*		14	93	92

Word	PoS	Freq	Ra	Di	Word	PoS	Freq	Ra	Di	Word	PoS	Freq	Ra	Di
raising		25	99	96	*reaching*		29	99	96	rebel	NoC	21	93	83
rally	NoC	16	89	82	react	Verb	26	100	96	*rebel*		8	85	81
rallies		3	61	79	*react*		13	100	95	*rebels*		12	89	83
rally		13	84	82	*reacted*		8	94	94	rebellion	NoC	11	93	89
Ralph	NoP	12	90	84	*reacting*		4	97	94	*rebellion*		10	93	89
Ralph		12	90	84	*reacts*		2	64	85	*rebellions*		1	40	84
Ralphs		0	5	34	reaction	NoC	76	100	92	rebuild	Verb	13	98	92
ram	NoC	10	87	78	*reaction*		56	100	92	*rebuild*		5	92	92
ram		9	81	76	*reactions*		21	98	90	*rebuilding*		2	75	91
rams		1	37	77	reactor	NoC	13	62	70	*rebuilds*		0	11	70
random	Adj	18	99	89	*reactor*		8	52	68	*rebuilt*		6	85	88
range	NoC	203	100	93	*reactors*		5	44	72	recall	Verb	57	100	95
range		196	100	93	read	Verb	284	100	86	*recall*		25	100	93
ranges		7	84	90	*read*		225	100	83	*recalled*		18	94	91
range	Verb	34	99	93	*reading*		49	100	95	*recalling*		5	95	92
range		9	89	92	*reads*		10	99	94	*recalls*		9	85	89
ranged		7	95	92	reader	NoC	88	99	90	receipt	NoC	19	100	90
ranges		4	79	90	*reader*		41	95	88	*receipt*		12	98	87
ranging		15	98	93	*readers*		47	98	90	*receipts*		7	93	89
ranger	NoC	14	75	77	readily	Adv	28	97	92	receive	Verb	247	100	95
ranger		1	55	85	reading	NoC	55	100	93	*receive*		75	100	94
rangers		12	55	75	*reading*		48	100	93	*received*		130	100	95
rank	NoC	34	100	94	*readings*		7	89	88	*receives*		13	93	92
rank		18	100	92	Reading	NoP	12	91	88	*receiving*		29	100	93
ranks		16	99	94	ready	Adj	102	100	95	receiver	NoC	20	98	88
rape	NoC	20	100	75	*readier*		0	16	74	*receiver*		16	97	88
rape		19	100	75	*ready*		102	100	95	*receivers*		4	71	81
rapes		1	33	74	Reagan	NoP	11	74	69	recent	Adj	158	100	94
rapid	Adj	36	97	93	*Reagan*		11	74	69	recently	Adv	123	100	95
rapidly	Adv	46	99	95	real	Adj	227	100	97	reception	NoC	26	100	94
rare	Adj	50	100	95	*real*		227	100	97	*reception*		24	100	93
rare		46	100	95	realise	Verb	98	99	92	*receptions*		1	52	86
rarer		2	75	91	*realise*		39	98	94	recession	NoC	39	93	87
rarest		1	52	79	*realised*		49	99	89	*recession*		38	93	87
rarely	Adv	42	100	94	*realises*		3	78	89	*recessions*		1	38	74
rat	NoC	24	97	81	*realising*		7	92	90	recipe	NoC	19	99	86
rat		11	93	86	realistic	Adj	19	100	94	*recipe*		12	98	85
rats		14	92	76	reality	NoC	74	100	94	*recipes*		7	83	85
rate	NoC	303	100	91	*realities*		8	94	92	recipient	NoC	11	93	91
rate		189	100	91	*reality*		65	100	94	*recipient*		7	90	90
rates		115	100	90	realize	Verb	59	96	92	*recipients*		5	81	89
rate	Verb	12	96	90	*realize*		22	93	91	reckon	Verb	40	100	88
rate		2	72	87	*realized*		31	94	89	*reckon*		21	96	82
rated		7	84	87	*realizes*		1	63	87	*reckoned*		10	98	93
rates		1	53	86	*realizing*		4	88	91	*reckoning*		1	50	88
rating		2	62	84	really	Adv	481	100	89	*reckons*		8	87	73
rather	Adv	213	100	96	realm	NoC	13	94	89	recognise	Verb	93	99	94
rather than	Conj	46	100	95	*realm*		11	93	89	*recognise*		36	99	92
rather than	Prep	169	100	94	*realms*		3	81	88	*recognised*		43	98	94
rating	NoC	17	96	84	rear	Adj	14	98	90	*recognises*		6	84	91
rating		10	91	87	*rear*		14	98	90	*recognising*		8	93	94
ratings		7	80	76	rear	NoC	12	96	92	recognition	NoC	58	99	91
ratio	NoC	37	88	86	*rear*		11	96	92	*recognition*		58	99	91
ratio		29	85	86	*rears*		0	14	74	*recognitions*		0	21	80
ratios		8	75	85	reason	NoC	289	100	96	recognize	Verb	60	97	93
rational	Adj	23	96	87	*reason*		181	100	97	*recognize*		21	97	93
raw	Adj	25	100	95	*reasons*		108	100	94	*recognized*		30	97	92
raw		25	100	95	reasonable	Adj	61	100	90	*recognizes*		4	68	87
Ray	NoP	18	95	88	reasonably	Adv	31	100	92	*recognizing*		5	84	91
reach	NoC	16	99	94	reasoning	NoC	10	93	87	recommend	Verb	59	100	94
reach		13	98	94	*reasoning*		10	93	87	*recommend*		18	100	94
reaches		3	87	92	reassure	Verb	14	97	93	*recommended*		32	100	93
reach	Verb	234	100	96	*reassure*		6	95	92	*recommending*		4	87	91
reach		68	100	97	*reassured*		5	89	90	*recommends*		5	81	89
reached		124	100	94	*reassures*		0	25	79	recommendation				
reaches		12	99	93	*reassuring*		3	83	91		NoC	40	99	92

Word	PoS	Freq	Ra	Di	Word	PoS	Freq	Ra	Di	Word	PoS	Freq	Ra	Di
recommendation		14	98	91	*reference*		77	100	90	registration	NoC	24	97	86
recommendations		26	89	92	*references*		20	99	91	*registration*		22	97	86
reconstruction	NoC	12	88	89	referendum	NoC	15	70	67	*registrations*		1	48	82
reconstruction		11	87	88	*referenda*		0	14	69	regret	Verb	18	100	93
reconstructions		1	43	82	*referendum*		14	70	67	*regret*		10	100	92
record	NoC	197	100	92	*referendums*		1	20	62	*regrets*		1	60	88
record		126	100	93	referral	NoC	12	70	70	*regretted*		5	95	92
records		71	100	89	*referral*		7	62	72	*regretting*		2	60	84
record	Verb	101	100	93	*referrals*		6	53	64	regular	Adj	75	100	95
record		23	100	92	reflect	Verb	113	99	95	regularly	Adv	39	100	94
recorded		57	100	92	*reflect*		38	98	93	regulate	Verb	18	89	91
recording		16	98	89	*reflected*		38	99	95	*regulate*		6	81	90
records		5	86	91	*reflecting*		15	98	94	*regulated*		6	84	90
recorder	NoC	12	98	90	*reflects*		22	93	93	*regulates*		1	56	82
recorder		9	97	91	reflection	NoC	25	99	95	*regulating*		4	73	89
recorders		3	70	81	*reflection*		20	99	95	regulation	NoC	68	100	91
recording	NoC	35	100	84	*reflections*		5	89	92	*regulation*		26	92	89
recording		25	99	85	reform	NoC	82	94	87	*regulations*		42	100	90
recordings		11	86	80	*reform*		54	94	88	regulatory	Adj	12	72	86
recover	Verb	51	100	94	*reforms*		28	86	85	rehearsal	NoC	10	94	89
recover		20	100	92	refuge	NoC	11	96	92	*rehearsal*		7	91	89
recovered		22	100	94	*refuge*		10	96	92	*rehearsals*		4	72	86
recovering		9	97	90	*refuges*		1	36	78	Reid	NoP	10	74	84
recovers		1	59	88	refugee	NoC	28	96	82	*Reid*		10	73	84
recovery	NoC	39	99	89	*refugee*		8	84	81	reign	NoC	18	95	85
recoveries		1	29	76	*refugees*		19	89	81	*reign*		18	95	85
recovery		38	99	89	refusal	NoC	20	96	89	*reigns*		1	27	76
recruit	Verb	20	100	93	*refusal*		19	96	89	reinforce	Verb	28	98	93
recruit		7	89	92	*refusals*		1	46	83	*reinforce*		9	90	92
recruited		9	94	92	refuse	Verb	106	100	95	*reinforced*		13	94	93
recruiting		4	86	89	*refuse*		22	100	94	*reinforces*		3	73	89
recruits		1	43	86	*refused*		63	100	94	*reinforcing*		3	81	90
recruitment	NoC	16	90	88	*refuses*		7	95	93	reject	Verb	64	100	92
recruitment		16	90	88	*refusing*		14	98	93	*reject*		15	99	92
red	Adj	126	100	95	regain	Verb	13	94	94	*rejected*		39	99	90
red		126	100	95	*regain*		6	93	94	*rejecting*		6	94	92
redder		1	34	82	*regained*		5	88	92	*rejects*		4	79	90
red	NoC	27	98	93	*regaining*		2	77	91	rejection	NoC	15	98	92
red		23	98	93	*regains*		0	27	82	*rejection*		15	96	92
reds		4	85	85	regard	NoC	17	97	88	*rejections*		0	32	83
reduce	Verb	178	100	93	regard	Verb	105	100	94	relate	Verb	134	100	92
reduce		71	100	93	*regard*		24	99	93	*relate*		26	98	92
reduced		66	100	94	*regarded*		70	99	94	*related*		57	100	91
reduces		12	83	90	*regarding*		4	91	93	*relates*		15	87	90
reducing		29	97	92	*regards*		7	96	93	*relating*		37	99	89
reduced	Adj	14	91	91	regarding	Prep	20	99	93	related	Adj	30	93	89
reduction	NoC	61	97	91	regardless	Adv	15	99	94	relation	NoC	140	100	88
reduction		48	96	91	regime	NoC	41	96	89	*relation*		28	100	87
reductions		13	81	88	*regime*		35	96	88	*relations*		112	100	87
redundancy	NoC	18	93	87	*regimes*		6	77	86	relationship	NoC	189	100	93
redundancies		6	72	86	regiment	NoC	15	93	81	*relationship*		129	100	94
redundancy		11	86	85	*regiment*		12	89	83	*relationships*		60	98	91
redundant	Adj	12	98	92	*regiments*		3	71	71	relative	Adj	39	99	90
ref	NoC	44	60	20	region	NoC	141	100	91	relative	NoC	36	100	92
ref		39	56	10	*region*		99	100	91	*relative*		9	100	93
ref.		4	16	19	*regions*		42	97	90	*relatives*		27	100	91
refs		1	20	39	regional	Adj	78	95	90	relative to	Prep	10	83	88
refer	Verb	138	100	91	register	NoC	27	99	88	relatively	Adv	79	100	92
refer		38	100	90	*register*		21	99	88	relax	Verb	33	100	91
referred		62	98	89	*registers*		6	76	85	*relax*		18	99	87
referring		18	99	93	register	Verb	35	100	92	*relaxed*		11	97	90
refers		20	95	91	*register*		10	99	91	*relaxes*		1	48	87
referee	NoC	14	85	83	*registered*		20	99	91	*relaxing*		3	89	92
referee		11	78	82	*registering*		3	91	92	relaxation	NoC	13	96	87
referees		3	58	79	*registers*		1	53	82	*relaxation*		12	96	88
reference	NoC	98	100	91	registered	Adj	14	95	80	*relaxations*		1	27	59

Word	PoS	Freq	Ra	Di	Word	PoS	Freq	Ra	Di	Word	PoS	Freq	Ra	Di
relaxed	Adj	14	100	94	reminder	NoC	13	99	95	*replaced*		57	100	92
release	NoC	53	100	89	*reminder*		10	99	94	*replaces*		5	81	90
release		48	100	89	*reminders*		2	84	92	*replacing*		15	98	91
releases		5	75	86	remote	Adj	30	100	93	replacement	NoC	29	100	93
release	Verb	79	100	93	*remote*		29	100	93	*replacement*		26	100	93
release		18	99	92	*remoter*		1	38	82	*replacements*		3	83	90
released		50	100	91	*remotest*		1	51	88	reply	NoC	36	100	93
releases		3	82	91	removal	NoC	22	98	92	*replies*		6	94	91
releasing		7	94	92	*removal*		21	98	92	*reply*		30	100	92
relevance	NoC	17	94	90	*removals*		1	30	60	reply	Verb	75	100	89
relevance		17	94	90	remove	Verb	115	100	95	*replied*		56	99	86
relevant	Adj	79	98	89	*remove*		39	100	94	*replies*		3	73	88
reliable	Adj	22	100	94	*removed*		59	99	96	*reply*		13	99	91
relief	NoC	68	100	94	*removes*		3	84	91	*replying*		3	78	91
relief		66	100	94	*removing*		14	98	94	report	NoC	325	100	88
reliefs		2	47	82	renaissance	NoC	11	89	83	*report*		248	100	86
relieve	Verb	15	100	95	*renaissance*		11	89	83	*reports*		77	100	91
relieve		8	100	94	render	Verb	22	97	92	report	Verb	189	100	89
relieved		5	87	90	*render*		7	90	90	*report*		29	100	95
relieves		1	45	86	*rendered*		9	93	93	*reported*		114	100	85
relieving		1	67	90	*rendering*		2	78	91	*reporting*		12	97	93
relieved	Adj	12	99	92	*renders*		3	66	89	*reports*		35	95	67
religion	NoC	51	100	87	renew	Verb	12	100	92	reportedly	Adv	15	67	63
religion		44	100	87	*renew*		5	96	90	reporter	NoC	19	98	90
religions		7	88	79	*renewed*		5	93	92	*reporter*		12	94	88
religious	Adj	66	100	90	*renewing*		2	71	90	*reporters*		7	93	87
reluctance	NoC	10	95	94	*renews*		0	29	83	reporting	NoC	12	89	84
reluctant	Adj	20	99	96	renewal	NoC	11	93	89	*reporting*		12	89	84
rely	Verb	54	100	92	*renewal*		11	92	89	represent	Verb	155	100	93
relied		13	97	89	*renewals*		0	21	78	*represent*		46	100	93
relies		6	83	91	renewed	Adj	11	95	89	*represented*		54	100	92
rely		27	100	92	rent	NoC	36	100	80	*representing*		23	97	92
relying		7	97	92	*rent*		28	100	76	*represents*		33	96	93
remain	Verb	268	100	95	*rents*		8	89	86	representation	NoC	51	96	90
remain		90	100	95	rent	Verb	14	100	94	*representation*		37	94	91
remained		91	97	93	*rent*		7	99	92	*representations*		14	87	83
remaining		12	98	95	*rented*		4	91	92	representative	Adj	15	88	91
remains		75	98	94	*renting*		2	79	89	representative	NoC	65	99	88
remainder	NoC	17	98	93	*rents*		0	27	83	*representative*		23	99	90
remainder		17	98	93	repair	NoC	26	100	91	*representatives*		43	95	85
remainders		0	13	64	*repair*		15	100	89	reproduce	Verb	16	96	91
remaining	Adj	41	97	93	*repairs*		11	98	91	*reproduce*		6	89	90
remains	NoC	15	95	93	repair	Verb	18	100	94	*reproduced*		7	87	90
remark	NoC	32	100	93	*repair*		8	100	93	*reproduces*		1	46	84
remark		12	98	91	*repaired*		5	98	93	*reproducing*		2	69	88
remarks		19	99	91	*repairing*		4	89	91	reproduction	NoC	13	93	86
remark	Verb	24	97	92	*repairs*		1	54	86	*reproduction*		11	90	85
remark		2	76	89	repay	Verb	11	98	94	*reproductions*		1	52	79
remarked		17	91	91	*repaid*		4	81	88	republic	NoC	58	97	78
remarking		1	70	90	*repay*		6	95	91	*republic*		43	96	81
remarks		3	79	89	*repaying*		1	47	86	*republics*		15	67	66
remarkable	Adj	35	100	94	*repays*		0	28	80	republican	NoC	17	82	80
remarkably	Adv	15	98	94	repayment	NoC	11	90	84	*republican*		12	76	78
remedy	NoC	24	92	80	*repayment*		7	79	82	*republicans*		5	58	81
remedies		10	87	81	*repayments*		4	69	82	reputation	NoC	39	100	95
remedy		13	85	78	repeat	Verb	68	100	92	*reputation*		37	100	95
remember	Verb	268	99	93	*repeat*		27	100	94	*reputations*		2	71	87
remember		191	99	92	*repeated*		32	98	94	request	NoC	51	99	93
remembered		54	99	90	*repeating*		6	100	95	*request*		38	99	92
remembering		15	99	90	*repeats*		2	75	87	*requests*		13	96	91
remembers		8	98	92	repeatedly	Adv	13	97	94	request	Verb	27	100	91
remind	Verb	55	100	93	repetition	NoC	11	97	88	*request*		7	97	89
remind		17	99	91	*repetition*		9	97	88	*requested*		15	98	91
reminded		24	100	90	*repetitions*		1	54	81	*requesting*		4	91	88
reminding		6	91	91	replace	Verb	111	100	93	*requests*		1	51	80
reminds		7	97	94	*replace*		34	100	95	require	Verb	284	100	92

Word	PoS	Freq	Ra	Di	Word	PoS	Freq	Ra	Di	Word	PoS	Freq	Ra	Di
require		69	100	92	resignation		22	96	72	restored		18	97	92
required		144	100	92	resignations		2	56	72	restores		1	46	83
requires		53	98	91	resist	Verb	35	100	96	restoring		4	86	90
requiring		18	94	91	resist		20	100	95	restraint	NoC	15	97	81
required	Adj	20	98	91	resisted		10	98	93	restraint		11	97	78
requirement	NoC	93	99	91	resisting		4	88	93	restraints		4	77	80
requirement		32	93	89	resists		1	52	84	restrict	Verb	40	99	92
requirements		60	97	91	resistance	NoC	38	98	92	restrict		11	89	90
rescue	NoC	17	100	91	resistance		37	98	92	restricted		21	97	93
rescue		17	100	91	resistances		1	26	70	restricting		5	84	91
rescues		0	29	78	resolution	NoC	44	98	85	restricts		2	65	86
rescue	Verb	17	100	93	resolution		37	97	86	restriction	NoC	40	97	88
rescue		7	96	93	resolutions		7	83	82	restriction		12	92	84
rescued		8	94	90	resolve	Verb	41	99	94	restrictions		27	94	88
rescues		1	93	89	resolve		15	96	93	result	NoC	334	100	94
rescuing		2	77	91	resolved		21	99	94	result		187	100	94
research	NoC	258	100	83	resolves		1	61	88	results		147	100	91
research		256	100	82	resolving		4	85	89	result	Verb	88	100	93
researches		2	70	87	resort	NoC	23	100	85	result		34	94	93
research	Verb	20	100	66	resort		19	99	86	resulted		29	96	92
research		14	94	51	resorts		5	69	79	resulting		18	90	91
researched		3	80	90	resource	NoC	128	100	92	results		7	86	91
researches		0	21	79	resource		22	88	90	resulting	Adj	14	85	92
researching		3	87	92	resources		105	100	92	resume	Verb	18	98	90
researcher	NoC	36	91	86	respect	NoC	64	100	95	resume		7	95	87
researcher		11	85	80	respect		49	100	96	resumed		9	93	89
researchers		25	88	85	respects		15	100	92	resumes		1	49	86
resemble	Verb	18	98	93	respect	Verb	19	100	95	resuming		1	65	89
resemble		6	93	91	respect		9	100	94	retail	Adj	20	88	90
resembled		4	86	92	respected		8	96	94	retailer	NoC	14	81	82
resembles		5	83	91	respecting		0	26	82	retailer		7	67	71
resembling		4	85	91	respects		1	67	88	retailers		7	88	87
resentment	NoC	11	95	93	respectable	Adj	12	99	92	retain	Verb	65	100	94
resentment		10	95	93	respective	Adj	12	96	92	retain		25	99	94
resentments		1	41	84	respectively	Adv	32	87	88	retained		24	97	93
reservation	NoC	16	97	90	respond	Verb	73	100	96	retaining		9	93	93
reservation		6	90	84	respond		35	100	95	retains		7	86	92
reservations		10	97	91	responded		22	96	94	retire	Verb	36	100	94
reserve	NoC	34	100	91	responding		11	97	94	retire		11	100	93
reserve		14	99	91	responds		4	86	91	retired		18	100	92
reserves		20	97	89	respondent	NoC	16	70	84	retires		2	75	87
reserve	Verb	19	100	92	respondent		5	52	72	retiring		4	97	91
reserve		5	91	89	respondents		11	70	86	retired	Adj	11	100	93
reserved		11	98	93	response	NoC	126	100	93	retirement	NoC	35	100	88
reserves		2	57	55	response		100	100	94	retirement		34	100	88
reserving		1	56	86	responses		26	98	91	retirements		1	42	85
reservoir	NoC	11	90	82	responsibility	NoC	122	100	94	retreat	NoC	11	94	92
reservoir		8	88	84	responsibilities		29	100	93	retreat		10	94	92
reservoirs		3	67	77	responsibility		93	100	94	retreats		1	40	80
residence	NoC	19	99	88	responsible	Adj	94	100	95	return	NoC	102	100	93
residence		17	99	88	rest	NoC	143	100	97	return		87	100	94
residences		1	60	86	rest		142	100	97	returns		15	98	88
resident	Adj	12	97	84	rests		1	67	87	return	Verb	225	100	96
resident	NoC	44	100	88	rest	Verb	48	100	94	return		78	100	96
resident		9	97	85	rest		20	100	94	returned		103	98	94
residents		35	99	88	rested		11	92	90	returning		33	99	95
residential	Adj	29	96	87	resting		10	97	90	returns		12	97	92
residue	NoC	10	90	71	rests		7	95	93	R/rev	NoC	11	89	87
residue		4	85	83	restaurant	NoC	51	100	88	R/rev		6	65	81
residues		6	53	61	restaurant		35	100	87	R/rev.		4	59	83
resign	Verb	33	99	81	restaurants		16	100	87	R/revs		1	33	72
resign		10	93	86	restoration	NoC	20	94	87	reveal	Verb	104	99	94
resigned		20	98	77	restoration		20	94	87	reveal		27	97	96
resigning		2	73	86	restorations		1	36	81	revealed		53	99	92
resigns		1	32	82	restore	Verb	40	98	93	revealing		8	96	94
resignation	NoC	24	96	72	restore		17	98	93	reveals		16	90	92

Word	PoS	Freq	Ra	Di	Word	PoS	Freq	Ra	Di	Word	PoS	Freq	Ra	Di
revelation	NoC	14	96	92	Richards	NoP	11	77	83	*risked*		3	84	90
revelation		9	95	91	Richardson	NoP	10	81	86	*risking*		3	87	93
revelations		5	90	89	*Richardson*		10	79	86	*risks*		1	52	87
revenge	NoC	11	96	92	*Richardsons*		0	8	58	ritual	NoC	14	98	89
revenge		11	96	92	rid	Verb	27	100	92	*ritual*		9	97	89
revenue	NoC	53	96	89	*rid*		26	100	92	*rituals*		5	85	87
revenue		41	93	89	*ridding*		0	34	84	rival	Adj	14	93	91
revenues		12	80	76	ride	NoC	20	99	91	rival	NoC	25	95	91
reverse	Verb	23	100	95	*ride*		17	99	92	*rival*		10	94	91
reverse		8	93	93	*rides*		3	78	87	*rivals*		15	94	90
reversed		11	100	95	ride	Verb	52	98	91	river	NoC	114	100	93
reverses		1	50	86	*ridden*		5	77	85	*river*		94	100	93
reversing		3	91	92	*ride*		17	96	90	*rivers*		20	99	87
review	NoC	89	99	91	*rides*		2	72	88	road	NoC	313	100	94
review		79	99	90	*riding*		17	97	91	*road*		273	100	93
reviews		10	92	92	*rode*		11	94	88	*roads*		39	100	93
review	Verb	42	97	93	rider	NoC	17	97	87	roar	Verb	10	87	87
review		17	92	92	*rider*		9	90	87	*roar*		1	48	86
reviewed		15	94	92	*riders*		8	86	85	*roared*		6	72	85
reviewing		7	89	92	ridge	NoC	17	96	86	*roaring*		3	70	88
reviews		3	72	90	*ridge*		13	91	85	*roars*		1	32	80
revise	Verb	12	99	93	*ridges*		4	70	81	Rob	NoP	12	74	79
revise		4	91	92	ridiculous	Adj	19	100	90	*Rob*		12	74	79
revised		6	88	92	rifle	NoC	11	86	89	rob	Verb	10	99	92
revises		0	13	70	*rifle*		7	80	88	*rob*		2	75	90
revising		2	70	89	*rifles*		3	72	89	*robbed*		6	94	89
revision	NoC	14	94	89	right	Adj	354	100	89	*robbing*		2	70	90
revision		11	91	89	*right*		354	100	89	*robs*		0	30	81
revisions		2	71	87	right	Adv	346	100	80	Robert	NoP	79	100	90
revival	NoC	12	88	91	right	NoC	299	100	93	Roberts	NoP	15	87	87
revival		12	88	91	*right*		169	100	94	Robin	NoP	19	97	86
revivals		0	30	81	*rights*		130	100	90	Robinson	NoP	16	95	87
revive	Verb	14	97	93	rightly	Adv	15	99	91	Robyn	NoP	12	23	25
revive		5	92	92	rigid	Adj	14	99	94	rock	NoC	93	100	91
revived		6	95	93	ring	NoC	52	100	94	*rock*		64	100	91
revives		0	27	81	*ring*		40	100	94	*rocks*		29	99	89
reviving		2	71	90	*rings*		12	95	90	rock	Verb	10	96	91
revolution	NoC	49	100	91	ring	Verb	74	100	90	*rock*		3	79	89
revolution		47	100	91	*rang*		27	95	88	*rocked*		4	76	87
revolutions		3	73	86	*ring*		29	97	89	*rocking*		3	79	89
revolutionary	Adj	24	93	86	*ringing*		9	94	90	*rocks*		0	16	74
reward	NoC	28	100	91	*rings*		4	92	92	rod	NoC	19	98	88
reward		17	100	92	*rung*		5	87	84	*rod*		14	95	87
rewards		11	94	88	riot	NoC	18	100	88	*rods*		5	83	87
reward	Verb	15	97	93	*riot*		9	99	89	Roger	NoP	26	100	91
reward		3	82	91	*riots*		9	92	85	role	NoC	210	100	93
rewarded		9	95	93	rip	Verb	12	97	91	*role*		182	100	93
rewarding		2	71	87	*rip*		3	85	91	*roles*		28	99	91
rewards		0	31	81	*ripped*		7	92	90	roll	NoC	23	100	93
Reynolds	NoP	11	87	84	*ripping*		2	65	87	*roll*		15	100	93
rhythm	NoC	21	98	86	*rips*		0	28	81	*rolls*		8	98	93
rhythm		15	97	89	rise	NoC	81	100	93	roll	Verb	49	100	92
rhythms		6	81	71	*rise*		72	100	93	*roll*		18	99	88
rib	NoC	12	93	86	*rises*		9	95	89	*rolled*		20	98	88
rib		5	77	71	rise	Verb	155	100	94	*rolling*		10	99	93
ribs		7	84	89	*rise*		34	100	93	*rolls*		1	72	89
ribbon	NoC	10	95	91	*risen*		17	97	93	rolling	Adj	11	97	92
ribbon		7	92	90	*rises*		9	94	92	Roman	Adj	44	100	93
ribbons		3	81	90	*rising*		36	100	95	Roman	NoC	15	97	82
rice	NoC	16	97	89	*rose*		59	100	89	*Roman*		7	79	65
rice		16	97	89	rising	Adj	11	100	94	*Romans*		9	88	84
rich	Adj	79	100	95	risk	NoC	129	100	91	romance	NoC	11	95	91
rich		67	100	95	*risk*		104	99	90	*romance*		10	93	90
richer		7	97	93	*risks*		25	99	92	*romances*		1	58	87
richest		5	86	91	risk	Verb	21	100	94	Romania	NoP	12	70	75
Richard	NoP	100	100	91	*risk*		15	100	93	romantic	Adj	21	96	92

1.1

Word	PoS	Freq	Ra	Di	Word	PoS	Freq	Ra	Di	Word	PoS	Freq	Ra	Di
Rome	NoP	34	100	89	rude	Adj	10	94	91	S	NoP	29	87	85
Rome		34	100	89	*rude*		10	94	90	*S*		10	70	68
Ron	NoP	13	89	88	*ruder*		0	19	78	*S.*		19	85	84
Ron		13	89	88	*rudest*		0	13	70	sack	NoC	12	97	88
roof	NoC	48	100	93	rug	NoC	14	79	55	*sack*		8	92	86
roof		41	100	93	*rug*		7	72	65	*sacks*		4	85	90
roofs		7	96	90	*rugs*		7	64	43	sack	Verb	13	99	90
room	NoC	364	100	92	rugby	NoC	29	95	76	*sack*		2	74	89
room		309	100	91	ruin	NoC	11	94	92	*sacked*		9	98	88
rooms		55	100	91	*ruin*		4	85	91	*sacking*		1	51	86
root	NoC	45	100	94	*ruins*		7	92	90	*sacks*		0	13	72
root		20	100	92	rule	NoC	187	100	91	sacred	Adj	13	99	90
roots		25	100	93	*rule*		82	100	90	sacrifice	NoC	11	97	91
root	Verb	10	99	93	*rules*		105	100	91	*sacrifice*		8	96	91
root		2	59	85	rule	Verb	41	100	93	*sacrifices*		3	87	90
rooted		7	97	93	*rule*		12	100	94	sad	Adj	36	100	94
rooting		1	55	84	*ruled*		24	98	91	*sad*		34	100	94
roots		0	17	74	*rules*		4	91	84	*sadder*		1	45	87
rope	NoC	22	95	90	*ruling*		1	48	86	*saddest*		1	50	87
rope		16	93	88	ruler	NoC	16	97	88	sadly	Adv	19	98	94
ropes		6	87	91	*ruler*		9	92	88	safe	Adj	78	100	95
rose	NoC	41	99	89	*rulers*		7	89	88	*safe*		66	100	95
rose		25	99	89	ruling	Adj	22	89	69	*safer*		9	98	87
roses		15	94	85	ruling	NoC	13	87	84	*safest*		3	90	92
Rose	NoP	28	95	80	*ruling*		12	86	83	safely	Adv	17	100	94
Ross	NoP	19	93	84	*rulings*		1	45	82	safety	NoC	86	100	93
Ross		19	93	84	rumour	NoC	20	100	93	*safety*		86	100	93
rough	Adj	35	100	94	*rumour*		7	98	93	sail	NoC	12	86	78
rough		34	100	94	*rumours*		13	98	92	*sail*		7	75	70
rougher		1	45	84	run	NoC	60	100	94	*sails*		5	80	86
roughest		0	29	81	*run*		47	100	94	sail	Verb	27	100	88
roughly	Adv	23	100	94	*runs*		13	97	86	*sail*		9	97	85
round	Adj	28	100	94	run	Verb	406	100	96	*sailed*		8	95	91
round		28	100	93	*ran*		87	100	91	*sailing*		10	95	84
rounder		0	25	77	*run*		174	100	96	*sails*		0	32	83
round	Adv	138	100	89	*runnin'*		0	12	63	sailor	NoC	12	95	88
round	NoC	47	99	87	*running*		104	100	95	*sailor*		5	84	89
round		35	99	86	*runs*		40	99	93	*sailors*		7	89	86
rounds		12	97	90	runner	NoC	15	95	87	saint	NoC	16	97	90
round	Prep	115	100	91	*runner*		7	90	89	*saint*		6	88	90
round	Verb	15	100	94	*runners*		8	80	85	*saints*		10	94	88
round		4	94	93	running	Adj	14	100	94	sake	NoC	33	100	91
rounded		7	96	93	running	NoC	22	100	95	*sake*		32	100	91
rounding		2	79	91	*running*		22	100	95	*sakes*		1	36	81
rounds		1	52	86	*runnings*		0	8	58	salad	NoC	14	83	88
route	NoC	78	100	92	rural	Adj	63	98	85	*salad*		11	83	87
route		56	100	92	rush	NoC	14	99	92	*salads*		3	62	84
routes		21	97	90	*rush*		13	99	92	salary	NoC	29	100	91
routine	NoC	35	100	94	*rushes*		2	51	84	*salaries*		9	92	91
routine		29	100	95	rush	Verb	33	100	92	*salary*		20	100	90
routines		6	91	87	*rush*		8	92	93	sale	NoC	192	100	89
Rover	NoP	13	83	78	*rushed*		15	98	90	*sale*		88	100	88
row	NoC	68	100	88	*rushes*		1	65	89	*sales*		104	100	89
row		48	100	90	*rushing*		8	94	92	Sally	NoP	15	88	78
rows		20	95	78	Russell	NoP	21	97	90	*Sally*		15	88	78
Roy	NoP	18	96	89	*Russell*		21	96	90	salmon	NoC	13	96	89
Roy		18	96	89	*Russells*		0	12	49	*salmon*		13	96	89
royal	Adj	147	100	92	Russia	NoP	43	99	85	salt	NoC	33	100	90
rub	Verb	23	97	90	*Russia*		43	99	85	*salt*		29	100	90
rub		6	88	91	Russian	Adj	52	100	85	*salts*		4	73	83
rubbed		9	87	86	Russian	NoC	16	94	88	salvation	NoC	11	97	87
rubbing		6	88	89	*Russian*		3	70	79	Sam	NoP	31	97	84
rubs		1	49	87	*Russians*		13	93	88	*Sam*		31	97	84
rubber	Adj	11	98	93	Ruth	NoP	30	90	66	same	DetP	615	100	98
rubbish	NoC	23	99	91	*Ruth*		30	90	66	sample	NoC	71	99	89
rubbish		23	99	91	S / s	Lett	74	100	87	*sample*		44	99	88

Word	PoS	Freq	Ra	Di	Word	PoS	Freq	Ra	Di	Word	PoS	Freq	Ra	Di
samples		27	98	85	*scattered*		11	98	94	*screaming*		12	96	89
Samuel	NoP	13	93	85	*scattering*		3	61	81	*screams*		1	46	86
San	NoP-	25	93	86	*scatters*		0	16	59	screen	NoC	57	100	90
sanction	NoC	16	89	83	scene	NoC	89	100	95	*screen*		48	100	89
sanction		4	77	89	*scene*		68	100	95	*screens*		9	98	91
sanctions		13	77	80	*scenes*		21	100	94	screen	Verb	11	96	88
sand	NoC	34	100	92	scent	NoC	11	88	88	*screen*		2	76	89
sand		30	100	92	*scent*		9	84	88	*screened*		5	91	91
sands		4	79	89	*scents*		2	53	81	*screening*		3	69	77
sandwich	NoC	19	98	90	schedule	NoC	30	99	89	*screens*		0	27	81
sandwich		10	94	90	*schedule*		24	99	88	screw	Verb	11	91	89
sandwiches		9	90	89	*schedules*		6	89	83	*screw*		3	77	88
Santa	NoP-	12	89	77	schedule	Verb	16	93	83	*screwed*		5	80	88
Sara	NoP	13	69	57	*schedule*		1	55	82	*screwing*		2	52	85
Sara		13	68	57	*scheduled*		14	93	81	*screws*		1	31	81
Sarah	NoP	35	94	84	*scheduling*		1	38	80	script	NoC	16	98	89
Sarah		35	94	84	scheme	NoC	170	100	92	*script*		12	98	88
satellite	NoC	22	97	81	*scheme*		119	100	92	*scripts*		4	76	87
satellite		17	97	84	*schemes*		51	99	92	scrutiny	NoC	12	95	92
satellites		5	78	70	scholar	NoC	18	96	88	*scrutinies*		0	10	56
satisfaction	NoC	30	100	93	*scholar*		7	94	87	*scrutiny*		12	95	92
satisfaction		29	100	94	*scholars*		11	87	87	sculpture	NoC	19	93	76
satisfactions		1	40	82	scholarship	NoC	11	93	89	*sculpture*		13	87	78
satisfactory	Adj	22	99	93	*scholarship*		9	91	88	*sculptures*		6	72	69
satisfied	Adj	31	100	93	*scholarships*		2	65	85	sea	NoC	139	100	94
satisfy	Verb	29	98	93	school	NoC	529	100	93	*sea*		130	100	94
satisfied		5	94	94	*school*		375	100	94	*seas*		9	97	91
satisfies		3	69	84	*schools*		154	100	89	seal	NoC	15	99	91
satisfy		20	98	93	science	NoC	127	100	87	*seal*		10	97	92
satisfying		2	76	90	*science*		106	100	86	*seals*		5	80	84
Saturday	NoP	87	100	89	*sciences*		21	88	84	seal	Verb	15	100	95
Saturday		83	99	89	scientific	Adj	59	98	89	*seal*		4	91	92
Saturdays		4	89	90	scientist	NoC	56	100	78	*sealed*		8	98	93
sauce	NoC	16	89	85	*scientist*		20	98	68	*sealing*		2	71	90
sauce		14	81	85	*scientists*		35	96	83	*seals*		1	47	85
sauces		2	55	81	scope	NoC	34	99	91	search	NoC	56	99	88
save	Verb	118	100	95	*scope*		34	99	91	*search*		51	99	88
save		67	100	95	*scopes*		0	9	66	*searches*		5	77	78
saved		32	100	94	score	NoC	45	100	92	search	Verb	43	100	94
saves		5	95	92	*score*		27	100	92	*search*		12	97	93
saving		14	100	95	*scores*		17	100	91	*searched*		11	98	91
saving	NoC	41	100	92	score	Verb	51	100	87	*searches*		1	35	73
saving		10	99	92	*score*		14	94	87	*searching*		19	99	93
savings		31	100	90	*scored*		28	100	85	season	NoC	122	100	87
say	Verb	3344	100	92	*scores*		1	59	86	*season*		109	100	87
said		2087	100	90	*scoring*		7	89	87	*seasons*		12	97	90
say		679	100	91	Scot	NoC	16	90	84	seat	NoC	109	100	91
sayed		0	3	42	*Scot*		3	76	86	*seat*		62	100	93
sayin'		1	15	62	*Scots*		12	84	82	*seats*		47	100	82
saying		180	100	91	Scotland	NoP	131	100	87	seat	Verb	11	94	89
says		398	100	88	*Scotland*		131	100	87	*seat*		0	23	80
scale	NoC	89	100	93	Scott	NoP	32	96	87	*seated*		9	91	88
scale		74	100	93	*Scott*		32	96	87	*seating*		1	64	87
scales		15	99	86	*Scotts*		0	19	68	*seats*		0	10	69
scan	Verb	12	97	90	Scottish	Adj	98	99	82	second	NoC	98	100	95
scan		3	78	84	scrap	NoC	10	99	93	*second*		56	100	95
scanned		4	80	88	*scrap*		6	93	92	*seconds*		42	100	93
scanning		4	84	88	*scraps*		4	91	92	second	Ord	358	100	96
scans		0	27	80	scratch	Verb	12	96	91	secondary	Adj	43	99	90
scandal	NoC	18	99	85	*scratch*		4	91	92	secondly	Adv	29	96	92
scandal		15	98	84	*scratched*		5	83	87	secret	Adj	36	100	93
scandals		3	76	83	*scratches*		0	17	75	secret	NoC	36	100	93
scarcely	Adv	17	92	92	*scratching*		3	82	90	*secret*		22	100	93
scared	Adj	12	92	89	scream	Verb	29	98	88	*secrets*		14	98	90
scatter	Verb	16	98	93	*scream*		5	82	87	secretary	NoC	162	100	86
scatter		2	75	89	*screamed*		11	80	84	*secretaries*		8	97	92

Word	PoS	Freq	Ra	Di	Word	PoS	Freq	Ra	Di	Word	PoS	Freq	Ra	Di
secretary		154	100	86	*sells*		9	96	90	*sergeant*		26	92	82
section	NoC	232	100	87	*sold*		84	100	94	*sergeants*		2	48	82
section		186	100	86	seller	NoC	24	92	61	series	NoC	144	100	93
sections		46	100	91	*seller*		19	84	56	serious	Adj	124	100	97
sector	NoC	110	97	90	*sellers*		5	79	78	seriously	Adv	57	100	97
sector		87	97	90	selling	NoC	12	95	88	serum	NoC	13	43	49
sectors		23	81	88	*selling*		12	95	88	*serum*		13	41	49
secure	Adj	18	100	94	semantic	Adj	13	61	70	*serums*		0	7	59
secure		18	100	94	semi-final	NoC	10	55	77	servant	NoC	48	100	93
secure	Verb	57	99	93	*semi-final*		6	44	75	*servant*		18	98	91
secure		28	99	93	*semi-finals*		4	48	79	*servants*		30	99	92
secured		19	97	93	seminar	NoC	19	94	86	serve	Verb	159	100	95
secures		1	53	85	*seminar*		12	88	86	*serve*		53	100	95
securing		9	90	91	*seminars*		8	82	84	*served*		64	100	94
security	NoC	158	100	88	senate	NoC	13	80	69	*serves*		17	100	92
securities		19	69	81	*senate*		13	80	69	*serving*		25	100	94
security		138	100	88	send	Verb	250	100	97	server	NoC	22	51	46
sediment	NoC	11	60	66	*send*		80	100	96	*server*		15	42	48
sediment		6	54	67	*sending*		26	100	96	*servers*		7	31	39
sediments		5	31	62	*sends*		6	98	93	service	NoC	549	100	93
see	Verb	1920	100	95	*sent*		137	100	97	*service*		300	100	94
saw		261	100	92	senior	Adj	82	100	92	*services*		249	100	91
see		1186	100	93	sensation	NoC	19	92	86	service	Verb	11	98	92
seeing		61	100	94	*sensation*		14	92	88	*service*		6	90	91
seen		376	100	97	*sensations*		5	80	80	*serviced*		3	84	90
sees		35	100	95	sense	NoC	229	100	95	*services*		0	22	79
seed	NoC	32	100	90	*sense*		213	100	95	*servicing*		3	74	90
seed		16	99	91	*senses*		16	97	90	session	NoC	66	100	91
seeds		16	99	91	sense	Verb	20	97	88	*session*		44	100	89
seek	Verb	169	100	94	*sense*		6	93	90	*sessions*		21	100	92
seek		54	98	94	*sensed*		10	84	85	set	NoC	140	100	95
seeking		46	98	95	*senses*		1	48	86	*set*		112	100	95
seeks		15	92	90	*sensing*		3	70	87	*sets*		29	100	93
sought		53	99	92	sensible	Adj	28	100	94	set	Verb	398	100	97
seem	Verb	624	100	96	sensitive	Adj	36	100	94	*set*		332	100	97
seem		170	99	97	sensitivity	NoC	17	98	88	*sets*		22	100	94
seemed		238	100	90	*sensitivities*		1	55	84	*setting*		45	100	96
seeming		4	86	86	*sensitivity*		16	98	88	setting	NoC	40	100	92
seems		212	100	96	sentence	NoC	86	100	89	*setting*		30	100	93
seemingly	Adv	12	97	95	*sentence*		58	100	90	*settings*		10	90	89
segment	NoC	15	91	82	*sentences*		29	98	87	settle	Verb	74	100	96
segment		7	80	80	sentence	Verb	14	85	82	*settle*		25	100	96
segments		8	86	83	*sentence*		0	11	67	*settled*		39	100	95
seize	Verb	26	97	93	*sentenced*		12	82	81	*settles*		2	82	92
seize		6	94	93	*sentencing*		1	37	79	*settling*		8	99	94
seized		17	96	92	sentiment	NoC	11	97	93	settlement	NoC	59	100	85
seizes		1	44	85	*sentiment*		6	93	92	*settlement*		46	98	85
seizing		2	77	89	*sentiments*		5	91	90	*settlements*		13	89	82
seldom	Adv	15	97	94	separate	Adj	77	100	95	seven	Num	176	100	91
select	Adj	12	95	83	separate	Verb	43	100	93	*seven*		173	100	91
select	Verb	58	100	92	*separate*		15	100	94	*sevens*		3	41	67
select		18	98	89	*separated*		21	99	93	seventeen	Num	18	100	88
selected		29	100	93	*separates*		3	79	91	*seventeen*		18	100	88
selecting		9	95	90	*separating*		5	96	92	seventeenth	Ord	12	91	87
selects		2	72	89	separately	Adv	18	100	93	seventh	Ord	15	100	92
selected	Adj	14	93	89	separation	NoC	19	98	91	seventy	Num	39	99	81
selection	NoC	63	100	92	*separation*		19	98	91	*seventies*		10	95	91
selection		60	100	92	*separations*		1	39	79	*seventy*		29	96	76
selections		2	68	88	Sept	NoP	32	50	46	several	DetP	240	100	96
selective	Adj	13	88	90	*Sept*		2	42	78	severe	Adj	47	100	92
self	NoC	38	100	93	*Sept.*		30	20	43	*severe*		46	100	92
self		36	100	92	September	NoP	104	100	90	*severest*		0	33	84
selves		2	75	90	sequence	NoC	56	98	83	severely	Adv	18	98	94
sell	Verb	213	100	95	*sequence*		42	98	86	sex	NoC	90	100	92
sell		76	100	94	*sequences*		14	77	75	*sex*		83	100	92
selling		43	100	94	sergeant	NoC	28	93	82	*sexes*		7	90	87

Word	PoS	Freq	Ra	Di	Word	PoS	Freq	Ra	Di	Word	PoS	Freq	Ra	Di
sexual	Adj	69	99	87	sheds		0	28	80	shoes		37	100	91
sexuality	NoC	14	89	83	sheep	NoC	30	99	91	shoot	Verb	77	100	94
sexualities		0	6	56	sheep		30	99	91	shoot		15	98	92
sexuality		14	89	83	sheer	Adj	21	100	95	shooting		11	95	93
sexually	Adv	10	97	88	sheer		21	100	95	shoots		2	71	90
shade	NoC	23	99	92	sheet	NoC	66	100	95	shot		49	100	92
shade		14	97	90	sheet		42	100	94	shooting	NoC	13	97	92
shades		9	97	90	sheets		24	98	94	shooting		12	97	92
shadow	NoC	45	100	91	Sheffield	NoP	21	91	87	shootings		1	38	80
shadow		30	100	92	Sheffield		21	91	87	shop	NoC	154	100	94
shadows		15	89	86	shelf	NoC	26	100	93	shop		102	100	93
shaft	NoC	13	97	90	shelf		14	100	93	shops		52	100	95
shaft		9	90	89	shelves		12	98	92	shop	Verb	16	98	92
shafts		4	81	89	shell	NoC	30	100	91	shop		5	95	92
Shah	NoP	11	46	32	shell		20	100	92	shopped		1	40	85
Shah		10	46	34	shells		10	98	89	shopping		10	94	90
Shahs		1	4	09	Shelley	NoP	12	64	40	shops		0	25	80
shake	Verb	93	100	85	Shelley		11	64	40	shopping	NoC	29	99	93
shake		13	98	91	shelter	NoC	16	100	94	shopping		29	99	93
shaken		8	94	90	shelter		14	100	93	shore	NoC	20	99	92
shakes		2	70	86	shelters		2	72	89	shore		15	96	91
shaking		18	95	86	shield	NoC	16	99	77	shores		5	86	89
shook		53	93	81	shield		10	99	84	short	Adj	198	100	97
Shakespeare	NoP	19	96	86	shields		6	73	63	short		177	100	98
Shakespeare		19	96	86	shift	NoC	34	100	93	shorter		18	100	94
shall	VMod	208	100	92	shift		26	100	93	shortest		3	89	92
sha~		5	57	83	shifts		8	99	91	short-term	Adj	17	91	91
shall		202	100	92	shift	Verb	37	100	95	shortage	NoC	21	98	93
shallow	Adj	15	100	93	shift		15	100	93	shortage		15	98	93
shallow		14	100	93	shifted		14	100	93	shortages		6	86	88
shallower		1	43	84	shifting		5	93	93	shortly	Adv	38	100	96
shallowest		0	10	70	shifts		3	80	90	shot	NoC	50	100	90
shame	NoC	19	98	92	shilling	NoC	10	92	87	shot		33	100	90
shame		19	98	92	shilling		4	78	85	shots		18	96	90
shape	NoC	82	100	94	shillings		6	86	87	should	VMod	1112	100	97
shape		62	100	94	shine	Verb	22	96	90	shoulder	NoC	88	98	87
shapes		19	99	92	shine		5	88	88	shoulder		46	97	88
shape	Verb	21	100	93	shined		0	11	71	shoulders		42	97	86
shape		6	97	92	shines		2	83	91	shout	Verb	59	100	88
shaped		11	98	91	shining		7	85	88	shout		10	96	90
shapes		0	27	80	shone		9	83	86	shouted		29	99	84
shaping		4	89	91	ship	NoC	70	100	92	shouting		17	98	90
share	NoC	161	100	86	ship		43	100	90	shouts		2	63	85
share		82	100	87	ships		27	100	91	show	NoC	105	100	92
shares		79	99	84	ship	Verb	16	99	72	show		87	100	91
share	Verb	116	100	97	ship		4	69	56	shows		18	100	92
share		54	100	96	shipped		5	92	84	show	Verb	598	100	95
shared		36	99	96	shipping		6	84	72	show		180	100	97
shares		5	89	91	ships		1	31	64	showed		107	100	94
sharing		21	100	95	shirt	NoC	36	98	89	showing		63	100	96
shared	Adj	15	97	92	shirt		28	96	88	shown		150	100	91
shareholder	NoC	39	89	81	shirts		8	94	92	shows		99	100	93
shareholder		8	74	81	shit	NoC	19	75	78	shower	NoC	19	95	91
shareholders		31	85	80	shit		19	73	78	shower		15	93	90
sharp	Adj	44	100	95	shits		0	22	79	showers		4	85	90
sharply	Adv	25	95	92	shiver	Verb	12	73	82	shrug	Verb	28	82	81
she	Pron	4888	100	86	shiver		2	38	82	shrug		2	66	88
'er		2	18	65	shivered		6	41	79	shrugged		24	73	80
her		1085	100	85	shivering		4	60	83	shrugging		1	37	79
she		3801	100	86	shivers		0	19	77	shrugs		1	36	81
shed	NoC	14	96	90	shock	NoC	45	100	93	shut	Verb	52	100	88
shed		10	90	88	shock		42	100	93	shut		47	100	87
sheds		4	89	90	shocks		3	83	85	shuts		1	59	88
shed	Verb	14	99	93	shocked	Adj	15	100	91	shutting		3	87	90
shed		12	98	93	shoe	NoC	48	100	91	shy	Adj	11	96	93
shedding		2	77	90	shoe		11	95	89	shy		11	96	93

Word	PoS	Freq	Ra	Di	Word	PoS	Freq	Ra	Di	Word	PoS	Freq	Ra	Di
shyer		0	8	64	*simple*		140	100	95	*size*	NoC	144	100	94
sick	Adj	44	100	93	*simpler*		10	96	93	*size*		127	100	94
sick		44	100	93	*simplest*		10	97	91	*sizes*		17	99	92
sicker		0	11	71	simply	Adv	177	100	96	sketch	NoC	12	99	92
sickness	NoC	12	99	91	simultaneously	Adv	18	99	93	*sketch*		6	94	93
sickness		12	99	91	sin	NoC	19	99	90	*sketches*		6	93	86
sicknesses		0	7	50	*sin*		13	99	89	skill	NoC	126	100	92
side	NoC	398	100	97	*sins*		6	90	89	*skill*		35	100	93
side		335	100	96	since	Adv	29	100	96	*skills*		91	99	91
sides		63	100	96	since	Conj	295	100	97	skilled	Adj	18	99	90
sigh	NoC	12	88	82	since	Prep	178	100	93	skin	NoC	75	99	92
sigh		11	85	81	sincerely	Adv	11	95	74	*skin*		69	99	91
sighs		1	44	85	sing	Verb	63	100	93	*skins*		6	91	87
sigh	Verb	25	78	81	*sang*		12	99	91	skirt	NoC	20	92	88
sigh		1	36	82	*sing*		21	98	91	*skirt*		14	87	88
sighed		21	64	80	*singin'*		0	9	64	*skirts*		6	78	87
sighing		2	45	82	*singing*		21	97	93	skull	NoC	14	98	88
sighs		1	48	82	*sings*		3	86	90	*skull*		11	97	87
sight	NoC	74	100	94	*sung*		5	86	90	*skulls*		2	62	83
sight		66	100	93	singer	NoC	20	97	89	sky	NoC	56	100	91
sights		8	93	92	*singer*		13	95	87	*skies*		6	91	92
sign	NoC	106	100	95	*singers*		7	88	86	*sky*		50	100	90
sign		59	100	93	single	Adj	177	100	95	slam	Verb	14	91	86
signs		47	100	95	single	NoC	15	90	83	*slam*		2	60	87
sign	Verb	93	100	90	*single*		6	84	77	*slammed*		9	76	84
sign		25	100	93	*singles*		8	73	84	*slamming*		2	54	84
signed		57	100	86	sink	NoC	13	97	89	*slams*		1	43	83
signing		9	98	90	*sink*		11	90	89	slave	NoC	17	99	86
signs		2	73	88	*sinks*		2	75	84	*slave*		9	98	84
signal	NoC	46	100	90	sink	Verb	32	100	92	*slaves*		8	88	86
signal		28	100	89	*sank*		11	93	87	sleep	NoC	39	98	82
signals		19	100	89	*sink*		8	98	93	*sleep*		39	98	82
signal	Verb	15	99	94	*sinking*		5	96	91	sleep	Verb	68	99	90
signal		4	90	90	*sinks*		1	48	86	·*sleep*		37	98	90
signalled		6	92	93	*sunk*		7	97	93	*sleeping*		11	97	91
signalling		3	86	91	sir	NoC	189	100	92	*sleeps*		2	70	88
signals		2	64	89	*sir*		188	100	92	*slept*		18	95	88
signature	NoC	15	100	90	*sirs*		1	23	66	sleeve	NoC	16	95	89
signature		11	100	88	sister	NoC	95	100	92	*sleeve*		10	91	88
signatures		4	91	90	*sister*		75	100	91	*sleeves*		7	87	89
significance	NoC	47	100	92	*sisters*		20	99	94	slice	NoC	15	96	92
significance		47	100	92	sit	Verb	300	100	90	*slice*		9	96	93
significances		0	11	61	*sat*		121	100	86	*slices*		6	87	89
significant	Adj	121	99	91	*sit*		86	100	91	slide	NoC	15	100	90
significantly	Adv	42	95	82	*sits*		12	99	93	*slide*		9	99	90
silence	NoC	57	100	86	*sitting*		81	100	91	*slides*		6	88	86
silence		56	100	86	site	NoC	155	100	91	slide	Verb	30	99	88
silences		1	48	84	*site*		97	100	92	*slid*		16	87	82
silent	Adj	38	100	88	*sites*		58	99	88	*slide*		7	94	92
silently	Adv	12	79	83	situate	Verb	20	99	88	*slides*		2	69	90
silk	NoC	24	97	90	*situate*		0	29	81	*sliding*		5	90	88
silk		22	97	90	*situated*		20	99	88	slight	Adj	39	100	94
silks		2	46	84	*situates*		0	6	34	*slight*		30	100	94
silly	Adj	29	96	88	*situating*		0	11	68	*slighter*		0	19	76
sillier		0	13	71	situation	NoC	198	100	95	*slightest*		9	99	92
silliest		0	19	77	*situation*		160	100	95	slightly	Adv	89	100	95
silly		28	96	88	*situations*		39	100	92	slim	Adj	13	98	91
silver	NoC	39	100	93	six	Num	305	100	93	*slim*		12	98	91
silver		39	100	93	*six*		303	100	93	*slimmer*		1	47	80
similar	Adj	184	100	94	*sixes*		1	44	79	*slimmest*		0	8	64
similarity	NoC	17	96	90	sixteen	Num	27	99	88	slip	NoC	12	98	91
similarities		9	90	91	*sixteen*		27	99	88	*slip*		9	97	90
similarity		8	92	89	sixth	Ord	25	100	92	*slips*		3	80	91
similarly	Adv	45	97	92	sixty	Num	57	98	82	slip	Verb	51	100	90
Simon	NoP	43	99	89	*sixties*		14	97	92	*slip*		14	97	92
simple	Adj	159	100	95	*sixty*		43	97	77	*slipped*		26	100	88

Word	PoS	Freq	Ra	Di	Word	PoS	Freq	Ra	Di	Word	PoS	Freq	Ra	Di
slipping		9	94	90	snake	NoC	12	94	89	solidarity	NoC	11	90	84
slips		2	84	91	*snake*		7	86	88	*solidarities*		0	5	34
slope	NoC	24	98	91	*snakes*		5	80	86	*solidarity*		11	90	83
slope		14	95	91	snap	Verb	28	98	86	solo	NoC	12	83	81
slopes		10	95	86	*snap*		5	90	90	*solo*		10	82	82
slow	Adj	56	100	96	*snapped*		19	92	83	*solos*		2	40	72
slow		48	100	96	*snapping*		2	66	87	solution	NoC	94	100	90
slower		7	98	93	*snaps*		1	48	83	*solution*		69	100	91
slowest		1	50	87	snatch	Verb	12	95	89	*solutions*		26	95	87
slow	Verb	23	99	94	*snatch*		3	79	89	solve	Verb	38	100	95
slow		8	99	94	*snatched*		7	86	87	*solve*		19	100	94
slowed		9	96	91	*snatches*		0	30	76	*solved*		12	98	95
slowing		4	94	94	*snatching*		2	56	86	*solves*		1	60	89
slows		2	74	90	sniff	Verb	11	85	85	*solving*		6	89	91
slowly	Adv	79	100	89	*sniff*		2	54	86	some	DetP	1712	100	98
small	Adj	518	100	97	*sniffed*		5	55	81	somebody	Pron	73	99	83
small		435	100	97	*sniffing*		4	71	81	somehow	Adv	45	100	91
smaller		73	100	96	*sniffs*		0	22	73	someone	Pron	187	100	93
smallest		11	99	95	snow	NoC	31	97	90	Somerset	NoP	13	92	87
smart	Adj	16	99	93	*snow*		30	97	89	something	Pron	526	100	92
smart		15	99	93	*snows*		1	43	84	sometimes	Adv	205	100	96
smarter		1	54	88	so	Adv	1893	100	93	somewhat	Adv	46	99	95
smartest		1	41	85	so	Conj	258	100	95	somewhere	Adv	70	100	91
smash	Verb	15	96	91	so-called	Adj	27	98	94	son	NoC	166	100	90
smash		3	84	91	so as	ClO	17	96	90	*son*		131	100	92
smashed		9	92	90	so long as	Conj	13	100	93	*sons*		35	100	83
smashes		0	33	83	so that	Conj	197	100	96	song	NoC	68	100	89
smashing		3	80	90	soap	NoC	15	99	92	*song*		40	100	90
smell	NoC	31	99	90	*soap*		13	98	91	*songs*		29	99	87
smell		26	99	89	*soaps*		2	61	85	soon	Adv	161	100	96
smells		5	84	90	soccer	NoC	13	75	79	sooner	Adv	18	100	93
smell	Verb	25	93	88	social	Adj	422	100	90	Sophie	NoP	13	71	55
smell		12	88	88	socialism	NoC	17	91	88	sophisticated	Adj	25	99	94
smelled		4	60	81	*socialism*		17	91	88	sorry	Adj	115	100	86
smelling		3	67	88	socialist	Adj	33	95	85	*sorrier*		0	14	73
smells		3	68	83	socially	Adv	15	98	89	*sorry*		114	100	86
smelt		4	69	84	society	NoC	282	100	93	sort	NoC	229	100	90
smile	NoC	69	99	82	*societies*		44	97	89	*sort*		199	100	90
smile		64	99	82	*society*		238	100	93	*sorts*		30	100	91
smiles		6	84	88	sociology	NoC	20	78	68	sort	Verb	38	99	91
smile	Verb	112	96	82	*sociology*		20	78	68	*sort*		19	98	90
smile		11	88	86	sock	NoC	12	94	89	*sorted*		13	98	90
smiled		76	91	80	*sock*		2	68	88	*sorting*		6	97	91
smiles		3	76	85	*socks*		10	92	88	*sorts*		0	30	83
smiling		22	88	82	sofa	NoC	12	88	86	sort of	Adv	59	93	74
Smith	NoP	86	100	89	*sofa*		10	85	86	soul	NoC	38	100	92
Smith		79	100	89	*sofas*		1	49	84	*soul*		30	99	92
Smiths		7	69	48	soft	Adj	66	100	93	*souls*		8	93	92
smoke	NoC	29	100	91	*soft*		61	100	93	sound	Adj	13	99	94
smoke		29	100	91	*softer*		4	89	92	*sound*		12	99	94
smokes		0	11	71	*softest*		0	33	84	*sounder*		0	29	81
smoke	Verb	29	100	91	softly	Adv	25	86	78	*soundest*		0	13	72
smoke		12	98	91	software	NoC	94	89	66	sound	NoC	129	100	91
smoked		5	90	88	soil	NoC	48	100	86	*sound*		102	100	92
smokes		1	56	83	*soil*		41	100	86	*sounds*		26	98	90
smoking		11	95	89	*soils*		7	60	79	sound	Verb	100	100	92
smoking	NoC	12	96	81	solar	Adj	13	95	81	*sound*		30	99	93
smooth	Adj	30	100	93	soldier	NoC	54	100	93	*sounded*		30	98	86
smooth		28	100	93	*soldier*		18	98	92	*sounding*		6	87	89
smoother		2	67	87	*soldiers*		36	100	91	*sounds*		34	99	92
smoothest		0	18	76	sole	Adj	22	100	91	soup	NoC	15	95	91
smooth	Verb	10	93	89	solely	Adv	17	96	93	*soup*		14	95	91
smooth		3	85	90	solicitor	NoC	58	100	81	*soups*		1	48	82
smoothed		4	66	85	*solicitor*		32	98	84	source	NoC	157	100	93
smoothing		3	64	84	*solicitors*		26	97	77	*source*		91	100	94
smooths		0	20	77	solid	Adj	35	100	95	*sources*		67	98	92

Word	PoS	Freq	Ra	Di	Word	PoS	Freq	Ra	Di	Word	PoS	Freq	Ra	Di
south	NoC	165	100	94	spectator	NoC	12	95	92	spiritual	Adj	23	97	88
south		165	100	94	*spectator*		5	89	89	spit	Verb	11	91	88
South	NoP-	67	100	87	*spectators*		7	87	91	*spat*		5	70	84
south-east	NoC	13	93	90	spectrum	NoC	20	94	81	*spit*		2	68	88
Southampton	NoP	12	88	87	*spectra*		3	32	51	*spits*		1	37	81
Southampton		12	88	87	*spectrum*		16	94	86	*spitting*		2	73	89
southern	Adj	55	100	92	speculation	NoC	19	99	91	splendid	Adj	17	98	93
sovereignty	NoC	12	77	83	*speculation*		17	99	91	split	Verb	32	100	96
sovereignty		12	77	83	*speculations*		2	62	88	*split*		25	100	96
Soviet	Adj	109	96	77	speech	NoC	89	100	92	*splits*		1	60	88
Soviet	NoC	10	76	69	*speech*		78	100	92	*splitting*		5	97	93
Soviet		7	45	56	*speeches*		10	97	90	spoil	Verb	15	99	94
Soviets		4	68	84	speed	NoC	78	100	93	*spoil*		6	96	92
space	NoC	140	100	95	*speed*		70	100	93	*spoiled*		4	87	91
space		125	100	96	*speeds*		9	84	84	*spoiling*		2	70	90
spaces		15	100	87	speed	Verb	18	100	95	*spoils*		1	52	87
Spain	NoP	45	99	90	*sped*		3	70	88	*spoilt*		3	89	92
Spain		45	99	90	*speed*		7	94	93	spokesman	NoC	42	95	82
Spanish	Adj	34	100	91	*speeded*		2	74	91	*spokesman*		40	92	81
Spanish		34	100	91	*speeding*		4	91	91	*spokesmen*		3	68	83
spare	Adj	19	100	95	*speeds*		2	70	88	sponsor	NoC	12	92	88
spare		19	100	95	spell	NoC	18	100	90	*sponsor*		5	83	89
spare	Verb	16	100	94	*spell*		13	99	91	*sponsors*		7	87	85
spare		10	98	93	*spells*		5	89	83	sponsor	Verb	16	96	91
spared		5	93	94	spell	Verb	21	100	91	*sponsor*		3	73	89
spares		0	21	78	*spell*		10	98	84	*sponsored*		11	89	90
sparing		1	44	86	*spelled*		3	82	89	*sponsoring*		2	72	90
spatial	Adj	12	66	82	*spelling*		2	77	88	*sponsors*		0	31	82
speak	Verb	261	100	94	*spells*		2	79	92	sponsorship	NoC	12	88	89
speak		94	100	94	*spelt*		4	94	91	*sponsorship*		12	88	89
speaking		54	100	96	spelling	NoC	10	87	80	*sponsorships*		0	24	78
speaks		14	100	94	*spelling*		9	86	80	spontaneous	Adj	10	96	89
spoke		70	100	91	*spellings*		1	36	75	sport	NoC	89	100	90
spoken		28	100	94	Spencer	NoP	14	93	87	*sport*		45	100	87
speaker	NoC	101	100	67	*Spencer*		13	93	87	*sports*		44	100	91
speaker		80	100	58	*Spencers*		0	11	61	sporting	Adj	11	94	88
speakers		22	97	85	spend	Verb	227	100	97	spot	NoC	54	100	95
special	Adj	220	100	96	*spend*		74	100	96	*spot*		41	100	94
specialise	Verb	12	90	91	*spending*		29	100	94	*spots*		12	98	93
specialise		3	70	87	*spends*		8	99	94	spot	Verb	23	99	93
specialised		3	78	91	*spent*		116	100	97	*spot*		7	98	93
specialises		3	67	88	spending	NoC	37	98	88	*spots*		0	32	84
specialising		3	71	90	*spending*		37	98	88	*spotted*		13	98	91
specialist	NoC	51	100	93	sphere	NoC	18	95	89	*spotting*		2	84	92
specialist		37	100	93	*sphere*		13	93	90	spread	NoC	18	100	92
specialists		14	90	92	*spheres*		5	79	88	*spread*		17	100	92
specially	Adv	20	100	95	spider	NoC	10	89	88	*spreads*		0	26	76
species	NoC	96	99	84	*spider*		7	87	88	spread	Verb	59	100	96
specific	Adj	113	100	92	*spiders*		4	70	84	*spread*		46	100	96
specifically	Adv	38	100	93	spill	Verb	14	99	92	*spreading*		9	98	95
specification	NoC	21	92	84	*spill*		4	90	90	*spreads*		4	94	90
specification		13	84	86	*spilled*		4	82	89	spring	NoC	63	100	95
specifications		8	87	80	*spilling*		3	80	88	*spring*		55	100	95
specified	Adj	12	82	76	*spills*		1	62	89	*springs*		8	97	90
specify	Verb	40	96	79	*spilt*		2	65	87	spring	Verb	18	100	93
specified		21	91	84	spin	Verb	18	97	91	*sprang*		7	83	88
specifies		3	65	80	*spin*		4	86	90	*spring*		5	95	94
specify		13	89	84	*spinning*		6	93	92	*springing*		2	78	92
specifying		4	71	80	*spins*		1	53	83	*springs*		1	63	90
specimen	NoC	25	90	80	*spun*		7	84	86	*sprung*		3	92	92
specimen		11	89	83	spine	NoC	15	90	84	spur	NoC	12	94	85
specimens		15	82	73	*spine*		10	88	87	*spur*		4	89	89
spectacle	NoC	12	96	92	*spines*		5	56	63	*spurs*		7	76	77
spectacle		6	92	92	spirit	NoC	84	100	88	squad	NoC	29	93	86
spectacles		6	84	87	*spirit*		65	100	85	*squad*		25	93	85
spectacular	Adj	19	99	92	*spirits*		19	99	91	*squads*		3	66	84

Word	PoS	Freq	Ra	Di	Word	PoS	Freq	Ra	Di	Word	PoS	Freq	Ra	Di
squadron	NoC	15	79	77	*stand*		19	100	94	*stayed*		34	99	93
squadron		13	73	76	*stands*		7	98	93	*staying*		28	100	93
squadrons		2	48	79	stand	Verb	326	100	92	*stays*		7	99	93
square	Adj	26	100	94	*stand*		92	100	96	steadily	Adv	17	96	94
square	NoC	51	100	95	*standing*		73	100	92	steady	Adj	26	100	96
square		42	100	95	*stands*		29	100	95	*steadier*		0	21	79
squares		9	99	87	*stood*		133	100	87	*steady*		25	100	96
squeeze	Verb	21	99	93	standard	Adj	72	100	91	steal	Verb	48	100	88
squeeze		7	94	92	standard	NoC	152	100	93	*steal*		9	95	93
squeezed		10	98	91	*standard*		56	100	93	*stealing*		9	97	86
squeezes		1	37	84	*standards*		96	100	92	*steals*		1	50	86
squeezing		3	82	89	standing	NoC	28	100	94	*stole*		9	88	84
St	NoC	15	98	89	*standing*		28	100	94	*stolen*		19	98	83
St		13	95	89	*standings*		0	12	71	steam	NoC	29	100	87
St.		2	58	77	Stanley	NoP	14	96	89	*steam*		28	100	87
St	NoP-	127	100	93	*Stanley*		14	96	89	*steams*		0	27	83
St		111	99	92	*Stanleys*		1	6	41	steel	NoC	38	100	94
St.		17	85	87	star	NoC	100	100	90	*steel*		37	100	94
stab	Verb	11	90	87	*star*		61	100	89	*steels*		0	22	77
stab		1	58	87	*stars*		39	100	90	steep	Adj	18	99	92
stabbed		7	82	83	stare	Verb	84	96	82	*steep*		16	99	92
stabbing		2	63	88	*stare*		8	80	84	*steeper*		2	58	87
stabs		0	20	79	*stared*		46	79	80	*steepest*		1	32	81
stability	NoC	22	94	91	*stares*		1	47	80	steer	Verb	12	100	93
stability		21	94	91	*staring*		29	95	83	*steer*		5	96	93
stable	Adj	31	100	93	start	NoC	86	100	96	*steered*		3	77	90
stadium	NoC	11	85	85	*start*		85	100	96	*steering*		3	83	91
stadia		1	23	72	*starts*		2	68	86	*steers*		1	30	71
stadium		10	85	85	start	Verb	414	100	96	stem	NoC	14	96	85
stadiums		1	33	82	*start*		153	100	94	*stem*		8	92	85
staff	NoC	227	100	93	*started*		175	100	95	*stems*		6	82	82
staff		226	100	93	*starting*		47	100	96	stem	Verb	14	97	93
staffs		1	62	86	*starts*		39	99	93	*stem*		5	91	92
staves		0	34	79	starting	NoC	17	98	93	*stemmed*		3	85	91
stage	NoC	203	100	95	*starting*		17	98	93	*stemming*		2	70	90
stage		162	100	96	state	NoC	440	100	90	*stems*		4	80	91
stages		41	99	93	*state*		364	100	90	step	NoC	139	100	96
stage	Verb	16	96	88	*states*		76	100	87	*step*		72	100	95
stage		3	73	86	state	Verb	103	100	91	*steps*		67	100	95
staged		9	84	88	*state*		26	98	92	step	Verb	57	100	91
stages		1	36	81	*stated*		48	99	88	*step*		16	100	95
staging		3	69	85	*states*		19	89	91	*stepped*		29	98	87
staircase	NoC	11	86	89	*stating*		10	95	90	*stepping*		9	95	78
staircase		9	84	88	statement	NoC	140	100	91	*steps*		2	83	91
staircases		2	54	87	*statement*		98	100	90	Stephen	NoP	49	98	81
stairs	NoC	40	98	87	*statements*		41	100	89	sterling	NoC	16	94	84
stair		4	68	82	States	NoP-	85	100	89	*sterling*		16	94	84
stairs		36	97	87	static	Adj	12	98	87	Steve	NoP	44	95	85
stake	NoC	29	99	89	station	NoC	137	100	91	*Steve*		43	95	85
stake		19	99	88	*station*		100	100	93	Steven	NoP	12	81	86
stakes		9	91	84	*stations*		37	99	86	steward	NoC	13	96	89
stall	NoC	14	97	91	statistical	Adj	21	85	87	*steward*		8	94	87
stall		7	93	88	statistics	NoC	32	99	90	*stewards*		6	85	88
stalls		7	92	92	statue	NoC	14	98	88	Stewart	NoP	21	94	88
stamp	NoC	17	100	88	*statue*		9	95	89	*Stewart*		21	92	88
stamp		11	100	84	*statues*		5	88	84	*Stewarts*		1	22	73
stamps		6	88	87	status	NoC	88	100	92	stick	NoC	26	98	92
stamp	Verb	12	100	88	statute	NoC	22	84	80	*stick*		19	97	92
stamp		3	89	90	*statute*		16	80	79	*sticks*		8	94	92
stamped		6	94	91	*statutes*		6	70	78	stick	Verb	61	100	93
stamping		2	73	89	statutory	Adj	37	95	86	*stick*		25	100	92
stamps		1	64	87	stay	NoC	13	100	93	*sticking*		9	97	93
stance	NoC	19	95	88	*stay*		11	99	92	*sticks*		4	90	92
stance		17	95	89	*stays*		2	75	89	*stuck*		22	97	91
stances		1	48	72	stay	Verb	183	100	94	stiff	Adj	16	98	93
stand	NoC	26	100	95	*stay*		114	100	93	*stiff*		15	97	92

Word	PoS	Freq	Ra	Di	Word	PoS	Freq	Ra	Di	Word	PoS	Freq	Ra	Di
stiffer		1	57	88	*straighten*		2	68	85	*stride*	Verb	12	79	84
stiffest		0	14	72	*straightened*		6	61	82	*stride*		1	48	84
still	Adj	29	99	93	*straightening*		2	45	84	*strides*		1	33	82
still		29	99	93	*straightens*		0	16	74	*striding*		3	59	84
still	Adv	718	100	97	straightforward	Adj	20	100	94	*strode*		7	57	82
stimulate	Verb	20	96	90	strain	NoC	29	100	92	strike	NoC	50	100	87
stimulate		10	93	91	*strain*		22	100	91	*strike*		39	100	87
stimulated		7	89	89	*strains*		7	95	89	*strikes*		11	93	85
stimulates		2	56	84	strain	Verb	13	100	91	strike	Verb	74	100	96
stimulating		1	60	88	*strain*		4	87	88	*strike*		18	100	95
stimulus	NoC	23	91	76	*strained*		5	87	88	*strikes*		6	99	94
stimuli		9	69	73	*straining*		4	82	86	*striking*		8	99	94
stimulus		15	88	76	*strains*		1	45	85	*struck*		42	100	94
stir	Verb	25	100	90	strand	NoC	14	96	88	striker	NoC	17	75	77
stir		10	94	87	*strand*		6	91	84	*striker*		13	48	73
stirred		9	88	87	*strands*		8	92	90	*strikers*		4	65	85
stirring		5	85	88	strange	Adj	68	100	92	striking	Adj	17	99	93
stirs		1	52	87	*strange*		64	100	92	string	NoC	41	100	87
Stirling	NoP	10	77	68	*stranger*		2	76	90	*string*		27	100	89
Stirling		10	76	67	*strangest*		1	66	89	*strings*		14	97	80
Stirlings		0	6	52	strangely	Adv	10	92	90	strip	NoC	24	100	94
stitch	NoC	16	84	51	stranger	NoC	23	98	90	*strip*		16	99	93
stitch		7	56	48	*stranger*		13	96	89	*strips*		8	97	91
stitches		9	81	53	*strangers*		10	94	92	strip	Verb	17	100	94
stock	NoC	92	100	93	strategic	Adj	30	94	89	*strip*		4	92	92
stock		76	100	92	strategy	NoC	89	99	91	*stripped*		9	98	93
stocks		16	98	90	*strategies*		27	86	88	*stripping*		3	87	91
stomach	NoC	31	98	89	*strategy*		62	99	92	*strips*		1	67	88
stomach		30	97	89	straw	NoC	15	98	93	strive	Verb	10	98	95
stomachs		2	67	86	*straw*		14	97	93	*strive*		4	90	93
stone	NoC	112	100	92	*straws*		1	58	86	*strived*		0	11	71
stone		79	100	93	stream	NoC	34	100	93	*striven*		1	44	86
stones		33	99	90	*stream*		25	100	94	*strives*		1	52	87
stool	NoC	11	85	78	*streams*		9	92	91	*striving*		3	92	93
stool		9	77	79	street	NoC	243	100	95	*strove*		2	68	89
stools		3	67	75	*street*		194	100	94	stroke	NoC	19	100	94
stop	NoC	24	100	94	*streets*		49	100	94	*stroke*		13	100	93
stop		20	100	94	strength	NoC	83	100	96	*strokes*		6	93	91
stops		4	88	90	*strength*		72	100	96	stroke	Verb	13	94	86
stop	Verb	255	100	93	*strengths*		11	92	92	*stroke*		3	77	89
stop		131	100	94	strengthen	Verb	30	98	93	*stroked*		5	60	81
stopped		96	100	90	*strengthen*		12	94	92	*strokes*		1	49	84
stopping		16	100	95	*strengthened*		10	95	92	*stroking*		3	61	84
stops		12	99	94	*strengthening*		6	86	90	strong	Adj	197	100	97
storage	NoC	30	99	88	*strengthens*		1	69	90	*strong*		160	100	97
storage		30	99	88	stress	NoC	42	100	89	*stronger*		26	100	97
store	NoC	59	100	93	*stress*		38	100	89	*strongest*		10	98	94
store		36	100	90	*stresses*		4	80	86	strongly	Adv	46	99	95
stores		23	100	93	stress	Verb	43	99	92	structural	Adj	27	87	90
store	Verb	33	100	91	*stress*		10	93	93	structure	NoC	181	100	91
store		8	99	91	*stressed*		22	98	90	*structure*		137	100	92
stored		19	97	90	*stresses*		5	75	91	*structures*		44	96	90
stores		1	59	87	*stressing*		5	88	90	struggle	NoC	44	100	92
storing		4	92	91	stretch	NoC	16	99	93	*struggle*		37	100	92
storm	NoC	27	100	93	*stretch*		12	99	93	*struggles*		7	91	86
storm		23	99	92	*stretches*		4	84	88	struggle	Verb	38	100	94
storms		5	92	92	stretch	Verb	47	100	90	*struggle*		7	99	94
story	NoC	184	100	95	*stretch*		13	100	76	*struggled*		14	97	91
stories		48	100	94	*stretched*		20	99	89	*struggles*		2	70	88
story		137	100	95	*stretches*		3	85	92	*struggling*		16	100	94
straight	Adj	32	100	93	*stretching*		11	99	93	Stuart	NoP	22	97	88
straight		31	100	95	strict	Adj	24	100	94	*Stuart*		21	96	87
straighter		1	44	86	*strict*		21	100	94	*Stuarts*		1	31	70
straightest		0	12	68	*stricter*		2	77	87	stuck	Adj	13	97	92
straight	Adv	59	99	92	*strictest*		1	58	88	student	NoC	222	100	88
straighten	Verb	10	87	85	strictly	Adv	20	99	94	*student*		77	100	89

Word	PoS	Freq	Ra	Di	Word	PoS	Freq	Ra	Di	Word	PoS	Freq	Ra	Di
students		146	100	87	substitute	Verb	13	98	91	*suggestion*	NoC	52	100	96
studio	NoC	84	100	53	*substitute*		5	87	92	*suggestion*		31	100	95
studio		76	99	48	*substituted*		5	92	89	*suggestions*		21	99	94
studios		8	85	86	*substitutes*		0	15	71	suicide	NoC	19	99	89
study	NoC	327	100	86	*substituting*		3	72	80	*suicide*		18	99	89
studies		136	100	84	subtle	Adj	18	99	92	*suicides*		1	52	86
study		192	100	87	suburb	NoC	11	96	92	suit	NoC	39	100	92
study	Verb	94	100	93	*suburb*		5	85	90	*suit*		31	100	92
studied		39	98	91	*suburbs*		7	94	91	*suits*		9	95	93
studies		1	50	83	succeed	Verb	54	99	95	suit	Verb	42	100	96
study		30	100	93	*succeed*		21	98	95	*suit*		20	99	94
studying		24	100	94	*succeeded*		26	98	93	*suited*		15	97	95
stuff	NoC	69	100	87	*succeeding*		3	88	92	*suiting*		0	21	80
stuff		69	99	87	*succeeds*		4	84	91	*suits*		7	99	94
stuffs		0	27	76	success	NoC	143	100	94	suitable	Adj	61	100	94
stuff	Verb	12	95	91	*success*		134	100	94	suite	NoC	15	99	90
stuff		3	82	89	*successes*		9	96	93	*suite*		13	98	90
stuffed		7	89	90	successful	Adj	108	100	95	*suites*		3	71	85
stuffing		2	62	88	successfully	Adv	34	98	92	sum	NoC	56	100	92
stuffs		0	17	77	succession	NoC	19	96	92	*sum*		41	100	91
stumble	Verb	11	93	87	*succession*		19	96	92	*sums*		15	100	91
stumble		2	67	89	*successions*		0	14	55	sum	Verb	14	99	94
stumbled		7	87	86	successive	Adj	19	92	92	*sum*		3	81	91
stumbles		0	31	83	successor	NoC	20	95	91	*summed*		6	94	93
stumbling		2	54	85	*successor*		14	94	90	*summing*		2	75	90
stupid	Adj	33	98	86	*successors*		5	79	90	*sums*		3	86	92
style	NoC	127	100	93	such	DetP	763	100	95	summarise	Verb	12	81	84
style		107	100	93	such as	Prep	321	100	93	*summarise*		3	68	88
styles		20	97	91	suck	Verb	16	97	89	*summarised*		6	76	76
subject	NoC	256	100	86	*suck*		4	84	89	*summarises*		2	53	85
subject		179	100	86	*sucked*		6	86	86	*summarising*		1	51	86
subjects		77	100	86	*sucking*		4	82	90	summary	NoC	30	98	88
subject	Verb	15	97	93	*sucks*		1	52	83	*summaries*		2	65	87
subject		1	71	89	sudden	Adj	39	100	90	*summary*		28	98	88
subjected		13	95	93	suddenly	Adv	118	100	88	summer	NoC	116	100	96
subjecting		1	62	89	Sue	NoP	16	91	88	*summer*		113	100	96
subjects		0	20	77	*Sue*		16	91	88	*summers*		3	71	89
subject to	Prep	51	97	88	sue	Verb	16	100	84	summit	NoC	27	94	81
subjective	Adj	12	80	85	*sue*		8	95	81	*summit*		25	93	80
submission	NoC	16	95	81	*sued*		5	83	83	*summits*		2	51	81
submission		11	95	82	*sueing*		0	8	42	summon	Verb	14	98	92
submissions		5	62	76	*sues*		1	32	82	*summon*		4	87	91
submit	Verb	39	99	88	*suing*		2	62	87	*summoned*		9	94	92
submit		12	98	90	suffer	Verb	123	100	95	*summoning*		2	59	87
submits		1	40	59	*suffer*		35	100	95	sun	NoC	115	100	85
submitted		22	95	86	*suffered*		54	100	94	*sun*		115	100	85
submitting		3	83	90	*suffering*		26	100	94	*suns*		1	35	79
subscription	NoC	11	86	89	*suffers*		8	92	92	Sunday	NoP	101	100	93
subscription		8	81	88	sufferer	NoC	13	86	65	*Sunday*		93	100	93
subscriptions		4	76	88	*sufferer*		6	65	50	*Sundays*		8	97	93
subsequent	Adj	43	95	92	*sufferers*		7	76	75	Sunderland	NoP	14	77	59
subsequently	Adv	37	96	91	suffering	NoC	14	100	92	*Sunderland*		14	77	58
subsidiary	NoC	18	86	80	*suffering*		13	100	92	sunlight	NoC	13	93	89
subsidiaries		6	64	82	*sufferings*		2	65	88	sunny	Adj	10	96	93
subsidiary		12	82	77	sufficient	Adj	59	100	93	*sunnier*		0	17	76
subsidy	NoC	18	84	88	sufficiently	Adv	26	98	93	*sunniest*		0	14	73
subsidies		11	76	85	Suffolk	NoP	12	89	82	*sunny*		10	95	93
subsidy		7	81	88	*Suffolk*		12	89	82	sunshine	NoC	13	97	92
substance	NoC	35	100	90	sugar	NoC	38	100	91	super	Adj	16	96	89
substance		22	99	92	*sugar*		36	100	91	superb	Adj	21	100	90
substances		13	92	86	*sugars*		2	53	85	superintendent	NoC	11	86	79
substantial	Adj	62	99	93	suggest	Verb	288	100	95	*superintendent*		10	85	78
substantially	Adv	17	89	92	*suggest*		89	100	94	*superintendents*		0	24	77
substitute	NoC	14	96	92	*suggested*		106	100	96	superior	Adj	20	99	94
substitute		10	94	91	*suggesting*		25	99	94	supermarket	NoC	16	100	92
substitutes		4	75	88	*suggests*		67	98	92	*supermarket*		11	100	92

Word	PoS	Freq	Ra	Di	Word	PoS	Freq	Ra	Di	Word	PoS	Freq	Ra	Di
supermarkets		6	86	90	surgeon		11	98	90	suspending		1	49	79
supervise	Verb	13	100	93	surgeons		6	88	87	suspends		0	24	81
supervise		5	95	91	surgery	NoC	28	99	87	suspension	NoC	15	96	89
supervised		6	94	92	surgeries		1	54	85	suspension		14	96	89
supervises		0	33	83	surgery		27	99	87	suspensions		1	32	72
supervising		2	82	91	surplus	NoC	13	92	87	suspicion	NoC	23	98	94
supervision	NoC	17	97	90	surprise	NoC	51	100	93	suspicion		16	98	94
supervision		17	97	90	surprise		48	100	92	suspicions		6	89	90
supervisor	NoC	11	93	88	surprises		4	95	93	suspicious	Adj	14	100	93
supervisor		8	90	87	surprise	Verb	14	100	91	Sussex	NoP	20	95	82
supervisors		4	72	87	surprise		6	87	91	sustain	Verb	29	98	94
supper	NoC	16	96	89	surprised		7	95	90	sustain		13	96	93
supper		15	96	88	surprises		1	57	89	sustained		12	97	93
suppers		1	37	83	surprising		1	32	81	sustaining		4	85	92
supplement	NoC	15	95	75	surprised	Adj	47	100	91	sustains		1	53	85
supplement		9	90	84	surprising	Adj	35	100	95	swallow	Verb	22	99	89
supplements		6	76	54	surprisingly	Adv	26	99	95	swallow		6	94	92
supplement	Verb	14	97	92	surrender	Verb	12	96	89	swallowed		13	98	85
supplement		6	93	92	surrender		5	90	90	swallowing		3	80	89
supplemented		6	86	90	surrendered		5	83	85	swallows		1	36	82
supplementing		1	56	87	surrendering		1	65	88	swear	Verb	23	98	90
supplements		0	32	83	surrenders		0	26	79	swear		9	87	87
supplier	NoC	32	97	89	Surrey	NoP	16	94	87	swearing		3	77	89
supplier		14	93	86	surround	Verb	45	100	96	swears		1	47	87
suppliers		18	90	90	surround		4	92	92	swore		5	78	87
supply	NoC	95	100	92	surrounded		24	100	95	sworn		6	83	77
supplies		25	100	91	surrounding		14	98	95	sweat	NoC	12	88	88
supply		69	100	89	surrounds		3	81	91	sweat		11	88	88
supply	Verb	76	100	91	surrounding	Adj	17	97	94	sweats		1	28	70
supplied		33	100	91	surroundings	NoC	12	96	93	Sweden	NoP	17	93	90
supplies		7	91	92	survey	NoC	98	100	91	sweep	Verb	31	100	93
supply		26	100	93	survey		79	100	91	sweep		5	95	93
supplying		9	97	93	surveys		19	86	89	sweeping		4	89	91
support	NoC	204	100	93	survey	Verb	12	99	93	sweeps		2	72	88
support		201	100	93	survey		3	83	90	swept		21	97	91
supports		3	81	90	surveyed		4	88	89	sweet	Adj	36	100	92
support	Verb	188	100	93	surveying		4	90	87	sweet		33	100	92
support		97	100	92	surveys		1	54	88	sweeter		1	58	88
supported		56	99	94	surveyor	NoC	12	90	80	sweetest		1	46	86
supporting		20	100	94	surveyor		7	77	78	swell	Verb	10	99	93
supports		14	89	81	surveyors		5	78	80	swell		2	82	91
supporter	NoC	44	99	90	survival	NoC	32	100	92	swelled		2	70	88
supporter		8	93	90	survival		31	100	92	swelling		2	76	88
supporters		37	97	89	survivals		1	33	83	swells		1	37	84
supporting	Adj	11	97	92	survive	Verb	72	100	95	swollen		3	77	91
suppose	Verb	121	99	91	survive		35	100	95	swiftly	Adv	12	95	88
suppose		107	99	90	survived		27	100	94	swim	Verb	25	97	92
supposed		11	96	90	survives		6	87	90	swam		4	79	87
supposes		1	48	86	surviving		4	91	93	swim		9	96	92
supposing		1	61	86	surviving	Adj	12	96	90	swimming		10	93	91
supposed	Adj	54	100	92	survivor	NoC	11	98	94	swims		1	49	83
suppress	Verb	14	96	94	survivor		4	87	91	swum		1	35	82
suppress		6	91	93	survivors		7	92	93	swimming	NoC	18	99	87
suppressed		6	91	93	Susan	NoP	21	89	82	swimming		18	99	87
suppresses		0	31	83	Susan		21	89	82	Swindon	NoP	21	69	48
suppressing		2	78	92	suspect	NoC	12	95	90	Swindon		21	69	48
supreme	Adj	33	99	73	suspect		8	94	89	swing	NoC	15	100	90
sure	Adj	241	100	92	suspects		4	75	88	swing		12	98	89
sure		240	100	92	suspect	Verb	41	100	95	swings		3	83	89
surer		0	32	83	suspect		20	100	94	swing	Verb	34	100	89
surest		1	35	84	suspected		16	97	93	swing		7	95	88
surely	Adv	63	99	93	suspecting		2	67	89	swinging		7	90	88
surface	NoC	103	100	92	suspects		3	82	91	swings		1	66	90
surface		90	100	92	suspend	Verb	24	99	87	swung		18	97	84
surfaces		14	95	89	suspend		4	86	84	Swiss	Adj	14	97	89
surgeon	NoC	17	99	90	suspended		18	98	87	switch	NoC	21	100	88

Word	PoS	Freq	Ra	Di	Word	PoS	Freq	Ra	Di	Word	PoS	Freq	Ra	Di
switch		17	100	88	*tale*	NoC	34	99	85	*taxation*		25	88	88
switches		4	78	85	*tale*		21	99	81	taxi	NoC	22	97	91
switch	Verb	46	100	95	*tales*		13	97	90	*taxi*		19	96	90
switch		16	100	93	talent	NoC	30	99	94	*taxis*		3	81	90
switched		20	100	93	*talent*		21	99	93	taxpayer	NoC	14	85	80
switches		3	83	89	*talents*		9	96	93	*taxpayer*		7	70	75
switching		6	100	92	talk	NoC	101	100	85	*taxpayers*		7	76	83
Switzerland	NoP	15	97	90	*talk*		41	100	95	Taylor	NoP	37	96	87
sword	NoC	19	98	86	*talks*		60	100	75	*Taylor*		36	96	87
sword		15	96	85	talk	Verb	308	100	92	*Taylors*		1	25	77
swords		4	83	88	*talk*		129	100	92	tea	NoC	88	100	90
Sydney	NoP	10	90	88	*talked*		44	100	92	*tea*		86	100	90
symbol	NoC	31	100	88	*talkin'*		1	21	70	*teas*		3	69	85
symbol		18	99	93	*talking*		128	100	90	teach	Verb	104	100	94
symbols		13	96	92	*talks*		7	94	93	*taught*		38	99	94
symbolic	Adj	14	98	89	tall	Adj	53	100	91	*teach*		28	99	94
sympathetic	Adj	15	99	95	*tall*		46	100	91	*teaches*		5	92	92
sympathy	NoC	24	100	95	*taller*		6	86	89	*teaching*		33	100	91
sympathies		3	79	89	*tallest*		2	65	85	teacher	NoC	203	100	90
sympathy		22	100	95	tank	NoC	48	100	78	*teacher*		87	100	90
symptom	NoC	37	100	82	*tank*		33	98	73	*teachers*		116	100	88
symptom		6	90	85	*tanks*		15	96	87	teaching	NoC	59	100	89
symptoms		31	100	81	tap	NoC	16	99	88	*teaching*		57	100	89
syndrome	NoC	13	97	84	*tap*		12	96	89	*teachings*		2	65	83
syndrome		12	97	84	*taps*		4	83	83	team	NoC	226	100	91
syndromes		1	20	70	tap	Verb	22	99	84	*team*		186	100	91
synthesis	NoC	12	79	76	*tap*		9	95	64	*teams*		39	98	91
syntheses		0	15	69	*tapped*		8	91	86	tear	NoC	49	100	88
synthesis		12	79	75	*tapping*		4	94	92	*·tear*		6	96	91
system	NoC	619	100	89	*taps*		1	45	83	*tears*		43	100	86
system		447	100	91	tape	NoC	60	100	88	tear	Verb	29	100	91
systems		173	100	80	*tape*		46	100	88	*tear*		6	91	91
systematic	Adj	17	88	90	*tapes*		14	100	86	*tearing*		5	88	89
T / t	Lett	60	99	84	target	NoC	91	100	90	*tears*		0	36	84
T	NoP	17	86	85	*target*		65	100	88	*tore*		7	85	87
T		5	65	77	*targets*		26	97	92	*torn*		10	100	91
T.		12	84	81	target	Verb	15	95	88	technical	Adj	68	100	93
T-shirt	NoC	10	88	90	*target*		3	82	88	technically	Adv	10	100	94
T-shirt		7	80	88	*targeted*		7	85	88	technique	NoC	105	100	92
T-shirts		4	78	88	*targeting*		4	75	86	*technique*		46	100	91
table	NoC	231	100	94	*targets*		0	18	69	*techniques*		59	97	91
table		201	100	94	*targetted*		0	8	41	technological	Adj	16	89	89
tables		29	100	95	*targetting*		0	10	62	technology	NoC	133	100	84
tablet	NoC	13	94	89	tariff	NoC	12	81	83	*technologies*		15	72	71
tablet		3	75	86	*tariff*		7	73	78	*technology*		118	100	85
tablets		9	91	88	*tariffs*		6	57	80	Ted	NoP	11	95	87
tackle	Verb	31	100	93	task	NoC	129	100	93	teenage	Adj	11	95	90
tackle		16	100	93	*task*		92	100	93	teenager	NoC	18	99	88
tackled		7	96	93	*tasks*		37	96	91	*teenager*		9	93	86
tackles		1	55	86	taste	NoC	43	100	95	*teenagers*		9	94	88
tackling		6	95	92	*taste*		34	100	95	tel	NoC	13	69	78
tactic	NoC	18	98	92	*tastes*		8	97	93	*tel*		12	68	77
tactic		4	84	91	taste	Verb	15	96	91	*tel.*		1	35	76
tactics		14	97	92	*taste*		7	91	89	telecommunica-				
tail	NoC	32	99	89	*tasted*		5	78	89	tion	NoC	13	75	67
tail		27	98	88	*tastes*		2	58	83	*telecommunication*		1	41	81
tails		5	89	89	*tasting*		1	47	85	*telecommunications*		13	74	66
take	Verb	1797	100	98	tax	NoC	184	100	88	telegraph	NoC	12	98	90
take		715	100	97	*tax*		156	100	88	*telegraph*		12	98	90
taken		355	100	98	*taxes*		28	98	88	*telegraphs*		0	15	73
takes		118	100	96	tax	Verb	14	98	84	telephone	NoC	72	100	94
taking		218	100	98	*tax*		7	88	80	*telephone*		67	100	94
took		391	100	95	*taxed*		6	86	84	*telephones*		5	95	91
takeover	NoC	15	85	81	*taxes*		0	10	66	telephone	Verb	23	100	92
takeover		11	81	81	*taxing*		1	51	87	*telephone*		14	99	90
takeovers		3	50	75	taxation	NoC	25	89	88	*telephoned*		7	91	89

Word	PoS	Freq	Ra	Di	Word	PoS	Freq	Ra	Di	Word	PoS	Freq	Ra	Di
telephones		0	21	79	*terminates*		1	41	82	*theme*		39	100	91
telephoning		2	72	87	*terminating*		1	67	89	*themes*		16	92	90
television	NoC	102	100	93	terrace	NoC	24	97	85	themselves	Pron	237	100	96
television		100	100	93	*terrace*		18	96	85	*theirselves*		0	12	67
televisions		1	60	87	*terraces*		6	85	82	*themselves*		237	100	96
tell	Verb	775	100	93	terrible	Adj	47	100	91	then	Adj	12	100	90
tell		307	100	90	terribly	Adv	13	97	91	then	Adv	1595	100	94
tellin'		0	12	64	territorial	Adj	12	93	85	theology	NoC	12	83	73
telling		58	100	92	territory	NoC	45	100	87	*theologies*		0	11	69
tells		37	99	95	*territories*		14	91	83	*theology*		11	83	73
told		372	100	93	*territory*		31	100	88	theoretical	Adj	30	88	88
temper	NoC	13	98	91	terror	NoC	16	98	91	theory	NoC	168	100	89
temper		12	95	87	*terror*		15	97	91	*theories*		37	98	87
tempers		2	68	88	*terrors*		1	60	88	*theory*		131	100	90
temperature	NoC	58	100	89	terrorist	NoC	15	92	86	therapy	NoC	21	96	86
temperature		44	100	89	*terrorist*		8	83	87	*therapies*		2	46	78
temperatures		14	93	87	*terrorists*		7	78	84	*therapy*		19	96	86
temple	NoC	21	95	85	Terry	NoP	25	96	89	there	Adv	746	100	88
temple		14	90	86	*Terry*		25	96	89	there	Ex	2532	100	97
temples		6	85	83	test	NoC	159	100	92	thereafter	Adv	14	95	91
temporarily	Adv	13	98	95	*test*		109	100	91	thereby	Adv	27	93	92
temporary	Adj	38	100	83	*tests*		50	100	92	therefore	Adv	232	100	93
tempt	Verb	16	100	95	test	Verb	70	100	94	these	DetP	1254	100	95
tempt		3	85	92	*test*		28	100	94	thesis	NoC	18	91	70
tempted		12	100	95	*tested*		26	100	93	*theses*		5	57	35
tempting		0	35	84	*testing*		14	100	94	*thesis*		13	88	82
tempts		0	23	80	*tests*		1	64	88	they	Pron	6081	100	95
temptation	NoC	13	99	94	testament	NoC	13	91	83	*'em*		16	85	85
temptation		11	99	94	*testament*		12	91	83	*them*		1733	100	96
temptations		2	67	89	*testaments*		1	36	84	*they*		4332	100	95
ten	Num	210	100	92	testing	NoC	20	97	91	thick	Adj	51	100	93
ten		203	100	92	*testing*		20	97	91	*thick*		46	100	92
tens		7	93	92	Texas	NoP	10	92	79	*thicker*		4	84	91
tenant	NoC	45	97	68	text	NoC	100	100	88	*thickest*		1	42	84
tenant		26	90	47	*text*		77	100	88	thief	NoC	17	98	86
tenants		20	95	89	*texts*		23	89	86	*thief*		8	86	89
tend	Verb	118	100	94	textile	NoC	13	91	90	*thieves*		10	88	78
tend		62	100	93	*textile*		7	85	88	thigh	NoC	15	83	83
tended		27	100	93	*textiles*		5	81	90	*thigh*		8	81	76
tending		4	91	91	texture	NoC	12	95	90	*thighs*		8	69	84
tends		24	98	92	*texture*		9	95	90	thin	Adj	56	100	92
tendency	NoC	36	100	92	*textures*		3	68	87	*thin*		51	100	92
tendencies		7	90	90	Thames	NoP	18	99	87	*thinner*		4	88	92
tendency		29	100	92	than	Conj	1033	100	98	*thinnest*		0	30	82
tender	Adj	13	100	93	thank	Verb	131	100	84	thing	NoC	776	100	92
tennis	NoC	28	98	82	*thank*		122	100	83	*thing*		352	100	91
tension	NoC	43	99	92	*thanked*		7	92	90	*things*		424	100	93
tension		33	99	92	*thanking*		2	77	90	think	Verb	1520	100	90
tensions		10	94	90	*thanks*		0	27	82	*think*		916	100	87
tent	NoC	16	96	88	thanks	NoC	62	100	92	*thinking*		92	100	92
tent		12	94	88	that	Adv	52	100	92	*thinks*		39	99	94
tents		4	85	88	that	Conj	7308	100	97	*thought*		473	100	91
tenth	Ord	11	100	91	that	DetP	3792	100	90	thinking	NoC	43	100	96
term	NoC	288	100	92	that is	Adv	46	100	93	*thinking*		43	100	96
term		123	100	92	Thatcher	NoP	34	94	83	third	Ord	211	100	95
terms		165	100	90	*Thatcher*		34	94	83	thirteen	Num	22	98	87
term	Verb	13	99	92	the	Det	61847	100	98	*thirteen*		22	98	87
term		2	75	90	theatre	NoC	65	100	92	thirty	Num	100	100	84
termed		10	93	91	*theatre*		59	100	92	*thirties*		8	93	92
terms		1	43	86	*theatres*		6	92	92	*thirty*		92	99	83
terminal	NoC	17	95	86	theft	NoC	20	98	83	this	DetP	4623	100	97
terminal		9	93	88	*theft*		17	97	82	Thomas	NoP	68	99	89
terminals		7	81	78	*thefts*		3	60	80	Thompson	NoP	14	90	88
terminate	Verb	11	97	89	their	Det	2608	100	97	*Thompson*		14	90	88
terminate		4	86	84	theirs	Pron	10	99	95	*Thompsons*		0	8	45
terminated		5	89	89	theme	NoC	55	100	92	thorough	Adj	11	98	94

Word	PoS	Freq	Ra	Di	Word	PoS	Freq	Ra	Di	Word	PoS	Freq	Ra	Di
thoroughly	Adv	21	100	95	*tie*		10	100	93	tin	NoC	26	99	92
those	DetP	888	100	96	*tied*		25	100	95	*tin*		20	98	91
thou	Pron	14	92	87	*ties*		3	88	92	*tins*		6	80	90
thee		7	86	83	*tying*		4	90	92	tiny	Adj	56	100	93
thou		7	84	85	tiger	NoC	13	95	83	*tinier*		0	9	66
though	Adv	99	99	86	*tiger*		9	92	83	*tiniest*		1	54	87
though	Conj	245	100	95	*tigers*		4	73	79	*tiny*		55	100	93
thought	NoC	142	100	93	tight	Adj	28	100	96	tip	NoC	31	100	94
thought		95	100	93	*tight*		23	100	95	*tip*		20	100	93
thoughts		47	98	91	*tighter*		5	97	94	*tips*		11	97	91
thousand	NoC	158	100	88	*tightest*		0	36	85	tip	Verb	17	99	94
thousand		104	100	82	tight	Adv	11	98	89	*tip*		5	94	91
thousands		55	100	93	tighten	Verb	15	99	88	*tipped*		8	96	92
thread	NoC	12	96	91	*tighten*		5	93	92	*tipping*		2	75	90
thread		8	94	91	*tightened*		8	89	82	*tips*		2	68	88
threads		4	85	89	*tightening*		2	73	88	tired	Adj	40	99	90
threat	NoC	70	99	94	*tightens*		0	36	85	tissue	NoC	29	97	81
threat		57	98	94	tightly	Adv	17	99	88	*tissue*		21	96	78
threats		14	98	93	tile	NoC	15	94	87	*tissues*		8	85	85
threaten	Verb	68	100	94	*tile*		4	70	84	title	NoC	118	100	82
threaten		9	99	93	*tiles*		12	93	88	*title*		97	100	79
threatened		37	100	92	till	Conj	24	96	87	*titles*		21	99	90
threatening		17	100	93	till	Prep	28	99	85	to	Inf	16470	100	99
threatens		6	89	89	Tim	NoP	34	96	80	*~na**		150	76	66
three	Num	800	100	95	*Tim*		34	96	80	*~ta**		36	59	64
three		797	100	95	timber	NoC	26	98	87	*to*		16284	100	99
threes		2	62	72	*timber*		23	97	86	to	Prep	9343	100	99
threshold	NoC	12	97	93	*timbers*		3	74	88	toast	NoC	10	88	88
threshold		10	96	93	time	NoC	1833	100	98	*toast*		10	85	88
thresholds		2	58	83	*time*		1542	100	98	*toasts*		1	36	83
throat	NoC	35	98	87	*times*		292	100	97	tobacco	NoC	15	100	84
throat		32	95	86	time	Verb	13	100	96	*tobacco*		15	100	84
throats		3	83	90	*time*		8	100	95	today	Adv	263	100	93
throne	NoC	13	99	90	*timed*		3	90	93	toe	NoC	17	96	92
throne		12	98	90	*times*		1	62	85	*toe*		6	94	91
thrones		1	31	79	*timing*		1	48	84	*toes*		10	95	91
through	Adv	95	100	95	timetable	NoC	14	97	90	together	Adv	308	100	98
through	Prep	743	100	98	*timetable*		11	97	89	toilet	NoC	20	97	90
throughout	Prep	116	100	95	*timetables*		2	85	89	*toilet*		15	95	89
throw	Verb	115	100	94	timing	NoC	18	100	94	*toilets*		5	89	90
threw		31	99	89	*timing*		17	100	94	Tokyo	NoP	11	82	83
throw		31	100	94	*timings*		1	47	79	tolerate	Verb	12	98	94
throwing		18	99	94						*tolerate*		6	98	94
thrown		30	100	95						*tolerated*		5	91	92
throws		5	98	93						*tolerates*		0	18	73
thrust	Verb	14	94	86						*tolerating*		0	34	84
thrust		12	91	86						Tom	NoP	55	100	89
thrusting		2	48	82						*Tom*		55	100	89
thrusts		0	30	81						*Toms*		0	23	78
thumb	NoC	14	98	92						tomato	NoC	15	91	85
thumb		11	96	91						*tomato*		7	77	85
thumbs		3	74	89						*tomatoes*		8	86	84
Thursday	NoP	39	99	89						Tommy	NoP	12	88	82
Thursday		37	99	89						*Tommies*		0	8	64
Thursdays		2	68	87						*Tommy*		12	86	82
thus	Adv	205	100	91						tomorrow	Adv	93	100	88
ticket	NoC	48	100	91						ton	NoC	17	99	91
ticket		22	99	93						*ton*		5	88	91
tickets		26	100	89						*tons*		12	97	88
tide	NoC	22	99	92						tone	NoC	51	100	90
tide		18	99	92						*tone*		42	99	90
tides		4	80	87						*tones*		9	90	90
tie	NoC	32	100	94						tongue	NoC	28	99	90
tie		19	98	91						*tongue*		24	99	89
ties		13	99	92						*tongues*		4	84	90
tie	Verb	42	100	96						tonight	Adv	69	96	87

Time periods
(frequencies per million words)

second	98	*fortnight*	15
minute	266	**month**	**398**
hour	**302**	**year**	**1639**
day	**940**	*decade*	62
weekend	73	*century*	233
week	**476**		

Broadly, this frequency list reflects the importance given to time periods founded on natural cycles (*year, day, week, month*) and the lesser status given to periods which are 'man-made' measuring devices multiplying or subdividing the other periods.

Times of day

morning 219; *afternoon* 89; *evening* 153. Other terms: *night* 393; *noon* 7; *day* 940; *dusk* 6; *dawn* 15; *sunset* 6

Word	PoS	Freq	Ra	Di	Word	PoS	Freq	Ra	Di	Word	PoS	Freq	Ra	Di
tonne	NoC	22	78	81	tourism	NoC	15	86	83	*train*		65	100	92
tonne		3	55	82	tourist	NoC	35	100	93	*trains*		19	97	89
tonnes		19	73	80	*tourist*		20	99	92	train	Verb	60	100	95
Tony	NoP	50	99	89	*tourists*		15	95	92	*train*		16	100	93
Tony		50	99	89	tournament	NoC	21	81	84	*trained*		30	100	95
too	Adv	701	100	95	*tournament*		16	74	84	*training*		11	99	92
tool	NoC	54	100	87	*tournaments*		4	63	82	*trains*		3	76	87
tool		22	97	87	toward	Prep	13	98	90	trainee	NoC	13	96	86
tools		32	100	86	towards	Prep	286	100	96	*trainee*		6	93	88
tooth	NoC	54	97	91	towel	NoC	13	92	90	*trainees*		7	75	82
teeth		47	97	90	*towel*		9	87	88	trainer	NoC	18	96	89
tooth		6	89	90	*towels*		4	79	90	*trainer*		10	81	85
top	Adj	112	100	93	tower	NoC	42	99	91	*trainers*		8	94	90
top	NoC	129	100	95	*tower*		34	99	92	training	NoC	194	100	91
top		120	100	95	*towers*		9	93	85	*training*		194	100	91
tops		9	95	92	town	NoC	221	100	93	transaction	NoC	44	98	80
top	Verb	15	100	92	*town*		180	100	92	*transaction*		23	92	75
top		5	97	92	*towns*		41	100	90	*transactions*		21	89	84
topped		7	92	91	toxic	Adj	12	88	78	transfer	NoC	59	100	87
topping		2	76	90	toy	NoC	21	98	91	*transfer*		51	99	86
tops		1	50	86	*toy*		9	96	92	*transfers*		8	83	87
topic	NoC	44	100	90	*toys*		12	95	89	transfer	Verb	57	100	92
topic		24	100	88	trace	NoC	19	100	93	*transfer*		18	99	90
topics		19	97	90	*trace*		12	98	91	*transferred*		31	100	92
torch	NoC	12	87	87	*traces*		8	94	93	*transferring*		7	95	92
torch		9	86	87	trace	Verb	27	100	95	*transfers*		1	52	86
torches		2	62	82	*trace*		11	99	93	transform	Verb	30	99	94
Tory	Adj	34	92	83	*traced*		10	97	94	*transform*		9	91	91
Tory	NoC	21	85	76	*traces*		2	70	89	*transformed*		16	99	94
Tories		20	79	75	*tracing*		4	93	93	*transforming*		4	82	91
Tory		1	47	81	track	NoC	76	100	92	*transforms*		2	58	87
toss	Verb	13	93	87	*track*		57	100	92	transformation	NoC	21	98	89
toss		3	74	87	*tracks*		19	99	91	*transformation*		17	98	90
tossed		8	81	85	trade	NoC	203	100	91	*transformations*		3	67	83
tosses		0	28	57	*trade*		191	100	91	transition	NoC	27	93	87
tossing		2	60	84	*trades*		12	93	90	*transition*		23	92	88
total	Adj	122	100	93	trade	Verb	27	100	91	*transitions*		3	60	70
total	NoC	53	99	91	*trade*		8	97	93	translate	Verb	22	99	94
total		51	99	91	*traded*		6	91	86	*translate*		6	95	92
totals		2	66	82	*trades*		1	43	84	*translated*		12	99	93
total	Verb	12	89	87	*trading*		12	95	90	*translates*		2	64	88
total		3	78	89	trader	NoC	18	98	91	*translating*		3	77	90
totalled		4	73	85	*trader*		6	86	85	translation	NoC	17	97	89
totalling		5	77	83	*traders*		12	96	91	*translation*		15	96	88
totals		1	45	86	trading	NoC	39	99	90	*translations*		3	73	86
totally	Adv	58	100	96	*trading*		39	99	90	transmission	NoC	16	93	89
touch	NoC	45	100	93	tradition	NoC	67	100	92	*transmission*		15	92	89
touch		41	100	91	*tradition*		51	99	92	*transmissions*		1	58	85
touches		4	90	92	*traditions*		16	95	90	transmit	Verb	14	97	91
touch	Verb	69	100	91	traditional	Adj	99	100	93	*transmit*		3	87	91
touch		26	99	91	traditionally	Adv	21	94	93	*transmits*		1	49	85
touched		30	99	88	traffic	NoC	67	100	90	*transmitted*		8	93	90
touches		3	91	91	*traffic*		67	100	90	*transmitting*		2	68	89
touching		10	93	90	tragedy	NoC	20	100	89	transport	NoC	82	100	92
tough	Adj	41	100	93	*tragedies*		2	74	90	*transport*		82	100	92
tough		32	100	93	*tragedy*		18	100	88	*transports*		0	25	65
tougher		6	90	89	tragic	Adj	12	98	92	transport	Verb	14	97	94
toughest		3	67	84	trail	NoC	15	97	91	*transport*		4	89	93
tour	NoC	67	100	91	*trail*		12	95	90	*transported*		7	97	93
tour		57	100	90	*trails*		3	77	89	*transporting*		3	84	91
tours		10	96	89	trail	Verb	11	95	89	*transports*		1	35	83
tour	Verb	14	94	90	*trail*		2	73	89	trap	NoC	17	100	92
tour		6	81	87	*trailed*		5	67	85	*trap*		13	99	92
toured		3	78	89	*trailing*		4	87	90	*traps*		4	86	90
touring		4	83	90	*trails*		1	43	85	trap	Verb	21	100	93
tours		0	29	82	train	NoC	84	100	92	*trap*		4	86	91

Word	PoS	Freq	Ra	Di	Word	PoS	Freq	Ra	Di	Word	PoS	Freq	Ra	Di
trapped		15	99	93	*trembled*		3	45	81	*trunk*		8	92	92
trapping		1	63	89	*trembles*		0	20	74	*trunks*		3	81	89
traps		0	34	84	*trembling*		9	72	82	trust	NoC	87	100	88
travel	NoC	40	100	93	tremendous	Adj	20	100	92	*trust*		74	100	89
travel		36	100	92	trend	NoC	47	95	92	*trusts*		14	84	79
travels		4	90	91	*trend*		26	93	93	trust	Verb	39	100	92
travel	Verb	88	100	96	*trends*		21	90	89	*trust*		28	100	92
travel		37	100	95	Trent	NoP	11	75	50	*trusted*		8	96	91
traveling		0	2	15	Trevor	NoP	12	89	87	*trusting*		2	73	90
travelled		22	99	94	*Trevor*		12	89	87	*trusts*		1	45	85
travelling		24	100	95	trial	NoC	86	100	91	trustee	NoC	21	88	74
travels		4	91	92	*trial*		65	100	90	*trustee*		9	73	74
traveller	NoC	25	100	88	*trials*		21	96	89	*trustees*		12	80	71
traveller		9	94	90	triangle	NoC	11	97	87	truth	NoC	87	100	94
travellers		16	98	85	*triangle*		8	97	88	*truth*		83	100	93
tray	NoC	18	91	89	*triangles*		3	65	79	*truths*		5	85	89
tray		14	88	87	tribe	NoC	14	92	87	try	NoC	17	92	83
trays		4	78	90	*tribe*		7	88	88	*tries*		5	60	78
treasure	NoC	14	97	89	*tribes*		6	81	83	*try*		11	90	85
treasure		9	93	87	tribunal	NoC	21	90	79	try	Verb	552	100	95
treasures		6	89	89	*tribunal*		16	85	83	*tried*		150	100	93
treasury	NoC·	27	97	89	*tribunals*		5	63	62	*tries*		15	99	94
treasuries		0	19	75	tribute	NoC	17	99	90	*try*		202	100	95
treasury		26	97	88	*tribute*		15	98	89	*trying*		185	100	94
treat	Verb	117	100	95	*tributes*		2	61	87	tube	NoC	30	100	90
treat		30	100	95	trick	NoC	23	100	94	*tube*		20	99	91
treated		69	100	93	*trick*		14	97	94	*tubes*		10	94	88
treating		13	100	95	*tricks*		8	96	93	tuck	Verb	15	97	89
treats		4	96	92	trigger	Verb	12	98	93	*tuck*		3	72	81
treatment	NoC	131	100	88	*trigger*		3	89	90	*tucked*		10	93	89
treatment		122	100	88	*triggered*		6	96	93	*tucking*		2	58	84
treatments		9	83	88	*triggering*		1	62	89	*tucks*		0	17	73
treaty	NoC	57	93	79	*triggers*		1	62	89	Tuesday	NoP	37	99	89
treaties		7	63	67	trip	NoC	56	100	94	*Tuesday*		36	99	89
treaty		50	92	80	*trip*		45	100	93	*Tuesdays*		2	63	88
tree	NoC	147	100	94	*trips*		11	97	92	tumour	NoC	16	79	63
tree		64	100	94	triumph	NoC	20	97	94	*tumour*		9	76	63
trees		83	100	93	*triumph*		17	97	94	*tumours*		7	51	63
tremble	Verb	15	83	83	*triumphs*		2	75	91	tune	NoC	18	100	93
tremble		3	52	84	troop	NoC	54	100	83	*tune*		14	100	94
					troop		5	83	80	*tunes*		4	76	86
					troops		48	99	83	tunnel	NoC	29	99	88
					trophy	NoC	16	92	86	*tunnel*		24	97	87
					trophies		3	75	87	*tunnels*		5	91	88
					trophy		13	85	85	Turkey	NoP	16	95	81
					tropical	Adj	18	94	81	*Turkey*		16	95	81
					trouble	NoC	99	100	95	Turkish	Adj	14	93	82
					trouble		89	100	94	turn	NoC	87	100	96
					troubles		10	98	93	*turn*		81	100	97
					trouble	Verb	12	99	91	*turns*		5	90	90
					trouble		4	88	89	turn	Verb	465	100	93
					troubled		6	95	91	*turn*		129	100	96
					troubles		1	59	89	*turned*		246	100	90
					troubling		1	55	88	*turning*		58	100	93
					trousers	NoC	26	98	90	*turns*		32	99	95
					trouser		3	63	85	Turner	NoP	12	92	90
					trousers		23	98	90	*Turner*		11	92	90
					truck	NoC	19	100	90	*Turners*		0	12	64
					truck		12	92	88	turnover	NoC	29	94	65
					trucks		7	94	89	*turnover*		29	94	64
					true	Adj	183	100	97	*turnovers*		0	20	75
					true		181	100	97	tutor	NoC	18	98	86
					truer		1	60	89	*tutor*		11	97	87
					truest		1	31	79	*tutors*		7	84	81
					truly	Adv	32	100	95	TV	NoC	66	97	88
					trunk	NoC	12	97	92	*T.V.*		1	30	74

Means of transport

The *car* (with 353 mentions per million words) is well established as Britain's favourite mode of transport, far outnumbering mentions of public and hired transport such as the *bus* (68), *train* (84) and *taxi* (22). Human-powered transport is mentioned even less: *bike* (which might also refer to motorbikes) gets 23 mentions per million words and *bicycle* 11. The maritime heritage is still strong with frequent references to *boat* (74) and *ship* (70) as well as to *ferry* (14) and *yacht* (10). Although a number of air-travel words (such as *flight* [64] and *plane* [45]) are ambiguous, there are quite frequent references to *aircraft* (62), with *helicopter* (16) also appearing. Forms of commercial transport that are mentioned include *van* (25) *lorry* (20) and *truck* (12).

Word	PoS	Freq	Ra	Di	Word	PoS	Freq	Ra	Di	Word	PoS	Freq	Ra	Di
TV		65	97	88	under	Adv	56	100	96	*unite*		5	89	92
twelve	Num	66	100	88	under	Prep	553	100	95	*united*		12	98	87
twelve		66	100	88	undergo	Verb	25	95	90	*unites*		1	49	87
twelves		1	20	53	*undergo*		6	88	92	*uniting*		1	62	89
twentieth	Ord	18	99	91	*undergoes*		1	53	86	united	Adj	68	99	86
twenty	Num	164	100	82	*undergoing*		6	89	90	*united*		68	99	86
twenties		7	92	92	*undergone*		6	90	91	United	NoP-	115	99	88
twenty		156	100	82	*underwent*		6	87	83	unity	NoC	29	94	88
twenty-five	Num	12	95	91	underground	Adj	11	97	91	*unities*		0	17	63
twenty-five		12	95	91	underline	Verb	13	99	93	*unity*		28	94	88
twice	Adv	63	100	97	*underline*		3	88	92	universal	Adj	26	98	91
twin	NoC	27	99	90	*underlined*		5	97	91	universe	NoC	27	96	80
twin		16	98	91	*underlines*		2	72	90	*universe*		26	96	80
twins		11	92	85	*underlining*		2	67	90	*universes*		1	26	67
twist	Verb	19	98	88	underlying	Adj	22	95	92	university	NoC	191	100	88
twist		4	85	90	undermine	Verb	21	98	92	*universities*		27	97	88
twisted		11	87	84	*undermine*		9	91	92	*university*		164	100	87
twisting		4	80	88	*undermined*		7	93	91	Unix	NoP	42	34	28
twists		1	37	83	*undermines*		1	59	88	*Unix*		42	34	28
two	Num	1563	100	97	*undermining*		3	84	91	*Unixes*		0	3	35
two		1561	100	97	underneath	Prep	10	98	90	unknown	Adj	43	100	73
twos		3	66	78	understand	Verb	238	100	96	unless	Conj	110	100	95
two-thirds	Num	12	90	89	*understand*		155	100	95	unlike	Prep	40	100	95
type	NoC	259	100	90	*understanding*		19	100	93	unlikely	Adj	57	100	95
type		170	100	88	*understands*		7	99	94	*unlikeliest*		0	17	77
types		89	100	92	*understood*		57	100	96	*unlikely*		56	100	95
type	Verb	11	96	84	understanding	NoC	77	100	92	unnecessary	Adj	19	99	94
type		3	63	81	*understanding*		75	100	92	unpleasant	Adj	13	97	93
typed		5	85	79	*understandings*		2	43	79	*unpleasant*		13	97	93
types		0	12	67	undertake	Verb	59	96	91	until	Conj	242	100	96
typing		3	74	82	*undertake*		17	95	91	until	Prep	167	100	95
typical	Adj	49	100	94	*undertaken*		27	95	90	unusual	Adj	41	100	96
typically	Adv	21	98	91	*undertakes*		2	64	80	unusually	Adv	10	95	94
tyre	NoC	14	99	90	*undertaking*		7	85	90	unwilling	Adj	10	96	95
tyre		6	95	89	*undertook*		6	84	87	up	Adv	1795	100	95
tyres		8	93	89	undertaking	NoC	16	94	80	up	Prep	83	100	91
U / u	Lett	21	87	77	*undertaking*		10	92	78	up to	Adv	94	100	92
ugly	Adj	14	99	92	*undertakings*		6	73	80	up to	Prep	152	100	96
uglier		0	25	81	undoubtedly	Adv	24	98	94	update	Verb	18	92	72
ugliest		0	26	80	unemployed	Adj	28	99	90	*update*		7	86	61
ugly		14	99	92	unemployment	NoC	64	99	88	*updated*		7	87	71
UK	NoP	177	92	89	unexpected	Adj	21	100	95	*updates*		1	36	83
U.K.		4	58	78	unfair	Adj	19	100	92	*updating*		3	72	87
UK		173	90	89	*unfair*		19	100	92	upon	Prep	234	100	94
ulcer	NoC	15	71	44	unfortunate	Adj	16	100	96	upper	Adj	54	99	93
ulcer		10	49	35	unfortunately	Adv	47	100	95	upset	Adj	18	100	92
ulcers		5	59	62	unhappy	Adj	19	100	93	upset	Verb	17	100	93
Ulster	NoP	24	76	68	*unhappier*		0	10	68	*upset*		14	99	93
Ulster		24	76	68	*unhappiest*		0	13	73	*upsets*		1	59	89
ultimate	Adj	25	100	94	*unhappy*		19	100	93	*upsetting*		2	84	91
ultimately	Adv	29	96	93	uniform	Adj	11	98	91	upstairs	Adv	25	93	86
UN	NoP	44	82	65	uniform	NoC	20	100	91	upwards	Adv	16	100	92
UN		44	81	65	*uniform*		15	100	90	urban	Adj	54	96	88
unable	Adj	64	100	96	*uniforms*		5	90	89	urge	Verb	39	98	93
unacceptable	Adj	12	91	93	union	NoC	211	100	88	*urge*		6	94	89
unaware	Adj	12	97	94	*union*		166	100	87	*urged*		23	97	91
uncertain	Adj	20	98	95	*unions*		45	94	89	*urges*		3	71	87
uncertainty	NoC	26	96	93	Union	NoP-	10	92	87	*urging*		8	95	92
uncertainties		4	84	91	unionist	NoC	11	77	77	urgent	Adj	22	100	95
uncertainty		22	96	93	*unionist*		2	53	78	*urgent*		22	100	95
unchanged	Adj	11	93	91	*unionists*		9	71	75	US	NoP	162	97	84
uncle	NoC	38	100	86	unique	Adj	43	99	93	*U.S.*		4	53	81
uncle		35	99	85	unit	NoC	180	100	93	*US*		158	97	84
uncles		2	76	88	*unit*		109	100	93	USA	NoP	52	92	81
uncomfortable	Adj	14	100	92	*units*		71	100	92	*U.S.A.*		2	44	79
unconscious	Adj	12	96	90	unite	Verb	19	100	91	*USA*		50	92	80

Word	PoS	Freq	Ra	Di	Word	PoS	Freq	Ra	Di	Word	PoS	Freq	Ra	Di
usage	NoC	13	95	88	variable	NoC	37	85	83	version	NoC	105	100	84
usage		12	94	89	*variable*		15	75	82	*version*		81	100	84
usages		1	43	71	*variables*		22	78	84	*versions*		24	95	82
use	NoC	328	100	93	variant	NoC	11	85	83	vertical	Adj	18	96	88
use		310	100	93	*variant*		4	77	87	very	Adj	65	100	96
uses		18	97	90	*variants*		6	69	79	*very*		65	100	96
use	Verb	1071	100	95	variation	NoC	53	99	90	very	Adv	1165	100	95
use		319	100	95	*variation*		27	93	87	vessel	NoC	29	98	86
used		469	100	95	*variations*		25	97	91	*vessel*		14	96	86
uses		36	100	93	varied	Adj	13	96	92	*vessels*		15	94	85
using		247	100	93	variety	NoC	102	100	93	via	Prep	45	100	91
used	Adj	45	100	97	*varieties*		15	92	87	vice-president	NoC	12	70	73
used (to)	Verb	156	100	83	*variety*		87	100	93	*vice-president*		11	70	74
useful	Adj	101	100	94	various	Adj	155	100	95	*vice-presidents*		1	26	69
useless	Adj	13	100	94	vary	Verb	63	100	92	victim	NoC	69	100	91
user	NoC	125	96	76	*varied*		16	97	92	*victim*		39	98	89
user		60	90	68	*varies*		13	88	91	*victims*		29	100	91
users		65	92	78	*vary*		30	95	92	Victoria	NoP	26	100	90
USSR	NoP	17	71	77	*varying*		4	78	90	*Victoria*		26	100	90
U.S.S.R.		0	13	59	varying	Adj	13	97	92	Victorian	Adj	25	99	92
USSR		17	70	76	vast	Adj	47	99	95	victory	NoC	63	100	89
usual	Adj	64	100	96	*vast*		47	99	95	*victories*		6	88	89
usually	Adv	191	100	95	*vaster*		0	15	72	*victory*		56	100	89
utility	NoC	16	92	86	VAT/vat	NoC	25	97	86	video	NoC	76	100	90
utilities		5	70	81	*V.A.T.*		0	8	59	*video*		65	100	89
utility		10	91	86	*VAT/vat*		24	95	85	*videos*		11	93	90
utterance	NoC	13	77	75	*VATs/vats*		1	33	82	video-taped	Adj	38	9	21
utterance		8	68	73	vegetable	NoC	28	100	91	Vienna	NoP	13	91	88
utterances		5	64	77	*vegetable*		10	98	91	Vietnam	NoP	18	88	79
utterly	Adv	13	98	92	*vegetables*		18	99	91	*Vietnam*		18	88	79
V / v	Lett	51	99	81	vegetation	NoC	10	82	85	view	NoC	289	100	95
V / v	Num	10	82	88	vehicle	NoC	73	100	88	*view*		214	100	95
v	Prep	87	83	64	*vehicle*		42	100	85	*views*		74	99	94
v		32	69	62	*vehicles*		31	100	90	view	Verb	44	100	92
v.		54	79	46	vein	NoC	15	96	88	*view*		16	100	88
vague	Adj	15	100	94	*vein*		8	94	86	*viewed*		21	96	92
valid	Adj	23	99	88	*veins*		8	87	86	*viewing*		5	90	90
validity	NoC	14	87	89	velocity	NoC	10	73	74	*views*		2	62	87
valley	NoC	52	98	92	*velocities*		1	29	64	viewer	NoC	13	88	90
valley		44	98	91	*velocity*		9	72	73	*viewer*		5	77	89
valleys		8	92	87	vendor	NoC	24	81	57	*viewers*		9	80	87
valuable	Adj	39	100	94	*vendor*		15	62	44	viewpoint	NoC	12	91	88
valuation	NoC	14	86	75	*vendors*		9	64	62	*viewpoint*		9	91	91
valuation		11	85	76	Venice	NoP	10	91	82	*viewpoints*		3	67	75
valuations		3	57	68	*Venice*		10	91	82	villa	NoC	21	91	85
value	NoC	250	100	92	venture	NoC	27	99	88	*villa*		17	89	83
value		175	100	93	*venture*		19	97	87	*villas*		3	61	85
values		75	98	90	*ventures*		8	85	87	village	NoC	137	100	93
value	Verb	19	100	94	venture	Verb	10	94	93	*village*		109	100	92
value		4	93	92	*venture*		4	88	93	*villages*		28	99	92
valued		13	99	93	*ventured*		4	81	88	violence	NoC	56	100	90
values		1	66	89	*ventures*		0	28	83	*violence*		56	100	90
valuing		2	59	85	*venturing*		1	59	90	violent	Adj	28	100	94
valve	NoC	12	89	83	venue	NoC	17	95	89	virgin	NoC	16	98	74
valve		7	77	81	*venue*		12	91	89	*virgin*		15	97	72
valves		4	72	83	*venues*		5	73	88	*virgins*		1	54	86
van	NoC	25	99	91	verb	NoC	14	84	75	Virginia	NoP	12	95	78
van		21	98	90	*verb*		9	76	74	*Virginia*		12	95	78
vans		4	82	89	*verbs*		5	59	74	virtually	Adv	44	100	95
Van	NoP-	22	94	90	verbal	Adj	15	98	90	virtue	NoC	26	99	91
vanish	Verb	16	98	89	verdict	NoC	16	96	87	*virtue*		19	95	90
vanish		3	87	86	*verdict*		14	95	87	*virtues*		7	94	92
vanished		11	92	88	*verdicts*		2	54	83	virus	NoC	20	93	82
vanishes		1	57	75	verse	NoC	20	98	89	*virus*		15	88	84
vanishing		1	42	83	*verse*		14	91	88	*viruses*		5	63	71
variable	Adj	13	92	88	*verses*		6	85	88	visible	Adj	29	99	94

Word	PoS	Freq	Ra	Di	Word	PoS	Freq	Ra	Di	Word	PoS	Freq	Ra	Di
vision	NoC	47	100	92	*Ws*		*0*	*14*	*53*	*wardrobes*		*2*	*49*	*80*
vision		*42*	*100*	*92*	wage	NoC	68	100	89	warehouse	NoC	14	99	90
visions		*5*	*89*	*92*	*wage*		*31*	*98*	*87*	*warehouse*		*10*	*97*	*91*
visit	NoC	104	100	90	*wages*		*37*	*100*	*91*	*warehouses*		*4*	*86*	*84*
visit		*76*	*100*	*88*	waist	NoC	15	93	88	warm	Adj	70	100	93
visits		*28*	*100*	*93*	*waist*		*14*	*92*	*87*	*warm*		*64*	*100*	*92*
visit	Verb	115	100	94	*waists*		*0*	*30*	*82*	*warmer*		*6*	*94*	*92*
visit		*50*	*100*	*91*	wait	Verb	213	100	91	*warmest*		*1*	*55*	*87*
visited		*43*	*98*	*90*	*wait*		*84*	*100*	*91*	warm	Verb	15	99	93
visiting		*18*	*100*	*95*	*waited*		*40*	*100*	*86*	*warm*		*6*	*87*	*91*
visits		*4*	*83*	*89*	*waiting*		*86*	*100*	*91*	*warmed*		*5*	*87*	*91*
visiting	Adj	11	99	94	*waits*		*3*	*81*	*91*	*warming*		*4*	*81*	*91*
visitor	NoC	70	100	93	waiter	NoC	10	87	86	*warms*		*1*	*57*	*89*
visitor		*22*	*97*	*90*	*waiter*		*8*	*79*	*85*	warmth	NoC	20	99	89
visitors		*48*	*100*	*93*	*waiters*		*3*	*64*	*86*	*warmth*		*20*	*99*	*89*
visual	Adj	34	95	87	waiting	NoC	10	97	89	warn	Verb	63	100	91
vital	Adj	51	100	94	*waiting*		*10*	*97*	*89*	*warn*		*11*	*100*	*93*
vitamin	NoC	13	85	82	wake	NoC	12	96	92	*warned*		*40*	*100*	*90*
vitamin		*8*	*77*	*79*	*wake*		*12*	*96*	*92*	*warning*		*6*	*93*	*88*
vitamins		*5*	*67*	*82*	*wakes*		*0*	*11*	*59*	*warns*		*6*	*76*	*84*
vivid	Adj	10	97	93	wake	Verb	41	99	89	warning	NoC	47	100	94
vocabulary	NoC	13	93	86	*wake*		*15*	*98*	*90*	*warning*		*39*	*100*	*94*
vocabularies		*0*	*23*	*76*	*wakes*		*2*	*71*	*89*	*warnings*		*8*	*98*	*92*
vocabulary		*12*	*93*	*85*	*waking*		*5*	*85*	*89*	warrant	NoC	11	96	87
vocational	Adj	10	75	78	*woke*		*14*	*93*	*86*	*warrant*		*7*	*89*	*82*
voice	NoC	203	100	88	*woken*		*5*	*79*	*87*	*warrants*		*3*	*67*	*80*
voice		*179*	*100*	*87*	Wales	NoP	93	100	90	warrior	NoC	11	93	85
voices		*24*	*99*	*92*	walk	NoC	51	100	91	*warrior*		*6*	*87*	*88*
voice	Verb	80	96	31	*walk*		*39*	*100*	*91*	*warriors*		*6*	*80*	*80*
voice		*74*	*84*	*25*	*walks*		*12*	*93*	*81*	wartime	NoC	10	93	91
voiced		*5*	*90*	*92*	walk	Verb	215	100	91	*wartime*		*10*	*93*	*91*
voices		*0*	*20*	*78*	*walk*		*66*	*100*	*92*	wash	Verb	49	100	93
voicing		*1*	*59*	*86*	*walked*		*94*	*100*	*87*	*wash*		*17*	*96*	*90*
vol	NoC	15	62	55	*walking*		*48*	*100*	*92*	*washed*		*19*	*99*	*92*
vol		*5*	*53*	*49*	*walks*		*7*	*97*	*92*	*washes*		*1*	*55*	*87*
vol.		*10*	*44*	*37*	Walker	NoP	21	91	89	*washing*		*11*	*97*	*93*
vols		*0*	*19*	*73*	*Walker*		*21*	*90*	*89*	washing	NoC	16	98	89
voltage	NoC	10	71	70	*Walkers*		*0*	*17*	*74*	*washing*		*15*	*98*	*89*
voltage		*9*	*71*	*70*	walking	NoC	17	97	89	*washings*		*0*	*11*	*63*
voltages		*1*	*17*	*67*	wall	NoC	175	100	93	Washington	NoP	33	97	88
volume	NoC	70	100	90	*wall*		*114*	*100*	*93*	*Washington*		*33*	*97*	*88*
volume		*54*	*100*	*90*	*walls*		*60*	*100*	*93*	*Washingtons*		*0*	*3*	*29*
volumes		*16*	*96*	*90*	Walter	NoP	19	96	88	waste	NoC	58	100	85
voluntary	Adj	39	98	90	wander	Verb	25	99	91	*waste*		*53*	*100*	*85*
volunteer	NoC	25	100	89	*wander*		*7*	*96*	*92*	*wastes*		*5*	*75*	*84*
volunteer		*6*	*89*	*91*	*wandered*		*10*	*85*	*87*	waste	Verb	33	100	93
volunteers		*19*	*97*	*87*	*wandering*		*8*	*94*	*92*	*waste*		*14*	*100*	*87*
von	NoP-	10	86	87	*wanders*		*1*	*58*	*88*	*wasted*		*10*	*100*	*95*
von		*10*	*86*	*87*	want~	Verb	945	100	91	*wastes*		*1*	*55*	*88*
vote	NoC	80	100	84	*wan~*		*26*	*61*	*62*	*wasting*		*7*	*99*	*92*
vote		*48*	*99*	*85*	*want*		*572*	*100*	*90*	watch	NoC	32	100	91
votes		*31*	*94*	*80*	*wanted*		*234*	*100*	*92*	*watch*		*29*	*100*	*91*
vote	Verb	53	100	88	*wantin'*		*0*	*6*	*54*	*watches*		*3*	*81*	*91*
vote		*23*	*98*	*90*	*wanting*		*24*	*100*	*93*	watch	Verb	202	100	91
voted		*23*	*93*	*84*	*wants*		*89*	*100*	*93*	*watch*		*67*	*100*	*91*
votes		*0*	*20*	*78*	war	NoC	297	100	94	*watched*		*67*	*100*	*88*
voting		*7*	*86*	*85*	*war*		*279*	*100*	*94*	*watches*		*3*	*79*	*89*
voter	NoC	23	87	83	*wars*		*19*	*99*	*93*	*watching*		*65*	*100*	*90*
voter		*3*	*55*	*79*	ward	NoC	26	100	85	water	NoC	372	100	94
voters		*20*	*85*	*83*	*ward*		*19*	*100*	*82*	*water*		*349*	*100*	*94*
voting	NoC	15	85	87	*wards*		*7*	*91*	*88*	*waters*		*22*	*99*	*92*
vulnerable	Adj	25	100	95	Ward	NoP	15	93	82	Watson	NoP	12	90	88
W / w	Lett	17	93	86	*Ward*		*15*	*92*	*82*	wave	NoC	59	100	91
W	NoP	24	87	82	*Wards*		*0*	*13*	*46*	*wave*		*32*	*100*	*92*
W		*8*	*71*	*78*	wardrobe	NoC	11	89	89	*waves*		*27*	*98*	*89*
W.		*16*	*86*	*78*	*wardrobe*		*10*	*89*	*89*	wave	Verb	27	99	87

Word	PoS	Freq	Ra	Di	Word	PoS	Freq	Ra	Di	Word	PoS	Freq	Ra	Di
wave		4	86	92	*weigh*		7	96	92	wheat	NoC	10	95	90
waved		15	92	84	*weighed*		8	100	95	*wheat*		10	95	91
waves		1	52	85	*weighing*		6	97	93	*wheats*		0	10	59
waving		8	91	88	*weighs*		3	87	90	wheel	NoC	41	99	92
way	NoC	1108	100	97	weight	NoC	94	100	93	*wheel*		26	99	91
way		958	100	97	*weight*		85	100	93	*wheels*		16	97	92
ways		149	100	95	*weights*		9	95	88	when	Adv	431	100	98
we	Pron	4202	100	93	weird	Adj	11	91	87	when	Conj	1712	100	97
us		623	100	96	welcome	Adj	27	100	94	whenever	Adv	32	100	96
we		3578	100	92	*welcome*		27	100	94	where	Adv	628	100	95
weak	Adj	45	100	95	welcome	NoC	11	100	94	where	Conj	458	100	96
weak		36	100	94	*welcome*		10	100	94	whereas	Conj	62	100	93
weaker		7	97	93	*welcomes*		0	19	78	whereby	Adv	20	95	92
weakest		2	83	92	welcome	Verb	57	100	90	wherever	Adv	23	99	96
weaken	Verb	14	100	94	*welcome*		28	99	86	whether	Conj	332	100	95
weaken		4	94	93	*welcomed*		23	98	91	whether or not	Conj	29	100	92
weakened		7	97	93	*welcomes*		3	78	88	which	DetP	3719	100	96
weakening		2	85	92	*welcoming*		3	85	91	while	Conj	503	100	97
weakens		1	47	87	welfare	NoC	48	100	91	while	NoC	63	100	91
weakness	NoC	27	100	95	*welfare*		48	100	91	*while*		63	100	91
weakness		17	98	94	well	Adj	42	100	94	whilst	Conj	58	100	93
weaknesses		10	93	92	*well*		42	100	94	whisky	NoC	19	95	87
wealth	NoC	38	98	92						*whiskies*		2	41	43
wealthy	Adj	16	98	94						*whisky*		17	95	87
wealthier		1	62	88						whisper	Verb	32	85	81
wealthiest		1	46	85						*whisper*		2	57	85
wealthy		14	98	94						*whispered*		25	70	80
weapon	NoC	60	100	89						*whispering*		4	70	85
weapon		20	100	91						*whispers*		1	41	78
weapons		40	100	85						white	Adj	207	100	95
wear	Verb	149	100	93						*white*		206	100	95
wear		43	100	92						*whiter*		1	41	80
wearing		50	100	92						*whitest*		0	11	70
wears		7	90	90						white	NoC	21	100	93
wore		30	97	89						*white*		12	98	93
worn		18	100	94						*whites*		9	94	86
weather	NoC	58	100	95						White	NoP	28	99	90
weather		57	100	95						WHO	NoP	11	88	81
weathers		1	46	87						*WHO*		10	88	81
weave	Verb	11	98	89						who	Pron	2055	100	98
weave		2	71	87						whoever	Pron	15	98	92
weaved		0	30	81						whole	Adj	216	100	97
weaves		1	47	88						whole	NoC	92	100	95
weaving		3	83	84						*whole*		91	100	95
wove		1	38	82						*wholes*		1	23	67
woven		4	80	86	well	Adv	1119	100	85	wholly	Adv	22	97	92
wedding	NoC	36	99	90	well	NoC	14	100	89	whom	Pron	129	100	95
wedding		33	99	90	*well*		9	99	91	whose	DetP	198	100	96
weddings		3	82	88	*wells*		5	81	82	why	Adv	509	100	92
Wednesday	NoP	46	98	88	well-known	Adj	15	96	94	wicked	Adj	11	96	87
Wednesday		44	98	88	Welsh	Adj	37	100	88	wicket	NoC	14	56	74
Wednesdays		2	70	89	west	NoC	127	100	94	*wicket*		6	51	76
wee	Adj	12	83	75	West	NoP-	88	100	90	*wickets*		8	34	72
week	NoC	476	100	94	*West*		88	100	90	wide	Adj	165	100	96
week		322	100	93	western	Adj	99	100	92	*wide*		113	100	96
weeks		154	100	95	Westminster	NoP	22	99	91	*wider*		49	100	93
weekend	NoC	73	100	90	*Westminster*		22	99	91	*widest*		3	82	92
weekend		63	100	89	wet	Adj	37	99	93	widely	Adv	56	97	93
weekends		10	99	94	*wet*		36	99	93	widen	Verb	14	97	94
weekly	Adj	23	100	93	*wetter*		1	42	81	*widen*		4	91	92
weep	Verb	12	92	86	*wettest*		1	31	82	*widened*		7	94	90
weep		3	62	81	whale	NoC	13	93	79	*widening*		2	88	93
weeping		3	64	83	*whale*		6	85	81	*widens*		1	52	87
weeps		0	29	79	*whales*		8	75	76	widespread	Adj	32	88	92
wept		5	76	86	what	DetP	2493	100	92	widow	NoC	20	100	92
weigh	Verb	24	100	95	whatever	DetP	132	100	95	*widow*		16	100	91

Weather
(occurrences per million words)

Britain is well-known for its cold, wet climate, so it is no surprise that *wind* (85), *rain* (64) and *cloud* (37) top the weather-related nouns, with *snow* (31) and *storm* (28) following close behind. In contrast, *sunshine* and *sunlight* each only receive 13 mentions per million words. The noun *sun* is more common than *rain*—with 115 mentions per million words—but it should be noted that this is also the name of a popular tabloid newspaper in Britain, hence many of these references will not be concerned with the weather. *Rain* is also the only weather verb to exceed 10 mentions per million words (14).

Word	PoS	Freq	Ra	Di	Word	PoS	Freq	Ra	Di	Word	PoS	Freq	Ra	Di
widows		4	85	86	*wire*	NoC	29	100	92	*woodlands*		3	72	87
width	NoC	13	99	88	*wire*		22	100	92	wool	NoC	18	99	92
width		12	98	89	*wires*		7	95	90	*wool*		18	99	92
widths		2	46	78	wisdom	NoC	15	99	94	*wools*		0	20	76
wife	NoC	190	100	93	*wisdom*		15	99	94	word	NoC	438	100	95
wife		171	100	93	*wisdoms*		0	11	68	*word*		193	100	94
wives		19	99	91	wise	Adj	24	100	95	*words*		244	100	95
wild	Adj	55	100	94	*wise*		20	100	95	work	NoC	653	100	96
wild		51	100	93	*wiser*		4	90	92	*work*		653	100	96
wilder		2	64	88	*wisest*		1	48	88	work	Verb	646	100	97
wildest		1	70	90	wish	NoC	30	100	96	*work*		260	100	96
wildlife	NoC	20	100	79	*wish*		16	100	95	*worked*		127	100	97
will	NoC	61	100	95	*wishes*		15	99	93	*working*		194	100	96
will		58	100	95	wish	Verb	170	100	96	*works*		63	100	95
wills		3	79	88	*wish*		103	100	95	*wrought*		2	76	91
Will	NoP	14	98	77	*wished*		37	100	92	worker	NoC	184	100	91
will	VMod	3357	100	96	*wishes*		15	100	92	*worker*		36	100	90
'll		726	100	85	*wishing*		15	98	95	*workers*		147	100	90
will		2470	100	95	wit	NoC	12	96	92	workforce	NoC	16	90	90
wo~		161	99	87	*wit*		8	93	91	*workforce*		15	90	90
William	NoP	84	100	88	*wits*		4	83	88	*workforces*		1	35	82
Williams	NoP	33	98	89	with	Prep	6575	100	99	working	Adj	60	100	92
Willie	NoP	13	79	53	with regard to	Prep	17	94	91	working	NoC	46	100	94
willing	Adj	39	100	97	with respect to	Prep	13	76	85	*working*		38	100	94
willingness	NoC	12	96	93	withdraw	Verb	47	100	92	*workings*		7	96	89
Wilson	NoP	40	96	89	*withdraw*		16	99	91	working-class	Adj	19	85	85
Wilson		40	95	88	*withdrawing*		4	90	89	works	NoC	82	100	87
Wilsons		0	16	71	*withdrawn*		17	97	92	workshop	NoC	32	100	91
Wimbledon	NoP	13	83	81	*withdraws*		1	61	89	*workshop*		18	100	91
win	NoC	29	91	81	*withdrew*		10	96	91	*workshops*		14	96	90
win		22	81	80	withdrawal	NoC	23	99	84	workstation	NoC	16	44	45
wins		7	76	83	*withdrawal*		20	99	84	*workstation*		7	34	49
win	Verb	241	100	90	*withdrawals*		2	56	79	*workstations*		8	39	40
win		83	100	90	within	Adv	13	99	94	world	NoC	600	100	96
winning		31	100	90	within	Prep	449	100	95	*world*		590	100	96
wins		9	95	90	without	Prep	456	100	98	*worlds*		10	95	92
won		117	100	90	witness	NoC	34	100	91	worldwide	Adj	10	86	85
wind	NoC	85	100	91	*witness*		18	99	89	worldwide	Adv	12	88	87
wind		71	100	91	*witnesses*		16	99	90	worm	NoC	12	94	79
winds		14	95	86	witness	Verb	21	100	95	*worm*		6	82	76
wind	Verb	23	100	95	*witness*		7	99	94	*worms*		7	80	77
wind		5	97	93	*witnessed*		11	100	95	worried	Adj	38	100	93
winded		0	27	79	*witnesses*		1	35	84	worry	NoC	19	100	95
winding		5	98	89	*witnessing*		2	86	92	*worries*		10	99	94
winds		2	78	89	wolf	NoC	12	94	89	*worry*		9	95	94
wound		10	100	92	*wolf*		5	80	87	worry	Verb	62	99	92
window	NoC	194	100	90	*wolves*		7	78	86	*worried*		8	98	92
window		106	100	91	woman	NoC	631	100	95	*worries*		3	86	91
windows		88	100	83	*woman*		232	100	92	*worry*		47	99	91
wine	NoC	74	100	90	*women*		399	100	93	*worrying*		4	87	91
wine		63	100	91	wonder	NoC	24	98	94	worrying	Adj	11	98	94
wines		11	89	75	*wonder*		19	98	93	worship	NoC	14	95	82
wing	NoC	53	100	92	*wonders*		4	88	91	*worship*		13	95	82
wing		28	100	92	wonder	Verb	124	100	90	*worships*		0	3	10
wings		24	100	89	*wonder*		46	100	91	worth	NoC	21	100	94
winner	NoC	52	100	87	*wondered*		48	98	85	*worth*		21	100	94
winner		32	99	87	*wondering*		25	98	88	worth	Prep	102	100	96
winners		20	94	87	*wonders*		4	94	92	worthwhile	Adj	15	100	94
winter	NoC	74	100	93	wonderful	Adj	49	99	94	worthy	Adj	13	100	95
winter		71	100	94	wood	NoC	67	100	93	*worthier*		0	9	66
winters		3	77	88	*wood*		52	100	92	*worthy*		13	100	95
wipe	Verb	24	99	91	*woods*		15	98	92	would	VMod	2904	100	96
wipe		7	95	91	Wood	NoP	22	99	88	*'d*		353	99	88
wiped		12	95	89	wooden	Adj	35	97	92	*would*		2551	100	97
wipes		1	38	84	woodland	NoC	13	91	89	wound	NoC	21	99	89
wiping		5	84	88	*woodland*		10	87	88	*wound*		11	91	86

Word	PoS	Freq	Ra	Di	Word	PoS	Freq	Ra	Di	Word	PoS	Freq	Ra	Di
wounds		10	98	88	*yacht*		10	85	81	*York*		99	100	88
wound	Verb	12	95	88	*yachts*		4	63	66	Yorkshire	NoP	44	100	86
wound		0	32	82	yard	NoC	69	100	93	*Yorkshire*		44	100	86
wounded		9	92	86	*yard*		33	100	91	you	Pron	6984	100	88
wounding		2	61	82	*yards*		37	100	93	*y'*		0	10	61
wounds		0	6	52	yarn	NoC	12	74	52	*ya*		14	57	63
wrap	Verb	24	98	92	*yarn*		9	61	51	*ye*		15	88	65
wrap		5	92	88	*yarns*		3	45	55	*you*		6954	100	88
wrapped		17	96	90	yeah	Int	834	80	64	young	Adj	379	100	96
wrapping		2	72	90	year	NoC	1639	100	96	*young*		315	100	96
wraps		1	40	84	*year*		737	100	94	*younger*		53	100	95
Wright	NoP	20	86	85	*years*		902	100	97	*youngest*		12	99	89
Wright		20	85	84	yell	Verb	12	82	83	Young	NoP	21	98	91
Wrights		0	7	59	*yell*		1	42	84	youngster	NoC	23	96	87
wrist	NoC	15	92	88	*yelled*		8	62	86	*youngster*		5	82	86
wrist		11	91	87	*yelling*		3	66	85	*youngsters*		17	95	86
wrists		5	77	86	*yells*		0	22	75	your	Det	1391	100	93
write	Verb	400	100	96	yellow	Adj	41	99	94	*yer*		8	52	73
write		109	100	96	*yellow*		41	99	94	*your*		1383	100	93
writes		26	99	89	Yeltsin	NoP	12	40	67	yours	Pron	42	99	88
writing		63	100	95	*Yeltsin*		12	40	67	yourself	Pron	107	99	92
written		103	100	96	yep	Int	13	44	68	youth	NoC	63	100	93
wrote		99	100	90	yes	Int	606	100	96	*youth*		54	100	94
writer	NoC	73	100	92	yesterday	Adv	195	98	79	*youths*		9	95	86
writer		37	100	92	yet	Adv	337	100	97	Yugoslavia	NoP	14	82	77
writers		36	98	91	yield	NoC	16	88	74	Z / z	Lett	11	82	82
writing	NoC	64	100	92	*yield*		11	86	69	Zealand	NoP-	26	96	86
writing		53	100	92	*yields*		5	65	83	*Zealand*		26	96	86
writings		11	89	89	yield	Verb	22	95	92	zero	Num	15	99	86
written	Adj	33	99	90	*yield*		10	94	91	*zero*		15	99	86
wrong	Adj	149	100	95	*yielded*		6	87	92	*zeros*		0	16	72
wrong		149	100	95	*yielding*		2	87	87	zone	NoC	37	100	90
X / x	Lett	61	99	86	*yields*		4	79	85	*zone*		26	100	91
Y / y	Lett	30	95	87	yo	Uncl	11	10	63	*zones*		12	86	85
yacht	NoC	14	89	77	York	NoP	99	100	88					

List 1.2. Rank frequency list for the whole corpus (not lemmatized)

PoS = Part of speech (grammatical word class)
Freq = Frequency per million words (in order from the most frequent word to a minimum frequency of 75)

Note that different spelling variants occur separately in the frequency list: e.g. *ie* and *i.e.*

Word	PoS	Freq	Word	PoS	Freq	Word	PoS	Freq
the	Det	61847	as	Prep	1774	're	Verb	835
of	Prep	29391	them	Pron	1733	yeah	Int	834
and	Conj	26817	some	DetP	1712	three	Num	797
a	Det	21626	when	Conj	1712	good	Adj	795
in	Prep	18214	could	VMod	1683	back	Adv	793
to	Inf	16284	him	Pron	1649	make	Verb	791
it	Pron	10875	into	Prep	1634	such	DetP	763
is	Verb	9982	its	Det	1632	on	Adv	756
to	Prep	9343	then	Adv	1595	there	Adv	746
was	Verb	9236	two	Num	1561	through	Prep	743
I	Pron	8875	out	Adv	1542	year	NoC	737
for	Prep	8412	time	NoC	1542	over	Prep	735
that	Conj	7308	my	Det	1525	'll	VMod	726
you	Pron	6954	about	Prep	1524	must	VMod	723
he	Pron	6810	did	Verb	1434	still	Adv	718
be*	Verb	6644	your	Det	1383	even	Adv	716
with	Prep	6575	now	Adv	1382	take	Verb	715
on	Prep	6475	me	Pron	1364	too	Adv	701
by	Prep	5096	no	Det	1343	more	DetP	699
at	Prep	4790	other	Adj	1336	here	Adv	699
have*	Verb	4735	only	Adv	1298	own	DetP	695
are	Verb	4707	just	Adv	1277	come	Verb	695
not	Neg	4626	more	Adv	1275	last	Ord	691
this	DetP	4623	these	DetP	1254	does	Verb	687
's	Gen	4599	also	Adv	1248	oh	Int	684
but	Conj	4577	people	NoC	1241	say	Verb	679
had	Verb	4452	know	Verb	1233	no	Int	662
they	Pron	4332	any	DetP	1220	going*	Verb	658
his	Det	4285	first	Ord	1193	'm	Verb	658
from	Prep	4134	see	Verb	1186	work	NoC	653
she	Pron	3801	very	Adv	1165	where	Adv	628
that	DetP	3792	new	Adj	1145	erm	Uncl	627
which	DetP	3719	may	VMod	1135	us	Pron	623
or	Conj	3707	well	Adv	1119	government	NoC	622
we	Pron	3578	should	VMod	1112	same	DetP	615
's	Verb	3490	her*	Pron	1085	man	NoC	614
an	Det	3430	like	Prep	1064	might	VMod	614
~n't	Neg	3328	than	Conj	1033	day	NoC	610
were	Verb	3227	how	Adv	1016	yes	Int	606
as	Conj	3006	get	Verb	995	however	Adv	605
do	Verb	2802	way	NoC	958	put	Verb	596
been	Verb	2686	one	Pron	953	world	NoC	590
their	Det	2608	our	Det	950	over	Adv	584
has	Verb	2593	made	Verb	943	another	DetP	581
would	VMod	2551	got	Verb	932	in	Adv	573
there	Ex	2532	after	Prep	927	want	Verb	572
what	DetP	2493	think	Verb	916	as	Adv	567
will	VMod	2470	between	Prep	903	life	NoC	566
all	DetP	2436	many	DetP	902	most	Adv	565
if	Conj	2369	years	NoC	902	against	Prep	562
can	VMod	2354	er	Uncl	896	again	Adv	561
her*	Det	2183	've	Verb	891	never	Adv	559
said	Verb	2087	those	DetP	888	under	Prep	553
who	Pron	2055	go	Verb	881	old	Adj	544
one	Num	1962	being	Verb	862	much	DetP	531
so	Adv	1893	because*	Conj	852	something	Pron	526
up	Adv	1795	down	Adv	845	Mr	NoC	524

Word	PoS	Freq	Word	PoS	Freq	Word	PoS	Freq
why	Adv	509	end	NoC	429	British	Adj	357
each	DetP	508	things	NoC	424	need	Verb	356
while	Conj	503	social	Adj	422	taken	Verb	355
house	NoC	501	most	DetP	422	done	Verb	354
part	NoC	496	find	Verb	420	right	Adj	354
number	NoC	493	group	NoC	414	'd [= would]	VMod	353
out of	Prep	491	quite	Adv	412	having	Verb	353
found*	Verb	489	mean	Verb	411	thing	NoC	352
off	Adv	486	five	Num	407	looked	Verb	352
different	Adj	484	party	NoC	403	London	NoP	351
went	Verb	483	every	Det	401	area	NoC	351
really	Adv	481	company	NoC	401	perhaps	Adv	350
'	Gen	479	women	NoC	399	head	NoC	350
thought	Verb	473	says	Verb	398	water	NoC	349
came	Verb	472	important	Adj	392	right	Adv	346
used	Verb	469	took	Verb	391	family	NoC	345
children	NoC	466	much	Adv	390	long	Adj	345
always	Adv	462	men	NoC	389	2	Num	344
four	Num	461	information	NoC	386	hand	NoC	344
where	Conj	458	1	Num	385	like	Verb	344
without	Prep	456	per cent	NoC	382	already	Adv	343
give	Verb	451	both	Adv	378	possible	Adj	342
few	DetP	450	national	Adj	376	nothing	Pron	341
within	Prep	449	often	Adv	376	yet	Adv	337
about	Adv	447	seen	Verb	376	large	Adj	337
system	NoC	447	given	Verb	375	left	Verb	336
local	Adj	445	school	NoC	375	side	NoC	335
place	NoC	443	fact	NoC	374	asked	Verb	334
great	Adj	442	money	NoC	374	set	Verb	332
during	Prep	440	told	Verb	372	whether	Conj	332
although	Conj	436	away	Adv	371	days	NoC	331
small	Adj	435	high	Adj	370	mm	Int	330
before	Prep	434	point	NoC	369	home	NoC	330
look	Verb	433	night	NoC	365	called	Verb	329
next	Ord	431	state	NoC	364	John	NoP	328
when	Adv	431	business	NoC	358	development	NoC	324
case	NoC	431	second	Ord	358	week	NoC	322
						such as	Prep	321
						use	Verb	319
						country	NoC	319
						power	NoC	318
						ca~	VMod	318
						later	Adv	317
						almost	Adv	316
						'd [= had]	Verb	315
						young	Adj	315
						council	NoC	313
						himself	Pron	311
						of course	Adv	310
						far	Adv	310
						both	DetP	310
						use	NoC	310
						room	NoC	309
						together	Adv	308
						tell	Verb	307
						little	Adj	306
						political	Adj	306
						before	Conj	305
						able	Adj	304
						become	Verb	304
						six	Num	303
						general	Adj	301
						service	NoC	300
						eyes	NoC	297
						members	NoC	297
						since	Conj	295

Word lengths

The American philologist George Zipf (1935, 1949) proposed a 'principle of least effort' for human language use. Among other things, this means that the words that people use *most often* will also prove to be the *shortest* and *simplest*. In a frequency list, we can see this principle at work by looking at the lengths of words in terms of how many (spoken) syllables they contain.

most common 1-syllable word: *the*	61,847 per million	
most common 2-syllable word: *into*	1,634 per million	(1,634)
most common 3-syllable word: *government*	622 per million	(817)
most common 4-syllable word: *information*	386 per million	(409)
most common 5-syllable word: *international*	221 per million	(204)
most common 6-syllable word: *responsibility*	93 per million	(102)

These frequencies follow the pattern predicted by Zipf's principle.

Note also that, with the exception of the most common word of all—*the*—the most frequent word in each length class is roughly twice as frequent as the most frequent word in the class below it. The figures in brackets on the right show this approximation.

Here, as a curiosity, is the longest (hyphenated) word in the corpus, which contains 133 characters and predictably occurs only once: *oral-aggressive-anal-retentive-come-and-see-me-five-times-a-week-for-years-at-vast-expense-or-how-do-i-know-you're-really-committed*. The longest scientific term contains 81 characters: *1-cyclopropyl-6-fluoro-1, 4-dihydro-4-oxo-y-(1-piperazinyl)-3-quinoline-carboxylic*. The longest proper noun is: *Llanfairpwllgwyngyllgogerychwyrndrobwllllantysiliogogogoch*.

1.2

Word	PoS	Freq	Word	PoS	Freq	Word	PoS	Freq
times	NoC	292	child	NoC	244	act	NoC	215
problem	NoC	290	less	Adv	243	around	Adv	215
anything	Pron	288	book	NoC	243	evidence	NoC	215
market	NoC	287	period	NoC	243	view	NoC	214
towards	Prep	286	until	Conj	242	better	Adj	214
court	NoC	285	several	DetP	240	off	Prep	214
public	Adj	285	sure	Adj	240	mind	NoC	213
others	NoC	282	father	NoC	239	sense	NoC	213
face	NoC	282	for example	Adv	239	rather	Adv	213
full	Adj	281	level	NoC	239	seems	Verb	212
doing	Verb	279	control	NoC	238	believe	Verb	212
war	NoC	279	known	Verb	238	morning	NoC	211
car	NoC	278	society	NoC	238	third	Ord	211
felt	Verb	278	major	Adj	238	else	Adv	209
police	NoC	278	seemed	Verb	238	half	DetP	209
keep	Verb	276	around	Prep	237	white	Adj	206
held	Verb	276	began	Verb	237	death	NoC	205
problems	NoC	275	itself	Pron	237	sometimes	Adv	205
road	NoC	273	themselves	Pron	237	thus	Adv	205
probably	Adv	273	minister	NoC	237	brought	Verb	204
help	Verb	272	economic	Adj	236	getting	Verb	203
interest	NoC	272	wanted	Verb	234	church	NoC	203
available	Adj	272	upon	Prep	234	ten	Num	203
law	NoC	270	areas	NoC	234	shall	VMod	202
best	Adj	266	after	Conj	233	try	Verb	202
form	NoC	266	therefore	Adv	232	behind	Prep	202
A / a	Lett	266	woman	NoC	232	heard	Verb	202
looking	Verb	264	England	NoP	231	God	NoP	202
early	Adj	264	city	NoC	231	table	NoC	201
making	Verb	264	community	NoC	231	change	NoC	201
today	Adv	263	only	Adj	231	4	Num	201
mother	NoC	262	including	Prep	230	support	NoC	201
saw	Verb	261	centre	NoC	230	back	NoC	200
knew	Verb	261	gave	Verb	229	sort	NoC	199
education	NoC	260	job	NoC	229	Mrs	NoC	198
work	Verb	260	among	Prep	229	whose	DetP	198
actually	Adv	260	position	NoC	228	industry	NoC	198
policy	NoC	260	effect	NoC	228	ago	Adv	198
ever	Adv	259	likely	Adj	227	free	Adj	198
so	Conj	258	real	Adj	227	care	NoC	198
at least	Adv	257	clear	Adj	227	so that	Conj	197
office	NoC	257	staff	NoC	226	order	NoC	197
am	Verb	256	black	Adj	225	century	NoC	197
research	NoC	256	kind	NoC	225	range	NoC	196
feel	Verb	256	read	Verb	225	European	Adj	195
big	Adj	255	provide	Verb	223	gone	Verb	195
body	NoC	255	particular	Adj	223	yesterday	Adv	195
door	NoC	254	became	Verb	223	training	NoC	194
let	Verb	253	line	NoC	221	working	Verb	194
Britain	NoP	251	moment	NoC	221	ask	Verb	194
3	Num	250	international	Adj	221	street	NoC	194
name	NoC	250	action	NoC	221	home	Adv	194
person	NoC	250	special	Adj	220	word	NoC	193
services	NoC	249	difficult	Adj	220	groups	NoC	193
months	NoC	248	certain	Adj	220	history	NoC	193
report	NoC	248	particularly	Adv	220	central	Adj	193
question	NoC	248	either	Adv	220	all	Adv	193
using	Verb	247	open	Adj	219	study	NoC	192
health	NoC	246	management	NoC	218	usually	Adv	191
turned	Verb	246	taking	Verb	218	remember	Verb	191
lot*	NoC	246	across	Prep	217	trade	NoC	191
million	NoC	245	idea	NoC	217	hundred	NoC	191
main	Adj	245	further*	Adj	216	programme	NoC	190
though	Conj	245	whole	Adj	216	food	NoC	190
words	NoC	244	age	NoC	216	committee	NoC	190
enough	Adv	244	process	NoC	215	air	NoC	189

Word	PoS	Freq	Word	PoS	Freq	Word	PoS	Freq
hours	NoC	189	systems	NoC	173	secretary	NoC	154
experience	NoC	189	herself	Pron	172	weeks	NoC	154
rate	NoC	189	practice	NoC	171	clearly	Adv	153
hands	NoC	188	wife	NoC	171	bad	Adj	153
indeed	Adv	188	price	NoC	170	art	NoC	153
sir	NoC	188	type	NoC	170	start	Verb	153
language	NoC	188	seem	Verb	170	up to	Prep	152
land	NoC	188	figure	NoC	170	include	Verb	152
result	NoC	187	former	DetP	170	poor	Adj	151
course	NoC	187	rather than	Prep	169	hospital	NoC	151
someone	Pron	187	lost	Verb	169	friends	NoC	151
everything	Pron	187	right	NoC	169	decided	Verb	151
certainly	Adv	186	need	NoC	169	~na*	Inf	150
based	Verb	186	matter	NoC	168	shown	Verb	150
team	NoC	186	decision	NoC	168	music	NoC	150
section	NoC	186	bank	NoC	168	month	NoC	150
10	Num	186	countries	NoC	168	English	Adj	150
leave	Verb	185	until	Prep	167	tried	Verb	150
trying	Verb	185	makes	Verb	166	game	NoC	150
coming	Verb	185	union	NoC	166	1990	Num	150
similar	Adj	184	terms	NoC	165	May	NoP	150
once	Adv	183	financial	Adj	165	anyone	Pron	150
minutes	NoC	183	needed	Verb	165	wrong	Adj	149
authority	NoC	183	south	NoC	165	ways	NoC	149
human	Adj	183	university	NoC	164	chapter	NoC	149
changes	NoC	183	club	NoC	164	followed	Verb	149
little	DetP	183	president	NoC	164	cost	NoC	149
cases	NoC	183	friend	NoC	164	play	Verb	149
common	Adj	182	parents	NoC	163	present	Adj	148
role	NoC	182	quality	NoC	163	love	NoC	148
data/datum	NoC	182	cos*	Conj	163	issue	NoC	148
true	Adj	181	building	NoC	163	at all	Adv	148
Europe	NoP	181	north	NoC	163	goes	Verb	148
necessary	Adj	181	stage	NoC	162	described	Verb	148
nature	NoC	181	meeting	NoC	162	more than*	Adv	148
class	NoC	181	wo~	VMod	161	award	NoC	148
reason	NoC	181	foreign	Adj	161	Mr.	NoC	148
long	Adv	181	soon	Adv	161	king	NoC	147
saying	Verb	180	strong	Adj	160	royal	Adj	147
town	NoC	180	situation	NoC	160	results	NoC	147
show	Verb	180	comes	Verb	160	workers	NoC	147
subject	NoC	179	late	Adj	159	April	NoP	147
voice	NoC	179	bed	NoC	159	expected	Verb	146
companies	NoC	178	recent	Adj	158	amount	NoC	146
since	Prep	178	date	NoC	158	students	NoC	146
because of	Prep	178	low	Adj	158	despite	Prep	146
simply	Adv	177	US	NoP	158	knowledge	NoC	146
especially	Adv	177	concerned	Adj	158	June	NoP	146
B / b	Lett	177	girl	NoC	158	moved	Verb	146
department	NoC	177	hard	Adj	157	news	NoC	145
single	Adj	177	American	Adj	157	light	NoC	145
short	Adj	177	David	NoP	157	March	NoP	145
personal	Adj	176	according to	Prep	157	approach	NoC	145
as well as	Prep	176	as if	Conj	157	lord	NoC	145
5	Num	176	twenty	Num	156	p.	NoC	145
pay	Verb	175	higher	Adj	156	cut	Verb	145
value	NoC	175	tax	NoC	156	basis	NoC	145
member	NoC	175	used (to)	VMod	156	hair	NoC	144
started	Verb	175	production	NoC	156	required	Verb	144
run	Verb	174	various	Adj	155	further	Adv	144
patients	NoC	173	understand	Verb	155	paid	Verb	144
paper	NoC	173	led	Verb	154	series	NoC	144
private	Adj	173	bring	Verb	154	better	Adv	143
seven	Num	173	schools	NoC	154	before	Adv	143
UK	NoP	173	ground	NoC	154	field	NoC	143
eight	Num	173	conditions	NoC	154	allowed	Verb	143

Word	PoS	Freq	Word	PoS	Freq	Word	PoS	Freq
easy	Adj	143	20	Num	131	treatment	NoC	122
kept	Verb	143	modern	Adj	131	energy	NoC	122
questions	NoC	143	theory	NoC	131	total	Adj	122
natural	Adj	142	books	NoC	131	thank	Verb	122
live	Verb	142	labour*	Adj	131	director	NoC	122
future	NoC	142	stop	Verb	131	12	Num	121
rest	NoC	142	in order	ClO	131	prime	Adj	121
project	NoC	141	legal	Adj	131	levels	NoC	121
greater	Adj	141	Scotland	NoP	131	significant	Adj	121
feet	NoC	141	material	NoC	131	issues	NoC	121
meet	Verb	141	son	NoC	131	sat	Verb	121
simple	Adj	140	received	Verb	130	income	NoC	120
died	Verb	140	model	NoC	130	top	NoC	120
for	Conj	139	chance	NoC	130	choice	NoC	120
happened	Verb	139	environment	NoC	130	away from	Prep	120
added	Verb	139	finally	Adv	130	costs	NoC	120
C / c	Lett	138	performance	NoC	130	design	NoC	119
manager	NoC	138	sea	NoC	130	pressure	NoC	119
computer	NoC	138	rights	NoC	130	scheme	NoC	119
security	NoC	138	growth	NoC	130	July	NoP	119
near	Prep	138	authorities	NoC	130	change	Verb	119
met	Verb	138	provided	Verb	130	a bit	Adv	119
evening	NoC	138	nice	Adj	129	list	NoC	118
means	Verb	138	whom	Pron	129	suddenly	Adv	118
round	Adv	138	produced	Verb	129	continue	Verb	118
carried	Verb	138	relationship	NoC	129	technology	NoC	118
hear	Verb	137	talk	Verb	129	hall	NoC	118
bit*	NoC	137	turn	Verb	129	takes	Verb	118
heart	NoC	137	built	Verb	129	ones	NoC	118
forward	Adv	137	final	Adj	129	details	NoC	117
sent	Verb	137	east	NoC	128	happy	Adj	117
above	Prep	137	1991	Num	128	consider	Verb	117
attention	NoC	137	talking	Verb	128	won	Verb	117
labour*	NoC	137	fine	Adj	127	defence	NoC	116
story	NoC	137	worked	Verb	127	following	Verb	116
structure	NoC	137	west	NoC	127	parts	NoC	116
move	Verb	136	parties	NoC	127	loss	NoC	116
agreed	Verb	136	size	NoC	127	industrial	Adj	116
nine	Num	136	record	NoC	126	activities	NoC	116
&	Conj	136	red	Adj	126	throughout	Prep	116
letter	NoC	136	close	Adj	126	spent	Verb	116
individual	Adj	136	property	NoC	125	outside	Prep	116
force	NoC	136	myself	Pron	125	teachers	NoC	116
studies	NoC	136	gon~	Verb	125	generally	Adv	116
movement	NoC	135	example	NoC	125	opened	Verb	115
account	NoC	135	space	NoC	125	floor	NoC	115
per	Prep	135	giving	Verb	125	round	Prep	115
call	Verb	135	normal	Adj	124	activity	NoC	115
6	Num	134	nor	Conj	124	hope	Verb	115
board	NoC	134	reached	Verb	124	points	NoC	115
success	NoC	134	buy	Verb	124	association	NoC	115
1989	Num	134	serious	Adj	124	nearly	Adv	115
French	Adj	134	quickly	Adv	124	United	NoP-	115
following	Adj	134	Peter	NoP	124	allow	Verb	115
considered	Verb	134	along	Prep	123	rates	NoC	115
current	Adj	133	plan	NoC	123	sun	NoC	115
everyone	Pron	133	behaviour	NoC	123	army	NoC	114
fire	NoC	133	France	NoP	123	sorry	Adj	114
agreement	NoC	133	recently	Adv	123	wall	NoC	114
please	Adv	133	term	NoC	123	hotel	NoC	114
boy	NoC	133	previous	Adj	123	forces	NoC	114
capital	NoC	133	couple	NoC	123	contract	NoC	114
stood	Verb	133	included	Verb	123	dead	Adj	114
analysis	NoC	132	pounds	NoC	123	30	Num	114
whatever	DetP	132	anyway	Adv	122	Paul	NoP	114
population	NoC	132	cup	NoC	122	stay	Verb	114

Word	PoS	Freq	Word	PoS	Freq	Word	PoS	Freq
reported	Verb	114	showed	Verb	107	wish	Verb	103
as well	Adv	113	style	NoC	107	opportunity	NoC	103
hour	NoC	113	7	Num	107	commission	NoC	102
difference	NoC	113	employment	NoC	107	1992	Num	102
meant	Verb	113	passed	Verb	107	oil	NoC	102
summer	NoC	113	appeared	Verb	107	sound	NoC	102
county	NoC	113	de*	NoP-	107	ready	Adj	102
specific	Adj	113	page	NoC	106	lines	NoC	102
numbers	NoC	113	hold	Verb	106	shop	NoC	102
wide	Adj	113	suggested	Verb	106	looks	Verb	102
appropriate	Adj	113	Germany	NoP	106	James	NoP	102
husband	NoC	112	continued	Verb	106	immediately	Adv	102
top	Adj	112	October	NoP	106	worth	Prep	102
played	Verb	112	offered	Verb	106	in terms of	Prep	102
relations	NoC	112	products	NoC	106	college	NoC	102
Dr	NoC	112	popular	Adj	106	press	NoC	102
figures	NoC	112	science	NoC	106	January	NoP	102
chairman	NoC	112	New	NoP-	106	fell	Verb	101
set	NoC	112	window	NoC	106	blood	NoC	101
lower	Adj	111	expect	Verb	106	goods	NoC	101
product	NoC	111	hon.	Adj	105	playing	Verb	101
colour	NoC	111	beyond	Prep	105	carry	Verb	101
ideas	NoC	111	resources	NoC	105	less	DetP	101
George	NoP	111	rules	NoC	105	film	NoC	101
St	NoP-	111	professional	Adj	105	prices	NoC	101
look	NoC	110	announced	Verb	105	useful	Adj	101
arms	NoC	110	economy	NoC	105	conference	NoC	101
obviously	Adv	110	picture	NoC	105	operation	NoC	100
unless	Conj	110	okay	Adv	105	follows	Verb	100
produce	Verb	110	needs	NoC	105	extent	NoC	100
changed	Verb	109	doctor	NoC	105	designed	Verb	100
season	NoC	109	maybe	Adv	105	application	NoC	100
developed	Verb	109	events	NoC	105	station	NoC	100
unit	NoC	109	a little	Adv	104	television	NoC	100
15	Num	109	direct	Adj	104	access	NoC	100
appear	Verb	109	gives	Verb	104	Richard	NoP	100
investment	NoC	109	advice	NoC	104	response	NoC	100
Soviet	Adj	109	running	Verb	104	degree	NoC	100
test	NoC	109	circumstances	NoC	104	majority	NoC	100
basic	Adj	109	sales	NoC	104			
write	Verb	109	risk	NoC	104			
village	NoC	109	interests	NoC	104			
reasons	NoC	108	September	NoP	104			
military	Adj	108	dark	Adj	104			
original	Adj	108	event	NoC	104			
successful	Adj	108	thousand	NoC	104			
garden	NoC	108	involved	Verb	103			
effects	NoC	108	written	Verb	103			
each other	Pron	108	park	NoC	103			
aware	Adj	108	1988	Num	103			
yourself	Pron	107	returned	Verb	103			
exactly	Adv	107	ensure	Verb	103			
help	NoC	107	America	NoP	103			
suppose	Verb	107	fish	NoC	103			

Past, present and future: *yesterday, today, tomorrow*

	Yesterday	Today	Tomorrow
Spoken English	177	503	234
Written English	197	236	76

In both speech and writing *today* is the commonest of these three words; but in speech there is preference for *tomorrow* rather than *yesterday*, while in writing this preference is reversed. Added together, the three terms are much more frequent in speech than in writing.

List 2.1. Alphabetical frequency list: speech v. writing (lemmatized)

(Words with a minimum lemma frequency of 160 per million words in either speech or writing)

FrS = Frequency (per million words) in spoken texts of the BNC
Ra = Range across spoken texts (up to a maximum of 10 sectors of the corpus)
Range across written texts (up to a maximum of 90 sectors of the corpus)
D1 = Dispersion in spoken texts: a value from 0 to 100 (Juilland's D)
LL = Log Likelihood, indicating the distinctiveness (or significance of the difference) between the frequencies in speech and writing
FrW = Rounded frequency (per million word tokens) in written texts
D2 = Dispersion in written texts, a value from 0 to 100 (Juilland's D)
+ = Higher frequency in speech
− = Higher frequency in writing

Note: Two kinds of words have very high distinctiveness values, because they normally occur in writing only, being avoided in transcriptions of speech. These are:

(*a*) Abbreviations, especially those containing full stops;
(*b*) Digital numbers (numbers are normally spelt out in spoken transcriptions)

In contrast, single letters (with the tag Lett) have high distinctiveness values for the opposite reason: they tend to occur only in speech, because the habit of transcribers is to represent spoken abbreviations or acronyms with letters spaced out as separate words, e.g. U S A, rather than USA.

Word	PoS	FrS Ra D1	LL	FrW Ra D2	Word	PoS	FrS Ra D1	LL	FrW Ra D2
'	Gen	141 10 82 –	3704	518 90 96	account	NoC	102 10 75 –	656	211 90 93
's	Gen	1606 10 95 –	29320	4945 90 97	*account*		72 10 76 –	403	142 90 93
1	Num	9 6 22 –	7560	429 90 91	accounts		30 10 70 –	256	69 90 88
1		9 6 22 –	7542	428 90 91	achieve	Verb	72 10 70 –	790	180 90 94
1s		0 0 00 –	18	1 28 66	*achieve*		39 9 69 –	160	71 90 94
2	Num	8 5 23 –	6715	384 90 91	*achieved*		24 10 70 –	590	86 90 94
2		8 5 23 –	6706	383 90 91	*achieves*		1 6 65 –	22	4 68 91
2s		0 1 00 –	10	1 26 65	*achieving*		8 8 67 –	87	20 89 93
3	Num	6 5 22 –	4910	279 90 92	across	Prep	173 10 93 –	108	222 90 95
3		6 5 22 –	4900	279 90 92	act	NoC	65 10 75 –	2154	269 90 88
3s		0 0 00 –	10	1 20 71	*act*		56 10 75 –	1876	234 90 87
4	Num	3 3 10 –	4059	224 90 93	*acts*		9 10 75 –	278	35 90 92
4		3 3 10 –	4049	224 90 93	action	NoC	98 10 74 –	1617	289 90 94
4s		0 0 00 –	10	1 24 75	*action*		88 10 73 –	1170	236 90 94
5	Num	5 3 08 –	3376	196 90 92	*actions*		10 10 74 –	493	53 90 93
5		5 3 08 –	3363	195 90 92	activity	NoC	64 10 75 –	1901	250 90 92
5s		0 0 00 –	13	1 23 67	*activities*		29 9 71 –	1031	126 90 93
10	Num	2 3 10 –	3850	208 90 91	*activity*		35 10 77 –	875	124 90 90
10		2 3 10 –	3823	207 90 91	actually	Adv	1239 10 89 +	25097	147 90 97
10s		0 0 00 –	26	1 35 70	add	Verb	155 10 81 –	707	289 90 96
1990	Num	6 3 25 –	2982	178 84 73	*add*		108 10 79 +	83	79 90 93
1990		5 3 24 –	2774	166 81 72	*added*		26 10 79 –	1557	152 90 94
1990s		0 1 00 –	210	11 77 89	*adding*		16 10 74 –	112	33 90 94
a	Det	18637 10 97 –	4991	21972 90 99	*adds*		6 10 82 –	186	24 87 91
A / a	Lett	424 10 82 +	911	250 90 93	after	Conj	126 10 95 –	665	245 90 96
a bit	Adv	496 10 87 +	8543	75 89 91	after	Prep	539 10 94 –	2180	972 90 96
able	Adj	339 10 90 +	45	300 90 97	again	Adv	836 10 96 +	1381	529 90 93
about	Adv	730 10 93 +	1785	414 90 98	against	Prep	257 10 77 –	2347	597 90 96
about	Prep	2730 10 95 +	9185	1384 90 96	age	NoC	171 10 95 –	335	261 90 94
absolutely	Adv	183 10 92 +	2104	44 90 94	*age*		124 10 95 –	528	226 90 94
accept	Verb	143 10 76 –	218	209 90 96	*ages*		47 10 77 +	36	35 89 94
accept		94 10 76 –	2	99 90 94	ago	Adv	259 10 94 +	200	191 90 93
accepted		37 10 72 –	320	84 90 96	agree	Verb	240 10 76 +	0	235 90 92
accepting		9 8 76 –	53	18 90 95	*agree*		144 10 79 +	455	75 90 86
accepts		4 9 74 –	27	9 81 92	*agreed*		85 10 69 –	258	142 90 91
according to	Prep	37 10 89 –	1478	171 90 93	*agreeing*		6 10 75 –	8	8 90 93

Word	PoS	FrS	Ra	D1	LL	FrW	Ra	D2
agrees		5	10	78 –	22	10	88	88
agreement	NoC	52	10	72 –	1117	172	90	84
agreement		42	10	73 –	949	143	90	84
agreements		10	7	66 –	168	29	80	85
ah	Int	712	10	73 +	22842	28	84	83
aha	Int	237	10	78 +	10125	1	41	83
ai~*	Verb	221	10	64 +	5909	15	78	74
air	NoC	86	10	89 –	812	203	90	95
air		86	10	89 –	803	201	90	95
airs		0	3	45 –	10	1	47	81
all	Adv	229	10	94 +	73	189	90	95
all	DetP	3644	10	96 +	6115	2297	90	98
allow	Verb	182	10	90 –	1022	360	90	95
allow		53	10	77 –	469	122	90	96
allowed		105	10	96 –	128	147	90	90
allowing		11	10	73 –	384	47	90	96
allows		13	10	77 –	288	45	90	91
almost	Adv	118	10	83 –	1831	339	90	97
already	Adv	267	10	89 –	210	352	90	98
alright*	Adj	366	10	73 +	15498	3	63	84
alright*	Adv	408	10	79 +	18179	1	38	80
also	Adv	556	10	79 –	5482	1328	90	95
although	Conj	160	10	83 –	2604	468	90	96
always	Adv	597	10	93 +	423	446	90	96
American	Adj	55	10	74 –	995	169	90	92
among	Prep	26	10	70 –	3242	252	90	96
amount	NoC	149	10	84 –	32	173	90	87
amount		138	10	85 –	5	147	90	85
amounts		11	10	76 –	102	26	90	92
an	Det	1846	10	89 –	10000	3613	90	98
and	Conj	25210	10	96 –	1134	27002	90	99
animal	NoC	66	10	79 –	710	163	90	90
animal		26	10	78 –	374	72	90	91
animals		40	10	78 –	342	91	90	89
another	DetP	640	10	97 +	66	575	90	98
any	DetP	1484	10	94 +	624	1189	90	96
anybody	Pron	249	10	93 +	5359	26	90	93
anything	Pron	633	10	94 +	3716	248	90	92
anyway	Adv	503	10	84 +	8512	78	90	89
appear	Verb	75	10	79 –	2823	333	90	97
appear		31	10	80 –	881	118	90	96
appeared		16	10	77 –	1328	117	90	96
appearing		6	9	71 –	73	15	90	95
appears		22	10	76 –	611	83	90	94
application	NoC	87	10	68 –	489	172	90	84
application		59	10	70 –	226	105	90	88
applications		27	8	62 –	281	67	83	76
apply	Verb	89	10	80 –	793	205	90	91
applied		20	10	84 –	493	72	90	93
applies		13	10	77 –	107	30	87	86
apply		46	10	77 –	188	83	90	90
applying		10	10	77 –	72	21	90	93
approach	NoC	53	10	71 –	1266	185	90	92
approach		48	10	71 –	994	156	90	93
approaches		5	6	52 –	287	29	87	90
area	NoC	498	10	78 –	154	595	90	93
area		356	10	79 +	0	351	90	91
areas		142	10	74 –	474	244	90	92
arm	NoC	63	10	89 –	1462	218	90	90
arm		36	10	84 –	496	98	90	88
arms		27	10	89 –	1002	120	90	91
around	Adv	196	10	94 +	20	217	90	96
around	Prep	137	10	87 –	572	249	90	96
art	NoC	59	10	66 –	1635	223	90	85
art		35	10	75 –	1487	166	90	83
arts		24	10	51 –	220	57	90	88
as	Adv	507	10	93 –	76	574	90	98
as	Conj	1558	10	87 –	9631	3174	90	98
as	Prep	916	10	81 –	5727	1873	90	96
as if	Conj	64	10	92 –	802	167	90	87
as well	Adv	516	10	92 +	9889	67	90	95
as well as	Prep	55	10	80 –	1268	190	90	95
ask	Verb	742	10	93 +	309	595	90	93
ask		399	10	93 +	1997	170	90	92
asked		218	10	94 –	528	348	90	91
asking		111	10	90 +	355	57	90	95
asks		14	10	89 –	18	20	90	91
at	Prep	4115	10	94 –	1147	4868	90	98
at all	Adv	270	10	94 +	961	134	90	94
at least	Adv	165	10	93 –	432	268	90	98
authority	NoC	190	10	69 –	644	327	90	92
authorities		72	10	68 –	350	136	90	91
authority		118	10	69 –	304	191	90	91
available	Adj	104	10	74 –	1531	291	90	93
award	NoC	20	10	70 –	2363	188	89	36
award		13	9	70 –	2288	163	89	27
awards		8	9	69 –	153	25	78	83
away	Adv	433	10	93 +	115	364	90	92
aye	Int	414	10	72 +	15007	10	54	77
B / b	Lett	352	10	85 +	1561	159	90	90
back	Adv	1211	10	95 +	2229	745	90	92
back	NoC	277	10	90 +	213	204	90	93
back		270	10	90 +	259	192	90	93
backs		7	10	82 –	30	12	88	93
bad	Adj	397	10	89 +	688	248	90	96
bad		296	10	87 +	1262	136	90	95
worse		71	10	92 +	5	64	90	94
worst		30	10	89 –	70	47	90	95
bank	NoC	103	10	93 –	1043	249	90	90
bank		85	10	91 –	565	177	90	90
banks		18	10	82 –	547	72	90	86
base	Verb	85	10	75 –	882	206	90	94
base		4	8	67 –	2	5	83	93
based		79	10	75 –	888	199	90	94
bases		0	0	00 –	15	1	46	86
basing		1	7	60 –	0	2	63	90
be*	Verb	57016	10	99 +	54270	40571	90	99
'm		2512	10	90 +	38492	443	90	86
're		4255	10	97 +	93216	439	90	88
's		15818	10	90 +	335636	1729	90	90
am		252	10	93 +	0	250	90	91
are		4663	10	93 –	4	4712	90	96
be		5790	10	93 –	1319	6742	90	97
been		2082	10	95 –	1693	2756	90	98
being		634	10	88 –	763	888	90	98
is		10164	10	94 +	37	9961	90	96
was		8097	10	93 –	1689	9368	90	96
were		2749	10	93 –	858	3282	90	97
because*	Conj	2039	10	92 +	14376	715	90	97
because of	Prep	142	10	86 –	87	182	90	97
become	Verb	214	10	78 –	4821	728	90	96
became		45	10	75 –	2381	244	90	94
become		109	10	78 –	1866	326	90	97
becomes		36	10	78 –	302	82	90	94
becoming		24	10	74 –	463	77	90	97
bed	NoC	194	10	77 +	12	178	90	89
bed		177	10	76 +	24	156	90	88
beds		17	10	82 –	11	22	88	93
before	Adv	230	10	93 +	529	133	90	93
before	Conj	316	10	95 +	4	304	90	96
before	Prep	220	10	92 –	1465	459	90	98
begin	Verb	99	10	81 –	4318	480	90	95

Word	PoS	FrS Ra D1	LL	FrW Ra D2	Word	PoS	FrS Ra D1	LL	FrW Ra D2
began		25 10 78 –	3462	262 90 91	business		225 10 81 –	643	373 90 93
begin		33 10 80 –	327	80 90 97	businesses		22 9 67 –	74	38 89 90
beginning		25 10 79 –	208	56 90 95	but	Conj	6366 10 98 +	7310	4370 90 97
begins		11 10 82 –	229	35 90 94	buy	Verb	523 10 82 +	2425	231 90 96
begun		5 9 68 –	578	47 90 96	bought		194 10 77 +	1068	79 90 96
behind	Prep	121 10 93 –	429	211 90 93	buy		261 10 83 +	1380	108 90 96
believe	Verb	290 10 87 –	114	354 90 97	buying		59 10 86 +	82	39 90 95
believe		257 10 88 +	105	207 90 95	buys		9 10 78 +	12	6 84 89
believed		17 10 75 –	839	90 90 96	by	Prep	1663 10 84 –	35309	5493 90 97
believes		11 10 68 –	326	43 90 97	C / c	Lett	453 10 83 +	5360	106 90 89
believing		5 8 71 –	90	15 90 95	call	Verb	643 10 93 +	239	523 90 97
better	Adv	197 10 86 +	215	137 90 95	call		290 10 94 +	1624	117 90 95
between	Prep	338 10 82 –	5239	968 90 96	called		306 10 91 –	20	332 90 97
big	Adj	659 10 88 +	2861	300 90 94	calling		30 10 87 –	35	42 90 94
big		549 10 87 +	3054	221 90 94	calls		18 10 88 –	73	32 90 94
bigger		76 10 86 +	406	31 90 95	can	VMod	4836 10 95 +	16812	2421 90 97
biggest		34 10 89 –	40	48 89 89	ca~		1248 10 85 +	19835	210 90 89
bit*	NoC	747 10 91 +	13606	104 90 92	can		3588 10 98 +	6572	2211 90 96
bit		635 10 92 +	12403	80 90 92	car	NoC	457 10 82 +	326	341 90 93
bits		112 10 89 +	1406	25 89 91	car		379 10 80 +	381	267 90 92
black	Adj	148 10 84 –	351	235 90 95	cars		78 10 88 +	1	75 90 89
black		147 10 84 –	351	234 90 95	care	NoC	95 10 72 –	749	210 90 90
blacker		1 5 63 +	0	1 35 84	care		95 10 72 –	741	209 90 90
blackest		0 1 00 –	1	1 35 84	cares		0 0 00 –	15	1 44 87
bloody	Adj	248 10 64 +	4945	30 90 87	carry	Verb	227 10 88 –	295	322 90 98
bloodiest		0 2 29 –	0	0 25 79	carried		69 10 74 –	470	146 90 97
bloody		247 10 64 +	4983	30 90 87	carries		9 10 87 –	70	19 90 94
board	NoC	112 10 85 –	197	168 90 92	carry		116 10 93 +	24	99 90 96
board		100 10 84 –	106	138 90 92	carrying		33 10 90 –	119	58 90 97
boards		12 10 84 –	136	30 90 88	case	NoC	314 10 80 –	2028	648 90 92
body	NoC	131 10 84 –	1695	347 90 96	case		243 10 80 –	1106	453 90 92
bodies		22 10 77 –	495	75 90 95	cases		71 10 76 –	1012	195 90 91
body		109 10 84 –	1217	272 90 95	cause	Verb	88 10 83 –	982	220 90 96
book	NoC	306 10 93 –	152	382 90 95	cause		29 10 84 –	201	61 90 94
book		220 10 92 –	27	246 90 95	caused		29 10 79 –	712	103 90 96
books		87 10 91 –	196	136 90 94	causes		11 10 81 –	48	21 89 93
both	Adv	111 10 85 –	2943	409 90 96	causing		18 10 78 –	89	34 90 95
both	DetP	189 10 91 –	626	324 90 98	central	Adj	71 10 79 –	1148	207 90 93
box	NoC	164 10 84 +	226	109 90 94	centre	NoC	151 10 79 –	833	297 90 93
box		129 10 84 +	201	83 90 95	centre		133 10 80 –	552	242 90 93
boxes		35 10 84 +	29	26 90 91	centres		18 10 70 –	330	56 89 90
boy	NoC	237 10 81 +	30	210 90 92	century	NoC	46 10 67 –	2512	255 90 92
boy		159 10 76 +	59	130 90 90	centuries		4 8 56 –	509	39 90 92
boys		78 10 88 –	1	81 90 94	century		42 10 68 –	2022	215 90 92
break	Verb	147 10 93 –	138	198 90 96	certain	Adj	169 10 83 –	147	226 90 96
break		59 10 92 +	0	58 90 97	certainly	Adv	299 10 79 +	682	173 90 97
breaking		21 10 89 –	29	31 90 96	chance	NoC	130 10 86 –	73	164 90 95
breaks		8 10 80 –	6	11 89 94	chance		109 10 89 –	42	133 90 95
broke		32 10 82 –	96	54 90 93	chances		21 10 71 –	39	32 90 92
broken		26 10 93 –	90	45 90 97	change	NoC	179 10 83 –	1544	408 90 93
bring	Verb	430 10 97 –	2	440 90 98	change		110 10 87 –	556	212 90 94
bring		216 10 96 +	259	147 90 98	changes		69 10 79 –	1056	196 90 92
bringing		45 10 91 –	2	49 90 97	change	Verb	326 10 95 +	115	267 90 98
brings		25 10 91 –	22	33 90 96	change		160 10 95 +	148	114 90 97
brought		143 10 94 –	230	211 90 97	changed		120 10 94 +	12	108 90 97
Britain	NoP	77 10 68 –	1857	271 90 92	changes		9 10 91 +	0	8 86 94
British	Adj	141 10 72 –	1921	382 90 93	changing		38 10 86 +	0	36 90 96
build	Verb	167 10 88 –	217	238 90 95	chapter	NoC	32 10 75 –	1878	185 90 91
build		61 10 85 –	9	69 90 95	chapter		30 10 74 –	1589	163 90 91
building		19 10 87 –	34	29 90 95	chapters		2 8 77 –	302	22 84 90
builds		5 9 75 –	1	6 78 90	child	NoC	497 10 82 –	814	734 90 94
built		83 10 86 –	214	134 90 94	child		130 10 79 –	725	257 90 91
building	NoC	144 10 85 –	412	239 90 94	children		367 10 83 –	261	477 90 95
building		122 10 85 –	125	167 90 95	choose	Verb	89 10 90 –	514	178 90 97
buildings		22 9 77 –	451	72 90 92	choose		50 10 91 –	62	70 90 95
business	NoC	248 10 80 –	717	411 90 93	chooses		3 10 66 –	24	7 89 92

Word	PoS	FrS Ra D1	LL	FrW Ra D2	Word	PoS	FrS Ra D1	LL	FrW Ra D2
choosing		7 10 89 –	84	18 90 94	*continues*		9 9 68 –	382	43 90 93
chose		13 10 84 –	115	30 90 96	*continuing*		9 9 67 –	79	21 90 95
chosen		16 10 83 –	335	53 90 97	contract	NoC	84 10 72 –	480	167 90 82
Christmas	NoC	194 10 74 +	1125	76 90 88	*contract*		64 10 70 –	305	120 90 81
church	NoC	127 10 76 –	712	251 90 91	*contracts*		21 10 78 –	180	47 89 83
church		107 10 79 –	615	214 90 91	control	NoC	90 10 80 –	1829	291 90 94
churches		19 8 47 –	96	37 89 86	*control*		83 10 80 –	1520	256 90 94
city	NoC	156 10 68 –	691	289 90 95	*controls*		7 10 75 –	330	35 90 87
cities		13 10 71 –	340	47 90 92	cos*	Conj	1535 10 78 +	68811	4 43 51
city		143 10 66 –	439	241 90 94	cost	NoC	180 10 73 –	380	279 90 93
claim	Verb	55 10 82 –	1482	205 90 92	*cost*		115 10 76 –	94	153 90 93
claim		26 10 82 –	130	50 90 94	*costs*		65 10 66 –	347	126 90 91
claimed		13 10 77 –	1008	91 90 89	could	VMod	1949 10 97 +	464	1653 90 95
claiming		9 10 75 –	119	24 90 91	council	NoC	470 10 70 +	452	334 90 89
claims		7 9 74 –	402	40 89 85	*council*		424 10 69 +	413	300 90 88
class	NoC	138 10 86 –	597	253 90 91	*councils*		46 10 71 +	39	33 84 88
class		108 10 86 –	390	189 90 91	country	NoC	261 10 79 –	1428	513 90 93
classes		30 10 79 –	216	64 90 91	*countries*		57 10 74 –	1115	180 90 89
clear	Adj	145 10 75 –	482	249 90 96	*country*		204 10 80 –	538	332 90 94
clear		140 10 75 –	443	237 90 96	county	NoC	267 10 60 +	1361	113 90 88
clearer		5 10 80 –	22	9 90 95	*counties*		9 9 73 –	39	16 85 89
clearest		1 4 49 –	26	3 76 92	*county*		258 10 59 +	1648	96 90 87
close	Adj	79 10 88 –	504	163 90 98	couple	NoC	227 10 92 +	563	128 90 94
close		67 10 88 –	367	132 90 98	*couple*		220 10 92 +	748	111 90 94
closer		9 10 83 –	95	22 90 96	*couples*		7 10 75 –	74	17 90 90
closest		3 9 74 –	52	8 90 94	course	NoC	177 10 81 –	391	277 90 90
club	NoC	110 10 91 –	573	212 90 88	*course*		143 10 81 –	128	192 90 93
club		90 10 93 –	460	173 90 87	*courses*		34 10 76 –	379	86 89 83
clubs		20 10 74 –	112	40 90 89	court	NoC	108 10 80 –	2506	372 90 86
come	Verb	3061 10 93 +	14641	1333 90 94	*court*		94 10 80 –	1961	307 90 85
came		473 10 91 +	0	471 90 94	*courts*		14 10 75 –	559	65 90 88
come		1737 10 90 +	13389	574 90 94	cover	Verb	136 10 87 –	204	198 90 96
comes		328 10 96 +	1637	140 90 96	*cover*		56 10 89 –	11	65 90 95
cometh		0 2 29 +	0	0 18 77	*covered*		53 10 85 –	107	82 90 96
comin'		0 0 00 –	21	1 29 77	*covering*		13 10 83 –	125	31 90 95
coming		522 10 92 +	5045	146 90 93	*covers*		13 10 85 –	23	20 90 93
committee	NoC	207 10 68 –	4	218 90 92	create	Verb	75 10 76 –	1392	233 90 94
committee		187 10 69 –	0	190 90 91	*create*		34 10 75 –	406	87 90 94
committees		21 8 66 –	18	28 85 89	*created*		23 10 75 –	705	92 90 94
common	Adj	67 10 83 –	1075	196 90 94	*creates*		6 10 73 –	69	15 86 92
community	NoC	139 10 71 –	902	288 90 92	*creating*		12 10 73 –	239	38 90 95
communities		14 8 67 –	280	45 81 89	cut	Verb	207 10 90 +	29	182 90 96
community		125 10 72 –	658	243 90 92	*cut*		165 10 89 +	33	142 90 96
company	NoC	232 10 78 –	3051	620 90 91	*cuts*		10 10 88 –	4	12 90 92
companies		74 10 72 –	893	190 90 90	*cutting*		32 10 88 +	4	28 90 95
company		158 10 80 –	2157	429 90 91	D / d	Lett	191 10 83 +	1631	59 90 90
computer	NoC	110 10 74 –	307	182 90 84	dad	NoC	270 10 67 +	3857	52 87 81
computer		85 10 80 –	277	145 90 84	*dad*		268 10 66 +	3870	51 86 81
computers		26 10 56 –	36	37 90 81	*dads*		2 10 72 +	6	1 39 81
concerned	Adj	134 10 76 –	44	160 90 95	data/datum*	NoC	51 9 55 –	1501	198 88 86
condition	NoC	78 10 78 –	1624	256 90 94	*data*		51 9 55 –	1494	197 88 86
condition		22 10 86 –	701	90 90 93	*datum*		0 0 00 –	12	1 31 81
conditions		56 10 73 –	937	165 90 93	date	NoC	96 10 86 –	503	187 90 76
consider	Verb	119 10 74 –	1453	309 90 94	*date*		80 10 85 –	541	167 90 74
consider		65 10 75 –	311	123 90 93	*dates*		17 10 85 –	3	19 90 93
considered		39 10 72 –	1037	144 90 95	day	NoC	1064 10 94 +	181	926 90 97
considering		10 9 72 –	140	28 90 94	*day*		746 10 93 +	330	594 90 97
considers		4 8 67 –	78	13 86 92	*days*		318 10 89 –	5	332 90 97
contain	Verb	30 9 72 –	2142	198 90 93	deal	Verb	170 10 77 +	0	167 90 94
contain		8 9 75 –	522	49 90 93	*deal*		80 10 77 +	30	65 90 94
contained		10 8 65 –	506	53 90 93	*dealing*		50 10 76 –	1	53 90 93
containing		4 6 61 –	616	45 90 90	*deals*		10 10 68 –	9	13 87 91
contains		8 7 72 –	518	50 90 93	*dealt*		29 10 76 –	10	36 90 93
continue	Verb	95 10 72 –	1900	305 90 97	death	NoC	64 10 86 –	1891	249 90 96
continue		66 10 72 –	304	124 90 95	*death*		57 10 87 –	1685	222 90 96
continued		10 10 68 –	1587	117 90 95	*deaths*		7 9 54 –	206	27 90 90

2.1

Word	PoS	FrS Ra D1	LL	FrW Ra D2
decide	Verb	169 10 89 –	301	254 90 98
decide		69 10 83 +	0	67 90 96
decided		89 10 92 –	338	158 90 97
decides		6 10 91 –	13	9 90 94
deciding		6 10 71 –	132	20 90 94
decision	NoC	134 10 73 –	664	256 90 92
decision		97 10 73 –	402	176 90 91
decisions		37 10 73 –	270	80 90 92
department	NoC	108 10 75 –	789	232 90 86
department		91 10 75 –	573	187 90 84
departments		17 9 73 –	227	45 88 89
describe	Verb	64 10 77 –	1980	256 90 94
describe		25 10 79 –	104	45 90 94
described		26 10 77 –	1725	162 90 93
describes		5 8 63 –	278	29 84 93
describing		9 8 70 –	81	20 90 94
despite	Prep	22 10 71 –	1846	160 90 96
detail	NoC	89 10 77 –	621	189 90 94
detail		45 10 72 –	53	63 90 94
details		44 10 82 –	676	126 90 93
develop	Verb	80 10 74 –	1573	255 90 93
develop		37 10 72 –	407	92 90 93
developed		26 10 78 –	1013	119 90 93
developing		15 9 72 –	126	33 90 92
develops		2 7 66 –	104	11 79 92
development	NoC	155 10 63 –	1873	401 90 92
development		142 9 62 –	1471	345 90 91
developments		13 9 62 –	441	56 90 92
die	Verb	140 10 92 –	384	230 90 93
die		41 10 94 –	34	55 90 93
died		79 10 89 –	350	147 90 90
dies		6 10 84 –	22	11 88 92
dying		13 10 79 –	10	17 90 93
difference	NoC	157 10 89 –	75	195 90 93
difference		136 10 91 +	52	111 90 94
differences		20 9 70 –	676	85 90 90
different	Adj	500 10 91 +	6	482 90 95
difficult	Adj	202 10 84 –	17 ·	222 90 96
director	NoC	57 10 66 –	1072	178 90 92

Word	PoS	FrS Ra D1	LL	FrW Ra D2
director		41 10 64 –	813	131 90 92
directors		16 10 61 –	260	47 88 89
do	Verb	16621 10 90 +175115		4318 90 94
d'		70 9 60 +	1249	10 50 78
did		3368 10 87 + 22872		1210 90 92
do		9594 10 90 +126017		2016 90 94
does		1549 10 94 +	9615	587 90 96
doing		943 10 94 +	12144	202 90 96
done		931 10 95 +	7898	288 90 97
doth		0 1 00 –	14	1 52 87
du~*		165 10 67 +	6150	3 33 56
dog	NoC	166 10 76 –	151	119 90 88
dog		128 10 75 +	282	75 90 87
dogs		38 10 81 –	8	44 89 89
door	NoC	296 10 81 –	1	302 90 87
door		255 10 81 +	0	253 90 86
doors		41 10 89 –	13	49 90 92
down	Adv	1472 10 90 +	4515	772 90 93
down	Prep	170 10 90 +	518	90 90 91
draw	Verb	136 10 87 –	459	234 90 98
draw		76 10 86 +	44	58 90 96
drawing		18 10 90 –	76	33 90 96
drawn		28 10 81 –	450	81 90 97
draws		4 10 79 –	68	12 86 93
drew		10 10 85 –	457	50 90 90
during	Prep	152 10 81 –	2833	473 90 95
E / e	Lett	273 10 86 +	4380	46 90 90
each	DetP	243 10 89 –	1947	539 90 95
early	Adj	135 10 88 –	1973	378 90 95
earlier		27 10 80 –	403	75 90 94
earliest		6 10 83 –	130	20 89 92
early		103 10 90 –	1442	283 90 95
easy	Adj	214 10 95 +	15	196 90 96
easier		65 10 93 +	69	45 90 96
easiest		13 10 85 +	29	7 88 93
easy		137 10 94 –	3	144 90 96
eat	Verb	254 10 71 +	805	131 90 92
ate		15 9 68 –	4	18 88 88
eat		170 10 70 +	1053	65 90 92
eaten		18 9 72 +	1	17 87 92
eating		41 10 74 +	42	29 88 92
eats		9 10 67 +	61	3 79 91
economic	Adj	53 10 65 –	2315	257 89 88
education	NoC	116 10 70 –	1146	277 90 90
education		115 10 70 –	1148	277 90 90
educations		0 1 00 +	0	0 10 68
effect	NoC	120 10 73 –	2070	361 90 93
effect		87 10 73 –	1282	244 90 93
effects		33 10 73 –	801	116 90 92
eh	Int	211 10 66 +	5626	14 67 82
eight	Num	611 10 94 +	8328	123 90 94
eight		606 10 94 +	8237	123 90 94
eights		5 7 61 +	101	0 24 75
eighty	Num	309 10 75 +	9068	16 88 87
eighties		13 10 72 +	25	8 77 84
eighty		296 10 75 + 10313		8 87 81
either	Adv	198 10 96 –	26	222 90 96
election	NoC	66 10 75 –	766	168 90 78
election		40 10 80 –	499	104 90 83
elections		26 8 65 –	267	63 84 66
else	Adv	475 10 95 +	2990	178 90 93
end	NoC	471 10 95 +	4	457 90 98
end		455 10 95 +	18	426 90 98
ends		16 10 86 –	80	31 90 94
end	Verb	100 10 93 –	280	164 90 88
end		61 10 94 +	6	55 90 96

Frequency of contracted verbs *have* and *be*

The contracted forms of the verbs BE and HAVE are much more frequent in speech than writing:

	SPEECH		Ratio*	WRITING		Ratio
'*m : am*	2512 :	252	9.97	443 :	250	1.77
'*re : are*	4255 :	4663	0.91	439 : 4712		0.09
'*s : is*	15818 : 10164		1.56	1729 : 9961		0.17
'*d : had*	575 :	2835	0.20	284 : 4639		0.06
'*s : has*	1844 :	1598	1.15	119 : 2708		0.04
'*ve : have*	4637 :	7488	0.62	440 : 4416		0.10

*The ratio is calculated by dividing the first (contracted) frequency by the second (uncontracted) frequency. A ratio of more than 1.00 indicates that the contracted form is commoner than the full form.

Notice that, for speech, all of the ratios are greater than those for writing and three exceed the 1.00 value—i.e., the contracted form is the commonest. A further ratio comes very close to 1.00.

Interestingly, even in writing, the contracted form '*m* is commoner than the uncontracted form *am*.

Word	PoS	FrS Ra D1	LL	FrW Ra D2	Word	PoS	FrS Ra D1	LL	FrW Ra D2
ended		23 10 88 –	522	78 90 75	*failing*		7 10 83 –	156	23 90 95
ending		6 9 77 –	80	15 90 93	*fails*		3 6 64 –	240	20 90 93
ends		10 10 86 –	20	16 90 94	fall	Verb	146 10 94 –	807	288 90 96
England	NoP	56 10 84 –	2136	252 90 93	*fall*		48 10 94 –	85	73 90 97
England		56 10 84 –	2135	252 90 93	*fallen*		18 10 89 –	127	38 90 95
English	Adj	52 10 85 –	969	161 90 94	*falling*		26 10 91 –	102	46 90 96
enough	Adv	241 10 93 –	0	244 90 95	*falls*		12 10 88 –	61	23 90 94
er	Uncl	8542 10 85 +390869	11 68 83		*fell*		42 10 86 –	503	108 90 94
erm	Uncl	6029 10 90 +281015	2 35 72		family	NoC	213 10 88 –	1499	453 90 95
especially	Adv	89 10 95 –	607	187 90 96	*families*		43 10 77 –	273	88 90 93
establish	Verb	39 9 69 –	1752	192 90 93	*family*		171 10 89 –	1226	365 90 95
establish		14 8 66 –	438	57 90 93	far	Adj	176 10 85 –	578	301 90 96
established		20 9 71 –	1062	108 90 93	*far*		111 10 91 +	263	63 90 95
establishes		0 3 45 –	48	4 70 89	*farther*		0 3 49 –	8	1 47 86
establishing		4 5 64 –	215	22 88 92	*farthest*		0 2 33 –	4	1 37 84
Europe	NoP	62 10 74 –	1189	195 90 91	*further**		63 10 68 –	1698	234 90 94
Europe		62 10 74 –	1188	195 90 91	*furthest*		2 8 72 –	0	2 62 90
European	Adj	69 10 68 –	1218	210 90 90	far	Adv	229 10 88 –	269	320 90 98
even	Adv	457 10 96 –	1226	746 90 97	father	NoC	151 10 79 –	541	263 90 91
event	NoC	53 10 75 –	1850	226 90 94	*father*		142 10 79 –	524	251 90 91
event		30 10 75 –	813	112 90 93	*fathers*		8 9 68 –	17	13 89 91
events		23 10 74 –	1048	114 90 95	feel	Verb	539 10 95 –	141	634 90 92
ever	Adv	275 10 94 +	12	257 90 95	*feel*		364 10 94 +	476	243 90 94
every	Det	456 10 96 +	85	395 90 97	*feeling*		38 10 90 –	87	60 90 89
everybody	Pron	267 10 95 +	4882	37 89 93	*feels*		30 10 93 –	2	33 90 94
everything	Pron	359 10 93 +	1493	167 90 93	*felt*		106 10 95 –	1567	298 90 90
evidence	NoC	82 10 68 –	1221	231 90 93	few	DetP	346 10 93 –	303	462 90 97
evidence		82 10 68 –	1218	230 90 93	field	NoC	82 10 85 –	1012	214 90 93
evidences		0 1 00 –	3	0 20 72	*field*		58 10 84 –	731	153 90 93
exactly	Adv	201 10 93 +	782	96 90 95	*fields*		24 10 79 –	281	62 90 93
example	NoC	101 10 76 –	637	207 90 92	fifteen	Num	208 10 93 +	3237	36 90 93
example		76 10 77 –	259	131 90 92	*fifteen*		207 10 93 +	3222	36 90 93
examples		25 9 72 –	440	76 88 91	fifty	Num	535 10 82 +	13056	45 90 90
expect	Verb	179 10 90 –	542	300 90 96	*fifties*		17 10 85 +	48	9 85 85
expect		119 10 90 +	17	104 90 96	*fifty*		519 10 81 +	13755	36 90 88
expected		35 10 81 –	1366	159 90 95	figure	NoC	203 10 65 –	279	291 90 94
expecting		22 10 89 +	0	21 90 92	*figure*		97 10 63 –	424	178 90 93
expects		3 8 75 –	135	15 87 78	*figures*		106 10 67 –	3	112 90 94
experience	NoC	116 10 81 –	707	235 90 94	financial	Adj	78 10 72 –	641	175 90 92
experience		103 10 82 –	532	198 90 94	find	Verb	785 10 94 –	527	1014 90 98
experiences		13 9 73 –	192	37 90 92	*find*		529 10 94 +	305	408 90 97
explain	Verb	109 10 84 –	492	202 90 97	*finding*		34 10 86 –	97	57 90 97
explain		67 10 83 –	23	81 90 96	*finds*		12 10 85 –	149	31 90 94
explained		25 10 85 –	451	76 90 96	*found*		209 10 94 –	2282	519 90 97
explaining		10 9 81 –	56	19 90 96	fine	Adj	191 10 94 +	122	145 90 95
explains		8 9 70 –	176	27 88 94	*fine*		187 10 94 +	293	120 90 95
eye	NoC	116 10 91 –	3006	423 90 87	*finer*		1 6 62 –	51	6 86 92
eye		53 10 94 –	247	100 90 94	*finest*		3 10 72 –	211	19 88 92
eyes		63 10 86 –	3032	324 90 84	finish	Verb	250 10 89 +	1288	105 90 94
face	NoC	114 10 89 –	1931	339 90 88	*finish*		80 10 90 +	738	23 90 94
face		103 10 88 –	1704	303 90 87	*finished*		155 10 88 +	680	70 90 93
faces		11 10 88 –	228	35 90 91	*finishes*		7 10 79 +	44	2 74 90
face	Verb	76 10 81 –	673	174 90 96	*finishing*		8 10 91 –	0	9 86 92
face		37 10 85 –	184	71 90 95	firm	NoC	58 10 84 –	1010	175 90 88
faced		16 10 76 –	286	49 90 97	*firm*		35 10 83 –	458	94 90 86
faces		3 10 74 –	131	15 88 88	*firms*		23 10 79 –	564	81 88 87
facing		20 10 77 –	120	40 90 96	first	Ord	957 10 93 –	572	1220 90 98
fact	NoC	513 10 81 +	191	416 90 96	five	Num	1318 10 94 +	15799	304 90 96
fact		492 10 81 +	396	360 90 96	*five*		1308 10 94 +	15609	303 90 95
facts		21 9 73 –	276	56 90 91	*fives*		10 9 77 +	221	1 37 75
factor	NoC	59 10 72 –	808	160 90 91	follow	Verb	134 10 82 –	3610	497 90 93
factor		26 9 73 –	303	67 90 90	*follow*		58 10 85 –	181	98 90 97
factors		32 8 70 –	507	93 86 91	*followed*		28 10 79 –	1658	163 90 97
fail	Verb	44 10 85 –	1333	175 90 96	*following*		32 10 78 –	974	126 90 93
fail		12 10 84 –	190	35 90 95	*follows*		16 10 71 –	1223	110 89 70
failed		23 10 82 –	774	96 90 95	food	NoC	122 10 88 –	506	221 90 94

2.1

Word	PoS	FrS Ra D1	LL	FrW Ra D2	Word	PoS	FrS Ra D1	LL	FrW Ra D2
food		117 10 88 –	374	198 90 94	give	Verb	1428 10 97 +	179	1268 90 98
foods		5 10 78 –	191	23 86 81	*gave*		148 10 94 –	381	239 90 95
foot	NoC	169 10 89 –	117	219 90 92	*give*		845 10 95 +	3270	405 90 97
feet		85 10 89 –	297	147 89 92	*given*		224 10 85 –	806	392 90 97
foot		84 10 86 +	18	72 90 93	*gives*		97 10 89 –	5	105 90 95
for	Prep	6239 10 96 –	7070	8664 90 98	*giveth*		0 0 00 –	2	0 10 69
for example	Adv	107 10 74 –	1037	254 90 92	*giving*		113 10 92 –	13	126 90 98
force	NoC	74 10 71 –	1923	270 90 90	go	Verb	5986 10 87 +	59897	1625 90 93
force		48 10 73 –	855	146 90 94	*go*		2885 10 87 +	35449	649 90 93
forces		26 9 65 –	1102	124 90 84	*goes*		503 10 80 +	6537	107 90 96
foreign	Adj	27 10 70 –	1909	177 90 83	*goin'**		0 0 00 –	82	4 34 67
forget	Verb	212 10 90 +	598	114 90 92	*going**		1263 10 87 +	16769	262 90 94
forget		117 10 93 +	471	55 90 92	*gone*		418 10 86 +	2299	170 90 91
forgets		2 6 50 +	0	2 61 87	*went*		917 10 85 +	3675	433 90 92
forgetting		8 10 87 +	0	8 88 91	God	NoP	305 10 86 +	536	190 90 89
forgot		43 10 77 +	393	13 88 87	going* (to)	Verb	2065 10 93 +	43787	226 90 90
forgotten		42 10 90 +	4	37 90 91	*going (to)*		911 10 90 +	10420	220 90 90
form	NoC	173 10 80 –	1413	387 90 93	*gon~*		1154 10 81 +	49873	6 58 82
form		133 10 83 –	921	282 90 94	good	Adj	2091 10 95 +	5164	1181 90 97
forms		40 10 72 –	508	105 90 91	*best*		217 10 94 –	113	272 90 96
form	Verb	50 10 76 –	1558	200 90 95	*better*		308 10 96 +	428	203 90 97
form		25 10 76 –	562	85 90 94	*good*		1566 10 93 +	6955	706 90 97
formed		15 10 75 –	704	77 90 94	government	NoC	312 10 70 –	2707	711 90 87
forming		4 8 73 –	177	19 90 95	*government*		295 10 70 –	2425	660 90 87
forms		5 9 66 –	132	19 86 93	*governments*		17 9 67 –	298	51 86 86
former	DetP	21 10 68 –	2312	187 90 89	great	Adj	430 10 88 –	856	659 90 97
forty	Num	396 10 92 +	9560	34 89 90	*great*		363 10 89 –	172	452 90 97
forties		8 10 84 +	20	5 77 90	*greater*		50 10 73 –	878	152 90 94
forty		388 10 92 +	9928	29 89 89	*greatest*		16 10 76 –	374	55 90 95
four	Num	1210 10 95 +	10078	379 90 96	ground	NoC	99 10 85 –	889	229 90 96
four		1199 10 95 +	9982	376 90 96	*ground*		80 10 86 –	484	163 90 96
fours		11 10 80 +	97	3 69 85	*grounds*		19 10 77 –	457	66 90 93
free	Adj	114 10 91 –	505	210 90 97	group	NoC	334 10 79 –	1670	639 90 94
free		113 10 91 –	489	208 90 97	*group*		249 10 79 –	871	433 90 94
freer		1 3 40 –	18	3 68 88	*groups*		85 10 79 –	871	206 90 93
freest		0 0 00 –	2	0 10 69	grow	Verb	110 10 90 –	462	201 90 96
friend	NoC	206 10 88 –	484	327 90 88	*grew*		12 10 80 –	398	50 90 95
friend		102 10 81 –	303	171 90 78	*grow*		44 10 90 –	25	56 90 94
friends		104 10 91 –	185	156 90 95	*growing*		24 10 88 –	43	36 90 96
from	Prep	2178 10 89 –	12708	4360 90 98	*grown*		24 10 83 –	115	45 90 95
full	Adj	209 10 94 –	281	298 90 98	*grows*		6 10 83 –	49	14 89 93
full		206 10 94 –	250	290 90 98	ha	Int	220 10 66 +	7090	8 77 86
fuller		2 7 68 –	34	6 87 93	half	DetP	440 10 92 +	2322	182 90 97
fullest		0 3 39 –	25	3 74 90	hand	NoC	315 10 96 –	1191	558 90 92
funny	Adj	164 10 72 +	2221	33 88 90	*hand*		221 10 95 –	576	358 90 92
funnier		1 5 55 +	1	1 26 79	*hands*		94 10 93 –	663	199 90 91
funniest		2 7 61 +	1	1 48 83	happen	Verb	577 10 90 +	1889	296 90 95
funny		161 10 72 +	2265	31 88 90	*happen*		156 10 84 –	515	80 90 95
future	NoC	100 10 75 –	260	162 90 94	*happened*		195 10 95 +	237	132 90 93
future		99 10 75 –	165	147 90 96	*happening*		86 10 86 +	482	35 90 94
futures		1 4 43 –	218	16 81 55	*happens*		140 10 88 +	984	49 90 96
G / g	Lett	188 10 75 +	3621	24 88 86	happy	Adj	187 10 92 +	261	123 90 94
game	NoC	151 10 80 –	223	219 90 90	*happier*		9 10 86 +	0	9 88 93
game		112 10 79 –	122	154 90 90	*happiest*		1 6 70 –	12	3 75 92
games		40 10 78 –	109	65 90 89	*happy*		176 10 92 +	298	110 90 94
general	Adj	162 10 77 –	882	317 90 93	hard	Adj	173 10 93 –	0	177 90 96
get	Verb	9230 10 88 +158951		1398 90 93	*hard*		153 10 92 –	1	158 90 96
get		3464 10 89 + 46650		709 90 94	*harder*		15 10 90 +	0	14 90 93
gets		204 10 87 +	1718	63 89 95	*hardest*		5 9 83 +	0	4 81 93
gettin'		0 0 00 –	23	1 25 70	have*	Verb	19689 10 97 + 27565		12957 90 98
getting		539 10 94 +	4647	165 90 95	*'ave*		0 2 24 –	18	2 17 60
got		5021 10 86 +117168		459 90 91	*'d*		575 10 89 +	2061	284 89 84
gotten		2 9 83 +	6	1 43 85	*'s*		1844 10 88 + 50198		119 88 86
girl	NoC	253 10 80 –	0	254 90 91	*'ve*		4735 10 95 +108766		446 90 89
girl		156 10 75 –	0	158 90 89	*had*		2835 10 94 –	7697	4639 90 94
girls		97 10 86 +	0	96 90 93	*has*		1598 10 88 –	5051	2708 90 95

Word	PoS	FrS Ra D1	LL	FrW Ra D2	Word	PoS	FrS Ra D1	LL	FrW Ra D2
have		7488 10 97 +	16057	4416 90 98	human	Adj	51 10 71 −	1515	199 90 94
having		452 10 96 +	299	341 90 98	hundred	NoC	1053 10 81 +	20229	136 90 89
*of**		162 10 67 +	7351	0 18 67	*hundred*		1023 10 80 +	23691	95 90 87
he	Pron	8628 10 84 +	34	8450 90 92	*hundreds*		31 10 89 −	26	41 90 93
'e		0 1 00 −	111	7 26 52	I / i	Lett	193 10 88 +	2743	37 90 89
'im		3 2 07 −	1	3 21 61	I	Pron	31893 10 90 +362616		7736 90 90
he		7277 10 84 +	364	6756 90 92	*i*		29448 10 90 +369238		6494 90 91
him		1348 10 84 −	676	1684 90 90	*me*	NoC	2444 10 87 +	8239	1239 90 89
head	NoC	188 10 92 −	1613	427 90 92	idea	NoC	323 10 89 −	1	328 90 96
head		164 10 91 −	1401	372 90 91	*idea*		253 10 92 +	66	213 90 96
heads		24 10 91 −	211	55 90 95	*ideas*		70 10 71 −	201	116 90 93
health	NoC	154 10 74 −	452	257 90 91	if	Conj	4544 10 96 +	18764	2118 90 97
health		154 10 74 −	452	257 90 91	important	Adj	280 10 76 −	411	405 90 95
hear	Verb	504 10 92 +	536	351 90 92	in	Adv	1307 10 93 +	8310	488 90 95
hear		254 10 89 +	935	124 90 91	in	Prep	11609 10 92 −	31394	18978 90 98
heard		232 10 93 +	48	199 90 91	*in*		11609 10 92 −	31394	18978 90 98
hearing		16 10 62 −	28	24 90 94	in~*	Verb	191 10 62 +	8523	1 22 74
hears		3 9 76 −	9	5 85 93	include	Verb	85 10 72 −	3280	384 90 93
heart	NoC	63 10 89 −	755	163 90 93	*include*		35 10 74 −	1453	165 90 93
heart		56 10 89 −	695	147 90 93	*included*		30 10 70 −	1140	133 90 93
hearts		7 10 85 −	61	16 88 92	*includes*		18 9 69 −	576	73 87 91
hello	Int	220 10 76 +	5546	17 81 86	*including*		2 6 65 −	113	12 87 93
help	Verb	332 10 93 +	207	426 90 97	including	Prep	45 10 79 −	2487	252 90 93
help		239 10 93 +	50	276 90 97	increase	Verb	89 10 72 −	778	204 90 93
helped		34 10 85 −	333	81 90 96	*increase*		44 10 74 −	149	76 90 93
helping		31 10 90 −	19	40 90 95	*increased*		23 10 71 −	533	79 90 92
helps		28 10 88 −	0	28 89 94	*increases*		6 7 64 −	138	21 79 91
her*	Det	644 10 82 −	16899	2362 90 87	*increasing*		16 9 67 −	54	27 90 94
here	Adv	1640 10 93 +	11087	590 90 93	indeed	Adv	166 10 77 −	32	191 90 95
herself	Pron	38 10 86 −	1723	187 90 84	industry	NoC	90 10 71 −	1401	259 90 91
high	Adj	268 10 87 −	2297	609 90 96	*industries*		13 9 67 −	321	47 83 90
high		185 10 89 −	1298	392 90 97	*industry*		77 10 71 −	1087	212 90 91
higher		66 10 80 −	755	167 90 93	information	NoC	206 10 76 −	1152	407 90 92
highest		18 10 85 −	268	51 90 95	*information*		206 10 76 −	1155	407 90 92
himself	Pron	87 10 87 −	2542	337 90 93	*informations*		0 2 29 +	1	0 10 68
his	Det	1333 10 92 −	31356	4628 90 94	interest	NoC	162 10 78 −	1753	401 90 94
'is		0 1 00 −	29	2 19 60	*interest*		133 10 79 −	1000	288 90 94
his		1333 10 92 −	31332	4627 90 94	*interests*		29 10 71 −	839	113 90 92
history	NoC	70 10 65 −	1273	216 90 92	international	Adj	38 10 69 −	2595	242 90 90
histories		1 3 43 −	124	9 79 87	into	Prep	1067 10 89 −	2560	1700 90 97
history		70 10 66 −	1176	207 90 92	involve	Verb	99 10 77 −	1065	244 90 94
hold	Verb	207 10 96 −	2248	512 90 96	*involve*		19 10 74 −	179	45 90 93
held		56 10 80 −	2920	302 90 94	*involved*		60 10 79 −	250	109 90 95
hold		110 10 90 +	1	106 90 97	*involves*		11 10 78 −	362	45 87 92
holding		31 10 91 −	328	77 90 94	*involving*		10 9 66 −	411	46 90 93
holds		9 10 92 −	168	28 90 95	issue	NoC	192 10 70 −	279	278 90 93
home	Adv	265 10 82 +	275	185 90 93	*issue*		112 10 69 −	108	152 90 93
home	NoC	286 10 90 −	349	402 90 94	*issues*		80 10 72 −	181	125 89 92
home		237 10 92 −	331	340 90 95	it	Pron	24508 10 93 +151834		9301 90 97
homes		49 10 70 −	25	62 90 91	*'t*		0 2 29 −	39	3 36 65
hope	Verb	259 10 92 +	79	215 90 94	*it*		24508 10 93 +151913		9298 90 97
hope		206 10 92 +	698	104 90 92	its	Det	338 10 84 −	17017	1782 90 95
hoped		10 10 76 −	561	56 90 95	itself	Pron	105 10 81 −	1052	252 90 96
hopes		4 9 74 −	178	20 86 85	job	NoC	496 10 90 +	908	306 90 95
hoping		39 10 90 −	4	35 89 91	*job*		382 10 91 +	1016	211 90 96
hospital	NoC	115 10 88 +	305	188 90 90	*jobs*		114 10 84 +	33	95 90 91
hospital		97 10 89 −	254	157 90 90	John	NoP	260 10 89 −	172	336 90 93
hospitals		19 10 75 −	51	31 88 87	join	Verb	110 10 88 −	312	182 90 96
hour	NoC	384 10 90 +	241	293 90 96	*join*		59 10 90 −	36	76 90 96
hour		194 10 89 +	559	104 90 94	*joined*		31 10 83 −	335	77 90 95
hours		191 10 88 +	0	189 90 96	*joining*		16 10 80 −	18	23 90 95
house	NoC	557 10 92 −	33	602 90 95	*joins*		3 10 81 −	18	6 85 91
house		460 10 91 −	40	506 90 94	just	Adv	3820 10 93 +	40726	982 90 94
houses		97 10 88 +	0	96 90 94	keep	Verb	660 10 93 +	505	487 90 96
how	Adv	1888 10 95 +	7106	915 90 96	*keep*		449 10 92 +	1068	256 90 96
however	Adv	90 10 74 −	7648	664 90 95	*keeping*		50 10 92 −	23	62 90 96

Word	PoS	FrS Ra D1	LL	FrW Ra D2	Word	PoS	FrS Ra D1	LL	FrW Ra D2
keeps		49 10 83 +	196	23 90 95	*letters*		59 10 93 −	66	81 90 95
kept		113 10 91 −	78	146 90 95	level	NoC	212 10 76 −	809	377 90 93
kill	Verb	89 10 90 −	390	165 90 93	*level*		164 10 75 −	301	247 90 94
kill		34 10 83 −	35	47 90 91	*levels*		48 10 79 −	641	129 90 92
killed		40 10 89 −	344	91 90 91	lie (/lay)	Verb	70 10 92 −	1226	212 90 94
killing		10 10 85 −	72	21 90 92	*lain*		0 0 00 −	71	4 70 88
kills		5 9 80 −	0	5 84 91	*lay*		10 10 91 −	789	71 90 90
kind	NoC	297 10 79 +	28	268 90 96	*lie*		23 10 87 −	126	45 90 95
kind		270 10 80 +	101	219 90 96	*lies*		9 10 82 −	390	44 90 94
kinds		27 10 69 −	109	49 90 92	*lying*		28 10 86 −	98	48 90 91
king	NoC	40 10 83 −	1492	177 90 93	life	NoC	333 10 87 −	2081	681 90 97
king		37 10 83 −	1338	160 90 92	*life*		293 10 88 −	1821	598 90 97
kings		3 7 72 −	155	16 88 89	*lifes*		0 0 00 −	14	1 20 63
know	Verb	6119 10 89 +	74360	1392 90 92	*lives*		41 10 78 −	251	83 90 96
knew		168 10 91 −	431	271 90 88	light	NoC	147 10 89 −	129	196 90 93
know		5550 10 89 +	104930	734 90 90	*light*		90 10 89 −	279	152 90 93
knowing		34 10 94 −	48	49 89 93	*lights*		57 10 85 +	28	45 88 91
known		92 10 90 −	1315	255 90 97	like	Adv	784 10 78 +	32469	7 77 84
knows		122 10 91 +	174	80 90 93	like	Prep	1762 10 89 +	4525	983 90 94
*~no**		152 10 66 +	5602	3 33 56	like	Verb	1170 10 91 +	10866	337 90 92
land	NoC	169 10 65 −	90	213 90 94	*like*		1070 10 92 +	12162	260 90 93
land		166 10 64 −	28	190 90 93	*liked*		52 10 87 −	4	57 89 89
lands		3 10 83 −	275	23 89 90	*likes*		45 10 73 +	261	18 89 93
language	NoC	88 10 84 −	1173	237 90 87	*liking*		3 10 73 −	0	3 69 88
language		79 10 85 −	914	200 90 87	likely	Adj	91 10 82 −	1205	244 90 95
languages		9 10 76 −	277	36 90 86	*likelier*		0 0 00 −	3	0 11 66
large	Adj	151 10 80 −	3331	508 90 96	*likeliest*		0 0 00 −	9	0 28 79
large		116 10 80 −	2195	363 90 96	*likely*		91 10 82 −	1197	243 90 95
larger		24 10 76 −	552	82 90 94	line	NoC	237 10 90 −	292	333 90 96
largest		11 9 71 −	624	63 90 93	*line*		181 10 88 −	92	226 90 96
last	Ord	788 10 95 +	150	680 90 92	*lines*		56 10 91 −	277	107 90 96
late	Adj	158 10 96 −	944	319 90 97	listen	Verb	204 10 87 +	611	108 90 91
late		102 10 92 −	272	166 90 97	*listen*		125 10 84 +	709	50 90 91
later		33 10 88 −	362	83 90 93	*listened*		14 10 90 −	46	25 87 88
latest		23 10 81 −	410	70 90 92	*listening*		62 10 72 +	208	31 89 91
later	Adv	179 10 96 −	809	333 90 97	*listens*		3 8 72 +	1	2 69 90
law	NoC	112 10 76 −	2003	342 90 91	little	Adj	700 10 88 +	4476	261 90 91
law		88 10 77 −	1863	291 90 89	little	DetP	37 10 85 −	1917	200 90 97
laws		24 10 64 −	171	51 90 93	live	Verb	357 10 91 +	26	326 90 96
lead	Verb	92 10 78 −	2783	362 90 97	*live*		167 10 94 +	49	139 90 96
lead		38 10 80 −	446	97 90 96	*lived*		81 10 81 −	0	82 90 95
leading		15 10 78 −	412	56 90 97	*lives*		35 10 82 +	30	26 88 92
leads		15 10 74 −	202	40 90 94	*living*		74 10 84 −	3	79 90 96
led		24 10 71 −	1901	170 90 96	local	Adj	301 10 74 −	602	462 90 93
leader	NoC	51 10 76 −	1215	178 90 86	London	NoP	132 10 90 −	2024	377 90 94
leader		36 10 77 −	513	99 90 86	*London*		132 10 90 −	2022	377 90 94
leaders		15 9 70 −	748	79 90 86	*Londons*		0 0 00 −	3	0 2 07
learn	Verb	151 10 88 −	113	198 90 96	long	Adj	409 10 97 +	8	390 90 97
learn		85 10 87 +	0	83 90 95	*long*		365 10 97 +	13	342 90 96
learned		12 10 79 −	407	50 90 94	*longer*		38 10 93 −	0	39 90 96
learning		24 10 87 −	63	39 89 92	*longest*		7 10 71 −	4	9 90 94
learns		2 9 80 −	26	5 83 90	long	Adv	153 10 91 −	49	184 90 96
learnt		28 10 91 +	21	21 90 95	look	NoC	233 10 89 +	913	111 90 91
leave	Verb	628 10 91 −	6	649 90 95	*look*		227 10 89 +	1120	97 90 90
leave		289 10 88 +	583	173 90 94	*looks*		7 10 86 −	47	14 86 91
leaves		18 10 91 −	50	30 89 96	look	Verb	1986 10 91 +	5912	1054 90 91
leaving		44 10 94 −	408	102 90 96	*look*		1123 10 88 +	9310	353 90 94
left		278 10 92 −	125	343 90 95	*looked*		209 10 90 −	771	368 90 86
less	Adv	119 10 85 −	888	258 90 95	*looking*		428 10 95 +	1009	245 90 93
let	Verb	422 10 93 +	685	268 90 92	*looks*		226 10 82 +	1353	87 90 95
let		390 10 92 +	753	237 90 91	lord	NoC	158 10 52 −	0	161 90 92
lets		13 10 88 +	17	9 86 90	*lord*		136 10 51 −	6	146 90 92
letting		19 10 91 −	6	22 90 92	*lords*		21 10 14 +	24	15 86 88
let's	Verb	401 10 93 +	8097	48 88 88	lose	Verb	258 10 96 −	16	280 90 96
letter	NoC	191 10 94 −	33	218 90 96	*lose*		70 10 95 +	5	64 90 96
letter		132 10 93 −	1	136 90 95	*loses*		5 10 76 −	15	9 87 94

Word	PoS	FrS Ra D1	LL	FrW Ra D2	Word	PoS	FrS Ra D1	LL	FrW Ra D2
losing		27 10 93 –	22	36 *90 95*	*meeting*		178 10 76 +	18	160 *90 90*
lost		155 10 95 –	13	171 *90 96*	*meetings*		53 10 77 –	0	54 *89 93*
loss	NoC	39 10 76 –	1368	168 *90 92*	member	NoC	309 10 72 –	729	490 *90 89*
loss		31 10 76 –	989	126 *90 93*	*member*		85 10 75 –	649	185 *90 84*
losses		8 9 70 –	382	42 *90 84*	*members*		224 10 71 –	222	305 *90 91*
lot*	NoC	992 10 91 +	16310	160 *90 95*	mention	Verb	170 10 84 +	329	103 *90 96*
lot		992 10 91 +	16309	160 *90 95*	*mention*		49 10 87 +	106	29 *90 95*
lots		0 2 33 +	3	0 *9 66*	*mentioned*		111 10 82 +	240	65 *90 95*
love	Verb	177 10 79 +	52	147 *89 90*	*mentioning*		8 10 79 +	12	5 *87 94*
love		132 10 76 +	249	81 *89 90*	*mentions*		3 9 69 –	6	4 *79 91*
loved		21 10 86 –	204	49 *89 89*	method	NoC	43 10 73 –	1693	196 *90 92*
loves		21 10 76 +	63	11 *85 92*	*method*		27 10 70 –	690	98 *90 92*
loving		3 9 70 –	15	6 *76 88*	*methods*		16 10 73 –	1034	98 *90 91*
lovely	Adj	231 10 74 +	3299	44 *89 91*	mhm	Int	722 10 71 +	33831	0 *2 13*
lovelier		0 2 33 –	0	0 *20 77*	might	VMod	809 10 91 +	657	592 *90 97*
loveliest		0 1 00 –	12	1 *43 84*	million	NoC	177 10 75 –	437	283 *90 88*
lovely		231 10 74 +	3379	43 *89 91*	*million*		157 10 73 –	417	256 *90 87*
low	Adj	143 10 86 –	1005	303 *90 95*	*millions*		20 10 82 –	24	28 *90 93*
low		91 10 87 –	384	166 *90 96*	mind	NoC	183 10 90 –	173	248 *90 94*
lower		42 10 83 –	630	119 *90 94*	*mind*		164 10 91 –	143	219 *90 94*
lowest		10 10 79 –	48	18 *89 93*	*minds*		20 10 82 –	32	29 *90 95*
M / m	Lett	251 10 82 +	5781	24 *89 87*	mind	Verb	256 10 77 +	3150	58 *89 88*
main	Adj	133 10 86 –	695	258 *90 96*	*mind*		246 10 76 +	3245	51 *89 88*
major	Adj	104 10 73 –	1082	254 *90 94*	*minded*		9 10 85 +	29	5 *84 93*
make	Verb	1902 10 94 –	382	2195 *90 98*	*minding*		1 7 70 –	0	1 *55 88*
made		539 10 91 –	2336	990 *90 98*	*minds*		0 2 33 –	2	0 *31 83*
make		977 10 94 +	477	769 *90 98*	mine	Pron	177 10 74 +	2739	31 *89 89*
makes		162 10 96 –	1	167 *90 96*	minister	NoC	72 10 71 –	2887	332 *90 77*
maketh		0 1 00 –	0	0 *10 66*	*minister*		56 10 69 –	2249	258 *90 75*
making		224 10 91 –	73	269 *90 98*	*ministers*		16 9 76 –	637	74 *87 79*
man	NoC	629 10 89 –	1843	1047 *90 94*	minute	NoC	472 10 90 +	1549	242 *90 94*
man		405 10 90 –	929	639 *90 93*	*minute*		219 10 86 +	1907	66 *90 92*
mans		1 4 49 +	1	0 *14 68*	*minutes*		253 10 88 +	278	175 *90 94*
men		223 10 79 –	947	408 *90 96*	mm	Int	3163 10 80 +	146051	3 *38 73*
management	NoC	102 10 70 –	880	233 *90 90*	model	NoC	51 10 76 –	1490	198 *90 91*
management		101 10 70 –	878	231 *90 90*	*model*		44 10 74 –	861	140 *90 91*
managements		1 5 58 –	2	2 *52 82*	*models*		7 10 81 –	697	58 *90 91*
manager	NoC	90 10 78 –	829	209 *90 90*	moment	NoC	295 10 86 +	74	249 *90 91*
manager		65 10 81 –	548	147 *90 89*	*moment*		285 10 87 +	196	214 *90 90*
managers		25 10 63 –	282	62 *89 90*	*moments*		10 9 63 –	238	35 *89 92*
many	DetP	654 10 91 –	870	931 *90 96*	money	NoC	637 10 96 +	1799	345 *90 95*
market	NoC	145 10 86 –	1688	369 *90 91*	*money*		637 10 96 +	1818	343 *90 95*
market		135 10 87 –	1147	305 *90 92*	*moneys*		0 3 45 –	12	2 *21 47*
markets		11 9 68 –	667	64 *88 89*	month	NoC	358 10 76 –	47	403 *90 94*
material	NoC	60 10 83 –	1510	215 *90 93*	*month*		147 10 91 –	·0	150 *90 93*
material		44 10 83 –	884	141 *90 93*	*months*		211 10 90 –	68	252 *90 95*
materials		16 10 78 –	641	74 *89 91*	more	Adv	624 10 87 –	4646	1351 *90 97*
matter	NoC	192 10 80 –	159	255 *90 94*	more	DetP	949 10 94 +	938	671 *90 98*
matter		145 10 84 –	38	171 *90 94*	morning	NoC	469 10 88 +	2580	190 *90 91*
matters		47 9 68 –	184	84 *90 92*	*morning*		459 10 88 +	2610	183 *90 91*
May	NoP	50 10 87 –	1007	162 *90 84*	*mornings*		11 10 86 +	8	8 *83 91*
May		50 10 87 –	1007	161 *90 84*	most	Adv	199 10 84 –	3559	607 *90 96*
Mays		0 1 00 –	0	0 *14 69*	most	DetP	261 10 86 –	814	441 *90 96*
may	VMod	480 10 80 –	5470	1211 *90 94*	mother	NoC	198 10 86 –	414	306 *90 92*
maybe	Adv	301 10 91 +	2996	82 *89 89*	*mother*		184 10 85 –	299	271 *90 91*
mean	Verb	2525 10 94 +	37448	463 *90 97*	*mothers*		14 10 81 –	155	35 *90 89*
mean		2250 10 93 +	53431	198 *90 93*	move	Verb	465 10 90 +	152	382 *90 96*
meaning		9 10 91 –	40	16 *90 95*	*move*		251 10 87 +	915	123 *90 97*
means		170 10 92 +	81	134 *90 95*	*moved*		106 10 92 –	133	150 *90 94*
meant		96 10 95 –	29	114 *90 96*	*moves*		11 10 83 –	52	21 *90 95*
meet	Verb	213 10 91 –	622	354 *90 97*	*moving*		96 10 88 +	6	88 *90 96*
meet		99 10 88 –	154	145 *90 97*	movement	NoC	55 10 74 –	1313	193 *90 94*
meeting		36 10 85 –	27	47 *90 94*	*movement*		48 10 72 –	840	145 *90 93*
meets		7 10 81 –	53	15 *90 94*	*movements*		7 10 72 –	517	48 *90 92*
met		70 10 92 –	461	146 *90 95*	Mr	NoC	570 10 66 –	190	685 *90 83*
meeting	NoC	231 10 77 –	14	213 *90 91*	*Mr*		565 10 65 +	37	519 *90 86*

Word	PoS	FrS Ra D1	LL	FrW Ra D2	Word	PoS	FrS Ra D1	LL	FrW Ra D2
Mr.		5 8 61 –	2751	164 85 40	number		531 10 87 +	34	488 90 95
Mrs	NoC	154 10 90 –	265	229 90 91	numbers		107 10 84 –	3	114 90 94
Mrs		150 10 89 –	147	204 90 90	O / o	Lett	255 10 87 +	6104	22 89 89
Mrs.		4 4 19 –	281	25 70 74	o'clock	Adv	188 10 89 +	3095	30 88 88
much	Adv	432 10 88 +	50	385 90 97	obviously	Adv	296 10 87 +	2620	89 89 96
much	DetP	764 10 97 +	1057	504 90 97	occur	Verb	44 10 77 –	1273	170 90 93
mum	NoC	418 10 63 +	8197	52 85 84	*occur*		17 10 77 –	433	61 90 92
mum		410 10 63 +	8323	48 85 83	*occurred*		16 10 79 –	427	59 90 93
mums		8 9 74 +	29	4 58 70	*occurring*		4 7 63 –	85	14 81 91
mummy	NoC	160 8 57 +	4271	11 75 74	*occurs*		7 8 70 –	334	36 87 91
mummies		1 4 42 +	5	1 25 73	of*	Prep	14550 10 87 –104519	31109 90 97
mummy		159 8 57 +	4312	10 74 73	of course	Adv	543 10 86 +	1695	283 90 94
must	VMod	589 10 93 –	305	739 90 96	off	Adv	831 10 86 +	2384	446 90 94
my	Det	2498 10 91 +	5790	1439 90 92	off	Prep	341 10 92 +	759	199 90 95
me		219 10 77 +	9843	1 2 02	offer	Verb	115 10 77 –	1583	313 90 96
mine		0 1 00 –	1	0 21 78	*offer*		42 10 80 –	470	105 90 95
my		2278 10 92 +	3796	1438 90 92	*offered*		52 10 62 –	389	112 90 97
N / n	Lett	162 10 84 +	2397	30 86 85	*offering*		15 10 78 –	263	45 90 94
name	NoC	367 10 92 +	55	322 90 95	*offers*		6 10 73 –	594	50 88 91
name		299 10 91 +	104	244 90 95	office	NoC	191 10 86 –	525	313 90 96
names		68 10 90 –	11	77 90 95	*office*		168 10 86 –	400	267 90 96
national	Adj	165 10 75 –	1698	401 90 91	*offices*		23 10 81 –	137	46 90 94
nature	NoC	63 10 71 –	1166	196 90 94	officer	NoC	166 10 70 –	15	183 90 94
nature		63 10 71 –	1150	195 90 94	*officer*		79 10 75 –	24	94 90 95
natures		0 1 00 –	19	1 45 75	*officers*		87 10 65 –	0	89 90 92
necessary	Adj	71 10 75 –	981	194 90 94	often	Adv	175 10 85 –	1517	399 90 95
need	NoC	172 10 74 –	498	285 90 95	oh	Int	5052 10 74 +166592	179 89 83
need		101 10 74 –	363	176 90 96	okay*	Adv	950 10 83 +	40074	7 66 83
needs		71 10 73 –	141	109 90 92	old	Adj	603 10 90 –	37	653 90 95
need	Verb	937 10 94 +	1561	592 90 97	*old*		529 10 90 –	4	545 90 94
need		749 10 94 +	3967	310 90 97	*older*		66 10 90 –	79	92 90 91
needed		77 10 86 –	662	175 90 98	*oldest*		7 10 87 –	51	16 90 94
needing		6 10 82 –	17	10 90 95	on	Adv	1849 10 88 +	13638	630 90 95
needs		104 10 91 +	6	96 90 96	on	Prep	5659 10 97 –	1235	6569 90 97
never	Adv	700 10 88 +	387	542 90 93	once	Adv	114 10 91 –	343	191 90 96
new	Adj	606 10 89 –	3568	1217 90 95	one	NoC	318 10 87 +	2856	94 90 96
new		603 10 89 –	3528	1208 90 95	one	Num	3034 10 94 +	5910	1839 90 98
newer		2 9 83 –	20	5 84 92	one	Pron	2532 10 88 +	21938	770 90 97
newest		1 7 70 –	21	4 82 91	only	Adj	244 10 97 +	8	229 90 98
next	Ord	594 10 98 +	645	412 90 95	only	Adv	1079 10 93 –	447	1323 90 98
nice	Adj	615 10 77 +	11858	79 90 90	ooh	Int	424 10 67 +	18553	2 54 84
nice		603 10 77 +	11893	74 90 90	open	Adj	155 10 92 –	234	226 90 95
nicer		9 9 73 +	87	3 63 88	open	Verb	150 10 90 –	399	245 90 95
nicest		3 9 80 +	5	2 54 84	*open*		81 10 87 +	3	76 90 96
night	NoC	494 10 82 +	279	381 90 92	*opened*		45 10 92 –	628	124 90 92
night		465 10 82 +	292	354 90 92	*opening*		15 10 87 –	67	28 90 96
nights		29 10 81 +	0	28 89 93	*opens*		9 10 87 –	51	18 90 92
nine	Num	576 10 95 +	10001	86 90 94	operation	NoC	65 10 80 –	835	172 90 93
nine		571 10 95 +	9860	86 90 94	*operation*		50 10 78 –	350	106 90 93
nines		5 8 57 +	169	0 16 75	*operations*		15 10 77 –	554	66 90 91
nineteen	Num	370 10 80 +	12917	10 88 86	opportunity	NoC	103 10 70 –	267	167 90 94
nineteen		370 10 80 +	12972	10 88 86	*opportunities*		28 10 67 –	219	62 90 92
nineteens		0 0 00 –	3	0 1 00	*opportunity*		75 10 71 –	91	106 90 94
ninety	Num	352 10 83 +	11873	11 87 86	or	Conj	3357 10 95 –	392	3747 90 95
nineties		10 10 79 +	51	4 70 86	order	NoC	141 10 79 –	632	262 90 91
ninety		342 10 83 +	12638	7 84 80	*order*		111 10 79 –	506	207 90 89
no	Det	1102 10 98 +	529	1371 90 98	*orders*		30 10 73 –	125	55 90 94
no	Int	4388 10 78 +128713	230 90 85	other	Adj	1313 10 94 –	4	1339 90 97
north	NoC	88 10 77 –	464	171 90 94	other	NoC	186 10 92 –	1242	388 90 97
not	Neg	17272 10 89 + 97115	6922 90 96	*other*		60 10 94 –	94	88 90 97
*~n~**		367 10 65 +	14924	4 40 62	*others*		126 10 88 –	1235	301 90 97
n't		12212 10 86 +177089	2300 90 88	our	Det	1253 10 85 +	1033	914 90 96
not		4693 10 97 +	11	4618 90 98	out	Adv	2316 10 93 +	3968	1452 90 96
nothing	Pron	403 10 92 +	125	333 90 92	out of	Prep	497 10 98 +	0	490 90 95
now	Adv	2864 10 97 +	14540	1211 90 96	over	Adv	443 10 96 –	423	600 90 89
number	NoC	638 10 87 +	20	602 90 95	over	Prep	543 10 96 –	627	757 90 98

Word	PoS	FrS Ra D1	LL	FrW Ra D2	Word	PoS	FrS Ra D1	LL	FrW Ra D2
own	DetP	443 10 91 –	1198	724 90 98	*pieces*		54 10 89 –	0	56 90 94
P / p	Lett	359 10 83 +	6868	47 83 82	place	NoC	444 10 95 –	185	545 90 98
p	NoC	0 0 00 –	3235	164 79 67	*place*		353 10 95 –	225	453 90 98
p		0 0 00 –	59	3 52 84	*places*		91 10 91 –	0	91 90 97
p.		0 0 00 –	3171	161 67 66	place	Verb	39 10 87 –	1298	163 90 97
ps		0 0 00 –	4	0 6 45	*place*		19 10 96 –	202	46 90 93
page	NoC	171 10 82 +	30	148 90 92	*placed*		17 10 74 –	910	94 90 97
page		137 10 81 +	93	103 90 90	*places*		1 7 68 –	77	7 85 92
pages		34 10 85 –	27	45 90 95	*placing*		2 7 63 –	172	16 90 96
paper	NoC	285 10 95 +	106	232 90 96	plan	NoC	204 10 69 –	14	222 90 93
paper		232 10 95 +	212	166 90 96	*plan*		155 10 66 +	87	120 90 92
papers		53 10 90 –	22	65 90 93	*plans*		49 10 75 –	325	102 90 93
parent	NoC	138 10 78 –	250	208 90 92	play	Verb	385 10 86 –	0	386 90 94
parent		27 10 71 –	38	39 90 90	*play*		194 10 85 +	150	143 90 94
parents		111 10 78 –	212	169 90 92	*played*		68 10 89 –	226	117 90 94
part	NoC	418 10 85 –	791	635 90 97	*playing*		108 10 84 +	4	100 90 93
part		355 10 85 –	510	512 90 97	*plays*		15 10 86 –	41	25 89 93
parts		63 10 85 –	328	122 90 95	please	Adv	361 10 86 +	3259	106 89 92
particular	Adj	209 10 76 –	10	225 90 93	point	NoC	747 10 79 +	1441	454 90 96
particularly	Adv	153 10 76 –	258	228 90 95	*point*		637 10 80 +	1887	338 90 96
party	NoC	263 10 83 –	1874	560 90 88	*points*		110 10 77 –	2	116 90 93
parties		36 10 77 –	1030	137 90 86	police	NoC	186 10 80 –	396	288 90 88
party		227 10 84 –	1035	423 90 88	*police*		186 10 80 –	396	288 90 88
pass	Verb	138 10 95 –	282	212 90 97	policy	NoC	280 10 61 –	162	356 90 91
pass		69 10 95 +	24	56 90 97	*policies*		58 10 62 –	139	92 87 90
passed		50 10 94 –	420	113 90 96	*policy*		223 10 61 –	63	264 90 90
passes		5 9 76 –	89	14 90 93	political	Adj	71 10 69 –	2928	333 90 90
passing		14 10 85 –	85	28 90 96	poor	Adj	108 10 95 –	262	172 90 96
past	Prep	168 10 82 +	1315	55 90 90	*poor*		100 10 96 –	220	157 90 96
patient	NoC	53 10 70 –	2423	264 90 72	*poorer*		5 9 70 –	24	9 84 92
patient		17 10 78 –	636	75 90 81	*poorest*		3 5 56 –	22	6 82 89
patients		36 10 65 –	1788	189 90 66	position	NoC	139 10 75 –	858	283 90 95
pattern	NoC	53 10 81 –	921	160 90 91	*position*		130 10 74 –	568	240 90 95
pattern		35 10 81 –	498	97 90 91	*positions*		9 9 77 –	397	43 90 92
patterns		18 10 74 –	430	63 89 90	possible	Adj	147 10 80 –	1595	364 90 96
pay	Verb	584 10 93 +	1097	357 90 95	pound	NoC	899 10 85 +	18746	101 90 75
paid		163 10 92 +	28	142 90 95	*pound*		327 10 83 +	7521	31 90 81
pay		309 10 92 +	982	160 90 94	*pounds*		572 10 76 +	11301	71 89 69
payed		1 7 64 +	33	0 11 70	power	NoC	151 10 77 –	2096	412 90 94
paying		95 10 92 +	473	41 90 95	*power*		130 10 78 –	1621	340 90 94
pays		15 10 89 +	0	15 89 94	*powers*		21 9 68 –	489	73 90 92
people	NoC	2071 10 87 +	5231	1162 90 96	practice	NoC	72 10 70 –	1467	233 90 92
people		2063 10 87 +	5371	1146 90 96	*practice*		62 10 71 –	1041	184 90 92
peoples		8 10 69 –	43	16 87 88	*practices*		10 9 62 –	455	49 90 89
per cent	NoC	69 10 65 –	4388	421 90 88	president	NoC	79 10 61 –	691	180 90 77
per cent		69 10 65 –	4353	418 90 88	*president*		76 10 61 –	660	174 89 76
percent	NoC	233 10 77 +	8348	6 76 83	*presidents*		2 4 34 –	32	6 76 78
percent		233 10 77 +	8355	6 76 83	price	NoC	178 10 85 –	415	282 90 91
perhaps	Adv	444 10 86 +	271	339 90 95	*price*		121 10 86 –	180	176 90 91
period	NoC	122 10 75 –	1313	302 90 93	*prices*		57 10 80 –	257	106 90 91
period		111 10 75 –	1020	258 90 93	private	Adj	69 10 82 –	920	185 90 94
periods		11 10 78 –	321	43 90 92	probably	Adv	585 10 95 +	3222	237 90 97
person	NoC	256 10 87 –	46	294 90 92	problem	NoC	568 10 83 +	0	564 90 95
person		244 10 87 –	1	250 90 93	*problem*		348 10 85 +	126	283 90 95
persons		12 9 68 –	297	43 90 87	*problems*		220 10 77 –	134	281 90 95
personal	Adj	65 10 81 –	1051	189 90 94	process	NoC	90 10 72 –	1821	290 90 92
pick	Verb	282 10 92 +	1099	134 90 93	*process*		78 10 72 –	1317	231 90 93
pick		171 10 91 +	1690	47 90 95	*processes*		12 7 70 –	534	58 87 89
picked		66 10 91 +	1	63 90 90	produce	Verb	131 10 73 –	1406	324 90 94
picking		33 10 91 +	74	19 89 93	*produce*		60 10 72 –	300	115 90 94
picks		11 10 84 +	43	5 85 92	*produced*		43 10 73 –	877	139 90 95
picture	NoC	131 10 91 +	59	162 90 95	*produces*		9 8 69 –	161	27 87 92
picture		91 10 93 –	23	107 90 95	*producing*		19 10 74 –	147	42 90 94
pictures		40 10 92 –	43	56 90 93	product	NoC	98 10 66 –	939	231 90 89
piece	NoC	174 10 91 +	51	145 90 95	*product*		58 9 60 –	344	117 90 89
piece		120 10 91 +	89	89 90 95	*products*		39 9 71 –	626	114 90 89

2.1

Word	PoS	FrS Ra D1	LL	FrW Ra D2	Word	PoS	FrS Ra D1	LL	FrW Ra D2
production	NoC	52 10 69 –	1130	174 90 92	*reasons*		74 10 74 –	136	112 90 94
production		50 10 68 –	1105	168 90 92	receive	Verb	100 10 75 –	1284	264 90 95
productions		3 5 55 –	27	6 79 89	*receive*		38 10 78 –	249	79 90 94
programme	NoC	159 10 78 –	475	266 90 92	*received*		46 10 71 –	828	140 90 95
programme		131 10 79 –	235	197 90 91	*receives*		3 8 67 –	116	14 85 92
programmes		28 10 69 –	301	69 90 92	*receiving*		13 10 75 –	132	31 90 93
project	NoC	109 10 76 –	532	207 90 88	recent	Adj	36 10 70 –	1540	173 90 94
project		84 10 76 –	314	148 90 86	record	NoC	99 10 88 –	684	209 90 92
projects		25 9 72 –	233	59 90 91	*record*		73 10 86 –	299	133 90 92
property	NoC	62 10 82 –	967	179 90 90	*records*		26 10 88 –	435	76 90 89
properties		18 10 73 –	191	44 89 91	reduce	Verb	72 10 75 –	909	190 90 93
property		45 10 82 –	781	135 90 88	*reduce*		30 10 73 –	334	76 90 93
prove	Verb	42 10 84 –	1196	161 90 96	*reduced*		25 10 80 –	377	71 90 94
prove		20 10 86 –	364	62 90 96	*reduces*		5 9 74 –	62	12 74 90
proved		14 10 79 –	723	75 90 96	*reducing*		13 9 67 –	137	31 88 92
proven		2 8 66 –	5	4 82 91	relationship	NoC	64 10 78 –	1251	203 90 93
proves		3 7 73 –	47	9 87 93	*relationship*		51 10 80 –	695	138 90 94
proving		3 8 75 –	95	12 90 94	*relationships*		13 8 71 –	598	65 90 91
provide	Verb	175 10 74 –	3268	544 90 94	remain	Verb	48 10 74 –	3076	293 90 96
provide		88 10 74 –	1205	239 90 94	*remain*		23 10 75 –	809	98 90 96
provided		38 10 72 –	999	140 90 94	*remained*		8 7 63 –	1406	101 90 94
provides		13 9 73 –	1016	92 87 92	*remaining*		4 8 63 –	88	13 90 95
providing		35 10 74 –	232	73 90 94	*remains*		13 8 70 –	860	82 90 94
public	Adj	102 10 72 –	1762	306 90 94	remember	Verb	544 10 91 +	2607	237 89 93
purpose	NoC	65 10 78 –	704	162 90 92	*remember*		513 10 91 +	4528	154 89 93
purpose		44 10 80 –	361	99 90 93	*remembered*		18 10 90 –	370	58 89 90
purposes		21 9 74 –	355	63 90 89	*remembering*		9 10 80 –	32	16 89 89
put (putt)	Verb	1827 10 91 +	15304	570 90 96	*remembers*		4 10 85 –	32	9 88 92
put		1640 10 90 +	15152	475 90 96	report	NoC	264 10 71 –	141	332 90 87
puts		35 10 91 +	12	28 89 95	*report*		215 10 70 –	50	251 90 85
putted		0 0 00 –	5	0 12 66	*reports*		48 10 75 –	142	80 90 90
putting		153 10 96 +	734	67 90 96	report	Verb	66 10 72 –	1214	204 90 88
quality	NoC	104 10 75 –	510	198 90 93	*report*		31 10 77 +	0	29 90 95
qualities		5 9 77 –	255	27 90 93	*reported*		22 10 71 –	1241	124 90 85
quality		99 10 74 –	337	170 90 93	*reporting*		7 8 70 –	31	13 89 93
question	NoC	463 10 80 +	150	382 90 95	*reports*		7 8 42 –	377	38 87 67
question		310 10 79 +	172	240 90 95	represent	Verb	66 10 73 –	734	166 90 94
questions		153 10 82 +	8	141 90 95	*represent*		24 10 69 –	135	48 90 93
quite	Adv	1050 10 95 +	8435	338 90 95	*represented*		16 10 75 –	416	58 90 93
raise	Verb	97 10 75 –	696	207 90 97	*representing*		11 8 72 –	92	24 89 92
raise		40 10 75 –	95	64 90 94	*represents*		16 9 68 –	132	35 87 93
raised		42 10 73 –	437	102 90 97	require	Verb	65 10 72 –	2760	309 90 93
raises		5 8 72 –	85	15 85 92	*require*		21 10 69 –	522	74 90 92
raising		10 9 73 –	128	27 90 97	*required*		30 10 72 –	1489	157 90 93
range	NoC	61 10 76 –	1540	219 90 93	*requires*		11 10 75 –	563	58 88 91
range		59 10 76 –	1471	211 90 93	*requiring*		3 7 64 –	207	20 87 91
ranges		2 6 61 –	69	8 78 90	research	NoC	59 10 64 –	2491	281 90 82
rate	NoC	137 10 80 –	1299	322 90 91	*research*		59 10 64 –	2461	279 90 82
rate		89 10 81 –	748	200 90 90	*researches*		0 2 29 –	31	3 68 88
rates		48 10 77 –	555	122 90 90	result	NoC	117 10 75 –	2137	359 90 94
rather	Adv	209 10 86 –	0	213 90 96	*result*		74 10 74 –	1007	200 90 95
rather than	Prep	101 10 83 –	373	177 90 94	*results*		43 10 78 –	1157	159 90 91
reach	Verb	57 10 83 –	2162	254 90 97	return	Verb	38 10 78 –	2652	247 90 97
reach		28 10 85 –	343	73 90 97	*return*		18 10 80 –	751	84 90 97
reached		18 10 77 –	1584	136 90 95	*returned*		12 8 70 –	1434	114 90 95
reaches		4 10 83 –	92	13 89 93	*returning*		6 9 76 –	385	36 90 96
reaching		7 9 73 –	276	32 90 96	*returns*		3 8 74 – *	116	13 89 92
read	Verb	314 10 96 +	34	281 90 85	right	Adj	1020 10 95 +	10194	277 90 88
read		260 10 96 +	60	221 90 80	*right*		1019 10 95 +	10192	277 90 88
reading		47 10 93 –	1	50 90 95	right	Adv	2209 10 90 +	62243	130 90 93
reads		7 10 87 –	10	10 89 94	right	NoC	115 10 80 –	1673	320 90 93
real	Adj	132 10 90 –	530	238 90 97	*right*		67 10 83 –	896	181 90 95
real		132 10 90 –	530	238 90 97	*rights*		48 10 75 –	778	139 90 90
really	Adv	1727 10 90 +	24300	337 90 94	ring	Verb	170 10 84 +	1106	63 90 89
reason	NoC	255 10 82 –	48	293 90 96	*rang*		40 10 77 –	67	25 85 86
reason		180 10 85 –	0	181 90 97	*ring*		88 10 85 +	934	23 87 90

Word	PoS	FrS Ra D1	LL	FrW Ra D2
ringing		18 10 81 +	84	8 84 89
rings		7 10 78 +	32	3 82 92
rung		17 10 69 +	222	4 77 86
rise	Verb	35 10 78 –	1534	169 90 94
rise		11 10 80 –	244	37 90 94
risen		7 7 61 –	79	18 90 93
rises		3 9 79 –	60	10 85 92
rising		9 10 78 –	313	39 90 96
rose		4 10 81 –	975	65 90 89
road	NoC	376 10 95 +	143	305 90 93
road		336 10 96 +	154	266 90 92
roads		41 10 80 +	0	39 90 92
role	NoC	73 10 70 –	1338	225 90 93
role		66 10 70 –	1105	196 90 93
roles		7 9 69 –	241	30 90 91
room	NoC	262 10 92 –	360	376 90 91
room		233 10 91 –	235	318 90 91
rooms		30 10 88 –	162	58 90 91
round	Adv	415 10 87 +	4467	106 90 90
round	Prep	245 10 89 +	1320	100 90 90
royal	Adj	38 10 75 –	1291	160 90 92
rule	NoC	84 10 80 –	805	199 90 90
rule		41 10 75 –	285	86 90 89
rules		43 10 80 –	527	112 90 90
run	Verb	359 10 96 –	66	411 90 95
ran		40 10 91 –	364	93 90 91
run		179 10 95 +	1	174 90 95
runnin'		0 0 00 –	4	0 12 63
running		113 10 96 +	7	103 90 94
runs		28 10 91 –	49	41 89 93
S / s	Lett	277 10 87 +	4124	51 90 87
same	DetP	651 10 95 +	24	611 90 97
say	Verb	6119 10 90 +	21998	3023 90 92
said		2685 10 79 +	1838	2018 90 89
say		2116 10 97 +	24125	512 90 94
sayin'		0 0 00 –	11	1 15 62
saying		577 10 94 +	6836	135 90 94
says		740 10 83 +	2804	358 90 87
scheme	NoC	110 10 72 –	272	177 90 92
scheme		78 10 73 –	190	124 90 91
schemes		33 9 69 –	82	53 90 91
school	NoC	549 10 87 +	8	527 90 93
school		431 10 88 –	94	368 90 93
schools		118 10 65 –	106	159 90 89
second	Ord	224 10 87 –	659	373 90 96
secretary	NoC	103 10 73 –	282	169 90 86
secretaries		7 10 66 –	3	8 87 91
secretary		96 10 74 –	284	161 90 85
section	NoC	106 10 77 –	978	247 90 87
section		89 10 78 –	715	197 90 85
sections		17 10 71 –	273	50 90 91
security	NoC	50 10 79 –	1121	170 90 88
securities		1 5 50 –	315	21 64 81
security		49 10 79 –	868	149 90 88
see	Verb	3162 10 92 +	7955	1776 90 95
saw		205 10 88 –	149	267 90 91
see		2507 10 92 +	13371	1033 90 93
seeing		61 10 95 –	0	61 90 94
seen		371 10 92 –	0	377 90 97
sees		19 10 89 –	100	37 90 95
seek	Verb	57 10 66 –	1131	182 90 94
seek		23 8 66 –	261	58 90 94
seeking		19 8 64 –	228	49 90 95
seeks		5 8 66 –	92	16 84 90
sought		9 9 69 –	634	58 90 92
seem	Verb	392 10 90 –	1132	651 90 96

Word	PoS	FrS Ra D1	LL	FrW Ra D2
seem		146 10 91 –	39	173 89 97
seemed		60 10 91 –	2144	259 90 90
seeming		0 4 59 –	64	5 82 86
seems		186 10 87 –	38	215 90 96
sell	Verb	234 10 90 +	21	211 90 94
sell		117 10 88 +	219	72 90 94
selling		47 10 82 +	3	43 90 94
sells		6 10 80 –	13	10 86 89
sold		63 10 86 –	65	87 90 94
send	Verb	280 10 95 +	40	247 90 97
send		137 10 96 +	386	74 90 96
sending		27 10 89 +	0	26 90 95
sends		7 10 87 +	0	6 88 93
sent		110 10 94 –	65	140 90 97
sense	NoC	163 10 75 –	238	236 90 95
sense		159 10 75 –	168	219 90 95
senses		4 8 60 –	144	17 89 90
serve	Verb	59 10 87 –	941	170 90 95
serve		24 10 86 –	231	57 90 95
served		19 10 82 –	492	69 90 94
serves		6 10 84 –	91	18 90 92
serving		9 10 75 –	145	27 90 94
service	NoC	343 10 78 –	1025	573 90 93
service		204 10 81 –	395	312 90 94
services		138 10 71 –	668	262 90 91
set	Verb	211 10 84 –	1213	420 90 98
set		174 10 84 –	1025	350 90 98
sets		11 10 77 –	76	23 90 94
setting		25 10 79 –	114	47 90 97
seven	Num	567 10 94 +	6769	131 90 95
seven		565 10 94 +	6896	128 90 95
sevens		2 7 68 –	3	3 34 64
seventy	Num	218 10 84 +	5331	18 89 90
seventies		14 10 81 +	20	9 85 90
seventy		204 10 84 +	6319	9 86 84
several	DetP	64 10 82 –	2057	260 90 97
shall	VMod	279 10 86 +	258	199 90 91
sha~		15 10 66 –	137	4 47 82
shall		264 10 87 +	201	195 90 90
share	NoC	48 10 76 –	1235	174 90 86
share		28 10 72 –	527	88 90 87
shares		19 10 75 –	723	86 89 84
she	Pron	4937 10 74 +	5	4882 90 85
'er		1 1 00 –	5	2 17 63
her		800 10 75 –	942	1118 90 84
she		4136 10 74 +	332	3762 90 85
shop	NoC	253 10 86 +	622	143 90 94
shop		188 10 85 +	687	92 90 93
shops		65 10 90 +	33	51 90 94
short	Adj	141 10 93 –	207	204 90 98
short		127 10 93 –	179	182 90 98
shorter		12 10 80 –	27	19 90 94
shortest		3 10 83 –	1	3 79 91
should	VMod	1173 10 95 –	38	1105 90 97
show	Verb	337 10 92 –	1538	629 90 95
show		169 10 94 –	7	181 90 97
showed		36 10 95 –	706	115 90 94
showing		52 10 71 –	23	64 90 96
shown		40 10 79 –	1283	163 90 91
shows		40 10 89 –	504	105 90 93
side	NoC	418 10 96 +	11	396 90 96
side		374 10 96 +	51	330 90 96
sides		44 10 86 –	72	65 90 96
similar	Adj	69 10 83 –	1059	198 90 94
simple	Adj	90 10 82 –	410	167 90 95
simple .		81 10 82 –	335	147 90 95

2.1

Word	PoS	FrS Ra D1	LL	FrW Ra D2	Word	PoS	FrS Ra D1	LL	FrW Ra D2
simpler		5 8 75 –	26	10 88 93	*spends*		6 10 80 –	2	8 89 93
simplest		4 10 72 –	56	11 87 91	*spent*		76 10 90 –	180	120 90 97
simply	Adv	98 10 73 –	488	187 90 97	staff	NoC	139 10 80 –	469	239 90 93
since	Conj	112 10 95 –	1681	316 90 97	*staff*		138 10 80 –	456	237 90 92
since	Prep	72 10 90 –	922	190 90 93	*staffs*		0 4 59 –	10	1 58 86
single	Adj	94 10 85 –	538	187 90 95	*staves*		0 1 00 –	9	1 33 79
sir	NoC	143 10 70 –	141	195 90 91	stage	NoC	140 10 81 –	252	210 90 95
sir		143 10 70 –	138	194 90 91	*stage*		126 10 81 –	98	166 90 96
sirs		0 1 00 –	9	1 22 66	*stages*		14 9 75 –	277	44 90 93
sit	Verb	419 10 84 +	485	287 90 89	stand	Verb	234 10 95 –	336	337 90 92
sat		76 10 79 –	215	126 90 85	*stand*		114 10 93 +	58	89 90 96
sit		209 10 82 +	1518	72 90 92	*standing*		63 10 90 –	16	74 90 91
sits		16 10 86 +	11	12 90 92	*stands*		21 10 90 –	30	30 90 95
sitting		117 10 88 +	163	77 90 90	*stood*		36 10 88 –	1119	144 90 87
situation	NoC	198 10 76 –	0	199 90 95	standard	NoC	68 10 78 –	667	162 90 93
situation		176 10 76 –	18	158 90 96	*standard*		32 10 82 –	132	58 90 93
situations		22 10 75 –	100	41 90 91	*standards*		36 10 74 –	571	103 90 93
six	Num	868 10 95 +	8520	240 90 95	start	Verb	743 10 94 +	2521	376 90 96
six		863 10 95 +	8443	239 90 95	*start*		365 10 94 +	2575	128 90 96
sixes		6 9 67 +	82	1 35 78	*started*		261 10 91 +	436	165 90 95
sixty	Num	308 10 85 +	7216	28 88 92	*starting*		57 10 92 +	21	46 90 96
sixties		15 10 81 +	0	13 87 91	*starts*		60 10 93 +	113	37 89 92
sixty		294 10 85 +	8781	15 87 87	state	NoC	128 10 73 –	3460	476 90 90
small	Adj	264 10 92 –	1730	548 90 97	*state*		108 10 76 –	2796	393 90 90
small		216 10 91 –	1525	460 90 97	*states*		20 10 48 –	666	83 90 87
smaller		42 10 93 –	175	77 90 95	stay	Verb	222 10 88 +	87	179 90 93
smallest		5 9 80 –	38	11 90 95	*stay*		146 10 88 +	95	110 90 93
so	Adv	5067 10 95 +	44484	1526 90 96	*stayed*		29 10 83 –	7	34 89 93
so	Conj	400 10 96 +	793	241 90 94	*staying*		34 10 79 +	14	27 90 92
so that	Conj	231 10 85 +	64	193 90 96	*stays*		12 10 90 +	30	7 89 93
social	Adj	115 10 75 –	3523	458 90 90	still	Adv	739 10 97 +	7	715 90 97
society	NoC	102 10 79 –	1712	303 90 93	stop	Verb	334 10 90 +	261	246 90 92
societies		13 9 71 –	340	47 88 89	*stop*		225 10 89 +	661	120 90 93
society		89 10 79 –	1379	256 90 93	*stopped*		70 10 90 –	85	99 90 89
some	DetP	1986 10 97 +	485	1681 90 98	*stopping*		22 10 89 +	28	15 90 94
somebody	Pron	409 10 96 +	9932	34 89 91	*stops*		16 10 88 +	12	12 89 94
someone	Pron	181 10 96 +	1	187 90 93	story	NoC	129 10 88 –	212	191 90 95
something	Pron	1290 10 96 +	9584	437 90 93	*stories*		34 10 84 –	50	49 90 94
sometimes	Adv	199 10 94 –	2	206 90 96	*story*		95 10 89 –	161	141 90 95
somewhere	Adv	173 10 93 +	1294	58 90 90	street	NoC	160 10 88 –	365	253 90 94
son	NoC	85 10 89 –	549	175 90 90	*street*		137 10 87 –	208	200 90 94
son		72 10 88 –	365	138 90 91	*streets*		23 10 81 –	200	52 90 94
sons		13 10 78 –	203	37 90 82	strong	Adj	95 10 90 –	747	209 90 97
soon	Adv	82 10 91 –	540	170 90 96	*strong*		77 10 90 –	606	170 90 97
sorry	Adj	431 10 91 +	6460	78 90 85	*stronger*		14 10 89 –	75	28 90 97
sorrier		0 0 00 –	3	0 14 74	*strongest*		3 8 66 –	76	11 90 94
sorry		431 10 91 +	6473	78 90 85	structure	NoC	89 10 64 –	654	191 90 91
sort	NoC	800 10 89 +	10829	163 90 95	*structure*		80 10 63 –	319	143 90 92
sort		712 10 90 +	9947	140 90 95	*structures*		9 7 69 –	459	48 89 90
sorts		88 10 83 +	927	23 90 96	student	NoC	73 10 69 –	1530	240 90 88
sort of	Adv	472 10 92 +	17161	11 83 82	*student*		25 10 78 –	526	82 90 89
source	NoC	31 10 76 –	1692	172 90 94	*students*		48 10 64 –	1004	157 90 87
source		19 10 78 –	942	99 90 94	study	NoC	56 10 79 –	3826	359 90 86
sources		12 8 64 –	752	73 90 92	*studies*		18 10 74 –	1801	149 90 84
south	NoC	103 10 77 –	308	172 90 94	*study*		38 10 80 –	2046	209 90 88
south		103 10 77 –	307	172 90 94	stuff	NoC	274 10 86 +	4406	46 90 90
speak	Verb	276 10 94 +	9	259 90 94	*stuff*		274 10 86 +	4430	45 89 90
speak		128 10 93 +	125	90 90 93	*stuffs*		0 2 33 –	1	0 25 75
speaking		68 10 88 +	36	53 90 96	subject	NoC	86 10 77 –	1727	276 90 88
speaks		10 10 87 –	15	15 90 94	*subject*		66 10 78 –	1059	192 90 86
spoke		43 10 92 –	129	73 90 90	*subjects*		19 10 66 –	693	84 90 86
spoken		26 10 89 –	1	29 90 93	such	DetP	225 10 91 –	5912	825 90 95
special	Adj	125 10 88 –	559	231 90 96	such as	Prep	43 10 73 –	4252	354 90 94
spend	Verb	214 10 91 –	8	228 90 97	suggest	Verb	157 10 75 –	803	303 90 95
spend		103 10 92 +	119	71 90 96	*suggest*		77 10 77 –	19	90 90 94
spending		28 10 83 –	0	30 90 96	*suggested*		42 10 74 –	569	114 90 96

2.1

Word	PoS	FrS Ra D1	LL	FrW Ra D2	Word	PoS	FrS Ra D1	LL	FrW Ra D2
suggesting		27 9 72 +	0	25 90 94	*test*		62 10 89 −	278	114 90 91
suggests		12 9 72 −	781	74 89 92	*tests*		20 10 78 −	262	53 90 92
support	NoC	106 10 71 −	645	215 90 93	than	Conj	683 10 95 −	1547	1074 90 98
support		104 10 71 −	636	212 90 93	thank	Verb	599 10 83 +	11499	77 90 89
supports		2 5 53 −	9	3 76 90	*thank*		595 10 83 +	12397	67 90 88
support	Verb	137 10 68 −	173	193 90 93	*thanked*		2 8 68 −	61	8 84 90
support		93 10 67 −	2	98 90 92	*thanking*		2 10 81 −	0	2 67 90
supported		23 9 68 −	293	60 90 94	*thanks*		0 3 45 +	0	0 24 81
supporting		15 10 76 −	16	20 90 93	thanks	NoC	162 10 92 +	1361	50 90 93
supports		6 8 55 −	60	15 81 80	that	Conj	7246 10 85 −	6	7315 90 97
suppose	Verb	282 10 89 +	1888	102 89 90	that	DetP	14252 10 95 +	213613	2581 90 95
suppose		275 10 89 +	2237	88 89 90	the	Det	39605 10 91 −	104720	64420 90 99
supposed		5 10 85 −	52	12 86 89	their	Det	1284 10 75 −	9386	2761 90 97
supposes		0 2 33 −	10	1 46 86	themselves	Pron	128 10 80 −	686	250 90 96
supposing		2 6 61 +	0	1 55 85	*theirselves*		4 9 80 +	147	0 3 43
sure	Adj	479 10 95 +	2185	213 90 92	*themselves*		124 10 80 −	732	250 90 96
sure		479 10 95 +	2211	212 90 92	then	Adv	3474 10 93 +	19911	1378 90 95
surer		0 0 00 −	10	1 32 84	theory	NoC	40 10 72 −	1585	183 90 89
surest		0 0 00 −	12	1 35 84	*theories*		4 9 68 −	510	40 89 87
system	NoC	232 10 76 −	3582	664 90 89	*theory*		35 10 70 −	1108	142 90 90
system		189 10 79 −	2141	476 90 91	there	Adv	2895 10 88 +	45274	498 90 92
systems		43 10 60 −	1558	188 90 80	*there*		2894 10 88 +	45269	498 90 92
T / t	Lett	255 10 91 +	4505	37 89 80	there	Ex	4067 10 95 +	9288	2354 90 98
table	NoC	176 10 91 −	163	237 90 94	therefore	Adv	152 10 73 −	356	241 90 92
table		148 10 90 −	176	208 90 94	these	DetP	1269 10 95 +	2	1252 90 95
tables		28 10 89 −	1	29 90 92	they	Pron	12517 10 95 +	62479	5337 90 97
take	Verb	2018 10 98 +	303	1771 90 98	*'em*		58 10 81 +	848	11 75 84
take		1149 10 97 +	2625	665 90 98	*them*		3126 10 93 +	10733	1572 90 96
taken		231 10 88 −	559	369 90 98	*they*		9333 10 95 +	52132	3754 90 97
takes		126 10 97 +	7	117 90 96	thing	NoC	2240 10 96 +	22464	607 90 94
taking		224 10 95 +	1	217 90 98	*thing*		1136 10 96 +	13670	261 90 92
took		287 10 91 −	351	404 90 95	*things*		1103 10 92 +	9183	346 90 95
talk	Verb	776 10 93 +	6061	254 90 92	think	Verb	5063 10 97 +	63854	1110 90 91
talk		266 10 92 +	1339	113 90 92	*think*		3977 10 97 +	71946	562 90 92
talked		68 10 85 +	125	42 90 91	*thinking*		179 10 94 +	771	82 90 92
talkin'		0 0 00 −	20	1 21 70	*thinks*		62 10 88 +	134	36 89 94
talking		428 10 94 +	5463	93 90 92	*thought*		845 10 83 +	2811	430 90 90
talks		14 10 89 +	67	6 84 93	third	Ord	132 10 85 −	391	220 90 95
tape	NoC	182 10 74 −	1987	46 90 92	thirty	Num	534 10 93 +	12312	50 90 92
tape		139 10 76 +	1502	35 90 92	*thirties*		14 10 76 +	50	7 83 92
tapes		44 10 67 +	484	11 90 90	*thirty*		520 10 93 +	12743	43 89 91
tax	NoC	118 10 87 −	316	192 90 87	this	DetP	5627 10 95 +	2379	4506 90 97
tax		107 10 87 −	197	162 90 87	those	DetP	1121 10 92 +	655	861 90 96
taxes		10 10 80 −	165	30 88 88	though	Adv	410 10 80 +	7013	63 89 93
tea	NoC	176 10 76 +	805	78 90 90	though	Conj	5 10 89 −	4885	273 90 96
tea		172 10 76 +	801	76 90 90	thousand	NoC	553 10 83 +	7468	113 90 90
teas		4 10 69 +	7	2 59 83	*thousand*		516 10 82 +	10998	56 90 86
teacher	NoC	134 10 74 −	305	211 90 89	*thousands*		37 10 80 −	75	57 90 92
teacher		67 10 84 −	58	90 90 90	three	Num	1735 10 95 +	9857	692 90 97
teachers		67 10 63 −	278	121 90 88	*three*		1721 10 95 +	9654	691 90 97
team	NoC	116 10 82 −	740	238 90 91	*threes*		14 10 64 +	375	1 52 87
team		93 10 83 −	651	197 90 91	through	Prep	615 10 92 −	271	758 90 98
teams		23 10 77 −	93	41 88 90	thus	Adv	8 10 75 −	3757	228 90 92
tell	Verb	1180 10 90 +	2156	728 90 92	time	NoC	2103 10 95 +	439	1802 90 98
tell		668 10 90 +	3824	265 90 89	*time*		1819 10 96 +	548	1509 90 98
tellin'		0 0 00 −	9	0 12 64	*times*		284 10 90 −	2	293 90 97
telling		108 10 88 +	401	53 90 92	to	Inf	16615 10 96 +	14	16453 90 99
tells		42 10 92 +	7	36 89 94	*~na**		1376 10 79 +	58868	8 66 83
told		362 10 88 −	3	373 90 92	*~ta**		326 10 75 +	13786	2 49 83
ten	Num	627 10 95 +	6680	161 90 96	*to*		14912 10 93 −	1371	16442 90 99
ten		616 10 95 +	6735	155 90 96	to	Prep	6950 10 94 −	7715	9620 90 99
tens		11 10 81 +	24	7 83 91	today	Adv	503 10 94 +	2058	236 90 92
term	NoC	178 10 78 −	555	301 90 91	together	Adv	262 10 92 −	84	313 90 98
term		102 10 82 −	43	125 90 92	tomorrow	Adv	234 10 80 +	1831	76 90 87
terms		76 10 72 −	681	176 90 89	tonight	Adv	178 10 81 +	1466	56 86 85
test	NoC	82 10 88 −	520	168 90 92	too	Adv	629 10 93 −	89	710 90 95

Word	PoS	FrS	Ra	D1	LL	FrW	Ra	D2
top	NoC	204	10	89 +	425	121	90	95
top		196	10	90 +	475	112	90	95
tops		7	10	82 –	4	9	85	91
towards	Prep	123	10	83 –	1331	305	90	96
town	NoC	171	10	84 –	138	227	90	93
town		159	10	84 –	30	182	90	92
towns		13	10	72 –	302	44	90	90
trade	NoC	131	10	67 –	334	211	90	91
trade		122	10	67 –	333	199	90	91
trades		9	8	49 –	5	12	85	91
training	NoC	156	10	73 –	93	198	90	91
training		156	10	73 –	93	198	90	91
true	Adj	177	10	94 –	2	184	90	97
true		177	10	94 –	1	182	90	97
truer		0	2	29 –	7	1	58	89
truest		0	1	00 –	5	1	30	79
try	Verb	824	10	97 +	1366	521	90	95
tried		107	10	96 –	159	155	90	93
tries		11	10	85 –	13	15	89	94
try		396	10	97 +	1728	180	90	96
trying		311	10	95 +	836	171	90	94
turn	Verb	358	10	93 –	307	477	90	93
turn		198	10	90 +	373	121	90	96
turned		100	10	92 –	1269	263	90	90
turning		34	10	94 –	137	61	90	93
turns		27	10	93 –	10	33	89	95
twelve	Num	280	10	94 +	4884	42	90	95
twelve		278	10	94 +	4881	41	90	95
twelves		1	8	68 –	11	0	12	38
twenty	Num	937	10	92 +	23421	74	90	91
twenties		13	10	82 +	38	7	82	91
twenty		925	10	92 +	23929	67	90	91
two	Num	2724	10	96 +	8369	1429	90	98
two		2710	10	96 +	8229	1428	90	98
twos		14	10	75 +	332	1	56	87
type	NoC	154	10	87 –	562	271	90	90
type		117	10	89 –	212	176	90	87
types		37	10	76 –	431	95	90	92
UK	NoP	0	2	29 –	3834	198	90	90
U.K.		0	0	00 –	82	4	58	79
UK		0	2	29 –	3746	193	88	90
under	Prep	234	10	91 –	2659	590	90	95
understand	Verb	236	10	86 –	0	238	90	96
understand		203	10	88 +	156	149	90	95
understanding		7	10	79 –	113	20	90	93
understands		3	10	80 –	22	7	89	94
understood		23	10	76 –	303	61	90	97
union	NoC	170	10	65 –	95	216	90	88
union		134	10	64 –	74	169	90	86
unions		36	9	64 –	21	46	85	89
unit	NoC	84	10	81 –	712	191	90	93
unit		48	10	85 –	485	116	90	93
units		36	10	73 –	231	74	90	91
university	NoC	87	10	43 –	806	203	90	87
universities		12	9	35 –	110	28	88	87
university		75	10	44 –	695	175	90	87
until	Conj	137	10	95 –	619	254	90	96
until	Prep	82	10	90 –	608	177	90	95
up	Adv	2891	10	91 +	6666	1668	90	95
up to	Prep	228	10	93 +	386	144	90	96
upon	Prep	80	10	73 –	1521	252	90	94
US	NoP	2	8	68 –	3319	181	89	84
U.S.		0	0	00 –	97	5	53	81
US		2	8	68 –	3220	176	89	84
use	NoC	106	10	82 –	2281	353	90	94
use		99	10	83 –	2204	334	90	94
uses		8	9	69 –	82	19	88	90
use	Verb	859	10	90 –	516	1095	90	95
use		455	10	92 +	605	303	90	95
used		225	10	87 –	1783	497	90	95
uses		22	10	90 –	76	38	90	92
using		157	10	85 –	430	257	90	93
used (to)	VMod	742	10	76 +	15000	88	90	94
usually	Adv	144	10	91 –	144	197	90	94
value	NoC	86	10	79 –	1637	269	90	92
value		70	10	81 –	919	187	90	93
values		15	8	70 –	786	82	90	90
various	Adj	101	10	76 –	242	161	90	95
very	Adv	2373	10	89 +	11530	1025	90	97
view	NoC	212	10	71 –	253	297	90	95
view		169	10	71 –	115	219	90	95
views		43	9	70 –	177	78	90	94
voice	NoC	56	10	89 –	1695	220	90	87
voice		48	10	89 –	1520	194	90	87
voices		8	10	84 –	176	26	89	92
wait	Verb	252	10	85 +	77	208	90	90
wait		166	10	83 +	755	74	90	91
waited		8	10	86 –	427	43	90	86
waiting		76	10	89 –	15	88	90	91
waits		2	7	63 –	7	3	74	91
walk	Verb	262	10	83 +	113	209	90	90
walk		122	10	83 +	461	59	90	92
walked		55	10	79 –	215	99	90	86
walking		74	10	84 +	138	45	90	91
walks		11	10	72 +	25	6	87	92
wall	NoC	98	10	85 –	450	183	90	93
wall		79	10	84 –	136	118	90	92
walls		19	10	86 –	436	65	90	93
want	Verb	2548	10	89 +	22687	760	90	93
wan~		231	10	70 +	9356	3	51	79
want		1776	10	89 +	20109	432	90	93
wanted		314	10	95 +	287	225	90	91
wantin'		0	0	00 –	2	0	6	54
wanting		31	10	94 +	19	23	90	93
wants		197	10	86 +	1185	76	90	93
war	NoC	181	10	74 –	604	311	90	94
war		170	10	74 –	556	291	90	94
wars		11	9	67 –	48	20	90	93
watch	Verb	243	10	77 +	91	197	90	90
watch		148	10	75 +	879	57	90	93
watched		31	10	75 –	274	71	90	87
watches		2	9	71 –	1	3	70	88
watching		62	10	81 –	1	66	90	90
water	NoC	285	10	84 –	251	382	90	94
water		278	10	84 –	180	358	90	94
waters		7	9	61 –	155	24	90	92
way	NoC	1358	10	95 +	614	1079	90	97
way		1252	10	96 +	956	925	90	97
ways		106	10	78 –	157	154	90	95
we	Pron	11507	10	93	+105361	3356	90	96
us		1059	10	92 +	2981	573	90	96
we		10448	10	93	+106914	2784	90	96
week	NoC	829	10	93 +	2548	435	90	94
week		631	10	92 +	2765	286	90	93
weeks		198	10	95 +	137	149	90	95
well	Adv	5310	10	87	+107026	634	90	95
what	DetP	7313	10	92 +	75414	1936	90	94
whatever	DetP	289	10	97 +	1663	114	90	96
when	Adv	530	10	92 +	248	420	90	98
when	Conj	2255	10	94 +	1836	1649	90	97
where	Adv	1380	10	94 +	8075	541	90	97
where	Conj	160	10	95 –	2907	492	90	96

Word	PoS	FrS	Ra	D1	LL	FrW	Ra	D2
whether	Conj	413	10	91 +	214	322	90	95
which	DetP	2208	10	82 –	8187	3893	90	96
while	Conj	156	10	95 –	3694	543	90	98
white	Adj	132	10	85 –	353	215	90	95
white		131	10	85 –	354	214	90	95
whiter		1	4	48 –	0	1	37	79
whitest		0	1	00 –	0	0	10	68
who	Pron	1780	10	94 –	443	2086	90	98
whole	Adj	248	10	92 +	52	212	90	97
whose	DetP	43	10	89 –	2013	216	90	97
why	Adv	1113	10	89 +	6453	439	90	92
wide	Adj	70	10	83 –	795	176	90	96
wide		48	10	84 –	529	120	90	96
wider		20	10	74 –	245	52	90	93
widest		1	5	61 –	22	3	77	92
wife	NoC	117	10	90 –	378	199	90	92
wife		107	10	90 –	315	178	90	92
wives		10	9	71 –	68	20	90	91
will	VMod	5508	10	94 +	13658	3108	90	96
'll		3066	10	86 +	53585	455	90	86
will		1890	10	88 –	1698	2537	90	94
wo~		552	10	82 +	7229	116	89	89
win	Verb	155	10	83 –	397	251	90	90
win		69	10	82 –	30	85	90	89
winning		13	10	82 –	162	34	90	89
wins		7	10	67 –	6	9	85	89
won		66	10	83 –	295	123	90	90
window	NoC	143	10	83 –	164	200	90	89
window		91	10	85 –	23	107	90	90
windows		52	10	76 –	195	92	90	82
wish	Verb	136	10	85 –	83	174	90	95
wish		113	10	85 +	10	101	90	95
wished		11	10	83 –	278	40	90	92
wishes		7	10	72 –	64	16	90	92
wishing		5	8	74 –	94	16	90	95
with	Prep	4446	10	97 +	8896	6821	90	99
within	Prep	253	10	74 –	1165	472	90	95
without	Prep	227	10	92 –	1611	483	90	98
woman	NoC	371	10	81 –	1434	661	90	94
woman		138	10	86 –	504	243	90	92
women		232	10	73 –	931	418	90	92
wonder	Verb	189	10	90 +	350	116	90	88
wonder		124	10	87 +	1111	37	90	92
wondered		32	10	91 –	77	50	88	84
wondering		30	10	94 –	12	24	88	87
wonders		3	10	84 –	5	4	84	92
word	NoC	419	10	89 –	9	440	90	94
word		214	10	88 +	24	191	90	94
words		205	10	88 –	76	249	90	94
work	NoC	601	10	92 –	48	659	90	95
work		601	10	92 –	48	659	90	95
work	Verb	931	10	91 +	1306	613	90	97
work		415	10	92 +	924	242	90	97
worked		152	10	85 –	53	124	90	97
working		282	10	91 +	412	184	90	97
works		82	10	94 +	65	61	90	95
wrought		0	1	00 –	36	2	75	92
worker	NoC	81	10	73 –	821	195	90	90
worker		18	10	80 –	135	39	90	89
workers		63	10	69 –	688	157	90	90
world	NoC	250	10	81 –	2954	640	90	96
world		248	10	80 –	2867	629	90	96
worlds		2	9	74 –	97	11	86	93
would	VMod	4472	10	94 +	8573	2722	90	96
'd		1194	10	92 +	15417	256	89	87
would		3278	10	92 +	2223	2467	90	97
write	Verb	432	10	90 +	29	396	90	96
write		206	10	88 +	828	97	90	95
writes		9	10	72 –	176	28	89	89
writing		63	10	86 +	0	63	90	95
written		94	10	88 –	11	105	90	96
wrote		61	10	93 –	195	103	90	89
wrong	Adj	263	10	95 +	841	136	90	95
wrong		263	10	95 +	841	136	90	95
yeah	Int	7890	10	78 +	356172	17	70	84
year	NoC	1507	10	90 –	126	1655	90	95
year		803	10	90 +	65	730	90	93
years		704	10	90 –	537	925	90	97
yes	Int	3840	10	93 +	107268	231	90	85
yesterday	Adv	177	10	83 –	19	197	88	77
yet	Adv	307	10	91 –	32	341	90	97
you	Pron	26077	10	92 +	387305	4774	90	90
y'		0	1	00 –	2	0	9	60
ya		117	10	67 +	4449	2	47	83
ye		3	7	69 –	173	17	81	64
you		25957	10	92 +	385328	4755	90	90
young	Adj	232	10	90 +	754	396	90	96
young		180	10	89 –	772	330	90	96
younger		43	10	90 –	20	54	90	95
youngest		9	10	86 –	11	12	89	88
your	Det	2860	10	92 +	14231	1221	90	93
yer		1	4	57 –	131	9	48	73
your		2859	10	92 +	14438	1212	90	93
yourself	Pron	182	10	95 +	509	99	89	91

List 2.2. Rank frequency list: spoken English (not lemmatized)

This list gives frequencies of word forms in the spoken part of the British National Corpus, comparing them with the written part, down to a minimum frequency of 10 per million words.

FrS = Rounded frequency (per million word tokens) in speech
LL = Log Likelihood, indicating the distinctiveness (or significance of the difference) between the frequencies in speech and writing
FrW = Rounded frequency (per million word tokens) in writing
+ = Higher frequency in speech
– = Higher frequency in writing

Word	PoS	FrS		LL	FrW	Word	PoS	FrS		LL	FrW
the	Det	39605	–	104720	64420	did	Verb	3368	+	22872	1210
I	Pron	29448	+	369238	6494	or	Conj	3357	–	392	3747
you	Pron	25957	+	385328	4755	would	VMod	3278	+	2223	2467
and	Conj	25210	–	1134	27002	mm	Int	3163	+	146051	3
it	Pron	24508	+	151913	9298	them	Pron	3126	+	10733	1572
a	Det	18637	–	4992	21972	'll	VMod	3066	+	53585	455
's	Verb	17677	+	384464	1848	one	Num	3034	+	5910	1839
to	Inf	14912	–	1371	16442	there	Adv	2894	+	45269	498
of	Prep	14550	–	104519	31109	up	Adv	2891	+	6666	1668
that	DetP	14252	–	213613	2581	go	Verb	2885	+	35449	649
~ n't	Neg	12212	+	177089	2300	now	Adv	2864	+	14540	1211
in	Prep	11609	–	31394	18978	your	Det	2859	+	14438	1212
we	Pron	10448	+	106914	2784	had	Verb	2835	–	7697	4639
is	Verb	10164	+	37	9961	were	Verb	2749	–	858	3282
do	Verb	9594	+	126017	2016	about	Prep	2730	+	9185	1384
they	Pron	9333	+	52132	3754	two	Num	2710	+	8229	1428
er	Uncl	8542	+	390864	11	said	Verb	2685	+	1838	2018
was	Verb	8097	–	1689	9368	one	Pron	2532	+	21938	770
yeah	Int	7890	+	356172	17	'm	Verb	2512	+	38492	443
have	Verb	7488	+	16057	4416	see	Verb	2507	+	13371	1033
what	DetP	7313	+	75414	1936	me	Pron	2444	+	8239	1239
he	Pron	7277	–	364	6756	very	Adv	2373	+	11530	1025
that	Conj	7246	–	6	7315	out	Adv	2316	+	3968	1452
to	Prep	6950	–	7715	9620	my	Det	2278	+	3796	1438
but	Conj	6366	+	7310	4370	when	Conj	2255	+	1836	1649
for	Prep	6239	–	7070	8664	mean	Verb	2250	+	53431	198
erm	Uncl	6029	+	281015	2	right	Adv	2209	+	62243	130
be	Verb	5790	–	1319	6742	which	DetP	2208	–	8187	3893
on	Prep	5659	–	1235	6569	from	Prep	2178	–	12708	4360
this	DetP	5627	+	2379	4506	going*	Verb	2174	+	27109	482
know	Verb	5550	+	104930	734	say	Verb	2116	+	24125	512
well	Adv	5310	+	107026	634	been	Verb	2082	–	1693	2756
so	Adv	5067	+	44484	1526	people	NoC	2063	+	5371	1146
oh	Int	5052	+	166592	179	because*	Conj	2039	+	14376	715
got	Verb	5025	+	117320	459	some	DetP	1986	+	485	1681
've	Verb	4735	+	108766	446	could	VMod	1949	+	464	1653
not	Neg	4693	+	11	4618	will	VMod	1890	–	1698	2537
are	Verb	4663	–	4	4713	how	Adv	1888	+	7106	915
if	Conj	4544	+	18764	2118	on	Adv	1849	+	13638	630
with	Prep	4446	–	8896	6821	an	Det	1846	–	10000	3613
no	Int	4388	+	128715	230	time	NoC	1819	+	548	1509
're	Verb	4255	+	93216	439	who	Pron	1780	–	443	2086
she	Pron	4136	+	332	3762	want	Verb	1776	+	20109	432
at	Prep	4115	–	1147	4868	like	Prep	1762	+	4525	983
there	Ex	4067	+	9288	2354	come	Verb	1737	+	13389	574
think	Verb	3977	+	71946	562	really	Adv	1727	+	24300	337
yes	Int	3840	+	107268	231	three	Num	1721	+	9654	691
just	Adv	3820	+	40726	982	by	Prep	1663	–	35309	5493
all	DetP	3644	+	6115	2297	here	Adv	1640	+	11087	590
can	VMod	3588	+	6572	2211	put	Verb	1640	+	15152	475
then	Adv	3474	+	19911	1378	's	Gen	1606	–	29320	4945
get	Verb	3464	+	46650	709	has	Verb	1598	–	5051	2708

Word	PoS	FrS		LL	FrW	Word	PoS	FrS		LL	FrW
good	Adj	1566	+	6955	706	mhm	Int	722	+	33831	0
as	Conj	1558	–	9631	3174	ah	Int	712	+	22842	28
does	Verb	1549	+	9615	587	sort	NoC	712	+	9947	140
cos*	Conj	1535	+	68811	4	years	NoC	704	–	537	925
any	DetP	1484	+	624	1189	never	Adv	700	+	387	542
down	Adv	1472	+	4515	772	little	Adj	700	+	4476	261
where	Adv	1380	+	8075	541	than	Conj	683	–	1547	1074
~na*	Inf	1376	+	58868	8	tell	Verb	668	+	3824	265
him	Pron	1348	–	676	1684	many	DetP	654	–	870	931
his	Det	1333	–	31332	4627	same	DetP	651	+	24	611
other	Adj	1313	–	4	1339	her*	Det	644	–	16899	2362
five	Num	1308	+	15609	303	another	DetP	640	+	66	575
in	Adv	1307	+	8310	488	money	NoC	637	+	1818	343
something	Pron	1290	+	9584	437	point	NoC	637	+	1887	338
their	Det	1284	–	9386	2761	bit*	NoC	635	+	12403	80
these	DetP	1269	+	2	1252	being	Verb	634	–	763	888
our	Det	1253	+	1033	914	anything	Pron	633	+	3716	248
way	NoC	1252	+	956	925	week	NoC	631	+	2765	286
ca~	VMod	1248	+	19835	210	too	Adv	629	–	89	710
actually	Adv	1239	+	25097	147	more	Adv	624	–	4646	1351
back	Adv	1211	+	2229	745	ten	Num	616	+	6735	155
four	Num	1199	+	9982	376	through	Prep	615	–	271	758
'd	VMod	1194	+	15417	256	eight	Num	606	+	8237	123
should	VMod	1173	+	38	1105	new	Adj	603	–	3528	1208
gon~	Verb	1154	+	49873	6	nice	Adj	603	+	11893	74
take	Verb	1149	+	2625	665	work	NoC	601	–	48	659
thing	NoC	1136	+	13670	261	always	Adv	597	+	423	446
look	Verb	1123	+	9310	353	thank	Verb	595	+	12397	67
those	DetP	1121	+	655	861	next	Ord	594	+	645	412
why	Adv	1113	+	6453	439	must	VMod	589	+	305	739
things	NoC	1103	+	9183	346	probably	Adv	585	+	3222	237
no	Det	1102	–	529	1371	saying	Verb	577	+	6836	135
only	Adv	1079	+	447	1323	'd	Verb	577	+	2075	285
like	Verb	1070	+	12162	260	pounds	NoC	572	+	11301	71
into	Prep	1067	–	2560	1700	nine	Num	571	+	9860	86
us	Pron	1059	+	2981	573	Mr	NoC	565	+	37	519
quite	Adv	1050	+	8435	338	seven	Num	565	+	6896	128
hundred	NoC	1023	+	23691	95	also	Adv	556	–	5482	1328
right	Adj	1019	+	10192	277	wo~	VMod	552	+	7229	116
lot*	NoC	992	+	16309	160	big	Adj	549	+	3054	221
make	Verb	977	+	477	769	over	Prep	543	–	627	757
first	Ord	957	–	572	1220	of course	Adv	543	+	1695	283
okay*	Adv	950	+	40074	7	getting	Verb	539	+	4647	165
more	DetP	949	+	938	671	made	Verb	539	–	2336	990
doing	Verb	943	+	12144	202	after	Prep	539	–	2180	972
done	Verb	931	+	7898	288	number	NoC	531	+	34	488
twenty	Num	925	+	23929	67	when	Adv	530	+	248	420
went	Verb	917	+	3675	433	old	Adj	529	–	4	545
as	Prep	916	–	5727	1873	find	Verb	529	+	305	408
six	Num	863	+	8443	239	coming	Verb	522	+	5045	146
give	Verb	845	+	3270	405	thirty	Num	520	+	12743	43
thought	Verb	845	+	2811	430	fifty	Num	519	+	13755	36
again	Adv	836	+	1381	529	as well	Adv	516	+	9892	67
off	Adv	831	+	2384	446	thousand	NoC	516	+	10998	56
might	VMod	809	+	657	592	remember	Verb	513	+	4528	154
year	NoC	803	+	65	730	as	Adv	507	–	76	574
her	Pron	800	–	942	1118	anyway	Adv	503	+	8512	78
last	Ord	788	+	150	680	goes	Verb	503	+	6537	107
like	Adv	784	+	32469	7	today	Adv	503	+	2058	236
much	DetP	764	+	1057	504	different	Adj	500	+	6	482
need	Verb	749	+	3967	310	out of	Prep	497	+	0	490
day	NoC	746	+	330	594	a bit	Adv	496	+	8543	75
used	VMod	742	+	15000	88	fact	NoC	492	+	396	360
says	Verb	740	+	2804	358	may	VMod	480	–	5470	1211
still	Adv	739	+	7	715	sure	Adj	479	+	2211	212
about	Adv	730	+	1785	414	else	Adv	475	+	2990	178

Word	PoS	FrS		LL	FrW	Word	PoS	FrS		LL	FrW
came	Verb	473	+	0	471	between	Prep	338	–	5239	968
sort of	Adv	472	+	17161	11	its	Det	338	–	17017	1782
night	NoC	465	+	292	354	B / b	Lett	337	+	1353	159
house	NoC	460	–	40	506	road	NoC	336	+	154	266
morning	NoC	459	+	2610	183	comes	Verb	328	+	1637	140
even	Adv	457	+	1226	746	pound	NoC	327	+	7521	31
every	Det	456	+	85	395	~ta*	Inf	326	+	13786	2
end	NoC	455	+	18	426	days	NoC	318	–	5	332
use	Verb	455	+	605	303	ones	NoC	318	+	2856	94
having	Verb	452	+	299	341	before	Conj	316	+	4	304
keep	Verb	449	+	1068	256	wanted	Verb	314	+	287	225
perhaps	Adv	444	+	271	339	trying	Verb	311	+	836	171
over	Adv	443	–	423	600	question	NoC	310	+	172	240
own	DetP	443	–	1198	724	pay	Verb	309	+	982	160
half	DetP	440	+	2322	182	better	Adj	308	+	428	203
away	Adv	433	+	115	364	yet	Adv	307	–	32	341
much	Adv	432	+	50	385	called	Verb	306	–	20	332
school	NoC	431	+	94	368	God	NoP	305	+	536	190
sorry	Adj	431	+	6473	78	local	Adj	301	+	602	462
C / c	Lett	431	+	4884	105	maybe	Adv	301	+	2996	82
talking	Verb	428	+	5463	93	certainly	Adv	299	+	682	173
looking	Verb	428	+	1009	245	name	NoC	299	+	104	244
council	NoC	424	+	413	300	bad	Adj	296	+	1262	136
ooh	Int	424	+	18553	2	eighty	Num	296	+	10313	8
gone	Verb	418	+	2299	170	obviously	Adv	296	+	2620	89
round	Adv	415	+	4467	106	government	NoC	295	–	2425	660
work	Verb	415	+	924	242	sixty	Num	294	+	8781	15
aye	Int	414	+	15007	10	life	NoC	293	+	1821	598
whether	Conj	413	+	214	322	call	Verb	290	+	1624	117
mum	NoC	410	+	8323	48	whatever	DetP	289	+	1663	114
though	Adv	410	+	7013	63	leave	Verb	289	+	583	173
somebody	Pron	409	+	9932	34	took	Verb	287	–	351	404
alright*	Adv	408	+	18179	1	moment	NoC	285	+	196	214
A / a	Lett	405	+	737	250	times	NoC	284	–	2	293
man	NoC	405	–	929	639	working	Verb	282	+	412	184
nothing	Pron	403	+	125	333	important	Adj	280	+	411	405
let's	Verb	401	+	8097	48	twelve	Num	278	+	4881	41
so	Conj	400	+	793	241	water	NoC	278	–	180	358
ask	Verb	399	+	1997	170	left	Verb	278	–	125	343
try	Verb	396	+	1728	180	ever	Adv	275	+	12	257
let	Verb	390	+	753	237	suppose	Verb	275	+	2237	88
forty	Num	388	+	9928	29	stuff	NoC	274	+	4430	45
job	NoC	382	+	1016	211	back	NoC	270	+	259	192
car	NoC	379	+	381	267	kind	NoC	270	+	101	219
side	NoC	374	+	51	330	at all	Adv	270	+	961	134
seen	Verb	371	–	0	377	dad	NoC	268	+	3870	51
nineteen	Num	370	+	12972	10	S / s	Lett	267	+	3846	51
~n~*	Neg	367	+	14924	4	everybody	Pron	267	+	4882	37
children	NoC	367	–	261	477	already	Adv	267	–	210	352
alright*	Adj	366	+	15498	3	talk	Verb	266	+	1339	113
start	Verb	365	+	2575	128	home	Adv	265	+	275	185
long	Adj	365	+	13	342	am	Verb	264	+	3	255
feel	Verb	364	+	476	243	shall	VMod	264	+	201	195
great	Adj	363	–	172	452	wrong	Adj	263	+	841	136
told	Verb	362	–	3	373	E / e	Lett	263	+	4180	44
please	Adv	361	+	3259	106	together	Adv	262	–	84	313
P / p	Lett	359	+	6865	47	buy	Verb	261	+	1380	108
everything	Pron	359	+	1493	167	started	Verb	261	+	436	165
area	NoC	356	+	0	351	most	DetP	261	–	814	441
part	NoC	355	–	510	512	John	NoP	260	–	172	336
place	NoC	353	–	225	453	read	Verb	260	+	60	221
problem	NoC	348	+	126	283	ago	Adv	259	+	200	191
few	DetP	346	–	303	462	county	NoC	258	+	1648	96
ninety	Num	342	+	12638	7	against	Prep	257	–	2347	597
off	Prep	341	+	759	199	believe	Verb	257	+	105	207
able	Adj	339	+	45	300	door	NoC	255	+	0	253

Word	PoS	FrS		LL	FrW	Word	PoS	FrS		LL	FrW
hear	Verb	254	+	935	124	small	Adj	216	–	1525	460
minutes	NoC	253	+	278	175	report	NoC	215	–	50	251
idea	NoC	253	+	66	213	word	NoC	214	+	24	191
within	Prep	253	–	1165	472	eh	Int	211	+	5626	14
move	Verb	251	+	915	123	months	NoC	211	–	68	252
group	NoC	249	–	871	433	sit	Verb	209	+	1518	72
anybody	Pron	249	+	5359	26	found	Verb	209	–	2304	521
world	NoC	248	–	2867	629	rather	Adv	209	–	0	213
whole	Adj	248	+	52	212	looked	Verb	209	–	771	368
bloody	Adj	247	+	4983	30	particular	Adj	209	–	10	225
mind	Verb	246	+	3245	51	fifteen	Num	207	+	3222	36
T / t	Lett	245	+	4186	37	hope	Verb	206	+	698	104
O / o	Lett	245	+	5747	22	write	Verb	206	+	828	97
round	Prep	245	+	1320	100	full	Adj	206	–	250	290
person	NoC	244	–	1	250	information	NoC	206	–	1155	407
only	Adj	244	+	8	229	saw	Verb	206	–	146	268
case	NoC	243	–	1106	453	words	NoC	205	–	76	249
each	DetP	243	–	1947	539	service	NoC	204	–	395	312
M / m	Lett	242	+	5455	24	country	NoC	204	–	538	332
enough	Adv	241	–	0	244	seventy	Num	204	+	6319	9
help	Verb	239	–	50	276	gets	Verb	204	+	1718	63
home	NoC	237	–	331	340	understand	Verb	203	+	156	149
aha	Int	237	+	10125	1	difficult	Adj	202	–	17	222
under	Prep	234	–	2659	590	exactly	Adv	201	+	782	96
tomorrow	Adv	234	+	1831	76	most	Adv	199	–	3559	607
percent	NoC	233	+	8355	6	sometimes	Adv	199	–	2	206
room	NoC	233	–	235	318	weeks	NoC	198	+	137	149
women	NoC	232	–	931	418	turn	Verb	198	+	373	121
paper	NoC	232	+	212	166	either	Adv	198	–	26	222
heard	Verb	232	+	48	199	better	Adv	197	+	215	137
taken	Verb	231	–	559	369	wants	Verb	197	+	1185	76
so that	Conj	231	+	64	193	top	NoC	196	+	475	112
lovely	Adj	231	+	3379	43	around	Adv	196	–	20	217
wan~	Verb	231	+	9356	3	happened	Verb	195	+	237	132
before	Adv	230	+	529	133	play	Verb	194	+	150	143
far	Adv	229	–	269	320	bought	Verb	194	+	1068	79
all	Adv	229	+	73	189	Christmas	NoC	194	+	1125	76
up to	Prep	228	+	386	144	hour	NoC	194	+	559	104
party	NoC	227	–	1035	423	I / i	Lett	193	+	2743	37
without	Prep	227	–	1611	483	in~*	Verb	191	+	8530	1
look	NoC	227	+	1120	97	hours	NoC	191	+	0	189
looks	Verb	226	+	1353	87	system	NoC	189	–	2141	476
stop	Verb	225	+	661	120	both	DetP	189	–	626	324
business	NoC	225	–	643	373	o'clock	Adv	188	+	3095	30
used	Verb	225	–	1783	497	shop	NoC	188	+	687	92
such	DetP	225	–	5912	825	fine	Adj	187	+	293	120
given	Verb	224	–	806	392	committee	NoC	187	–	0	190
making	Verb	224	–	73	269	seems	Verb	186	–	38	215
members	NoC	224	–	222	305	police	NoC	186	–	396	288
second	Ord	224	–	659	373	high	Adj	185	–	1298	392
taking	Verb	224	+	1	217	mother	NoC	184	–	299	271
men	NoC	223	–	947	408	absolutely	Adv	183	+	2104	44
policy	NoC	223	–	63	264	D / d	Lett	183	+	1469	59
ai~*	Uncl	221	+	5909	15	yourself	Pron	182	+	509	99
hand	NoC	221	–	576	358	G / g	Lett	182	+	3422	24
couple	NoC	220	+	748	111	someone	Pron	181	–	1	187
before	Prep	220	–	1465	459	line	NoC	181	–	92	226
hello	Int	220	+	5546	17	young	Adj	180	–	772	330
problems	NoC	220	–	134	281	reason	NoC	180	–	0	181
ha	Int	220	+	7090	8	later	Adv	179	–	809	333
book	NoC	220	–	27	246	thinking	Verb	179	+	771	82
me*	Det	219	+	9843	1	run	Verb	179	+	1	174
minute	NoC	219	+	1907	66	meeting	NoC	178	+	18	160
asked	Verb	218	–	528	348	tonight	Adv	178	+	1466	56
best	Adj	217	–	114	272	yesterday	Adv	177	–	19	197
bring	Verb	216	+	259	147	bed	NoC	177	+	24	156

Word	PoS	FrS		LL	FrW	Word	PoS	FrS		LL	FrW
mine	Pron	177	+	2739	31	hard	Adj	153	−	1	158
true	Adj	177	−	1	182	putting	Verb	153	+	734	67
happy	Adj	176	+	298	110	questions	NoC	153	+	8	141
situation	NoC	176	+	18	158	during	Prep	152	−	2833	473
often	Adv	175	−	1517	399	therefore	Adv	152	−	356	241
set	Verb	174	−	1025	350	~no*	Verb	152	+	5602	3
across	Prep	173	−	108	222	worked	Verb	152	+	53	124
somewhere	Adv	173	+	1294	58	forward	Adv	151	+	16	135
tea	NoC	172	+	801	76	up	Prep	151	+	539	75
pick	Verb	171	+	1690	47	chairman	NoC	151	+	146	107
family	NoC	171	−	1226	365	Friday	NoP	150	+	1357	44
war	NoC	170	−	556	291	Mrs	NoC	150	−	147	204
down	Prep	170	+	518	90	that	Adv	150	+	1506	40
means	Verb	170	+	81	134	table	NoC	148	−	176	208
eat	Verb	170	+	1053	65	afternoon	NoC	148	+	473	77
view	NoC	169	−	115	219	bye	Int	148	+	5794	2
show	Verb	169	−	7	181	watch	Verb	148	+	879	57
certain	Adj	169	−	147	226	gave	Verb	148	−	381	239
knew	Verb	168	−	431	271	month	NoC	147	−	0	150
office	NoC	168	−	400	267	black	Adj	147	−	351	234
past	Prep	168	+	1315	55	possible	Adj	147	−	1595	364
live	Verb	167	+	49	139	Saturday	NoP	147	+	471	76
land	NoC	166	−	28	190	seem	Verb	146	−	39	173
wait	Verb	166	+	755	74	fire	NoC	146	+	14	131
indeed	Adv	166	−	32	191	stay	Verb	146	+	95	110
cut	Verb	165	+	33	142	interesting	Adj	146	+	255	91
national	Adj	165	−	1698	401	matter	NoC	145	−	38	171
at least	Adv	165	−	432	268	usually	Adv	144	−	144	197
du~*	Verb	165	+	6150	3	phone	NoC	144	+	805	58
level	NoC	164	−	301	247	nobody	Pron	144	+	944	53
head	NoC	164	−	1401	372	agree	Verb	144	+	455	75
mind	NoC	164	−	143	219	Sunday	NoP	143	+	277	87
paid	Verb	163	+	28	142	city	NoC	143	−	439	241
of*	Verb	162	+	7351	0	on to	Prep	143	+	288	86
thanks	NoC	162	+	1361	50	course	NoC	143	−	128	192
makes	Verb	162	−	1	167	brought	Verb	143	−	230	211
general	Adj	162	−	882	317	sir	NoC	143	−	138	194
funny	Adj	161	+	2265	31	father	NoC	142	−	524	251
where	Conj	160	−	2907	492	in terms of	Prep	142	+	169	97
although	Conj	160	−	2604	468	because of	Prep	142	−	87	182
change	Verb	160	+	148	114	areas	NoC	142	−	474	244
boy	NoC	159	+	59	130	development	NoC	142	−	1471	345
sense	NoC	159	−	168	219	'	Gen	141	−	3704	518
myself	Pron	159	+	97	122	British	Adj	141	−	1921	382
mummy	NoC	159	+	4312	10	clear	Adj	140	−	443	237
town	NoC	159	−	30	182	happens	Verb	140	+	984	49
company	NoC	158	−	2157	429	tape	NoC	139	+	1502	35
N / n	Lett	157	+	2274	30	woman	NoC	138	−	504	243
million	NoC	157	−	417	256	amount	NoC	138	−	5	147
dear	Int	157	+	2762	23	staff	NoC	138	−	456	237
using	Verb	157	−	430	257	services	NoC	138	−	668	262
happen	Verb	156	+	515	80	trouble	NoC	138	+	265	84
girl	NoC	156	−	0	158	David	NoP	138	−	28	159
while	Conj	156	−	3694	543	street	NoC	137	−	208	200
training	NoC	156	−	93	198	page	NoC	137	+	93	103
through	Adv	155	+	376	88	send	Verb	137	−	386	74
open	Adj	155	−	234	226	around	Prep	137	−	572	249
lost	Verb	155	−	13	171	until	Conj	137	−	619	254
finished	Verb	155	+	680	70	easy	Adj	137	−	3	144
plan	NoC	155	−	87	120	difference	NoC	136	+	52	111
health	NoC	154	−	452	257	lord	NoC	136	−	6	146
eleven	Num	154	+	2566	24	rest	NoC	136	−	3	142
R / r	Lett	154	+	1556	41	market	NoC	135	−	1147	305
long	Adv	153	−	49	184	union	NoC	134	−	74	169
particularly	Adv	153	−	258	228	basically	Adv	134	+	2390	19
York	NoP	153	+	300	93	concerned	Adj	134	−	44	160

2.2

Word	PoS	FrS		LL	FrW	Word	PoS	FrS		LL	FrW
form	NoC	133	–	921	282	labour*	Adj	118	–	16	133
supposed	Adj	133	+	1004	45	hell	NoC	118	+	680	46
main	Adj	133	–	695	258	district	NoC	118	+	242	70
centre	NoC	133	–	552	242	anyone	Pron	118	–	84	153
U / u	Lett	133	+	3745	8	extra	Adj	117	+	77	89
interest	NoC	133	–	1000	288	type	NoC	117	–	212	176
fair	Adj	133	+	282	78	bottom	NoC	117	+	589	50
real	Adj	132	+	530	238	sell	Verb	117	+	219	72
London	NoP	132	–	2022	377	sitting	Verb	117	+	163	77
third	Ord	132	–	391	220	forget	Verb	117	+	471	55
letter	NoC	132	–	1	136	ya	Pron	117	+	4449	2
love	Verb	132	+	249	81	food	NoC	117	–	374	198
white	Adj	131	–	354	214	yep	Int	117	+	4760	1
eighteen	Num	131	+	2416	18	Paul	NoP	116	+	0	114
programme	NoC	131	–	235	197	carry	Verb	116	+	24	99
once	Conj	131	+	186	86	large	Adj	116	–	2195	363
Monday	NoP	130	+	982	44	education	NoC	115	–	1148	277
child	NoC	130	–	725	257	social	Adj	115	–	3523	458
position	NoC	130	–	568	240	cost	NoC	115	–	94	153
power	NoC	130	–	1621	340	once	Adv	114	–	343	191
ready	Adj	130	+	79	99	love	NoC	114	–	97	152
box	NoC	129	+	201	83	fucking	Adj	114	+	3088	7
okay*	Adj	129	+	4259	4	fairly	Adv	114	–	323	62
dog	NoC	128	+	282	75	news	NoC	114	–	84	149
plus	Prep	128	+	469	63	jobs	NoC	114	+	33	95
speak	Verb	128	+	125	90	stand	Verb	114	+	58	89
short	Adj	127	–	179	182	worth	Prep	114	+	16	100
nearly	Adv	127	+	13	114	pardon	NoC	114	+	3483	5
takes	Verb	126	+	7	117	list	NoC	114	–	1	118
stage	NoC	126	–	98	166	traffic	NoC	114	+	325	61
after	Conj	126	–	665	245	free	Adj	113	–	489	208
lots	Pron	126	+	1190	36	giving	Verb	113	–	13	126
others	NoC	126	–	1235	301	kept	Verb	113	–	78	146
community	NoC	125	–	658	243	half	NoC	113	+	228	67
red	Adj	125	–	0	126	running	Verb	113	+	7	103
enough	DetP	125	+	230	77	wish	Verb	113	+	10	101
special	Adj	125	–	559	231	issue	NoC	112	–	108	152
listen	Verb	125	+	709	50	cup	NoC	112	–	9	123
themselves	Pron	124	–	732	250	bits	NoC	112	+	1406	25
wonder	Verb	124	+	1111	37	since	Conj	112	–	1681	316
X / x	Lett	124	+	639	52	normally	Adv	112	+	109	79
age	NoC	124	–	528	226	quarter	NoC	112	+	192	70
ought	VMod	123	+	592	54	actual	Adj	112	+	271	63
towards	Prep	123	–	1331	305	game	NoC	112	–	122	154
H / h	Lett	123	+	1157	35	parents	NoC	111	–	212	169
till	Prep	122	+	2271	17	hair	NoC	111	–	94	148
building	NoC	122	–	125	167	order	NoC	111	–	506	207
unless	Conj	122	+	15	109	period	NoC	111	–	1020	258
walk	Verb	122	+	461	59	far	Adj	111	+	263	63
knows	Verb	122	+	174	80	mentioned	Verb	111	+	240	65
trade	NoC	122	–	333	199	both	Adv	111	–	2943	409
behind	Prep	121	–	429	211	asking	Verb	111	+	355	57
price	NoC	121	–	180	176	change	NoC	110	–	556	212
F / f	Lett	121	+	1390	29	points	NoC	110	–	2	116
changed	Verb	120	+	12	108	interested	Adj	110	+	62	85
piece	NoC	120	+	89	89	hold	Verb	110	+	1	106
less	Adv	119	–	888	258	sent	Verb	110	–	65	140
answer	NoC	119	+	87	89	budget	NoC	110	–	104	78
kids	NoC	119	+	1081	35	cold	Adj	109	+	13	97
motion	NoC	119	+	963	38	become	Verb	109	–	1866	326
expect	Verb	119	+	17	104	chance	NoC	109	–	42	133
almost	Adv	118	–	1831	339	body	NoC	109	–	1217	272
everyone	Pron	118	–	20	135	telling	Verb	108	+	401	53
schools	NoC	118	–	106	159	state	NoC	108	–	2796	393
authority	NoC	118	–	304	191	fourteen	Num	108	+	1745	18
along	Adv	118	+	325	64	class	NoC	108	–	390	189

Word	PoS	FrS		LL	FrW		Word	PoS	FrS		LL	FrW
pretty	Adv	108	+	559	45		over there	Adv	97	+	2271	9
evening	NoC	108	–	83	142		girls	NoC	97	+	0	96
add	Verb	108	+	83	79		hospital	NoC	97	–	254	157
playing	Verb	108	+	4	100		houses	NoC	97	+	0	96
church	NoC	107	–	615	214		figure	NoC	97	–	424	178
shut	Verb	107	+	687	40		bag	NoC	97	+	341	48
clearly	Adv	107	–	177	159		a lot	Adv	96	+	681	34
tax	NoC	107	–	197	162		moving	Verb	96	+	6	88
for example	Adv	107	–	1037	254		secretary	NoC	96	–	284	161
numbers	NoC	107	–	3	114		hot	Adj	96	+	2	90
wife	NoC	107	–	315	178		colour	NoC	96	–	26	113
sixteen	Num	107	+	1734	17		care	NoC	95	–	741	209
tried	Verb	107	–	159	155		dinner	NoC	95	+	168	59
felt	Verb	106	–	1567	298		planning	NoC	95	–	0	96
ways	NoC	106	–	157	154		front	NoC	95	+	29	79
moved	Verb	106	–	133	150		floor	NoC	95	–	43	118
figures	NoC	106	–	3	112		story	NoC	95	–	161	141
doctor	NoC	106	+	0	105		paying	Verb	95	+	473	41
daddy	NoC	106	+	2174	12		straight	Adv	95	+	214	55
hang	Verb	106	+	1384	22		onto	Prep	95	+	177	58
itself	Pron	105	–	1052	252		card	NoC	95	+	241	53
allowed	Verb	105	–	128	147		Wednesday	NoP	95	+	525	38
size	NoC	105	–	47	129		K / k	Lett	94	+	1413	17
support	NoC	104	–	636	212		basis	NoC	94	–	228	150
councillor	NoC	104	+	1795	16		bus	NoC	94	–	292	49
needs	Verb	104	+	6	96		worry	Verb	94	+	440	41
friends	NoC	104	–	185	156		hands	NoC	94	–	663	199
major	Adj	104	–	1082	254		accept	Verb	94	–	2	99
available	Adj	104	–	1531	291		written	Verb	94	–	11	105
early	Adj	103	–	1442	283		single	Adj	94	–	538	187
spend	Verb	103	+	119	71		court	NoC	94	–	1961	307
god	NoC	103	+	1027	28		support	Verb	93	–	2	98
face	NoC	103	–	1704	303		L / l	Lett	93	+	1012	24
south	NoC	103	–	307	172		baby	NoC	93	+	0	90
experience	NoC	103	–	532	198		imagine	Verb	93	+	174	57
meant	Verb	103	–	11	114		team	NoC	93	–	651	197
quid	NoC	103	+	3232	4		known	Verb	93	–	1313	255
yo	Uncl	103	+	4822	0		bloody	Adv	92	+	1790	12
friend	NoC	102	–	303	171		Oxford	NoP	92	+	6	85
term	NoC	102	–	43	125		fucking	Adv	92	+	3032	3
V / v	Lett	102	+	486	44		definitely	Adv	92	+	928	25
public	Adj	102	–	1762	306		weekend	NoC	92	+	135	60
late	Adj	102	–	272	166		awful	Adj	92	+	970	24
management	NoC	101	–	878	231		window	NoC	91	–	23	107
various	Adj	101	–	242	161		department	NoC	91	–	573	187
need	NoC	101	–	363	176		places	NoC	91	–	0	91
matter	Verb	101	+	876	30		quick	Adj	91	+	193	54
rather than	Prep	101	–	373	177		likely	Adj	91	–	1197	243
board	NoC	100	–	106	138		ball	NoC	91	+	41	72
poor	Adj	100	–	220	157		picture	NoC	91	–	23	107
Jesus	NoP	100	+	351	50		low	Adj	91	–	384	166
turned	Verb	100	–	1269	263		region	NoC	91	–	8	100
meet	Verb	99	–	154	145		coffee	NoC	90	+	90	64
use	NoC	99	–	2204	334		reckon	Verb	90	+	1601	13
future	NoC	99	–	165	147		settlement	NoC	90	+	399	41
quality	NoC	99	–	337	170		light	NoC	90	–	279	152
go	NoC	98	+	1978	12		however	Adv	90	–	7648	664
lady	NoC	98	+	0	97		club	NoC	90	–	460	173
simply	Adv	98	–	488	187		society	NoC	89	–	1379	256
gives	Verb	97	–	5	105		especially	Adv	89	–	607	187
further	Adv	97	–	195	150		decided	Verb	89	–	338	158
holiday	NoC	97	+	60	74		rate	NoC	89	–	748	200
thirteen	Num	97	+	1816	13		section	NoC	89	–	715	197
yours	Pron	97	+	623	36		Thursday	NoP	88	+	620	31
bet	Verb	97	+	1947	12		quickly	Adv	88	–	128	128
decision	NoC	97	–	402	176		chair	NoC	88	+	17	76

Word	PoS	FrS		LL	FrW	Word	PoS	FrS		LL	FrW
law	NoC	88	–	1863	291	completely	Adv	80	–	5	87
normal	Adj	88	–	134	129	issues	NoC	80	–	181	125
green	Adj	88	–	13	100	structure	NoC	80	–	319	143
north	NoC	88	–	464	171	wall	NoC	79	–	136	118
minus	Prep	88	+	2636	4	died	Verb	79	–	350	147
sorts	NoC	88	+	927	23	based	Verb	79	–	888	199
garden	NoC	88	–	43	110	anywhere	Adv	79	+	331	37
action	NoC	88	–	1170	236	football	NoC	79	+	23	66
possibly	Adv	88	+	34	71	space	NoC	79	–	220	130
provide	Verb	88	–	1205	239	along	Prep	79	–	209	129
ring	Verb	88	+	934	23	help	NoC	79	–	94	110
near	Prep	88	–	242	144	language	NoC	79	–	914	200
otherwise	Adv	88	–	0	88	officer	NoC	79	–	24	94
station	NoC	87	–	19	102	hit	Verb	79	–	13	90
Michael	NoP	87	–	7	96	financial	Adj	78	–	641	175
machine	NoC	87	+	1	84	cars	NoC	78	+	1	75
instead of	Prep	87	+	37	70	television	NoC	78	–	59	103
effect	NoC	87	–	1282	244	hall	NoC	78	–	172	122
officers	NoC	87	–	0	89	totally	Adv	78	+	73	56
Peter	NoP	87	–	139	128	radio	NoC	78	–	12	89
books	NoC	87	–	196	136	site	NoC	78	–	45	99
himself	Pron	87	–	2542	337	wear	Verb	78	+	264	39
blue	Adj	86	–	3	92	boys	NoC	78	–	1	81
middle	NoC	86	+	126	56	sounds	Verb	78	+	509	29
happening	Verb	86	+	482	35	process	NoC	78	–	1317	231
air	NoC	86	–	803	201	scheme	NoC	78	–	190	124
well	Adj	86	+	437	36	housing	NoC	77	+	22	65
aware	Adj	86	–	55	110	Richard	NoP	77	–	63	102
corner	NoC	85	+	16	73	industry	NoC	77	–	1087	212
bank	NoC	85	–	565	177	suggest	Verb	77	–	19	90
learn	Verb	85	+	0	83	Britain	NoP	77	–	1857	271
groups	NoC	85	–	871	206	strong	Adj	77	–	606	170
feet	NoC	85	–	297	147	needed	Verb	77	–	662	175
member	NoC	85	–	649	185	odd	Adj	77	+	222	41
agreed	Verb	85	–	258	142	birthday	NoC	77	+	522	27
terrible	Adj	85	+	292	42	president	NoC	76	–	660	174
while	NoC	85	+	78	60	music	NoC	76	–	502	159
computer	NoC	85	–	277	145	terms	NoC	76	–	681	176
and so on	Adv	84	+	251	45	sat	Verb	76	–	215	126
foot	NoC	84	+	18	72	park	NoC	76	–	90	107
cost	Verb	84	+	128	54	draw	Verb	76	+	44	58
project	NoC	84	–	314	148	waiting	Verb	76	–	15	88
Tuesday	NoP	83	+	565	30	bigger	Adj	76	+	406	31
control	NoC	83	–	1520	256	spent	Verb	76	–	180	120
save	Verb	83	+	40	65	example	NoC	76	–	259	131
built	Verb	83	–	214	134	opportunity	NoC	75	–	91	106
stupid	Adj	83	+	640	27	check	Verb	75	+	83	52
works	Verb	82	+	65	61	slightly	Adv	75	–	24	90
until	Prep	82	–	608	177	course*	Adv	75	+	2925	1
soon	Adv	82	–	540	170	tend	Verb	75	+	29	61
miles	NoC	82	–	31	100	post	NoC	75	–	24	90
earlier	Adv	82	–	28	98	afford	Verb	75	+	191	42
evidence	NoC	82	–	1218	230	kitchen	NoC	75	+	8	83
open	Verb	81	+	3	76	proper	Adj	75	+	16	64
whole	NoC	81	–	13	92	university	NoC	75	–	695	175
lived	Verb	81	–	0	82	reasons	NoC	74	–	136	112
simple	Adj	81	–	335	147	Yorkshire	NoP	74	+	208	40
upon	Prep	80	–	1521	252	beginning	NoC	74	+	2	70
finish	Verb	80	+	738	23	walking	Verb	74	+	138	45
ground	NoC	80	–	484	163	living	Verb	74	–	3	79
income	NoC	80	–	172	125	result	NoC	74	–	1007	200
husband	NoC	80	–	116	116	companies	NoC	74	–	893	190
involved	Adj	80	–	31	98	brother	NoC	73	–	19	87
deal	Verb	80	+	30	65	record	NoC	73	–	299	133
away from	Prep	80	–	174	125	video	NoC	73	+	12	64
date	NoC	80	–	541	167	statement	NoC	73	–	82	101

Word	PoS	FrS		LL	FrW	Word	PoS	FrS		LL	FrW
rid	Verb	73	+	680	21	bill	NoC	68	–	69	93
properly	Adv	73	+	49	55	item	NoC	68	+	229	34
start	NoC	73	–	19	86	talked	Verb	68	+	125	42
brilliant	Adj	73	+	375	31	less	DetP	68	–	142	105
hey	Int	73	+	1238	11	safety	NoC	68	–	49	88
apparently	Adv	73	–	4	78	close	Adj	67	–	367	132
college	NoC	72	–	108	105	common	Adj	67	–	1075	196
choice	NoC	72	–	258	126	shit	NoC	67	+	959	13
pressure	NoC	72	–	249	125	teacher	NoC	67	–	58	90
double	Adj	72	+	44	55	bloke	NoC	67	+	1484	7
since	Prep	72	–	922	190	right	NoC	67	–	896	181
account	NoC	72	–	403	142	a little	Adv	67	–	174	109
seventeen	Num	72	+	1165	12	explain	Verb	67	–	23	81
authorities	NoC	72	–	350	136	teachers	NoC	67	–	278	121
colleagues	NoC	72	+	49	54	even if	Conj	67	–	61	90
son	NoC	72	–	365	138	ourselves	Pron	67	+	104	43
per	Prep	72	–	406	142	won	Verb	66	–	295	123
bar	NoC	71	–	4	78	wonderful	Adj	66	+	66	47
necessary	Adj	71	–	981	194	continue	Verb	66	–	304	124
central	Adj	71	–	1148	207	subject	NoC	66	–	1059	192
political	Adj	71	–	2928	333	public	NoC	66	–	117	99
none	Pron	71	–	26	86	gas	NoC	66	–	8	74
needs	NoC	71	–	141	109	silly	Adj	66	+	442	24
miss	Verb	71	+	341	31	role	NoC	66	–	1105	196
cases	NoC	71	–	1012	195	picked	Verb	66	+	1	63
worse	Adj	71	+	5	64	film	NoC	66	–	158	105
depends	Verb	70	+	89	47	older	Adj	66	–	79	92
set	NoC	70	–	199	116	client	NoC	66	+	4	60
stopped	Verb	70	–	85	99	higher	Adj	66	–	755	167
lunch	NoC	70	+	55	52	bedroom	NoC	65	+	112	41
Chris	NoP	70	+	149	42	consider	Verb	65	–	311	123
lose	Verb	70	+	5	64	Christ	NoP	65	+	74	45
d'	Verb	70	+	1249	10	sales	NoC	65	–	191	109
met	Verb	70	–	461	146	shops	NoC	65	+	33	51
drink	NoC	70	+	98	46	careful	Adj	65	+	34	51
value	NoC	70	–	919	187	hate	Verb	65	+	467	23
environment	NoC	70	–	377	137	manager	NoC	65	–	548	147
benefit	NoC	70	–	9	79	insurance	NoC	65	–	5	71
deal	NoC	70	–	44	90	employment	NoC	65	–	219	112
Y / y	Lett	70	+	488	25	costs	NoC	65	–	347	126
pull	Verb	70	+	212	37	outside	Prep	65	–	304	122
history	NoC	70	–	1176	207	personal	Adj	65	–	1051	189
ideas	NoC	70	–	201	116	easier	Adj	65	+	69	45
beautiful	Adj	70	–	41	89	present	Adj	65	–	680	158
all right*	Adv	70	+	5	64	serious	Adj	64	–	396	131
Mark	NoP	70	+	2	66	top	Adj	64	–	276	118
European	Adj	69	–	1218	210	flats	NoC	64	+	839	14
expensive	Adj	69	–	21	57	appropriate	Adj	64	–	280	118
similar	Adj	69	–	1059	198	loads	NoC	64	+	1179	9
carried	Verb	69	–	470	146	correct	Adj	64	+	4	58
pass	Verb	69	+	24	56	advice	NoC	64	–	204	109
west	NoC	69	–	362	134	east	NoC	64	–	449	136
private	Adj	69	–	920	185	outside	Adv	64	+	23	52
summer	NoC	69	–	229	118	whereas	Conj	64	+	0	62
changes	NoC	69	–	1056	196	da	Uncl	64	+	2339	1
per cent	NoC	69	–	4353	418	as if	Conj	64	–	802	167
pension	NoC	69	+	130	42	bother	Verb	64	–	643	17
win	Verb	69	–	30	85	Dave	NoP	64	+	446	22
conference	NoC	69	–	130	104	as to	Prep	64	–	14	74
fish	NoC	69	–	146	107	till	Conj	64	+	531	20
decide	Verb	69	+	0	67	several	DetP	64	–	2057	260
played	Verb	68	–	226	117	contract	NoC	64	–	305	120
pence	NoC	68	+	1515	7	sold	Verb	63	–	65	87
speaking	Verb	68	+	36	53	ours	Pron	63	+	927	12
names	NoC	68	–	11	77	milk	NoC	63	+	53	46
stick	Verb	68	+	612	20	parts	NoC	63	–	328	122

Word	PoS	FrS		LL	FrW	Word	PoS	FrS		LL	FrW
nature	NoC	63	–	1150	195	range	NoC	59	–	1471	211
workers	NoC	63	–	688	157	research	NoC	59	–	2461	279
eyes	NoC	63	–	3032	324	join	Verb	59	–	36	76
standing	Verb	63	–	16	74	buying	Verb	59	+	82	39
upstairs	Adv	63	+	487	21	application	NoC	59	–	226	105
guy	NoC	63	+	530	20	break	Verb	59	+	0	58
front	Adj	63	–	6	70	realize	Verb	59	+	500	18
further*	Adj	63	–	1698	234	village	NoC	59	–	312	114
dead	Adj	63	–	313	120	eventually	Adv	59	–	152	95
writing	Verb	63	+	0	63	afraid	Adj	59	–	0	60
ring	NoC	63	+	125	38	letters	NoC	59	–	66	81
weight	NoC	63	–	76	88	Jim	NoP	58	+	56	41
play	NoC	62	–	4	68	field	NoC	58	–	731	153
twice	Adv	62	–	0	63	product	NoC	58	–	344	117
positive	Adj	62	–	65	86	Tony	NoP	58	+	15	49
Greater	NoP-	62	+	1249	8	clothes	NoC	58	–	37	75
congress	NoC	62	+	11	54	follow	Verb	58	–	181	98
sick	Adj	62	+	79	42	past	NoC	58	–	118	89
busy	Adj	62	+	35	48	labour*	NoC	58	–	657	146
in front of	Prep	62	–	2	66	weather	NoC	58	+	0	57
sort	Verb	62	–	787	14	'em	Pron	58	+	848	11
watching	Verb	62	–	1	66	current	Adj	58	–	619	142
second	NoC	62	+	7	55	specific	Adj	58	–	375	119
Europe	NoP	62	–	1188	195	policies	NoC	58	–	139	92
surely	Adv	62	–	0	64	useful	Adj	58	–	248	106
thinks	Verb	62	+	134	36	drive	Verb	57	+	42	43
practice	NoC	62	–	1041	184	capital	NoC	57	–	615	141
James	NoP	62	–	209	107	responsibility	NoC	57	–	180	97
listening	Verb	62	+	208	31	lucky	Adj	57	+	65	39
comments	NoC	62	+	103	39	prices	NoC	57	–	257	106
as long as	Conj	62	+	328	25	starting	Verb	57	+	21	46
fill	Verb	62	+	137	36	death	NoC	57	–	1685	222
each other	Pron	62	–	265	113	increase	NoC	57	–	212	100
test	NoC	62	+	278	114	lights	NoC	57	+	28	45
transport	NoC	61	–	63	84	sites	NoC	57	–	0	58
horse	NoC	61	–	41	79	plenty	Pron	57	+	25	45
sister	NoC	61	–	29	76	extent	NoC	57	–	256	105
June	NoP	61	–	710	156	individual	Adj	57	–	669	145
press	NoC	61	–	214	106	discussion	NoC	57	–	124	89
like	Conj	61	+	432	21	countries	NoC	57	–	1115	180
end	Verb	61	+	6	55	lines	NoC	56	–	277	107
conversation	NoC	61	+	8	54	paragraph	NoC	56	+	316	23
wrote	Verb	61	–	195	103	George	NoP	56	–	370	117
build	Verb	61	–	9	69	missed	Verb	56	+	61	39
call	NoC	61	+	0	60	heart	NoC	56	–	695	147
honest	Adj	61	+	300	26	heavy	Adj	56	–	205	99
seeing	Verb	61	–	0	61	England	NoP	56	–	2135	252
necessarily	Adv	61	+	3	56	horrible	Adj	56	+	712	12
sector	NoC	61	–	103	90	act	NoC	56	–	1876	234
boat	NoC	61	+	9	53	debate	NoC	56	–	32	71
bread	NoC	61	+	139	35	reasonable	Adj	56	–	5	62
produce	Verb	60	–	300	115	cover	Verb	56	–	11	65
apart from	Prep	60	–	4	66	hopefully	Adv	56	+	578	15
cheap	Adj	60	+	112	37	cat	NoC	56	+	71	37
starts	Verb	60	+	113	37	fit	Verb	56	+	30	43
recently	Adv	60	–	453	130	held	Verb	56	–	2920	302
coal	NoC	60	+	17	50	Jane	NoP	56	+	46	41
born	Verb	60	–	74	84	conditions	NoC	56	–	937	165
seemed	Verb	60	–	2144	259	train	NoC	56	–	15	66
other	NoC	60	–	94	88	minister	NoC	56	–	2249	258
answer	Verb	60	+	10	52	care	Verb	55	+	3	51
involved	Verb	60	–	250	109	throw	Verb	55	+	186	28
wee	Adj	59	+	1303	6	walked	Verb	55	–	215	99
pay	NoC	59	+	50	43	as well as	Prep	55	–	1268	190
generally	Adv	59	–	378	122	earth	NoC	55	–	239	102
resources	NoC	59	–	271	111	Nottingham	NoP	55	+	450	18

Word	PoS	FrS		LL	FrW	Word	PoS	FrS		LL	FrW
enjoy	Verb	55	–	21	67	majority	NoC	51	–	333	105
American	Adj	55	–	995	169	attention	NoC	51	–	805	147
pleased	Adj	55	+	16	46	glad	Adj	51	+	26	39
sun	NoC	55	–	437	121	relationship	NoC	51	–	695	138
telephone	NoC	55	–	27	68	data	NoC	51	–	1494	197
united	Adj	55	–	33	70	human	Adj	51	–	1515	199
rubbish	NoC	55	+	394	19	function	NoC	51	–	123	81
excellent	Adj	55	–	28	69	basic	Adj	51	–	442	116
chap	NoC	55	+	730	11	scale	NoC	50	–	99	77
a little bit	Adv	54	+	1610	3	dealing	Verb	50	–	1	53
in order	ClO	54	–	653	140	passed	Verb	50	–	420	113
darling	NoC	54	+	387	19	greater	Adj	50	–	878	152
pair	NoC	54	–	7	61	used	Adj	50	+	7	44
argument	NoC	54	–	131	86	regional	Adj	50	–	131	81
pieces	NoC	54	–	0	56	operation	NoC	50	–	350	106
final	Adj	54	–	625	137	coat	NoC	50	+	73	33
provision	NoC	54	–	169	91	English	NoC	50	–	157	85
total	Adj	54	–	543	130	May	NoP	50	–	1007	161
daughter	NoC	54	–	234	99	cor	Int	50	+	1815	1
excuse	Verb	54	+	848	9	choose	Verb	50	–	62	70
warm	Adj	54	–	18	65	Steve	NoP	50	+	10	43
investment	NoC	54	–	392	115	driving	Verb	50	+	35	37
worried	Adj	54	+	69	36	keeping	Verb	50	–	23	62
for instance	Adv	54	–	68	76	modern	Adj	50	–	752	141
feeling	NoC	54	–	62	75	charge	NoC	50	–	241	94
unfortunately	Adv	53	+	11	46	Brian	NoP	50	+	5	44
more than*	Adv	53	–	902	159	production	NoC	50	–	1105	168
meetings	NoC	53	–	0	54	manage	Verb	50	+	20	40
sheet	NoC	53	+	33	41	leg	NoC	50	–	3	54
eye	NoC	53	–	247	100	Martin	NoP	50	–	2	53
shoes	NoC	53	+	78	35	homes	NoC	49	–	25	62
America	NoP	53	–	331	109	tree	NoC	49	–	39	65
covered	Verb	53	–	107	82	phoned	Verb	49	+	766	9
phone	Verb	53	+	790	10	copy	NoC	49	–	0	51
nil	Pron	53	+	1475	3	tt	Int	49	+	1884	1
allow	Verb	53	–	469	122	above	Prep	49	+	838	147
papers	NoC	53	–	22	65	mention	Verb	49	+	106	29
economic	Adj	53	–	2315	257	plans	NoC	49	–	325	102
load	NoC	52	+	257	23	drink	Verb	49	+	93	30
previous	Adj	52	–	583	131	access	NoC	49	–	361	106
Ann	NoP	52	+	464	16	horses	NoC	49	+	0	49
cake	NoC	52	+	199	25	noticed	Verb	49	–	3	53
note	NoC	52	–	11	61	Jean	NoP	49	+	112	28
means	NoC	52	–	271	101	easily	Adv	49	–	349	104
quiet	Adj	52	–	18	63	sing	Verb	49	+	317	18
early	Adv	52	–	98	79	circumstances	NoC	49	–	414	111
ordinary	Adj	52	–	46	70	security	NoC	49	–	868	149
windows	NoC	52	–	195	92	sex	NoC	49	–	188	87
cards	NoC	52	+	45	38	very	Adj	49	–	53	67
English	Adj	52	–	969	161	comment	NoC	49	+	66	32
fund	NoC	52	–	2	56	Bill	NoP	49	+	0	47
turn	NoC	52	–	141	85	keeps	Verb	49	+	196	23
lane	NoC	52	+	17	43	truth	NoC	49	–	186	86
offered	Verb	52	–	389	112	environmental	Adj	48	–	202	88
liked	Verb	52	–	4	57	presumably	Adv	48	+	73	31
showing	Verb	52	–	23	64	division	NoC	48	–	262	95
legs	NoC	51	–	36	67	fall	Verb	48	–	85	73
bottle	NoC	51	+	28	40	wide	Adj	48	–	529	120
fourth	Num	51	–	17	62	trees	NoC	48	–	198	87
as soon as	Conj	51	+	9	44	rates	NoC	48	–	555	122
Mary	NoP	51	–	71	73	unit	NoC	48	–	485	116
amendment	NoC	51	+	494	14	W / w	Lett	48	+	494	13
existing	Adj	51	–	271	99	reports	NoC	48	–	142	80
greenbelt	NoC	51	+	2263	0	levels	NoC	48	–	641	129
blood	NoC	51	–	348	107	yellow	Adj	48	+	12	41
show	NoC	51	–	204	92	any	Adv	48	+	328	17

Word	PoS	FrS		LL	FrW	Word	PoS	FrS		LL	FrW
throughout	Prep	48	–	574	124	mate	NoC	45	+	398	13
surprised	Adj	48	+	0	47	responsible	Adj	45	–	366	100
movement	NoC	48	–	840	145	catch	Verb	45	+	1	42
voice	NoC	48	–	1520	194	chicken	NoC	45	+	266	17
students	NoC	48	–	1004	157	no one*	Pron	45	–	219	85
force	NoC	48	–	855	146	population	NoC	45	–	873	142
tired	Adj	48	+	16	39	property	NoC	45	–	781	135
finally	Adv	48	–	775	140	huge	Adj	45	–	201	83
proposals	NoC	48	–	78	71	became	Verb	45	–	2381	244
married	Adj	48	–	8	55	original	Adj	44	–	544	115
oil	NoC	48	–	410	109	cheaper	Adj	44	+	182	21
approach	NoC	48	–	994	156	run	NoC	44	–	1	47
rights	NoC	48	–	778	139	hole	NoC	44	–	0	46
ahead	Adv	48	–	45	64	April	NoP	44	–	1108	159
Alan	NoP	47	–	5	53	success	NoC	44	–	910	144
up to	Adv	47	–	323	100	rich	Adj	44	–	100	70
Scotland	NoP	47	–	796	140	notes	NoC	44	–	36	59
document	NoC	47	–	3	51	sides	NoC	44	–	72	65
ages	NoC	47	+	36	35	purpose	NoC	44	–	361	99
inside	Prep	47	–	131	77	model	NoC	44	–	861	140
reading	Verb	47	–	1	50	details	NoC	44	–	676	126
cash	NoC	47	–	198	86	grow	Verb	44	–	25	56
selling	Verb	47	+	3	43	wages	NoC	44	+	14	36
matters	NoC	47	–	184	84	nought	Pron	44	+	1605	1
self	NoC	47	+	35	35	urgh	Int	44	+	1922	0
speed	NoC	47	–	98	73	competition	NoC	44	–	378	100
mouth	NoC	47	–	324	99	successful	Adj	44	–	551	115
caught	Verb	47	–	251	91	increase	Verb	44	–	149	76
extremely	Adv	47	–	88	71	contact	NoC	44	–	66	64
push	Verb	46	+	86	28	tapes	NoC	44	+	484	11
bothered	Verb	46	+	548	11	stone	NoC	44	–	217	84
concern	NoC	46	–	360	102	bath	NoC	44	+	117	24
army	NoC	46	–	593	122	energy	NoC	44	–	749	131
drop	Verb	46	+	79	29	leaving	Verb	44	–	408	102
glass	NoC	46	–	355	101	chocolate	NoC	44	+	235	18
flat	NoC	46	–	0	47	file	NoC	44	–	35	58
benefits	NoC	46	–	134	77	Q / q	Lett	44	+	330	15
councils	NoC	46	+	39	33	material	NoC	44	–	884	141
Tim	NoP	46	+	45	33	hill	NoC	43	–	41	59
apply	Verb	46	–	188	83	sound	NoC	43	–	488	109
managed	Verb	46	–	146	78	equal	Adj	43	–	62	63
sale	NoC	46	–	273	93	spoke	Verb	43	–	129	73
pub	NoC	46	+	17	37	out	Prep	43	+	835	6
hardly	Adv	46	–	282	93	garage	NoC	43	–	231	18
received	Verb	46	–	828	140	natural	Adj	43	–	1060	154
bringing	Verb	45	–	2	49	obvious	Adj	43	–	284	90
suddenly	Adv	45	–	655	126	rules	NoC	43	–	527	112
prepared	Adj	45	–	11	53	Mike	NoP	43	+	0	43
due	Adj	45	–	154	78	younger	Adj	43	–	20	54
guess	Verb	45	+	174	22	such as	Prep	43	–	4252	354
sleep	Verb	45	+	22	36	March	NoP	43	–	1109	157
afterwards	Adv	45	–	0	46	forgot	Verb	43	+	393	13
including	Prep	45	–	2487	252	systems	NoC	43	–	1558	188
notice	Verb	45	+	28	34	left	NoC	43	+	24	33
Margaret	NoP	45	+	15	37	address	NoC	43	–	14	52
sea	NoC	45	–	832	140	views	NoC	43	–	177	78
wood	NoC	45	–	9	52	economy	NoC	43	–	535	112
clean	Adj	45	–	2	49	response	NoC	43	–	468	106
opened	Verb	45	–	628	124	exercise	NoC	43	–	81	65
vote	NoC	45	–	2	49	produced	Verb	43	–	877	139
September	NoP	45	–	478	111	branch	NoC	43	–	24	54
North	NoP-	45	–	16	55	results	NoC	43	–	1157	159
likes	Verb	45	+	261	18	goal	NoC	43	–	59	61
accident	NoC	45	–	73	66	spirit	NoC	43	–	97	67
detail	NoC	45	–	53	63	whose	DetP	43	–	2013	216
married	Verb	45	–	1	48	separate	Adj	43	–	204	80

2.2

Word	PoS	FrS		LL	FrW	Word	PoS	FrS		LL	FrW
honestly	Adv	43	+	449	11	January	NoP	41	−	534	109
families	NoC	43	−	273	88	rule	NoC	41	−	285	86
Freud	NoP	43	+	379	13	cream	NoC	41	+	30	30
strange	Adj	42		94	66	additional	Adj	41	−	200	77
shame	NoC	42	+	255	16	cheese	NoC	41	+	83	24
seriously	Adv	42	−	47	59	lives	NoC	41	−	251	83
sorted	Verb	42	+	541	9	pictures	NoC	40	−	43	56
lower	Adj	42	−	630	119	toilet	NoC	40	+	342	13
immediately	Adv	42	−	507	109	doo	Uncl	40	+	1654	0
Andrew	NoP	42	−	1	45	commission	NoC	40	−	550	110
character	NoC	42	−	314	91	direction	NoC	40	−	351	92
agreement	NoC	42	−	949	143	entirely	Adv	40	−	158	72
base	NoC	42	−	316	92	agenda	NoC	40	+	117	22
suggested	Verb	42	−	569	114	over here	Adv	40	+	746	6
smaller	Adj	42	−	175	77	rang	Verb	40	+	67	25
fell	Verb	42	−	503	108	sixth	Ord	40	+	87	24
ladies	NoC	42	+	28	32	shows	Verb	40	−	504	105
telly	NoC	42	+	907	4	France	NoP	40	−	851	133
advance	NoC	42	+	9	36	wash	Verb	40	+	274	14
offer	Verb	42	−	470	105	key	Adj	40	−	229	80
lad	NoC	42	+	229	17	animals	NoC	40	−	342	91
complete	Adj	42	−	413	100	raise	Verb	40	−	95	64
Tom	NoP	42	−	40	57	killed	Verb	40	−	344	91
century	NoC	42	−	2022	215	shown	Verb	40	−	1283	163
everywhere	Adv	42	+	30	31	ran	Verb	40	−	364	93
degree	NoC	42	−	488	106	attitude	NoC	40	−	88	62
waste	NoC	42	−	28	54	talk	NoC	40	−	0	41
enjoyed	Verb	42	−	20	52	forms	NoC	40	−	508	105
cover	NoC	42	−	8	48	close	Verb	40	+	6	35
tells	Verb	42	+	7	36	squared	Verb	40	+	1248	2
miss*	NoC	42	−	377	96	election	NoC	40	−	499	104
rain	NoC	42	−	85	64	fully	Adv	40	−	395	95
forgotten	Verb	42	+	4	37	panel	NoC	40	+	2	37
etcetera	Adv	42	+	1520	1	estate	NoC	40	−	49	56
raised	Verb	42	−	437	102	straight	Adj	40	+	22	30
Ian	NoP	42	−	32	55	games	NoC	40	−	109	65
meal	NoC	42	−	0	43	French	Adj	40	−	1031	145
Robert	NoP	41	−	247	84	for	Conj	40	−	1120	151
as it were	Adv	41	+	686	7	safe	Adj	40	−	143	69
noise	NoC	41	−	6	47	dropped	Verb	40	−	70	59
washing	NoC	41	+	370	12	winter	NoC	40	−	186	74
February	NoP	41	−	299	89	dark	Adj	39	−	591	111
eating	Verb	41	+	42	29	significant	Adj	39	−	835	130
wind	NoC	41	−	168	75	Terry	NoP	39	+	79	24
die	Verb	41	−	34	55	skills	NoC	39	−	424	97
legal	Adj	41	−	944	141	farm	NoC	39	−	165	72
good	NoC	41	+	110	23	Sarah	NoP	39	+	6	34
ill	Adj	41	−	6	47	products	NoC	39	−	626	114
break	NoC	41	+	8	35	either	DetP	39	−	78	60
discuss	Verb	41	−	50	58	future	Adj	39	−	346	90
organization	NoC	41	−	101	66	referred	Verb	39	−	111	65
direct	Adj	41	−	564	112	considered	Verb	39	−	1037	144
fault	NoC	41	+	15	33	achieve	Verb	39	−	160	71
stuck	Verb	41	+	148	20	wine	NoC	39	−	118	66
library	NoC	41	−	287	87	stock	NoC	39	−	247	80
dear	Adj	41	+	7	36	share	Verb	39	−	50	55
science	NoC	41	−	589	113	wedding	NoC	39	+	10	33
fuck	Verb	41	+	750	6	pain	NoC	39	−	217	77
director	NoC	41	−	813	131	sugar	NoC	39	+	2	36
roads	NoC	41	+	0	39	association	NoC	39	−	760	124
meat	NoC	41	+	7	35	hoping	Verb	39	+	4	35
message	NoC	41	−	158	73	notice	NoC	39	−	70	59
opinion	NoC	41	−	216	79	background	NoC	39	−	111	64
dry	Adj	41	−	41	56	trust	NoC	39	−	225	78
doors	NoC	41	−	13	49	step	NoC	39	−	209	76
hm	Int	41	+	1626	1	ability	NoC	39	−	435	97

Word	PoS	FrS		LL	FrW	Word	PoS	FrS		LL	FrW
review	NoC	39	–	283	83	Bob	NoP	37	–	3	41
goods	NoC	39	–	571	109	season	NoC	37	–	722	118
favour	NoC	39	+	87	22	Nick	NoP	37	+	29	27
reference	NoC	39	–	272	82	decisions	NoC	37	–	270	80
middle	Adj	38	–	188	73	thick	Adj	37	–	22	47
mainly	Adv	38	–	202	74	press	Verb	37	+	20	29
faith	NoC	38	–	48	54	wearing	Verb	37	–	41	51
provided	Verb	38	–	999	140	Andy	NoP	37	+	30	27
goodness	NoC	38	+	308	12	maths	NoC	37	+	550	7
dogs	NoC	38	–	8	44	develop	Verb	37	–	407	92
admit	Verb	38	+	0	37	Phil	NoP	37	+	141	18
improve	Verb	38	–	120	65	sentence	NoC	37	–	98	60
feeling	Verb	38	–	87	60	boring	Adj	37	+	238	14
study	NoC	38	–	2046	209	hi	Int	37	+	610	6
Jack	NoP	38	–	76	59	theatre	NoC	37	–	108	61
under	Adv	38	–	69	58	face	Verb	37	–	184	71
chips	NoC	38	+	198	16	facilities	NoC	37	–	273	80
shopping	NoC	38	+	34	27	difficulty	NoC	37	–	148	66
cope	Verb	38	–	1	40	personally	Adv	37	+	41	25
appointment	NoC	38	–	11	45	ensure	Verb	37	–	636	111
royal	Adj	38	–	1291	160	Charlotte	NoP	37	+	253	13
engine	NoC	38	–	35	51	thousands	NoC	37	–	75	57
procedure	NoC	38	–	88	60	glasses	NoC	37	+	56	24
song	NoC	38	–	1	40	profit	NoC	37	–	83	58
receive	Verb	38	–	249	79	breakfast	NoC	37	–	13	44
key	NoC	38	–	29	50	king	NoC	37	–	1338	160
equipment	NoC	38	–	424	95	accepted	Verb	37	–	320	84
hotel	NoC	38	–	775	123	items	NoC	37	–	190	71
July	NoP	38	–	843	128	parliament	NoC	37	–	551	104
hurt	Verb	38	+	0	38	tiny	Adj	37	–	77	57
stayed	Verb	38	–	8	44	collect	Verb	37	+	25	27
inside	Adv	38	–	34	51	knowledge	NoC	37	–	1314	158
memory	NoC	38	–	266	80	patients	NoC	36	–	1788	189
balance	NoC	38	–	319	86	sign	Verb	36	+	56	23
recording	Verb	38	+	259	14	becomes	Verb	36	–	302	82
duty	NoC	38	–	321	86	fifth	Ord	36	+	0	35
even though	Conj	38	–	99	61	October	NoP	36	–	694	114
lead	Verb	38	–	446	97	ee	Int	36	+	1164	1
independent	Adj	38	–	542	105	resolution	NoC	36	–	0	37
route	NoC	38	–	79	59	unions	NoC	36	–	21	46
longer	Adj	38	–	0	39	showed	Verb	36	–	706	115
Sue	NoP	38	+	276	13	clever	Adj	36	+	69	22
industrial	Adj	38	–	804	125	growth	NoC	36	–	1061	141
changing	Verb	38	+	0	36	match	NoC	36	–	210	72
parish	NoC	38	–	0	39	dirty	Adj	36	+	37	25
strategy	NoC	38	–	123	64	bags	NoC	36	+	92	20
minus	NoC	38	+	1143	2	in case	Conj	36	+	89	21
best	Adv	38	–	327	86	meeting	Verb	36	–	27	47
technology	NoC	38	–	836	127	negative	Adj	36	–	23	46
international	Adj	38	–	2595	242	recent	Adj	36	–	1540	173
herself	Pron	38	–	1723	187	performance	NoC	36	–	1065	141
element	NoC	38	–	77	58	pen	NoC	36	+	127	18
vote	Verb	37	+	94	21	Simon	NoP	36	–	12	44
speaker	NoC	37	–	313	84	length	NoC	36	–	244	76
little	DetP	37	–	1917	200	units	NoC	36	–	231	74
November	NoP	37	–	495	100	ever so	Adv	36	+	921	3
relief	NoC	37	–	170	70	bike	NoC	36	+	168	16
pulled	Verb	37	–	205	73	bridge	NoC	36	–	110	61
Wales	NoP	37	–	485	99	chairman	NoC	36	+	1474	0
according to	Prep	37	–	1478	171	arm	NoC	36	–	496	98
holidays	NoC	37	+	28	27	membership	NoC	36	–	69	55
Germany	NoP	37	–	675	114	nose	NoC	36	–	15	44
distance	NoC	37	–	173	70	cross	NoC	36	–	14	44
impact	NoC	37	–	259	79	leader	NoC	36	–	513	99
mortgage	NoC	37	+	26	28	in relation to	Prep	36	–	30	48
types	NoC	37	–	431	95	stood	Verb	36	–	1119	144

Word	PoS	FrS		LL	FrW	Word	PoS	FrS		LL	FrW
seat	NoC	36	–	150	65	doctors	NoC	34	–	32	46
advertising	NoC	36	–	7	41	gentleman	NoC	34	–	75	54
risk	NoC	36	–	677	112	courses	NoC	34	–	379	86
possibility	NoC	36	–	245	75	pages	NoC	34	–	27	45
parties	NoC	36	–	1030	137	kill	Verb	34	–	35	47
spell	Verb	36	+	516	7	driver	NoC	34	–	92	56
United	NoP-	36	–	838	124	working	Adj	34	–	149	63
standards	NoC	36	–	571	103	Ken	NoP	34	+	5	30
conservative*	Adj	36	–	169	67	staying	Verb	34	+	14	27
dangerous	Adj	36	–	114	61	shh	Int	34	+	1435	0
deep	Adj	35	–	345	84	biggest	Adj	34	–	40	48
lives	Verb	35	+	30	26	regular	Adj	34	–	319	80
December	NoP	35	–	534	100	Gary	NoP	34	+	44	23
pattern	NoC	35	–	498	97	factory	NoC	34	–	38	47
medical	Adj	35	–	525	100	campaign	NoC	34	–	530	98
peasants	NoC	35	+	182	15	queen	NoC	34	–	342	82
prefer	Verb	35	–	0	37	behaviour	NoC	34	–	1013	133
sleep	NoC	35	–	4	40	last	Verb	34	+	13	27
theory	NoC	35	–	1108	142	grant	NoC	34	–	7	39
effort	NoC	35	–	330	83	helped	Verb	34	–	333	81
sad	Adj	35	+	0	34	closed	Verb	34	–	364	84
gold	NoC	35	–	286	79	principle	NoC	34	–	404	87
firm	NoC	35	–	458	94	hold	NoC	34	+	7	29
include	Verb	35	–	1453	165	calls	NoC	34	+	2	31
boxes	NoC	35	+	29	26	fingers	NoC	34	–	132	61
tremendous	Adj	35	+	113	18	knowing	Verb	34	–	48	49
Neil	NoP	35	+	7	30	create	Verb	34	–	406	87
context	NoC	35	–	434	92	effectively	Adv	34	–	70	52
expected	Verb	35	–	1366	159	eggs	NoC	34	–	3	38
river	NoC	35	–	547	101	unemployment	NoC	34	–	197	68
criteria	NoC	35	–	5	40	present	NoC	34	–	16	42
keen	Adj	35	–	0	37	now that	Conj	34	+	4	30
knock	Verb	35	+	340	10	voluntary	Adj	34	–	8	40
sheep	NoC	35	+	8	30	stories	NoC	34	–	50	49
lads	NoC	35	+	232	13	next to	Prep	34	+	5	30
procedures	NoC	35	–	77	55	colours	NoC	34	–	32	46
design	NoC	35	–	927	129	on top of	Prep	34	+	26	25
touch	Verb	35	+	35	25	past	Adj	34	–	508	95
doubt	NoC	35	–	183	68	turning	Verb	34	–	137	61
thought	NoC	35	–	567	102	affect	Verb	34	–	53	49
providing	Verb	35	–	232	73	helpful	Adj	33	+	1	32
series	NoC	35	–	1323	156	joint	Adj	33	–	205	68
mayor	NoC	35	+	86	20	Jonathan	NoP	33	+	172	14
effective	Adj	35	–	628	107	advantage	NoC	33	–	309	78
stairs	NoC	35	–	0	37	whilst	Conj	33	–	143	61
style	NoC	35	–	739	115	later	Adj	33	–	362	83
mad	Adj	35	+	4	31	begin	Verb	33	–	327	80
league	NoC	35	–	408	89	proposal	NoC	33	–	23	43
mess	NoC	35	+	103	19	sound	Verb	33	+	5	29
total	NoC	35	–	64	53	picking	Verb	33	+	74	19
as though	Conj	35	–	88	56	professional	Adj	33	–	751	113
beyond	Prep	35	–	719	114	da	NoC	33	+	1062	1
art	NoC	35	–	1487	166	tickets	NoC	33	+	21	25
protection	NoC	35	–	374	86	dear	NoC	33	+	181	14
crime	NoC	35	–	265	76	carrying	Verb	33	–	119	58
count	Verb	35	+	84	20	consideration	NoC	33	–	108	57
puts	Verb	35	+	12	28	funding	NoC	33	–	11	40
hmm	Int	35	+	826	3	pretty	Adj	33	+	11	27
States	NoP	35	–	430	90	sum	NoC	33	–	17	42
living	NoC	35	–	33	47	sake	NoC	33	+	0	32
activity	NoC	35	–	875	124	furniture	NoC	33	–	1	36
remind	Verb	35	+	155	15	grass	NoC	33	–	20	42
Birmingham	NoP	35	+	0	34	supply	NoC	33	–	265	74
roof	NoC	35	–	14	42	strategic	Adj	33	+	2	30
mark	NoC	34	+	0	33	pocket	NoC	33	–	1	36
finding	Verb	34	–	97	57	egg	NoC	33	+	27	24

Word	PoS	FrS		LL	FrW
hard	Adv	33	–	287	76
van	NoC	33	+	70	20
wet	Adj	33		2	36
knocked	Verb	33	+	41	22
bathroom	NoC	33	+	27	24
perfectly	Adv	33	–	37	46
fancy	Verb	33	+	314	9
Harrogate	NoP	33	+	623	4
point	Verb	33	+	0	33
countryside	NoC	33	–	12	40
button	NoC	33	+	153	15
effects	NoC	33	–	801	116
Colin	NoP	33	+	29	24
defence	NoC	33	–	939	126
drive	NoC	33	–	54	49
iron	NoC	33	–	44	47
Ben	NoP	33	+	0	32
Leeds	NoP	33	–	64	50
teeth	NoC	33	–	58	49
walk	NoC	33	–	11	39
technical	Adj	33	–	257	72
schemes	NoC	33	–	82	53
Harlow	NoP	33	+	881	2
relevant	Adj	33	–	398	85
chief	Adj	33	–	346	80
acid	NoC	33	–	71	51
saved	Verb	33	+	0	32
skin	NoC	33	–	272	73
massive	Adj	32	–	36	45
writing	NoC	32	–	106	56
factors	NoC	32	–	507	93
survey	NoC	32	–	398	84
standard	Adj	32	–	308	76
bottom	Adj	32	+	109	16
bear	Verb	32	–	49	47
pink	Adj	32	+	2	30
empty	Adj	32	–	114	56
square	NoC	32	–	28	43
hat	NoC	32	+	0	31
Christopher	NoP	32	+	41	22
honourable	Adj	32	+	466	6
broke	Verb	32	–	96	54
edge	NoC	32	–	345	80
electricity	NoC	32	–	10	39
railway	NoC	32	–	320	77
degrees	NoC	32	+	0	31
average	Adj	32	–	191	65
beat	Verb	32	–	48	47
savings	NoC	32	+	0	30
borrow	Verb	32	+	192	12
flat	Adj	32	–	6	37
marks	NoC	32	+	5	28
trousers	NoC	32	+	40	22
standard	NoC	32	–	132	58
Emma	NoP	32	+	185	13
assume	Verb	32	–	24	42
wherever	Adv	32	+	38	22
refer	Verb	32	–	11	39
metal	NoC	32	–	57	48
marvellous	Adj	32	+	98	17
exam	NoC	32	+	459	6
legislation	NoC	32	–	292	74
consultation	NoC	32	+	24	23
enormous	Adj	32	–	31	43
following	Verb	32	–	974	126
fruit	NoC	32	–	27	42
record	Verb	32	+	35	22
agricultural	Adj	32	–	24	42
carefully	Adv	32	–	321	76
neck	NoC	32	–	142	59
mile	NoC	32	–	0	32
cutting	Verb	32	+	4	28
wondered	Verb	32	–	77	50
mistake	NoC	32	–	10	38
altogether	Adv	31	–	0	32
Liverpool	NoP	31	–	137	58
welcome	Verb	31	+	5	27
Joe	NoP	31	–	41	45
somehow	Adv	31	–	51	46
rough	Adj	31	–	2	34
executive	NoC	31	–	404	83
Geoff	NoP	31	+	259	10
charge	Verb	31	+	187	12
holding	Verb	31	–	328	77
helping	Verb	31	–	19	40
reduction	NoC	31	–	78	50
petrol	NoC	31	+	25	23
fun	NoC	31	–	3	35
compared	Verb	31	…	554	95
race	NoC	31	–	362	79
fortnight	NoC	31	+	171	13
joined	Verb	31	–	335	77
Jenny	NoP	31	+	100	16
treatment	NoC	31	–	1086	133
lead*	NoC	31	–	138	57
potatoes	NoC	31	+	121	15
cupboard	NoC	31	+	174	12
y'know	Int	31	+	824	2
cheque	NoC	31	+	63	19
in particular	Adv	31	–	269	71
respect	NoC	31	–	89	51
light	Adj	31	–	216	66
loss	NoC	31	–	989	126
flowers	NoC	31	–	129	56
watched	Verb	31	–	274	71
annual	Adj	31	–	453	86
option	NoC	31	–	134	57
speech	NoC	31	–	422	84
wanting	Verb	31	+	19	23
prime	Adj	31	–	1074	131
track	NoC	31	–	165	60
individuals	NoC	31	–	446	86
appear	Verb	31	–	881	118
standing	NoC	31	+	3	28
absolute	Adj	31	–	5	35
Oxfordshire	NoP	31	+	134	14
just about	Adv	31	+	169	12
suggestion	NoC	31	–	0	31
hundreds	NoC	31	–	26	41
watch	NoC	31	+	1	29
Manchester	NoP	31	–	98	52
originally	Adv	31	–	58	47
brown	Adj	31	–	58	47
nasty	Adj	31	+	87	16
report	Verb	31	+	0	29
works	NoC	31	–	481	88
Fox	NoP	31	+	178	12
along with	Prep	31	–	105	53
amongst	Prep	31	–	63	47
ice	NoC	31	–	29	41
demand	NoC	30	–	577	95
switch	Verb	30	+	115	15

Word	PoS	FrS		LL	FrW	Word	PoS	FrS		LL	FrW
realise	Verb	30	–	23	40	perfect	Adj	29	–	180	59
aid	NoC	30	–	432	84	discussed	Verb	29	–	345	75
plastic	NoC	30	–	31	42	blah	Int	29	+	853	2
peace	NoC	30	–	580	95	cause	Verb	29	–	201	61
August	NoP	30	–	446	85	underneath	Prep	29	+	292	8
Easter	NoC	30	+	90	16	contribution	NoC	29	–	151	56
accounts	NoC	30	–	256	69	rent	NoC	29	+	0	28
reduce	Verb	30	–	334	76	cold	NoC	29	+	15	23
wondering	Verb	30	+	12	24	drugs	NoC	29	–	152	56
yard	NoC	30	–	1	33	longer	Adv	29	–	6	34
required	Verb	30	–	1489	157	southern	Adj	29	–	169	58
Tory	Adj	30	–	5	35	clients	NoC	29	–	105	51
avoid	Verb	30	–	453	85	his*	Pron	29	–	108	51
event	NoC	30	–	813	112	master	NoC	29	–	242	65
amazing	Adj	30	+	70	17	reform	NoC	29	–	159	57
orders	NoC	30	–	125	55	credit	NoC	29	–	360	76
back	Adj	30	+	71	17	virtually	Adv	29	–	67	46
seconds	NoC	30	–	39	43	recorded	Verb	29	–	195	61
calling	Verb	30	–	35	42	following	Adj	29	–	1348	146
respond	Verb	30	–	9	36	star	NoC	29	–	238	65
customer	NoC	30	–	76	49	confidence	NoC	29	–	352	75
primary	Adj	30	–	543	92	interview	NoC	29	–	59	44
fresh	Adj	30	–	303	72	kid	NoC	29	+	94	15
outside	Adj	30	–	14	37	funds	NoC	29	–	256	66
forest	NoC	30	–	332	75	will	NoC	29	–	206	61
feels	Verb	30	–	2	33	difficulties	NoC	29	–	333	73
strike	NoC	30	–	27	40	reading	NoC	29	–	99	50
worst	Adj	30	–	70	47	left	Adj	29	–	710	102
comment	Verb	30	+	57	18	alone	Adj	29	–	168	57
classes	NoC	30	–	216	64	Ireland	NoP	29	–	735	104
still	Adj	30	+	0	29	times	Prep	29	+	605	3
carpet	NoC	30	–	16	23	fight	Verb	29	–	40	41
laugh	Verb	30	+	37	20	summat	Pron	29	+	760	2
chapter	NoC	30	–	1589	163	past	Adv	29	+	29	20
clean	Verb	30	+	109	15	gun	NoC	29	–	13	36
ridiculous	Adj	30	+	64	18	commitment	NoC	29	–	193	60
northern	Adj	30	–	282	70	super	Adj	29	+	96	15
rooms	NoC	30	–	162	58	encourage	Verb	29	–	136	54
included	Verb	30	–	1140	133	rural	Adj	29	–	263	66
homework	NoC	30	+	411	6	row	NoC	29	–	107	50
danger	NoC	30	–	216	64	sign	NoC	29	–	217	62
session	NoC	30	–	62	46	biscuits	NoC	29	+	260	8
appreciate	Verb	30	+	4	26	spending	Verb	28	–	0	30
plate	NoC	30	–	38	42	sensible	Adj	28	+	0	27
stop	NoC	30	+	43	19	helps	Verb	28	–	0	28
Leicester	NoP	29	+	63	17	senior	Adj	28	–	534	89
presentation	NoC	29	–	2	32	plant	NoC	28	–	417	80
activities	NoC	29	–	1031	126	laughing	Verb	28	+	8	24
dealt	Verb	29	–	10	36	share	NoC	28	–	527	88
aspects	NoC	29	–	379	78	whoever	Pron	28	+	117	13
article	NoC	29	–	311	72	Selby	NoP	28	+	864	1
Stuart	NoP	29	+	34	20	split	Verb	28	+	3	25
interests	NoC	29	–	839	113	singing	Verb	28	+	22	21
understanding	NoC	29	–	413	81	requirements	NoC	28	–	241	64
customers	NoC	29	–	312	72	taught	Verb	28	–	31	39
desk	NoC	29	–	72	47	bound	Verb	28	–	97	49
caused	Verb	29	–	712	103	learnt	Verb	28	+	21	21
no longer	Adv	29	–	601	95	machines	NoC	28	–	107	50
cut	NoC	29	+	0	29	salt	NoC	28	–	0	29
sports	NoC	29	–	60	45	reach	Verb	28	–	343	73
brothers	NoC	29	–	15	37	oi	Int	28	+	790	2
across	Adv	29	–	11	36	licence	NoC	28	–	19	37
answers	NoC	29	–	2	32	impression	NoC	28	–	61	44
introduced	Verb	29	–	568	92	essentially	Adv	28	–	23	37
nights	NoC	29	+	0	28	thinking	NoC	28	–	64	44
neighbours	NoC	29	–	2	32	buses	NoC	28	+	115	13

Word	PoS	FrS		LL	FrW	Word	PoS	FrS		LL	FrW
sweet	Adj	28	–	10	34	weird	Adj	27	+	208	9
ticket	NoC	28	+	19	21	holy	Adj	27	–	3	30
microphone	NoC	28	+	411	5	losing	Verb	27	–	22	36
West	NoP-	28	–	624	95	elderly	Adj	27	–	141	52
granddad	NoC	28	+	1196	0	um	Int	27	+	439	4
lay	Verb	28	–	694	100	divided	Verb	27	–	55	41
opportunities	NoC	28	–	219	62	attack	NoC	27	–	492	83
grandma	NoC	28	+	668	2	planning	Verb	27	–	150	53
directly	Adv	28	–	626	95	asleep	Adj	27	+	2	24
jump	Verb	28	+	78	15	employers	NoC	27	–	74	44
ship	NoC	28	–	68	45	caravan	NoC	27	+	242	8
enter	Verb	28	–	160	56	downstairs	Adv	27	+	52	16
media	NoC	28	–	506	86	ya	Int	27	+	957	1
vehicle	NoC	28	–	63	44	highly	Adv	27	–	710	99
programmes	NoC	28	–	301	69	practical	Adj	27	–	494	83
golf	NoC	28	–	14	35	councillors	NoC	27	+	24	19
angle	NoC	28	+	5	24	J / j	Lett	27	+	96	13
move	NoC	28	–	342	72	identify	Verb	27	–	148	53
damage	NoC	28	–	388	76	filled	Verb	27	–	170	55
followed	Verb	28	–	1658	163	pop	Verb	27	+	233	8
sport	NoC	28	–	89	47	suspect	Verb	27	+	22	20
lying	Verb	28	–	98	48	parent	NoC	27	–	38	39
target	NoC	28	–	303	69	decent	Adj	27	+	37	18
control	Verb	28	–	162	55	turns	Verb	27	–	10	33
electric	Adj	28	–	14	35	blind	Adj	27	+	0	26
revolution	NoC	28	–	102	49	teaching	NoC	27	–	224	60
St	NoP-	28	–	999	120	fridge	NoC	27	+	265	7
shape	NoC	28	–	276	66	guidance	NoC	27	–	11	33
tables	NoC	28	–	1	30	server	NoC	27	+	90	13
channel	NoC	28	–	49	41	assessment	NoC	27	–	358	72
claim	NoC	28	–	322	70	smoke	Verb	27	+	173	10
unemployed	Adj	28	–	0	28	suggesting	Verb	27	+	0	25
wage	NoC	28	–	5	32	introduce	Verb	27	–	25	36
stuck	Adj	28	+	154	11	sending	Verb	27	+	0	26
runs	Verb	28	–	49	41	briefly	Adv	27	–	14	34
drawn	Verb	28	–	450	81	shot	NoC	27	–	14	33
enquiry	NoC	27	+	55	17	earlier	Adj	27	–	403	75
whenever	Adv	27	–	7	32	lack	NoC	27	–	703	98
laid	Verb	27	–	236	62	mostly	Adv	27	–	55	41
civil	Adj	27	–	619	93	rail	NoC	26	–	56	41
applications	NoC	27	–	281	67	tin	NoC	26	+	20	19
square	Adj	27	+	1	26	developed	Verb	26	–	1013	119
huh	Int	27	+	586	3	steps	NoC	26	–	359	72
luck	NoC	27	–	8	32	recall	Verb	26	+	0	25
finger	NoC	27	–	8	33	block	NoC	26	–	32	37
opposite	Adj	27	–	8	33	on behalf of	Prep	26	–	0	27
band	NoC	27	–	346	72	seconded	Verb	26	+	554	3
la	Fore	27	+	42	18	related	Verb	26	–	233	60
straight away	Adv	27	+	336	6	below	Prep	26	–	212	58
popular	Adj	27	–	932	115	heat	NoC	26	–	195	57
method	NoC	27	–	690	98	forces	NoC	26	–	1102	124
lesson	NoC	27	+	9	22	factor	NoC	26	–	303	67
arms	NoC	27	–	1002	120	farmers	NoC	26	–	159	53
network	NoC	27	–	416	78	birds	NoC	26	–	231	60
currently	Adv	27	–	390	75	spare	Adj	26	+	26	18
in favour of	Prep	27	–	24	37	reaction	NoC	26	–	218	59
guilty	Adj	27	–	69	44	spoken	Verb	26	–	1	29
willing	Adj	27	–	47	41	clear	Verb	26	+	2	24
other than	Prep	27	–	76	45	whom	Pron	26	–	1368	141
relatively	Adv	27	–	514	85	prepared	Verb	26	–	177	55
kinds	NoC	27	–	109	49	physical	Adj	26	–	791	103
nor	Conj	27	–	1247	136	elections	NoC	26	–	267	63
just	Adj	27	+	38	18	lecture	NoC	26	+	46	16
Arthur	NoP	27	–	0	29	Frank	NoP	26	–	42	39
foreign	Adj	27	–	1909	177	argue	Verb	26	–	86	45
charges	NoC	27	–	251	63	task	NoC	26	–	741	100

2.2

Word	PoS	FrS		LL	FrW	Word	PoS	FrS		LL	FrW
claim	Verb	26	–	130	50	Steven	NoP	25	+	133	10
salary	NoC	26	+	19	19	butter	NoC	25	+	8	20
essential	Adj	26	–	663	94	form	Verb	25	–	562	85
exciting	Adj	26	–	19	34	motor	NoC	25	–	90	44
western	Adj	26	–	852	107	progress	NoC	25	–	528	82
nevertheless	Adv	26	–	445	78	camera	NoC	25	–	2	27
complicated	Adj	26	–	4	29	root	NoC	25	+	10	20
dozen	NoC	26	–	0	27	liberal*	Adj	25	–	222	57
address	Verb	26	+	22	19	reduced	Verb	25	–	377	71
animal	NoC	26	–	374	72	occasion	NoC	25	–	207	56
urban	Adj	26	–	207	57	dress	NoC	25	–	90	43
among	Prep	26	–	3242	252	player	NoC	25	–	257	60
soft	Adj	26	–	296	66	newspaper	NoC	25	–	180	53
computers	NoC	26	–	36	37	bright	Adj	25	–	227	58
occasions	NoC	26	–	55	40	equals	Verb	25	+	408	4
roughly	Adv	26	+	3	23	boss	NoC	25	–	20	33
Derek	NoP	26	+	20	19	describe	Verb	25	–	104	45
broken	Verb	26	–	90	45	packet	NoC	25	+	125	10
trial	NoC	26	–	342	69	gosh	Int	25	+	717	1
solicitor	NoC	26	–	13	32	temperature	NoC	25	–	111	46
brain	NoC	26	–	136	50	revenue	NoC	25	–	82	43
analysis	NoC	26	–	1437	145	green	NoC	25	–	13	31
gate	NoC	26	–	34	37	famous	Adj	25	–	375	70
Alex	NoP	26	+	25	18	identified	Verb	25	–	324	66
Africa	NoP	26	–	539	84	sheets	NoC	25	+	0	24
chest	NoC	26	–	51	39	arrangements	NoC	25	–	274	62
realized	Verb	26	–	10	31	literally	Adv	25	+	12	19
falling	Verb	26	–	102	46	brings	Verb	25	–	22	33
poll	NoC	26	–	3	29	objectives	NoC	25	–	109	46
added	Verb	26	–	1557	152	Major	NoP	25	–	87	43
described	Verb	26	–	1725	162	agency	NoC	25	–	292	63
records	NoC	26	–	435	76	managers	NoC	25	–	282	62
clock	NoC	26	–	3	29	violence	NoC	25	–	253	60
badly	Adv	26	–	97	45	priority	NoC	25	–	33	35
costs	Verb	26	–	17	33	explained	Verb	25	–	451	76
kind of	Adv	26	+	481	3	considerable	Adj	24	–	855	104
Smith	NoP	26	–	549	85	Pete	NoP	24	+	103	11
alive	Adj	26	–	90	44	youth	NoC	24	–	231	58
average	NoC	25	–	37	37	suitable	Adj	24	–	318	65
requirement	NoC	25	–	18	33	location	NoC	24	–	82	42
teach	Verb	25	–	3	29	grand	Adj	24	–	140	49
protect	Verb	25	–	183	54	arts	NoC	24	–	220	57
definition	NoC	25	–	148	51	represent	Verb	24	–	135	48
folk	NoC	25	+	9	21	pack	NoC	24	–	0	26
elsewhere	Adv	25	–	247	60	becoming	Verb	24	–	463	77
employed	Verb	25	–	152	51	specifically	Adv	24	–	60	39
secondly	Adv	25	–	4	29	Dennis	NoP	24	+	57	14
joke	NoC	25	+	8	21	heads	NoC	24	–	211	55
peasant	NoC	25	+	47	15	New	NoP-	24	–	1023	115
assembly	NoC	25	–	216	57	variety	NoC	24	–	717	95
importance	NoC	25	–	847	105	Christian	Adj	24	–	337	66
student	NoC	25	–	526	82	recommenda-tion	NoC	24	+	75	13
projects	NoC	25	–	233	59						
Kevin	NoP	25	+	1	23	learning	Verb	24	–	63	39
examples	NoC	25	–	440	76	blame	Verb	24	+	0	23
setting	Verb	25	–	114	47	growing	Verb	24	–	43	36
comfortable	Adj	25	–	70	41	options	NoC	24	–	62	39
nowadays	Adv	25	+	49	15	brief	Adj	24	–	158	50
due to	Prep	25	–	547	84	bearing	Verb	24	+	2	22
fast	Adj	25	–	14	32	reasonably	Adv	24	–	16	31
smell	Verb	25	+	136	10	partly	Adv	24	–	273	61
Sally	NoP	25	+	69	14	led	Verb	24	–	1901	170
beginning	Verb	25	–	208	56	fields	NoC	24	–	281	62
version	NoC	25	–	601	88	Pat	NoP	24	+	26	17
hanging	Verb	25	+	1	23	active	Adj	24	–	494	78
began	Verb	25	–	3462	262	nowhere	Adv	24	+	0	24

Word	PoS	FrS		LL	FrW	Word	PoS	FrS		LL	FrW
achieved	Verb	24	–	590	86	occasionally	Adv	23	–	93	42
minor	Adj	24	–	149	49	quarters	NoC	23	+	16	17
grown	Verb	24	–	112	45	crap	NoC	23	+	312	5
doubt	Verb	24	+	4	21	Karen	NoP	23	+	33	15
prison	NoC	24	–	372	69	fox	NoC	23	+	183	8
aspect	NoC	24	–	117	46	marketing	NoC	23	–	195	52
ta	Int	24	+	245	6	wow	Int	23	+	487	3
capacity	NoC	24	–	294	63	terribly	Adv	23	+	84	11
round	NoC	24	–	42	36	nursery	NoC	23	+	16	17
Mick	NoP	24	+	54	14	awkward	Adj	23	+	35	15
larger	Adj	24	–	552	82	feed	Verb	23	–	0	25
arrived	Verb	24	–	742	96	latest	Adj	23	–	410	70
keys	NoC	24	+	0	22	spread	Verb	23	–	157	49
audience	NoC	24	–	249	58	reality	NoC	23	–	406	70
solution	NoC	24	–	440	74	sufficient	Adj	23	–	326	63
recognize	Verb	24	+	4	21	signed	Verb	23	–	300	61
serve	Verb	24	–	231	57	failed	Verb	23	–	774	96
laws	NoC	24	–	171	51	lie	Verb	23	–	126	45
cook	Verb	24	+	33	16	migration	NoC	23	+	67	12
Clare	NoP	24	+	3	21	seek	Verb	23	–	261	58
trip	NoC	24	–	140	48	pool	NoC	23	–	149	47
sky	NoC	24	–	192	53	professor	NoC	23	–	229	55
gentlemen	NoC	24	+	54	14	streets	NoC	23	–	200	52
limit	NoC	24	–	37	35	worth	NoC	23	+	1	21
committed	Verb	24	–	147	48	ended	Verb	23	–	522	78
districts	NoC	24	+	22	17	spending	NoC	23	–	66	38
Helen	NoP	24	–	5	28	mark	Verb	23	–	2	25
hope	NoC	24	–	262	59	fat	Adj	23	–	9	28
score	NoC	24	–	6	28	tenants	NoC	23	+	6	19
trust	Verb	24	–	9	29	engineering	NoC	23	–	219	54
expenditure	NoC	24	–	259	59	organisations	NoC	23	–	216	54
disgusting	Adj	24	+	255	6	missing	Verb	23	–	16	30
pulling	Verb	24	–	0	24	recommenda- tions	NoC	23	–	3	26
commercial	Adj	24	–	596	85	understood	Verb	23	–	303	61
heating	NoC	24	+	7	20	teams	NoC	23	–	93	41
spot	NoC	24	–	101	43	pushing	Verb	23	–	0	24
dictionary	NoC	24	+	14	18	events	NoC	23	–	1048	114
organisation	NoC	24	–	673	90	increased	Verb	23	–	533	79
moon	NoC	24	–	12	30	drop	NoC	23	+	0	22
German	Adj	24	–	918	107	lessons	NoC	23	–	0	23
impossible	Adj	24	–	477	76	screen	NoC	23	–	181	51
proposed	Adj	24	–	81	41	firms	NoC	23	–	564	81
detailed	Adj	24	–	332	65	Fred	NoP	23	+	1	21
recognise	Verb	24	–	59	38	release	NoC	23	–	188	51
in general	Adv	24	–	105	44	C. / c.	Lett	23	+	648	1
overall	Adj	24	–	327	64	pie	NoC	23	+	101	10
visit	Verb	24	–	203	54	acceptable	Adj	23	–	68	38
image	NoC	24	–	538	81	offices	NoC	23	–	137	46
carbon	NoC	24	–	0	25	uncle	NoC	23	–	59	37
teaching	Verb	24	–	36	34	Matthew	NoP	23	–	4	26
act	Verb	24	–	310	63	ideal	Adj	23	–	175	50
Sussex	NoP	24	+	7	19	blow	Verb	23	+	73	12
created	Verb	23	–	705	92	late	Adv	23	–	113	43
Marks	NoP	23	+	194	7	status	NoC	23	–	769	95
ho	Int	23	+	579	2	offer	NoC	23	–	343	64
slow	Adj	23	–	181	51	supported	Verb	23	–	293	60
trained	Verb	23	–	16	30	friendly	Adj	23	–	87	40
grateful	Adj	23	–	7	28	ps	Lett	23	+	1065	0
conclusion	NoC	23	–	210	54	journey	NoC	23	–	186	51
proportion	NoC	23	–	374	68	exist	Verb	23	–	269	58
return	NoC	23	–	741	95	speakers	NoC	23	+	0	22
Graham	NoP	23	–	113	44	substantial	Adj	23	–	375	67
aircraft	NoC	23	–	357	66	phrase	NoC	23	–	24	31
grey	Adj	23	–	173	50	remain	Verb	23	–	809	98
Lee	NoP	23	–	58	38	penny	NoC	23	+	87	11
propose	Verb	23	+	60	13						

Word	PoS	FrS		LL	FrW
dream	NoC	23	–	87	40
stress	NoC	23	–	86	40
traditional	Adj	23	–	958	108
frightened	Adj	23	+	1	21
magazine	NoC	23	–	176	50
jacket	NoC	23	–	23	31
forced	Verb	23	–	560	80
pushed	Verb	23	–	220	54
condition	NoC	22	–	701	90
ow	Int	22	+	1056	0
pot	NoC	22	+	5	19
pit	NoC	22	+	15	17
male	Adj	22	+	795	96
zero	Num	22	+	42	14
concentrate	Verb	22	–	28	32
link	NoC	22	–	101	42
Claire	NoP	22	+	100	10
businesses	NoC	22	–	74	38
payment	NoC	22	–	269	58
equally	Adv	22	–	431	71
limited	Adj	22	–	411	69
stopping	Verb	22	+	28	15
tall	Adj	22	–	166	48
documents	NoC	22	–	144	46
conscious	Adj	22	–	29	32
instead	Adv	22	–	570	81
rise	NoC	22	–	523	77
naughty	Adj	22	+	268	5
bodies	NoC	22	–	495	75
except	Conj	22	–	118	43
boundary	NoC	22	+	1	20
database	NoC	22	–	54	35
policeman	NoC	22	+	0	21
thin	Adj	22	–	237	54
buildings	NoC	22	–	451	72
strength	NoC	22	–	528	77
pleasure	NoC	22	–	252	56
invited	Verb	22	–	130	44
accommodation	NoC	22	–	149	46
fixed	Adj	22	–	68	37
expecting	Verb	22	+	0	21
gap	NoC	22	–	58	36
spring	NoC	22	–	287	59
fit	Adj	22	–	26	31
uses	Verb	22	–	76	38
reported	Verb	22	–	1241	124
introduction	NoC	22	–	453	71
stick	NoC	22	+	6	18
bird	NoC	22	–	72	38
shower	NoC	22	+	34	14
tied	Verb	22	–	5	26
democracy	NoC	22	–	134	45
confident	Adj	22	–	44	34
appears	Verb	22	–	611	83
travel	Verb	22	–	81	39
tools	NoC	22	–	40	33
photograph	NoC	22	–	3	25
OK*	Adv	22	+	8	18
objective	NoC	22	–	24	30
heaven	NoC	22	–	3	25
seats	NoC	22	–	187	50
pensions	NoC	22	+	4	19
cause	NoC	22	–	547	78
K. / k.	Lett	22	+	1024	0
players	NoC	22	–	696	89
unusual	Adj	22	–	125	43

Word	PoS	FrS		LL	FrW
situations	NoC	22	–	100	41
maintenance	NoC	22	–	113	42
path	NoC	22	–	399	67
Scottish	Adj	22	–	979	107
travel	NoC	22	–	73	37
communist	Adj	22	–	130	44
measure	Verb	22	+	7	18
checked	Verb	22	–	6	26
that is	Adv	22	–	177	48
religious	Adj	22	–	447	71
chairs	NoC	22	+	2	20
Joan	NoP	22	+	3	19
tablets	NoC	22	+	143	8
usual	Adj	22	–	422	69
recommend	Verb	22	+	7	18
communication	NoC	22	–	382	66
Sam	NoP	22	–	39	32
concept	NoC	22	–	428	69
thrown	Verb	22	–	33	31
South	NoP	22	–	467	72
typical	Adj	22	–	215	52
Billy	NoP	22	–	0	22
despite	Prep	22	–	1846	160
present	Verb	22	–	54	35
whether or not	Conj	22	–	22	30
as opposed to	Prep	21	+	14	16
regulations	NoC	21	–	141	45
Amy	NoP	21	+	176	7
percentage	NoC	21	–	19	29
sight	NoC	21	–	460	71
Scott	NoP	21	–	43	33
apple	NoC	21	–	11	27
real	Adv	21	+	459	2
inspector	NoC	21	–	26	30
breaking	Verb	21	–	29	31
loves	Verb	21	+	63	11
suffer	Verb	21	–	68	36
lords	NoC	21	+	24	15
shot	Verb	21	–	226	53
shopping	Verb	21	+	123	8
politics	NoC	21	–	593	81
deliver	Verb	21	–	0	22
verse	NoC	21	+	40	13
marriage	NoC	21	–	660	85
former	DetP	21	–	2312	187
tends	Verb	21	–	4	25
allowance	NoC	21	–	0	22
opening	NoC	21	–	242	54
plants	NoC	21	–	555	78
domestic	Adj	21	–	507	74
inflation	NoC	21	–	175	48
closed	Adj	21	+	0	20
powers	NoC	21	–	489	73
slowly	Adv	21	–	671	86
seventh	Ord	21	+	28	14
local	NoC	21	+	4	18
coast	NoC	21	–	191	49
near	Adv	21	+	14	16
repeat	Verb	21	–	14	27
elements	NoC	21	–	435	69
previously	Adv	21	–	506	74
rock	NoC	21	–	432	69
French	NoC	21	–	68	36
boot	NoC	21	+	29	14
published	Verb	21	–	998	107
sweets	NoC	21	+	201	6

2.2

Word	PoS	FrS		LL	FrW	Word	PoS	FrS		LL	FrW
roll	NoC	21	+	28	14	Thomas	NoP	20	–	515	73
shock	NoC	21	–	142	44	nicely	Adv	20	+	109	8
underneath	Adv	21	+	161	7	lordship	NoC	20	+	171	6
purposes	NoC	21	–	355	63	discussions	NoC	20	–	49	33
permission	NoC	21	–	50	34	Julie	NoP	20	+	26	14
facts	NoC	21	–	276	56	fighting	Verb	20	–	93	38
suit	NoC	21	–	39	32	backwards	Adv	20	+	3	18
critical	Adj	21	–	344	62	organizations	NoC	20	–	39	31
disease	NoC	21	–	842	97	scene	NoC	20	–	518	74
package	NoC	21	–	336	61	code	NoC	20	–	282	56
shirt	NoC	21	–	22	29	temporary	Adj	20	–	115	40
nurse	NoC	21	–	46	33	aunty	NoC	20	+	721	1
metres	NoC	21	–	65	35	stations	NoC	20	–	102	39
working	NoC	21	–	106	40	Thatcher	NoP	20	–	69	35
treated	Verb	21	–	514	74	cow	NoC	20	+	31	13
familiar	Adj	21	–	339	61	William	NoP	20	–	779	91
employees	NoC	21	–	359	63	inner	Adj	20	–	190	48
snow	NoC	21	–	34	31	recession	NoC	20	–	112	40
tight	Adj	21	–	3	24	X. / x.	Lett	20	+	951	0
chain	NoC	21	–	91	39	applied	Verb	20	–	493	72
individual	NoC	21	–	311	59	level	Adj	20	–	11	26
clue	NoC	21	+	81	10	need*	VMod	20	–	68	35
plaintiff	NoC	21	–	34	31	wider	Adj	20	–	245	52
designed	Verb	21	–	1043	110	surface	NoC	20	–	882	98
cross	Verb	21	–	1	23	ignore	Verb	20	–	10	25
text	NoC	21	–	642	83	presents	NoC	20	+	125	8
Banbury	NoP	21	+	260	5	hungry	Adj	20	+	1	18
chances	NoC	21	–	39	32	pupils	NoC	20	–	741	88
constant	Adj	21	–	214	51	inch	NoC	20	+	3	17
back	Verb	21	+	89	9	charged	Verb	20	–	214	50
require	Verb	21	–	522	74	prove	Verb	20	–	364	62
earn	Verb	21	+	0	20	cuts	NoC	20	–	37	30
maintain	Verb	21	–	307	58	clubs	NoC	20	–	112	40
committees	NoC	21	–	18	28	holes	NoC	20	–	20	27
strongly	Adv	21	–	196	49	profits	NoC	20	–	369	62
lorry	NoC	21	+	40	13	tests	NoC	20	–	262	53
Jackie	NoP	21	+	119	8	stand	NoC	20	+	0	19
purely	Adv	21	–	11	26	orange	NoC	20	+	42	12
formal	Adj	21	–	454	69	bin	NoC	20	+	156	7
except	Prep	21	–	38	31	enable	Verb	20	–	234	51
ear	NoC	21	–	28	30	graph	NoC	20	+	88	9
bid	NoC	21	–	42	32	extension	NoC	20	–	88	37
lump	NoC	21	+	73	10	Lisa	NoP	20	+	39	12
stands	Verb	21	–	30	30	owe	Verb	20	+	43	12
contracts	NoC	21	–	180	47	survive	Verb	20	–	87	37
treat	Verb	21	–	40	31	washed	Verb	20	+	0	19
fat	NoC	21	+	2	18	biscuit	NoC	20	+	264	4
lift	Verb	21	+	1	19	disabled	Adj	20	–	52	32
plain	Adj	21	–	30	30	ears	NoC	20	–	45	31
functions	NoC	21	–	269	55	religion	NoC	20	–	187	47
potential	Adj	21	–	482	71	invite	Verb	20	+	46	11
loved	Verb	21	–	204	49	feelings	NoC	20	–	310	57
boots	NoC	21	–	13	26	shout	Verb	20	+	88	9
attractive	Adj	21	–	272	55	minds	NoC	20	–	32	29
quote	Verb	21	+	96	9	mill	NoC	20	–	65	34
goals	NoC	20	–	219	50	madam	NoC	20	+	145	7
contact	Verb	20	–	152	44	allocation	NoC	20	+	1	18
differences	NoC	20	–	676	85	once again	Adv	20	–	109	39
residents	NoC	20	–	78	36	duck	NoC	20	+	56	11
fast	Adv	20	–	178	47	justice	NoC	20	–	519	73
pudding	NoC	20	+	134	7	yards	NoC	20	–	106	39
Anne	NoP	20	–	176	47	drug	NoC	20	–	268	54
tenth	Ord	20	+	69	10	newspapers	NoC	20	–	91	37
Edinburgh	NoP	20	–	393	64	sure	Adv	20	+	271	4
socks	NoC	20	+	100	9	replace	Verb	20	–	80	36
description	NoC	20	–	271	55	states	NoC	20	–	666	83

Word	PoS	FrS		LL	FrW	Word	PoS	FrS		LL	FrW
fuel	NoC	20	–	155	44	circle	NoC	19	–	85	36
publicity	NoC	20	–	15	26	selection	NoC	19	–	428	65
bid	Verb	20	+	136	7	Dr	NoC	19	–	1305	122
established	Verb	20	–	1062	108	mixed	Verb	19	–	7	24
steel	NoC	20	–	112	39	sees	Verb	19	–	100	37
check	NoC	20	+	1	18	pensioners	NoC	19	+	25	13
thoughts	NoC	20	–	225	50	like	Adj	19	+	6	16
fence	NoC	20	+	6	16	abroad	Adv	19	–	143	42
presented	Verb	20	–	725	87	expert	NoC	19	–	149	42
facing	Verb	20	–	120	40	subjects	NoC	19	–	693	84
diagram	NoC	20	+	39	12	Russell	NoP	19	–	1	21
proud	Adj	20	–	59	33	nan	NoC	19	+	287	3
proposed	Verb	20	–	204	48	answered	Verb	19	–	127	40
beer	NoC	20	–	72	35	twelfth	Num	19	+	103	8
diary	NoC	20	–	0	20	A. / a.	Lett	19	+	823	0
millions	NoC	20	–	24	28	adults	NoC	19	–	80	35
cleared	Verb	20	–	22	27	wake	Verb	19	+	15	14
Irish	Adj	20	–	399	63	appeal	NoC	19	–	941	100
Linda	NoP	20	+	49	11	fear	NoC	19	–	495	70
formula	NoC	20	–	23	27	efficient	Adj	19	–	152	42
statements	NoC	20	–	161	44	accent	NoC	19	+	18	14
parking	NoC	20	+	17	14	building	Verb	19	–	34	29
paint	NoC	20	–	3	23	babies	NoC	19	–	14	25
Lucy	NoP	20	–	27	28	intention	NoC	19	–	245	51
films	NoC	20	–	91	37	mental	Adj	19	–	397	62
rightly	Adv	20	+	15	14	retirement	NoC	19	–	89	36
airport	NoC	20	–	40	30	taste	NoC	19	–	93	36
bottles	NoC	20	+	1	18	retired	Verb	19	+	0	18
Danny	NoP	20	+	113	8	complaints	NoC	19	–	30	28
organized	Verb	20	–	0	20	dead	Adv	19	+	84	9
guys	NoC	19	+	47	11	swear	Verb	19	+	115	7
divide	Verb	19	+	47	11	tough	Adj	19	–	70	34
affected	Verb	19	–	331	58	multiply	Verb	19	+	256	4
Australia	NoP	19	–	270	53	involve	Verb	19	–	179	45
fed up	Adj	19	+	196	5	joking	Verb	19	+	175	6
formally	Adv	19	–	3	22	copies	NoC	19	–	97	37
plane	NoC	19	–	87	36	nuclear	Adj	19	–	775	88
shares	NoC	19	–	723	86	half way	Adv	19	+	281	3
bills	NoC	19	–	51	32	being	NoC	19	–	35	29
upset	Adj	19	+	2	17	finance	NoC	19	–	361	60
rude	Adj	19	+	87	9	Charlie	NoP	19	–	37	29
bastard	NoC	19	+	22	13	charity	NoC	19	–	104	37
files	NoC	19	–	43	31	fetch	Verb	19	+	38	11
producing	Verb	19	–	147	42	rather than	Conj	19	–	238	50
desperate	Adj	19	–	21	27	cell	NoC	19	–	360	59
opposition	NoC	19	–	931	99	initially	Adv	19	–	136	40
churches	NoC	19	–	96	37	source	NoC	19	–	942	99
map	NoC	19	–	147	42	walls	NoC	19	–	436	65
touch	NoC	19	–	161	44	complex	Adj	19	–	624	78
chemistry	NoC	19	–	0	20	roll	Verb	19	+	0	18
signs	NoC	19	–	242	51	patch	NoC	19	+	6	15
bear	NoC	19	+	44	11	photographs	NoC	19	–	80	35
fashion	NoC	19	–	211	48	tape	Verb	19	+	539	1
and so forth	Adv	19	+	257	4	pregnant	Adj	19	–	5	23
dressed	Verb	19	–	112	39	served	Verb	19	–	492	69
minimum	Adj	19	–	48	31	exams	NoC	19	+	166	6
in touch with	Prep	19	+	29	12	shared	Verb	19	–	117	38
conflict	NoC	19	–	358	60	bugger	NoC	19	+	339	3
battery	NoC	19	+	29	12	arguments	NoC	19	–	140	41
mirror	NoC	19	–	121	40	daft	Adj	19	+	174	5
daily	Adj	19	–	351	59	trading	NoC	19	–	143	41
seeking	Verb	19	–	228	49	crisis	NoC	19	–	420	64
motorway	NoC	19	+	49	11	youngsters	NoC	19	+	1	17
distribution	NoC	19	–	467	68	hectares	NoC	19	+	142	6
emergency	NoC	19	–	147	42	bible	NoC	19	–	0	20
swimming	NoC	19	+	1	18	birth	NoC	19	–	319	56

Word	PoS	FrS		LL	FrW	Word	PoS	FrS		LL	FrW
shouting	Verb	19	+	1	17	clerk	NoC	18	–	0	20
lost	Adj	19	–	19	26	title	NoC	18	–	1071	106
broad	Adj	19	–	275	52	collection	NoC	18	–	753	85
store	NoC	19	–	113	38	shoulder	NoC	18	–	245	49
Kelly	NoP	19	–	3	22	copy	Verb	18	+	78	8
instructions	NoC	19	–	111	38	representatives	NoC	18	–	202	45
Keith	NoP	19	–	42	29	truly	Adv	18	–	81	34
agent	NoC	19	–	203	46	centres	NoC	18	–	330	56
Dan	NoP	19	+	80	9	shortly	Adv	18	–	150	41
conservatives*	NoC	19	–	11	24	test	Verb	18	–	45	29
grounds	NoC	19	–	457	66	residential	Adj	18	–	57	31
curtains	NoC	19	–	1	20	hers	Pron	18	–	25	26
measure	NoC	19	–	244	50	welcome	Adj	18	–	38	28
fee	NoC	19	–	49	30	kettle	NoC	18	+	82	8
advise	Verb	19	–	2	21	eaten	Verb	18	+	1	17
discovered	Verb	19	–	500	69	sets	NoC	18	–	50	30
elected	Verb	19	–	224	48	citizens	NoC	18	–	89	35
Tories	NoC	19	–	1	20	banks	NoC	18	–	547	72
cancer	NoC	19	–	186	45	studies	NoC	18	–	1801	149
input	NoC	19	–	76	34	China	NoP	18	–	250	49
suggestions	NoC	19	–	3	21	laugh	NoC	18	+	0	17
hospitals	NoC	19	–	51	31	highest	Adj	18	–	268	51
pint	NoC	19	+	32	12	includes	Verb	18	–	576	73
kick	Verb	19	+	75	9	fallen	Verb	18	–	127	38
Roger	NoP	19	–	24	27	compare	Verb	18	–	20	25
capable	Adj	19	–	287	53	reached	Verb	18	–	1584	136
place	Verb	19	–	202	46	patterns	NoC	18	–	430	63
coke	NoC	19	+	207	5	handy	Adj	18	+	79	8
dance	NoC	19	–	55	31	branches	NoC	18	–	82	34
volume	NoC	19	–	346	58	administration	NoC	18	–	555	72
handle	Verb	19	–	27	27	sore	Adj	18	+	99	7
letting	Verb	19	–	6	22	merely	Adv	18	–	715	83
dwellings	NoC	19	+	111	7	causing	Verb	18	–	89	34
'cos*	Conj	18	+	315	3	learning	NoC	18	–	373	59
objection	NoC	18	+	24	12	apart	Adv	18	–	116	37
employer	NoC	18	–	61	32	lift	NoC	18	–	20	25
batteries	NoC	18	+	137	6	statutory	Adj	18	–	143	40
discussing	Verb	18	–	1	20	chat	NoC	18	+	82	8
no doubt	Adv	18	–	130	39	favourite	Adj	18	–	90	34
toast	NoC	18	+	71	9	partner	NoC	18	–	298	53
depending on	Prep	18	–	10	23	tip	NoC	18	–	2	20
ego	NoC	18	+	75	9	blank	Adj	18	+	7	14
chip	NoC	18	+	0	18	yourselves	Pron	18	+	206	4
Rob	NoP	18	+	30	12	drivers	NoC	18	–	32	27
drinking	Verb	18	–	1	20	statistics	NoC	18	–	85	34
Ron	NoP	18	+	19	13	pencil	NoC	18	+	34	11
bowl	NoC	18	–	10	23	visit	NoC	18	–	723	83
gradually	Adv	18	–	128	39	vast	Adj	18	–	270	51
cheerio	Int	18	+	688	0	relate	Verb	18	–	33	27
attend	Verb	18	–	119	38	wheel	NoC	18	–	30	27
Soviet	Adj	18	–	1291	119	drawing	Verb	18	–	76	33
island	NoC	18	–	543	72	partnership	NoC	18	–	114	37
Jimmy	NoP	18	–	17	25	tie	Verb	18	+	52	9
Lancashire	NoP	18	+	0	17	properties	NoC	18	–	191	44
booked	Verb	18	+	32	11	Stephen	NoP	18	–	291	52
beef	NoC	18	+	6	15	exchange	NoC	18	–	822	89
leaves	Verb	18	–	50	30	expressed	Verb	18	–	605	75
abuse	NoC	18	–	96	35	diet	NoC	18	–	184	43
belt	NoC	18	–	5	22	knife	NoC	18	–	40	28
eighth	Ord	18	+	24	12	return	Verb	18	–	751	84
beg	Verb	18	+	109	7	worker	NoC	18	–	135	39
damn	Adj	18	+	160	5	delivery	NoC	18	–	131	38
junction	NoC	18	+	0	18	wooden	Adj	18	–	124	38
cabinet	NoC	18	–	534	71	atmosphere	NoC	18	–	293	52
inches	NoC	18	–	13	24	recording	NoC	18	–	25	25
ringing	Verb	18	+	84	8	permanent	Adj	18	–	248	48

Word	PoS	FrS		LL	FrW	Word	PoS	FrS		LL	FrW
noble	Adj	18	+	13	13	cottage	NoC	17	−	90	33
educational	Adj	18	−	443	63	sections	NoC	17	−	273	50
throat	NoC	18	−	90	34	bored	Adj	17	+	7	14
intend	Verb	18	−	5	21	brochure	NoC	17	+	59	9
remembered	Verb	18	−	370	58	disaster	NoC	17	−	59	30
twelfths	Num	18	+	817	0	whatsoever	DetP	17	+	54	9
operate	Verb	18	−	184	43	behind	Adv	17	−	119	36
brackets	NoC	18	+	158	5	Ryedale	NoP	17	+	523	1
delighted	Adj	18	−	36	27	flow	NoC	17	−	252	48
East	NoP-	18	−	287	51	dee	Uncl	17	+	677	0
alarm	NoC	18	−	6	21	fellow	NoC	17	−	2	19
freedom	NoC	18	−	476	65	somewhat	Adv	17	−	276	50
Gordon	NoP	18	−	34	27	slight	Adj	17	−	71	31
calls	Verb	18	−	73	32	beds	NoC	17	−	11	22
lock	NoC	18	+	3	15	ninth	Ord	17	+	55	9
plan	Verb	18	−	38	27	Tracey	NoP	17	+	186	4
solid	Adj	18	−	123	37	challenge	NoC	17	−	366	57
premises	NoC	18	−	164	41	jury	NoC	17	−	19	24
Welsh	Adj	18	−	148	40	approval	NoC	17	−	181	42
wicked	Adj	18	+	39	10	initiative	NoC	17	−	147	39
tank	NoC	17	−	100	35	arrange	Verb	17	−	18	23
Ruth	NoP	17	−	74	32	acting	Verb	17	−	207	44
gorgeous	Adj	17	+	164	5	judge	NoC	17	−	258	48
believed	Verb	17	−	839	90	agents	NoC	17	−	159	40
placed	Verb	17	−	910	94	bungalow	NoC	17	+	185	4
dust	NoC	17	−	36	27	locally	Adv	17	−	0	18
bomb	NoC	17	−	43	28	naturally	Adv	17	−	227	46
influence	NoC	17	−	798	87	pack	Verb	17	+	64	8
own	Verb	17	+	1	16	taping	Verb	17	+	593	0
knocking	Verb	17	+	74	8	channels	NoC	17	−	1	19
bell	NoC	17	−	0	18	surprise	NoC	17	−	295	51
generation	NoC	17	−	307	53	disappointed	Adj	17	−	8	21
conversations	NoC	17	+	45	10	Lord	NoP	17	−	4	20
complete	Verb	17	−	111	36	beans	NoC	17	+	10	13
firstly	Adv	17	+	0	17	rung	Verb	17	+	222	4
match	Verb	17	−	45	28	disk	NoC	17	−	44	27
internal	Adj	17	−	587	73	expression	NoC	17	−	729	81
links	NoC	17	−	125	37	assurance	NoC	17	−	1	18
unlikely	Adj	17	−	416	61	rugby	NoC	17	−	63	30
Cambridge	NoP	17	−	139	39	Wendy	NoP	17	+	98	7
recorder	NoC	17	+	72	8	ward	NoC	17	−	2	19
military	Adj	17	−	1317	119	half	Adv	17	+	0	16
users	NoC	17	−	559	71	note	Verb	17	−	277	50
oven	NoC	17	+	11	13	nurses	NoC	17	−	35	26
improvement	NoC	17	−	209	45	threat	NoC	17	−	435	61
attached	Verb	17	−	138	38	surgery	NoC	17	−	49	28
talks	NoC	17	−	477	65	alternative	Adj	17	−	346	55
jumper	NoC	17	+	209	4	incident	NoC	17	−	158	39
wire	NoC	17	−	11	22	boundaries	NoC	17	−	28	25
smoke	NoC	17	−	58	30	battle	NoC	17	−	544	69
Glasgow	NoP	17	−	210	45	departments	NoC	17	−	227	45
gift	NoC	17	−	67	31	switched	Verb	17	−	7	21
belong	Verb	17	−	7	21	Susan	NoP	17	−	8	21
dare	VMod	17	+	28	11	Joyce	NoP	17	+	11	13
boom	NoC	17	+	1	16	fifties	Num	17	+	48	9
associated	Verb	17	−	696	80	implications	NoC	17	−	266	48
neither	Adv	17	−	384	58	sexual	Adj	17	−	641	75
debt	NoC	17	−	385	58	governments	NoC	17	−	298	51
beauty	NoC	17	−	218	45	villages	NoC	17	−	62	29
checking	Verb	17	+	0	16	attempt	NoC	17	−	982	97
Kuwait	NoP	17	+	0	16	sample	NoC	17	−	251	47
anyhow	Adv	17	+	246	3	dates	NoC	17	−	3	19
failure	NoC	17	−	771	85	hunting	NoC	17	−	1	18
fight	NoC	17	−	65	30	males	NoC	17	−	18	23
output	NoC	17	−	447	63	one another	Pron	17	−	57	29
relations	NoC	17	−	1396	123	borough	NoC	17	−	3	19

Word	PoS	FrS		LL	FrW	Word	PoS	FrS		LL	FrW
bum	NoC	17	+	264	3	responsibilities	NoC	16	–	74	30
indicate	Verb	17	–	215	44	kick	NoC	16	+	5	13
software	NoC	17	–	1085	103	materials	NoC	16	–	641	74
occur	Verb	17	–	433	61	smart	Adj	16	+	1	15
arse	NoC	17	+	177	4	eastern	Adj	16	–	494	64
chief	NoC	17	–	168	40	occurred	Verb	16	–	427	59
targets	NoC	17	–	46	27	arguing	Verb	16	–	2	18
vital	Adj	17	–	354	55	hurry	Verb	16	+	54	8
Nigel	NoP	17	–	123	36	below	Adv	16	–	995	96
Angela	NoP	17	+	31	10	adopted	Verb	16	–	371	55
patient	NoC	17	–	636	75	Pam	NoP	16	+	189	4
meals	NoC	17	–	28	25	illness	NoC	16	–	121	35
visitors	NoC	17	–	312	52	follows	Verb	16	–	1223	110
precisely	Adv	17	–	138	37	loose	Adj	16	–	52	27
bonus	NoC	17	+	5	14	driving	NoC	16	+	4	13
skill	NoC	17	–	137	37	faced	Verb	16	–	286	49
cats	NoC	17	+	0	16	stops	Verb	16	+	12	12
prevent	Verb	17	–	621	74	Barbara	NoP	16	–	0	17
crown	NoC	17	–	361	55	greatest	Adj	16	–	375	55
chuck	Verb	16	+	296	2	salad	NoC	16	+	19	11
sisters	NoC	16	–	9	21	named	Verb	16	–	259	47
Edward	NoP	16	–	647	75	resistance	NoC	16	–	173	40
Tesco	NoP	16	+	191	4	settlements	NoC	16	+	7	13
in respect of	Prep	16	–	73	30	automatically	Adv	16	–	69	29
narrow	Adj	16	–	326	53	co-op	NoC	16	+	261	3
depend	Verb	16	–	139	37	completed	Verb	16	–	433	59
lunchtime	NoC	16	+	54	8	planned	Verb	16	–	269	47
measures	NoC	16	–	585	71	medicine	NoC	16	–	69	29
guess	NoC	16	+	113	6	balls	NoC	16	+	0	15
height	NoC	16	–	174	40	mixed	Adj	16	–	10	20
aargh	Int	16	+	726	0	ends	NoC	16	–	80	31
continuous	Adj	16	–	50	28	stomach	NoC	16	–	87	31
secondary	Adj	16	–	250	47	false	Adj	16	–	164	39
nanny	NoC	16	+	134	5	dry	Verb	16	+	13	12
landlords	NoC	16	+	79	7	directors	NoC	16	–	260	47
Brighton	NoP	16	+	1	15	vegetables	NoC	16	–	3	18
wonder	NoC	16	–	5	20	lectures	NoC	16	+	1	14
near	Adj	16	–	2	19	male	NoC	16	–	19	22
ministers	NoC	16	–	637	74	wise	Adj	16	–	9	20
owned	Verb	16	–	149	38	Michelle	NoP	16	+	134	5
increasing	Adj	16	–	425	60	shed	NoC	16	+	38	9
order	Verb	16	–	2	19	mail	NoC	16	–	127	35
ordered	Verb	16	–	330	53	fuck	NoC	16	+	200	3
wee	NoC	16	+	456	1	sandwiches	NoC	16	+	51	8
equals	NoC	16	+	328	2	sits	Verb	16	+	11	12
soup	NoC	16	+	6	13	define	Verb	16	–	39	25
potential	NoC	16	–	289	50	regularly	Adv	16	–	197	41
joining	Verb	16	–	18	23	proposing	Verb	16	+	64	7
growing	Adj	16	–	493	64	Laura	NoP	16	–	48	27
smell	NoC	16	–	45	27	increasing	Verb	16	–	54	27
Dawn	NoP	16	+	65	8	shift	Verb	16	+	0	15
fun	Adj	16	–	0	17	immediate	Adj	16	–	534	66
premium	NoC	16	+	12	12	hearing	Verb	16	–	28	24
appeared	Verb	16	–	1328	117	initial	Adj	16	–	554	68
solicitors	NoC	16	–	50	27	estimate	NoC	16	–	1	17
pipe	NoC	16	–	25	24	fella	NoC	16	+	396	1
Barry	NoP	16	–	4	19	engineer	NoC	16	–	24	23
prize	NoC	16	–	94	32	sticking	Verb	16	+	44	9
entitled	Adj	16	–	50	27	indication	NoC	16	–	32	24
features	NoC	16	–	861	88	removed	Verb	16	–	501	64
career	NoC	16	–	793	84	draft	NoC	16	–	49	27
Ray	NoP	16	–	2	19	bone	NoC	16	–	36	25
tail	NoC	16	–	54	28	broken	Adj	16	–	80	30
fiver	NoC	16	+	194	4	Robin	NoP	16	–	8	20
submission	NoC	16	+	25	10	satisfied	Adj	16	–	101	32
chosen	Verb	16	–	335	53	fly	Verb	16	–	84	31

2.2

Word	PoS	FrS		LL	FrW	Word	PoS	FrS		LL	FrW
flying	Verb	16	–	23	23	dining	NoC	15	–	0	16
closely	Adv	16	–	443	60	powerful	Adj	15	–	734	79
sleeping	Verb	16	+	16	11	issued	Verb	15	–	467	61
methods	NoC	16	–	1034	98	train	Verb	15	–	0	16
frankly	Adv	16	+	35	9	beach	NoC	15	–	196	41
reply	NoC	16	–	98	32	print	NoC	15	–	20	22
female	Adj	16	–	519	65	pays	Verb	15	+	0	15
proof	NoC	16	–	61	28	composite	Adj	15	+	106	5
knee	NoC	16	–	13	21	pile	NoC	15	–	1	17
benefit	Verb	16	–	94	32	improved	Verb	15	–	72	29
shift	NoC	16	–	50	27	confirm	Verb	15	–	60	27
Ipswich	NoP	16	+	9	12	excuse	NoC	15	–	2	17
sharp	Adj	16	–	275	47	burnt	Verb	15	+	26	10
represented	Verb	16	–	416	58	fees	NoC	15	–	89	31
paint	Verb	16	+	6	13	Les*	NoP	15	+	3	13
drove	Verb	16	–	173	39	Adam	NoP	15	–	164	38
nineteenth	Ord	16	–	125	35	resource	NoC	15	–	29	23
preparation	NoC	16	–	130	35	B. / b.	Lett	15	+	716	0
outer	Adj	16	–	42	25	nervous	Adj	15	–	111	33
juice	NoC	16	–	0	17	fishing	NoC	15	–	123	34
bypass	NoC	16	+	151	4	subject to	Prep	15	–	394	55
boats	NoC	16	–	11	20	vehicles	NoC	15	–	109	33
accurate	Adj	16	–	87	31	regard	Verb	15	–	42	25
scored	Verb	16	–	78	30	pleasant	Adj	15	–	67	28
surprising	Adj	16	–	156	37	pity	NoC	15	–	3	18
adding	Verb	16	–	112	33	packed	Verb	15	–	7	19
net	Adj	16	–	232	44	locked	Verb	15	–	56	27
competitive	Adj	16	–	177	39	cycle	NoC	15	–	122	34
represents	Verb	16	–	132	35	earning	Verb	15	+	12	11
forever	Adv	16	–	5	19	bang	Verb	15	+	176	4
feature	NoC	16	–	427	59	Z / z	Lett	15	+	15	11
handed	Verb	16	–	160	38	accidents	NoC	15	–	13	20
swimming	Verb	16	+	34	9	collecting	Verb	15	–	0	15
throwing	Verb	16	–	2	18	leaders	NoC	15	–	748	79
sand	NoC	16	–	94	32	trains	NoC	15	–	11	20
Maggie	NoP	16	–	62	28	exception	NoC	15	–	94	31
microwave	NoC	16	+	114	5	running	NoC	15	–	24	22
leather	NoC	16	–	52	27	nations	NoC	15	–	249	44
whisky	NoC	16	–	2	17	entry	NoC	15	–	401	56
mood	NoC	16	–	129	35	alone	Adv	15	–	771	80
Wilson	NoP	16	–	215	42	Christine	NoP	15	+	14	11
inside	NoC	16	+	13	11	presume	Verb	15	+	136	4
prior to	Prep	16	–	110	33	nation	NoC	15	–	285	47
poem	NoC	16	–	44	26	travelling	Verb	15	–	47	25
deputy	NoC	16	–	203	41	bedrooms	NoC	15	–	0	16
all of a sudden	Adv	16	+	238	3	relating	Verb	15	–	186	39
concerns	NoC	16	–	50	26	fantastic	Adj	15	+	10	11
Russia	NoP	16	–	265	46	calcium	NoC	15	+	5	12
mouse	NoC	16	–	2	18	bacon	NoC	15	+	48	8
Italy	NoP	16	–	379	55	ministry	NoC	15	–	374	54
Elizabeth	NoP	16	–	168	38	increased	Adj	15	–	492	62
potato	NoC	15	+	49	8	oxygen	NoC	15	–	10	19
little	NoC	15	+	713	0	compensation	NoC	15	–	119	33
values	NoC	15	–	786	82	routes	NoC	15	–	23	22
manufacturing	NoC	15	–	247	45	tennis	NoC	15	–	84	30
flower	NoC	15	–	24	23	object	NoC	15	–	424	57
Trevor	NoP	15	+	11	11	official	Adj	15	–	834	84
culture	NoC	15	–	974	94	drinks	NoC	15	–	24	22
formed	Verb	15	–	704	77	alternative	NoC	15	–	175	38
settle	Verb	15	–	46	26	dreadful	Adj	15	+	0	14
park	Verb	15	+	198	3	offering	Verb	15	–	263	45
appendix	NoC	15	–	3	18	pointed	Verb	15	–	503	62
songs	NoC	15	–	82	30	leading	Verb	15	–	412	56
crowd	NoC	15	–	264	46	enterprise	NoC	15	–	264	45
camp	NoC	15	–	113	33	ate	Verb	15	–	4	18
wild	Adj	15	–	392	56	plays	Verb	15	–	41	25

Word	PoS	FrS		LL	FrW	Word	PoS	FrS		LL	FrW
Lewis	NoP	15	–	198	40	arrive	Verb	15	–	101	31
fortune	NoC	15	–	23	22	Johnny	NoP	15	–	0	15
lounge	NoC	15	+	0	14	topic	NoC	15	–	53	26
cooker	NoC	15	+	140	4	definite	Adj	15	–	1	16
touched	Verb	15	–	107	32	guarantee	Verb	15	+	0	14
fundamental	Adj	15	–	307	49	sixties	Num	15	+	0	13
beside	Prep	15	–	506	63	developing	Verb	15	–	126	33
orange	Adj	15	+	1	14	harder	Adj	15	+	0	14
cheers	Int	15	+	213	3	physics	NoC	15	–	11	19
concrete	NoC	15	+	35	9	nearest	Adj	15	–	19	21
cleaned	Verb	15	+	16	10	smoking	Verb	15	+	16	10
electrical	Adj	15	–	36	24	treasurer	NoC	15	+	35	8
operations	NoC	15	–	554	66	twentieth	Num	15	–	10	19
sandwich	NoC	15	+	30	9	Shirley	NoP	14	+	46	7
bricks	NoC	15	+	27	9	leaflet	NoC	14	+	6	12
Lawrence	NoP	15	–	26	22	reproductive	Adj	14	+	75	6
Chinese	Adj	15	–	231	43	least	Adv	14	–	310	48
intended	Verb	15	–	710	76	listened	Verb	14	–	46	25
assignment	NoC	15	+	10	11	bucket	NoC	14	+	21	9
regions	NoC	15	–	267	45	cleaning	Verb	14	+	7	11
rice	NoC	15	–	0	16	expense	NoC	14	–	83	29
guide	NoC	15	–	339	51	establish	Verb	14	–	438	57
pizza	NoC	15	+	164	4	careers	NoC	14	–	4	17
guidelines	NoC	15	–	40	24	approximately	Adv	14	–	94	30
Roy	NoP	15	–	5	18	drawing	NoC	14	–	58	26
sha~	VMod	15	+	137	4	print	Verb	14	+	16	10
Philip	NoP	15	–	229	42	organize	Verb	14	+	44	8
sin	NoC	15	+	4	12	mountain	NoC	14	–	235	42
memories	NoC	15	–	68	28	express	Verb	14	–	133	34
moral	Adj	15	–	424	57	stores	NoC	14	–	39	24
approved	Verb	15	–	224	42	washing	Verb	14	+	10	11
shoe	NoC	15	+	12	11	jam	NoC	14	+	41	8
awake	Adj	15	+	2	13	feedback	NoC	14	+	2	13
restaurant	NoC	15	–	171	37	threes	Num	14	+	375	1
taxi	NoC	15	–	10	19	asks	Verb	14	–	18	20
with regard to	Prep	15	–	2	17	summary	NoC	14	–	97	30
opening	Verb	15	–	67	28	enjoying	Verb	14	–	33	23
freezer	NoC	15	+	193	3	appointed	Verb	14	–	572	66
Milton	NoP	15	–	0	16	breath	NoC	14	–	409	55
supporting	Verb	15	–	16	20	quote	NoC	14	+	157	4
cooking	NoC	15	–	1	16	thirties	Num	14	+	50	7
sergeant	NoC	15	–	68	28	loud	Adj	14	–	1	16
maximum	Adj	15	–	169	37	gardens	NoC	14	–	197	39
threw	Verb	15	–	117	33	ma	NoC	14	+	93	5
confused	Adj	15	–	13	20	pitch	NoC	14	–	78	28
silver	NoC	15	–	219	41	wool	NoC	14	–	8	18
jumped	Verb	15	–	50	25	colleague	NoC	14	–	3	17
unable	Adj	15	–	612	69	gear	NoC	14	–	12	19
marked	Verb	15	–	196	39	stronger	Adj	14	–	75	28
cricket	NoC	15	–	145	35	alcohol	NoC	14	–	118	32
Midlands	NoP	15	–	2	17	Bobby	NoP	14	+	20	9
drunk	Adj	15	–	1	16	consequences	NoC	14	–	309	48
platform	NoC	15	–	63	27	leisure	NoC	14	–	100	30
referring	Verb	15	–	7	18	prepare	Verb	14	–	117	32
less than	Adv	15	–	234	43	severe	Adj	14	–	335	50
Jo	NoP	15	+	47	8	ladder	NoC	14	+	1	13
in between	Adv	15	+	47	8	tie	NoC	14	–	14	19
head	Adj	15	–	0	15	adult	NoC	14	–	329	49
cakes	NoC	15	–	24	9	Nottingham-shire	NoP	14	+	101	5
leads	Verb	15	–	202	40						
involvement	NoC	15	–	269	45	Carl	NoP	14	+	11	10
advert	NoC	15	+	172	3	sooner	Adv	14	–	10	19
wipe	Verb	15	+	67	6	at first	Adv	14	–	269	45
tap	NoC	15	+	4	12	ceiling	NoC	14	–	46	24
sectors	NoC	15	–	40	24	dish	NoC	14	–	1	16
differentiate	Verb	15	+	144	4	defined	Verb	14	–	471	59

2.2

Word	PoS	FrS		LL	FrW
Malcolm	NoP	14	–	10	19
whereby	Adv	14	–	18	20
Bryony	NoP	14	+	271	2
Sandra	NoP	14	+	63	6
guns	NoC	14	–	20	21
unfair	Adj	14	–	16	20
ay	Int	14	+	358	1
conferences	NoC	14	+	5	12
devil	NoC	14	–	6	17
agriculture	NoC	14	–	231	42
settled	Verb	14	–	234	42
representation	NoC	14	–	202	39
Dee	NoP	14	+	141	4
timber	NoC	14	–	42	24
Spain	NoP	14	–	318	48
Eric	NoP	14	–	16	20
engines	NoC	14	–	14	19
Catherine	NoP	14	–	3	17
essay	NoC	14	–	2	16
blimey	Int	14	+	419	1
appointments	NoC	14	–	0	15
say	NoC	14	+	87	5
informed	Verb	14	–	148	35
emphasis	NoC	14	–	476	59
living	Adj	14	–	197	39
straightforward	Adj	14	–	20	20
dig	Verb	14	+	25	9
upper	Adj	14	–	461	58
valuable	Adj	14	–	233	42
armed	Adj	14	–	203	39
mistakes	NoC	14	–	2	16
bollocks	NoC	14	+	284	2
mission	NoC	14	–	78	28
mothers	NoC	14	–	155	35
hide	Verb	14	–	41	24
pig	NoC	14	+	0	13
household	NoC	14	–	244	42
fifteenth	Ord	14	+	59	7
aim	NoC	14	–	408	54
monthly	Adj	14	–	16	20
offspring	NoC	14	+	21	9
pure	Adj	14	–	168	36
upset	Verb	14	+	0	14
piano	NoC	14	–	19	20
equation	NoC	14	–	60	26
entire	Adj	14	–	378	52
Sharon	NoP	14	+	63	6
matches	NoC	14	–	43	24
remove	Verb	14	–	244	42
proved	Verb	14	–	723	75
theirs	Pron	14	+	14	10
roundabout	NoC	14	+	169	3
concert	NoC	14	–	14	19
quarry	NoC	14	+	20	9
recognition	NoC	14	–	534	63
leaves	NoC	14	–	202	39
courts	NoC	14	–	559	65
Henry	NoP	14	–	819	81
seventies	Num	14	+	20	9
brick	NoC	14	–	12	19
bars	NoC	14	–	54	25
counter	NoC	14	–	8	18
complain	Verb	14	+	0	14
approach	Verb	14	–	7	18
angry	Adj	14	–	288	46
aggressive	Adj	14	–	18	20
employee	NoC	14	–	132	33
Matt	NoP	14	+	54	7
partners	NoC	14	–	242	42
voted	Verb	14	–	46	24
exhibition	NoC	14	–	473	59
extend	Verb	14	–	134	33
negotiations	NoC	14	–	207	39
leave	NoC	14	–	35	23
blooming	Adj	14	+	475	0
chancellor	NoC	14	–	208	39
net	NoC	14	–	61	26
parked	Verb	14	+	1	13
dot	NoC	14	+	7	11
weak	Adj	14	–	194	38
objections	NoC	14	+	1	13
arranged	Verb	14	–	250	43
motions	NoC	14	+	74	6
blokes	NoC	14	+	246	2
kiss	NoC	14	–	0	15
kind	Adj	14	–	0	14
wardrobe	NoC	14	+	19	9
fix	Verb	14	+	2	12
delegates	NoC	14	–	2	16
contributions	NoC	14	–	104	30
videos	NoC	14	+	8	11
differently	Adv	14	–	2	16
twos	Num	14	+	332	1
directions	NoC	14	–	39	23
cigarettes	NoC	14	+	0	13
error	NoC	14	–	233	41
connected	Verb	14	–	130	33
expenses	NoC	14	–	25	21
passing	Verb	14	–	85	28
cloth	NoC	14	–	22	20
corridor	NoC	14	–	32	22
addressed	Verb	14	–	92	29
gain	Verb	14	–	219	40
solve	Verb	14	–	20	20
stars	NoC	14	–	250	42
calculator	NoC	14	+	214	2
communities	NoC	14	–	280	45
gross	Adj	14	–	44	24
audit	NoC	14	–	39	23
dollars	NoC	14	–	7	17
Darwin	NoP	14	+	5	11
released	Verb	14	–	422	55
increasingly	Adv	14	–	695	73
invest	Verb	14	–	3	16
captain	NoC	14	–	474	58
crossed	Verb	14	–	132	32
Liz	NoP	14	–	7	17
fitted	Verb	14	–	164	35
supporters	NoC	14	–	214	39
Bernard	NoP	14	–	31	22
display	NoC	14	–	317	47
stroke	NoC	14	+	0	13
struck	Verb	14	–	293	45
fractions	NoC	14	+	129	4
talks	Verb	14	+	67	6
philosophy	NoC	14	–	191	37
fixed	Verb	14	–	109	30
bet	NoC	14	+	48	7
dock	NoC	14	+	2	12
Norman	NoP	14	–	56	25
but	Prep	14	–	41	23
promised	Verb	14	–	256	42

Word	PoS	FrS		LL	FrW	Word	PoS	FrS		LL	FrW
coach	NoC	14	–	111	30	manner	NoC	13	–	607	66
judgement	NoC	14	–	71	26	assistance	NoC	13	–	323	47
deposit	NoC	14	–	9	18	warning	NoC	13	–	260	42
Paula	NoP	14	+	8	10	billion	NoC	13	–	390	51
stages	NoC	14	–	277	44	teddy	NoC	13	+	165	3
double	NoC	14	+	8	10	Shakespeare	NoP	13	–	19	19
hydrogen	NoC	14	+	2	12	covering	Verb	13	–	125	31
encouraged	Verb	14	–	359	50	handle	NoC	13	+	1	12
Trent	NoP	13	+	5	11	chose	Verb	13	–	115	30
covers	Verb	13	–	23	20	in charge of	Prep	13	–	8	17
persuade	Verb	13	–	63	25	och	Int	13	+	365	1
entrance	NoC	13	–	144	33	experiences	NoC	13	–	192	37
crisps	NoC	13	+	183	3	criterion	NoC	13	+	0	13
written	Adj	13	–	170	35	de*	NoP	13	–	1461	117
fed	Verb	13	–	40	23	Americans	NoC	13	–	111	30
Notts	NoP	13	+	178	3	announced	Verb	13	–	1430	116
healthy	Adj	13	–	207	38	dentist	NoC	13	+	87	5
promote	Verb	13	–	151	34	wash	NoC	13	+	35	7
Walsall	NoP	13	+	242	2	aids	NoC	13	–	157	34
ultimately	Adv	13	–	116	31	skirt	NoC	13	–	1	14
agencies	NoC	13	–	217	39	outstanding	Adj	13	–	135	32
magazines	NoC	13	–	10	18	adequate	Adj	13	–	210	38
minimum	NoC	13	–	30	21	cells	NoC	13	–	890	84
developments	NoC	13	–	441	56	painted	Verb	13	–	69	26
diamond	NoC	13	+	4	11	priorities	NoC	13	–	30	21
payments	NoC	13	–	339	48	border	NoC	13	–	272	43
shoot	Verb	13	–	1	15	shillings	NoC	13	+	64	6
leading	Adj	13	–	614	67	drawer	NoC	13	+	13	9
incredible	Adj	13	+	1	12	live	Adj	13	–	120	31
Derby	NoP	13	+	1	12	string	NoC	13	–	102	29
posh	Adj	13	+	161	3	tower	NoC	13	–	182	36
request	NoC	13	–	242	41	cancel	Verb	13	+	20	8
provides	Verb	13	–	1016	92	brush	NoC	13	–	0	13
employ	Verb	13	–	8	17	Abingdon	NoP	13	+	135	3
soap	NoC	13	+	0	13	festival	NoC	13	–	144	33
scared	Adj	13	+	2	12	mud	NoC	13	–	24	20
cool	Adj	13	–	142	33	claimed	Verb	13	–	1008	91
format	NoC	13	–	34	22	straw	NoC	13	–	0	14
tour	NoC	13	–	546	62	Albert	NoP	13	–	50	23
remains	Verb	13	–	860	82	pass	NoC	13	–	16	18
suffered	Verb	13	–	489	59	lets	Verb	13	+	17	9
Anthony	NoP	13	–	60	25	frame	NoC	13	–	157	34
linked	Verb	13	–	269	43	females	NoC	13	–	29	21
rare	Adj	13	–	368	50	largely	Adv	13	–	841	80
Harry	NoP	13	–	359	50	mixture	NoC	13	–	172	35
since	Adv	13	–	116	31	harm	NoC	13	–	56	24
crazy	Adj	13	–	14	18	Oliver	NoP	13	–	54	24
content	NoC	13	–	344	49	suite	NoC	13	+	0	13
affairs	NoC	13	–	816	80	tradition	NoC	13	–	451	56
allows	Verb	13	–	288	45	funeral	NoC	13	–	43	22
farmer	NoC	13	–	41	23	relationships	NoC	13	–	598	65
proceed	Verb	13	–	38	22	developing	Adj	13	–	144	33
injury	NoC	13	–	366	50	expertise	NoC	13	–	93	28
parliamentary	Adj	13	–	321	47	stones	NoC	13	–	174	35
rely	Verb	13	–	99	29	eighties	Num	13	+	25	8
oops	Int	13	+	431	1	fraction	NoC	13	–	2	15
allowances	NoC	13	+	0	12	classroom	NoC	13	–	53	24
dying	Verb	13	–	10	17	flipping	Adj	13	+	393	1
industries	NoC	13	–	321	47	cinema	NoC	13	–	27	20
exact	Adj	13	–	46	23	efforts	NoC	13	–	535	61
tiles	NoC	13	+	2	12	duties	NoC	13	–	256	41
applies	Verb	13	–	107	30	rapidly	Adv	13	–	364	49
bom	NoC	13	+	480	0	driving	Adj	13	+	0	13
wheels	NoC	13	–	4	16	murder	NoC	13	–	495	58
carrots	NoC	13	+	119	4	curriculum	NoC	13	–	487	58
physically	Adv	13	–	28	21	sons	NoC	13	–	203	37

Word	PoS	FrS		LL	FrW		Word	PoS	FrS		LL	FrW
constantly	Adv	13	–	146	33		poverty	NoC	13	–	158	33
stall	NoC	13	+	40	7		painting	NoC	13	–	258	41
excited	Adj	13	–	8	17		species	NoC	13	–	1277	106
claims	NoC	13	–	479	57		hurts	Verb	13	+	115	4
scientific	Adj	13	–	591	65		winning	Verb	13	–	162	34
penalty	NoC	13	–	98	28		lawn	NoC	13	+	3	11
coloured	Adj	13	–	23	19		Brenda	NoP	13	+	76	5
collected	Verb	13	–	183	36		facility	NoC	13	–	56	24
nerves	NoC	13	+	0	12		towns	NoC	13	–	302	44
even when	Conj	13	–	72	26		Caroline	NoP	13	–	25	19
Charles	NoP	13	–	1173	100		contacts	NoC	13	–	41	22
copper	NoC	13	–	16	18		White	NoP	13	–	122	30
name	Verb	13	–	0	13		struggle	NoC	13	–	247	40
dark	NoC	13	–	150	33		easiest	Adj	13	+	29	7
prince	NoC	13	–	589	64		wore	Verb	13	–	146	32
intelligent	Adj	13	–	24	20		regarded	Verb	13	–	799	77
menu	NoC	13	–	7	16		India	NoP	13	–	401	51
female	NoC	13	–	42	22		refers	Verb	13	–	32	20
crucial	Adj	13	–	353	48		knees	NoC	13	–	94	27
nowt	Pron	13	+	311	1		flexibility	NoC	13	–	33	21
indicated	Verb	13	–	335	47		exists	Verb	13	–	171	34
arising	Verb	13	–	52	23		construction	NoC	13	–	673	69
mean	Adj	13	–	84	27		democratic	Adj	13	–	609	65
racing	Verb	13	–	61	24		cooked	Verb	13	+	15	9
earnings	NoC	13	–	167	34		reducing	Verb	13	–	137	31
brand new	Adj	13	+	96	4		Adrian	NoP	13	+	11	9
gather	Verb	13	–	5	16		officials	NoC	13	–	646	67
enquiries	NoC	13	–	10	17		practically	Adv	13	–	1	14
carers	NoC	13	+	0	12		bench	NoC	13	–	35	21
supply	Verb	13	–	96	28		basket	NoC	13	–	0	14
historical	Adj	13	–	532	60		twenties	Num	13	+	38	7
locks	NoC	13	+	18	8		pollution	NoC	13	–	309	45
corporate	Adj	13	–	373	50		Raymond	NoP	13	+	18	8
arrangement	NoC	13	–	178	35		exceptions	NoC	13	–	3	15
Sheila	NoP	13	+	11	9		book	Verb	13	+	105	4
slate	NoC	13	+	63	6		changing	Adj	13	–	78	26
shows	NoC	13	–	18	19		mam	NoC	13	+	93	4
sharing	Verb	13	–	45	22		commitments	NoC	13	–	0	13
object	Verb	13	+	5	10		Gulf	NoP	13	–	77	26
engineers	NoC	13	–	85	27		ride	NoC	13	–	14	17
registration	NoC	13	–	54	23		eleventh	Num	13	+	52	6
directory	NoC	13	–	4	15		operating	Verb	13	–	107	28
impressed	Adj	13	–	9	17		cousin	NoC	13	–	21	19
up to date	Adj	13	+	54	6		bless	Verb	13	+	72	5
mix	Verb	13	+	0	12		jeans	NoC	13	–	0	13
explanation	NoC	13	–	400	51		wing	NoC	13	–	127	30
signal	NoC	13	–	113	29		clarify	Verb	13	+	12	9
dreams	NoC	13	–	80	26		suit	Verb	13	–	33	20
crew	NoC	13	–	136	31		reflect	Verb	13	–	263	41
directive	NoC	13	–	15	18		budgets	NoC	13	–	0	13
burn	Verb	13	+	0	12		lend	Verb	13	–	0	13
corn	NoC	13	+	0	12		plates	NoC	13	–	70	25
cities	NoC	13	–	340	47		redundancy	NoC	13	+	1	11
delivered	Verb	13	–	154	33		Midland	NoP	13	–	3	15
societies	NoC	13	–	340	47		ride	Verb	12	–	12	17
training	Verb	13	+	4	10		flight	NoC	12	–	480	56
ships	NoC	13	–	106	29		Daniel	NoP	12	–	6	15
award	NoC	13	–	2288	163		Kate	NoP	12	–	72	25
steam	NoC	13	–	122	30		expansion	NoC	12	–	231	39
loan	NoC	13	–	257	41		guarantee	NoC	12	–	9	16
promotion	NoC	13	–	186	36		selling	NoC	12	+	0	12
sensitive	Adj	13	–	231	39		filling	Verb	12	–	4	15
pairs	NoC	13	–	43	22		jolly	Adv	12	+	143	3
receiving	Verb	13	–	132	31		valid	Adj	12	–	64	24
headquarters	NoC	13	–	113	29		Lincoln	NoP	12	+	11	9
crying	Verb	13	–	0	14		by now	Adv	12	–	55	23

Word	PoS	FrS		LL	FrW	Word	PoS	FrS		LL	FrW
catalogue	NoC	12	–	74	25	Swindon	NoP	12	–	46	22
kicked	Verb	12	–	10	16	soul	NoC	12	–	156	32
consultants	NoC	12	–	7	16	cheeky	Adj	12	+	166	2
pressures	NoC	12	–	108	28	Betty	NoP	12	–	1	14
personnel	NoC	12	–	194	36	quietly	Adv	12	–	323	45
secure	Adj	12	–	23	19	hay	NoC	12	+	21	8
goodbye	Int	12	+	6	10	cups	NoC	12	+	0	12
seminar	NoC	12	+	0	12	mine	NoC	12	–	15	17
stays	Verb	12	+	30	7	regarding	Prep	12	–	44	21
bones	NoC	12	–	64	24	meaning	NoC	12	–	740	72
ambulance	NoC	12	–	15	17	Douglas	NoP	12	–	82	25
granny	NoC	12	+	56	6	candidate	NoC	12	–	296	43
dancing	NoC	12	+	0	12	grants	NoC	12	–	36	20
gates	NoC	12	–	33	20	easier	Adv	12	–	0	12
alter	Verb	12	–	31	20	allocated	Verb	12	–	19	18
examination	NoC	12	–	425	52	constitution	NoC	12	–	298	43
magistrates	NoC	12	–	48	22	search	NoC	12	–	475	55
rabbit	NoC	12	–	3	15	controlled	Verb	12	–	244	39
swap	Verb	12	+	83	4	study	Verb	12	–	158	32
choir	NoC	12	+	5	10	neighbourhood	NoC	12	–	5	15
bleeding	Adj	12	+	37	7	cry	Verb	12	–	17	17
returned	Verb	12	–	1434	114	Dick	NoP	12	–	1	13
evolution	NoC	12	–	87	26	ducks	NoC	12	+	31	7
faster	Adv	12	–	19	18	seconder	NoC	12	+	462	0
consistent	Adj	12	–	165	33	pursue	Verb	12	–	38	20
heck	NoC	12	+	305	1	landlord	NoC	12	–	118	29
certificate	NoC	12	–	134	31	raining	Verb	12	+	65	5
universities	NoC	12	–	110	28	muscle	NoC	12	–	24	18
Rebecca	NoP	12	+	49	6	trustees	NoC	12	+	0	12
saving	Verb	12	–	1	14	victory	NoC	12	–	574	61
wording	NoC	12	+	22	8	Skelton	NoP	12	+	226	2
assets	NoC	12	–	349	47	moderator	NoC	12	+	309	1
Patrick	NoP	12	–	149	32	spelling	NoC	12	+	14	8
specialist	NoC	12	–	248	40	approached	Verb	12	–	148	31
worn	Verb	12	–	27	19	behave	Verb	12	–	22	18
persons	NoC	12	–	297	43	judge	Verb	12	–	41	21
landscape	NoC	12	–	188	35	riding	Verb	12	–	22	18
on board	Adv	12	–	2	14	refused	Verb	12	–	700	69
amendments	NoC	12	+	6	10	entertainment	NoC	12	–	44	21
automatic	Adj	12	–	66	24	flu	NoC	12	+	57	5
weekends	NoC	12	+	3	10	glory	NoC	12	–	17	17
rose	NoC	12	–	95	27	maximum	NoC	12	–	12	16
rotten	Adj	12	+	22	8	promise	Verb	12	–	8	16
bitch	NoC	12	+	14	8	sums	NoC	12	–	7	15
off of	Prep	12	+	256	1	nonsense	NoC	12	–	14	17
related	Adj	12	–	147	32	Northern	NoP-	12	–	356	47
switch	NoC	12	–	15	17	depressed	Adj	12	–	7	15
Portsmouth	NoP	12	+	14	8	cigarette	NoC	12	–	72	24
disagree	Verb	12	+	30	7	welfare	NoC	12	–	439	52
personality	NoC	12	–	141	31	mechanism	NoC	12	–	151	31
Newark	NoP	12	+	241	2	convinced	Adj	12	–	93	26
specially	Adv	12	–	37	21	blocks	NoC	12	–	54	22
recommended	Verb	12	–	178	34	column	NoC	12	–	140	30
pop	NoC	12	+	55	23	woke	Verb	12	–	3	14
discount	NoC	12	–	28	19	cooking	Verb	12	+	1	11
manual	NoC	12	+	0	12	primarily	Adv	12	–	180	34
criticism	NoC	12	–	422	52	deliberately	Adv	12	–	133	30
museum	NoC	12	–	775	74	useless	Adj	12	–	1	13
characters	NoC	12	–	282	42	complaint	NoC	12	–	29	19
sources	NoC	12	–	752	73	worrying	Adj	12	+	1	11
sink	NoC	12	+	2	11	scope	NoC	12	–	222	37
Essex	NoP	12	–	69	24	stamps	NoC	12	+	63	5
fail	Verb	12	–	190	35	grew	Verb	12	–	398	50
suffering	Verb	12	–	109	28	assuming	Verb	12	–	35	20
transfer	NoC	12	–	475	55	testing	Verb	12	–	3	14
outcome	NoC	12	–	253	40	joy	NoC	12	–	86	25

Word	PoS	FrS		LL	FrW	Word	PoS	FrS		LL	FrW
lighting	NoC	12	–	22	18	potentially	Adv	12	–	95	26
aside	Adv	12	–	244	39	learned	Verb	12	–	407	50
forgive	Verb	12	–	3	14	transferred	Verb	12	–	180	33
Maxwell	NoP	12	–	1	13	tube	NoC	12	–	45	21
printer	NoC	12	–	17	17	trainers	NoC	12	+	21	7
processes	NoC	12	–	534	58	granted	Verb	12	–	416	50
railways	NoC	12	–	33	20	slept	Verb	12	–	27	18
cattle	NoC	12	–	106	27	incidentally	Adv	12	+	1	10
existence	NoC	12	–	754	72	studying	Verb	11	–	93	26
whichever	DetP	12	+	11	8	sub-committee	NoC	11	+	72	4
significantly	Adv	12	–	339	45	owners	NoC	11	–	279	41
theme	NoC	12	–	288	42	gloves	NoC	11	+	2	10
Jan*	NoP	12	–	4	14	blowing	Verb	11	+	2	10
mid	Adj	12	–	7	15	booklet	NoC	11	+	2	10
toys	NoC	12	+	0	12	midnight	NoC	11	–	38	20
anxiety	NoC	12	–	118	28	perform	Verb	11	–	191	34
thoroughly	Adv	12	–	55	22	argued	Verb	11	–	745	71
shorter	Adj	12	–	27	19	worthwhile	Adj	11	–	9	15
overtime	NoC	12	+	103	4	techniques	NoC	11	–	646	65
above	Adv	12	–	1280	103	grade	NoC	11	–	42	20
Ricky	NoP	12	+	88	4	mass	NoC	11	–	255	39
architecture	NoC	12	–	141	30	improvements	NoC	11	–	95	26
Victoria	NoP	12	–	105	27	Lynn	NoP	11	+	56	5
extraordinary	Adj	12	–	154	31	wasting	Verb	11	+	24	7
creating	Verb	12	–	239	38	left	Adv	11	+	63	5
estimates	NoC	12	–	37	20	politicians	NoC	11	–	215	36
interviews	NoC	12	–	92	26	laying	Verb	11	–	1	13
messing	Verb	12	+	184	2	firm	Adj	11	–	235	37
housing	Verb	12	–	144	30	soldiers	NoC	11	–	251	38
lately	Adv	12	+	11	8	shoulders	NoC	11	–	358	46
boards	NoC	12	–	136	30	processing	NoC	11	–	169	32
auditors	NoC	12	–	0	12	Lock	NoP	11	+	123	3
grammar	NoC	12	–	91	26	bearings	NoC	11	+	122	3
neither	DetP	12	–	142	30	whoops	Int	11	+	408	0
Carol	NoP	12	+	1	10	beings	NoC	11	–	29	18
Aaron	NoP	12	+	162	2	reminds	Verb	11	+	20	7
Norwich	NoP	12	–	7	15	annoying	Adj	11	+	111	3
heading	NoC	12	+	2	10	periods	NoC	11	–	321	43
abbey	NoC	12	–	36	20	except for	Prep	11	–	53	21
falls	Verb	12	–	61	23	advantages	NoC	11	–	163	32
exercise	Verb	12	–	86	25	steady	Adj	11	–	111	27
owner	NoC	12	–	477	54	causes	Verb	11	–	48	21
workforce	NoC	12	–	10	16	urgent	Adj	11	–	66	23
score	Verb	12	–	3	14	testing	NoC	11	–	48	21
suggests	Verb	12	–	781	74	cleaner	NoC	11	+	22	7
photo	NoC	12	–	0	13	pace	NoC	11	–	179	33
dancing	Verb	12	–	1	13	picks	Verb	11	+	43	5
democrats	NoC	12	–	47	21	pad	NoC	11	+	25	7
approved	Adj	12	+	3	10	votes	NoC	11	–	191	34
costing	Verb	12	+	4	9	rings	NoC	11	–	0	12
principles	NoC	12	–	599	62	golden	Adj	11	–	297	42
pretend	Verb	12	–	0	12	boiler	NoC	11	+	29	6
machinery	NoC	12	–	93	26	largest	Adj	11	–	624	63
spoon	NoC	12	+	23	7	factories	NoC	11	–	20	17
attendance	NoC	12	–	31	19	relatives	NoC	11	–	124	28
Janet	NoP	12	+	3	9	sounded	Verb	11	–	173	32
unfortunate	Adj	12	–	16	17	disappeared	Verb	11	–	215	35
hardware	NoC	12	–	55	22	realistic	Adj	11	–	38	19
sauce	NoC	12	–	5	14	combination	NoC	11	–	396	48
overnight	Adv	12	–	0	12	expectations	NoC	11	–	215	35
carbonate	NoC	12	+	83	4	Westminster	NoP	11	–	68	23
freezing	Adj	12	+	8	9	demands	NoC	11	–	499	55
finds	Verb	12	–	149	31	Joy	NoP	11	+	56	5
consumer	NoC	12	–	375	47	outside of	Prep	11	+	16	7
Kim	NoP	12	–	2	13	tongue	NoC	11	–	99	26
correctly	Adv	12	–	39	20	phoning	Verb	11	+	147	2

Word	PoS	FrS		LL	FrW	Word	PoS	FrS		LL	FrW
no-one*	Pron	11	–	57	22	interpretation	NoC	11	–	388	47
integrate	Verb	11	+	18	7	kit	NoC	11	–	35	19
lamb	NoC	11	+	0	10	starting	NoC	11	–	25	17
trolley	NoC	11	+	23	7	reductions	NoC	11	–	4	13
amounts	NoC	11	–	102	26	considerably	Adv	11	–	167	31
attended	Verb	11	–	243	38	framework	NoC	11	–	319	43
wish	NoC	11	–	15	16	all the same	Adv	11	+	1	10
odds	NoC	11	–	13	16	lorries	NoC	11	+	24	6
mayor	NoP	11	+	453	0	fog	NoC	11	+	0	10
institutions	NoC	11	–	760	71	corporation	NoC	11	–	249	37
least	DetP	11	+	3	9	stamp	NoC	11	–	0	11
representative	NoC	11	–	81	24	believes	Verb	11	–	326	43
emotional	Adj	11	–	260	39	boyfriend	NoC	11	–	0	11
psychology	NoC	11	–	120	28	nails	NoC	11	–	5	14
tune	NoC	11	–	4	14	scenario	NoC	11	+	16	7
envelope	NoC	11	–	7	15	zero	NoC	11	+	11	8
tens	Num	11	+	24	7	kingdom	NoC	11	–	74	23
admitted	Verb	11	–	602	62	allowing	Verb	11	–	384	47
increases	NoC	11	–	82	24	constable	NoC	11	–	40	19
genuine	Adj	11	–	222	36	dole	NoC	11	+	66	4
Bristol	NoP	11	–	155	31	rub	Verb	11	+	33	6
schedule	NoC	11	–	92	25	ugh	Int	11	+	251	1
Grant	NoP	11	–	83	24	react	Verb	11	–	3	13
anniversary	NoC	11	–	58	22	log	NoC	11	–	0	11
Newcastle	NoP	11	–	128	28	attitudes	NoC	11	–	469	52
highway	NoC	11	+	3	9	fans	NoC	11	–	230	36
reception	NoC	11	–	101	26	winner	NoC	11	–	204	34
ratio	NoC	11	–	156	31	neighbour	NoC	11	–	34	19
slide	NoC	11	+	4	9	na	Int	11	+	355	0
hook	NoC	11	+	0	10	avenue	NoC	11	–	20	17
troops	NoC	11	–	463	53	assure	Verb	11	+	1	10
remarks	NoC	11	–	46	20	gang	NoC	11	–	14	15
everyday	Adj	11	–	65	22	ugly	Adj	11	–	6	14
forecast	NoC	11	+	5	9	phase	NoC	11	–	437	50
stewards	NoC	11	+	43	5	surplus	NoC	11	–	3	13
fall	NoC	11	–	346	45	Geoffrey	NoP	11	–	28	18
contribute	Verb	11	–	131	28	plus	NoC	11	+	8	8
institute	NoC	11	–	544	58	miners	NoC	11	–	36	19
witness	NoC	11	–	34	19	threatened	Verb	11	–	280	40
Bicester	NoP	11	+	206	1	productivity	NoC	11	–	51	21
jumping	Verb	11	+	7	8	generous	Adj	11	–	92	25
encouraging	Adj	11	–	66	22	dun~	Verb	11	+	440	0
raw	Adj	11	–	105	26	tone	NoC	11	–	367	45
perception	NoC	11	–	73	23	shelf	NoC	11	–	10	15
thingy	NoC	11	+	427	0	dishes	NoC	11	–	9	14
external	Adj	11	–	486	54	dare	Verb	11	+	1	9
wished	Verb	11	–	278	40	printed	Verb	11	–	37	19
Cathy	NoP	11	+	61	4	restrictions	NoC	11	–	149	29
Alison	NoP	11	–	5	14	red	NoC	11	–	87	24
depth	NoC	11	–	184	33	umm	Int	11	+	351	0
justify	Verb	11	–	59	22	loo	NoC	11	+	92	3
tins	NoC	11	+	40	5	grief	NoC	11	–	10	15
studio	NoC	11	–	969	83	determine	Verb	11	–	322	42
anxious	Adj	11	–	194	33	palace	NoC	11	–	412	48
closure	NoC	11	–	48	20	cotton	NoC	11	–	82	24
eighteenth	Ord	11	–	58	21	frequently	Adv	11	–	647	63
tunnel	NoC	11	–	98	25	maintained	Verb	11	–	324	42
creation	NoC	11	–	453	52	vision	NoC	11	–	376	46
hand	Verb	11	+	3	9	petition	NoC	11	–	2	13
feeding	Verb	11	–	35	19	efficiency	NoC	11	–	286	40
acceleration	NoC	11	+	28	6	German	NoC	11	–	20	16
moves	Verb	11	–	52	21	aunt	NoC	11	–	193	33
literature	NoC	11	–	535	57	muscles	NoC	11	–	62	22
leadership	NoC	11	–	466	52	fits	Verb	11	+	2	9
mister	NoC	11	+	46	5	shell	NoC	11	–	54	21
sets	Verb	11	–	76	23	shadow	NoC	11	–	183	32

2.2

Word	PoS	FrS		LL	FrW	Word	PoS	FrS		LL	FrW
Saint	NoP-	11	+	35	5	fourteenth	Num	11	+	27	6
tested	Verb	11	−	133	28	mornings	NoC	11	+	8	8
core	NoC	11	−	241	37	brigade	NoC	11	−	1	12
waste	Verb	11	−	10	15	blow	NoC	11	−	60	21
fours	Num	11	+	97	3	deny	Verb	11	−	90	24
lemon	NoC	11	−	1	12	pints	NoC	11	+	54	4
junior	Adj	11	−	151	30	privatization	NoC	11	+	5	8
embarrassed	Adj	11	−	5	13	taped	Verb	11	+	167	2
rise	Verb	11	−	244	37	preparing	Verb	11	−	129	27
terrific	Adj	11	+	26	6	apples	NoC	11	+	4	8
Mickey	NoP	11	+	42	5	in between	Prep	11	+	161	2
violent	Adj	11	−	153	30	discipline	NoC	11	−	604	60
user	NoC	11	−	685	66	hitting	Verb	11	−	0	11
crap	Adj	11	+	289	1	ownership	NoC	11	−	209	34
tidy	Adj	11	+	16	7	evaluation	NoC	11	−	162	30
stated	Verb	11	−	467	52	tanks	NoC	11	−	15	15
spaces	NoC	11	−	15	16	purple	Adj	11	−	0	12
chamber	NoC	11	−	171	31	complaining	Verb	11	+	2	9
rope	NoC	11	−	20	16	fortunate	Adj	11	−	5	13
quiz	NoC	11	+	56	4	drama	NoC	11	−	275	38
trick	NoC	11	−	12	15	passage	NoC	11	−	347	44
weapons	NoC	11	−	335	43	extreme	Adj	11	−	230	35
walks	Verb	11	+	25	6	builders	NoC	11	+	0	10
faces	NoC	11	−	228	35	squeeze	Verb	11	+	16	7
delay	NoC	11	−	91	24	begins	Verb	11	−	229	35
supper	NoC	11	−	16	16	boxing	NoC	11	−	2	12
genes	NoC	11	−	67	22	carpets	NoC	11	+	0	10
unique	Adj	11	−	398	47	Holland	NoP	11	−	21	16
tries	Verb	11	−	13	15	requires	Verb	11	−	563	58
posts	NoC	11	−	83	23	assess	Verb	11	−	144	29
valley	NoC	11	−	400	47	wars	NoC	11	−	48	20
pits	NoC	11	+	2	9	cloud	NoC	11	−	70	22
burning	Verb	11	−	6	14	tyres	NoC	11	+	8	8
T. / t.	Lett	11	+	503	0	superb	Adj	11	−	71	22
retain	Verb	11	−	123	27	concentration	NoC	10	−	335	42
bearing	NoC	11	+	24	6	pensioner	NoC	10	+	30	6
navy	NoC	11	−	61	21	owt	Pron	10	+	303	1
peculiar	Adj	11	−	12	15	Brussels	NoP	10	−	17	16
mass	Adj	11	−	260	38	servants	NoC	10	−	190	32
belief	NoC	11	−	531	56	harvest	NoC	10	+	0	10
spreadsheet	NoC	11	+	36	5	appraisal	NoC	10	−	0	11
representing	Verb	11	−	92	24	bay	NoC	10	−	250	37
worship	NoC	11	−	7	14	blue	NoC	10	−	3	13
involves	Verb	11	−	362	45	fraud	NoC	10	−	43	19
presence	NoC	11	−	1074	89	carriage	NoC	10	−	61	21
nah	Int	11	+	216	1	pray	Verb	10	−	12	15
advised	Verb	11	−	116	26	grab	Verb	10	+	5	8
select	Verb	11	−	41	19	correlation	NoC	10	−	10	14
questionnaire	NoC	11	−	1	12	black	NoC	10	−	4	13
rolls	NoC	11	+	9	8	nuts	NoC	10	+	3	9
guard	NoC	11	−	117	26	assist	Verb	10	−	126	27
volunteers	NoC	11	−	46	19	cheapest	Adj	10	+	41	5
Bruce	NoP	11	−	31	18	farms	NoC	10	−	43	19
preference	NoC	11	−	80	23	old fashioned	Adj	10	+	153	2
Jason	NoP	11	+	0	11	drinking	NoC	10	−	17	15
dramatic	Adj	11	−	321	42	logical	Adj	10	−	100	25
experience	Verb	11	−	120	27	taxes	NoC	10	−	165	30
receipt	NoC	11	−	1	12	fortunately	Adv	10	−	29	17
replaced	Verb	11	−	638	62	connection	NoC	10	−	269	38
pipes	NoC	11	−	0	12	strict	Adj	10	−	70	22
Indian	Adj	11	−	309	41	Hugh	NoP	10	−	70	22
walkman	NoC	11	+	278	1	peas	NoC	10	+	26	6
confusion	NoC	11	−	170	31	drawings	NoC	10	−	99	25
markets	NoC	11	−	667	64	depression	NoC	10	−	92	24
premiums	NoC	11	+	20	6	tendency	NoC	10	−	183	32
technique	NoC	11	−	445	50	behalf	NoC	10	−	8	14

2.2

Word	PoS	FrS		LL	FrW	Word	PoS	FrS		LL	FrW
heavily	Adv	10	–	362	44	Iraq	NoP	10	–	222	34
cancelled	Verb	10	–	1	12	advertised	Verb	10	+	14	7
measured	Verb	10	–	189	32	powder	NoC	10	–	7	13
Hill	NoP	10	–	9	14	flexible	Adj	10	–	113	26
buttons	NoC	10	+	2	9	closing	Verb	10	–	14	15
honey	NoC	10	–	0	11	lake	NoC	10	–	339	42
landed	Verb	10	–	43	19	investigation	NoC	10	–	551	56
amazed	Adj	10	+	3	9	crossing	NoC	10	+	0	10
redundant	Adj	10	–	3	12	Marie	NoP	10	–	47	19
Anna	NoP	10	–	161	30	Debbie	NoP	10	+	35	5
thirds	Num	10	+	43	5	yum	Int	10	+	373	0
categories	NoC	10	–	245	36	Italian	Adj	10	–	360	44
burden	NoC	10	–	137	28	contained	Verb	10	–	506	53
continued	Verb	10	–	1587	117	secret	Adj	10	–	290	39
E. / e.	Lett	10	+	205	1	lamp	NoC	10	–	11	14
seed	NoC	10	–	23	16	blown	Verb	10	–	3	12
recycling	NoC	10	+	10	7	guild	NoC	10	+	9	7
influence	Verb	10	–	127	27	dispute	NoC	10	–	199	32
relates	Verb	10	–	15	15	banana	NoC	10	+	39	5
nursing	NoC	10	–	7	13	ends	Verb	10	–	20	16
adopt	Verb	10	–	122	26	voucher	NoC	10	+	77	3
defend	Verb	10	–	72	22	sizes	NoC	10	–	40	18
lid	NoC	10	–	0	11	commit	Verb	10	–	12	14
spelt	Verb	10	+	69	4	forwards	Adv	10	–	10	14
step	Verb	10	–	27	17	considering	Verb	10	–	140	28
directed	Verb	10	–	256	37	editor	NoC	10	–	341	42
salvation	NoC	10	–	1	11	nationally	Adv	10	+	2	8
tutor	NoC	10	–	0	11	sixpence	NoC	10	+	142	2
recognized	Verb	10	–	192	32	victim	NoC	10	–	347	43
lies	NoC	10	–	4	13	Kyle	NoP	10	+	128	2
united	Verb	10	–	4	13	Tommy	NoP	10	–	2	12
actions	NoC	10	–	493	53	demonstrate	Verb	10	–	116	26
alteration	NoC	10	+	17	6	fives	Num	10	+	221	1
limits	NoC	10	–	192	32	O. / o.	Lett	10	+	475	0
replacement	NoC	10	–	143	28	Russian	Adj	10	–	571	57
singer	NoC	10	–	9	14	cheek	NoC	10	–	58	20
Kath	NoP	10	+	185	1	kicking	Verb	10	+	2	8
Kingdom	NoP-	10	–	419	48	lock	Verb	10	+	19	6
plays	NoC	10	–	2	12	desire	NoC	10	–	540	55
Commons	NoP	10	–	237	35	quoted	Verb	10	–	120	26
accused	Verb	10	–	325	42	embarrassing	Adj	10	–	0	11
grace	NoC	10	–	22	16	raising	Verb	10	–	128	27
sympathy	NoC	10	–	82	23	gravy	NoC	10	+	151	2
retire	Verb	10	–	0	11	pond	NoC	10	–	38	18
criminal	Adj	10	–	427	48	assumption	NoC	10	–	213	33
Thames	NoP	10	–	49	19	operating	NoC	10	–	208	33
ham	NoC	10	+	9	7	defendant	NoC	10	–	247	36
autumn	NoC	10	–	340	43	clothing	NoC	10	–	83	23
saving	NoC	10	+	0	10	cows	NoC	10	–	4	12
drew	Verb	10	–	457	50	save	Prep	10	+	100	3
driven	Verb	10	–	195	32	independence	NoC	10	–	435	49
Spencers	NoP	10	+	338	0	appeal	Verb	10	–	55	20
storage	NoC	10	–	192	32	sometime	Adv	10	+	30	5
rush	Verb	10	+	4	8	chair	Verb	10	+	173	2
S. / s.	Lett	10	+	480	0	pump	NoC	10	–	0	10
at present	Adv	10	–	184	31	issue	Verb	10	–	31	17
in addition to	Prep	10	–	265	37	Mansfield	NoP	10	+	82	3
Suffolk	NoP	10	–	2	12	extended	Verb	10	–	354	43
dependent	Adj	10	–	310	40	apologies	NoC	10	+	39	5
spider	NoC	10	+	19	6	reputation	NoC	10	–	315	40
expand	Verb	10	–	42	19	nineties	Num	10	+	51	4
express	NoC	10	–	0	11	structural	Adj	10	–	162	29
concentrating	Verb	10	–	2	12	chapel	NoC	10	–	68	21
offence	NoC	10	–	307	40	pet	NoC	10	–	10	14
speaks	Verb	10	–	15	15	affecting	Verb	10	–	40	18
Pauline	NoP	10	+	20	6	painful	Adj	10	–	61	20

Word	PoS	FrS		LL	FrW	Word	PoS	FrS		LL	FrW
entered	Verb	10	–	702	65	quantity	NoC	10	–	120	25
fan	NoC	10	–	19	15	dioxide	NoC	10	–	16	15
visual	Adj	10	–	265	37	soil	NoC	10	–	385	45
visits	NoC	10	–	166	30	locations	NoC	10	–	21	15
miserable	Adj	10	–	3	12	force	Verb	10	–	92	23
reserves	NoC	10	–	68	21	Japan	NoP	10	–	822	72
sorting	Verb	10	+	20	6	considerations	NoC	10	–	118	25
constituency	NoC	10	–	56	20	castle	NoC	10	–	495	52
weekly	Adj	10	–	103	24	lists	NoC	10	–	95	23
prayer	NoC	10	–	80	22	illegal	Adj	10	–	130	26
counting	Verb	10	+	2	8	pointing	Verb	10	–	97	23
comma	NoC	10	+	213	1	girlfriend	NoC	10	–	4	12
taste	Verb	10	+	13	7	achievement	NoC	10	–	228	34
pressed	Verb	10	–	189	31	wishes	NoC	10	–	21	15
taxation	NoC	10	–	131	27	then	Adj	10	–	5	12
novel	NoC	10	–	210	33	cleaning	NoC	10	–	5	12
accounting	NoC	10	–	129	27	guests	NoC	10	–	267	37
collar	NoC	10	–	14	14	involving	Verb	10	–	411	46
plug	NoC	10	+	39	5	tray	NoC	10	–	19	15
muck	NoC	10	+	103	3	deals	Verb	10	–	9	13
disability	NoC	10	–	21	16	artist	NoC	10	–	379	44
traditionally	Adv	10	–	77	22	convenient	Adj	10	–	76	21
absence	NoC	10	–	672	63	at last	Adv	10	–	442	48
consultant	NoC	10	–	31	17	trend	NoC	10	–	156	28
lazy	Adj	10	+	4	8	hoped	Verb	10	–	561	56
deserve	Verb	10	–	8	13	given that	Conj	10	–	6	12
noted	Verb	10	–	730	67	altered	Verb	10	–	36	17
assumed	Verb	10	–	389	45	tent	NoC	10	–	4	12
tended	Verb	10	–	166	29	arrested	Verb	10	–	283	37
comprehensive	Adj	10	–	286	38	arise	Verb	10	–	257	36
noisy	Adj	10	–	0	10	blocked	Verb	10	–	10	13
federal	Adj	10	–	335	42	Germans	NoC	10	–	137	27
delays	NoC	10	–	0	11	explaining	Verb	10	–	56	19
moments	NoC	10	–	238	35	wives	NoC	10	–	68	20
associations	NoC	10	–	75	22	pupil	NoC	10	–	115	25
supermarket	NoC	10	–	0	11	agreements	NoC	10	–	168	29
affects	Verb	10	–	15	14	cuts	Verb	10	–	4	12
federation	NoC	10	–	90	23	Israel	NoP	10	–	247	35
ahead of	Prep	10	–	149	28	applying	Verb	10	–	72	21
provisions	NoC	10	–	387	45	victims	NoC	10	–	200	32
purchase	NoC	10	–	214	33	final	NoC	10	–	178	30
curve	NoC	10	–	133	27	geography	NoC	10	–	37	17
killing	Verb	10	–	72	21	practices	NoC	10	–	455	49
spiritual	Adj	10	–	114	25	grandfather	NoC	10	–	28	16
continuing	Adj	10	–	262	36	occupation	NoC	10	–	108	24
recovery	NoC	10	–	335	41	confirmed	Verb	10	–	516	53
consequence	NoC	10	–	273	37	dramatically	Adv	10	–	29	16
buyer	NoC	10	–	164	29	pan	NoC	10	–	6	12
discover	Verb	10	–	247	35	submitted	Verb	10	–	99	23
land	Verb	10	–	8	13	cast	Verb	10	–	207	32
cutting	NoC	10	–	0	11	fired	Verb	10	–	73	21
script	NoC	10	–	6	13	lowest	Adj	10	–	48	18
accommodate	Verb	10	–	15	14	oak	NoC	10	–	35	17
tackle	Verb	10	–	28	16	toes	NoC	10	–	0	10
determined	Verb	10	–	737	67	detective	NoC	10	–	50	18
climate	NoC	10	–	179	30	damp	Adj	10	–	52	19
messages	NoC	10	–	71	21	breast	NoC	10	–	41	18
Kent	NoP	10	–	152	28	destroyed	Verb	10	–	235	34
constraints	NoC	10	–	66	20	Taylor	NoP	10	–	313	39
gifts	NoC	10	–	42	18						

List 2.3. Rank frequency list: written English (not lemmatized)

This list gives frequencies of word forms in the written part of the British National Corpus, comparing them with those of the spoken part (minimum frequency: 20 per million in the written part)

FrS = Rounded frequency (per million word tokens) in spoken English
LL = Log Likelihood, indicating the distinctiveness (or significance of the difference) between the frequencies in speech and writing
FrW = Rounded frequency (per million word tokens) in written English
+ = Higher frequency in speech
− = Higher frequency in writing

Word	PoS	FrS		LL	FrW	Word	PoS	FrS		LL	FrW
the	Det	39605	−	104720	64420	said	Verb	2685	+	1838	2018
of	Prep	14550	−	104519	31109	do	Verb	9594	+	126017	2016
and	Conj	25210	−	1134	27002	what	DetP	7313	+	75414	1936
a	Det	18637	−	4992	21972	as	Prep	916	−	5727	1873
in	Prep	11609	−	31394	18978	's	Verb	17677	+	384464	1848
to	Inf	14912	−	1371	16442	one	Num	3034	+	5910	1839
is	Verb	10164	+	37	9961	its	Det	338	−	17017	1782
to	Prep	6950	−	7715	9620	into	Prep	1067	−	2560	1700
was	Verb	8097	−	1689	9368	him	Pron	1348	−	676	1684
it	Pron	24508	+	151913	9298	some	DetP	1986	+	485	1681
for	Prep	6239	−	7070	8664	up	Adv	2891	+	6666	1668
that	Conj	7246	−	6	7315	could	VMod	1949	+	464	1653
with	Prep	4446	−	8896	6821	when	Conj	2255	+	1836	1649
he	Pron	7277	+	364	6756	them	Pron	3126	+	10733	1572
be	Verb	5790	−	1319	6742	so	Adv	5067	+	44484	1526
on	Prep	5659	−	1235	6569	time	NoC	1819	+	548	1509
I	Pron	29448	+	369238	6494	out	Adv	2316	+	3968	1452
by	Prep	1663	−	35309	5493	my	Det	2278	+	3796	1438
's	Gen	1606	−	29320	4945	two	Num	2710	+	8229	1428
at	Prep	4115	−	1147	4868	about	Prep	2730	+	9185	1384
you	Pron	25957	+	385328	4755	then	Adv	3474	+	19911	1378
are	Verb	4663	−	4	4713	no	Det	1102	−	529	1371
had	Verb	2835	−	7697	4639	more	Adv	624	−	4646	1351
his	Det	1333	−	31332	4627	other	Adj	1313	−	4	1339
not	Neg	4693	+	11	4618	also	Adv	556	−	5482	1328
this	DetP	5627	+	2379	4506	only	Adv	1079	−	447	1323
have	Verb	7488	+	16057	4416	these	DetP	1269	+	2	1252
but	Conj	6366	+	7310	4370	me	Pron	2444	+	8239	1239
from	Prep	2178	−	12708	4360	first	Ord	957	−	572	1220
which	DetP	2208	−	8187	3893	your	Det	2859	+	14438	1212
she	Pron	4136	+	332	3762	may	VMod	480	−	5470	1211
they	Pron	9333	+	52132	3754	now	Adv	2864	+	14540	1211
or	Conj	3357	−	392	3747	did	Verb	3368	+	22872	1210
an	Det	1846	−	10000	3613	new	Adj	603	−	3528	1208
were	Verb	2749	−	858	3282	any	DetP	1484	+	624	1189
as	Conj	1558	−	9631	3174	people	NoC	2063	+	5371	1146
we	Pron	10448	+	106914	2784	her	Pron	800	−	942	1118
their	Det	1284	−	9386	2761	should	VMod	1173	+	38	1105
been	Verb	2082	−	1693	2756	than	Conj	683	−	1547	1074
has	Verb	1598	−	5051	2708	see	Verb	2507	+	13371	1033
that	DetP	14252	+	213613	2581	very	Adv	2373	+	11530	1025
will	VMod	1890	−	1698	2537	made	Verb	539	−	2336	990
would	VMod	3278	+	2223	2467	like	Prep	1762	+	4525	983
her*	Det	644	−	16899	2362	just	Adv	3820	+	40726	982
there	Ex	4067	+	9288	2354	after	Prep	539	−	2180	972
~ n't	Neg	12212	+	177089	2300	between	Prep	338	−	5239	968
all	DetP	3644	+	6115	2297	many	DetP	654	−	870	931
can	VMod	3588	+	6572	2211	years	NoC	704	−	537	925
if	Conj	4544	+	18764	2118	way	NoC	1252	+	956	925
who	Pron	1780	−	443	2086	how	Adv	1888	+	7106	915

Word	PoS	FrS		LL	FrW	Word	PoS	FrS		LL	FrW
our	Det	1253	+	1033	914	without	Prep	227	−	1611	483
being	Verb	634	−	763	888	going*	Verb	2174	+	27109	482
those	DetP	1121	+	655	861	different	Adj	500	+	6	482
such	DetP	225	−	5912	825	children	NoC	367	−	261	477
down	Adv	1472	+	4515	772	system	NoC	189	−	2141	476
one	Pron	2532	+	21938	770	put	Verb	1640	+	15152	475
make	Verb	977	+	477	769	during	Prep	152	−	2833	473
through	Prep	615	−	271	758	within	Prep	253	−	1165	472
over	Prep	543	−	627	757	came	Verb	473	+	0	471
even	Adv	457	−	1226	746	although	Conj	160	−	2604	468
back	Adv	1211	+	2229	745	few	DetP	346	−	303	462
must	VMod	589	−	305	739	local	Adj	301	−	602	462
know	Verb	5550	+	104930	734	small	Adj	216	−	1525	460
year	NoC	803	+	65	730	before	Prep	220	−	1465	459
own	DetP	443	−	1198	724	got	Verb	5025	+	117320	459
still	Adv	739	+	7	715	social	Adj	115	−	3523	458
because*	Conj	2039	+	14376	715	'll	VMod	3066	+	53585	455
too	Adv	629	−	89	710	place	NoC	353	−	225	453
get	Verb	3464	+	46650	709	case	NoC	243	−	1106	453
good	Adj	1566	+	6955	706	great	Adj	363	−	172	452
three	Num	1721	+	9654	691	off	Adv	831	+	2384	446
last	Num	788	+	150	680	always	Adv	597	+	423	446
more	DetP	949	+	938	671	've	Verb	4735	+	108766	446
take	Verb	1149	+	2625	665	'm	Verb	2512	+	38492	443
however	Adv	90	−	7648	664	most	DetP	261	−	814	441
government	NoC	295	−	2425	660	're	Verb	4255	+	93216	439
work	NoC	601	−	48	659	why	Adv	1113	+	6453	439
go	Verb	2885	+	35449	649	something	Pron	1290	+	9584	437
man	NoC	405	−	929	639	group	NoC	249	−	871	433
well	Adv	5310	+	107026	634	went	Verb	917	+	3675	433
on	Adv	1849	+	13638	630	want	Verb	1776	+	20109	432
world	NoC	248	−	2867	629	thought	Verb	845	+	2811	430
same	DetP	651	+	24	611	company	NoC	158	−	2157	429
most	Adv	199	−	3559	607	1	Num	9	−	7542	428
over	Adv	443	−	423	600	end	NoC	455	+	18	426
life	NoC	293	−	1821	598	party	NoC	227	−	1035	423
against	Prep	257	−	2347	597	when	Adv	530	+	248	420
day	NoC	746	+	330	594	per cent	NoC	69	−	4353	418
might	VMod	809	+	657	592	women	NoC	232	−	931	418
under	Prep	234	−	2659	590	about	Adv	730	+	1785	414
here	Adv	1640	+	11087	590	next	Ord	594	+	645	412
does	Verb	1549	+	9615	587	both	Adv	111	−	2943	409
another	DetP	640	+	66	575	men	NoC	223	−	947	408
come	Verb	1737	+	13389	574	find	Verb	529	+	305	408
as	Adv	507	−	76	574	information	NoC	206	−	1155	407
us	Pron	1059	+	2981	573	important	Adj	280	−	411	405
think	Verb	3977	+	71946	562	give	Verb	845	+	3270	405
old	Adj	529	−	4	545	took	Verb	287	−	351	404
while	Conj	156	−	3694	543	national	Adj	165	−	1698	401
never	Adv	700	+	387	542	often	Adv	175	−	1517	399
where	Adv	1380	+	8075	541	every	Det	456	+	85	395
each	DetP	243	−	1947	539	state	NoC	108	−	2796	393
again	Adv	836	+	1381	529	given	Verb	224	−	806	392
found	Verb	209	−	2304	521	high	Adj	185	−	1298	392
Mr	NoC	565	+	37	519	much	Adv	432	+	50	385
'	Gen	141	−	3704	518	2	Num	8	−	6706	383
part	NoC	355	−	510	512	British	Adj	141	−	1921	382
say	Verb	2116	+	24125	512	seen	Verb	371	−	0	377
house	NoC	460	−	40	506	London	NoP	132	−	2022	377
much	DetP	764	+	1057	504	four	Num	1199	+	9982	376
there	Adv	2894	+	45269	498	told	Verb	362	−	3	373
used	Verb	225	−	1783	497	second	Ord	224	−	659	373
where	Conj	160	−	2907	492	business	NoC	225	−	643	373
out of	Prep	497	+	0	490	head	NoC	164	−	1401	372
in	Adv	1307	+	8310	488	taken	Verb	231	−	559	369
number	NoC	531	+	34	488	school	NoC	431	+	94	368

Word	PoS	FrS		LL	FrW	Word	PoS	FrS		LL	FrW
looked	Verb	209	–	771	368	times	NoC	284	–	2	293
family	NoC	171	–	1226	365	war	NoC	170	–	556	291
possible	Adj	147	–	1595	364	available	Adj	104	–	1531	291
away	Adv	433	+	115	364	law	NoC	88	–	1863	291
large	Adj	116	–	2195	363	full	Adj	206	–	250	290
fact	NoC	492	+	396	360	police	NoC	186	–	396	288
hand	NoC	221	–	576	358	interest	NoC	133	–	1000	288
says	Verb	740	+	2804	358	done	Verb	931	+	7898	288
water	NoC	278	–	180	358	week	NoC	631	+	2765	286
such as	Prep	43	–	4252	354	'd	Verb	577	+	2075	285
night	NoC	465	+	292	354	of course	Adv	543	+	1695	283
look	Verb	1123	+	9310	353	problem	NoC	348	+	126	283
already	Adv	267	–	210	352	early	Adj	103	–	1442	283
area	NoC	356	+	0	351	form	NoC	133	–	921	282
set	Verb	174	–	1025	350	problems	NoC	220	–	134	281
asked	Verb	218	–	528	348	research	NoC	59	–	2461	279
things	NoC	1103	+	9183	346	3	Num	6	–	4900	279
development	NoC	142	–	1471	345	right	Adj	1019	+	10192	277
left	Verb	278	–	343	343	education	NoC	115	–	1148	277
money	NoC	637	+	1818	343	help	Verb	239	–	50	276
long	Adj	365	+	13	342	though	Conj	5	–	4885	273
having	Verb	452	+	299	341	best	Adj	217	–	114	272
yet	Adv	307	–	32	341	body	NoC	109	–	1217	272
home	NoC	237	–	331	340	knew	Verb	168	–	431	271
power	NoC	130	–	1621	340	mother	NoC	184	–	299	271
perhaps	Adv	444	+	271	339	Britain	NoP	77	–	1857	271
almost	Adv	118	–	1831	339	making	Verb	224	–	73	269
point	NoC	637	+	1887	338	at least	Adv	165	–	432	268
quite	Adv	1050	+	8435	338	saw	Verb	206	–	146	268
himself	Pron	87	–	2542	337	office	NoC	168	–	400	267
really	Adv	1727	+	24300	337	car	NoC	379	+	381	267
John	NoP	260	–	172	336	road	NoC	336	+	154	266
use	NoC	99	–	2204	334	tell	Verb	668	+	3824	265
nothing	Pron	403	+	125	333	policy	NoC	223	–	63	264
later	Adv	179	–	809	333	turned	Verb	100	–	1269	263
political	Adj	71	–	2928	333	began	Verb	25	–	3462	262
called	Verb	306	–	20	332	services	NoC	138	–	668	262
country	NoC	204	–	538	332	thing	NoC	1136	+	13670	261
days	NoC	318	–	5	332	little	Adj	700	+	4476	261
young	Adj	180	–	772	330	several	DetP	64	–	2057	260
side	NoC	374	+	51	330	like	Verb	1070	+	12162	260
become	Verb	109	–	1866	326	seemed	Verb	60	–	2144	259
both	DetP	189	–	626	324	period	NoC	111	–	1020	258
eyes	NoC	63	–	3032	324	main	Adj	133	–	695	258
whether	Conj	413	+	214	322	less	Adv	119	–	888	258
far	Adv	229	–	269	320	minister	NoC	56	–	2249	258
room	NoC	233	–	235	318	child	NoC	130	–	725	257
general	Adj	162	–	882	317	using	Verb	157	–	430	257
since	Conj	112	–	1681	316	health	NoC	154	–	452	257
together	Adv	262	–	84	313	ever	Adv	275	+	12	257
service	NoC	204	–	395	312	economic	Adj	53	--	2315	257
need	Verb	749	+	3967	310	control	NoC	83	–	1520	256
court	NoC	94	–	1961	307	keep	Verb	449	+	1068	256
public	Adj	102	–	1762	306	million	NoC	157	–	417	256
members	NoC	224	–	222	305	'd	VMod	1194	+	15417	256
market	NoC	135	–	1147	305	society	NoC	89	–	1379	256
towards	Prep	123	–	1331	305	am	Verb	264	+	3	255
before	Conj	316	+	4	304	known	Verb	93	–	1313	255
face	NoC	103	–	1704	303	until	Conj	137	–	619	254
use	Verb	455	+	605	303	for example	Adv	107	–	1037	254
five	Num	1308	+	15609	303	major	Adj	104	–	1082	254
held	Verb	56	–	2920	302	door	NoC	255	+	0	253
others	NoC	126	–	1235	301	months	NoC	211	–	68	252
council	NoC	424	+	413	300	itself	Pron	105	–	1052	252
able	Adj	339	+	45	300	among	Prep	26	–	3242	252
felt	Verb	106	–	1567	298	including	Prep	45	–	2487	252

Word	PoS	FrS		LL	FrW	Word	PoS	FrS		LL	FrW
upon	Prep	80	–	1521	252	third	Num	132	–	391	220
England	NoP	56	–	2135	252	view	NoC	169	–	115	219
report	NoC	215	–	50	251	kind	NoC	270	+	101	219
father	NoC	142	–	524	251	sense	NoC	159	–	168	219
person	NoC	244	–	1	250	mind	NoC	164	–	143	219
A / a	Lett	405	+	737	250	around	Adv	196	–	20	217
themselves	Pron	124	–	732	250	taking	Verb	224	+	1	217
around	Prep	137	–	572	249	whose	DetP	43	–	2013	216
words	NoC	205	–	76	249	century	NoC	42	–	2022	215
anything	Pron	633	+	3716	248	seems	Verb	186	–	38	215
level	NoC	164	–	301	247	white	Adj	131	–	354	214
book	NoC	220	–	27	246	moment	NoC	285	+	196	214
looking	Verb	428	+	1009	245	church	NoC	107	–	615	214
after	Conj	126	–	665	245	rather	Adv	209	–	0	213
enough	Adv	241	–	0	244	idea	NoC	253	+	66	213
effect	NoC	87	–	1282	244	industry	NoC	77	–	1087	212
name	NoC	299	+	104	244	whole	Adj	248	+	52	212
areas	NoC	142	–	474	244	sure	Adj	479	+	2211	212
became	Verb	45	–	2381	244	support	NoC	104	–	636	212
likely	Adj	91	–	1197	243	change	NoC	110	–	556	212
feel	Verb	364	+	476	243	behind	Prep	121	–	429	211
community	NoC	125	–	658	243	range	NoC	59	–	1471	211
woman	NoC	138	–	504	243	job	NoC	382	+	1016	211
international	Adj	38	–	2595	242	brought	Verb	143	–	230	211
work	Verb	415	+	924	242	ca~	VMod	1248	+	19835	210
centre	NoC	133	–	552	242	European	Adj	69	–	1218	210
therefore	Adv	152	–	356	241	care	NoC	95	–	741	209
city	NoC	143	–	439	241	study	NoC	38	–	2046	209
so	Conj	400	+	793	241	free	Adj	113	–	489	208
question	NoC	310	+	172	240	table	NoC	148	–	176	208
position	NoC	130	–	568	240	order	NoC	111	–	506	207
gave	Verb	148	–	381	239	history	NoC	70	–	1176	207
provide	Verb	88	–	1205	239	10	Num	2	–	3823	207
six	Num	863	+	8443	239	central	Adj	71	–	1148	207
real	Adj	132	–	530	238	believe	Verb	257	+	105	207
let	Verb	390	+	753	237	groups	NoC	85	–	871	206
clear	Adj	140	–	443	237	sometimes	Adv	199	–	2	206
probably	Adv	585	+	3222	237	Mrs	NoC	150	–	147	204
staff	NoC	138	–	456	237	better	Adj	308	+	428	203
action	NoC	88	–	1170	236	doing	Verb	943	+	12144	202
today	Adv	503	+	2058	236	air	NoC	86	–	803	201
black	Adj	147	–	351	234	language	NoC	79	–	914	200
further*	Adj	63	–	1698	234	street	NoC	137	–	208	200
act	NoC	56	–	1876	234	result	NoC	74	–	1007	200
special	Adj	125	–	559	231	rate	NoC	89	–	748	200
yes	Int	3840	+	107268	231	little	DetP	37	–	1917	200
process	NoC	78	–	1317	231	hands	NoC	94	–	663	199
management	NoC	101	–	878	231	trade	NoC	122	–	333	199
no	Int	4388	+	128715	230	off	Prep	341	+	759	199
evidence	NoC	82	–	1218	230	based	Verb	79	–	888	199
only	Adj	244	+	8	229	heard	Verb	232	+	48	199
particularly	Adv	153	–	258	228	human	Adj	51	–	1515	199
thus	Adv	8	–	3757	228	experience	NoC	103	–	532	198
age	NoC	124	–	528	226	mean	Verb	2250	+	53431	198
certain	Adj	169	–	147	226	training	NoC	156	–	93	198
open	Adj	155	–	234	226	food	NoC	117	–	374	198
line	NoC	181	–	92	226	similar	Adj	69	–	1059	198
wanted	Verb	314	+	287	225	data	NoC	51	–	1494	197
particular	Adj	209	–	10	225	team	NoC	93	–	651	197
4	Num	3	–	4049	224	yesterday	Adv	177	–	19	197
difficult	Adj	202	–	17	222	section	NoC	89	–	715	197
death	NoC	57	–	1685	222	usually	Adv	144	–	144	197
either	Adv	198	–	26	222	programme	NoC	131	–	235	197
across	Prep	173	–	108	222	changes	NoC	69	–	1056	196
big	Adj	549	+	3054	221	common	Adj	67	–	1075	196
read	Verb	260	+	60	221	role	NoC	66	–	1105	196

Word	PoS	FrS		LL	FrW	Word	PoS	FrS		LL	FrW
cases	NoC	71	–	1012	195	price	NoC	121	–	180	176
5	Num	5	–	3363	195	US	NoP	2	–	3220	176
Europe	NoP	62	–	1188	195	terms	NoC	76	–	681	176
shall	VMod	264	+	201	195	minutes	NoC	253	+	278	175
nature	NoC	63	–	1150	195	financial	Adj	78	–	641	175
voice	NoC	48	–	1520	194	needed	Verb	77	–	662	175
necessary	Adj	71	–	981	194	university	NoC	75	–	695	175
sir	NoC	143	–	138	194	president	NoC	76	–	660	174
so that	Conj	231	+	64	193	run	Verb	179	+	1	174
UK	NoP	0	–	3746	193	certainly	Adv	299	+	682	173
subject	NoC	66	–	1059	192	leave	Verb	289	+	583	173
back	NoC	270	+	259	192	recent	Adj	36	–	1540	173
course	NoC	143	–	128	192	club	NoC	90	–	460	173
once	Adv	114	–	343	191	seem	Verb	146	–	39	173
indeed	Adv	166	–	32	191	south	NoC	103	–	307	172
word	NoC	214	+	24	191	north	NoC	88	–	464	171
ago	Adv	259	+	200	191	friend	NoC	102	–	303	171
authority	NoC	118	–	304	191	according to	Prep	37	–	1478	171
companies	NoC	74	–	893	190	matter	NoC	145	–	38	171
since	Prep	72	–	922	190	lost	Verb	155	–	13	171
land	NoC	166	–	28	190	trying	Verb	311	+	836	171
committee	NoC	187	–	0	190	soon	Adv	82	–	540	170
God	NoP	305	+	536	190	quality	NoC	99	–	337	170
as well as	Prep	55	–	1268	190	ask	Verb	399	+	1997	170
patients	NoC	36	–	1788	189	strong	Adj	77	–	606	170
class	NoC	108	–	390	189	gone	Verb	418	+	2299	170
personal	Adj	65	–	1051	189	led	Verb	24	–	1901	170
hours	NoC	191	+	0	189	union	NoC	134	–	74	169
all	Adv	229	+	73	189	parents	NoC	111	–	212	169
systems	NoC	43	–	1558	188	American	Adj	55	–	995	169
herself	Pron	38	–	1723	187	production	NoC	50	–	1105	168
especially	Adv	89	–	607	187	as if	Conj	64	–	802	167
someone	Pron	181	–	1	187	date	NoC	80	–	541	167
value	NoC	70	–	919	187	building	NoC	122	–	125	167
department	NoC	91	–	573	187	makes	Verb	162	–	1	167
former	DetP	21	–	2312	187	everything	Pron	359	+	1493	167
simply	Adv	98	–	488	187	higher	Adj	66	–	755	167
single	Adj	94	–	538	187	art	NoC	35	–	1487	166
home	Adv	265	+	275	185	paper	NoC	232	+	212	166
private	Adj	69	–	920	185	stage	NoC	126	–	98	166
member	NoC	85	–	649	185	1990	Num	5	–	2774	166
working	Verb	282	+	412	184	late	Adj	102	–	272	166
practice	NoC	62	–	1041	184	low	Adj	91	–	384	166
long	Adv	153	–	49	184	conditions	NoC	56	–	937	165
morning	NoC	459	+	2610	183	include	Verb	35	–	1453	165
town	NoC	159	–	30	182	started	Verb	261	+	436	165
short	Adj	127	–	179	182	getting	Verb	539	+	4647	165
half	DetP	440	+	2322	182	Mr.	NoC	5	–	2751	164
true	Adj	177	–	1	182	award	NoC	13	–	2288	163
because of	Prep	142	–	87	182	shown	Verb	40	–	1283	163
show	Verb	169	–	7	181	chapter	NoC	30	–	1589	163
reason	NoC	180	–	0	181	followed	Verb	28	–	1658	163
right	NoC	67	–	896	181	ground	NoC	80	–	484	163
countries	NoC	57	–	1115	180	described	Verb	26	–	1725	162
try	Verb	396	+	1728	180	tax	NoC	107	–	197	162
oh	Int	5052	+	166592	179	p.	NoC	0	–	3171	161
else	Adv	475	+	2990	178	English	Adj	52	–	969	161
wife	NoC	107	–	315	178	various	Adj	101	–	242	161
figure	NoC	97	–	424	178	May	NoP	50	–	1007	161
rather than	Prep	101	–	373	177	secretary	NoC	96	–	284	161
bank	NoC	85	–	565	177	concerned	Adj	134	–	44	160
until	Prep	82	–	608	177	king	NoC	37	–	1338	160
foreign	Adj	27	–	1909	177	despite	Prep	22	–	1846	160
type	NoC	117	–	212	176	royal	Adj	38	–	1291	160
need	NoC	101	–	363	176	pay	Verb	309	+	982	160
decision	NoC	97	–	402	176	lot*	NoC	992	+	16309	160

2.3

Word	PoS	FrS		LL	FrW	Word	PoS	FrS		LL	FrW
meeting	NoC	178	+	18	160	actually	Adv	1239	+	25097	147
results	NoC	43	−	1157	159	simple	Adj	81	−	335	147
expected	Verb	35	−	1366	159	20	Num	1	−	2748	146
David	NoP	138	−	28	159	kept	Verb	113	−	78	146
more than	Adv	53	−	902	159	met	Verb	70	−	461	146
April	NoP	44	−	1108	159	coming	Verb	522	+	5045	146
clearly	Adv	107	−	177	159	force	NoC	48	−	855	146
B / b	Lett	337	+	1353	159	lord	NoC	136	−	6	146
schools	NoC	118	−	106	159	labour*	NoC	58	−	657	146
music	NoC	76	−	502	159	following	Adj	29	−	1348	146
knowledge	NoC	37	−	1314	158	carried	Verb	69	−	470	146
present	Adj	65	−	680	158	meet	Verb	99	−	154	145
situation	NoC	176	+	18	158	movement	NoC	48	−	840	145
hard	Adj	153	−	1	158	individual	Adj	57	−	669	145
girl	NoC	156	−	0	158	analysis	NoC	26	−	1437	145
decided	Verb	89	−	338	158	computer	NoC	85	−	277	145
required	Verb	30	−	1489	157	French	Adj	40	−	1031	145
students	NoC	48	−	1004	157	considered	Verb	39	−	1037	144
hospital	NoC	97	−	254	157	success	NoC	44	−	910	144
poor	Adj	100	−	220	157	near	Prep	88	−	242	144
workers	NoC	63	−	688	157	stood	Verb	36	−	1119	144
March	NoP	43	−	1109	157	up to	Prep	228	+	386	144
bed	NoC	177	+	24	156	easy	Adj	137	−	3	144
approach	NoC	48	−	994	156	agreement	NoC	42	−	949	143
friends	NoC	104	−	185	156	play	Verb	194	+	150	143
series	NoC	35	−	1323	156	structure	NoC	80	−	319	143
June	NoP	61	−	710	156	1991	Num	3	−	2472	142
tried	Verb	107	−	159	155	agreed	Verb	85	−	258	142
ten	Num	616	+	6735	155	rest	NoC	136	−	3	142
ways	NoC	106	−	157	154	theory	NoC	35	−	1108	142
game	NoC	112	−	122	154	cut	Verb	165	+	33	142
remember	Verb	513	+	4528	154	account	NoC	72	−	403	142
natural	Adj	43	−	1060	154	current	Adj	58	−	619	142
anyone	Pron	118	−	84	153	per	Prep	72	−	406	142
field	NoC	58	−	731	153	population	NoC	45	−	873	142
cost	NoC	115	−	94	153	paid	Verb	163	+	28	142
issue	NoC	112	−	108	152	evening	NoC	108	−	83	142
love	NoC	114	−	97	152	story	NoC	95	−	161	141
added	Verb	26	−	1557	152	questions	NoC	153	+	8	141
light	NoC	90	−	279	152	capital	NoC	57	−	615	141
greater	Adj	50	−	878	152	legal	Adj	41	−	944	141
&	Conj	7	−	2402	151	whom	Pron	26	−	1368	141
for	Conj	40	−	1120	151	material	NoC	44	−	884	141
bases	NoC	94	−	228	150	performance	NoC	36	−	1065	141
month	NoC	147	−	0	150	modern	Adj	50	−	752	141
moved	Verb	106	−	133	150	growth	NoC	36	−	1061	141
further	Adv	97	−	195	150	Scotland	NoP	47	−	796	140
understand	Verb	203	+	156	149	model	NoC	44	−	861	140
studies	NoC	18	−	1801	149	received	Verb	46	−	828	140
6	Num	5	−	2518	149	sent	Verb	110	−	65	140
1989	Num	1	−	2830	149	provided	Verb	38	−	999	140
news	NoC	114	−	84	149	comes	Verb	328	+	1637	140
security	NoC	49	−	868	149	in order	ClO	54	−	653	140
weeks	NoC	198	+	137	149	sort	NoC	712	+	9947	140
hair	NoC	111	−	94	148	sea	NoC	45	−	832	140
project	NoC	84	−	314	148	finally	Adv	48	−	775	140
feet	NoC	85	−	297	147	rights	NoC	48	−	778	139
allowed	Verb	105	−	128	147	produced	Verb	43	−	877	139
bring	Verb	216	+	259	147	live	Verb	167	+	49	139
amount	NoC	138	−	5	147	board	NoC	100	−	106	138
above	Prep	49	−	838	147	relationship	NoC	51	−	695	138
manager	NoC	65	−	548	147	son	NoC	72	−	365	138
attention	NoC	51	−	805	147	parties	NoC	36	−	1030	137
died	Verb	79	−	350	147	final	Adj	54	−	625	137
heart	NoC	56	−	695	147	environment	NoC	70	−	377	137
future	NoC	99	−	165	147	better	Adv	197	+	215	137

2.3

Word	PoS	FrS		LL	FrW	Word	PoS	FrS		LL	FrW
letter	NoC	132	–	1	136	industrial	Adj	38	–	804	125
books	NoC	87	–	196	136	pressure	NoC	72	–	249	125
reached	Verb	18	–	1584	136	away from	Prep	80	–	174	125
authorities	NoC	72	–	350	136	forces	NoC	26	–	1102	124
bad	Adj	296	+	1262	136	activity	NoC	35	–	875	124
wrong	Adj	263	+	841	136	worked	Verb	152	+	53	124
east	NoC	64	–	449	136	reported	Verb	22	–	1241	124
nor	Conj	27	–	1247	136	scheme	NoC	78	–	190	124
forward	Adv	151	+	16	135	hear	Verb	254	+	935	124
everyone	Pron	118	–	20	135	continue	Verb	66	–	304	124
12	Num	1	–	2494	135	United	NoP-	36	–	838	124
property	NoC	45	–	781	135	association	NoC	39	–	760	124
saying	Verb	577	+	6836	135	throughout	Prep	48	–	574	124
means	Verb	170	+	81	134	opened	Verb	45	–	628	124
at all	Adv	270	+	961	134	cup	NoC	112	–	9	123
built	Verb	83	–	214	134	move	Verb	251	+	915	123
west	NoC	69	–	362	134	consider	Verb	65	–	311	123
behaviour	NoC	34	–	1013	133	relations	NoC	17	–	1396	123
included	Verb	30	–	1140	133	hotel	NoC	38	–	775	123
before	Adv	230	+	529	133	won	Verb	66	–	295	123
chance	NoC	109	–	42	133	eight	Num	606	+	8237	123
labour*	Adj	118	–	16	133	Dr	NoC	19	–	1305	122
France	NoP	40	–	851	133	parts	NoC	63	–	328	122
record	NoC	73	–	299	133	rates	NoC	48	–	555	122
treatment	NoC	31	–	1086	133	hall	NoC	78	–	172	122
happened	Verb	195	+	237	132	army	NoC	46	–	593	122
close	Adj	67	–	367	132	generally	Adv	59	–	378	122
fire	NoC	146	+	14	131	allow	Verb	53	–	469	122
prime	Adj	31	–	1074	131	15	Num	1	–	2236	122
energy	NoC	44	–	749	131	myself	Pron	159	+	97	122
previous	Adj	52	–	583	131	outside	Prep	65	–	304	122
director	NoC	41	–	813	131	sun	NoC	55	–	437	121
serious	Adj	64	–	396	131	teachers	NoC	67	–	278	121
example	NoC	76	–	259	131	turn	Verb	198	+	373	121
recently	Adv	60	–	453	130	spent	Verb	76	–	180	120
significant	Adj	39	–	835	130	St	NoP-	28	–	999	120
space	NoC	79	–	220	130	stop	Verb	225	+	661	120
right	Adv	2209	+	62243	130	wide	Adj	48	–	529	120
total	Adj	54	–	543	130	fine	Adj	187	+	293	120
boy	NoC	159	+	59	130	dead	Adj	63	–	313	120
levels	NoC	48	–	641	129	contract	NoC	64	–	305	120
size	NoC	105	–	47	129	arms	NoC	27	–	1002	120
design	NoC	35	–	927	129	plan	NoC	155	+	87	120
along	Prep	79	–	209	129	Soviet	Adj	18	–	1291	119
normal	Adj	88	–	134	129	specific	Adj	58	–	375	119
July	NoP	38	–	843	128	lower	Adj	42	–	630	119
Peter	NoP	87	–	139	128	7	Num	3	–	2065	119
start	Verb	365	+	2575	128	military	Adj	17	–	1317	119
quickly	Adv	88	–	128	128	developed	Verb	26	–	1013	119
seven	Num	565	+	6896	128	list	NoC	114	–	1	118
technology	NoC	38	–	836	127	wall	NoC	79	–	136	118
30	Num	2	–	2275	127	summer	NoC	69	–	229	118
costs	NoC	65	–	347	126	appropriate	Adj	64	–	280	118
suddenly	Adv	45	–	655	126	appear	Verb	31	–	881	118
following	Verb	32	–	974	126	top	Adj	64	–	276	118
defence	NoC	33	–	939	126	season	NoC	37	–	722	118
giving	Verb	113	–	13	126	floor	NoC	95	–	43	118
activities	NoC	29	–	1031	126	hon.	Adj	0	–	2293	118
details	NoC	44	–	676	126	de*	NoP	13	–	1461	117
choice	NoC	72	–	258	126	continued	Verb	10	–	1587	117
loss	NoC	31	–	989	126	played	Verb	68	–	226	117
sat	Verb	76	–	215	126	product	NoC	58	–	344	117
red	Adj	125	–	0	126	George	NoP	56	–	370	117
issues	NoC	80	–	181	125	appeared	Verb	16	–	1328	117
term	NoC	102	–	43	125	takes	Verb	126	+	7	117
income	NoC	80	–	172	125	call	Verb	290	+	1624	117

2.3

Word	PoS	FrS		LL	FrW	Word	PoS	FrS		LL	FrW
set	NoC	70	–	199	116	sound	NoC	43	–	488	109
effects	NoC	33	–	801	116	advice	NoC	64	–	204	109
wo~	VMod	552	+	7229	116	immediately	Adv	42	–	507	109
unit	NoC	48	–	485	116	a little	Adv	67	–	174	109
husband	NoC	80	–	116	116	needs	NoC	71	–	141	109
ideas	NoC	70	–	201	116	America	NoP	53	–	331	109
announced	Verb	13	–	1430	116	January	NoP	41	–	534	109
basic	Adj	51	–	442	116	oil	NoC	48	–	410	109
points	NoC	110	–	2	116	unless	Conj	122	+	15	109
investment	NoC	54	–	392	115	goods	NoC	39	–	571	109
successful	Adj	44	–	551	115	sales	NoC	65	–	191	109
original	Adj	44	–	544	115	involved	Verb	60	–	250	109
New	NoP-	24	–	1023	115	established	Verb	20	–	1062	108
produce	Verb	60	–	300	115	fell	Verb	42	–	503	108
showed	Verb	36	–	706	115	changed	Verb	120	+	12	108
style	NoC	35	–	739	115	buy	Verb	261	+	1380	108
1988	Num	0	–	2207	115	8	Num	3	–	1845	108
popular	Adj	27	–	932	115	traditional	Adj	23	–	958	108
meant	Verb	103	–	11	114	window	NoC	91	–	23	107
test	NoC	62	–	278	114	published	Verb	21	–	998	107
village	NoC	59	–	312	114	Scottish	Adj	22	–	979	107
Germany	NoP	37	–	675	114	lines	NoC	56	–	277	107
October	NoP	36	–	694	114	blood	NoC	51	–	348	107
whatever	DetP	289	+	1663	114	western	Adj	26	–	852	107
1992	Num	1	–	2138	114	chairman	NoC	151	+	146	107
change	Verb	160	+	148	114	goes	Verb	503	+	6537	107
events	NoC	23	–	1048	114	effective	Adj	35	–	628	107
suggested	Verb	42	–	569	114	German	Adj	24	–	918	107
products	NoC	39	–	626	114	fish	NoC	69	–	146	107
returned	Verb	12	–	1434	114	picture	NoC	91	–	23	107
Paul	NoP	116	+	0	114	park	NoC	76	–	90	107
numbers	NoC	107	–	3	114	James	NoP	62	–	209	107
nearly	Adv	127	+	13	114	response	NoC	43	–	468	106
beyond	Prep	35	–	719	114	degree	NoC	42	–	488	106
science	NoC	41	–	589	113	please	Adv	361	+	3259	106
professional	Adj	33	–	751	113	press	NoC	61	–	214	106
passed	Verb	50	–	420	113	operation	NoC	50	–	350	106
each other	Pron	62	–	265	113	prices	NoC	57	–	257	106
talk	Verb	266	+	1339	113	hold	Verb	110	+	1	106
colour	NoC	96	–	26	113	round	Adv	415	+	4467	106
interests	NoC	29	–	839	113	access	NoC	49	–	361	106
figures	NoC	106	–	3	112	title	NoC	18	–	1071	106
offered	Verb	52	–	389	112	opportunity	NoC	75	–	91	106
event	NoC	30	–	813	112	useful	Adj	58	–	248	106
rules	NoC	43	–	527	112	species	NoC	13	–	1277	106
reasons	NoC	74	–	136	112	shows	Verb	40	–	504	105
economy	NoC	43	–	535	112	importance	NoC	25	–	847	105
risk	NoC	36	–	677	112	extent	NoC	57	–	256	105
direct	Adj	41	–	564	112	majority	NoC	51	–	333	105
employment	NoC	65	–	219	112	offer	Verb	42	–	470	105
top	NoC	196	+	475	112	gives	Verb	97	–	5	105
couple	NoC	220	+	748	111	forms	NoC	40	–	508	105
dark	Adj	39	–	591	111	college	NoC	72	–	108	105
September	NoP	45	–	478	111	application	NoC	59	–	226	105
ensure	Verb	37	–	636	111	film	NoC	66	–	158	105
difference	NoC	136	+	52	111	less	DetP	68	–	142	105
resources	NoC	59	–	271	111	independent	Adj	38	–	542	105
circumstances	NoC	49	–	414	111	C / c	Lett	431	+	4884	105
help	NoC	79	–	94	110	written	Verb	94	–	11	105
happy	Adj	176	+	298	110	doctor	NoC	106	+	0	105
stay	Verb	146	+	95	110	easily	Adv	49	–	349	104
aware	Adj	86	–	55	110	considerable	Adj	24	–	855	104
follows	Verb	16	–	1223	110	hope	Verb	206	+	698	104
garden	NoC	88	–	43	110	expect	Verb	119	+	17	104
commission	NoC	40	–	550	110	conference	NoC	69	–	130	104
designed	Verb	21	–	1043	110	election	NoC	40	–	499	104

2.3

Word	PoS	FrS		LL	FrW	Word	PoS	FrS		LL	FrW
hour	NoC	194	+	559	104	earlier	Adv	82	–	28	98
Ireland	NoP	29	–	735	104	follow	Verb	58	–	181	98
parliament	NoC	37	–	551	104	method	NoC	27	–	690	98
wrote	Verb	61	–	195	103	methods	NoC	16	–	1034	98
standards	NoC	36	–	571	103	support	Verb	93	–	2	98
caused	Verb	29	–	712	103	campaign	NoC	34	–	530	98
above	Adv	12	–	1280	103	involved	Adj	80	–	31	98
physical	Adj	26	–	791	103	arm	NoC	36	–	496	98
running	Verb	113	+	7	103	surface	NoC	20	–	882	98
software	NoC	17	–	1085	103	lack	NoC	27	–	703	98
11	Num	1	–	1919	103	remain	Verb	23	–	809	98
page	NoC	137	+	93	103	cold	Adj	109	+	13	97
television	NoC	78	–	59	103	write	Verb	206	+	828	97
Richard	NoP	77	–	63	102	ability	NoC	39	–	435	97
leaving	Verb	44	–	408	102	pattern	NoC	35	–	498	97
plans	NoC	49	–	325	102	skills	NoC	39	–	424	97
left	Adj	29	–	710	102	look	NoC	227	+	1120	97
thought	NoC	35	–	567	102	responsibility	NoC	57	–	180	97
raised	Verb	42	–	437	102	lady	NoC	98	+	0	97
concern	NoC	46	–	360	102	in terms of	Prep	142	+	169	97
station	NoC	87	–	19	102	attempt	NoC	17	–	982	97
earth	NoC	55	–	239	102	disease	NoC	21	–	842	97
wish	Verb	113	+	10	101	lead	Verb	38	–	446	97
statement	NoC	73	–	82	101	miss*	NoC	42	–	377	96
glass	NoC	46	–	355	101	below	Adv	16	–	995	96
river	NoC	35	–	547	101	male	Adj	22	–	795	96
means	NoC	52	–	271	101	planning	NoC	95	–	0	96
remained	Verb	8	–	1406	101	exactly	Adv	201	+	782	96
increase	NoC	57	–	212	100	houses	NoC	97	+	0	96
playing	Verb	108	+	4	100	failed	Verb	23	–	774	96
November	NoP	37	–	495	100	county	NoC	258	+	1648	96
December	NoP	35	–	534	100	girls	NoC	97	+	0	96
worth	Prep	114	+	16	100	needs	Verb	104	+	6	96
green	Adj	88	–	13	100	Michael	NoP	87	–	7	96
round	Prep	245	+	1320	100	arrived	Verb	24	–	742	96
Charles	NoP	13	–	1173	100	I / i	Num	0	–	1816	96
competition	NoC	44	–	378	100	peace	NoC	30	–	580	95
responsible	Adj	45	–	366	100	demand	NoC	30	–	577	95
region	NoC	91	–	8	100	status	NoC	23	–	769	95
complete	Adj	42	–	413	100	equipment	NoC	38	–	424	95
lay	Verb	28	–	694	100	eventually	Adv	59	–	152	95
miles	NoC	82	–	31	100	no longer	Adv	29	–	601	95
eye	NoC	53	–	247	100	past	Adj	34	–	508	95
medical	Adj	35	–	525	100	jobs	NoC	114	+	33	95
appeal	NoC	19	–	941	100	fully	Adv	40	–	395	95
task	NoC	26	–	741	100	West	NoP-	28	–	624	95
up to	Adv	47	–	323	100	hundred	NoC	1023	+	23691	95
opposition	NoC	19	–	931	99	division	NoC	48	–	262	95
carry	Verb	116	+	24	99	compared	Verb	31	–	554	95
existing	Adj	51	–	271	99	directly	Adv	28	–	626	95
public	NoC	66	–	117	99	variety	NoC	24	–	717	95
leader	NoC	36	–	513	99	1987	Num	0	–	1807	95
Wales	NoP	37	–	485	99	return	NoC	23	–	741	95
site	NoC	78	–	45	99	types	NoC	37	–	431	95
daughter	NoC	54	–	234	99	ones	NoC	318	+	2856	94
source	NoC	19	–	942	99	charge	NoC	50	–	241	94
highly	Adv	27	–	710	99	essential	Adj	26	–	663	94
purpose	NoC	44	–	361	99	placed	Verb	17	–	910	94
walked	Verb	55	–	215	99	firm	NoC	35	–	458	94
ready	Adj	130	+	79	99	officer	NoC	79	–	24	94
stopped	Verb	70	–	85	99	culture	NoC	15	–	974	94
heavy	Adj	56	–	205	99	civil	Adj	27	–	619	93
yourself	Pron	182	+	509	99	factors	NoC	32	–	507	93
mouth	NoC	47	–	324	99	hardly	Adv	46	–	282	93
accept	Verb	94	–	2	99	talking	Verb	428	+	5463	93
II / ii	Num	0	–	1893	98	ran	Verb	40	–	364	93

Word	PoS	FrS		LL	FrW	Word	PoS	FrS		LL	FrW
bill	NoC	68	–	69	93	nuclear	Adj	19	–	775	88
York	NoP	153	+	300	93	through	Adv	155	+	376	88
sale	NoC	46	–	273	93	moving	Verb	96	+	6	88
blue	Adj	86	–	3	92	works	NoC	31	–	481	88
introduced	Verb	29	–	568	92	features	NoC	16	–	861	88
older	Adj	66	–	79	92	1986	Num	1	–	1652	88
direction	NoC	40	–	351	92	safety	NoC	68	–	49	88
whole	NoC	81	–	13	92	environmental	Adj	48	–	202	88
created	Verb	23	–	705	92	used	VMod	742	+	15000	88
primary	Adj	30	–	543	92	share	NoC	28	–	527	88
shop	NoC	188	+	687	92	otherwise	Adv	88	–	0	88
windows	NoC	52	–	195	92	weight	NoC	63	–	76	88
develop	Verb	37	–	407	92	families	NoC	43	–	273	88
policies	NoC	58	–	139	92	version	NoC	25	–	601	88
provides	Verb	13	–	1016	92	waiting	Verb	76	–	15	88
context	NoC	35	–	434	92	suppose	Verb	275	+	2237	88
show	NoC	51	–	204	92	other	NoC	60	–	94	88
base	NoC	42	–	316	92	looks	Verb	226	+	1353	87
places	NoC	91	–	0	91	trees	NoC	48	–	198	87
character	NoC	42	–	314	91	principle	NoC	34	–	404	87
provision	NoC	54	–	169	91	create	Verb	34	–	406	87
William	NoP	20	–	779	91	Sunday	NoP	143	+	277	87
killed	Verb	40	–	344	91	sex	NoC	49	–	188	87
caught	Verb	47	–	251	91	library	NoC	41	–	287	87
animals	NoC	40	–	342	91	influence	NoC	17	–	798	87
interesting	Adj	146	+	255	91	sold	Verb	63	–	65	87
claimed	Verb	13	–	1008	91	completely	Adv	80	–	5	87
suggest	Verb	77	–	19	90	brother	NoC	73	–	19	87
States	NoP	35	–	430	90	presented	Verb	20	–	725	87
speak	Verb	128	+	125	90	annual	Adj	31	–	453	86
baby	NoC	93	+	0	90	argument	NoC	54	–	131	86
sector	NoC	61	–	103	90	truth	NoC	49	–	186	86
slightly	Adv	75	–	24	90	rule	NoC	41	–	285	86
condition	NoC	22	–	701	90	best	Adv	38	–	327	86
hot	Adj	96	+	2	90	nine	Num	571	+	9860	86
organisation	NoC	24	–	673	90	shares	NoC	19	–	723	86
obvious	Adj	43	–	284	90	latter	DetP	5	–	1272	86
future	Adj	39	–	346	90	start	NoC	73	–	19	86
post	NoC	75	–	24	90	none	Pron	71	–	26	86
18	Num	2	–	1592	90	on to	Prep	143	+	288	86
even if	Conj	67	–	61	90	25	Num	2	–	1527	86
deal	NoC	70	–	44	90	slowly	Adv	21	–	671	86
teacher	NoC	67	–	58	90	positive	Adj	62	–	65	86
down	Prep	170	+	518	90	media	NoC	28	–	506	86
16	Num	2	–	1594	90	individuals	NoC	31	–	446	86
hit	Verb	79	–	13	90	duty	NoC	38	–	321	86
believed	Verb	17	–	839	90	protection	NoC	35	–	374	86
past	NoC	58	–	118	89	once	Conj	131	+	186	86
piece	NoC	120	+	89	89	cash	NoC	47	–	198	86
stand	Verb	114	+	58	89	courses	NoC	34	–	379	86
exchange	NoC	18	–	822	89	balance	NoC	38	–	319	86
league	NoC	35	–	408	89	achieved	Verb	24	–	590	86
officers	NoC	87	–	0	89	avoid	Verb	30	–	453	85
senior	Adj	28	–	534	89	collection	NoC	18	–	753	85
February	NoP	41	–	299	89	interested	Adj	110	+	62	85
extra	Adj	117	+	77	89	marriage	NoC	21	–	660	85
beautiful	Adj	70	–	41	89	relatively	Adv	27	–	514	85
players	NoC	22	–	696	89	no one*	Pron	45	–	219	85
obviously	Adv	296	+	2620	89	August	NoP	30	–	446	85
14	Num	1	–	1597	89	commercial	Adj	24	–	596	85
answer	NoC	119	+	87	89	Smith	NoP	26	–	549	85
9	Num	2	–	1550	89	turn	NoC	52	–	141	85
presence	NoC	11	–	1074	89	win	Verb	69	–	30	85
discussion	NoC	57	–	124	89	relevant	Adj	33	–	398	85
radio	NoC	78	–	12	89	form	Verb	25	–	562	85
pupils	NoC	20	–	741	88	Oxford	NoP	92	+	6	85

Word	PoS	FrS		LL	FrW	Word	PoS	FrS		LL	FrW
differences	NoC	20	–	676	85	politics	NoC	21	–	593	81
English	NoC	50	–	157	85	explain	Verb	67	–	23	81
failure	NoC	17	–	771	85	drawn	Verb	28	–	450	81
smiled	Verb	3	–	1383	84	function	NoC	51	–	123	81
return	Verb	18	–	751	84	instead	Adv	22	–	570	81
13	Num	1	–	1516	84	image	NoC	24	–	538	81
speaker	NoC	37	–	313	84	love	Verb	132	+	249	81
survey	NoC	32	–	398	84	separate	Adj	43	–	204	80
deep	Adj	35	–	345	84	largely	Adv	13	–	841	80
Africa	NoP	26	–	539	84	forced	Verb	23	–	560	80
born	Verb	60	–	74	84	reports	NoC	48	–	142	80
transport	NoC	61	–	63	84	alone	Adv	15	–	771	80
career	NoC	16	–	793	84	memory	NoC	38	–	266	80
aid	NoC	30	–	432	84	stock	NoC	39	–	247	80
official	Adj	15	–	834	84	chief	Adj	33	–	346	80
due to	Prep	25	–	547	84	regular	Adj	34	–	319	80
machine	NoC	87	+	1	84	associated	Verb	17	–	696	80
closed	Verb	34	–	364	84	key	Adj	40	–	229	80
accepted	Verb	37	–	320	84	knows	Verb	122	+	174	80
speech	NoC	31	–	422	84	bit*	NoC	635	+	12403	80
trouble	NoC	138	+	265	84	begin	Verb	33	–	327	80
matters	NoC	47	–	184	84	happen	Verb	156	+	515	80
cells	NoC	13	–	890	84	decisions	NoC	37	–	270	80
subjects	NoC	19	–	693	84	affairs	NoC	13	–	816	80
stone	NoC	44	–	217	84	facilities	NoC	37	–	273	80
Robert	NoP	41	–	247	84	plant	NoC	28	–	417	80
review	NoC	39	–	283	83	edge	NoC	32	–	345	80
studio	NoC	11	–	969	83	opinion	NoC	41	–	216	79
kitchen	NoC	75	–	8	83	add	Verb	108	+	83	79
apply	Verb	46	–	188	83	horse	NoC	61	–	41	79
executive	NoC	31	–	404	83	normally	Adv	112	+	109	79
text	NoC	21	–	642	83	race	NoC	31	–	362	79
huge	Adj	45	–	201	83	increased	Verb	23	–	533	79
attack	NoC	27	–	492	83	early	Adv	52	–	98	79
practical	Adj	27	–	494	83	leaders	NoC	15	–	748	79
appears	Verb	22	–	611	83	receive	Verb	38	–	249	79
box	NoC	129	+	201	83	benefit	NoC	70	–	9	79
later	Adj	33	–	362	83	living	Verb	74	–	3	79
effort	NoC	35	–	330	83	front	NoC	95	+	29	79
visit	NoC	18	–	723	83	impact	NoC	37	–	259	79
lives	NoC	41	–	251	83	bought	Verb	194	+	1068	79
learn	Verb	85	+	0	83	powerful	Adj	15	–	734	79
states	NoC	20	–	666	83	gold	NoC	35	–	286	79
merely	Adv	18	–	715	83	active	Adj	24	–	494	78
student	NoC	25	–	526	82	apparently	Adv	73	–	4	78
lived	Verb	81	–	0	82	ended	Verb	23	–	522	78
larger	Adj	24	–	552	82	due	Adj	45	–	154	78
remains	Verb	13	–	860	82	fair	Adj	133	+	282	78
voice	Verb	1	–	1482	82	budget	NoC	110	+	104	78
progress	NoC	25	–	528	82	complex	Adj	19	–	624	78
queen	NoC	34	–	342	82	anyway	Adv	503	+	8512	78
1985	Num	1	–	1530	82	cause	NoC	22	–	547	78
reference	NoC	39	–	272	82	managed	Verb	46	–	146	78
maybe	Adv	301	+	2996	82	advantage	NoC	33	–	309	78
values	NoC	15	–	786	82	views	NoC	43	–	177	78
becomes	Verb	36	–	302	82	aspects	NoC	29	–	379	78
covered	Verb	53	–	107	82	plants	NoC	21	–	555	78
thinking	Verb	179	+	771	82	sorry	Adj	431	+	6473	78
letters	NoC	59	–	66	81	nevertheless	Adv	26	–	445	78
regional	Adj	50	–	131	81	network	NoC	27	–	416	78
expression	NoC	17	–	729	81	trust	NoC	39	–	225	78
firms	NoC	23	–	564	81	bar	NoC	71	–	4	78
helped	Verb	34	–	333	81	inside	Prep	47	–	131	77
Henry	NoP	14	–	819	81	names	NoC	68	–	11	77
boys	NoC	78	–	1	81	additional	Adj	41	–	200	77
understanding	NoC	29	–	413	81	railway	NoC	32	–	320	77

Word	PoS	FrS		LL	FrW	Word	PoS	FrS		LL	FrW
rise	NoC	22	–	523	77	domestic	Adj	21	–	507	74
strength	NoC	22	–	528	77	standing	Verb	63	–	16	74
100	Num	2	–	1338	77	winter	NoC	40	–	186	74
sitting	Verb	117	+	163	77	museum	NoC	12	–	775	74
scale	NoC	50	–	99	77	treated	Verb	21	–	514	74
pain	NoC	39	–	217	77	legislation	NoC	32	–	292	74
enough	DetP	125	+	230	77	previously	Adv	21	–	506	74
regarded	Verb	13	–	799	77	ministers	NoC	16	–	637	74
joined	Verb	31	–	335	77	holiday	NoC	97	+	60	74
benefits	NoC	46	–	134	77	as to	Prep	64	–	14	74
afternoon	NoC	148	+	473	77	wait	Verb	166	+	755	74
formed	Verb	15	–	704	77	send	Verb	137	+	386	74
holding	Verb	31	–	328	77	materials	NoC	16	–	641	74
smaller	Adj	42	–	175	77	no	NoC	0	–	1452	74
becoming	Verb	24	–	463	77	gas	NoC	66	–	8	74
standard	Adj	32	–	308	76	solution	NoC	24	–	440	74
carefully	Adv	32	–	321	76	supply	NoC	33	–	265	74
tomorrow	Adv	234	+	1831	76	suggests	Verb	12	–	781	74
Christmas	NoC	194	+	1125	76	prevent	Verb	17	–	621	74
records	NoC	26	–	435	76	scene	NoC	20	–	518	74
chair	NoC	88	+	17	76	Mary	NoP	51	–	71	73
sister	NoC	61	–	29	76	corner	NoC	85	+	16	73
damage	NoC	28	–	388	76	pulled	Verb	37	–	205	73
wants	Verb	197	+	1185	76	includes	Verb	18	–	576	73
impossible	Adj	24	–	477	76	skin	NoC	33	–	272	73
examples	NoC	25	–	440	76	Thomas	NoP	20	–	515	73
increase	Verb	44	–	149	76	middle	Adj	38	–	188	73
tea	NoC	172	+	801	76	difficulties	NoC	29	–	333	73
intended	Verb	15	–	710	76	providing	Verb	35	–	232	73
step	NoC	39	–	209	76	internal	Adj	17	–	587	73
explained	Verb	25	–	451	76	reach	Verb	28	–	343	73
for instance	Adv	54	–	68	76	powers	NoC	21	–	489	73
length	NoC	36	–	244	76	message	NoC	41	–	158	73
join	Verb	59	–	36	76	sources	NoC	12	–	752	73
crime	NoC	35	–	265	76	TV	NoC	1	–	1291	73
Saturday	NoP	147	+	471	76	justice	NoC	20	–	519	73
open	Verb	81	+	3	76	spoke	Verb	43	–	129	73
reduce	Verb	30	–	334	76	increasingly	Adv	14	–	695	73
hard	Adv	33	–	287	76	speed	NoC	47	–	98	73
credit	NoC	29	–	360	76	fall	Verb	48	–	85	73
currently	Adv	27	–	390	75	fresh	Adj	30	–	303	72
earlier	Adj	27	–	403	75	match	NoC	36	–	210	72
possibility	NoC	36	–	245	75	24	Num	2	–	1253	72
proved	Verb	14	–	723	75	move	NoC	28	–	342	72
sexual	Adj	17	–	641	75	entirely	Adv	40	–	158	72
Edward	NoP	16	–	647	75	ball	NoC	91	+	41	72
bodies	NoC	22	–	495	75	technical	Adj	33	–	257	72
50	Num	1	–	1328	75	existence	NoC	12	–	754	72
a bit	Adv	496	+	8543	75	sit	Verb	209	+	1518	72
forest	NoC	30	–	332	75	meaning	NoC	12	–	740	72
dog	NoC	128	+	282	75	article	NoC	29	–	311	72
up	Prep	151	+	539	75	customers	NoC	29	–	312	72
EC	NoP	0	–	1468	75	cultural	Adj	8	–	900	72
clothes	NoC	58	–	37	75	animal	NoC	26	–	374	72
confidence	NoC	29	–	352	75	band	NoC	27	–	346	72
feeling	NoC	54	–	62	75	South	NoP-	22	–	467	72
expressed	Verb	18	–	605	75	administration	NoC	18	–	555	72
wind	NoC	41	–	168	75	foot	NoC	84	+	18	72
discussed	Verb	29	–	345	75	assessment	NoC	27	–	358	72
patient	NoC	17	–	636	75	farm	NoC	39	–	165	72
cars	NoC	78	+	1	75	sell	Verb	117	+	219	72
agree	Verb	144	+	455	75	Japan	NoP	10	–	822	72
units	NoC	36	–	231	74	buildings	NoC	22	–	451	72
require	Verb	21	–	522	74	island	NoC	18	–	543	72
mainly	Adv	38	–	202	74	applied	Verb	20	–	493	72
nice	Adj	603	+	11893	74	steps	NoC	26	–	359	72

Word	PoS	FrS		LL	FrW	Word	PoS	FrS		LL	FrW
banks	NoC	18	–	547	72	joint	Adj	33	–	205	68
institutions	NoC	11	–	760	71	proportion	NoC	23	–	374	68
introduction	NoC	22	–	453	71	distribution	NoC	19	–	467	68
sight	NoC	21	–	460	71	contrast	NoC	7	–	868	68
insurance	NoC	65	–	5	71	doubt	NoC	35	–	183	68
potential	Adj	21	–	482	71	unemployment	NoC	34	–	197	68
debate	NoC	56	–	32	71	play	NoC	62	–	4	68
watched	Verb	31	–	274	71	initial	Adj	16	–	554	68
possibly	Adv	88	+	34	71	half	NoC	113	+	228	67
argued	Verb	11	–	745	71	twenty	Num	925	+	23929	67
achieve	Verb	39	–	160	71	very	Adj	49	–	53	67
users	NoC	17	–	559	71	officials	NoC	13	–	646	67
in particular	Adv	31	–	269	71	spirit	NoC	43	–	97	67
items	NoC	37	–	190	71	path	NoC	22	–	399	67
measures	NoC	16	–	585	71	thank	Verb	595	+	12397	67
cabinet	NoC	18	–	534	71	conservative*	Adj	36	–	169	67
extremely	Adv	47	–	88	71	enjoy	Verb	55	–	21	67
religious	Adj	22	–	447	71	Paris	NoP	8	–	793	67
proposals	NoC	48	–	78	71	leading	Adj	13	–	614	67
equally	Adv	22	–	431	71	legs	NoC	51	–	36	67
face	Verb	37	–	184	71	as well	Adv	516	+	9892	67
pounds	NoC	572	+	11301	71	determined	Verb	10	–	737	67
spend	Verb	103	+	119	71	substantial	Adj	23	–	375	67
reduced	Verb	25	–	377	71	factor	NoC	26	–	303	67
17	Num	1	–	1263	70	noted	Verb	10	–	730	67
choose	Verb	50	–	62	70	decide	Verb	69	+	0	67
claim	NoC	28	–	322	70	applications	NoC	27	–	281	67
latest	Adj	23	–	410	70	putting	Verb	153	+	734	67
finished	Verb	155	+	680	70	rural	Adj	29	–	263	66
smile	NoC	6	–	957	70	aircraft	NoC	23	–	357	66
quarter	NoC	112	+	192	70	strange	Adj	42	–	94	66
famous	Adj	25	–	375	70	Christian	Adj	24	–	337	66
district	NoC	118	+	242	70	accident	NoC	45	–	73	66
reality	NoC	23	–	406	70	difficulty	NoC	37	–	148	66
northern	Adj	30	–	282	70	minute	NoC	219	+	1907	66
united	Adj	55	–	33	70	funds	NoC	29	–	256	66
ordinary	Adj	52	–	46	70	immediate	Adj	16	–	534	66
instead of	Prep	87	+	37	70	shape	NoC	28	–	276	66
distance	NoC	37	–	173	70	grounds	NoC	19	–	457	66
beginning	NoC	74	+	2	70	manner	NoC	13	–	607	66
relief	NoC	37	–	170	70	apart from	Prep	60	–	4	66
fear	NoC	19	–	495	70	in front of	Prep	62	–	2	66
rich	Adj	44	–	100	70	appointed	Verb	14	–	572	66
front	Adj	63	–	6	70	organization	NoC	41	–	101	66
formal	Adj	21	–	454	69	identified	Verb	25	–	324	66
safe	Adj	40	–	143	69	user	NoC	11	–	685	66
obtained	Verb	7	–	909	69	train	NoC	56	–	15	66
unable	Adj	15	–	612	69	watching	Verb	62	–	1	66
refused	Verb	12	–	700	69	operations	NoC	15	–	554	66
build	Verb	61	–	9	69	Mark	NoP	70	+	2	66
trial	NoC	26	–	342	69	wine	NoC	39	–	118	66
discovered	Verb	19	–	500	69	football	NoC	79	+	23	66
served	Verb	19	–	492	69	light	Adj	31	–	216	66
concept	NoC	22	–	428	69	communication	NoC	22	–	382	66
elements	NoC	21	–	435	69	soft	Adj	26	–	296	66
construction	NoC	13	–	673	69	sides	NoC	44	–	72	65
programmes	NoC	28	–	301	69	freedom	NoC	18	–	476	65
limited	Adj	22	–	411	69	rose	Verb	4	–	975	65
prison	NoC	24	–	372	69	master	NoC	29	–	242	65
target	NoC	28	–	303	69	tree	NoC	49	–	39	65
battle	NoC	17	–	544	69	fig.	NoC	0	–	1282	65
rock	NoC	21	–	432	69	save	Verb	83	+	40	65
usual	Adj	22	–	422	69	seat	NoC	36	–	150	65
accounts	NoC	30	–	256	69	relationships	NoC	13	–	598	65
excellent	Adj	55	–	28	69	talks	NoC	17	–	477	65
telephone	NoC	55	–	27	68	entered	Verb	10	–	702	65

2.3

Word	PoS	FrS		LL	FrW	Word	PoS	FrS		LL	FrW
selection	NoC	19	–	428	65	patterns	NoC	18	–	430	63
suitable	Adj	24	–	318	65	quiet	Adj	52	–	18	63
mentioned	Verb	111	+	240	65	recognition	NoC	14	–	534	63
papers	NoC	53	–	22	65	act	Verb	24	–	310	63
exercise	NoC	43	–	81	65	1981	Num	1	–	1159	63
female	Adj	16	–	519	65	40	Num	2	–	1087	63
games	NoC	40	–	109	65	plus	Prep	128	+	469	63
deal	Verb	80	+	30	65	output	NoC	17	–	447	63
walls	NoC	19	–	436	65	beside	Prep	15	–	506	63
average	Adj	32	–	191	65	picked	Verb	66	+	1	63
democratic	Adj	13	–	609	65	equal	Adj	43	–	62	63
techniques	NoC	11	–	646	65	detail	NoC	45	–	53	63
improve	Verb	38	–	120	65	employees	NoC	21	–	359	63
referred	Verb	39	–	111	65	purposes	NoC	21	–	355	63
detailed	Adj	24	–	332	65	writing	Verb	63	+	0	63
1984	Num	2	–	1101	65	21	Num	1	–	1128	63
warm	Adj	54	–	18	65	though	Adv	410	+	7013	63
cover	Verb	56	–	11	65	capacity	NoC	24	–	294	63
housing	NoC	77	+	22	65	twice	Adv	62	–	0	63
star	NoC	29	–	238	65	laid	Verb	27	–	236	62
courts	NoC	14	–	559	65	mental	Adj	19	–	397	62
scientific	Adj	13	–	591	65	pointed	Verb	15	–	503	62
eat	Verb	170	+	1053	65	attitude	NoC	40	–	88	62
strategy	NoC	38	–	123	64	replaced	Verb	11	–	638	62
background	NoC	39	–	111	64	replied	Verb	5	–	885	62
growing	Adj	16	–	493	64	tour	NoC	13	–	546	62
ahead	Adv	48	–	45	64	principles	NoC	12	–	599	62
overall	Adj	24	–	327	64	managers	NoC	25	–	282	62
Edinburgh	NoP	20	–	393	64	sign	NoC	29	–	217	62
offer	NoC	23	–	343	64	profits	NoC	20	–	369	62
markets	NoC	11	–	667	64	whereas	Conj	64	+	0	62
prince	NoC	13	–	589	64	reasonable	Adj	56	–	5	62
along	Adv	118	+	325	64	silence	NoC	8	–	733	62
lose	Verb	70	+	5	64	fourth	Ord	51	–	17	62
worse	Adj	71	+	5	64	increased	Adj	15	–	492	62
rain	NoC	42	–	85	64	homes	NoC	49	–	25	62
eastern	Adj	16	–	494	64	critical	Adj	21	–	344	62
classes	NoC	30	–	216	64	Darlington	NoP	2	–	1032	62
Inc	Adj	0	–	1257	64	prove	Verb	20	–	364	62
requirements	NoC	28	–	241	64	pp.	NoC	0	–	1211	62
contact	NoC	44	–	66	64	admitted	Verb	11	–	602	62
removed	Verb	16	–	501	64	widely	Adv	8	–	722	62
video	NoC	73	+	12	64	arrangements	NoC	25	–	274	62
showing	Verb	52	–	23	64	keeping	Verb	50	–	23	62
coffee	NoC	90	+	90	64	opportunities	NoC	28	–	219	62
proper	Adj	75	+	16	64	fields	NoC	24	–	281	62
all right*	Adv	70	+	5	64	fairly	Adv	114	+	323	62
crisis	NoC	19	–	420	64	even though	Conj	38	–	99	61
danger	NoC	30	–	216	64	theatre	NoC	37	–	108	61
raise	Verb	40	–	95	64	will	NoC	29	–	206	61
surely	Adv	62	–	0	64	seeing	Verb	61	–	0	61
1983	Num	1	–	1107	64	cause	Verb	29	–	201	61
actual	Adj	112	+	271	63	signed	Verb	23	–	300	61
Irish	Adj	20	–	399	63	victory	NoC	12	–	574	61
sufficient	Adj	23	–	326	63	goal	NoC	43	–	59	61
frequently	Adv	11	–	647	63	understood	Verb	23	–	303	61
far	Adj	111	+	263	63	traffic	NoC	114	+	325	61
educational	Adj	18	–	443	63	whilst	Conj	33	–	143	61
elections	NoC	26	–	267	63	threat	NoC	17	–	435	61
charges	NoC	27	–	251	63	familiar	Adj	21	–	339	61
absence	NoC	10	–	672	63	issued	Verb	15	–	467	61
gets	Verb	204	+	1718	63	unlikely	Adj	17	–	416	61
largest	Adj	11	–	624	63	package	NoC	21	–	336	61
agency	NoC	25	–	292	63	pair	NoC	54	–	7	61
working	Adj	34	–	149	63	partly	Adv	24	–	273	61
1993	Num	1	–	1154	63	efforts	NoC	13	–	535	61

2.3

Word	PoS	FrS		LL	FrW	Word	PoS	FrS		LL	FrW
turning	Verb	34	–	137	61	processes	NoC	12	–	534	58
occur	Verb	17	–	433	61	below	Prep	26	–	212	58
fingers	NoC	34	–	132	61	correct	Adj	64	+	4	58
recorded	Verb	29	–	195	61	draw	Verb	76	+	44	58
tend	Verb	75	+	29	61	shook	Verb	3	–	913	58
note	NoC	52	–	11	61	debt	NoC	17	–	385	58
dangerous	Adj	36	–	114	61	apparent	Adj	7	–	706	58
works	Verb	82	+	65	61	somewhere	Adv	173	+	1294	58
1979	Num	1	–	1096	61	audience	NoC	24	–	249	58
bridge	NoC	36	–	110	61	neither	Adv	17	–	384	58
historical	Adj	13	–	532	60	carrying	Verb	33	–	119	58
elsewhere	Adv	25	–	247	60	rooms	NoC	30	–	162	58
related	Verb	26	–	233	60	murder	NoC	13	–	495	58
v.	Prep	0	–	1185	60	onto	Prep	95	+	177	58
while	NoC	85	+	78	60	maintain	Verb	21	–	307	58
player	NoC	25	–	257	60	upper	Adj	14	–	461	58
procedure	NoC	38	–	88	60	standard	NoC	32	–	132	58
client	NoC	66	+	4	60	captain	NoC	14	–	474	58
feeling	Verb	38	–	87	60	sought	Verb	9	–	634	58
teaching	NoC	27	–	224	60	exist	Verb	23	–	269	58
birds	NoC	26	–	231	60	southern	Adj	29	–	169	58
sentence	NoC	37	–	98	60	models	NoC	7	–	697	58
discipline	NoC	11	–	604	60	affected	Verb	19	–	331	58
track	NoC	31	–	165	60	Corp	NoC	1	–	1065	58
supported	Verb	23	–	293	60	phone	NoC	144	+	805	58
call	NoC	61	+	0	60	element	NoC	38	–	77	58
either	DetP	39	–	78	60	revealed	Verb	7	–	692	58
commitment	NoC	29	–	193	60	seek	Verb	23	–	261	58
conflict	NoC	19	–	358	60	remembered	Verb	18	–	370	58
closely	Adv	16	–	443	60	sites	NoC	57	–	0	58
weekend	NoC	92	+	135	60	break	Verb	59	+	0	58
afraid	Adj	59	–	0	60	1980	Num	1	–	1071	58
violence	NoC	25	–	253	60	represented	Verb	16	–	416	58
appearance	NoC	8	–	669	60	Liverpool	NoP	31	–	137	58
finance	NoC	19	–	361	60	discuss	Verb	41	–	50	58
increasing	Adj	16	–	425	60	file	NoC	44	–	35	58
completed	Verb	16	–	433	59	profit	NoC	37	–	83	58
22	Num	1	–	1058	59	curriculum	NoC	13	–	487	58
occurred	Verb	16	–	427	59	payment	NoC	22	–	269	58
dropped	Verb	40	–	70	59	volume	NoC	19	–	346	58
cell	NoC	19	–	360	59	under	Adv	38	–	69	58
perfect	Adj	29	–	180	59	bright	Adj	25	–	227	58
daily	Adj	19	–	351	59	youth	NoC	24	–	231	58
19	Num	0	–	1127	59	institute	NoC	11	–	544	58
emphasis	NoC	14	–	476	59	requires	Verb	11	–	563	58
dinner	NoC	95	+	168	59	1982	Num	1	–	1029	57
defined	Verb	14	–	471	59	lead*	NoC	31	–	138	57
hope	NoC	24	–	262	59	urban	Adj	26	–	207	57
walk	Verb	122	+	461	59	alone	Adj	29	–	168	57
reaction	NoC	26	–	218	59	expensive	Adj	69	+	21	57
hill	NoC	43	–	41	59	liberal*	Adj	25	–	222	57
individual	NoC	21	–	311	59	assembly	NoC	25	–	216	57
projects	NoC	25	–	233	59	watch	Verb	148	+	879	57
expenditure	NoC	24	–	259	59	Russian	Adj	10	–	571	57
Jack	NoP	38	–	76	59	feelings	NoC	20	–	310	57
notes	NoC	44	–	36	59	nodded	Verb	1	–	1008	57
neck	NoC	32	–	142	59	claims	NoC	13	–	479	57
seriously	Adv	42	–	47	59	establish	Verb	14	–	438	57
learning	NoC	18	–	373	59	asking	Verb	111	+	355	57
exhibition	NoC	14	–	473	59	object	NoC	15	–	424	57
suffered	Verb	13	–	489	59	weather	NoC	58	+	0	57
spring	NoC	22	–	287	59	option	NoC	31	–	134	57
D / d	Lett	183	+	1469	59	imagine	Verb	93	+	174	57
route	NoC	38	–	79	59	consideration	NoC	33	–	108	57
notice	NoC	39	–	70	59	heat	NoC	26	–	195	57
feature	NoC	16	–	427	59	reform	NoC	29	–	159	57

2.3

Word	PoS	FrS		LL	FrW	Word	PoS	FrS		LL	FrW
liked	Verb	52	–	4	57	treaty	NoC	8	–	616	55
finding	Verb	34	–	97	57	forget	Verb	117	+	471	55
literature	NoC	11	–	535	57	professor	NoC	23	–	229	55
thousands	NoC	37	–	75	57	filled	Verb	27	–	170	55
tiny	Adj	37	–	77	57	attractive	Adj	21	–	272	55
moral	Adj	15	–	424	57	demands	NoC	11	–	499	55
Tom	NoP	42	–	40	57	search	NoC	12	–	475	55
serve	Verb	24	–	231	57	procedures	NoC	35	–	77	55
ltd	Adj	0	–	1084	57	breath	NoC	14	–	409	55
arts	NoC	24	–	220	57	Italy	NoP	16	–	379	55
challenge	NoC	17	–	366	57	vital	Adj	17	–	354	55
empty	Adj	32	–	114	56	double	Adj	72	+	44	55
31	Num	1	–	977	56	die	Verb	41	–	34	55
pass	Verb	69	+	24	56	past	Prep	168	+	1315	55
flowers	NoC	31	–	129	56	functions	NoC	21	–	269	55
facts	NoC	21	–	276	56	orders	NoC	30	–	125	55
contribution	NoC	29	–	151	56	prepared	Verb	26	–	177	55
drugs	NoC	29	–	152	56	married	Adj	48	–	8	55
necessarily	Adv	61	+	3	56	end	Verb	61	+	6	55
investigation	NoC	10	–	551	56	properly	Adv	73	+	49	55
leading	Verb	15	–	412	56	description	NoC	20	–	271	55
beginning	Verb	25	–	208	56	alternative	Adj	17	–	346	55
Japanese	Adj	8	–	644	56	membership	NoC	36	–	69	55
flight	NoC	12	–	480	56	Ian	NoP	42	–	32	55
middle	NoC	86	+	126	56	released	Verb	14	–	422	55
as though	Conj	35	–	88	56	North	NoP-	45	–	16	55
III / iii	Num	0	–	1074	56	thin	Adj	22	–	237	54
driver	NoC	34	–	92	56	protect	Verb	25	–	183	54
tonight	Adv	178	+	1466	56	owner	NoC	12	–	477	54
thousand	NoC	516	+	10998	56	aim	NoC	14	–	408	54
belief	NoC	11	–	531	56	e.g.	Adv	0	–	1050	54
occasion	NoC	25	–	207	56	cost	Verb	84	+	128	54
grow	Verb	44	–	25	56	branch	NoC	43	–	24	54
birth	NoC	19	–	319	56	faith	NoC	38	–	48	54
estate	NoC	40	–	49	56	broke	Verb	32	–	96	54
totally	Adv	78	+	73	56	engineering	NoC	23	–	219	54
pieces	NoC	54	–	0	56	conclusion	NoC	23	–	210	54
centres	NoC	18	–	330	56	waste	NoC	42	–	28	54
USA	NoP	0	–	1069	56	institution	NoC	8	–	582	54
entry	NoC	15	–	401	56	quick	Adj	91	+	193	54
dry	Adj	41	–	41	56	conversation	NoC	61	+	8	54
pleasure	NoC	22	–	252	56	encourage	Verb	29	–	136	54
pictures	NoC	40	–	43	56	external	Adj	11	–	486	54
wild	Adj	15	–	392	56	realised	Verb	8	–	580	54
enter	Verb	28	–	160	56	organisations	NoC	23	–	216	54
hoped	Verb	10	–	561	56	pushed	Verb	23	–	220	54
fund	NoC	52	–	2	56	congress	NoC	62	+	11	54
code	NoC	20	–	282	56	colleagues	NoC	72	+	49	54
tradition	NoC	13	–	451	56	ministry	NoC	15	–	374	54
developments	NoC	13	–	441	56	opening	NoC	21	–	242	54
writing	NoC	32	–	106	56	drug	NoC	20	–	268	54
28	Num	0	–	1033	55	leg	NoC	50	–	3	54
subject to	Prep	15	–	394	55	younger	Adj	43	–	20	54
greatest	Adj	16	–	375	55	visit	Verb	24	–	203	54
crown	NoC	17	–	361	55	gentleman	NoC	34	–	75	54
control	Verb	28	–	162	55	ought	VMod	123	+	592	54
etc	Adv	7	–	652	55	meetings	NoC	53	–	0	54
heads	NoC	24	–	211	55	tests	NoC	20	–	262	53
lips	NoC	6	–	696	55	dealing	Verb	50	–	1	53
second	NoC	62	+	7	55	prepared	Adj	45	–	11	53
ancient	Adj	8	–	634	55	noticed	Verb	49	–	3	53
desire	NoC	10	–	540	55	laughed	Verb	9	–	537	53
transfer	NoC	12	–	475	55	IBM	NoP	0	–	1045	53
share	Verb	39	–	50	55	contained	Verb	10	–	506	53
straight	Adv	95	+	214	55	Martin	NoP	50	–	2	53
adopted	Verb	16	–	371	55	Australia	NoP	19	–	270	53

Word	PoS	FrS		LL	FrW	Word	PoS	FrS		LL	FrW
boat	NoC	61	+	9	53	his*	Pron	29	–	108	51
farmers	NoC	26	–	159	53	wearing	Verb	37	–	41	51
newspaper	NoC	25	–	180	53	academic	Adj	8	–	559	51
23	Num	1	–	961	53	employed	Verb	25	–	152	51
planning	Verb	27	–	150	53	India	NoP	13	–	401	51
along with	Prep	31	–	105	53	attempts	NoC	6	–	615	51
capable	Adj	19	–	287	53	surprise	NoC	17	–	295	51
beneath	Prep	3	–	785	53	enable	Verb	20	–	234	51
partner	NoC	18	–	298	53	release	NoC	23	–	188	51
card	NoC	95	+	241	53	acid	NoC	33	–	71	51
speaking	Verb	68	+	36	53	laws	NoC	24	–	171	51
chosen	Verb	16	–	335	53	observed	Verb	4	–	708	51
sky	NoC	24	–	192	53	shops	NoC	65	+	33	51
generation	NoC	17	–	307	53	clients	NoC	29	–	105	51
identify	Verb	27	–	148	53	significance	NoC	9	–	492	51
nobody	Pron	144	+	944	53	inside	Adv	38	–	34	51
Alan	NoP	47	–	5	53	definition	NoC	25	–	148	51
schemes	NoC	33	–	82	53	governments	NoC	17	–	298	51
actions	NoC	10	–	493	53	guide	NoC	15	–	339	51
telling	Verb	108	+	401	53	copy	NoC	49	–	0	51
meanwhile	Adv	8	–	558	53	highest	Adj	18	–	268	51
narrow	Adj	16	–	326	53	care	Verb	55	+	3	51
ordered	Verb	16	–	330	53	journey	NoC	23	–	186	51
troops	NoC	11	–	463	53	signs	NoC	19	–	242	51
confirmed	Verb	10	–	516	53	careful	Adj	65	+	34	51
hence	Adv	6	–	643	53	S / s	Lett	267	+	3846	51
total	NoC	35	–	64	53	dad	NoC	268	+	3870	51
shot	Verb	21	–	226	53	Jones	NoP	9	–	507	51
effectively	Adv	34	–	70	52	constant	Adj	21	–	214	51
welfare	NoC	12	–	439	52	vast	Adj	18	–	270	51
streets	NoC	23	–	200	52	intention	NoC	19	–	245	51
marketing	NoC	23	–	195	52	screen	NoC	23	–	181	51
broad	Adj	19	–	275	52	grey	Adj	23	–	173	50
leadership	NoC	11	–	466	52	row	NoC	29	–	107	50
wood	NoC	45	–	9	52	thanks	NoC	162	+	1361	50
attitudes	NoC	11	–	469	52	offers	Verb	6	–	594	50
elderly	Adj	27	–	141	52	i.e.	Adv	5	–	652	50
Manchester	NoP	31	–	98	52	wondered	Verb	32	–	77	50
wider	Adj	20	–	245	52	goals	NoC	20	–	219	50
entire	Adj	14	–	378	52	rare	Adj	13	–	368	50
examination	NoC	12	–	425	52	phase	NoC	11	–	437	50
Stephen	NoP	18	–	291	52	drew	Verb	10	–	457	50
outside	Adv	64	+	23	52	contains	Verb	8	–	518	50
atmosphere	NoC	18	–	293	52	technique	NoC	11	–	445	50
check	Verb	75	+	83	52	reduction	NoC	31	–	78	50
stated	Verb	11	–	467	52	brief	Adj	24	–	158	50
X / x	Lett	124	+	639	52	granted	Verb	12	–	416	50
enjoyed	Verb	42	–	20	52	encouraged	Verb	14	–	359	50
lunch	NoC	70	+	55	52	Leeds	NoP	33	–	64	50
visitors	NoC	17	–	312	52	key	NoC	38	–	29	50
typical	Adj	22	–	215	52	brain	NoC	26	–	136	50
criticism	NoC	12	–	422	52	obtain	Verb	9	–	501	50
address	NoC	43	–	14	52	Jesus	NoP	100	+	351	50
castle	NoC	10	–	495	52	injury	NoC	13	–	366	50
answer	Verb	60	+	10	52	machines	NoC	28	–	107	50
creation	NoC	11	–	453	52	thoughts	NoC	20	–	225	50
explanation	NoC	13	–	400	51	somewhat	Adv	17	–	276	50
readers	NoC	7	–	574	51	measure	NoC	19	–	244	50
stared	Verb	1	–	876	51	claim	Verb	26	–	130	50
billion	NoC	13	–	390	51	bottom	NoC	117	+	589	50
engine	NoC	38	–	35	51	coal	NoC	60	+	17	50
East	NoP-	18	–	287	51	ideal	Adj	23	–	175	50
respect	NoC	31	–	89	51	reading	Verb	47	–	1	50
mind	Verb	246	+	3245	51	reading	NoC	29	–	99	50
slow	Adj	23	–	181	51	severe	Adj	14	–	335	50
document	NoC	47	–	3	51	Harry	NoP	13	–	359	50

Word	PoS	FrS		LL	FrW	Word	PoS	FrS		LL	FrW
sections	NoC	17	–	273	50	tall	Adj	22	–	166	48
listen	Verb	125	+	709	50	lying	Verb	28	–	98	48
rather than	Conj	19	–	238	50	27	Num	0	–	910	48
magazine	NoC	23	–	176	50	judge	NoC	17	–	258	48
learned	Verb	12	–	407	50	structures	NoC	9	–	459	48
note	Verb	17	–	277	50	Spain	NoP	14	–	318	48
corporate	Adj	13	–	373	50	moreover	Adv	1	–	834	48
potential	NoC	16	–	289	50	busy	Adj	62	+	35	48
charged	Verb	20	–	214	50	represent	Verb	24	–	135	48
grew	Verb	12	–	398	50	movements	NoC	7	–	517	48
seats	NoC	22	–	187	50	fashion	NoC	19	–	211	48
index	NoC	9	–	486	49	bag	NoC	97	+	341	48
contain	Verb	8	–	522	49	cover	NoC	42	–	8	48
China	NoP	18	–	250	49	least	Adv	14	–	310	48
seeking	Verb	19	–	228	49	elected	Verb	19	–	224	48
similarly	Adv	7	–	561	49	Kingdom	NoP-	10	–	419	48
little	Adv	3	–	762	49	metal	NoC	32	–	57	48
rapidly	Adv	13	–	364	49	biggest	Adj	34	–	40	48
UN	NoP	1	–	904	49	proposed	Verb	20	–	204	48
affect	Verb	34	–	53	49	author	NoC	5	–	591	48
minor	Adj	24	–	149	49	flow	NoC	17	–	252	48
loved	Verb	21	–	204	49	Roman	Adj	9	–	463	48
in addition	Adv	5	–	644	49	republic	NoC	6	–	569	48
teeth	NoC	33	–	58	49	consequences	NoC	14	–	309	48
bus	NoC	94	+	292	49	unknown	Adj	5	–	592	48
via	Prep	8	–	521	49	married	Verb	45	–	1	48
stories	NoC	34	–	50	49	inflation	NoC	21	–	175	48
adult	NoC	14	–	329	49	trip	NoC	24	–	140	48
bringing	Verb	45	–	2	49	let's	Verb	401	+	8097	48
coast	NoC	21	–	191	49	BBC	NoP	0	–	889	48
shoulder	NoC	18	–	245	49	inner	Adj	20	–	190	48
happens	Verb	140	+	984	49	in relation to	Prep	36	–	30	48
kinds	NoC	27	–	109	49	subsequent	Adj	5	–	597	48
bound	Verb	28	–	97	49	pool	NoC	23	–	149	47
doors	NoC	41	–	13	49	worst	Adj	30	–	70	47
contemporary	Adj	4	–	671	49	factory	NoC	34	–	38	47
launched	Verb	8	–	514	49	sharp	Adj	16	–	275	47
knowing	Verb	34	–	48	49	meeting	Verb	36	–	27	47
practices	NoC	10	–	455	49	consumer	NoC	12	–	375	47
horses	NoC	49	+	0	49	African	Adj	8	–	486	47
Tony	NoP	58	+	15	49	valley	NoC	11	–	400	47
faced	Verb	16	–	286	49	depends	Verb	70	+	89	47
strongly	Adv	21	–	196	49	planned	Verb	16	–	269	47
objects	NoC	8	–	498	49	bear	Verb	32	–	49	47
clean	Adj	45	–	2	49	thick	Adj	37	–	22	47
grand	Adj	24	–	140	49	societies	NoC	13	–	340	47
revolution	NoC	28	–	102	49	unique	Adj	11	–	398	47
drive	NoC	33	–	54	49	cities	NoC	13	–	340	47
26	Num	1	–	867	49	declared	Verb	6	–	552	47
content	NoC	13	–	344	49	recognised	Verb	6	–	567	47
fundamental	Adj	15	–	307	49	flat	NoC	46	–	0	47
vote	NoC	45	–	2	49	amongst	Prep	31	–	63	47
independence	NoC	10	–	435	49	contracts	NoC	21	–	180	47
spread	Verb	23	–	157	49	run	NoC	44	–	1	47
customer	NoC	30	–	76	49	gallery	NoC	7	–	524	47
permanent	Adj	18	–	248	48	interpretation	NoC	11	–	388	47
that is	Adv	22	–	177	48	indicated	Verb	13	–	335	47
payments	NoC	13	–	339	48	sample	NoC	17	–	251	47
committed	Verb	24	–	147	48	sport	NoC	28	–	89	47
palace	NoC	11	–	412	48	nation	NoC	15	–	285	47
crucial	Adj	13	–	353	48	noise	NoC	41	–	6	47
implications	NoC	17	–	266	48	visited	Verb	8	–	494	47
combination	NoC	11	–	396	48	kill	Verb	34	–	35	47
mum	NoC	410	+	8323	48	Unix	NoP	2	–	760	47
at last	Adv	10	–	442	48	display	NoC	14	–	317	47
criminal	Adj	10	–	427	48	desk	NoC	29	–	72	47

Word	PoS	FrS		LL	FrW	Word	PoS	FrS		LL	FrW
iron	NoC	33	–	44	47	pages	NoC	34	–	27	45
assistance	NoC	13	–	323	47	badly	Adv	26	–	97	45
surprised	Adj	48	+	0	47	tone	NoC	11	–	367	45
assets	NoC	12	–	349	47	regions	NoC	15	–	267	45
Northern	NoP-	12	–	356	47	representatives	NoC	18	–	202	45
parliamentary	Adj	13	–	321	47	departments	NoC	17	–	227	45
setting	Verb	25	–	114	47	enterprise	NoC	15	–	264	45
religion	NoC	20	–	187	47	significantly	Adv	12	–	339	45
living	NoC	35	–	33	47	struck	Verb	14	–	293	45
general	NoC	7	–	514	47	beauty	NoC	17	–	218	45
pick	Verb	171	+	1690	47	lie	Verb	23	–	126	45
wonderful	Adj	66	+	66	47	offering	Verb	15	–	263	45
industries	NoC	13	–	321	47	stuff	NoC	274	+	4430	45
beat	Verb	32	–	48	47	walking	Verb	74	+	138	45
allowing	Verb	11	–	384	47	describe	Verb	25	–	104	45
named	Verb	16	–	259	47	assumed	Verb	10	–	389	45
begun	Verb	5	–	578	47	sports	NoC	29	–	60	45
P / p	Lett	359	+	6865	47	distinction	NoC	9	–	420	45
proceedings	NoC	7	–	512	47	grown	Verb	24	–	112	45
fast	Adv	20	–	178	47	provisions	NoC	10	–	387	45
ill	Adj	41	–	6	47	involvement	NoC	15	–	269	45
tears	NoC	7	–	516	47	Andrew	NoP	42	–	1	45
Bill	NoP	49	+	0	47	containing	Verb	4	–	616	45
secondary	Adj	16	–	250	47	massive	Adj	32	–	36	45
directors	NoC	16	–	260	47	pretty	Adv	108	+	559	45
J.	NoP	0	–	914	47	plenty	Pron	57	+	25	45
brown	Adj	31	–	58	47	reader	NoC	5	–	557	45
originally	Adv	31	–	58	47	easier	Adj	65	+	69	45
Anne	NoP	20	–	176	47	extensive	Adj	6	–	531	45
negative	Adj	36	–	23	46	Christ	NoP	65	+	74	45
hell	NoC	118	+	680	46	quietly	Adv	12	–	323	45
doctors	NoC	34	–	32	46	decline	NoC	7	–	496	45
Russia	NoP	16	–	265	46	long-term	Adj	8	–	448	45
somehow	Adv	31	–	51	46	Glasgow	NoP	17	–	210	45
agent	NoC	19	–	203	46	manufacturing	NoC	15	–	247	45
accommodation	NoC	22	–	149	46	other than	Prep	27	–	76	45
involving	Verb	10	–	411	46	broken	Verb	26	–	90	45
starting	Verb	57	+	21	46	supposed	Adj	133	+	1004	45
falling	Verb	26	–	102	46	improvement	NoC	17	–	209	45
crowd	NoC	15	–	264	46	cancer	NoC	19	–	186	45
unions	NoC	36	–	21	46	ship	NoC	28	–	68	45
sequence	NoC	8	–	458	46	involves	Verb	11	–	362	45
drink	NoC	70	+	98	46	Joe	NoP	31	–	41	45
documents	NoC	22	–	144	46	lights	NoC	57	+	28	45
shoulders	NoC	11	–	358	46	and so on	Adv	84	+	251	45
offices	NoC	23	–	137	46	argue	Verb	26	–	86	45
vision	NoC	11	–	376	46	29	Num	0	–	831	45
milk	NoC	63	+	53	46	regulations	NoC	21	–	141	45
temperature	NoC	25	–	111	46	communities	NoC	14	–	280	45
60	Num	1	–	799	46	involve	Verb	19	–	179	45
place	Verb	19	–	202	46	at first	Adv	14	–	269	45
afterwards	Adv	45	–	0	46	soil	NoC	10	–	385	45
session	NoC	30	–	62	46	pollution	NoC	13	–	309	45
perfectly	Adv	33	–	37	46	fall	NoC	11	–	346	45
rarely	Adv	9	–	431	46	remaining	Adj	7	–	473	45
colours	NoC	34	–	32	46	democracy	NoC	22	–	134	45
aspect	NoC	24	–	117	46	allows	Verb	13	–	288	45
unfortunately	Adv	53	+	11	46	artists	NoC	6	–	525	45
virtually	Adv	29	–	67	46	nations	NoC	15	–	249	44
hole	NoC	44	–	0	46	alive	Adj	26	–	90	44
naturally	Adv	17	–	227	46	interview	NoC	29	–	59	44
objectives	NoC	25	–	109	46	dogs	NoC	38	–	8	44
pleased	Adj	55	+	16	46	as soon as	Conj	51	+	9	44
angry	Adj	14	–	288	46	V / v	Lett	102	+	486	44
close	Adv	9	–	429	45	towns	NoC	13	–	302	44
appointment	NoC	38	–	11	45	breakfast	NoC	37	–	13	44

Word	PoS	FrS		LL	FrW		Word	PoS	FrS		LL	FrW
Friday	NoP	150	+	1357	44		lovely	Adj	231	+	3379	43
Brian	NoP	50	+	5	44		extended	Verb	10	–	354	43
invited	Verb	22	–	130	44		pay	NoC	59	+	50	43
thinking	NoC	28	–	64	44		conventional	Adj	6	–	470	43
heavily	Adv	10	–	362	44		positions	NoC	9	–	397	43
Graham	NoP	23	–	113	44		Major	NoP	25	–	87	43
indicate	Verb	17	–	215	44		program	NoC	8	–	405	43
contact	Verb	20	–	152	44		seconds	NoC	30	–	39	43
gently	Adv	8	–	441	44		constitution	NoC	12	–	298	43
E / e	Lett	263	+	4180	44		operate	Verb	18	–	184	43
shock	NoC	21	–	142	44		relative	Adj	9	–	382	43
principal	Adj	4	–	578	44		selling	Verb	47	+	3	43
employers	NoC	27	–	74	44		thirty	Num	520	+	12743	43
stayed	Verb	38	–	8	44		sudden	Adj	8	–	425	43
artist	NoC	10	–	379	44		border	NoC	13	–	272	43
nose	NoC	36	–	15	44		believes	Verb	11	–	326	43
stages	NoC	14	–	277	44		Steve	NoP	50	+	10	43
Co/CO	NoC	3	–	669	44		candidate	NoC	12	–	296	43
used	Adj	50	+	7	44		meal	NoC	42	–	0	43
guilty	Adj	27	–	69	44		victim	NoC	10	–	347	43
formation	NoC	4	–	602	44		liability	NoC	8	–	416	43
acting	Verb	17	–	207	44		arranged	Verb	14	–	250	43
absolutely	Adv	183	+	2104	44		ourselves	Pron	67	+	104	43
identity	NoC	6	–	508	44		Chinese	Adj	15	–	231	43
net	Adj	16	–	232	44		less than	Adv	15	–	234	43
unlike	Prep	6	–	519	44		Mike	NoP	43	+	0	43
firmly	Adv	7	–	481	44		revenue	NoC	25	–	82	43
impression	NoC	28	–	61	44		drive	Verb	57	+	42	43
vehicle	NoC	28	–	63	44		autumn	NoC	10	–	340	43
statements	NoC	20	–	161	44		lane	NoC	52	+	17	43
warned	Verb	7	–	458	44		framework	NoC	11	–	319	43
cross	NoC	36	–	14	44		concentration	NoC	10	–	335	42
communist	Adj	22	–	130	44		promised	Verb	14	–	256	42
motor	NoC	25	–	90	44		maintained	Verb	11	–	324	42
properties	NoC	18	–	191	44		Philip	NoP	15	–	229	42
lies	Verb	9	–	390	44		lake	NoC	10	–	339	42
candidates	NoC	9	–	387	44		Wilson	NoP	16	–	215	42
Monday	NoP	130	+	982	44		grass	NoC	33	–	20	42
spokesman	NoC	5	–	538	44		efficient	Adj	19	–	152	42
Italian	Adj	10	–	360	44		editor	NoC	10	–	341	42
in general	Adv	24	–	105	44		terrible	Adj	85	+	292	42
limited	Verb	9	–	394	44		1980s	Num	0	–	832	42
ref	NoC	1	–	740	44		determine	Verb	11	–	322	42
establishment	NoC	9	–	399	44		producing	Verb	19	–	147	42
touch	NoC	19	–	161	44		remove	Verb	14	–	244	42
fuel	NoC	20	–	155	44		household	NoC	14	–	244	42
passage	NoC	11	–	347	44		stars	NoC	14	–	250	42
Simon	NoP	36	–	12	44		fruit	NoC	32	–	27	42
dress	NoC	25	–	90	43		catch	Verb	45	+	1	42
fit	Verb	56	+	30	43		mountain	NoC	14	–	235	42
late	Adv	23	–	113	43		present	NoC	34	–	16	42
unusual	Adj	22	–	125	43		map	NoC	19	–	147	42
square	NoC	32	–	28	43		expert	NoC	19	–	149	42
waited	Verb	8	–	427	43		roof	NoC	35	–	14	42
periods	NoC	11	–	321	43		assume	Verb	32	–	24	42
proposal	NoC	33	–	23	43		video-taped	Adj	0	–	813	42
diet	NoC	18	–	184	43		warning	NoC	13	–	260	42
except	Conj	22	–	118	43		location	NoC	24	–	82	42
enormous	Adj	32	–	31	43		maintenance	NoC	22	–	113	42
studied	Verb	6	–	496	43		rejected	Verb	9	–	362	42
performed	Verb	6	–	473	43		partners	NoC	14	–	242	42
persons	NoC	12	–	297	43		calling	Verb	30	–	35	42
continues	Verb	9	–	382	43		emergency	NoC	19	–	147	42
linked	Verb	13	–	269	43		plate	NoC	30	–	38	42
spot	NoC	24	–	101	43		wealth	NoC	6	–	461	42
weapons	NoC	11	–	335	43		pension	NoC	69	+	130	42

Word	PoS	FrS		LL	FrW	Word	PoS	FrS		LL	FrW
occasionally	Adv	23	–	93	42	decade	NoC	7	–	429	41
reflected	Verb	8	–	408	42	Bob	NoP	37	–	3	41
characters	NoC	12	–	282	42	acquired	Verb	4	–	530	41
approved	Verb	15	–	224	42	arguments	NoC	19	–	140	41
afford	Verb	75	+	191	42	situations	NoC	22	–	100	41
dramatic	Adj	11	–	321	42	proposed	Adj	24	–	81	41
sum	NoC	33	–	17	42	writer	NoC	9	–	358	41
losses	NoC	8	–	382	42	sheet	NoC	53	+	33	41
sick	Adj	62	+	79	42	shortly	Adv	18	–	150	41
settled	Verb	14	–	234	42	demanded	Verb	3	–	576	41
approval	NoC	17	–	181	42	Jane	NoP	56	+	46	41
abroad	Adv	19	–	143	42	yellow	Adj	48	+	12	41
Chris	NoP	70	+	149	42	willing	Adj	27	–	47	41
plastic	NoC	30	–	31	42	paying	Verb	95	+	473	41
golden	Adj	11	–	297	42	beach	NoC	15	–	196	41
theme	NoC	12	–	288	42	denied	Verb	6	–	436	41
link	NoC	22	–	101	42	owners	NoC	11	–	279	41
silent	Adj	6	–	462	42	settlement	NoC	90	+	399	41
accused	Verb	10	–	325	42	that	Adv	150	+	1506	40
valuable	Adj	14	–	233	42	initially	Adv	19	–	136	40
emerged	Verb	4	–	546	42	reputation	NoC	10	–	315	40
1978	Num	0	–	803	42	examine	Verb	7	–	393	40
agricultural	Adj	32	–	24	42	dependent	Adj	10	–	310	40
federal	Adj	10	–	335	42	temporary	Adj	20	–	115	40
lifted	Verb	9	–	357	42	gained	Verb	8	–	389	40
agriculture	NoC	14	–	231	42	claims	Verb	7	–	402	40
talked	Verb	68	+	125	42	friendly	Adj	23	–	87	40
divided	Verb	27	–	55	41	working	NoC	21	–	106	40
comfortable	Adj	25	–	70	41	theories	NoC	4	–	510	40
duties	NoC	13	–	256	41	strike	NoC	30	–	27	40
deputy	NoC	16	–	203	41	cope	Verb	38	–	1	40
runs	Verb	28	–	49	41	Yorkshire	NoP	74	+	208	40
recovery	NoC	10	–	335	41	height	NoC	16	–	174	40
channel	NoC	28	–	49	41	offence	NoC	10	–	307	40
Jim	NoP	58	+	56	41	occasions	NoC	26	–	55	40
ice	NoC	31	–	29	41	funding	NoC	33	–	11	40
regularly	Adv	16	–	197	41	struggle	NoC	13	–	247	40
Brown	NoP	9	–	368	41	dream	NoC	23	–	87	40
silver	NoC	15	–	219	41	tasks	NoC	9	–	327	40
teams	NoC	23	–	93	41	song	NoC	38	–	1	40
advertising	NoC	36	–	7	41	countryside	NoC	33	–	12	40
R / r	Lett	154	+	1556	41	stress	NoC	23	–	86	40
fight	Verb	29	–	40	41	Lewis	NoP	15	–	198	40
worry	Verb	94	+	440	41	answered	Verb	19	–	127	40
error	NoC	14	–	233	41	realise	Verb	30	–	23	40
reflect	Verb	13	–	263	41	chief	NoC	17	–	168	40
painting	NoC	13	–	258	41	1976	Num	0	–	784	40
lifespan	NoC	1	–	715	41	shut	Verb	107	+	687	40
rail	NoC	26	–	56	41	subsequently	Adv	9	–	329	40
twelve	Num	278	+	4881	41	gain	Verb	14	–	219	40
odd	Adj	77	+	222	41	radical	Adj	8	–	352	40
focus	NoC	9	–	344	41	facing	Verb	20	–	120	40
premises	NoC	18	–	164	41	helping	Verb	31	–	19	40
request	NoC	13	–	242	41	recession	NoC	20	–	112	40
characteristics	NoC	9	–	358	41	sleep	NoC	35	–	4	40
hundreds	NoC	31	–	26	41	bottle	NoC	51	+	28	40
Indian	Adj	11	–	309	41	leads	Verb	15	–	202	40
loan	NoC	13	–	257	41	manage	Verb	50	+	20	40
trading	NoC	19	–	143	41	clubs	NoC	20	–	112	40
bedroom	NoC	65	+	112	41	criteria	NoC	35	–	5	40
mostly	Adv	27	–	55	41	efficiency	NoC	11	–	286	40
talk	NoC	40	–	0	41	outcome	NoC	12	–	253	40
1977	Num	0	–	768	41	wished	Verb	11	–	278	40
publication	NoC	5	–	487	41	agents	NoC	17	–	159	40
deeply	Adv	7	–	400	41	empire	NoC	7	–	396	40
foundation	NoC	7	–	400	41	statutory	Adj	18	–	143	40

2.3

Word	PoS	FrS		LL	FrW	Word	PoS	FrS		LL	FrW
Middlesbrough	NoP	3	–	579	40	awareness	NoC	8	–	335	39
Welsh	Adj	18	–	148	40	electricity	NoC	32	–	10	39
notion	NoC	9	–	325	40	initiative	NoC	17	–	147	39
resistance	NoC	16	–	173	40	yards	NoC	20	–	106	39
mirror	NoC	19	–	121	40	dressed	Verb	19	–	112	39
specialist	NoC	12	–	248	40	false	Adj	16	–	164	39
threatened	Verb	11	–	280	40	refer	Verb	32	–	11	39
voluntary	Adj	34	–	8	40	aside	Adv	12	–	244	39
at once	Adv	8	–	348	40	travel	Verb	22	–	81	39
clause	NoC	9	–	328	39	Cambridge	NoP	17	–	139	39
glad	Adj	51	+	26	39	expansion	NoC	12	–	231	39
incident	NoC	17	–	158	39	scientists	NoC	9	–	326	39
wear	Verb	78	+	264	39	Luke	NoP	7	–	373	39
Belfast	NoP	8	–	356	39	remarkable	Adj	8	–	346	39
marked	Verb	15	–	196	39	chain	NoC	21	–	91	39
parish	NoC	38	–	0	39	worker	NoC	18	–	135	39
learning	Verb	24	–	63	39	Frank	NoP	26	–	42	39
islands	NoC	5	–	450	39	parent	NoC	27	–	38	39
walk	NoC	33	–	11	39	healthy	Adj	13	–	207	38
chest	NoC	26	–	51	39	soldiers	NoC	11	–	251	38
grant	NoC	34	–	7	39	drama	NoC	11	–	275	38
chancellor	NoC	14	–	208	39	attached	Verb	17	–	138	38
Taylor	NoP	10	–	313	39	Elizabeth	NoP	16	–	168	38
supporters	NoC	14	–	214	39	businesses	NoC	22	–	74	38
competitive	Adj	16	–	177	39	shared	Verb	19	–	117	38
negotiations	NoC	14	–	207	39	convention	NoC	5	–	455	38
centuries	NoC	4	–	509	39	intelligence	NoC	9	–	322	38
lucky	Adj	57	+	65	39	fallen	Verb	18	–	127	38
armed	Adj	14	–	203	39	adequate	Adj	13	–	210	38
rapid	Adj	5	–	463	39	comprehensive	Adj	10	–	286	38
options	NoC	24	–	62	39	delivery	NoC	18	–	131	38
agencies	NoC	13	–	217	39	weak	Adj	14	–	194	38
global	Adj	8	–	342	39	Wednesday	NoP	95	+	525	38
steel	NoC	20	–	112	39	spending	NoC	23	–	66	38
relating	Verb	15	–	186	39	alternative	NoC	15	–	175	38
representation	NoC	14	–	202	39	pale	Adj	9	–	302	38
no doubt	Adv	18	–	130	39	acceptable	Adj	23	–	68	38
writers	NoC	7	–	393	39	creating	Verb	12	–	239	38
longer	Adj	38	–	0	39	arrival	NoC	3	–	515	38
tired	Adj	48	+	16	39	uses	Verb	22	–	76	38
taught	Verb	28	–	31	39	fighting	Verb	20	–	93	38
once again	Adv	20	–	109	39	1970s	Num	0	–	745	38
missed	Verb	56	+	61	39	mistake	NoC	32	–	10	38
gardens	NoC	14	–	197	39	regime	NoC	8	–	330	38
sensitive	Adj	13	–	231	39	attend	Verb	18	–	119	38
specifically	Adv	24	–	60	39	owned	Verb	16	–	149	38
examined	Verb	6	–	408	39	experienced	Verb	9	–	299	38
images	NoC	6	–	407	39	connection	NoC	10	–	269	38
administrative	Adj	5	–	463	39	inquiry	NoC	7	–	356	38
drove	Verb	16	–	173	39	handed	Verb	16	–	160	38
leaves	NoC	14	–	202	39	recognise	Verb	24	–	59	38
currency	NoC	4	–	521	39	store	NoC	19	–	113	38
co-operation	NoC	4	–	486	39	mass	Adj	11	–	260	38
comments	NoC	62	+	103	39	communications	NoC	9	–	292	38
buying	Verb	59	+	82	39	reports	Verb	7	–	377	38
controlled	Verb	12	–	244	39	motion	NoC	119	+	963	38
roads	NoC	41	+	0	39	instructions	NoC	19	–	111	38
stations	NoC	20	–	102	39	1975	Num	0	–	726	38
gradually	Adv	18	–	128	39	ring	NoC	63	+	125	38
aimed	Verb	8	–	350	39	cards	NoC	52	+	45	38
rising	Verb	9	–	313	39	hurt	Verb	38	+	0	38
secret	Adj	10	–	290	39	Adam	NoP	15	–	164	38
200	Num	1	–	643	39	eggs	NoC	34	–	3	38
emotional	Adj	11	–	260	39	attended	Verb	11	–	243	38
living	Adj	14	–	197	39	bird	NoC	22	–	72	38
mass	NoC	11	–	255	39	Lee	NoP	23	–	58	38

Word	PoS	FrS		LL	FrW	Word	PoS	FrS		LL	FrW
darkness	NoC	4	–	461	38	pull	Verb	70	+	212	37
wooden	Adj	18	–	124	38	keen	Adj	35	–	0	37
surprising	Adj	16	–	156	37	brothers	NoC	29	–	15	37
restaurant	NoC	15	–	171	37	supreme	Adj	5	–	435	37
admit	Verb	38	+	0	37	partnership	NoC	18	–	114	37
cat	NoC	56	+	71	37	starts	Verb	60	+	113	37
arrested	Verb	10	–	283	37	stairs	NoC	35	–	0	37
command	NoC	8	–	344	37	films	NoC	20	–	91	37
T / t	Lett	245	+	4186	37	anywhere	Adv	79	+	331	37
sons	NoC	13	–	203	37	imposed	Verb	8	–	308	37
travel	NoC	22	–	73	37	gate	NoC	26	–	34	37
minority	NoC	9	–	287	37	copies	NoC	19	–	97	37
electronic	Adj	7	–	364	37	derived	Verb	3	–	522	37
literary	Adj	3	–	502	37	guests	NoC	10	–	267	37
philosophy	NoC	14	–	191	37	licence	NoC	28	–	19	37
sees	Verb	19	–	100	37	core	NoC	11	–	241	37
outside	Adj	30	–	14	37	successfully	Adv	9	–	282	37
corporation	NoC	11	–	249	37	panel	NoC	40	+	2	37
links	NoC	17	–	125	37	in favour of	Prep	27	–	24	37
flat	Adj	32	–	6	37	bay	NoC	10	–	250	37
essentially	Adv	28	–	23	37	duke	NoC	6	–	395	37
maximum	Adj	15	–	169	37	paintings	NoC	4	–	473	36
championship	NoC	4	–	487	37	growing	Verb	24	–	43	36
precisely	Adv	17	–	138	37	chemical	Adj	7	–	340	36
in addition to	Prep	10	–	265	37	continuing	Adj	10	–	262	36
firm	Adj	11	–	235	37	well	Adj	86	+	437	36
pub	NoC	46	+	17	37	thinks	Verb	62	+	134	36
fixed	Adj	22	–	68	37	returning	Verb	6	–	385	36
solid	Adj	18	–	123	37	greatly	Adv	7	–	333	36
skill	NoC	17	–	137	37	suffer	Verb	21	–	68	36
enemy	NoC	6	–	385	37	languages	NoC	9	–	277	36
forgotten	Verb	42	+	4	37	residents	NoC	20	–	78	36
computers	NoC	26	–	36	37	category	NoC	9	–	284	36
I / i	Lett	193	+	2743	37	occurs	Verb	7	–	334	36
block	NoC	26	–	32	37	1974	Num	0	–	667	36
prefer	Verb	35	–	0	37	taste	NoC	19	–	93	36
no.	NoC	0	–	729	37	categories	NoC	10	–	245	36
consequence	NoC	10	–	273	37	pure	Adj	14	–	168	36
charity	NoC	19	–	104	37	supplied	Verb	9	–	277	36
insisted	Verb	5	–	443	37	comparison	NoC	9	–	274	36
accompanied	Verb	2	–	587	37	wages	NoC	44	+	14	36
Margaret	NoP	45	+	15	37	findings	NoC	5	–	411	36
apart	Adv	18	–	116	37	behind	Adv	17	–	119	36
depend	Verb	16	–	139	37	Washington	NoP	7	–	354	36
driving	Verb	50	+	35	37	V / v	Prep	0	–	709	36
newspapers	NoC	20	–	91	37	tells	Verb	42	+	7	36
result	Verb	6	–	383	37	French	NoC	21	–	68	36
mere	Adj	5	–	418	37	plane	NoC	19	–	87	36
everybody	Pron	267	+	4882	37	classical	Adj	4	–	458	36
scope	NoC	12	–	222	37	advanced	Adj	6	–	363	36
churches	NoC	19	–	96	37	yours	Pron	97	+	623	36
visual	Adj	10	–	265	37	wet	Adj	33	–	2	36
Rome	NoP	5	–	436	37	complete	Verb	17	–	111	36
extension	NoC	20	–	88	37	round	NoC	24	–	42	36
DNA	NoC	0	–	711	37	fans	NoC	11	–	230	36
resolution	NoC	36	–	0	37	lots	Pron	126	+	1190	36
survive	Verb	20	–	87	37	fill	Verb	62	+	137	36
wonder	Verb	124	+	1111	37	Nigel	NoP	17	–	123	36
uncle	NoC	23	–	59	37	tower	NoC	13	–	182	36
anger	NoC	4	–	446	37	changing	Verb	38	+	0	36
average	NoC	25	–	37	37	introduce	Verb	27	–	25	36
Spanish	Adj	9	–	291	37	losing	Verb	27	–	22	36
directed	Verb	10	–	256	37	genuine	Adj	11	–	222	36
experiences	NoC	13	–	192	37	retirement	NoC	19	–	89	36
cheap	Adj	60	+	112	37	tension	NoC	7	–	334	36
rise	Verb	11	–	244	37	gap	NoC	22	–	58	36

Word	PoS	FrS		LL	FrW
worried	Adj	54	+	69	36
affair	NoC	9	–	280	36
respond	Verb	30	–	9	36
sugar	NoC	39	+	2	36
fifteen	Num	207	+	3222	36
defendant	NoC	10	–	247	36
collected	Verb	13	–	183	36
politicians	NoC	11	–	215	36
advance	NoC	42	+	9	36
replace	Verb	20	–	80	36
furniture	NoC	33	–	1	36
pocket	NoC	33	–	1	36
personnel	NoC	12	–	194	36
fifty	Num	519	+	13755	36
arise	Verb	10	–	257	36
respectively	Adv	2	–	531	36
sleep	Verb	45	+	22	36
Williams	NoP	7	–	321	36
dealt	Verb	29	–	10	36
module	NoC	3	–	499	36
gun	NoC	29	–	13	36
socialist	Adj	7	–	340	36
dear	Adj	41	+	7	36
circle	NoC	19	–	85	36
judgment	NoC	7	–	333	36
across	Adv	29	–	11	36
promotion	NoC	13	–	186	36
MP	NoC	1	–	622	36
consumption	NoC	7	–	332	36
written	Adj	13	–	170	35
metres	NoC	21	–	65	35
expectations	NoC	11	–	215	35
disappeared	Verb	11	–	215	35
Commons	NoP	10	–	237	35
widespread	Adj	7	–	337	35
meat	NoC	41	+	7	35
faces	NoC	11	–	228	35
catholic	Adj	6	–	362	35
Gloucester	NoP	6	–	349	35
abuse	NoC	18	–	96	35
represents	Verb	16	–	132	35
database	NoC	22	–	54	35
Oct.	NoP	0	–	693	35
numerous	Adj	6	–	358	35
fitted	Verb	14	–	164	35
discover	Verb	10	–	247	35
mail	NoC	16	–	127	35
estimated	Verb	7	–	325	35
extreme	Adj	11	–	230	35
mothers	NoC	14	–	155	35
break	NoC	41	+	8	35
consent	NoC	9	–	276	35
preparation	NoC	16	–	130	35
begins	Verb	11	–	229	35
ignored	Verb	7	–	314	35
acts	NoC	9	–	278	35
fifth	Ord	36	+	0	35
tape	NoC	139	+	1502	35
cricket	NoC	15	–	145	35
H / h	Lett	123	+	1157	35
priority	NoC	25	–	33	35
absolute	Adj	31	–	5	35
stones	NoC	13	–	174	35
Thatcher	NoP	20	–	69	35
distinct	Adj	7	–	331	35
arrangement	NoC	13	–	178	35
experts	NoC	9	–	266	35
mixture	NoC	13	–	172	35
repeated	Verb	7	–	318	35
golf	NoC	28	–	14	35
fail	Verb	12	–	190	35
landscape	NoC	12	–	188	35
Israel	NoP	10	–	247	35
bread	NoC	61	+	139	35
need*	VMod	20	–	68	35
adults	NoC	19	–	80	35
mood	NoC	16	–	129	35
by	Adv	3	–	486	35
limit	NoC	24	–	37	35
illness	NoC	16	–	121	35
components	NoC	8	–	304	35
kids	NoC	119	–	1081	35
hoping	Verb	39	+	4	35
champion	NoC	7	–	312	35
moments	NoC	10	–	238	35
Jan.	NoP	0	–	682	35
present	Verb	22	–	54	35
tank	NoC	17	–	100	35
electric	Adj	28	–	14	35
Tory	Adj	30	–	5	35
ages	NoC	47	+	36	35
fun	NoC	31	–	3	35
intervention	NoC	7	–	307	35
shoes	NoC	53	+	78	35
nineteenth	Num	16	–	125	35
informed	Verb	14	–	148	35
happening	Verb	86	+	482	35
controls	NoC	7	–	330	35
beer	NoC	20	–	72	35
citizens	NoC	18	–	89	35
photographs	NoC	19	–	80	35
concluded	Verb	3	–	456	35
Johnson	NoP	8	–	299	35
organised	Verb	8	–	296	35
close	Verb	40	+	6	35
self	NoC	47	+	35	35
wave	NoC	7	–	322	34
alliance	NoC	5	–	365	34
notice	Verb	45	+	28	34
teaching	Verb	24	–	36	34
prospect	NoC	9	–	256	34
favourite	Adj	18	–	90	34
causing	Verb	18	–	89	34
earnings	NoC	13	–	167	34
somebody	Pron	409	+	9932	34
sad	Adj	35	+	0	34
Birmingham	NoP	35	+	0	34
survival	NoC	7	–	313	34
pilot	NoC	8	–	295	34
item	NoC	68	+	229	34
exists	Verb	13	–	171	34
rough	Adj	31	–	2	34
Sarah	NoP	39	+	6	34
Iraq	NoP	10	–	222	34
shareholders	NoC	5	–	392	34
recommended	Verb	12	–	178	34
territory	NoC	7	–	298	34
given	Adj	9	–	260	34
exciting	Adj	26	–	19	34
symptoms	NoC	8	–	289	34
mill	NoC	20	–	65	34
throat	NoC	18	–	90	34

Word	PoS	FrS		LL	FrW	Word	PoS	FrS		LL	FrW
fishing	NoC	15	–	123	34	Scott	NoP	21	–	43	33
attacks	NoC	9	–	243	34	clinical	Adj	4	–	400	33
perform	Verb	11	–	191	34	aunt	NoC	11	–	193	33
sweet	Adj	28	–	10	34	novel	NoC	10	–	210	33
winner	NoC	11	–	204	34	proud	Adj	20	–	59	33
aids	NoC	13	–	157	34	contents	NoC	7	–	301	33
destroyed	Verb	10	–	235	34	conducted	Verb	7	–	292	33
promote	Verb	13	–	151	34	operating	NoC	10	–	208	33
frame	NoC	13	–	157	34	point	Verb	33	+	0	33
cycle	NoC	15	–	122	34	purchase	NoC	10	–	214	33
statistics	NoC	18	–	85	34	employee	NoC	14	–	132	33
Asia	NoP	2	–	491	34	glanced	Verb	1	–	571	33
achievement	NoC	10	–	228	34	nurse	NoC	21	–	46	33
a lot	Adv	96	+	681	34	yard	NoC	30	–	1	33
input	NoC	19	–	76	34	cool	Adj	13	–	142	33
votes	NoC	11	–	191	34	guidance	NoC	27	–	11	33
fewer	DetP	8	–	287	34	feels	Verb	30	–	2	33
constitutional	Adj	5	–	366	34	pace	NoC	11	–	179	33
ownership	NoC	11	–	209	34	boss	NoC	25	–	20	33
express	Verb	14	–	133	34	opposite	Adj	27	–	8	33
primarily	Adv	12	–	180	34	nervous	Adj	15	–	111	33
inevitably	Adv	7	–	288	34	depth	NoC	11	–	184	33
branches	NoC	18	–	82	34	drawing	Verb	18	–	76	33
longer	Adv	29	–	6	34	constantly	Adv	13	–	146	33
confident	Adj	22	–	44	34	threw	Verb	15	–	117	33
tough	Adj	19	–	70	34	festival	NoC	13	–	144	33
truly	Adv	18	–	81	34	developing	Adj	13	–	144	33
winning	Verb	13	–	162	34	wedding	NoC	39	+	10	33
permission	NoC	21	–	50	34	1973	Num	0	–	616	33
1960s	Num	0	–	634	34	prisoners	NoC	7	–	287	33
briefly	Adv	27	–	14	34	cried	Verb	6	–	318	33
adding	Verb	16	–	112	33	vehicles	NoC	15	–	109	33
profession	NoC	9	–	250	33	Nov.	NoP	0	–	639	33
councils	NoC	46	+	39	33	dismissed	Verb	4	–	405	33
shot	NoC	27	–	14	33	finger	NoC	27	–	8	33
perspective	NoC	8	–	267	33	turns	Verb	27	–	10	33
assumption	NoC	10	–	213	33	setting	NoC	9	–	228	33
anxious	Adj	11	–	194	33	Tim	NoP	46	+	45	33
concerning	Prep	7	–	295	33	connected	Verb	14	–	130	33
left	NoC	43	+	24	33	coat	NoC	50	+	73	33
stable	Adj	9	–	239	33	discussions	NoC	20	–	49	33
breach	NoC	7	–	304	33	points	Verb	5	–	361	33
dominant	Adj	5	–	370	33	defeat	NoC	4	–	400	33
cottage	NoC	17	–	90	33	vary	Verb	9	–	232	33
poverty	NoC	13	–	158	33	Sam	NoP	22	–	39	32
consistent	Adj	12	–	165	33	luck	NoC	27	–	8	32
compensation	NoC	15	–	119	33	crossed	Verb	14	–	132	32
theoretical	Adj	3	–	443	33	presentation	NoC	29	–	2	32
hills	NoC	9	–	231	33	prize	NoC	16	–	94	32
fault	NoC	41	+	15	33	satisfied	Adj	16	–	101	32
Sept.	NoP	0	–	652	33	disabled	Adj	20	–	52	32
developing	Verb	15	–	126	33	resulted	Verb	4	–	398	32
transferred	Verb	12	–	180	33	sounded	Verb	11	–	173	32
entrance	NoC	13	–	144	33	Joseph	NoP	8	–	258	32
camp	NoC	15	–	113	33	visible	Adj	4	–	388	32
mark	NoC	34	+	0	33	comment	NoC	49	+	66	32
et al	Adv	0	–	599	33	conduct	NoC	4	–	387	32
requirement	NoC	25	–	18	33	port	NoC	9	–	236	32
prior to	Prep	16	–	110	33	whenever	Adv	27	–	7	32
brings	Verb	25	–	22	33	sake	NoC	33	+	0	32
extend	Verb	14	–	134	33	altogether	Adv	31	–	0	32
Moscow	NoP	5	–	352	33	dispute	NoC	10	–	199	32
delivered	Verb	13	–	154	33	provided	Conj	7	–	287	32
dark	NoC	13	–	150	33	answers	NoC	29	–	2	32
tools	NoC	22	–	40	33	soul	NoC	12	–	156	32
costs	Verb	26	–	17	33	furthermore	Adv	3	–	434	32

Word	PoS	FrS		LL	FrW	Word	PoS	FrS		LL	FrW
solicitor	NoC	26	–	13	32	treat	Verb	21	–	40	31
study	Verb	12	–	158	32	crew	NoC	13	–	136	31
hearing	NoC	9	–	227	32	observation	NoC	7	–	261	31
impressive	Adj	8	–	263	32	funny	Adj	161	+	2265	31
processing	NoC	11	–	169	32	extraordinary	Adj	12	–	154	31
shadow	NoC	11	–	183	32	ears	NoC	20	–	45	31
alcohol	NoC	14	–	118	32	realized	Verb	26	–	10	31
reply	NoC	16	–	98	32	Bush	NoP	6	–	311	31
wore	Verb	13	–	146	32	holder	NoC	5	–	331	31
driven	Verb	10	–	195	32	presumably	Adv	48	+	73	31
recognized	Verb	10	–	192	32	pressed	Verb	10	–	189	31
limits	NoC	10	–	192	32	reasonably	Adv	24	–	16	31
servants	NoC	10	–	190	32	IV / iv	Num	0	–	591	31
outstanding	Adj	13	–	135	32	mechanism	NoC	12	–	151	31
articles	NoC	7	–	276	32	instruments	NoC	6	–	297	31
stepped	Verb	5	–	332	32	reducing	Verb	13	–	137	31
reaching	Verb	7	–	276	32	at present	Adv	10	–	184	31
prepare	Verb	14	–	117	32	listening	Verb	62	+	208	31
fought	Verb	9	–	221	32	stomach	NoC	16	–	87	31
saved	Verb	33	+	0	32	economics	NoC	7	–	256	31
touched	Verb	15	–	107	32	monetary	Adj	3	–	422	31
measured	Verb	10	–	189	32	routine	NoC	9	–	215	31
enthusiasm	NoC	8	–	237	32	considerably	Adv	11	–	167	31
calls	Verb	18	–	73	32	precise	Adj	9	–	217	31
distant	Adj	5	–	327	32	phrase	NoC	23	–	24	31
poetry	NoC	6	–	291	32	hat	NoC	32	+	0	31
experiments	NoC	7	–	271	32	device	NoC	8	–	236	31
princess	NoC	8	–	234	32	approached	Verb	12	–	148	31
origin	NoC	5	–	340	32	calls	NoC	34	+	2	31
suit	NoC	21	–	39	32	possession	NoC	6	–	289	31
storage	NoC	10	–	192	32	suggestion	NoC	31	–	0	31
Greek	Adj	5	–	343	32	minimum	Adj	19	–	48	31
Ruth	NoP	17	–	74	32	covering	Verb	13	–	125	31
alongside	Prep	6	–	309	32	except	Prep	21	–	38	31
cast	Verb	10	–	207	32	Thursday	NoP	88	+	620	31
mile	NoC	32	–	0	32	bigger	Adj	76	+	406	31
bid	NoC	21	–	42	32	protein	NoC	6	–	307	31
fast	Adj	25	–	14	32	satisfaction	NoC	7	–	251	31
hung	Verb	9	–	212	32	slight	Adj	17	–	71	31
neighbours	NoC	29	–	2	32	chamber	NoC	11	–	171	31
shouted	Verb	9	–	224	32	mad	Adj	35	+	4	31
Patrick	NoP	12	–	149	32	personality	NoC	12	–	141	31
bills	NoC	19	–	51	32	organizations	NoC	20	–	39	31
ladies	NoC	42	+	28	32	dance	NoC	19	–	55	31
staring	Verb	4	–	390	32	everywhere	Adv	42	+	30	31
benefit	Verb	16	–	94	32	fears	NoC	8	–	233	31
wage	NoC	28	–	5	32	green	NoC	25	–	13	31
Dec.	NoP	0	–	622	32	escape	Verb	7	–	271	31
sand	NoC	16	–	94	32	discovery	NoC	5	–	318	31
musical	Adj	7	–	281	32	implementation	NoC	7	–	259	31
rocks	NoC	7	–	275	32	receiving	Verb	13	–	132	31
conscious	Adj	22	–	29	32	gift	NoC	17	–	67	31
chances	NoC	21	–	39	32	exception	NoC	15	–	94	31
Canada	NoP	8	–	255	32	remote	Adj	9	–	208	31
employer	NoC	18	–	61	32	jacket	NoC	23	–	23	31
helpful	Adj	33	+	1	32	smooth	Adj	5	–	307	31
Ben	NoP	33	+	0	32	Kong	NoP-	5	–	342	31
related	Adj	12	–	147	32	plaintiff	NoC	21	–	34	31
concentrate	Verb	22	–	28	32	sentences	NoC	9	–	210	31
advantages	NoC	11	–	163	32	degrees	NoC	32	+	0	31
tendency	NoC	10	–	183	32	selected	Verb	8	–	219	31
attacked	Verb	7	–	273	32	snow	NoC	21	–	34	31
victims	NoC	10	–	200	32	Hong	NoP-	4	–	356	31
turnover	NoC	7	–	270	32	frequency	NoC	3	–	384	31
thrown	Verb	22	–	33	31	accurate	Adj	16	–	87	31
gentle	Adj	6	–	291	31	mine	Pron	177	+	2739	31

Word	PoS	FrS		LL	FrW	Word	PoS	FrS		LL	FrW
confusion	NoC	11	–	170	31	taxes	NoC	10	–	165	30
designs	NoC	5	–	311	31	summary	NoC	14	–	97	30
A.	NoP	0	–	604	31	strategies	NoC	4	–	359	30
arrive	Verb	15	–	101	31	White	NoP	13	–	122	30
fit	Adj	22	–	26	31	contributions	NoC	14	–	104	30
in spite of	Prep	5	–	321	31	steam	NoC	13	–	122	30
ultimately	Adv	13	–	116	31	responsibilities	NoC	16	–	74	30
residential	Adj	18	–	57	31	Berlin	NoP	4	–	335	30
finds	Verb	12	–	149	31	evaluation	NoC	11	–	162	30
miss	Verb	71	+	341	31	songs	NoC	15	–	82	30
attracted	Verb	6	–	272	31	psychological	Adj	9	–	195	30
mountains	NoC	8	–	226	31	Tuesday	NoP	83	+	565	30
ratio	NoC	11	–	156	31	Ken	NoP	34	+	5	30
bishop	NoC	5	–	323	31	aged	Prep	3	–	390	30
fees	NoC	15	–	89	31	stands	Verb	21	–	30	30
fly	Verb	16	–	84	31	drink	Verb	49	+	93	30
determination	NoC	4	–	355	31	approximately	Adv	14	–	94	30
readily	Adv	6	–	289	31	leaves	Verb	18	–	50	30
pound	NoC	327	+	7521	31	roles	NoC	7	–	241	30
files	NoC	19	–	43	31	manufacturers	NoC	7	–	249	30
unity	NoC	7	–	248	31	scored	Verb	16	–	78	30
since	Adv	13	–	116	31	rugby	NoC	17	–	63	30
brilliant	Adj	73	+	375	31	final	NoC	10	–	178	30
breaking	Verb	21	–	29	31	Americans	NoC	13	–	111	30
Bristol	NoP	11	–	155	31	missing	Verb	23	–	16	30
live	Adj	13	–	120	31	plain	Adj	21	–	30	30
hospitals	NoC	19	–	51	31	smoke	NoC	17	–	58	30
certificate	NoC	12	–	134	31	combined	Verb	4	–	338	30
ends	NoC	16	–	80	31	now that	Conj	34	+	4	30
childhood	NoC	9	–	209	31	founded	Verb	5	–	316	30
cuts	NoC	20	–	37	30	newly	Adv	5	–	313	30
straight	Adj	40	+	22	30	Anna	NoP	10	–	161	30
leisure	NoC	14	–	100	30	mode	NoC	5	–	289	30
fight	NoC	17	–	65	30	violent	Adj	11	–	153	30
in respect of	Prep	16	–	73	30	sheep	NoC	35	+	8	30
secure	Verb	8	–	225	30	dominated	Verb	5	–	323	30
matter	Verb	101	+	876	30	variation	NoC	5	–	295	30
housing	Verb	12	–	144	30	sets	NoC	18	–	50	30
trained	Verb	23	–	16	30	deliberately	Adv	12	–	133	30
savings	NoC	32	+	0	30	modules	NoC	2	–	449	30
relation	NoC	8	–	232	30	boards	NoC	12	–	136	30
holy	Adj	27	–	3	30	loans	NoC	7	–	251	30
coach	NoC	14	–	111	30	investors	NoC	6	–	278	30
peak	NoC	8	–	214	30	disaster	NoC	17	–	59	30
architecture	NoC	12	–	141	30	Feb.	NoP	0	–	582	30
column	NoC	12	–	140	30	junior	Adj	11	–	151	30
Rose	NoP	6	–	294	30	1972	Num	0	–	582	30
wing	NoC	13	–	127	30	N / n	Lett	157	+	2274	30
protest	NoC	6	–	269	30	moon	NoC	24	–	12	30
Pacific	NoP	3	–	404	30	next to	Prep	34	+	5	30
reforms	NoC	5	–	297	30	infection	NoC	6	–	268	30
climate	NoC	10	–	179	30	laboratory	NoC	5	–	316	30
inevitable	Adj	5	–	300	30	ear	NoC	21	–	28	30
broken	Adj	16	–	80	30	critics	NoC	5	–	306	30
airport	NoC	20	–	40	30	whether or not	Conj	22	–	22	30
neither	DetP	12	–	142	30	samples	NoC	9	–	181	30
round	Adj	7	–	238	30	bloody	Adj	247	+	4983	30
fee	NoC	19	–	49	30	spending	Verb	28	–	0	30
objective	NoC	22	–	24	30	guitar	NoC	5	–	302	30
inspector	NoC	21	–	26	30	tennis	NoC	15	–	84	30
o'clock	Adv	188	+	3095	30	tables	NoC	28	–	1	30
cream	NoC	41	+	30	30	demonstrated	Verb	4	–	323	30
chose	Verb	13	–	115	30	applies	Verb	13	–	107	30
Neil	NoP	35	+	7	30	visits	NoC	10	–	166	30
fixed	Verb	14	–	109	30	undertaken	Verb	6	–	255	30
strategic	Adj	33	+	2	30	waves	NoC	5	–	295	30

Word	PoS	FrS		LL	FrW	Word	PoS	FrS		LL	FrW
pink	Adj	32	+	2	30	evident	Adj	3	–	364	29
70	Num	1	–	521	29	Zealand	NoP–	6	–	266	29
participation	NoC	6	–	254	29	causes	NoC	5	–	282	29
survived	Verb	7	–	235	29	excitement	NoC	6	–	248	29
villages	NoC	17	–	62	29	landlord	NoC	12	–	118	29
m.	NoC	0	–	578	29	responses	NoC	7	–	231	29
Keith	NoP	19	–	42	29	cut	NoC	29	+	0	29
pride	NoC	8	–	206	29	comfort	NoC	5	–	274	29
restrictions	NoC	11	–	149	29	Howard	NoP	8	–	197	29
signal	NoC	13	–	113	29	building	Verb	19	–	34	29
above	Adj	2	–	432	29	watch	NoC	31	+	1	29
tended	Verb	10	–	166	29	imagination	NoC	8	–	190	29
complicated	Adj	26	–	4	29	deaf	Adj	8	–	190	29
concepts	NoC	4	–	320	29	press	Verb	37	+	20	29
sound	Verb	33	+	5	29	overseas	Adj	7	–	238	29
minds	NoC	20	–	32	29	assess	Verb	11	–	144	29
reveal	Verb	3	–	361	29	Arthur	NoP	27	–	0	29
headquarters	NoC	13	–	113	29	occasional	Adj	5	–	276	29
structural	Adj	10	–	162	29	0	Num	1	–	449	29
automatically	Adv	16	–	69	29	spoken	Verb	26	–	1	29
salt	NoC	28	–	0	29	sounds	Verb	78	+	509	29
attempted	Verb	5	–	296	29	teach	Verb	25	–	3	29
medicine	NoC	16	–	69	29	universities	NoC	12	–	110	28
experiment	NoC	9	–	174	29	helps	Verb	28	–	0	28
so-called	Adj	7	–	244	29	push	Verb	46	+	86	28
report	Verb	31	+	0	29	circuit	NoC	9	–	177	28
thereby	Adv	5	–	309	29	Aug.	NoP	0	–	558	28
agreements	NoC	10	–	168	29	surprisingly	Adv	5	–	297	28
abandoned	Verb	4	–	350	29	contribute	Verb	11	–	131	28
buyer	NoC	10	–	164	29	pressures	NoC	12	–	108	28
host	NoC	6	–	260	29	operating	Verb	13	–	107	28
test	Verb	18	–	45	29	sounds	NoC	7	–	219	28
secondly	Adv	25	–	4	29	universal	Adj	4	–	337	28
forty	Num	388	+	9928	29	universe	NoC	8	–	185	28
hold	NoC	34	+	7	29	consciousness	NoC	4	–	329	28
eating	Verb	41	+	42	29	treasury	NoC	8	–	203	28
Charlie	NoP	19	–	37	29	illustrated	Verb	2	–	398	28
still	Adj	30	+	0	29	succeeded	Verb	4	–	325	28
80	Num	0	–	544	29	occupied	Verb	6	–	254	28
drop	Verb	46	+	79	29	Newcastle	NoP	11	–	128	28
headed	Verb	8	–	195	29	holds	Verb	9	–	168	28
1970	Num	0	–	535	29	puts	Verb	35	+	12	28
percentage	NoC	21	–	19	29	Jean	NoP	49	+	112	28
engaged	Verb	9	–	170	29	state	Verb	8	–	202	28
mention	Verb	49	+	106	29	penalty	NoC	13	–	98	28
F / f	Lett	121	+	1390	29	MPs	NoC	3	–	364	28
acceptance	NoC	6	–	245	29	anxiety	NoC	12	–	118	28
acquisition	NoC	3	–	375	29	relatives	NoC	11	–	124	28
describes	Verb	5	–	278	29	match	Verb	17	–	45	28
trust	Verb	24	–	9	29	replacement	NoC	10	–	143	28
deep	Adv	7	–	218	29	pleasant	Adj	15	–	67	28
clock	NoC	26	–	3	29	component	NoC	5	–	293	28
addressed	Verb	14	–	92	29	fellow	Adj	8	–	195	28
approaches	NoC	5	–	287	29	welcome	Adj	18	–	38	28
marry	Verb	9	–	182	29	pitch	NoC	14	–	78	28
improved	Verb	15	–	72	29	trend	NoC	10	–	156	28
expense	NoC	14	–	83	29	tested	Verb	11	–	133	28
shirt	NoC	21	–	22	29	fat	Adj	23	–	9	28
one another	Pron	17	–	57	29	writes	Verb	9	–	176	28
being	NoC	19	–	35	29	consists	Verb	4	–	302	28
string	NoC	13	–	102	29	passing	Verb	14	–	85	28
rely	Verb	13	–	99	29	suffering	Verb	12	–	109	28
instrument	NoC	5	–	283	29	throw	Verb	55	+	186	28
1971	Num	0	–	541	29	commonly	Adv	4	–	324	28
poll	NoC	26	–	3	29	Maggie	NoP	16	–	62	28
ships	NoC	13	–	106	29	proof	NoC	16	–	61	28

Word	PoS	FrS		LL	FrW	Word	PoS	FrS		LL	FrW
bomb	NoC	17	–	43	28	variations	NoC	8	–	195	27
ahead of	Prep	10	–	149	28	gathered	Verb	9	–	161	27
Lucy	NoP	20	–	27	28	holes	NoC	20	–	20	27
complaints	NoC	19	–	30	28	last	Verb	34	+	13	27
whispered	Verb	1	–	492	28	NHS	NoP	0	–	538	27
Kent	NoP	10	–	152	28	confirm	Verb	15	–	60	27
ah	Int	712	+	22842	28	sensible	Adj	28	+	0	27
surgery	NoC	17	–	49	28	dozen	NoC	26	–	0	27
researchers	NoC	2	–	401	28	solicitors	NoC	16	–	50	27
supply	Verb	13	–	96	28	paused	Verb	1	–	459	27
mission	NoC	14	–	78	28	birthday	NoC	77	+	522	27
god	NoC	103	+	1027	28	linguistic	Adj	1	–	423	27
overcome	Verb	9	–	157	28	holidays	NoC	37	+	28	27
knife	NoC	18	–	40	28	cleared	Verb	20	–	22	27
tail	NoC	16	–	54	28	judges	NoC	7	–	204	27
summit	NoC	3	–	341	28	entitled	Adj	16	–	50	27
marks	NoC	32	+	5	28	increasing	Verb	16	–	54	27
Alexander	NoP	6	–	253	28	plan	Verb	18	–	38	27
grateful	Adj	23	–	7	28	preparing	Verb	11	–	129	27
committees	NoC	21	–	18	28	collect	Verb	37	+	25	27
nights	NoC	29	+	0	28	Nick	NoP	37	+	29	27
influenced	Verb	6	–	232	28	repeat	Verb	21	–	14	27
slipped	Verb	7	–	206	28	formula	NoC	20	–	23	27
expertise	NoC	13	–	93	28	loose	Adj	16	–	52	27
passengers	NoC	6	–	229	28	pretty	Adj	33	+	11	27
unemployed	Adj	28	–	0	28	edition	NoC	8	–	177	27
35	Num	0	–	513	28	on behalf of	Prep	26	–	0	27
score	NoC	24	–	6	28	listed	Verb	8	–	189	27
burden	NoC	10	–	137	28	knees	NoC	13	–	94	27
stronger	Adj	14	–	75	28	judicial	Adj	2	–	405	27
attempt	Verb	7	–	203	28	awarded	Verb	5	–	276	27
mortgage	NoC	37	+	26	28	attract	Verb	9	–	155	27
tenant	NoC	7	–	223	28	stream	NoC	6	–	230	27
zone	NoC	6	–	236	28	constructed	Verb	3	–	351	27
injuries	NoC	7	–	217	28	camera	NoC	25	–	2	27
classic	Adj	8	–	192	28	cattle	NoC	12	–	106	27
cutting	Verb	32	+	4	28	targets	NoC	17	–	46	27
as for	Prep	6	–	239	28	stupid	Adj	83	+	640	27
authors	NoC	3	–	372	28	qualities	NoC	5	–	255	27
sufficiently	Adv	6	–	228	28	equivalent	Adj	9	–	164	27
rent	NoC	29	+	0	28	supplies	NoC	6	–	222	27
solutions	NoC	7	–	206	28	delighted	Adj	18	–	36	27
psychology	NoC	11	–	120	28	retain	Verb	11	–	123	27
regulation	NoC	8	–	178	28	generated	Verb	7	–	194	27
San	NoP-	3	–	349	28	Victoria	NoP	12	–	105	27
existed	Verb	6	–	241	28	welcome	Verb	31	+	5	27
conservation	NoC	6	–	241	28	consequently	Adv	8	–	188	27
closer	Adv	9	–	154	28	decades	NoC	4	–	293	27
memories	NoC	15	–	68	28	steady	Adj	11	–	111	27
considering	Verb	10	–	140	28	apple	NoC	21	–	11	27
continuous	Adj	16	–	50	28	located	Verb	9	–	159	27
millions	NoC	20	–	24	28	ultimate	Adj	7	–	194	27
flesh	NoC	7	–	223	28	fear	Verb	9	–	148	27
Helen	NoP	24	–	5	28	dust	NoC	17	–	36	27
squad	NoC	7	–	202	28	medieval	Adj	7	–	206	27
sergeant	NoC	15	–	68	28	assumptions	NoC	7	–	209	27
opening	Verb	15	–	67	28	creative	Adj	7	–	191	27
sharply	Adv	1	–	455	28	Andy	NoP	37	+	30	27
standing	NoC	31	+	3	28	risks	NoC	7	–	203	27
displayed	Verb	2	–	373	27	serving	Verb	9	–	145	27
shopping	NoC	38	+	34	27	assist	Verb	10	–	126	27
intellectual	Adj	5	–	272	27	relate	Verb	18	–	33	27
disk	NoC	17	–	44	27	Victorian	Adj	9	–	161	27
Francis	NoP	6	–	246	27	coalition	NoC	2	–	377	27
staying	Verb	34	+	14	27	handle	Verb	19	–	27	27
softly	Adv	1	–	429	27	drivers	NoC	18	–	32	27

2.3

Word	PoS	FrS		LL	FrW	Word	PoS	FrS		LL	FrW
1968	Num	0	–	528	27	purely	Adv	21	–	11	26
platform	NoC	15	–	63	27	amounts	NoC	11	–	102	26
rose	NoC	12	–	95	27	convinced	Adj	12	–	93	26
produces	Verb	9	–	161	27	illegal	Adj	10	–	130	26
layer	NoC	8	–	167	27	Australian	Adj	8	–	177	26
locked	Verb	15	–	56	27	nurses	NoC	17	–	35	26
smell	NoC	16	–	45	27	informal	Adj	6	–	221	26
Durham	NoP	5	–	246	27	sending	Verb	27	+	0	26
influence	Verb	10	–	127	27	raw	Adj	11	–	105	26
desperate	Adj	19	–	21	27	500	Num	1	–	449	26
completion	NoC	6	–	217	27	bitter	Adj	8	–	159	26
roots	NoC	9	–	147	27	appreciate	Verb	30	+	4	26
mean	Adj	13	–	84	27	90	Num	0	–	479	26
aims	NoC	7	–	191	27	texts	NoC	1	–	416	26
shift	NoC	16	–	50	27	voices	NoC	8	–	176	26
Gordon	NoP	18	–	34	27	hers	Pron	18	–	25	26
engineers	NoC	13	–	85	27	La	NoP-	2	–	392	26
draft	NoC	16	–	49	27	calculated	Verb	6	–	216	26
backed	Verb	8	–	179	27	publicity	NoC	20	–	15	26
native	Adj	2	–	384	27	drawing	NoC	14	–	58	26
experience	Verb	11	–	120	27	ruled	Verb	5	–	243	26
Ulster	NoP	2	–	364	27	journal	NoC	3	–	325	26
leather	NoC	16	–	52	27	lawyers	NoC	6	–	227	26
taxation	NoC	10	–	131	27	frequent	Adj	3	–	338	26
ban	NoC	5	–	273	27	honest	Adj	61	+	300	26
etc.	Adv	4	–	286	27	undoubtedly	Adv	8	–	173	26
raising	Verb	10	–	128	27	conclusions	NoC	8	–	159	26
Germans	NoC	10	–	137	27	quoted	Verb	10	–	120	26
deaths	NoC	7	–	206	27	blind	Adj	27	+	0	26
Laura	NoP	16	–	48	27	q.v.	Uncl	0	–	509	26
imperial	Adj	3	–	327	27	recommenda-tions	NoC	23	–	3	26
colleges	NoC	9	–	142	27						
curve	NoC	10	–	133	27	experimental	Adj	3	–	303	26
wheel	NoC	18	–	30	27	potentially	Adv	12	–	95	26
climbed	Verb	4	–	281	27	once more	Adv	4	–	273	26
accounting	NoC	10	–	129	27	tongue	NoC	11	–	99	26
possibilities	NoC	8	–	176	27	reception	NoC	11	–	101	26
surrounded	Verb	5	–	257	27	machinery	NoC	12	–	93	26
explains	Verb	8	–	176	27	interviews	NoC	12	–	92	26
vulnerable	Adj	8	–	178	27	checked	Verb	22	–	6	26
Roger	NoP	19	–	24	27	wings	NoC	9	–	147	26
Nicholas	NoP	6	–	232	27	collective	Adj	4	–	276	26
beliefs	NoC	3	–	317	26	equation	NoC	14	–	60	26
adopt	Verb	10	–	122	26	settle	Verb	15	–	46	26
concerns	NoC	16	–	50	26	account	Verb	7	–	187	26
integration	NoC	6	–	223	26	net	NoC	14	–	61	26
hopes	NoC	7	–	196	26	versions	NoC	4	–	261	26
anybody	Pron	249	+	5359	26	transition	NoC	4	–	285	26
attempting	Verb	6	–	234	26	lives	Verb	35	+	30	26
sophisticated	Adj	9	–	140	26	improvements	NoC	11	–	95	26
promise	NoC	7	–	183	26	tied	Verb	22	–	5	26
guard	NoC	11	–	117	26	concentrated	Verb	5	–	229	26
shrugged	Verb	0	–	469	26	boxes	NoC	35	+	29	26
Alice	NoP	9	–	138	26	poem	NoC	16	–	44	26
judgement	NoC	14	–	71	26	even when	Conj	13	–	72	26
boots	NoC	21	–	13	26	offences	NoC	5	–	231	26
medium	NoC	8	–	171	26	intense	Adj	4	–	266	26
advised	Verb	11	–	116	26	destruction	NoC	6	–	222	26
cathedral	NoC	6	–	224	26	lost	Adj	19	–	19	26
revolutionary	Adj	7	–	186	26	grammar	NoC	12	–	91	26
retained	Verb	5	–	256	26	demonstrate	Verb	10	–	116	26
Matthew	NoP	23	–	4	26	investigate	Verb	6	–	197	26
dreams	NoC	13	–	80	26	topic	NoC	15	–	53	26
notably	Adv	1	–	402	26	square	Adj	27	+	1	26
300	Num	0	–	466	26	changing	Adj	13	–	78	26
evolution	NoC	12	–	87	26	level	Adj	20	–	11	26

Word	PoS	FrS		LL	FrW	Word	PoS	FrS		LL	FrW
argues	Verb	3	–	305	26	Diana	NoP	5	–	224	25
announcement	NoC	9	–	128	26	bone	NoC	16	–	36	25
flexible	Adj	10	–	113	26	acted	Verb	4	–	255	25
Gulf	NoP	13	–	77	26	guest	NoC	6	–	190	25
studying	Verb	11	–	93	26	suggesting	Verb	27	+	0	25
interaction	NoC	4	–	260	26	photograph	NoC	22	–	3	25
pack	NoC	24	–	0	26	bars	NoC	14	–	54	25
painted	Verb	13	–	69	26	boundaries	NoC	17	–	28	25
buried	Verb	7	–	171	26	hero	NoC	7	–	184	25
VAT / vat	NoC	9	–	135	26	modest	Adj	7	–	176	25
exposure	NoC	3	–	329	25	qualifications	NoC	9	–	123	25
hotels	NoC	8	–	164	25	urged	Verb	3	–	322	25
outer	Adj	16	–	42	25	Anthony	NoP	13	–	60	25
discourse	NoC	1	–	437	25	instruction	NoC	9	–	136	25
joy	NoC	12	–	86	25	lift	NoC	18	–	20	25
departure	NoC	3	–	320	25	consumers	NoC	6	–	193	25
recording	NoC	18	–	25	25	contributed	Verb	5	–	218	25
reminded	Verb	9	–	138	25	Kate	NoP	12	–	72	25
travelling	Verb	15	–	47	25	tends	Verb	21	–	4	25
as long as	Conj	62	+	328	25	earl	NoC	3	–	292	25
mark	Verb	23	–	2	25	historic	Adj	8	–	142	25
rang	Verb	40	+	67	25	admission	NoC	5	–	227	25
persuade	Verb	13	–	63	25	pupil	NoC	10	–	115	25
composition	NoC	5	–	221	25	Jimmy	NoP	18	–	17	25
Douglas	NoP	12	–	82	25	definitely	Adv	92	+	928	25
leaned	Verb	0	–	466	25	plates	NoC	13	–	70	25
quantity	NoC	10	–	120	25	transaction	NoC	6	–	195	25
professionals	NoC	6	–	201	25	meals	NoC	17	–	28	25
tickets	NoC	33	+	21	25	carbon	NoC	24	–	0	25
recall	Verb	26	+	0	25	on top of	Prep	34	+	26	25
dirty	Adj	36	+	37	25	Dutch	Adj	8	–	143	25
indicates	Verb	6	–	212	25	province	NoC	2	–	342	25
define	Verb	16	–	39	25	punishment	NoC	5	–	222	25
ethnic	Adj	5	–	226	25	bits	NoC	112	+	1406	25
personally	Adv	37	+	41	25	glance	NoC	4	–	271	25
jumped	Verb	15	–	50	25	laughter	NoC	2	–	342	25
entitled	Verb	7	–	180	25	mortality	NoC	5	–	227	25
tunnel	NoC	11	–	98	25	Y / y	Lett	70	+	488	25
rational	Adj	7	–	172	25	customs	NoC	4	–	242	25
Mrs.	NoC	4	–	281	25	Norman	NoP	14	–	56	25
passion	NoC	5	–	246	25	logical	Adj	10	–	100	25
prominent	Adj	5	–	224	25	45	Num	1	–	420	25
ignore	Verb	20	–	10	25	drawings	NoC	10	–	99	25
inadequate	Adj	5	–	221	25	generous	Adj	11	–	92	25
Lloyd	NoP	4	–	276	25	ruling	Adj	2	–	321	25
barely	Adv	3	–	291	25	listened	Verb	14	–	46	25
exercise	Verb	12	–	86	25	Arab	Adj	2	–	340	25
considerations	NoC	10	–	118	25	touch	Verb	35	+	35	25
deficit	NoC	8	–	143	25	mutual	Adj	5	–	238	25
accordingly	Adv	5	–	218	25	feed	Verb	23	–	0	25
cake	NoC	52	+	199	25	lit	Verb	7	–	160	25
acute	Adj	3	–	291	25	plays	Verb	15	–	41	25
excluded	Verb	8	–	144	25	logic	NoC	9	–	119	25
babies	NoC	19	–	14	25	heaven	NoC	22	–	3	25
PC/pc	NoC	1	–	437	25	awards	NoC	8	–	153	25
schedule	NoC	11	–	92	25	wholly	Adv	5	–	216	24
flew	Verb	9	–	130	25	smiling	Verb	4	–	250	24
governor	NoC	8	–	158	25	wondering	Verb	30	+	12	24
welcomed	Verb	7	–	186	25	reliable	Adj	5	–	210	24
catalogue	NoC	12	–	74	25	confined	Verb	4	–	246	24
opera	NoC	7	–	171	25	pulling	Verb	24	–	0	24
Dublin	NoP	7	–	164	25	stressed	Verb	5	–	227	24
spiritual	Adj	10	–	114	25	eleven	Num	154	+	2566	24
compare	Verb	18	–	20	25	resignation	NoC	1	–	378	24
split	Verb	28	+	3	25	C.	NoP	0	–	479	24
regard	Verb	15	–	42	25	complex	NoC	7	–	162	24

2.3

Word	PoS	FrS		LL	FrW	Word	PoS	FrS		LL	FrW
avoided	Verb	3	–	301	24	curious	Adj	6	–	177	24
asleep	Adj	27	+	2	24	prospects	NoC	8	–	146	24
storm	NoC	7	–	174	24	visitor	NoC	5	–	218	24
liable	Adj	6	–	203	24	bones	NoC	12	–	64	24
ceiling	NoC	14	–	46	24	underlying	Adj	5	–	200	24
indication	NoC	16	–	32	24	managing	Adj	8	–	146	24
weekly	Adj	10	–	103	24	Jewish	Adj	8	–	141	24
representing	Verb	11	–	92	24	pipe	NoC	16	–	25	24
entering	Verb	7	–	176	24	electrical	Adj	15	–	36	24
racing	Verb	13	–	61	24	Oliver	NoP	13	–	54	24
Owen	NoP	4	–	257	24	charter	NoC	8	–	139	24
Atlantic	NoP	4	–	244	24	awful	Adj	92	+	970	24
guidelines	NoC	15	–	40	24	inches	NoC	18	–	13	24
humour	NoC	5	–	207	24	claiming	Verb	9	–	119	24
Latin	Adj	3	–	283	24	identical	Adj	5	–	213	24
habit	NoC	9	–	114	24	devices	NoC	6	–	170	24
mystery	NoC	7	–	161	24	sheets	NoC	25	+	0	24
delay	NoC	11	–	91	24	variables	NoC	4	–	248	24
nearby	Adj	3	–	282	24	Colin	NoP	33	+	29	24
bare	Adj	7	–	160	24	hearing	Verb	16	–	28	24
silk	NoC	5	–	203	24	clear	Verb	26	+	2	24
explore	Verb	8	–	136	24	timber	NoC	14	–	42	24
Grant	NoP	11	–	83	24	stores	NoC	14	–	39	24
phenomenon	NoC	3	–	310	24	uncertainty	NoC	6	–	179	24
cheese	NoC	41	+	83	24	coverage	NoC	9	–	107	24
sole	Adj	5	–	217	24	Terry	NoP	39	+	79	24
honour	NoC	5	–	223	24	California	NoP	6	–	190	24
Essex	NoP	12	–	69	24	M / m	Lett	242	+	5455	24
representative	NoC	11	–	81	24	gaze	NoC	1	–	402	24
increases	NoC	11	–	82	24	substance	NoC	7	–	152	24
cigarette	NoC	12	–	72	24	matches	NoC	14	–	43	24
G / g	Lett	182	+	3422	24	sixth	Ord	40	+	87	24
J	NoP	0	–	473	24	assault	NoC	5	–	224	24
bath	NoC	44	+	117	24	strain	NoC	7	–	148	24
participants	NoC	4	–	251	24	win	NoC	9	–	110	24
egg	NoC	33	+	27	24	tool	NoC	8	–	139	24
profile	NoC	9	–	119	24	laughing	Verb	28	+	8	24
occupation	NoC	10	–	108	24	tight	Adj	21	+	3	24
identification	NoC	6	–	177	24	classroom	NoC	13	–	53	24
poet	NoC	6	–	190	24	Ford	NoP	7	–	163	24
harm	NoC	13	–	56	24	glasses	NoC	37	+	56	24
valid	Adj	12	–	64	24	Great	NoP-	6	–	191	24
bathroom	NoC	33	+	27	24	hide	Verb	14	–	41	24
angle	NoC	28	+	5	24	jury	NoC	17	–	19	24
deny	Verb	11	–	90	24	cotton	NoC	11	–	82	24
red	NoC	11	–	87	24	emperor	NoC	1	–	368	24
fate	NoC	4	–	239	24	nowhere	Adv	24	+	0	24
obligation	NoC	6	–	189	24	mixed	Verb	19	–	7	24
waters	NoC	7	–	155	24	facility	NoC	13	–	56	24
divisions	NoC	6	–	176	24	L / l	Lett	93	+	1012	24
adds	Verb	6	–	186	24	gross	Adj	14	–	44	24
multiple	Adj	8	–	141	24	pushing	Verb	23	+	0	24
sectors	NoC	15	–	40	24	canal	NoC	4	–	238	24
damages	NoC	5	–	223	24	viewed	Verb	2	–	340	23
Egypt	NoP	6	–	191	24	libraries	NoC	5	–	212	23
Rachel	NoP	8	–	145	24	consultation	NoC	32	+	24	23
voted	Verb	14	–	46	24	secret	NoC	7	–	164	23
automatic	Adj	12	–	66	24	posts	NoC	11	–	83	23
lawyer	NoC	6	–	196	24	wanting	Verb	31	+	19	23
depression	NoC	10	–	92	24	registration	NoC	13	–	54	23
silly	Adj	66	+	442	24	stability	NoC	5	–	221	23
Van/van	NoP	3	–	284	24	recovered	Verb	5	–	218	23
responded	Verb	5	–	218	24	finish	Verb	80	+	738	23
travelled	Verb	7	–	149	24	sign	Verb	36	+	56	23
distinctive	Adj	2	–	318	24	presidential	Adj	3	–	261	23
conservatives*	NoC	19	–	11	24	Louis	NoP	2	–	328	23

Word	PoS	FrS		LL	FrW	Word	PoS	FrS		LL	FrW
pointing	Verb	10	–	97	23	unexpected	Adj	3	–	260	23
Wood	NoP	9	–	106	23	dear	Int	157	+	2762	23
farming	NoC	8	–	130	23	exclusive	Adj	4	–	218	23
Albert	NoP	13	–	50	23	sessions	NoC	9	–	110	23
titles	NoC	5	–	204	23	force	Verb	10	–	92	23
arrange	Verb	17	–	18	23	Westminster	NoP	11	–	68	23
restricted	Verb	5	–	210	23	errors	NoC	6	–	178	23
Young	NoP	3	–	263	23	1967	Num	0	–	401	23
marginal	Adj	7	–	148	23	controversial	Adj	7	–	135	23
publishing	NoC	6	–	184	23	focus	Verb	8	–	115	23
bowl	NoC	18	–	10	23	Sheffield	NoP	9	–	103	23
assessed	Verb	7	–	152	23	kingdom	NoC	11	–	74	23
sighed	Verb	0	–	434	23	cross	Verb	21	–	1	23
submitted	Verb	10	–	99	23	fabric	NoC	8	–	133	23
era	NoC	4	–	228	23	priest	NoC	6	–	162	23
sets	Verb	11	–	76	23	maintaining	Verb	7	–	153	23
arising	Verb	13	–	52	23	flying	Verb	16	–	23	23
transactions	NoC	5	–	215	23	succeed	Verb	9	–	111	23
namely	Adv	8	–	136	23	talent	NoC	5	–	211	23
Maria	NoP	5	–	203	23	but	Prep	14	–	41	23
observations	NoC	7	–	151	23	horror	NoC	8	–	131	23
trials	NoC	3	–	273	23	gains	NoC	5	–	211	23
satisfactory	Adj	9	–	104	23	bent	Verb	6	–	162	23
hanging	Verb	25	+	1	23	capitalist	Adj	2	–	323	23
depending on	Prep	18	–	10	23	sympathy	NoC	10	–	82	23
official	NoC	5	–	193	23	demand	Verb	7	–	141	23
oral	Adj	5	–	217	23	prosecution	NoC	6	–	180	23
typically	Adv	5	–	191	23	petrol	NoC	31	+	25	23
refuse	Verb	8	–	127	23	pop	NoC	12	–	55	23
interpreted	Verb	4	–	236	23	concentrations	NoC	2	–	290	23
chemicals	NoC	9	–	112	23	crash	NoC	7	–	134	23
disposal	NoC	6	–	172	23	separated	Verb	5	–	198	23
lists	NoC	10	–	95	23	urgent	Adj	11	–	66	23
resource	NoC	15	–	29	23	enjoying	Verb	14	–	33	23
album	NoC	9	–	103	23	improved	Adj	6	–	173	23
reflects	Verb	8	–	133	23	Walker	NoP	2	–	294	23
generations	NoC	6	–	179	23	Poland	NoP	4	–	225	23
connections	NoC	4	–	249	23	effectiveness	NoC	3	–	250	23
gastric	Adj	0	–	454	23	creatures	NoC	3	–	272	23
engineer	NoC	16	–	24	23	audit	NoC	14	–	39	23
organic	Adj	4	–	222	23	clothing	NoC	10	–	83	23
Kevin	NoP	25	+	1	23	foods	NoC	5	–	191	23
electoral	Adj	9	–	113	23	good	NoC	41	+	110	23
carpet	NoC	30	+	16	23	lands	NoC	3	–	275	23
exact	Adj	13	–	46	23	trends	NoC	7	–	148	23
perception	NoC	11	–	73	23	marked	Adj	6	–	172	23
continued	Adj	5	–	215	23	enables	Verb	8	–	121	23
federation	NoC	10	–	90	23	Davies	NoP	2	–	301	23
failing	Verb	7	–	156	23	in part	Adv	4	–	218	23
ideology	NoC	3	–	262	23	removal	NoC	8	–	115	23
conversion	NoC	6	–	160	23	tale	NoC	7	–	152	23
by now	Adv	12	–	55	23	cold	NoC	29	+	15	23
lessons	NoC	23	–	0	23	falls	Verb	12	–	61	23
preference	NoC	11	–	80	23	resolved	Verb	8	–	126	23
cm	NoC	0	–	452	23	farmer	NoC	13	–	41	23
statistical	Adj	4	–	220	23	lease	NoC	6	–	154	23
collapse	NoC	3	–	262	23	paragraph	NoC	56	+	316	23
males	NoC	17	–	18	23	flower	NoC	15	–	24	23
keeps	Verb	49	+	196	23	expected	Adj	8	–	114	23
roughly	Adv	26	+	3	23	scenes	NoC	5	–	193	23
directions	NoC	14	–	39	23	persuaded	Verb	6	–	154	23
blame	Verb	24	+	0	23	ring	Verb	88	+	934	23
preferred	Verb	4	–	233	23	fed	Verb	13	–	40	23
sorts	NoC	88	+	927	23	declined	Verb	3	–	278	23
Gary	NoP	34	+	44	23	emerge	Verb	4	–	233	23
desirable	Adj	5	–	201	23	guardian	NoC	5	–	184	23

Word	PoS	FrS		LL	FrW		Word	PoS	FrS		LL	FrW
sciences	NoC	6	–	168	23		formerly	Adv	1	–	353	22
banking	NoC	6	–	166	23		blocks	NoC	12	–	54	22
innocent	Adj	8	–	127	23		O / o	Lett	245	+	5747	22
injured	Verb	8	–	117	23		clever	Adj	36	+	69	22
hate	Verb	65	+	467	23		Miller	NoP	4	–	224	22
paint	NoC	20	–	3	23		reluctant	Adj	6	–	163	22
leave	NoC	14	–	35	23		actor	NoC	6	–	163	22
swept	Verb	4	–	235	23		superb	Adj	11	–	71	22
joining	Verb	16	–	18	23		marine	Adj	2	–	299	22
load	NoC	52	+	257	23		uncertain	Adj	3	–	249	22
pregnant	Adj	19	–	5	23		Stewart	NoP	8	–	105	22
resigned	Verb	3	–	261	23		gesture	NoC	4	–	214	22
specified	Verb	3	–	246	23		closer	Adj	9	–	95	22
establishing	Verb	4	–	215	22		addition	NoC	9	–	100	22
conviction	NoC	3	–	242	22		converted	Verb	6	–	168	22
permitted	Verb	4	–	225	22		Baker	NoP	2	–	276	22
wire	NoC	17	–	11	22		traditionally	Adv	10	–	77	22
sheer	Adj	6	–	157	22		diplomatic	Adj	3	–	252	22
romantic	Adj	4	–	231	22		composed	Verb	3	–	244	22
funeral	NoC	13	–	43	22		institutional	Adj	2	–	284	22
Dave	NoP	64	+	446	22		Jackson	NoP	5	–	181	22
humans	NoC	3	–	252	22		bands	NoC	7	–	128	22
formally	Adv	19	–	3	22		cloud	NoC	11	–	70	22
favour	NoC	39	+	87	22		beds	NoC	17	–	11	22
gene	NoC	7	–	142	22		naked	Adj	8	–	116	22
everyday	Adj	11	–	65	22		stretched	Verb	6	–	162	22
register	NoC	9	–	92	22		winners	NoC	7	–	143	22
keys	NoC	24	+	0	22		fortune	NoC	15	–	23	22
exposed	Verb	3	–	251	22		32	Num	0	–	383	22
encouraging	Adj	11	–	66	22		chapters	NoC	2	–	302	22
hidden	Verb	6	–	170	22		registered	Verb	7	–	127	22
male	NoC	16	–	19	22		pairs	NoC	13	–	43	22
experienced	Adj	9	–	104	22		1969	Num	0	–	383	22
reactions	NoC	6	–	170	22		ease	NoC	3	–	258	22
Lawrence	NoP	15	–	26	22		gender	NoC	2	–	279	22
sharing	Verb	13	–	45	22		speakers	NoC	23	+	0	22
operated	Verb	8	–	120	22		Iran	NoP	3	–	258	22
export	NoC	5	–	177	22		genes	NoC	11	–	67	22
withdrawal	NoC	4	–	215	22		defend	Verb	10	–	72	22
full-time	Adj	7	–	134	22		installed	Verb	4	–	222	22
practitioners	NoC	1	–	345	22		acquire	Verb	4	–	218	22
knocked	Verb	33	+	41	22		tissue	NoC	9	–	93	22
declaration	NoC	4	–	218	22		strict	Adj	10	–	70	22
running	NoC	15	–	24	22		routes	NoC	15	–	23	22
warmth	NoC	5	–	193	22		justified	Verb	7	–	133	22
correspondent	NoC	3	–	276	22		discrimination	NoC	4	–	208	22
1950s	Num	0	–	424	22		wildlife	NoC	3	–	238	22
lesson	NoC	27	+	9	22		publications	NoC	3	–	246	22
magnificent	Adj	3	–	241	22		guess	Verb	45	+	174	22
prayer	NoC	10	–	80	22		corridor	NoC	14	–	32	22
daughters	NoC	8	–	108	22		bulk	NoC	9	–	99	22
hang	Verb	106	+	1384	22		hardware	NoC	12	–	55	22
fighting	NoC	7	–	129	22		print	NoC	15	–	20	22
friendship	NoC	3	–	241	22		distributed	Verb	8	–	106	22
asset	NoC	5	–	173	22		Hugh	NoP	10	–	70	22
letting	Verb	19	–	6	22		mechanisms	NoC	5	–	175	22
proceed	Verb	13	–	38	22		Billy	NoP	22	–	0	22
plans	Verb	3	–	243	22		references	NoC	9	–	95	22
scientist	NoC	6	–	160	22		wherever	Adv	32	+	38	22
established	Adj	4	–	226	22		drop	NoC	23	+	0	22
count	NoC	9	–	96	22		record	Verb	32	+	35	22
thoroughly	Adv	12	–	55	22		Clarke	NoP	9	–	87	22
drinks	NoC	15	–	24	22		recover	Verb	7	–	127	22
magistrates	NoC	12	–	48	22		commented	Verb	4	–	223	22
female	NoC	13	–	42	22		bearing	Verb	24	+	2	22
graphics	NoC	5	–	177	22		contacts	NoC	13	–	41	22

Word	PoS	FrS		LL	FrW	Word	PoS	FrS		LL	FrW
R.	NoP	0	–	427	22	navy	NoC	11	–	61	21
in accordance with	Prep	8	–	102	22	voters	NoC	5	–	187	21
						functional	Adj	7	–	134	21
Microsoft	NoP	5	–	182	22	biological	Adj	7	–	127	21
in response to	Prep	6	–	156	22	securities	NoC	1	–	315	21
no-one*	Pron	11	–	57	22	heritage	NoC	6	–	143	21
rest	Verb	8	–	103	22	capitalism	NoC	4	–	215	21
deliver	Verb	21	–	0	22	Marx	NoP	3	–	225	21
and/or	Conj	0	–	403	22	Emily	NoP	7	–	127	21
reflection	NoC	7	–	126	22	bonds	NoC	3	–	236	21
Christopher	NoP	32	+	41	22	rolled	Verb	7	–	125	21
craft	NoC	7	–	120	22	minimum	NoC	13	–	30	21
known	Adj	3	–	232	22	de*	Fore	4	–	195	21
anniversary	NoC	11	–	58	22	policeman	NoC	22	+	0	21
sociology	NoC	3	–	262	22	generate	Verb	8	–	108	21
protected	Verb	7	–	134	22	controversy	NoC	4	–	208	21
trousers	NoC	32	+	40	22	disappointed	Adj	17	–	8	21
destroy	Verb	8	–	108	22	passenger	NoC	8	–	96	21
justify	Verb	11	–	59	22	alarm	NoC	18	–	6	21
Swindon	NoP	12	–	46	22	venture	NoC	3	–	246	21
associations	NoC	10	–	75	22	killing	Verb	10	–	72	21
forests	NoC	2	–	283	22	suggestions	NoC	19	–	3	21
agenda	NoC	40	+	117	22	required	Adj	8	–	95	21
format	NoC	13	–	34	22	fiction	NoC	7	–	126	21
allowance	NoC	21	–	0	22	commander	NoC	6	–	155	21
dollar	NoC	8	–	104	22	worth	NoC	23	+	1	21
distinguish	Verb	5	–	164	22	tracks	NoC	4	–	216	21
Lords	NoP	3	–	253	22	mathematics	NoC	8	–	111	21
Bernard	NoP	14	–	31	22	increases	Verb	6	–	138	21
doubts	NoC	5	–	164	22	Fred	NoP	23	+	1	21
Clinton	NoP	5	–	189	22	escaped	Verb	5	–	176	21
belt	NoC	18	–	5	22	intend	Verb	18	–	5	21
rows	NoC	7	–	135	22	Russell	NoP	19	–	1	21
tourist	NoC	8	–	109	22	rid	Verb	73	+	680	21
digital	Adj	2	–	268	22	blow	NoC	11	–	60	21
superior	Adj	4	–	213	22	mentally	Adv	9	–	87	21
muscles	NoC	11	–	62	22	weapon	NoC	9	–	84	21
Kelly	NoP	19	–	3	22	chapel	NoC	10	–	68	21
Wright	NoP	3	–	241	22	Harris	NoP	6	–	152	21
estates	NoC	6	–	139	22	ensuring	Verb	5	–	172	21
equity	NoC	4	–	205	21	Moore	NoP	2	–	260	21
convenient	Adj	10	–	76	21	Susan	NoP	17	–	8	21
imports	NoC	2	–	267	21	inspection	NoC	8	–	95	21
restoration	NoC	3	–	259	21	reserves	NoC	10	–	68	21
murmured	Verb	0	–	421	21	colonel	NoC	5	–	170	21
damaged	Verb	8	–	109	21	ticket	NoC	28	+	19	21
styles	NoC	5	–	173	21	breeding	NoC	3	–	222	21
eighteenth	Ord	11	–	58	21	Clare	NoP	24	+	3	21
lightly	Adv	3	–	235	21	entertainment	NoC	12	–	44	21
mechanical	Adj	7	–	125	21	outlined	Verb	6	–	135	21
belong	Verb	17	–	7	21	Korea	NoP	4	–	201	21
artificial	Adj	8	–	100	21	democrats	NoC	12	–	47	21
rivers	NoC	7	–	127	21	shapes	NoC	6	–	151	21
resist	Verb	7	–	123	21	vote	Verb	37	+.	94	21
finance	Verb	5	–	180	21	deposits	NoC	2	–	285	21
S.	NoP	0	–	420	21	invasion	NoC	5	–	180	21
situated	Verb	3	–	227	21	knee	NoC	16	–	13	21
retail	Adj	7	–	116	21	escape	NoC	4	–	191	21
like	Conj	61	+	432	21	computing	NoC	5	–	158	21
strictly	Adv	7	–	124	21	desperately	Adv	8	–	91	21
implies	Verb	6	–	144	21	messages	NoC	10	–	71	21
regarding	Prep	12	–	44	21	cap	NoC	9	–	77	21
ocean	NoC	9	–	79	21	learnt	Verb	28	+	21	21
expecting	Verb	22	+	0	21	applying	Verb	10	–	72	21
spectacular	Adj	3	–	233	21	states	Verb	4	–	188	21
except for	Prep	11	–	53	21	champagne	NoC	5	–	163	21

Word	PoS	FrS		LL	FrW	Word	PoS	FrS		LL	FrW
exports	NoC	2	–	258	21	successive	Adj	3	–	239	21
snapped	Verb	3	–	223	21	frightened	Adj	23	+	1	21
stolen	Verb	7	–	118	21	productivity	NoC	11	–	51	21
assistant	NoC	8	–	107	21	quantities	NoC	5	–	170	21
carriage	NoC	10	–	61	21	display	Verb	4	–	200	21
fired	Verb	10	–	73	21	acknowledged	Verb	3	–	220	21
seller	NoC	1	–	303	21	refusal	NoC	3	–	227	21
joke	NoC	25	+	8	21	in case	Conj	36	+	89	21
Eliot	NoP	3	–	249	21	1945	Num	0	–	380	20
abstract	Adj	5	–	170	21	topics	NoC	9	–	83	20
jurisdiction	NoC	2	–	274	21	earned	Verb	9	–	79	20
satisfy	Verb	9	–	82	21	Pope	NoC	1	–	295	20
upstairs	Adv	63	+	487	21	wives	NoC	10	–	68	20
doubt	Verb	24	+	4	21	virtue	NoC	5	–	169	20
bench	NoC	13	–	35	21	beaten	Verb	7	–	111	20
availability	NoC	6	–	137	21	understanding	Verb	7	–	113	20
causes	Verb	11	–	48	21	deciding	Verb	6	–	132	20
RAF	NoP	2	–	278	21	constraints	NoC	10	–	66	20
C	NoP	0	–	362	21	secured	Verb	3	–	215	20
emotions	NoC	5	–	154	21	pursue	Verb	12	–	38	20
legislative	Adj	3	–	225	21	chemistry	NoC	19	–	0	20
testing	NoC	11	–	48	21	comparable	Adj	4	–	189	20
networks	NoC	4	–	192	21	butter	NoC	25	+	8	20
part-time	Adj	8	–	91	21	eg	Adv	0	–	401	20
stored	Verb	5	–	177	21	asks	Verb	14	–	18	20
Ross	NoP	4	–	189	21	creature	NoC	4	–	205	20
expenses	NoC	14	–	25	21	initiatives	NoC	8	–	102	20
working-class	Adj	0	–	408	21	suit	Verb	13	–	33	20
sisters	NoC	16	–	9	21	fails	Verb	3	–	240	20
folk	NoC	25	+	9	21	mixed	Adj	16	–	10	20
searching	Verb	3	–	228	21	Evans	NoP	3	–	214	20
associated	Adj	4	–	194	21	supporting	Verb	15	–	16	20
switched	Verb	17	–	7	21	straightforward	Adj	14	–	20	20
m	NoC	0	–	407	21	unhappy	Adj	8	–	89	20
moves	Verb	11	–	52	21	separation	NoC	3	–	221	20
obligations	NoC	5	–	165	21	cloth	NoC	14	–	22	20
recognize	Verb	24	+	4	21	refers	Verb	13	–	32	20
Asian	Adj	6	–	142	21	therapy	NoC	8	–	100	20
fleet	NoC	3	–	231	21	boats	NoC	16	–	11	20
cheaper	Adj	44	+	182	21	painful	Adj	10	–	61	20
stake	NoC	6	–	135	21	recalled	Verb	1	–	333	20
sadly	Adv	7	–	114	21	isolation	NoC	4	–	181	20
physically	Adv	13	–	28	21	remarks	NoC	11	–	46	20
nearest	Adj	15	–	19	21	influential	Adj	2	–	264	20
tube	NoC	12	–	45	21	curtains	NoC	19	–	1	20
judge	Verb	12	–	41	21	courage	NoC	8	–	94	20
singing	Verb	28	+	22	21	opposed	Verb	7	–	107	20
B.	NoP	0	–	406	21	duration	NoC	2	–	268	20
priorities	NoC	13	–	30	21	discussing	Verb	18	–	1	20
advise	Verb	19	–	2	21	invitation	NoC	8	–	101	20
1,000	Num	0	–	375	21	origins	NoC	3	–	235	20
refugees	NoC	6	–	144	21	debts	NoC	6	–	143	20
shell	NoC	11	–	54	21	incorporated	Verb	5	–	161	20
guns	NoC	14	–	20	21	accidents	NoC	15	–	13	20
designer	NoC	4	–	192	21	bags	NoC	36	+	92	20
compete	Verb	8	–	101	21	prevented	Verb	3	–	213	20
equivalent	NoC	8	–	103	21	Walter	NoP	4	–	187	20
continuing	Verb	9	–	79	21	150	Num	1	–	338	20
flexibility	NoC	13	–	33	21	autonomy	NoC	0	–	351	20
explicit	Adj	5	–	171	21	closure	NoC	11	–	48	20
spirits	NoC	6	–	127	21	conception	NoC	4	–	192	20
discretion	NoC	6	–	145	21	tonnes	NoC	5	–	166	20
feared	Verb	2	–	273	21	grants	NoC	12	–	36	20
specially	Adv	12	–	37	21	stuck	Verb	41	+	148	20
succession	NoC	2	–	260	21	complained	Verb	7	–	114	20
females	NoC	13	–	29	21	drinking	Verb	18	–	1	20

Word	PoS	FrS		LL	FrW	Word	PoS	FrS		LL	FrW
cheek	NoC	10	–	58	20	alter	Verb	12	–	31	20
gates	NoC	12	–	33	20	Cardiff	NoP	4	–	168	20
whereby	Adv	14	–	18	20	enabled	Verb	5	–	165	20
cinema	NoC	13	–	27	20	Eric	NoP	14	–	16	20
tip	NoC	18	–	2	20	limitations	NoC	3	–	219	20
wise	Adj	16	–	9	20	Robin	NoP	16	–	8	20
piano	NoC	14	–	19	20	collections	NoC	3	–	234	20
grade	NoC	11	–	42	20	desert	NoC	6	–	125	20
describing	Verb	9	–	81	20	assuming	Verb	12	–	35	20
diary	NoC	20	–	0	20	abbey	NoC	12	–	36	20
harbour	NoC	3	–	207	20	mayor	NoC	35	+	86	20
covers	Verb	13	–	23	20	cable	NoC	7	–	112	20
random	Adj	4	–	175	20	organized	Verb	20	–	0	20
merchant	NoC	3	–	217	20	flying	Adj	8	–	85	20
impose	Verb	9	–	78	20	appeal	Verb	10	–	55	20
past	Adv	29	+	29	20	questioned	Verb	4	–	178	20
resort	NoC	6	–	138	20	suspended	Verb	3	–	214	20
Stuart	NoP	29	+	34	20	count	Verb	35	+	84	20
laugh	Verb	30	+	37	20	hopes	Verb	4	–	178	20
unnecessary	Adj	5	–	161	20	analysed	Verb	0	–	340	20
burst	Verb	6	–	138	20	earliest	Adj	6	–	130	20
signals	NoC	6	–	127	20	earn	Verb	21	+	0	20
boundary	NoC	22	+	1	20	lifetime	NoC	7	–	113	20
launch	NoC	6	–	131	20	assured	Verb	7	–	101	20
E.	NoP	0	–	394	20	consensus	NoC	5	–	145	20
masters	NoC	4	–	177	20	achieving	Verb	8	–	87	20
Tories	NoC	19	–	1	20	midnight	NoC	11	–	38	20
economies	NoC	7	–	115	20	Dean	NoP	7	–	108	20
restored	Verb	3	–	227	20	wars	NoC	11	–	48	20
producers	NoC	4	–	171	20	Jews	NoC	6	–	132	20
estimates	NoC	12	–	37	20	diseases	NoC	7	–	101	20
stick	Verb	68	+	612	20	concrete	Adj	1	–	296	20
purchaser	NoC	2	–	259	20	liberation	NoC	4	–	186	20
correctly	Adv	12	–	39	20	van	NoC	33	+	70	20
solve	Verb	14	–	20	20	reign	NoC	1	–	301	20
rape	NoC	9	–	66	20	grinned	Verb	0	–	347	20
Lord	NoP	17	–	4	20	heading	Verb	8	–	81	20
root	NoC	25	+	10	20	intelligent	Adj	13	–	24	20
aggressive	Adj	14	–	18	20	delight	NoC	3	–	205	20
terrace	NoC	5	–	159	20	heating	NoC	24	+	7	20
Morgan	NoP	4	–	188	20	differ	Verb	6	–	129	20
till	Conj	64	+	531	20	wonder	NoC	16	–	5	20
closed	Adj	21	+	0	20	demanding	Verb	5	–	136	20
surveys	NoC	7	–	108	20	clerk	NoC	18	–	0	20
genetic	Adj	4	–	178	20	railways	NoC	12	–	33	20
confused	Adj	15	–	13	20	journalists	NoC	4	–	182	20
demonstration	NoC	7	–	108	20	guy	NoC	63	+	530	20
requiring	Verb	3	–	207	20	necessity	NoC	6	–	134	20
swung	Verb	2	–	280	20	IRA	NoP	0	–	384	20
unfair	Adj	14	–	16	20	kissed	Verb	3	–	219	20
elegant	Adj	2	–	244	20	essence	NoC	7	–	109	20
giant	Adj	3	–	200	20	subtle	Adj	6	–	131	20
mud	NoC	13	–	24	20	Pakistan	NoP	3	–	230	20
Bishop	NoP	5	–	158	20	monthly	Adj	14	–	16	20
trains	NoC	15	–	11	20	release	Verb	7	–	101	20
parallel	Adj	2	–	244	20	visiting	Verb	8	–	92	20
interior	NoC	2	–	275	20	skilled	Adj	6	–	124	20
bible	NoC	19	–	0	20	suspect	Verb	27	+	22	20
constituency	NoC	10	–	56	20	suppliers	NoC	4	–	169	20
producer	NoC	3	–	224	20	chairs	NoC	22	+	2	20
Vietnam	NoP	5	–	147	20	shaking	Verb	6	–	121	20
resulting	Verb	2	–	251	20	officially	Adv	5	–	155	20
1964	Num	0	–	377	20	simultaneously	Adv	3	–	229	20

List 2.4. Distinctiveness list contrasting speech and writing

(Ordered by Log Likelihood; not lemmatized; minimum log likelihood of 1000).

PoS = Part of speech
FrS = Rounded frequency (per million word tokens) in the spoken part of the BNC
LL = Log Likelihood, indicating the distinctiveness (or significance of the difference) between the frequencies in speech and writing
FrW = Rounded frequency (per million word tokens) in the written part of the BNC
+ = Higher frequency in speech
− = Higher frequency in writing

Word	PoS	FrS	LL	FrW	Word	PoS	FrS	LL	FrW
er	Uncl	8542 +	390869	11	ah	Int	712 +	22842	28
you	Pron	25957 +	385328	4755	one	Pron	2532 +	21938	770
's	Verb	17677 +	384464	1848	want	Verb	1776 +	20109	432
I	Pron	29448 +	369238	6494	then	Adv	3474 +	19911	1378
yeah	Int	7890 +	356172	17	ca~	VMod	1248 +	19835	210
erm	Uncl	6029 +	281015	2	if	Conj	4544 +	18764	2118
that	DetP	14252 +	213613	2581	ooh	Int	424 +	18553	2
~ n't	Neg	12212 +	177089	2300	alright*	Adv	408 +	18179	1
oh	Int	5052 +	166592	179	sort of	Adv	472 +	17161	11
it	Pron	24508 +	151913	9298	its	Det	338 −	17017	1782
mm	Int	3163 +	146051	3	her*	Det	644 −	16899	2362
no	Int	4388 +	128715	230	lot*	NoC	992 +	16309	160
do	Verb	9594 +	126017	2016	have*	Verb	7488 +	16057	4416
got	Verb	5025 +	117320	459	five	Num	1308 +	15609	303
've	Verb	4735 +	108766	446	alright*	Adj	366 +	15498	3
yes	Int	3840 +	107268	231	'd	VMod	1194 +	15417	256
well	Adv	5310 +	107026	634	put	Verb	1640 +	15152	475
we	Pron	10448 +	106914	2784	aye	Int	414 +	15007	10
know	Verb	5550 +	104930	734	used	VMod	742 +	15000	88
the	Det	39605 −	104720	64420	~n~*	Neg	367 +	14924	4
of*	Prep	14550 −	104519	31109	now	Adv	2864 +	14540	1211
're	Verb	4255 +	93216	439	your	Det	2859 +	14438	1212
what	DetP	7313 +	75414	1936	because*	Conj	2039 +	14376	715
think	Verb	3977 +	71946	562	~ta*	Inf	326 +	13786	2
cos*	Conj	1535 +	68811	4	fifty	Num	519 +	13755	36
right	Adv	2209 +	62243	130	thing	NoC	1136 +	13670	261
~na*	Inf	1376 +	58868	8	on	Adv	1849 +	13638	630
'll	VMod	3066 +	53585	455	come	Verb	1737 +	13389	574
mean	Verb	2250 +	53431	198	see	Verb	2507 +	13371	1033
they	Pron	9333 +	52132	3754	nineteen	Num	370 +	12972	10
gon~	Verb	1154 +	49873	6	thirty	Num	520 +	12743	43
get	Verb	3464 +	46650	709	from	Prep	2178 −	12708	4360
there	Adv	2894 +	45269	498	ninety	Num	342 +	12638	7
so	Adv	5067 +	44484	1526	bit*	NoC	635 +	12403	80
just	Adv	3820 +	40726	982	thank	Verb	595 +	12397	67
okay*	Adv	950 +	40074	7	like	Verb	1070 +	12162	260
'm	Verb	2512 +	38492	443	doing	Verb	943 +	12144	202
go	Verb	2885 +	35449	649	nice	Adj	603 +	11893	74
by	Prep	1663 −	35309	5493	very	Adv	2373 +	11530	1025
mhm	Int	722 +	33831	0	pounds	NoC	572 +	11301	71
like	Adv	784 +	32469	7	here	Adv	1640 +	11087	590
in	Prep	11609 −	31394	18978	thousand	NoC	516 +	10998	56
his	Det	1333 −	31332	4627	them	Pron	3126 +	10733	1572
's	Gen	1606 −	29320	4945	eighty	Num	296 +	10313	8
going*	Verb	2174 +	27109	482	right	Adj	1019 +	10192	277
actually	Adv	1239 +	25097	147	aha	Int	237 +	10125	1
really	Adv	1727 +	24300	337	an	Det	1846 −	10000	3613
say	Verb	2116 +	24125	512	four	Num	1199 +	9982	376
twenty	Num	925 +	23929	67	sort	NoC	712 +	9947	140
hundred	NoC	1023 +	23691	95	somebody	Pron	409 +	9932	34
did	Verb	3368 +	22872	1210	forty	Num	388 +	9928	29

2.4

Word	PoS	FrS		LL	FrW	Word	PoS	FrS		LL	FrW
as well	Adv	516	+	9892	67	may	VMod	480	–	5470	1211
nine	Num	571	+	9860	86	talking	Verb	428	+	5463	93
me*	Det	219	+	9843	1	M / m	Lett	242	+	5455	24
three	Num	1721	+	9654	691	people	NoC	2063	+	5371	1146
as	Conj	1558	–	9631	3174	anybody	Pron	249	+	5359	26
does	Verb	1549	+	9615	587	between	Prep	338	–	5239	968
something	Pron	1290	+	9584	437	has	Verb	1598	–	5051	2708
their	Det	1284	–	9386	2761	coming	Verb	522	+	5045	146
wan~	Verb	231	+	9356	3	a	Det	18637	–	4992	21972
look	Verb	1123	+	9310	353	bloody	Adj	247	+	4983	30
there	Ex	4067	+	9288	2354	3	Num	6	–	4900	279
about	Prep	2730	+	9185	1384	though	Conj	5	–	4885	273
things	NoC	1103	+	9183	346	C / c	Lett	431	+	4884	105
with	Prep	4446	–	8896	6821	everybody	Pron	267	+	4882	37
sixty	Num	294	+	8781	15	twelve	Num	278	+	4881	41
a bit	Adv	496	+	8543	75	yo	Uncl	103	+	4822	0
in	Verb	191	+	8530	1	yep	Int	117	+	4760	1
anyway	Adv	503	+	8512	78	getting	Verb	539	+	4647	165
six	Num	863	+	8443	239	more	Adv	624	–	4646	1351
quite	Adv	1050	+	8435	338	remember	Verb	513	+	4528	154
percent*	NoC	233	+	8355	6	like	Prep	1762	+	4525	983
mum	NoC	410	+	8323	48	down	Adv	1472	+	4515	772
in	Adv	1307	+	8310	488	little	Adj	700	+	4476	261
me	Pron	2444	+	8239	1239	round	Adv	415	+	4467	106
eight	Num	606	+	8237	123	ya	Pron	117	+	4449	2
two	Num	2710	+	8229	1428	stuff	NoC	274	+	4430	45
which	DetP	2208	+	8187	3893	per cent*	NoC	69	–	4353	418
let's	VMod	401	+	8097	48	mummy	NoC	159	+	4312	10
where	Adv	1380	+	8075	541	okay*	Adj	129	+	4259	4
done	Verb	931	+	7898	288	such as	Prep	43	–	4252	354
to	Prep	6950	+	7715	9620	T / t	Lett	245	+	4186	37
had	Verb	2835	–	7697	4639	E / e	Lett	263	+	4180	44
however	Adv	90	–	7648	664	4	Num	3	–	4049	224
1	Num	9	–	7542	428	out	Adv	2316	+	3968	1452
pound	NoC	327	+	7521	31	need	Verb	749	+	3967	310
of*	Verb	162	+	7351	0	dad	NoC	268	+	3870	51
but	Conj	6366	+	7310	4370	S / s	Lett	267	+	3846	51
wo~	VMod	552	+	7229	116	tell	Verb	668	+	3824	265
how	Adv	1888	+	7106	915	10	Num	2	–	3823	207
ha	Int	220	+	7090	8	my	Det	2278	+	3796	1438
for	Prep	6239	–	7070	8664	thus	Adv	8	–	3757	228
though	Adv	410	+	7013	63	UK	NoP	0	–	3746	193
good	Adj	1566	+	6955	706	U / u	Lett	133	+	3745	8
seven	Num	565	+	6896	128	anything	Pron	633	+	3716	248
P / p	Lett	359	+	6865	47	'	Gen	141	–	3704	518
saying	Verb	577	+	6836	135	while	Conj	156	–	3694	543
ten	Num	616	+	6735	155	went	Verb	917	+	3675	433
2	Num	8	–	6706	383	most	Adv	199	–	3559	607
up	Adv	2891	+	6666	1668	new	Adj	603	–	3528	1208
can	VMod	3588	+	6572	2211	social	Adj	115	–	3523	458
goes	Verb	503	+	6537	107	pardon	NoC	114	+	3483	5
sorry	Adj	431	+	6473	78	began	Verb	25	–	3462	262
why	Adv	1113	+	6453	439	G / g	Lett	182	+	3422	24
seventy	Num	204	+	6319	9	lovely	Adj	231	+	3379	43
du~*	Verb	165	+	6150	3	5	Num	5	–	3363	195
all	DetP	3644	+	6115	2297	give	Verb	845	+	3270	405
such	DetP	225	–	5912	825	please	Adv	361	+	3259	106
one	Num	3034	+	5910	1839	mind	Verb	246	+	3245	51
ai~*	Verb	221	+	5909	15	among	Prep	26	–	3242	252
bye	Int	148	+	5794	2	quid	NoC	103	+	3232	4
O / o	Lett	245	+	5747	22	probably	Adv	585	+	3222	237
as	Prep	916	–	5727	1873	fifteen	Num	207	+	3222	36
eh	Int	211	+	5626	14	US	NoP	2	–	3220	176
no	Verb	152	+	5602	3	p.	NoC	0	–	3171	161
hello	Int	220	+	5546	17	o'clock	Adv	188	–	3095	30
also	Adv	556	–	5482	1328	fucking	Adj	114	+	3088	7

2.4

Word	PoS	FrS		LL	FrW	Word	PoS	FrS		LL	FrW
big	Adj	549	+	3054	221	minister	NoC	56	–	2249	258
eyes	NoC	63	–	3032	324	suppose	Verb	275	+	2237	88
fucking	Adv	92	+	3032	3	15	Num	1	–	2236	122
maybe	Adv	301	+	2996	82	back	Adv	1211	+	2229	745
else	Adv	475	+	2990	178	would	VMod	3278	+	2223	2467
us	Pron	1059	+	2981	573	sure	Adj	479	+	2211	212
both	Adv	111	–	2943	409	1988	Num	0	–	2207	115
political	Adj	71	–	2928	333	use	NoC	99	–	2204	334
course*	Adv	75	+	2925	1	large	Adj	116	–	2195	363
held	Verb	56	–	2920	302	after	Prep	539	–	2180	972
where	Conj	160	–	2907	492	daddy	NoC	106	+	2174	12
world	NoC	248	–	2867	629	company	NoC	158	–	2157	429
ones	NoC	318	+	2856	94	seemed	Verb	60	–	2144	259
during	Prep	152	–	2833	473	system	NoC	189	–	2141	476
1989	Num	1	–	2830	149	1992	Num	1	–	2138	114
thought	Verb	845	+	2811	430	England	NoP	56	–	2135	252
says	Verb	740	+	2804	358	absolutely	Adv	183	+	2104	44
state	NoC	108	–	2796	393	'd	Verb	577	+	2075	285
int	Uncl	59	+	2778	0	7	Num	3	–	2065	119
1990	Num	5	–	2774	166	today	Adv	503	+	2058	236
week	NoC	631	+	2765	286	several	DetP	64	–	2057	260
dear	Int	157	+	2762	23	study	NoC	38	–	2046	209
Mr.	NoC	5	–	2751	164	London	NoP	132	–	2022	377
20	Num	1	–	2748	146	century	NoC	42	–	2022	215
I / i	Lett	193	+	2743	37	whose	DetP	43	–	2013	216
mine	Pron	177	+	2739	31	ask	Verb	399	+	1997	170
under	Prep	234	–	2659	590	go	NoC	98	+	1978	12
minus	Prep	88	+	2636	4	court	NoC	94	–	1961	307
ha	Uncl	56	+	2633	0	bet	Verb	97	+	1947	12
take	Verb	1149	+	2625	665	each	DetP	243	–	1947	539
obviously	Adv	296	+	2620	89	urgh	Int	44	+	1922	0
morning	NoC	459	+	2610	183	British	Adj	141	–	1921	382
although	Conj	160	–	2604	468	11	Num	1	–	1919	103
international	Adj	38	–	2595	242	little	DetP	37	–	1917	200
start	Verb	365	+	2575	128	foreign	Adj	27	–	1909	177
eleven	Num	154	+	2566	24	minute	NoC	219	+	1907	66
into	Prep	1067	–	2560	1700	led	Verb	24	–	1901	170
himself	Pron	87	–	2542	337	II / ii	Num	0	–	1893	98
6	Num	5	–	2518	149	point	NoC	637	–	1887	338
12	Num	1	–	2494	135	in~*	Verb	40	+	1885	0
including	Prep	45	–	2487	252	tt	Int	49	+	1884	1
1991	Num	3	–	2472	142	act	NoC	56	–	1876	234
research	NoC	59	–	2461	279	become	Verb	109	–	1866	326
government	NoC	295	–	2425	660	law	NoC	88	–	1863	291
eighteen	Num	131	+	2416	18	Britain	NoP	77	–	1857	271
&	Conj	7	–	2402	151	despite	Prep	22	–	1846	160
basically	Adv	134	+	2390	19	8	Num	3	–	1845	108
off	Adv	831	+	2384	446	said	Verb	2685	+	1838	2018
became	Verb	45	–	2381	244	when	Conj	2255	+	1836	1649
this	DetP	5627	+	2379	4506	tomorrow	Adv	234	+	1831	76
against	Prep	257	–	2347	597	almost	Adv	118	–	1831	339
da	Uncl	64	+	2339	1	life	NoC	293	–	1821	598
made	Verb	539	–	2336	990	money	NoC	637	+	1818	343
half	DetP	440	+	2322	182	I / i	Num	0	–	1816	96
economic	Adj	53	–	2315	257	thirteen	Num	97	+	1816	13
former	DetP	21	–	2312	187	cor	Int	50	+	1815	1
found	Verb	209	–	2304	521	1987	Num	0	–	1807	95
gone	Verb	418	+	2299	170	studies	NoC	18	–	1801	149
hon.	Adj	0	–	2293	118	councillor	NoC	104	+	1795	16
award	NoC	13	–	2288	163	bloody	Adv	92	+	1790	12
30	Num	2	–	2275	127	patients	NoC	36	–	1788	189
N / n	Lett	157	+	2274	30	about	Adv	730	+	1785	414
till	Prep	122	+	2271	17	used	Verb	225	–	1783	497
over there	Adv	97	+	2271	9	public	Adj	102	–	1762	306
funny	Adj	161	+	2265	31	fourteen	Num	108	+	1745	18
greenbelt	NoC	51	+	2263	0	sixteen	Num	107	+	1734	17

Word	PoS	FrS		LL	FrW	Word	PoS	FrS		LL	FrW
try	Verb	396	+	1728	180	development	NoC	142	–	1471	345
described	Verb	26	–	1725	162	D / d	Lett	183	+	1469	59
herself	Pron	38	–	1723	187	EC	NoP	0	–	1468	75
gets	Verb	204	+	1718	63	tonight	Adv	178	+	1466	56
face	NoC	103	–	1704	303	before	Prep	220	–	1465	459
national	Adj	165	–	1698	401	de*	NoP	13	–	1461	117
will	VMod	1890	–	1698	2537	include	Verb	35	–	1453	165
further*	Adj	63	–	1698	234	no	NoC	0	–	1452	74
of course	Adv	543	+	1695	283	early	Adj	103	–	1442	283
been	Verb	2082	–	1693	2756	analysis	NoC	26	–	1437	145
pick	Verb	171	+	1690	47	shh	Int	34	+	1435	0
was	Verb	8097	–	1689	9368	returned	Verb	12	–	1434	114
death	NoC	57	–	1685	222	announced	Verb	13	–	1430	116
since	Conj	112	–	1681	316	K / k	Lett	94	+	1413	17
whatever	DetP	289	+	1663	114	bits	NoC	112	+	1406	25
followed	Verb	28	–	1658	163	remained	Verb	8	–	1406	101
doo	Uncl	40	+	1654	0	head	NoC	164	–	1401	372
1986	Num	1	–	1652	88	relations	NoC	17	–	1396	123
county	NoC	258	+	1648	96	F / f	Lett	121	+	1390	29
comes	Verb	328	+	1637	140	hang	Verb	106	+	1384	22
hm	Int	41	+	1626	1	smiled	Verb	3	–	1383	84
call	Verb	290	+	1624	117	again	Adv	836	+	1381	529
power	NoC	130	–	1621	340	buy	Verb	261	+	1380	108
without	Prep	227	–	1611	483	society	NoC	89	–	1379	256
a little bit	Adv	54	+	1610	3	to	Inf	14912	–	1371	16442
nought	Pron	44	+	1605	1	whom	Pron	26	–	1368	141
reckon	Verb	90	+	1601	13	expected	Verb	35	–	1366	159
14	Num	1	–	1597	89	la	Uncl	43	+	1362	2
possible	Adj	147	–	1595	364	thanks	NoC	162	+	1361	50
16	Num	2	–	1594	90	Friday	NoP	150	+	1357	44
18	Num	2	–	1592	90	looks	Verb	226	+	1353	87
chapter	NoC	30	–	1589	163	B / b	Lett	337	+	1353	159
continued	Verb	10	–	1587	117	following	Adj	29	–	1348	146
reached	Verb	18	–	1584	136	talk	Verb	266	+	1339	113
felt	Verb	106	–	1567	298	100	Num	2	–	1338	77
added	Verb	26	–	1557	152	king	NoC	37	–	1338	160
systems	NoC	43	–	1558	188	towards	Prep	123	–	1331	305
R / r	Lett	154	+	1556	41	appeared	Verb	16	–	1328	117
9	Num	2	–	1550	89	50	Num	1	–	1328	75
than	Conj	683	–	1547	1074	series	NoC	35	–	1323	156
recent	Adj	36	–	1540	173	round	Prep	245	+	1320	100
available	Adj	104	–	1531	291	be	Verb	5790	–	1319	6742
1985	Num	1	–	1530	82	process	NoC	78	–	1317	231
25	Num	2	–	1527	86	military	Adj	17	–	1317	119
small	Adj	216	–	1525	460	past	Prep	168	+	1315	55
upon	Prep	80	–	1521	252	knowledge	NoC	37	–	1314	158
etcetera	Adv	42	+	1520	1	known	Verb	93	–	1313	255
control	NoC	83	–	1520	256	Dr	NoC	19	–	1305	122
voice	NoC	48	–	1520	194	wee	Adj	59	+	1303	6
sit	Verb	209	+	1518	72	high	Adj	185	–	1298	392
often	Adv	175	–	1517	399	somewhere	Adv	173	+	1294	58
13	Num	1	–	1516	84	TV	NoC	1	–	1291	73
pence	NoC	68	+	1515	7	royal	Adj	38	–	1291	160
human	Adj	51	–	1515	199	Soviet	Adj	18	–	1291	119
that	Adv	150	+	1506	40	shown	Verb	40	–	1283	163
tape	NoC	139	+	1502	35	fig.	NoC	0	–	1282	65
data	NoC	51	–	1494	197	effect	NoC	87	–	1282	244
everything	Pron	359	+	1493	167	above	Adv	12	–	1280	103
required	Verb	30	–	1489	157	species	NoC	13	–	1277	106
art	NoC	35	–	1487	166	latter	DetP	5	–	1272	86
bloke	NoC	67	+	1484	7	turned	Verb	100	–	1269	263
voice	Verb	1	–	1482	82	as well as	Prep	55	–	1268	190
according to	Prep	37	–	1478	171	17	Num	1	–	1263	70
nil	Pron	53	+	1475	3	bad	Adj	296	+	1262	136
chairman	NoP	36	+	1474	0	Inc	Adj	0	–	1257	64
range	NoC	59	–	1471	211	24	Num	2	–	1253	72

Word	PoS	FrS		LL	FrW	Word	PoS	FrS		LL	FrW
d'	Verb	70	+	1249	10	Ltd	Adj	0	–	1084	57
Greater	NoP-	62	+	1249	8	major	Adj	104	–	1082	254
squared	Verb	40	+	1248	2	kids	NoC	119	+	1081	35
nor	Conj	27	–	1247	136	common	Adj	67	–	1075	196
reported	Verb	22	–	1241	124	prime	Adj	31	–	1074	131
hey	Int	73	+	1238	11	presence	NoC	11	–	1074	89
on	Prep	5659	–	1235	6569	III / iii	Num	0	–	1074	56
others	NoC	126	–	1235	301	1980	Num	1	–	1071	58
family	NoC	171	–	1226	365	title	NoC	18	–	1071	106
even	Adv	457	–	1226	746	USA	NoP	0	–	1069	56
follows	Verb	16	–	1223	110	bought	Verb	194	+	1068	79
European	Adj	69	–	1218	210	keep	Verb	449	+	1068	256
evidence	NoC	82	–	1218	230	performance	NoC	36	–	1065	141
body	NoC	109	–	1217	272	Corp	NoC	1	–	1065	58
pp.	NoC	0	–	1211	62	Ps / ps	Lett	23	+	1065	0
provide	Verb	88	–	1205	239	da	NoC	33	+	1062	1
own	DetP	443	–	1198	724	established	Verb	20	–	1062	108
likely	Adj	91	–	1197	243	growth	NoC	36	–	1061	141
granddad	NoC	28	+	1196	0	natural	Adj	43	–	1060	154
lots	Pron	126	+	1190	36	subject	NoC	66	–	1059	192
Europe	NoP	62	–	1188	195	similar	Adj	69	–	1059	198
v.	Prep	0	–	1185	60	22	Num	1	–	1058	59
wants	Verb	197	+	1185	76	much	DetP	764	+	1057	504
loads	NoC	64	+	1179	9	changes	NoC	69	–	1056	196
history	NoC	70	–	1176	207	ow	Int	22	+	1056	0
Charles	NoP	13	–	1173	100	eat	Verb	170	+	1053	65
action	NoC	88	–	1170	236	itself	Pron	105	–	1052	252
seventeen	Num	72	+	1165	12	personal	Adj	65	–	1051	189
within	Prep	253	–	1165	472	e.g.	Adv	0	–	1050	54
ee	Int	36	+	1164	1	events	NoC	23	–	1048	114
1981	Num	1	–	1159	63	IBM	NoP	0	–	1045	53
H / h	Lett	123	+	1157	35	designed	Verb	21	–	1043	110
results	NoC	43	–	1157	159	practice	NoC	62	–	1041	184
information	NoC	206	–	1155	407	considered	Verb	39	–	1037	144
1993	Num	1	–	1154	63	for example	Adv	107	–	1037	254
nature	NoC	63	–	1150	195	party	NoC	227	–	1035	423
education	NoC	115	–	1148	277	methods	NoC	16	–	1034	98
central	Adj	71	–	1148	207	28	Num	0	–	1033	55
at	Prep	4115	–	1147	4868	our	Det	1253	+	1033	914
market	NoC	135	–	1147	305	Darlington	NoP	2	–	1032	62
minus	NoC	38	+	1143	2	activities	NoC	29	–	1031	126
included	Verb	30	–	1140	133	French	Adj	40	–	1031	145
and	Conj	25210	–	1134	27002	parties	NoC	36	–	1030	137
21	Num	1	–	1128	63	1982	Num	1	–	1029	57
19	Num	0	–	1127	59	god	NoC	103	+	1027	28
Christmas	NoC	194	+	1125	76	set	Verb	174	–	1025	350
for	Conj	40	–	1120	151	K. / k.	Lett	22	+	1024	0
look	NoC	227	+	1120	97	New	NoP-	24	–	1023	115
stood	Verb	36	–	1119	144	period	NoC	111	–	1020	258
countries	NoC	57	–	1115	180	provides	Verb	13	–	1016	92
wonder	Verb	124	+	1111	37	job	NoC	382	+	1016	211
March	NoP	43	–	1109	157	behaviour	NoC	34	–	1013	133
theory	NoC	35	–	1108	142	developed	Verb	26	–	1013	119
April	NoP	44	–	1108	159	cases	NoC	71	–	1012	195
1983	Num	1	–	1107	64	L / l	Lett	93	+	1012	24
case	NoC	243	–	1106	453	looking	Verb	428	+	1009	245
role	NoC	66	–	1105	196	claimed	Verb	13	–	1008	91
production	NoC	50	–	1105	168	nodded	Verb	1	–	1008	57
forces	NoC	26	–	1102	124	result	NoC	74	–	1007	200
1984	Num	2	–	1101	65	May	NoP	50	–	1007	161
1979	Num	1	–	1096	61	supposed	Adj	133	+	1004	45
40	Num	2	–	1087	63	students	NoC	48	–	1004	157
industry	NoC	77	–	1087	212	arms	NoC	27	–	1002	120
treatment	NoC	31	–	1086	133	interest	NoC	133	–	1000	288
software	NoC	17	–	1085	103						

List 3.1 Alphabetical frequency list: conversational v. task-oriented speech (lemmatized)

Comparing the demographically sampled and context-governed parts of the spoken BNC

FrC = Rounded frequency (per million word tokens) in demographically sampled conversational speech
R = Range across conversational speech (maximum of 4 sectors)
  Range across task-oriented speech (maximum of 6 sectors)
DD = Dispersion (Juilland's D) in demographically sampled conversational speech
LL = Log Likelihood, indicating the distinctiveness (or significance of the difference) between the frequencies in conversational speech and task-oriented speech
FrT = Rounded frequency (per million word tokens) in context-governed speech (task-oriented)
DG = Dispersion (Juilland's D) in context-governed speech (task-oriented)
+ = Higher frequency in conversational speech
− = Higher frequency in task-oriented speech

Note: The list is restricted to lemmas with a frequency of 120 per million or more in one of the two speech subcorpora

Word	PoS	FrC	R	DD		LL	FrT	R	DG
'	Gen	74	4	92	−	250	188	6	85
's	Gen	1604	4	98	−	0	1608	6	91
a	Det	17056	4	98	−	962	19719	6	98
a		17055	4	98	−	962	19719	6	98
A / a	Lett	252	4	82	−	532	542	6	82
a		235	4	82	−	541	521	6	82
a.		16	4	81	−	3	21	6	76
a	Uncl	158	4	88	−	54	222	6	76
a bit	Adv	711	4	96	+	647	349	6	89
able	Adj	226	4	96	−	283	417	6	93
about	Adv	842	4	96	+	118	654	6	89
about	Prep	2274	4	97	−	552	3042	6	98
absolutely	Adv	161	4	92	−	19	198	6	88
accept	Verb	36	4	87	−	681	217	6	84
accept		26	4	88	−	407	140	6	84
accepted		7	4	85	−	204	57	6	79
accepting		1	2	36	−	57	14	6	93
accepts		1	3	50	−	7	6	6	79
account	NoC	30	4	95	−	425	152	6	81
account		22	4	87	−	287	106	6	83
accounts		8	4	80	−	138	46	6	74
across	Prep	135	4	94	−	61	199	6	93
action	NoC	21	4	79	−	525	151	6	83
action		18	4	72	−	489	136	6	81
actions		3	4	47	−	39	15	6	79
actual	Adj	56	4	94	−	215	150	6	93
actually	Adv	790	4	90	+	1221	1546	6	95
add	Verb	66	4	90	−	406	216	6	86
add		45	4	90	−	287	150	6	83
added		12	4	87	−	60	35	6	90
adding		6	4	62	−	51	22	6	78
adds		3	4	70	−	9	8	6	83
after	Conj	121	4	94	−	1	130	6	90
after	Prep	453	4	95	−	99	598	6	93
afternoon	NoC	174	4	91	+	19	140	6	85
afternoon		167	4	92	+	15	136	6	84
afternoons		8	4	85	+	6	46	6	76
again	Adv	839	4	97	+	0	835	6	93
against	Prep	79	4	95	−	1028	379	6	84
age	NoC	194	4	96	+	21	155	6	94
age		109	4	97	−	12	134	6	94
ages		85	4	87	+	210	21	6	89
ago	Adv	233	4	92	−	19	277	6	92
agree	Verb	63	4	89	−	1108	361	6	85
agree		47	4	90	−	534	210	6	88
agreed		11	4	88	−	585	135	6	78
agreeing		2	4	79	−	19	8	6	75
agrees		2	4	52	−	14	8	6	83
ah	Int	1394	4	91	+	4663	246	6	80
aha	Int	270	4	89	+	34	213	6	59
ai~*	Verb	500	4	85	+	2697	30	6	76
all	Adv	273	4	96	+	58	199	6	95
all	DetP	4027	4	96	+	282	3383	6	97
allow	Verb	128	4	93	−	117	219	6	93
allow		15	4	76	−	223	79	6	86
allowed		108	4	91	+	0	103	6	96
allowing		2	4	89	−	61	17	6	82
allows		3	4	64	−	72	21	6	90
almost	Adv	54	4	92	−	276	162	6	89
along	Adv	103	4	95	−	14	128	6	92
already	Adv	190	4	93	−	164	319	6	89
alright*	Adj	714	4	95	+	2355	129	6	84
alright*	Adv	703	4	96	+	1493	206	6	81
also	Adv	160	4	90	−	2370	827	6	91
although	Conj	66	4	89	−	442	224	6	92
always	Adv	670	4	98	+	62	547	6	90
amount	NoC	66	4	93	−	367	206	6	96
amount		63	4	93	−	321	190	6	95
amounts		3	4	81	−	50	17	6	83
an	Det	1149	4	95	+	1985	2323	6	96
and	Conj	21569	4	98	−	3800	27701	6	97
and so on	Adv	18	4	93	−	455	130	6	82
another	DetP	639	4	95	−	0	640	6	95
answer	NoC	75	4	83	−	277	198	6	94
answer		54	4	82	−	284	164	6	92
answers		22	4	80	−	13	34	6	92
answer	Verb	41	4	84	−	210	124	6	88
answer		23	4	89	−	180	85	6	86
answered		14	4	78	−	11	23	6	83
answering		1	4	67	−	34	10	6	83

Word	PoS	FrC R DD	LL	FrT R DG	Word	PoS	FrC R DD	LL	FrT R DG
answers		3 3 62 –	6	7 6 76	*'s*		21385 4 99 +	13596	12010 6 96
any	DetP	1223 4 98 –	332	1662 6 94	*am*		270 4 91 +	9	239 6 89
anybody	Pron	201 4 95 –	65	281 6 93	*are*		3929 4 97 –	837	5166 6 92
anyone	Pron	96 4 74 –	29	132 6 94	*be*		4558 4 98 –	1914	6633 6 95
anything	Pron	710 4 96 +	65	581 6 90	*been*		1762 4 95 –	355	2300 6 95
anyway	Adv	785 4 97 +	1094	311 6 87	*being*		370 4 95 –	834	814 6 93
application	NoC	6 4 77 –	714	141 6 79	*is*		8343 4 99 –	2368	11409 6 94
application		6 4 72 –	454	96 6 81	*was*		8272 4 97 +	26	7977 6 88
applications		1 2 36 –	266	46 6 71	*were*		2508 4 96 –	151	2914 6 88
apply	Verb	30 4 85 –	318	130 6 89	because*	Conj	1494 4 94 –	1071	2411 6 98
applied		10 4 78 –	38	27 6 90	because of	Prep	73 4 95 –	264	190 6 95
applies		3 4 73 –	71	20 6 88	become	Verb	48 4 86 –	1110	328 6 92
apply		12 4 86 –	208	69 6 86	*became*		8 4 80 –	273	70 6 86
applying		5 4 75 –	17	13 6 77	*become*		29 4 88 –	491	163 6 88
area	NoC	133 4 80 –	2269	748 6 89	*becomes*		8 4 77 –	187	56 6 92
area		112 4 81 –	1393	524 6 89	*becoming*		3 4 60 –	171	39 6 88
areas		21 4 72 –	928	225 6 87	bed	NoC	352 4 93 +	898	87 6 88
around	Adv	219 4 91 +	18	180 6 94	*bed*		330 4 94 +	931	73 6 87
around	Prep	84 4 91 –	157	173 6 89	*beds*		22 4 67 +	9	14 6 89
as	Adv	385 4 97 –	215	590 6 97	bedroom	NoC	130 4 81 +	207	47 6 74
as	Conj	851 4 97 –	2457	2040 6 97	*bedroom*		110 4 84 +	207	35 6 70
as	Prep	298 4 97 –	3439	1339 6 95	*bedrooms*		20 4 66 +	11	12 6 85
as well	Adv	657 4 96 +	267	420 6 92	before	Adv	263 4 92 +	33	208 6 93
ask	Verb	602 4 95 –	192	838 6 94	before	Conj	303 4 92 –	3	324 6 94
ask		339 4 94 –	65	440 6 92	before	Prep	169 4 95 –	87	255 6 94
asked		179 4 97 –	50	244 6 95	begin	Verb	47 4 95 –	217	135 6 84
asking		74 4 88 –	88	135 6 97	*began*		9 4 67 –	77	36 6 82
asks		9 4 80 –	13	18 6 94	*begin*		13 4 91 –	102	48 6 87
at	Prep	3274 4 96 –	1253	4691 6 96	*beginning*		15 4 82 –	32	32 6 77
at all	Adv	241 4 95 –	22	290 6 93	*begins*		9 4 74 –	2	12 6 75
at least	Adv	147 4 97 –	13	177 6 90	*begun*		1 3 62 –	27	8 6 72
authority	NoC	10 4 94 –	1664	312 6 82	behind	Prep	139 4 95 +	17	109 6 91
authorities		4 4 77 –	634	118 6 80	believe	Verb	177 4 92 –	336	368 6 89
authority		7 4 88 –	1030	194 6 82	*believe*		169 4 93 –	223	317 6 89
available	Adj	18 4 86 –	640	163 6 87	*believed*		5 4 56 –	81	26 6 84
aware	Adj	14 4 89 –	527	134 6 89	*believes*		2 3 57 –	70	17 6 76
away	Adv	488 4 97 +	48	396 6 88	*believing*		1 2 29 –	26	7 6 81
aye	Int	539 4 81 +	261	329 6 38	benefit	NoC	31 4 80 –	534	175 6 87
B / b	Lett	210 4 88 –	432	449 6 88	*benefit*		25 4 71 –	240	101 6 86
b		201 4 88 –	413	429 6 88	*benefits*		6 4 79 –	322	74 6 88
b.		9 4 84 –	19	19 6 67	bet	Verb	212 4 92 +	959	22 6 89
baby	NoC	153 4 91 –	102	84 6 61	*bet*		211 4 92 +	1002	19 6 90
babies		14 4 92 –	10	23 6 63	*betting*		1 3 62 –	1	2 4 64
baby		139 4 91 +	154	62 6 59	better	Adv	297 4 93 +	344	130 6 97
back	Adv	1408 4 97 +	225	1076 6 95	between	Prep	125 4 94 –	1096	485 6 93
back	NoC	366 4 95 +	199	216 6 91	big	Adj	890 4 95 +	561	501 6 85
back		361 4 95 +	212	208 6 90	*big*		772 4 95 +	623	397 6 85
backs		5 4 73 –	3	8 6 80	*bigger*		93 4 81 +	25	64 6 79
bad	Adj	538 4 93 +	348	300 6 91	*biggest*		26 4 82 –	14	40 6 89
bad		431 4 93 +	420	205 6 89	birthday	NoC	154 4 87 +	498	29 6 68
worse		83 4 90 +	14	62 6 90	*birthday*		150 4 88 +	504	26 6 64
worst		25 4 81 –	6	34 6 87	*birthdays*		4 4 57 +	3	2 4 52
bag	NoC	250 4 90 +	736	52 6 73	bit*	NoC	955 4 97 +	404	605 6 92
bag		191 4 90 +	655	32 6 72	*bit*		807 4 97 +	324	517 6 92
bags		60 4 91 +	106	20 6 74	*bits*		148 4 93 +	81	87 6 88
base	Verb	14 4 71 –	517	132 6 89	black	Adj	219 4 90 +	231	100 6 84
base		1 2 40 –	16	6 6 69	*black*		218 4 90 +	232	99 6 84
based		13 4 75 –	494	124 6 90	bloke	NoC	167 4 86 +	661	22 6 73
basing		0 1 00 –	8	2 6 63	*bloke*		140 4 85 +	570	18 6 70
basically	Adv	80 4 68 –	161	170 6 92	*blokes*		27 4 79 +	92	5 6 78
basis	NoC	11 4 86 –	672	151 6 81	bloody	Adj	559 4 87 +	2990	35 6 82
basis		11 4 86 –	672	151 6 81	*bloody*		559 4 87 +	3002	34 6 82
bases		0 2 66 –	1	1 5 76	bloody	Adv	212 4 89 +	1207	10 6 84
be*	Verb	59412 4 99 –	711	55376 6 99	blue	Adj	134 4 82 +	181	54 6 85
'm		3334 4 95 +	1865	1950 6 95	board	NoC	90 4 87 –	31	127 6 79
're		4681 4 98 +	300	3963 6 97	*board*		79 4 88 –	34	115 6 78

Word	PoS	FrC	R	DD	LL	FrT	R	DG
boards		11	4	77 −	0	12	6	77
body	NoC	75	4	85 +	177	168	6	87
bodies		6	4	82 −	104	33	6	88
body		70	4	85 −	103	135	6	84
book	NoC	345	4	94 +	35	279	6	89
book		252	4	92 +	33	197	6	88
books		93	4	97 +	3	82	6	85
both	Adv	61	4	95 −	169	144	6	88
both	DetP	146	4	94 −	71	218	6	91
bother	Verb	195	4	92 +	356	64	6	85
bother		100	4	95 +	141	39	6	82
bothered		84	4	85 +	210	21	6	87
bothering		9	4	88 +	23	2	6	74
bothers		3	4	73 +	0	2	5	62
bottle	NoC	121	4	90 +	247	37	6	77
bottle		93	4	90 +	230	23	6	78
bottles		29	4	90 +	29	13	5	73
bottom	NoC	149	4	89 +	39	105	6	88
bottom		139	4	89 +	27	102	6	88
bottoms		10	4	81 +	27	2	4	55
box	NoC	243	4	85 +	259	111	6	93
box		201	4	84 +	276	80	6	94
boxes		42	4	72 +	8	31	6	81
boy	NoC	388	4	93 +	666	134	6	82
boy		291	4	92 +	759	70	6	79
boys		98	4	93 +	34	64	6	81
break	Verb	152	4	93 +	1	144	6	88
break		60	4	84 +	0	59	6	90
breaking		16	4	88 −	8	25	6	87
breaks		9	4	62 +	0	8	6	74
broke		41	4	85 +	14	27	6	70
broken		26	4	92 +	0	26	6	89
bring	Verb	414	4	96 −	3	440	6	97
bring		234	4	96 +	9	205	6	95
bringing		34	4	95 −	21	53	6	94
brings		20	4	91 −	6	28	6	92
brought		127	4	89 −	12	154	6	95
British	Adj	48	4	86 −	494	204	6	76
brother	NoC	125	4	86 +	34	87	6	71
brother		102	4	81 +	79	54	6	73
brothers		23	4	74 −	11	34	6	68
budget	NoC	14	4	74 −	902	197	6	71
budget		12	4	80 −	811	177	6	72
budgets		1	2	21 −	91	20	6	68
build	Verb	98	4	88 −	216	215	6	93
build		31	4	86 −	110	81	6	92
building		12	4	89 −	20	24	6	90
builds		3	4	77 −	8	6	6	75
built		53	4	87 −	81	103	6	86
building	NoC	68	4	93 −	318	197	6	92
building		62	4	93 −	229	163	6	90
buildings		6	4	82 −	103	33	6	89
bus	NoC	166	4	83 +	107	93	6	69
bus		149	4	83 +	217	57	6	72
buses		17	4	78 −	32	36	6	59
business	NoC	103	4	92 −	674	347	6	86
business		98	4	91 −	570	312	6	86
businesses		5	3	59 −	116	34	6	71
but	Conj	6561	4	98 −	42	6232	6	97
buy	Verb	860	4	94 +	1508	293	6	88
bought		348	4	89 +	850	89	6	83
buy		415	4	94 +	626	156	6	89
buying		83	4	86 +	64	43	6	91
buys		15	4	85 +	30	4	6	83
by	Prep	783	4	94 −	3652	2265	6	92
bye	Int	264	4	91 +	629	69	6	71
C / c	Lett	226	4	82 −	884	609	6	88
C		217	4	82 −	824	577	6	88
C.		9	4	81 −	61	32	6	82
cake	NoC	131	4	90 +	446	23	6	75
cake		104	4	89 +	374	17	6	73
cakes		27	4	90 +	74	6	5	62
call	NoC	56	4	96 −	123	122	6	82
call		40	4	90 −	53	75	6	82
calls		16	4	89 −	78	47	6	82
call	Verb	555	4	96 −	86	704	6	90
call		243	4	96 −	56	322	6	92
called		271	4	96 −	27	329	6	86
calling		26	4	90 −	3	33	6	80
calls		15	4	92 −	2	19	6	80
can	VMod	5573	4	98 +	786	4332	6	96
ca~		1919	4	98 +	2503	789	6	94
can		3654	4	99 +	8	3543	6	96
car	NoC	738	4	92 +	1201	265	6	90
car		639	4	92 +	1245	201	6	89
cars		99	4	96 +	39	64	6	82
card	NoC	236	4	81 +	375	86	6	84
card		158	4	84 +	296	51	6	85
cards		78	4	75 +	86	35	6	81
care	NoC	31	4	78 −	357	139	6	75
carry	Verb	146	4	89 −	215	283	6	91
carried		21	4	78 −	279	102	6	79
carries		6	4	78 −	4	10	6	85
carry		95	4	87 −	26	130	6	95
carrying		23	4	90 −	21	40	6	92
case	NoC	96	4	97 −	1251	462	6	91
case		78	4	94 −	925	356	6	89
cases		18	4	89 −	329	106	6	85
cat	NoC	138	4	89 +	425	27	6	65
cat		111	4	90 +	387	18	6	69
cats		28	4	69 +	50	9	6	44
catch	Verb	140	4	95 +	83	80	6	90
catch		62	4	86 +	44	33	6	85
catches		4	4	71 +	0	3	6	88
catching		10	4	77 +	0	9	6	85
caught		64	4	93 +	44	35	6	88
cause	Verb	39	4	89 −	213	121	6	89
cause		20	4	76 −	20	35	6	82
caused		9	4	84 −	119	43	6	89
causes		4	4	86 −	35	16	6	87
causing		6	4	78 −	66	26	6	86
centre	NoC	56	4	93 −	490	217	6	86
centre		53	4	92 −	389	188	6	86
centres		3	4	73 −	115	29	6	78
certain	Adj	66	4	91 −	509	240	6	96
certainly	Adv	102	4	86 −	1071	434	6	87
chair	NoC	126	4	80 +	17	99	6	75
chair		94	4	79 +	2	85	6	72
chairs		33	4	82 +	37	14	6	85
chairman	NoC	5	4	66 −	1429	252	6	62
chairman		5	4	66 −	1418	251	6	62
chairmen		0	0	00 −	10	2	5	70
chance	NoC	93	4	93 −	77	155	6	83
chance		83	4	94 −	44	126	6	86
chances		9	4	79 −	48	29	6	69
change	NoC	90	4	86 −	348	241	6	87
change		78	4	86 −	71	133	6	86
changes		12	4	82 −	420	108	6	87
change	Verb	270	4	96 −	70	365	6	97
change		136	4	98 −	24	175	6	96
changed		103	4	94 −	18	132	6	94
changes		6	4	82 −	5	11	6	91

3.1

Word	PoS	FrC R DD	LL	FrT R DG	Word	PoS	FrC R DD	LL	FrT R DG
changing		25 4 94 –	32	46 6 88	*conference*		9 4 30 –	469	109 6 85
cheap	Adj	185 4 90 +	293	67 6 92	*conferences*		1 1 00 –	120	23 6 49
cheap		98 4 86 +	164	34 6 91	consider	Verb	24 4 88 –	669	184 6 84
cheaper		71 4 92 +	113	26 6 89	*consider*		15 4 76 –	327	99 6 84
cheapest		15 4 78 +	16	7 6 76	*considered*		5 4 87 –	264	62 6 84
check	Verb	104 4 87 –	8	124 6 87	*considering*		2 3 58 –	51	15 6 78
check		67 4 89 –	6	81 6 84	*considers*		0 2 42 –	32	7 6 76
checked		23 4 85 +	1	20 6 86	continue	Verb	12 4 73 –	664	152 6 83
checking		13 4 75 –	8	20 6 86	*continue*		9 4 68 –	458	106 6 84
checks		1 2 40 –	2	3 6 75	*continued*		1 4 100 –	81	17 6 77
child	NoC	267 4 92 –	821	655 6 82	*continues*		1 3 59 –	68	15 6 77
child		61 4 96 –	288	178 6 79	*continuing*		1 3 42 –	57	14 6 74
children		206 4 91 –	539	477 6 83	contract	NoC	31 4 76 –	271	120 6 74
Christmas	NoC	345 4 81 +	824	91 6 74	*contract*		21 4 68 –	238	93 6 72
church	NoC	126 4 43 –	0	127 6 75	*contracts*		10 4 87 –	39	28 6 78
church		99 4 54 –	5	113 6 74	control	NoC	34 4 78 –	275	128 6 87
churches		27 2 02 +	22	14 6 82	*control*		32 4 78 –	256	118 6 87
city	NoC	26 4 76 –	963	245 6 74	*controls*		3 4 48 –	19	9 6 77
cities		4 4 87 –	56	19 6 73	conversation	NoC	131 4 68 +	250	42 6 89
city		23 4 72 –	911	226 6 72	*conversation*		100 4 72 +	171	34 6 86
class	NoC	100 4 88 –	77	164 6 84	*conversations*		32 4 55 +	83	8 6 86
class		88 4 86 –	25	121 6 80	cos*	Conj	2705 4 95 +	6251	734 6 78
classes		11 4 79 –	92	43 6 86	cost	NoC	35 4 88 –	1030	279 6 81
clear	Adj	45 4 86 –	581	214 6 81	*cost*		27 4 86 –	575	175 6 85
clear		42 4 87 –	573	207 6 80	*costs*		7 4 86 –	471	104 6 73
clearer		3 4 70 –	7	7 6 80	cost	Verb	133 4 96 +	7	115 6 87
clearly	Adv	6 4 81 –	926	176 6 76	*cost*		100 4 94 +	21	73 6 90
client	NoC	4 4 85 –	868	157 6 78	*costing*		10 4 83 –	1	13 6 78
client		2 4 79 –	624	110 6 74	*costs*		22 4 89 –	3	28 6 79
clients		2 3 65 –	246	48 6 82	could	VMod	1922 4 96 –	2	1967 6 95
coat	NoC	121 4 76 +	506	14 6 77	council	NoC	68 4 77 –	3128	745 6 79
coat		108 4 75 +	498	10 6 73	*council*		65 4 77 –	2746	670 6 78
coats		13 4 79 +	24	4 6 80	*councils*		3 4 64 –	395	76 6 85
coffee	NoC	154 4 91 +	294	49 6 79	councillor	NoC	3 4 81 –	1290	219 6 53
coffee		153 4 91 +	299	48 6 80	*councillor*		2 4 80 –	1040	174 6 43
cold	Adj	205 4 92 +	510	51 6 84	*councillors*		1 3 59 –	251	44 6 79
cold		197 4 92 +	493	50 6 83	country	NoC	109 4 85 –	709	365 6 84
colder		7 4 48 +	19	2 5 70	*countries*		19 4 73 –	208	82 6 79
colleague	NoC	3 3 55 –	818	143 6 74	*country*		90 4 86 –	507	283 6 85
colleague		1 2 21 –	109	23 6 83	county	NoC	17 4 59 –	2287	438 6 67
colleagues		1 3 62 –	717	120 6 69	*counties*		3 3 46 –	36	13 6 78
colour	NoC	195 4 88 +	228	85 6 90	*county*		14 4 60 –	2269	425 6 66
colour		145 4 86 +	175	62 6 87	couple	NoC	270 4 88 +	56	198 6 95
colours		50 4 90 +	53	23 6 86	*couple*		267 4 88 +	68	189 6 94
come	Verb	3799 4 98 +	1237	2557 6 94	*couples*		3 4 77 –	15	9 6 74
came		480 4 94 +	0	469 6 84	course	NoC	66 4 83 –	564	253 6 91
come		2303 4 95 +	1282	1349 6 95	*course*		57 4 83 –	415	202 6 88
comes		358 4 95 +	18	308 6 97	*courses*		9 4 78 –	154	51 6 84
coming		657 4 98 +	242	430 6 95	court	NoC	40 4 93 –	348	154 6 86
comment	NoC	25 4 73 –	573	169 6 79	*court*		37 4 94 –	269	132 6 86
comment		10 4 65 –	265	75 6 79	*courts*		2 3 62 –	91	22 6 89
comments		15 4 71 –	307	94 6 77	cover	Verb	83 4 87 –	156	172 6 91
committee	NoC	26 4 72 –	1452	331 6 77	*cover*		38 4 89 –	44	68 6 90
committee		25 4 71 –	1276	297 6 77	*covered*		28 4 85 –	90	70 6 91
committees		1 2 40 –	180	34 6 75	*covering*		8 4 65 –	15	17 6 86
community	NoC	14 4 73 –	1049	224 6 83	*covers*		9 4 75 –	12	17 6 86
communities		1 2 36 –	122	23 6 77	cup	NoC	200 4 86 +	323	72 6 60
community		14 4 75 –	929	202 6 84	*cup*		178 4 86 +	268	67 6 57
company	NoC	84 4 83 –	771	333 6 84	*cups*		22 4 85 +	59	5 6 81
companies		13 4 76 –	447	115 6 81	cut	Verb	262 4 91 +	102	169 6 87
company		71 4 82 –	381	218 6 84	*cut*		217 4 90 +	110	130 6 87
computer	NoC	84 4 81 –	47	129 6 63	*cuts*		9 4 78 –	0	10 6 84
computer		69 4 81 –	20	95 6 70	*cutting*		35 4 85 +	3	29 6 80
computers		15 4 73 –	37	34 6 43	D / d	Lett	126 4 76 –	161	235 6 83
concerned	Adj	30 4 86 –	689	204 6 87	*d*		118 4 76 –	171	227 6 83
conference	NoC	10 4 28 –	587	133 6 81	*d.*		9 4 70 +	0	8 6 60

Word	PoS	FrC	R	DD	LL	FrT	R	DG
da	Uncl	145	4	82 +	790	8	6	80
dad	NoC	600	4	95 +	3057	44	6	64
dad		598	4	95 +	3082	42	6	63
dads		2	4	58 +	0	2	6	70
daddy	NoC	258	4	81 +	1782	3	5	60
daddy		256	4	81 +	1782	3	5	65
darling	NoC	130	4	76 +	848	3	6	79
darling		130	4	76 +	849	3	6	79
date	NoC	58	4	99 −	113	122	6	87
date		49	4	93 −	90	101	6	85
dates		9	4	67 −	23	22	6	91
David	NoP	146	4	84 +	3	132	6	87
day	NoC	1132	4	97 +	30	1018	6	88
day		876	4	97 +	159	657	6	91
days		256	4	95 −	89	361	6	84
deal	Verb	40	4	92 −	852	259	6	87
deal		19	4	95 −	397	122	6	89
dealing		13	4	84 −	235	76	6	84
deals		1	4	81 −	64	15	6	75
dealt		6	4	54 −	156	45	6	88
dear	Int	324	4	91 +	1297	42	6	82
decide	Verb	107	4	96 −	172	212	6	92
decide		33	4	85 −	140	93	6	89
decided		65	4	95 −	45	105	6	94
decides		5	4	91 −	1	6	6	88
deciding		3	4	56 −	12	8	6	68
decision	NoC	24	4	83 −	807	210	6	83
decision		17	4	81 −	585	152	6	83
decisions		7	4	85 −	221	58	6	83
definitely	Adv	121	4	91 +	61	72	6	89
department	NoC	15	4	92 −	721	171	6	89
department		14	4	91 −	581	144	6	89
departments		1	3	59 −	146	28	6	90
detail	NoC	25	4	94 −	388	133	6	87
detail		7	4	77 −	289	71	6	81
details		18	4	94 −	124	62	6	91
develop	Verb	13	4	65 −	501	126	6	87
develop		5	4	56 −	252	59	6	83
developed		6	4	58 −	133	40	6	93
developing		1	3	42 −	111	24	6	84
develops		0	2	42 −	10	3	5	70
development	NoC	9	4	68 −	1360	255	6	71
development		8	3	65 −	1241	233	6	71
developments		1	3	67 −	119	22	6	70
die	Verb	131	4	90 −	4	146	6	87
die		40	4	86 −	0	42	6	95
died		72	4	87 −	4	84	6	82
dies		5	4	74 −	0	6	6	79
dying		14	4	84 +	0	13	6	65
difference	NoC	102	4	90 −	142	194	6	93
difference		100	4	90 −	70	161	6	93
differences		2	4	50 −	158	33	6	82
different	Adj	356	4	97 −	308	599	6	95
difficult	Adj	95	4	89 −	443	275	6	93
dinner	NoC	205	4	92 +	816	27	6	81
dinner		198	4	91 +	808	25	6	81
dinners		7	4	83 +	13	2	4	65
discuss	Verb	16	4	87 −	526	139	6	87
discuss		8	4	78 −	229	64	6	91
discussed		3	4	66 −	212	47	6	80
discussing		5	4	74 −	89	28	6	83
discussion	NoC	11	4	58 −	505	122	6	78
discussion		9	4	65 −	359	89	6	79
discussions		2	3	26 −	147	33	6	72
district	NoC	15	4	34 −	1060	228	6	65
district		13	4	38 −	865	189	6	67
districts		2	1	00 −	197	39	6	54
do	Verb	22196	4	99 +	12983	12807	6	94
d'		145	4	65 +	575	19	5	48
did		4805	4	98 +	4247	2386	6	88
do		12854	4	100 +	7687	7365	6	94
does		1852	4	98 +	414	1342	6	96
doing		1106	4	94 +	196	832	6	94
done		1077	4	95 +	161	831	6	94
du~*		357	4	85 +	1669	33	6	75
doctor	NoC	113	4	83 −	38	159	6	73
doctor		83	4	79 −	36	122	6	65
doctors		30	4	82 −	3	37	6	81
dog	NoC	301	4	89 +	766	74	6	92
dog		241	4	89 +	706	51	6	93
dogs		60	4	86 +	84	24	6	83
door	NoC	463	4	90 +	658	181	6	88
door		414	4	89 +	688	146	6	88
doors		49	4	92 +	12	35	6	82
down	Adv	1934	4	97 +	1009	1155	6	89
down	Prep	206	4	93 +	52	146	6	85
draw	Verb	91	4	82 −	110	167	6	90
draw		51	4	82 −	59	93	6	87
drawing		15	4	77 −	2	19	6	92
drawn		13	4	80 −	62	38	6	87
draws		3	4	77 −	3	5	6	74
drew		8	4	73 −	3	12	6	85
drink	NoC	163	4	93 +	510	32	6	79
drink		137	4	92 +	460	24	6	79
drinks		26	4	80 +	55	7	5	71
drink	Verb	158	4	92 +	527	28	6	80
drank		8	4	73 +	21	2	4	62
drink		98	4	91 +	341	16	6	80
drinking		33	4	88 +	77	9	6	71
drinks		8	4	74 +	49	0	1	00
drunk		13	4	93 +	55	1	3	55
drive	Verb	196	4	93 +	159	100	6	88
drive		83	4	89 +	78	40	6	87
driven		7	4	86 −	7	12	6	84
drives		10	4	82 +	14	4	6	82
driving		71	4	94 +	62	35	6	81
drove		25	4	88 +	38	9	6	76
drop	Verb	144	4	93 +	115	74	6	92
drop		68	4	94 +	70	31	6	85
dropped		55	4	90 +	43	29	6	90
dropping		11	4	75 +	3	8	6	88
drops		9	4	81 +	2	6	6	90
during	Prep	53	4	84 −	526	220	6	93
E / e	Lett	174	4	73 −	271	341	6	88
e		167	4	73 −	261	328	6	88
e.		7	4	75 −	10	13	6	72
each	DetP	160	4	96 −	209	299	6	92
early	Adj	85	4	93 −	138	170	6	92
earlier		10	4	92 −	80	38	6	86
earliest		3	4	66 −	8	7	6	86
early		72	4	91 −	70	124	6	92
easy	Adj	192	4	96 −	15	229	6	93
easier		57	4	97 −	6	70	6	90
easiest		10	4	76 −	4	14	6	76
easy		125	4	91 −	6	144	6	95
eat	Verb	509	4	90 +	1855	79	6	77
ate		30	4	80 +	111	5	5	56
eat		347	4	90 +	1337	49	6	79
eaten		35	4	91 +	113	6	5	65
eating		78	4	91 +	234	16	6	71
eats		19	4	76 +	66	3	5	77
education	NoC	27	4	66 −	591	177	6	75

3.1

Word	PoS	FrC	R	DD		LL	FrT	R	DG	Word	PoS	FrC	R	DD		LL	FrT	R	DG
education		27	4	66	–	589	176	6	75	*f.*		2	4	65	–	3	4	6	70
effect	NoC	22	4	81	–	718	188	6	83	face	NoC	154	4	96	+	102	86	6	93
effect		16	4	83	–	521	136	6	82	*face*		144	4	96	+	117	74	6	92
effects		6	4	73	–	196	51	6	82	*faces*		10	4	77	–	0	11	6	83
egg	NoC	121	4	87	+	299	31	6	76	fact	NoC	180	4	90	–	1759	740	6	90
egg		61	4	80	+	167	14	6	77	*fact*		177	4	90	–	1633	707	6	90
eggs		59	4	90	+	133	17	6	73	*facts*		3	3	51	–	144	34	6	87
eh	Int	461	4	88	+	2202	41	6	67	fair	Adj	130	4	97	–	1	138	6	95
eight	Num	590	4	89	–	5	625	6	91	*fair*		129	4	97	–	0	135	6	95
eight		580	4	89	–	8	624	6	91	*fairer*		1	3	59	–	5	3	4	60
eights		9	4	68	+	37	1	3	54	fairly	Adv	37	4	83	–	423	166	6	96
eighteen	Num	105	4	93	–	37	149	6	90	fall	Verb	167	4	96	+	21	132	6	93
eighteen		105	4	93	–	37	149	6	90	*fall*		53	4	94	+	3	45	6	92
eighty	Num	167	4	94	–	501	406	6	71	*fallen*		17	4	84	–	0	19	6	83
eighties		3	4	73	–	61	20	6	79	*falling*		29	4	92	+	3	23	6	87
eighty		164	4	94	–	452	387	6	71	*falls*		8	4	92	–	9	14	6	89
either	Adv	183	4	97	–	7	207	6	94	*fell*		60	4	89	+	50	30	6	88
eleven	Num	178	4	92	+	23	140	6	93	family	NoC	134	4	91	–	219	267	6	90
eleven		176	4	91	+	21	139	6	93	*families*		12	4	87	–	183	63	6	86
else	Adv	499	4	97	+	8	458	6	92	*family*		122	4	89	–	101	204	6	89
end	NoC	394	4	95	–	92	524	6	97	far	Adj	86	4	93	–	359	238	6	92
end		381	4	95	–	88	507	6	97	*far*		78	4	95	–	72	133	6	94
ends		13	4	69	–	3	18	6	84	*further**		6	4	63	–	487	102	6	77
enjoy	Verb	128	4	87	+	10	106	6	90	*furthest*		2	4	80	+	0	2	5	67
enjoy		61	4	82	+	4	51	6	90	far	Adv	135	4	95	–	288	292	6	94
enjoyed		45	4	87	+	2	39	6	87	father	NoC	117	4	88	–	54	174	6	69
enjoying		18	4	92	+	5	12	6	75	*father*		116	4	88	–	36	161	6	68
enjoys		4	4	74	+	0	4	6	71	*fathers*		1	3	67	–	49	13	6	74
enough	Adv	281	4	93	+	47	213	6	94	feel	Verb	474	4	91	–	56	583	6	96
enough	DetP	152	4	98	+	40	107	6	93	*feel*		305	4	90	–	68	404	6	96
er	Uncl	5075	4	93	–	10677	10913	6	86	*feeling*		49	4	95	+	19	31	6	87
erm	Uncl	3946	4	89	–	5387	7454	6	96	*feels*		30	4	87	+	0	30	6	92
even	Adv	463	4	94	+	0	453	6	95	*felt*		89	4	93	–	20	118	6	97
evening	NoC	95	4	95	–	24	128	6	83	few	DetP	278	4	88	–	96	392	6	95
evening		87	4	95	–	28	122	6	83	fifteen	Num	229	4	85	+	16	193	6	96
evenings		8	4	91	+	0	7	6	89	*fifteen*		228	4	85	+	15	192	6	96
ever	Adv	287	4	93	+	3	267	6	91	fifty	Num	433	4	96	–	143	606	6	72
every	Det	442	4	95	–	3	466	6	94	*fifties*		12	4	80	–	10	20	6	83
everybody	Pron	240	4	96	–	19	285	6	94	*fifty*		421	4	96	–	133	585	6	72
everyone	Pron	126	4	60	+	3	113	6	94	figure	NoC	33	4	84	–	1284	319	6	71
everything	Pron	433	4	97	+	105	309	6	92	*figure*		15	4	85	–	618	152	6	67
evidence	NoC	13	4	62	–	519	129	6	76	*figures*		17	4	77	–	666	167	6	74
evidence		13	4	62	–	518	129	6	76	fill	Verb	126	4	93	+	29	91	6	89
exactly	Adv	188	4	85	–	6	210	6	92	*fill*		76	4	95	+	24	52	6	86
example	NoC	19	4	59	–	586	157	6	90	*filled*		29	4	84	+	1	25	6	91
example		17	4	58	–	388	116	6	89	*filling*		15	4	94	+	4	11	6	82
examples		2	3	57	–	212	41	6	86	*fills*		6	4	86	+	3	3	6	78
expect	Verb	146	4	89	–	44	202	6	88	film	NoC	125	4	85	+	128	58	6	81
expect		110	4	89	–	4	125	6	85	*film*		103	4	87	+	148	40	6	83
expected		14	4	73	–	107	50	6	90	*films*		22	4	73	–	1	18	6	72
expecting		20	4	82	–	0	23	6	85	financial	Adj	11	4	88	–	529	125	6	82
expects		2	3	62	–	1	4	5	68	find	Verb	652	4	98	–	164	876	6	95
experience	NoC	39	4	90	–	417	168	6	92	*find*		441	4	95	–	106	590	6	94
experience		37	4	88	–	342	148	6	93	*finding*		20	4	86	–	46	44	6	91
experiences		2	3	51	–	83	21	6	85	*finds*		9	4	84	–	4	13	6	80
explain	Verb	49	4	83	–	261	150	6	92	*found*		181	4	98	–	27	229	6	93
explain		29	4	76	–	170	93	6	93	fine	Adj	186	4	92	–	1	196	6	90
explained		13	4	93	–	39	32	6	89	*fine*		180	4	92	–	1	192	6	90
explaining		4	3	61	–	26	13	6	88	*finest*		4	4	53	+	3	2	6	81
explains		3	3	63	–	28	11	6	71	finish	Verb	328	4	93	+	168	197	6	86
extra	Adj	100	4	89	–	18	129	6	89	*finish*		103	4	90	+	45	65	6	89
eye	NoC	148	4	92	+	60	95	6	93	*finished*		206	4	95	+	115	120	6	81
eye		58	4	94	+	3	50	6	92	*finishes*		11	4	80	+	17	4	6	83
eyes		90	4	91	+	79	45	6	90	*finishing*		8	4	77	+	0	8	6	88
F / f	Lett	58	4	78	–	273	169	6	85	fire	NoC	127	4	80	–	30	170	6	91
f		56	4	77	–	270	165	6	86	*fire*		123	4	80	–	27	162	6	91

3.1

Word	PoS	FrC	R	DD	LL	FrT	R	DG	Word	PoS	FrC	R	DD	LL	FrT	R	DG
fires		5	4	64 −	3	8	5	70	funny	Adj	326	4	91 +	1154	53	6	84
first	Ord	715	4	97 −	452	1123	6	97	*funniest*		3	4	66 +	12	0	3	55
fish	NoC	121	4	69 +	249	36	6	72	*funny*		321	4	92 +	1133	52	6	84
fish		117	4	68 +	240	35	6	72	further	Adv	48	4	92 −	192	131	6	90
fishes		4	4	77 +	9	1	2	18	future	NoC	19	4	85 −	588	156	6	88
five	Num	1241	4	96 −	32	1371	6	90	*future*		19	4	85 −	576	154	6	88
five		1224	4	96 −	38	1365	6	90	*futures*		0	0	00 −	13	2	4	47
fives		16	4	78 +	24	6	5	65	G / g	Lett	76	4	80 −	533	265	6	79
flat	NoC	59	4	86 −	182	145	6	57	*g*		72	4	79 −	532	257	6	79
flat		44	4	88 −	1	48	6	62	*g.*		4	4	65 −	5	8	5	66
flats		16	4	74 −	314	98	6	45	game	NoC	173	4	89 +	21	136	6	64
floor	NoC	146	4	90 +	139	70	6	83	*game*		124	4	95 +	9	103	6	62
floor		140	4	90 +	147	64	6	85	*games*		49	4	69 +	15	33	6	69
floors		6	4	74 +	0	6	6	64	garden	NoC	161	4	81 +	234	62	6	90
follow	Verb	54	4	90 −	376	188	6	91	*garden*		146	4	81 +	268	48	6	91
follow		30	4	82 −	106	77	6	92	*gardens*		15	4	75 +	0	14	6	78
followed		10	4	88 −	92	40	6	86	general	Adj	33	4	91 −	898	250	6	90
following		11	4	94 −	106	46	6	84	get	Verb	13069	4	98 +	11068	6604	6	91
follows		3	4	77 −	91	25	6	79	*get*		4712	4	97 +	3118	2611	6	92
food	NoC	131	4	88 +	4	115	6	80	*gets*		297	4	93 +	295	140	6	94
food		126	4	88 +	5	110	6	80	*getting*		633	4	95 +	114	475	6	94
foods		5	4	49 −	0	6	6	74	*got*		7425	4	98 +	7978	3376	6	91
foot	NoC	223	4	89 +	117	132	6	90	*gotten*		2	4	86 −	0	2	5	67
feet		106	4	88 +	35	71	6	86	girl	NoC	431	4	94 +	871	131	6	86
foot		117	4	87 +	88	62	6	89	*girl*		295	4	95 +	881	61	6	85
for	Prep	5366	4	96 −	883	6837	6	98	*girls*		135	4	86 +	106	70	6	83
for example	Adv	13	4	79 −	762	171	6	88	give	Verb	1334	4	99 −	44	1492	6	96
forget	Verb	280	4	98 +	152	165	6	90	*gave*		154	4	93 +	2	143	6	91
forget		134	4	93 +	16	106	6	89	*give*		923	4	98 +	49	793	6	95
forgets		3	3	39 +	9	1	3	50	*given*		106	4	93 −	485	305	6	93
forgetting		10	4	94 +	4	7	6	79	*gives*		61	4	92 −	102	122	6	94
forgot		80	4	97 +	218	18	6	87	*giving*		89	4	95 −	35	129	6	92
forgotten		53	4	95 +	21	34	6	90	glass	NoC	143	4	93 +	305	42	6	85
form	NoC	70	4	91 −	493	244	6	87	*glass*		70	4	90 +	87	30	6	83
form		58	4	91 −	334	185	6	89	*glasses*		73	4	89 +	255	12	6	85
forms		12	4	84 −	166	59	6	76	go	NoC	158	4	78 +	212	63	6	95
forty	Num	321	4	94 −	103	448	6	91	*go*		153	4	77 +	209	61	6	95
forties		7	4	70 −	2	10	6	90	*goes*		4	4	54 +	3	2	4	65
forty		314	4	93 −	101	438	6	91	go	Verb	8740	4	97 +	8780	4102	6	92
forward	Adv	50	4	94 −	561	221	6	82	*go*		4192	4	98 +	4105	1990	6	92
four	Num	1161	4	91 −	14	1243	6	92	*goes*		802	4	78 +	1227	299	6	96
four		1147	4	90 −	16	1234	6	91	*going**		1823	4	96 +	1721	880	6	94
fours		14	4	85 +	4	9	6	65	*gone*		622	4	92 +	688	279	6	97
fourteen	Num	80	4	96 −	57	129	6	88	*went*		1302	4	92 +	1118	654	6	80
fourteen		79	4	96 −	56	128	6	88	god	NoC	205	4	94 +	632	40	6	66
free	Adj	93	4	89 −	28	128	6	91	*god*		203	4	93 +	697	34	6	65
free		93	4	89 −	26	127	6	91	*gods*		2	3	51 −	11	6	5	38
Friday	NoP	233	4	95 +	270	102	6	91	God	NoP	418	4	85 +	292	227	6	77
Friday		225	4	94 +	257	99	6	91	going (to)*	Verb	2560	4	97 +	825	1727	6	93
Fridays		8	4	84 +	14	2	4	62	*going*		642	4	89 −	592	1096	6	92
friend	NoC	228	4	82 +	15	192	6	82	*gon~*		1918	4	93 +	3526	631	6	83
friend		123	4	82 +	29	88	6	68	good	Adj	2429	4	99 +	383	1859	6	95
friends		104	4	81 +	0	104	6	89	*best*		196	4	93 −	13	230	6	94
from	Prep	1315	4	98 −	2593	2769	6	95	*better*		350	4	99 +	40	279	6	96
fuck	Verb	124	4	54 +	899	1	3	50	*good*		1883	4	99 +	447	1349	6	93
fuck		100	4	53 +	737	0	2	37	government	NoC	29	4	88 −	2430	505	6	82
fucked		12	4	44 +	83	0	1	00	*government*		28	4	87 −	2292	478	6	82
fucking		10	4	53 +	67	0	1	00	*governments*		1	2	40 −	138	27	6	77
fucking	Adj	278	4	62 +	1998	2	4	50	great	Adj	259	4	95 −	513	546	6	92
fucking	Adv	226	4	50 +	1677	0	3	55	*great*		250	4	95 −	264	441	6	90
full	Adj	185	4	87 −	19	225	6	94	*greater*		5	4	80 −	384	81	6	86
full		183	4	87 −	18	222	6	94	*greatest*		4	4	59 −	72	24	6	86
fuller		1	3	57 −	1	2	4	58	ground	NoC	54	4	87 −	160	130	6	89
fund	NoC	8	4	86 −	608	130	6	63	*ground*		46	4	88 −	110	104	6	89
fund		6	4	82 −	382	83	6	54	*grounds*		7	4	83 −	55	26	6	80
funds		3	4	83 −	225	47	6	74	group	NoC	92	4	76 −	1476	500	6	93

Word	PoS	FrC	R	DD		LL	FrT	R	DG
group		70	4	78	–	1078	372	6	92
groups		22	4	70	–	398	128	6	92
H / h	Lett	68	4	88	–	214	168	6	74
H		64	4	88	–	222	164	6	75
H.		4	4	76	–	0	4	5	33
ha	Int	499	4	94	+	2728	29	6	71
hair	NoC	231	4	90	+	810	38	6	69
hair		222	4	90	+	787	36	6	69
hairs		9	4	66	+	24	2	5	71
half	DetP	590	4	99	+	354	337	6	95
half	NoC	101	4	93	–	15	127	6	84
half		98	4	93	–	14	123	6	83
halves		2	4	74	–	2	4	6	72
hand	NoC	307	4	90	–	1	319	6	95
hand		219	4	90	–	0	222	6	93
hands		89	4	84	–	1	97	6	93
hang	Verb	221	4	91	+	286	91	6	86
hang		165	4	87	+	229	65	6	84
hanging		39	4	89	+	57	15	6	83
hangs		6	4	69	+	8	2	6	78
hung		11	4	82	+	2	8	6	81
happen	Verb	373	4	93	–	541	717	6	94
happen		74	4	90	–	338	212	6	92
happened		170	4	94	–	23	213	6	95
happening		47	4	91	–	136	113	6	90
happens		82	4	89	–	179	179	6	93
happy	Adj	158	4	88	–	32	206	6	91
happier		6	4	78	–	9	12	6	86
happiest		1	1	00	–	2	2	5	70
happy		151	4	88	–	25	193	6	90
hard	Adj	171	4	93	–	0	174	6	88
hard		154	4	94	+	0	152	6	87
harder		12	4	83	–	3	16	6	89
hardest		4	3	56	–	0	5	6	83
hate	Verb	154	4	78	+	510	28	6	86
hate		130	4	75	+	463	21	6	85
hated		11	4	90	+	14	4	6	77
hates		14	4	87	+	52	2	4	63
have*	Verb	21938	4	97	+	1803	18151	6	99
'd		712	4	91	+	228	481	6	80
's		2595	4	95	+	2117	1331	6	96
've		5528	4	97	+	930	4192	6	95
had		3081	4	94	+	149	2667	6	89
has		1098	4	99	–	1160	1940	6	88
have		8093	4	98	+	343	7074	6	97
having		488	4	94	+	20	427	6	96
*of**		343	4	87	+	1487	38	6	58
he	Pron	13583	4	96	+	19749	5239	6	89
'im		6	1	00	+	36	0	1	00
he		11465	4	96	+	16728	4412	6	88
him		2111	4	95	+	2996	826	6	89
head	NoC	226	4	92	+	54	162	6	91
head		206	4	91	+	76	135	6	90
heads		20	4	85	–	5	27	6	90
health	NoC	37	4	89	–	761	234	6	84
hear	Verb	574	4	86	+	68	456	6	94
hear		306	4	81	+	74	218	6	89
heard		258	4	89	+	20	214	6	93
hearing		8	4	88	–	29	21	6	83
hears		2	4	62	–	0	3	6	71
hell	NoC	235	4	94	+	831	38	6	94
hell		234	4	94	+	829	38	6	94
hello	Int	392	4	85	+	939	103	6	79
help	Verb	254	4	92	+	135	386	6	96
help		193	4	91	–	62	270	6	94
helped		20	4	84	–	46	44	6	89
helping		23	4	90	–	15	37	6	90
helps		18	4	91	–	28	36	6	91
her*	Det	1052	4	96	+	1793	365	6	96
here	Adv	2003	4	97	+	561	1391	6	94
hey	Int	151	4	87	+	620	19	6	85
high	Adj	156	4	91	–	361	346	6	91
high		123	4	93	–	152	227	6	91
higher		22	4	79	–	239	96	6	89
highest		10	4	76	–	24	23	6	87
his	Det	1556	4	94	+	260	1181	6	88
his		1556	4	94	+	260	1181	6	88
hit	Verb	136	4	90	+	119	68	6	87
hit		112	4	89	+	95	56	6	88
hits		9	4	82	+	7	5	6	75
hitting		15	4	86	+	15	7	6	81
hold	Verb	207	4	98	+	0	207	6	93
held		23	4	86	–	157	79	6	86
hold		149	4	98	+	95	84	6	96
holding		27	4	91	–	3	34	6	88
holds		7	4	83	–	2	10	6	93
holiday	NoC	155	4	95	+	21	120	6	80
holiday		122	4	94	+	45	80	6	79
holidays		32	4	87	–	4	41	6	81
home	Adv	436	4	96	+	766	148	6	89
home	NoC	217	4	96	–	122	334	6	88
home		209	4	96	–	24	256	6	89
homes		9	4	72	–	301	77	6	77
hope	Verb	225	4	94	+	32	282	6	88
hope		182	4	94	–	20	223	6	88
hoped		4	4	86	–	28	14	6	78
hopes		2	4	65	–	5	5	5	70
hoping		37	4	82	–	0	40	6	87
horse	NoC	90	4	76	–	28	125	6	81
horse		60	4	74	–	0	62	6	80
horses		30	4	71	–	55	62	6	79
hospital	NoC	104	4	93	–	7	123	6	81
hospital		98	4	93	+	0	96	6	81
hospitals		6	4	85	–	68	27	6	79
hot	Adj	163	4	90	+	295	54	6	82
hot		160	4	91	+	299	52	6	82
hotter		2	4	40	+	0	2	4	63
hour	NoC	441	4	88	+	58	346	6	87
hour		249	4	87	+	110	156	6	91
hours		192	4	89	+	0	190	6	82
house	NoC	644	4	92	+	94	497	6	90
house		568	4	92	+	177	386	6	90
houses		75	4	85	–	34	111	6	84
housing	NoC	10	4	80	–	541	124	6	80
housing		10	4	80	–	540	124	6	80
how	Adv	1989	4	95	+	38	1818	6	93
however	Adv	16	4	80	–	538	140	6	86
hundred	NoC	735	4	95	–	715	1271	6	75
hundred		712	4	95	–	701	1235	6	74
hundreds		23	4	85	–	15	36	6	87
I / i	Lett	116	4	85	–	231	246	6	94
I	Pron	43353	4	99	+	28571	24053	6	95
I		39817	4	99	+	25333	22356	6	94
me		3536	4	96	+	3378	1698	6	95
idea	NoC	206	4	91	–	315	402	6	94
idea		186	4	92	–	128	298	6	96
ideas		20	4	87	–	301	104	6	75
if	Conj	4120	4	98	–	284	4835	6	94
important	Adj	48	4	89	–	1718	439	6	90
in	Adv	1576	4	94	+	387	1122	6	91
in	Prep	8506	4	97	–	6113	13731	6	95
in~*	Verb	452	4	89	+	2859	13	6	73

Word	PoS	FrC R DD	LL	FrT R DG	Word	PoS	FrC R DD	LL	FrT R DG
in terms of	Prep	7 4 75 −	1262	235 6 86	*kind*		109 4 88 −	771	381 6 87
include	Verb	15 4 83 −	505	133 6 81	*kinds*		6 4 87 −	140	42 6 74
include		7 4 89 −	192	54 6 83	kitchen	NoC	139 4 89 +	328	37 6 85
included		6 4 66 −	169	46 6 77	*kitchen*		136 4 90 +	356	33 6 86
includes		2 3 58 −	124	29 6 79	*kitchens*		2 4 65 −	2	4 4 68
including		0 0 00 −	24	4 6 77	knock	Verb	129 4 94 +	134	60 6 92
income	NoC	27 4 54 −	328	125 6 85	*knock*		56 4 92 +	83	21 6 84
income		26 4 53 −	299	117 6 84	*knocked*		50 4 94 +	57	22 6 89
incomes		1 2 36 −	31	8 6 73	*knocking*		21 4 88 +	5	15 6 84
increase	Verb	16 4 72 −	528	139 6 81	*knocks*		3 4 83 +	0	2 4 52
increase		11 4 69 −	212	67 6 82	know	Verb	8304 4 97 +	5415	4624 6 90
increased		3 4 73 −	166	37 6 82	*knew*		196 4 95 +	33	149 6 84
increases		1 2 36 −	45	10 6 72	*know*		7527 4 97 +	4883	4198 6 90
increasing		2 3 46 −	113	25 6 73	*knowing*		29 4 96 −	5	37 6 94
indeed	Adv	49 4 76 −	682	245 6 85	*known*		59 4 91 −	91	115 6 95
industry	NoC	13 4 43 −	611	144 6 82	*knows*		161 4 97 +	85	95 6 93
industries		2 3 42 −	84	21 6 75	*~no**		332 4 86 +	1601	29 6 76
industry		10 4 42 −	527	123 6 82	L / l	Lett	71 4 69 −	65	121 6 80
information	NoC	36 4 87 −	1258	323 6 90	*l*		68 4 67 −	48	110 6 82
information		35 4 87 −	1259	323 6 90	*l.*		3 4 73 −	27	11 5 39
int	Uncl	135 4 68 +	760	7 6 80	labour*	Adj	29 4 69 −	572	178 6 77
interest	NoC	50 4 94 −	649	239 6 86	lady	NoC	139 4 90 −	0	140 6 88
interest		45 4 94 −	474	193 6 87	*ladies*		28 4 74 −	36	52 6 87
interests		5 4 78 −	190	46 6 79	*lady*		112 4 93 +	13	88 6 87
interested	Adj	60 4 92 −	177	145 6 90	land	NoC	35 4 80 −	925	261 6 68
interesting	Adj	79 4 90 −	233	191 6 89	*land*		34 4 80 −	921	257 6 68
into	Prep	670 4 95 −	1116	1339 6 96	*lands*		1 4 80 −	6	4 6 90
involve	Verb	24 4 95 −	486	150 6 89	large	Adj	55 4 93 −	497	217 6 87
involve		4 4 78 −	102	29 6 83	*large*		44 4 92 −	361	165 6 87
involved		16 4 86 −	270	89 6 91	*larger*		9 4 84 −	81	35 6 81
involves		3 4 73 −	51	16 6 91	*largest*		3 3 44 −	58	17 6 78
involving		1 3 57 −	64	15 6 73	last	Ord	876 4 96 +	69	727 6 94
involved	Adj	17 4 84 −	432	124 6 91	late	Adj	163 4 94 +	1	155 6 95
issue	NoC	10 4 65 −	1709	317 6 83	*late*		127 4 94 +	45	84 6 91
issue		5 4 59 −	1029	186 6 81	*later*		21 4 86 −	34	42 6 92
issues		5 4 78 −	681	131 6 86	*latest*		14 4 80 −	24	29 6 79
it	Pron	30417 4 99 +	9929	20465 6 96	later	Adv	177 4 98 −	0	181 6 93
it		30417 4 99 +	9928	20465 6 96	laugh	Verb	139 4 90 +	524	20 6 95
item	NoC	13 4 58 −	735	167 6 77	*laugh*		62 4 91 +	254	8 6 87
item		5 4 52 −	547	110 6 70	*laughed*		17 4 87 +	49	4 6 78
items		8 4 60 −	200	56 6 89	*laughing*		57 4 81 +	213	9 6 87
its	Det	218 4 60 −	318	420 6 88	law	NoC	29 4 89 −	525	169 6 86
itself	Pron	33 4 88 −	412	154 6 94	*law*		26 4 91 −	373	131 6 87
Jesus	NoP	58 4 69 −	137	129 6 80	*laws*		3 4 56 −	160	38 6 69
job	NoC	369 4 94 −	239	583 6 89	lead	Verb	25 4 89 −	402	137 6 89
job		316 4 93 −	82	428 6 87	*lead*		12 4 87 −	148	56 6 91
jobs		53 4 93 −	257	156 6 91	*leading*		5 4 73 −	57	22 6 87
John	NoP	232 4 80 −	22	280 6 85	*leads*		6 4 70 −	40	20 6 74
join	Verb	68 4 89 −	118	138 6 93	*led*		3 4 53 −	174	39 6 84
join		40 4 91 −	45	72 6 95	learn	Verb	106 4 94 −	99	182 6 88
joined		17 4 75 −	51	41 6 85	*learn*		57 4 93 −	67	104 6 87
joining		9 4 95 −	23	21 6 79	*learned*		5 4 89 −	25	16 6 81
joins		2 4 74 −	1	4 6 76	*learning*		21 4 88 −	3	27 6 82
just	Adv	4621 4 96 +	1171	3273 6 95	*learns*		1 3 67 −	4	2 6 83
K / k	Lett	49 4 82 −	312	162 6 82	*learnt*		22 4 89 −	11	33 6 92
k		37 4 90 −	279	133 6 83	leave	Verb	812 4 97 +	371	503 6 93
k.		12 4 53 −	36	29 6 78	*leave*		403 4 97 +	311	211 6 91
keep	Verb	782 4 94 +	157	576 6 90	*leaves*		20 4 82 +	0	17 6 89
keep		539 4 94 +	126	387 6 89	*leaving*		48 4 94 +	3	41 6 92
keeping		39 4 90 −	15	57 6 94	*left*		341 4 93 +	101	234 6 90
keeps		76 4 95 −	108	30 6 91	leg	NoC	162 4 84 +	252	60 6 84
kept		127 4 94 +	13	103 6 84	*leg*		72 4 86 +	72	34 6 81
kid	NoC	217 4 88 +	223	100 6 82	*legs*		89 4 79 +	193	26 6 78
kid		48 4 88 +	88	16 6 69	less	Adv	60 4 90 −	231	160 6 92
kids		169 4 82 +	145	85 6 81	let	Verb	517 4 93 +	148	357 6 94
kind	NoC	115 4 88 +	900	422 6 86	*let*		481 4 93 +	148	328 6 94

Word	PoS	FrC	R	DD	LL	FrT	R	DG	Word	PoS	FrC	R	DD	LL	FrT	R	DG
lets		13	4	91 +	0	13	6	81	lot*	NoC	840	4	95 −	168	1096	6	89
letting		22	4	88 +	4	16	6	92	*lot*		840	4	95 −	168	1096	6	89
let's	Verb	345	4	94 −	56	439	6	93	lots	Pron	107	4	86 −	21	139	6	80
letter	NoC	189	4	96 −	0	192	6	90	love	NoC	189	4	88 +	333	64	6	70
letter		127	4	95 −	1	136	6	88	*love*		188	4	88 +	333	64	6	70
letters		62	4	92 +	1	56	6	90	love	Verb	307	4	93 +	677	87	6	81
level	NoC	54	4	88 −	1008	320	6	86	*love*		246	4	94 +	702	54	6	84
level		39	4	88 −	814	249	6	84	*loved*		21	4	81 +	0	20	6	79
levels		14	4	88 −	196	71	6	91	*loves*		38	4	92 +	89	10	6	63
life	NoC	202	4	94 −	388	423	6	90	*loving*		2	4	88 −	0	3	5	54
life		185	4	95 −	296	366	6	91	lovely	Adj	437	4	91 +	1303	90	6	88
lives		17	4	70 −	108	57	6	81	*lovely*		437	4	91 +	1306	90	6	88
light	NoC	194	4	95 +	106	114	6	88	low	Adj	74	4	94 −	251	189	6	92
light		116	4	94 +	54	72	6	86	*low*		52	4	94 −	125	117	6	91
lights		78	4	93 +	53	43	6	76	*lower*		19	4	89 −	99	58	6	88
like	Adv	1332	4	86 +	2666	410	6	88	*lowest*		3	4	60 −	36	14	6	88
like	Prep	2400	4	94 +	1604	1325	6	91	M / m	Lett	109	4	82 −	636	349	6	90
like	Verb	1512	4	96 +	694	936	6	94	*m*		104	4	81 −	621	336	6	89
like		1349	4	96 +	506	879	6	93	*m.*		5	4	95 −	16	12	6	81
liked		71	4	94 +	48	39	6	84	machine	NoC	124	4	92 +	4	109	6	73
likes		89	4	94 +	302	15	6	81	*machine*		107	4	94 +	32	74	6	74
liking		3	3	57 +	0	3	6	61	*machines*		17	4	80 −	34	36	6	71
likely	Adj	40	4	88 −	229	126	6	88	main	Adj	66	4	94 −	263	179	6	95
line	NoC	150	4	92 −	237	296	6	96	major	Adj	15	4	82 −	683	165	6	85
line		107	4	90 −	227	231	6	96	make	Verb	1517	4	97 −	568	2166	6	96
lines		43	4	90 −	21	65	6	92	*made*		372	4	95 −	385	653	6	96
list	NoC	73	4	92 −	155	158	6	85	*make*		814	4	97 −	196	1089	6	95
list		69	4	92 −	133	144	6	85	*makes*		172	4	99 +	4	155	6	94
lists		4	4	79 −	24	13	6	84	*making*		159	4	94 −	140	269	6	94
listen	Verb	258	4	85 +	99	167	6	82	man	NoC	541	4	86 −	87	688	6	85
listen		183	4	84 +	188	85	6	87	*man*		436	4	83 +	17	383	6	86
listened		16	4	83 +	1	13	6	90	*men*		105	4	97 −	491	304	6	81
listening		54	4	87 −	6	67	6	55	management	NoC	7	4	78 −	857	168	6	82
listens		4	4	65 +	5	2	6	64	*management*		7	4	79 −	854	166	6	82
little	Adj	974	4	94 +	743	513	6	90	manager	NoC	31	4	89 −	315	130	6	84
live	Verb	340	4	92 −	5	369	6	88	*manager*		26	4	93 −	187	92	6	87
live		157	4	91 −	4	174	6	93	*managers*		5	4	65 −	140	38	6	75
lived		68	4	86 −	15	90	6	75	many	DetP	457	4	92 −	438	788	6	93
lives		56	4	92 +	78	22	6	91	Mark	NoP	120	4	79 +	255	35	6	76
living		60	4	83 −	18	83	6	83	market	NoC	78	4	87 −	242	191	6	92
load	NoC	195	4	92 −	367	63	6	84	*market*		76	4	88 −	196	175	6	93
load		79	4	90 +	95	34	6	80	*markets*		2	3	59 −	63	17	6	75
loads		116	4	91 +	291	29	6	82	matter	NoC	96	4	87 −	372	257	6	80
local	Adj	41	4	86 −	2053	479	6	87	*matter*		88	4	84 −	167	184	6	83
London	NoP	109	4	91 −	29	148	6	89	*matters*		8	3	42 −	294	74	6	73
long	Adj	416	4	94 +	0	404	6	97	matter	Verb	149	4	98 +	100	82	6	93
long		376	4	94 +	2	357	6	97	*matter*		141	4	98 +	112	73	6	92
longer		34	4	87 −	2	40	6	90	*mattered*		0	2	42 −	3	2	5	57
longest		6	4	75 −	0	7	6	59	*matters*		7	4	88 +	0	7	6	88
long	Adv	190	4	94 +	59	129	6	91	may	VMod	151	4	87 −	1866	705	6	92
look	NoC	314	4	94 +	192	178	6	90	maybe	Adv	236	4	91 −	103	345	6	90
look		304	4	94 +	183	174	6	90	mean	Verb	2922	4	94 +	439	2252	6	94
looks		10	4	89 +	9	5	6	91	*mean*		2675	4	93 +	560	1960	6	93
look	Verb	2591	4	96 +	1280	1572	6	96	*meaning*		9	4	81 +	0	8	6	90
look		1581	4	95 +	1293	810	6	95	*means*		129	4	92 −	73	198	6	95
looked		255	4	94 +	69	178	6	97	*meant*		110	4	96 +	15	86	6	93
looking		379	4	98 −	40	461	6	95	meet	Verb	144	4	94 −	164	259	6	95
looks		377	4	98 +	697	123	6	91	*meet*		58	4	93 −	129	127	6	95
lord	NoC	28	4	84 −	951	247	6	53	*meeting*		20	4	76 −	52	47	6	89
lord		26	4	81 −	784	212	6	52	*meets*		4	4	63 −	11	9	6	85
lords		2	4	73 −	174	35	6	12	*met*		62	4	98 −	7	76	6	88
lose	Verb	251	4	93 −	1	262	6	94	meeting	NoC	48	4	85 −	1266	357	6	90
lose		76	4	87 +	3	67	6	95	*meeting*		39	4	80 −	947	273	6	88
loses		3	4	75 −	5	7	6	70	*meetings*		9	4	86 −	320	83	6	92
losing		23	4	86 −	5	30	6	91	member	NoC	29	4	68 −	2396	500	6	85
lost		149	4	94 −	1	159	6	91	*member*		15	4	74 −	502	132	6	85

Word	PoS	FrC	R	DD	LL	FrT	R	DG	Word	PoS	FrC	R	DD	LL	FrT	R	DG
members		14	4	54 –	1931	368	6	85	*mums*		13	4	70 +	21	4	5	73
mention	Verb	72	4	92 –	452	237	6	95	mummy	NoC	390	4	83 +	2792	3	4	46
mention		28	4	87 –	69	64	6	95	*mummies*		2	3	47 +	9	0	1	00
mentioned		40	4	89 –	369	159	6	95	*mummy*		388	4	83 +	2790	2	4	49
mentioning		3	4	63 –	26	11	6	88	must	VMod	716	4	97 +	191	502	6	95
mentions		1	3	57 –	5	4	6	65	my	Det	3220	4	95 +	1451	2004	6	90
mhm	Int	392	4	89 –	1158	947	6	70	*me*		362	4	89 +	648	122	6	61
might	VMod	856	4	95 +	19	777	6	97	*my*		2857	4	93 +	1025	1882	6	91
million	NoC	52	4	80 –	735	262	6	82	myself	Pron	177	4	92 +	14	147	6	95
million		42	4	78 –	719	236	6	80	N / n	Lett	87	4	82 –	266	213	6	87
millions		10	4	84 –	33	26	6	82	*n*		84	4	82 –	258	207	6	87
mind	NoC	125	4	97 –	139	224	6	93	*n.*		2	4	74 –	7	6	6	63
mind		117	4	97 –	97	195	6	92	name	NoC	418	4	90 +	49	332	6	88
minds		8	4	82 –	61	28	6	91	*name*		354	4	91 +	73	260	6	87
mind	Verb	463	4	92 +	1171	115	6	86	*names*		63	4	83 –	2	71	6	86
mind		454	4	92 +	1239	104	6	84	national	Adj	34	4	91 –	915	255	6	85
minded		6	4	96 –	5	11	6	82	nearly	Adv	185	4	88 +	187	87	6	88
mine	Pron	344	4	95 +	1127	63	6	93	need	NoC	36	4	89 –	941	265	6	83
minute	NoC	569	4	94 +	140	405	6	84	*need*		28	4	87 –	436	150	6	80
minute		322	4	95 +	338	148	6	88	*needs*		7	4	84 –	538	114	6	87
minutes		247	4	86 –	1	257	6	81	need	Verb	804	4	94 –	135	1028	6	92
miss	Verb	192	4	90 +	73	124	6	89	*need*		675	4	95 –	53	800	6	91
miss		92	4	86 +	44	56	6	76	*needed*		43	4	98 –	112	100	6	89
missed		72	4	92 +	29	46	6	91	*needing*		3	4	71 –	12	8	6	90
misses		3	4	60 +	6	1	4	63	*needs*		83	4	86 –	31	119	6	90
missing		25	4	97 +	1	21	6	89	never	Adv	978	4	98 +	762	510	6	88
mm	Int	5202	4	91 +	9146	1768	6	73	new	Adj	457	4	92 –	270	709	6	87
moment	NoC	185	4	95 –	310	370	6	88	*new*		454	4	93 –	271	705	6	87
moment		183	4	95 –	272	355	6	88	*newer*		2	3	58 +	0	2	6	91
moments		1	3	67 –	66	16	6	69	*newest*		1	2	42 –	0	2	5	63
Monday	NoP	197	4	97 –	205	91	6	86	news	NoC	71	4	94 –	122	143	6	65
Monday		191	4	98 +	199	88	6	87	next	Ord	572	4	97 –	6	609	6	97
Mondays		6	4	63 +	5	3	5	65	nice	Adj	1121	4	95 +	2945	268	6	90
money	NoC	678	4	94 +	18	609	6	94	*nice*		1101	4	95 +	2901	262	6	90
money		678	4	94 +	18	609	6	94	*nicer*		18	4	87 +	52	4	5	71
month	NoC	294	4	92 –	84	402	6	89	*nicest*		3	4	81 +	0	2	5	66
month		140	4	97 –	3	153	6	84	night	NoC	792	4	95 +	1249	290	6	85
months		154	4	87 –	111	249	6	90	*night*		749	4	95 +	1207	270	6	86
more	Adv	342	4	97 –	979	818	6	95	*nights*		43	4	86 +	45	20	6	74
more	DetP	827	4	97 –	112	1032	6	91	nine	Num	605	4	94 +	10	556	6	90
morning	NoC	648	4	94 +	469	347	6	90	*nine*		594	4	95 +	7	554	6	90
morning		634	4	94 +	465	339	6	90	*nines*		11	4	60 +	43	1	4	62
mornings		13	4	89 +	4	9	6	76	nineteen	Num	111	4	93 –	1515	548	6	93
most	Adv	92	4	89 –	456	273	6	91	ninety	Num	248	4	91 –	227	423	6	79
most	DetP	140	4	96 –	427	343	6	93	*nineties*		5	4	60 –	17	13	6	80
mother	NoC	239	4	91 +	59	170	6	73	*ninety*		243	4	91 –	212	410	6	78
mother		232	4	91 +	89	150	6	71	no	Det	1105	4	98 +	0	1101	6	96
mothers		6	4	66 –	33	19	6	85	no	Int	7830	4	99 +	18948	2034	6	86
motion	NoC	5	3	24 –	1231	220	6	76	nobody	Pron	156	4	94 +	7	136	6	93
motion		4	3	28 –	1108	197	6	75	north	NoC	36	4	95 –	243	124	6	80
motions		1	1	00 –	123	23	6	82	not	Neg	24332	4	98 +	20006	12442	6	97
move	Verb	360	4	94 –	171	536	6	88	*~n~**		836	4	91 +	4617	46	6	79
move		195	4	92 –	92	289	6	83	*~n't*		18418	4	97 +	21862	7967	6	94
moved		91	4	87 –	15	117	6	91	*not*		5078	4	96 +	222	4429	6	96
moves		8	4	81 –	4	13	6	77	note	NoC	56	4	83 –	129	124	6	88
moving		66	4	93 –	70	117	6	88	*note*		36	4	90 –	38	63	6	91
Mr	NoC	158	4	79 –	2518	853	6	66	*notes*		20	4	69 –	103	61	6	81
Mr		156	4	79 –	2498	845	6	66	nothing	Pron	521	4	96 +	239	322	6	96
Mr.		2	2	32 –	20	8	6	61	now	Adv	2761	4	96 –	26	2935	6	96
Mrs	NoC	145	4	79 –	3	159	6	88	number	NoC	352	4	92 –	987	834	6	96
Mrs		145	4	79 –	1	153	6	88	*number*		299	4	91 –	773	690	6	94
Mrs.		0	1	00 –	31	6	3	18	*numbers*		52	4	93 –	218	144	6	89
much	Adv	289	4	95 –	350	529	6	90	O / o	Lett	162	4	85 –	255	319	6	88
much	DetP	829	4	97 +	39	719	6	96	*o*		155	4	86 –	245	306	6	88
mum	NoC	964	4	92 +	5580	44	6	61	*o.*		6	4	66 –	10	13	6	89
mum		951	4	92 +	5615	39	6	57	o'clock	Adv	253	4	94 +	157	143	6	87

3.1

Word	PoS	FrC	R	DD	±	LL	FrT	R	DG
obviously	Adv	160	4	91	–	482	389	6	93
of	Prep	7989	4	98	–	22702	19038	6	95
of course	Adv	288	4	90	–	920	717	6	92
off	Adv	1243	4	96	+	1419	549	6	91
off	Prep	439	4	97	+	195	274	6	95
offer	Verb	49	4	89	–	298	160	6	79
offer		18	4	95	–	108	58	6	84
offered		24	4	88	–	113	70	6	56
offering		4	4	57	–	63	22	6	89
offers		3	4	83	–	18	9	6	75
office	NoC	118	4	95	–	210	241	6	86
office		107	4	94	–	163	209	6	85
offices		10	4	81	–	54	31	6	86
officer	NoC	21	4	68	–	1154	264	6	80
officer		16	4	60	–	433	121	6	85
officers		5	4	95	–	752	143	6	74
often	Adv	93	4	91	–	297	232	6	89
oh	Int	9884	4	99	+	33062	1746	6	82
okay*	Adj	115	4	86	–	10	138	6	84
okay*	Adv	618	4	71	–	871	1177	6	81
old	Adj	746	4	89	+	237	505	6	86
old		663	4	88	+	233	438	6	87
older		77	4	91	+	12	59	6	83
oldest		7	4	71	–	0	8	6	80
on	Adv	2618	4	95	+	2214	1323	6	97
on	Prep	5245	4	96	–	217	5943	6	98
on to	Prep	85	4	97	–	179	183	6	91
once	Adv	141	4	94	+	43	96	6	89
once	Conj	120	4	94	–	6	138	6	92
one	NoC	451	4	93	+	382	228	6	91
one	Num	2540	4	95	–	581	3372	6	93
one	Pron	3542	4	95	+	2795	1841	6	94
only	Adj	234	4	96	–	2	250	6	95
only	Adv	1331	4	95	+	408	907	6	98
ooh	Int	917	4	88	+	4268	87	6	70
open	Adj	131	4	93	–	27	172	6	91
open	Verb	196	4	90	+	98	119	6	92
open		115	4	91	+	96	58	6	88
opened		54	4	89	+	12	39	6	91
opening		18	4	81	+	4	13	6	86
opens		9	4	85	+	0	9	6	78
opportunity	NoC	15	4	79	–	681	164	6	79
opportunities		2	4	80	–	235	46	6	77
opportunity		13	4	75	–	454	118	6	80
or	Conj	2800	4	97	–	670	3738	6	96
order	NoC	62	4	91	–	349	196	6	80
order		51	4	89	–	252	152	6	80
orders		11	4	82	–	99	43	6	77
other	Adj	1016	4	99	–	491	1517	6	97
other	NoC	137	4	93	–	94	219	6	95
other		56	4	93	–	2	62	6	90
others		81	4	92	–	119	157	6	91
ought	VMod	108	4	81	–	13	134	6	89
our	Det	666	4	91	–	2117	1655	6	91
out	Adv	2846	4	99	+	844	1954	6	94
out of	Prep	509	4	97	+	2	488	6	97
over	Adv	496	4	97	+	44	407	6	96
over	Prep	479	4	97	–	55	588	6	95
over there	Adv	169	4	95	+	376	48	6	91
own ·	DetP	315	4	96	–	273	530	6	94
Oxford	NoP	14	4	69	–	608	146	6	08
P / p	Lett	224	4	91	–	384	452	6	80
P		224	4	91	–	383	452	6	80
page	NoC	90	4	92	–	297	227	6	83
page		68	4	93	–	268	184	6	82
pages		22	4	90	–	34	43	6	84

Word	PoS	FrC	R	DD	±	LL	FrT	R	DG
paper	NoC	279	4	91	–	0	289	6	92
paper		237	4	93	+	0	229	6	92
papers		42	4	78	–	17	61	6	90
pardon	NoC	189	4	95	+	344	63	6	83
pardon		189	4	95	+	346	62	6	83
parent	NoC	69	4	82	–	268	185	6	77
parent		8	4	72	–	111	40	6	75
parents		61	4	79	–	173	146	6	77
part	NoC	187	4	96	–	1007	576	6	97
part		156	4	95	–	885	491	6	96
parts		32	4	87	–	123	85	6	92
particular	Adj	35	4	84	–	1294	328	6	90
particularly	Adv	36	4	95	–	768	234	6	86
party	NoC	138	4	95	–	455	348	6	87
parties		12	4	84	–	133	52	6	86
party		126	4	94	–	340	296	6	86
pass	Verb	121	4	91	–	15	149	6	95
pass		68	4	92	–	0	70	6	93
passed		43	4	89	–	8	56	6	94
passes		3	3	35	–	6	6	6	79
passing		7	4	77	–	24	18	6	85
past	Prep	270	4	95	+	428	98	6	83
Paul	NoP	158	4	69	+	106	87	6	74
pay	Verb	681	4	90	+	113	517	6	92
paid		189	4	88	+	28	145	6	89
pay		368	4	90	+	78	268	6	91
payed		1	3	59	–	1	2	4	52
paying		106	4	85	+	8	88	6	94
pays		18	4	85	+	2	14	6	88
pension	NoC	38	4	59	–	243	127	6	72
pension		35	4	58	–	129	92	6	70
pensions		3	4	68	–	146	35	6	76
people	NoC	1116	4	91	–	3387	2725	6	95
people		1114	4	91	–	3358	2712	6	95
peoples		2	4	65	–	35	12	6	74
percent	NoC	81	4	77	–	805	337	6	83
perhaps	Adv	247	4	88	–	668	579	6	92
period	NoC	25	4	81	–	670	189	6	87
period		23	4	79	–	616	171	6	85
periods		3	4	76	–	54	17	6	90
person	NoC	155	4	83	–	301	325	6	91
person		153	4	82	–	254	306	6	92
persons		2	3	65	–	78	19	6	77
phone	NoC	190	4	88	+	70	124	6	86
phone		181	4	88	+	64	119	6	86
phones		9	4	77	+	6	5	6	74
phone	Verb	204	4	86	+	455	57	6	85
phone		89	4	81	+	168	29	6	87
phoned		93	4	92	+	268	20	6	89
phones		5	4	68	+	10	1	4	63
phoning		17	4	74	+	20	7	6	61
pick	Verb	362	4	98	+	161	226	6	96
pick		224	4	98	+	117	134	6	94
picked		79	4	88	+	19	57	6	90
picking		42	4	92	+	14	28	6	92
picks		17	4	86	+	18	8	6	86
picture	NoC	142	4	96	+	6	124	6	91
picture		95	4	99	+	1	88	6	88
pictures		47	4	89	+	8	36	6	86
piece	NoC	194	4	89	+	16	161	6	86
piece		132	4	89	+	8	112	6	85
pieces		62	4	86	+	8	49	6	84
place	NoC	376	4	97	–	76	491	6	95
place		309	4	96	–	38	383	6	95
places		66	4	93	–	49	108	6	92
plan	NoC	32	4	83	–	1307	322	6	76

Word	PoS	FrC	R	DD		LL	FrT	R	DG	Word	PoS	FrC	R	DD		LL	FrT	R	DG
plan		19	4	80	–	1103	248	6	74	public	Adj	11	4	97	–	759	164	6	85
plans		13	4	86	–	224	74	6	83	pull	Verb	187	4	96	+	125	104	6	87
planning	NoC	8	4	66	–	759	155	6	73	*pull*		94	4	92	+	58	53	6	89
play	Verb	560	4	94	+	550	266	6	87	*pulled*		49	4	91	+	25	29	6	80
play		298	4	95	+	378	124	6	89	*pulling*		33	4	88	+	27	17	6	81
played		79	4	91	+	11	61	6	82	*pulls*		11	4	78	+	18	4	6	89
playing		165	4	94	+	213	68	6	86	put (putt)	Verb	2361	4	93	+	1084	1462	6	95
plays		19	4	79	+	7	12	6	83	*put*		2168	4	93	+	1181	1278	6	94
please	Adv	495	4	91	+	343	269	6	81	*puts*		41	4	91	+	9	30	6	86
plus	Prep	89	4	87	–	86	154	6	81	*putting*		152	4	92	–	0	154	6	95
point	NoC	291	4	81	–	2245	1059	6	85	quality	NoC	28	4	79	–	468	156	6	82
point		258	4	79	–	1800	896	6	85	*qualities*		1	3	57	–	24	8	6	87
points		32	4	67	–	462	164	6	84	*quality*		27	4	78	–	444	148	6	81
police	NoC	77	4	92	–	507	260	6	86	quarter	NoC	155	4	95	+	20	122	6	82
policy	NoC	12	4	77	–	2555	464	6	70	*quarter*		139	4	94	+	45	93	6	84
policies		4	4	73	–	493	94	6	70	*quarters*		16	4	92	–	15	28	6	72
policy		9	4	63	–	2064	369	6	70	question	NoC	155	4	84	–	1689	674	6	90
position	NoC	28	4	93	–	777	215	6	85	*question*		94	4	83	–	1259	459	6	89
position		26	4	91	–	728	201	6	84	*questions*		61	4	86	–	443	216	6	92
positions		2	4	73	–	49	13	6	94	quick	Adj	131	4	94	+	56	83	6	93
possible	Adj	52	4	86	–	496	212	6	87	*quick*		122	4	94	+	71	70	6	93
possibly	Adv	39	4	85	–	215	121	6	93	*quicker*		9	4	91	–	0	9	6	87
pound	NoC	796	4	90	–	84	969	6	77	*quickest*		0	1	00	–	9	3	6	81
pound		490	4	87	+	568	215	6	85	quid	NoC	214	4	86	+	859	28	6	84
pounds		306	4	92	–	954	754	6	72	*quid*		212	4	86	+	854	28	6	83
power	NoC	42	4	79	–	665	226	6	86	quite	Adv	897	4	96	–	161	1155	6	97
power		40	4	78	–	511	191	6	86	R / r	Lett	113	4	79	–	97	190	6	92
powers		1	3	57	–	178	35	6	79	*r*		109	4	78	–	95	184	6	91
president	NoC	5	4	79	–	672	129	6	68	*r.*		4	4	76	–	2	6	6	75
president		5	4	73	–	655	125	6	68	raise	Verb	16	4	68	–	610	152	6	88
presidents		0	1	00	–	17	4	3	34	*raise*		8	4	61	–	224	62	6	86
pressure	NoC	28	4	84	–	316	123	6	90	*raised*		5	4	92	–	302	67	6	87
pressure		27	4	83	–	229	103	6	90	*raises*		1	2	36	–	34	8	6	82
pressures		1	1	00	–	108	20	6	84	*raising*		2	3	29	–	54	16	6	83
price	NoC	133	4	89	–	84	209	6	80	rate	NoC	48	4	88	–	474	198	6	90
price		100	4	87	–	27	136	6	80	*rate*		32	4	88	–	293	127	6	92
prices		33	4	95	–	74	73	6	77	*rates*		16	4	85	–	181	71	6	83
probably	Adv	686	4	97	+	123	515	6	97	rather	Adv	142	4	88	–	160	255	6	84
problem	NoC	228	4	93	–	1629	800	6	92	rather than	Prep	38	4	88	–	309	143	6	94
problem		167	4	93	–	735	471	6	94	read	Verb	310	4	97	–	0	316	6	93
problems		61	4	88	–	965	329	6	88	*read*		251	4	96	–	2	266	6	93
process	NoC	9	4	55	–	691	145	6	86	*reading*		53	4	92	+	5	43	6	89
process		8	4	53	–	578	125	6	84	*reads*		6	4	74	–	0	8	6	84
processes		0	1	00	–	117	20	6	85	ready	Adj	199	4	89	+	254	82	6	94
produce	Verb	14	4	85	–	990	212	6	86	*ready*		199	4	89	+	255	82	6	94
produce		6	4	88	–	467	98	6	85	real	Adj	94	4	94	–	82	159	6	92
produced		4	4	72	–	326	69	6	87	really	Adv	2175	4	86	+	808	1420	6	96
produces		1	2	36	–	69	14	6	81	reason	NoC	100	4	98	–	751	360	6	92
producing		3	4	70	–	128	31	6	87	*reason*		89	4	98	–	355	242	6	93
product	NoC	6	4	70	–	846	160	6	75	*reasons*		11	4	94	–	491	118	6	88
product		2	3	58	–	536	97	6	68	receive	Verb	23	4	73	–	504	152	6	88
products		3	3	53	–	313	64	6	83	*receive*		11	4	72	–	162	57	6	93
programme	NoC	85	4	87	–	264	209	6	76	*received*		8	4	63	–	275	71	6	81
programme		70	4	88	–	218	173	6	78	*receives*		0	2	42	–	21	5	6	79
programmes		15	4	79	–	46	37	6	63	*receiving*		4	4	71	–	52	19	6	80
project	NoC	22	4	68	–	613	168	6	88	reckon	Verb	207	4	91	+	699	36	6	84
project		19	4	66	–	424	128	6	86	*reckon*		178	4	90	+	616	30	6	81
projects		2	3	62	–	200	41	6	86	*reckoned*		10	4	84	+	21	3	5	73
proposal	NoC	2	3	47	–	777	135	6	74	*reckons*		18	4	89	+	70	3	6	79
proposal		2	3	46	–	291	55	6	68	record	NoC	66	4	84	–	83	122	6	91
proposals		0	2	42	–	492	80	6	76	*record*		48	4	79	–	67	91	6	87
provide	Verb	24	4	85	–	1175	277	6	87	*records*		18	4	86	–	16	31	6	87
provide		12	4	70	–	600	140	6	89	record	Verb	152	4	65	+	186	64	6	85
provided		5	4	79	–	256	61	6	84	*record*		47	4	66	+	48	21	6	80
provides		1	3	57	–	100	22	6	87	*recorded*		34	4	78	+	7	25	6	88
providing		6	4	82	–	219	55	6	85	*recording*		68	4	57	+	172	17	6	72

3.1

Word	PoS	FrC	R	DD	LL	FrT	R	DG
records		2	3	58 +	5	1	2	26
red	Adj	202	4	86 +	323	73	6	89
red		201	4	86 +	322	73	6	89
refer	Verb	9	4	84 –	769	160	6	75
refer		5	4	82 –	210	51	6	78
referred		1	2	36 –	391	66	6	70
referring		3	4	76 –	83	23	6	80
refers		1	3	67 –	110	21	6	71
region	NoC	5	4	55 –	934	174	6	74
region		4	4	60 –	822	150	6	71
regions		1	3	42 –	114	24	6	82
remember	Verb	623	4	98 +	79	490	6	83
remember		592	4	98 +	84	459	6	83
remembered		21	4	93 +	5	15	6	87
remembering		5	4	75 –	17	12	6	82
remembers		5	4	80 –	4	4	6	77
report	NoC	28	4	65 –	1969	425	6	84
report		19	4	64 –	1707	350	6	83
reports		9	4	66 –	277	75	6	86
resource	NoC	7	4	72 –	569	120	6	86
resource		2	3	42 –	102	24	6	89
resources		5	4	69 –	468	96	6	83
rest	NoC	124	4	94 –	7	144	6	94
rest		123	4	94 –	7	144	6	94
result	NoC	24	4	91 –	634	180	6	86
result		11	4	80 –	484	117	6	85
results		14	4	93 –	165	63	6	86
Richard	NoP	124	4	66 +	195	45	6	76
right	Adj	1160	4	95 +	135	924	6	94
right		1160	4	95 +	136	923	6	94
right	Adv	2304	4	90 +	29	2144	6	84
right	NoC	41	4	94 –	390	165	6	88
right		33	4	90 –	139	91	6	88
rights		8	4	80 –	292	74	6	86
ring	Verb	261	4	92 +	329	109	6	79
rang		74	4	95 +	199	17	6	91
ring		122	4	91 +	94	64	6	77
ringing		21	4	86 +	3	16	6	64
rings		12	4	81 +	16	5	6	70
rung		31	4	71 +	87	7	6	70
road	NoC	352	4	97 –	11	393	6	92
road		328	4	97 –	1	341	6	94
roads		24	4	92 –	50	52	6	76
room	NoC	326	4	94 +	107	219	6	92
room		301	4	93 +	139	186	6	93
rooms		25	4	95 –	5	33	6	83
round	Adv	578	4	94 +	445	304	6	85
round	Prep	326	4	94 +	186	189	6	90
rule	NoC	26	4	94 –	331	124	6	91
rule		10	4	79 –	198	62	6	83
rules		16	4	95 –	138	62	6	90
run	Verb	353	4	98 –	0	362	6	92
ran		49	4	91 +	13	34	6	85
run		169	4	95 –	3	185	6	91
running		111	4	91 –	0	114	6	95
runs		25	4	88 –	2	30	6	86
S / s	Lett	181	4	76 –	247	343	6	92
s		175	4	75 –	235	330	6	92
s.		6	4	82 –	12	13	6	87
same	DetP	545	4	96 –	125	723	6	95
Saturday	NoP	245	4	90 +	353	95	6	84
Saturday		232	4	90 +	346	88	6	85
Saturdays		13	4	83 +	9	7	6	57
save	Verb	129	4	97 –	3	142	6	85
save		82	4	93 –	0	84	6	87
saved		23	4	84 –	23	39	6	66
saves		11	4	86 +	5	7	6	81
saving		13	4	88 +	0	12	6	80
say	Verb	8230	4	96 +	5054	4675	6	97
said		4617	4	90 +	9714	1363	6	95
say		2021	4	95 –	30	2182	6	97
saying		554	4	94 –	6	593	6	91
says		1038	4	77 +	828	537	6	88
scheme	NoC	13	4	79 –	804	177	6	84
scheme		10	4	71 –	536	124	6	85
schemes		2	3	58 –	271	54	6	80
school	NoC	504	4	91 –	26	580	6	79
school		480	4	91 +	38	398	6	80
schools		24	4	79 –	649	182	6	68
second	Ord	136	4	94 –	260	284	6	89
secretary	NoC	18	4	76 –	619	161	6	84
secretaries		1	4	100 –	45	11	6	72
secretary		17	4	75 –	574	150	6	84
section	NoC	27	4	79 –	498	160	6	87
section		25	4	80 –	381	132	6	88
sections		2	4	65 –	126	28	6	82
sector	NoC	8	4	28 –	564	121	6	52
sector		7	4	28 –	448	98	6	56
sectors		1	2	24 –	117	24	5	32
see	Verb	3913	4	98 +	1240	2649	6	90
saw		286	4	95 +	225	149	6	94
see		3079	4	98 +	909	2116	6	88
seeing		56	4	99 –	2	64	6	93
seen		473	4	94 +	195	301	6	97
sees		19	4	90 –	0	20	6	81
seem	Verb	283	4	91 –	226	467	6	91
seem		108	4	89 –	73	172	6	92
seemed		53	4	82 –	5	64	6	91
seems		122	4	94 –	166	230	6	87
sell	Verb	243	4	89 +	2	227	6	83
sell		125	4	92 +	3	112	6	79
selling		39	4	87 –	8	52	6	74
sells		9	4	82 +	10	4	6	73
sold		70	4	73 +	4	59	6	85
send	Verb	266	4	93 –	4	290	6	92
send		135	4	94 –	0	138	6	93
sending		19	4	90 –	13	31	6	90
sends		6	4	80 –	1	7	6	82
sent		106	4	90 –	1	113	6	88
sense	NoC	42	4	86 –	763	246	6	82
sense		41	4	85 –	743	240	6	83
senses		1	2	29 –	19	6	6	62
service	NoC	84	4	92 –	1676	520	6	90
service		68	4	90 –	753	298	6	95
services		16	4	89 –	1003	222	6	83
set	Verb	106	4	95 –	407	283	6	89
set		91	4	92 –	309	232	6	89
sets		4	4	52 –	41	16	6	86
setting		11	4	87 –	63	35	6	82
settlement	NoC	2	3	37 –	1066	177	6	45
settlement		2	3	37 –	895	150	6	44
settlements		0	0	00 –	173	27	6	48
seven	Num	526	4	89 –	21	595	6	91
seven		521	4	89 –	23	594	6	91
sevens		5	4	82 +	18	1	3	50
seventy	Num	148	4	88 –	168	266	6	81
seventies		8	4	72 –	19	18	6	82
seventy		140	4	87 –	150	248	6	80
shall	VMod	392	4	87 +	319	201	6	91
sha~		29	4	70 +	92	5	6	86
shall		363	4	88 +	260	196	6	91
she	Pron	9544	4	97 +	30651	1786	6	90

Word	PoS	FrC	R	DD		LL	FrT	R	DG
'er		3	1	00	+	21	0	0	00
her		1531	4	97	+	4740	301	6	94
she		8010	4	97	+	25899	1485	6	89
shit	NoC	162	4	67	+	1036	4	6	62
shit		160	4	67	+	1032	4	6	63
shoe	NoC	130	4	94	+	400	26	6	58
shoe		25	4	80	+	53	7	6	62
shoes		104	4	91	+	352	18	6	56
shop	NoC	303	4	95	+	69	219	6	74
shop		232	4	95	+	72	158	6	70
shops		71	4	95	+	3	61	6	83
short	Adj	112	4	95	-	42	161	6	92
short		101	4	94	-	39	145	6	93
shorter		10	4	86	-	2	13	6	69
shortest		2	4	80	-	1	3	6	77
should	VMod	1047	4	99	-	96	1259	6	93
show	Verb	272	4	94	-	92	382	6	92
show		158	4	93	-	5	177	6	92
showed		37	4	91	+	0	36	6	95
showing		33	4	89	-	51	64	6	63
shown		15	4	82	-	121	57	6	84
shows		29	4	85	-	24	48	6	90
shut	Verb	232	4	81	+	864	35	6	90
shut		220	4	79	+	861	30	6	87
shuts		5	4	82	+	11	1	3	53
shutting		7	4	67	+	6	3	6	83
side	NoC	405	4	98	-	2	427	6	93
side		370	4	97	-	0	377	6	93
sides		35	4	85	-	13	50	6	81
silly	Adj	125	4	87	+	362	26	6	90
silly		124	4	87	+	358	26	6	90
simple	Adj	34	4	85	-	280	128	6	94
simple		30	4	90	-	256	115	6	94
simpler		3	2	12	-	10	7	6	84
simplest		1	4	80	-	14	6	6	80
simply	Adv	15	4	69	-	631	154	6	84
since	Conj	98	4	93	-	11	121	6	96
sing	Verb	144	4	91	+	243	51	6	91
sang		8	4	80	+	3	5	6	82
sing		85	4	89	+	186	24	6	82
singing		45	4	94	+	69	17	6	72
sings		3	4	92	+	6	1	4	55
sung		3	3	56	-	0	4	6	70
single	Adj	49	4	85	-	161	124	6	91
sir	NoC	98	4	17	-	107	174	6	72
sir		98	4	17	-	107	174	6	72
sit	Verb	661	4	97	+	965	254	6	96
sat		131	4	91	+	275	39	6	87
sit		342	4	92	+	584	119	6	93
sits		22	4	82	+	17	12	6	91
sitting		165	4	94	+	136	84	6	95
site	NoC	26	4	54	-	775	209	6	79
site		20	4	60	-	364	118	6	82
sites		6	4	33	-	431	92	6	71
situation	NoC	41	4	83	-	1086	305	6	87
situation		37	4	81	-	954	271	6	86
situations		4	4	82	-	132	34	6	88
six	Num	788	4	92	-	53	924	6	93
six		779	4	91	-	58	920	6	93
sixes		9	4	60	+	12	3	5	49
sixty	Num	206	4	90	-	250	378	6	84
sixties		7	4	69	-	33	20	6	87
sixty		200	4	90	-	223	358	6	83
size	NoC	121	4	91	+	2	110	6	91
size		112	4	91	+	4	99	6	90
sizes		9	4	84	-	1	11	6	83
sleep	Verb	132	4	92	+	287	38	6	82
sleep		82	4	88	+	204	20	6	82
sleeping		23	4	92	+	26	10	6	78
sleeps		7	4	68	+	25	1	5	74
slept		20	4	82	+	42	6	6	73
small	Adj	195	4	90	-	131	311	6	94
small		155	4	87	-	127	258	6	94
smaller		35	4	85	-	7	47	6	96
smallest		5	3	58	-	0	6	6	75
so	Adv	5121	4	96	+	4	5029	6	93
so	Conj	405	4	97	+	0	396	6	94
so that	Conj	113	4	95	-	473	312	6	93
social	Adj	22	4	89	-	665	179	6	88
society	NoC	29	4	86	-	434	152	6	92
societies		5	4	69	-	36	18	6	71
society		24	4	84	-	402	134	6	91
some	DetP	1856	4	96	-	61	2076	6	97
somebody	Pron	431	4	98	+	8	393	6	94
someone	Pron	200	4	85	+	13	168	6	86
something	Pron	1433	4	95	+	111	1192	6	96
sometimes	Adv	184	4	94	-	7	209	6	90
somewhere	Adv	209	4	92	+	53	148	6	92
sorry	Adj	441	4	90	+	1	424	6	86
sorry		441	4	90	+	1	424	6	86
sort	NoC	519	4	97	-	741	992	6	93
sort		473	4	98	-	599	875	6	94
sorts		46	4	87	-	157	117	6	85
sort	Verb	145	4	92	+	54	94	6	81
sort		83	4	93	+	46	48	6	77
sorted		52	4	91	+	16	35	6	84
sorting		9	4	88	-	0	10	6	80
sort of	Adv	549	4	93	+	86	420	6	87
sound	Verb	166	4	95	+	95	96	6	93
sound		42	4	93	+	13	28	6	96
sounded		18	4	88	+	29	7	6	86
sounding		2	4	80	-	0	2	5	68
sounds		104	4	93	+	63	59	6	89
south	NoC	43	4	85	-	273	143	6	79
speak	Verb	220	4	91	-	80	314	6	96
speak		113	4	89	-	12	138	6	92
speaking		42	4	83	-	72	86	6	90
speaks		9	4	82	-	2	11	6	81
spoke		33	4	90	-	16	50	6	92
spoken		23	4	88	-	3	29	6	84
special	Adj	75	4	90	-	147	159	6	92
spend	Verb	164	4	93	-	82	247	6	91
spend		85	4	95	-	23	116	6	92
spending		17	4	88	-	37	37	6	83
spends		6	4	73	+	0	6	6	69
spent		56	4	89	-	35	89	6	90
staff	NoC	40	4	86	-	583	206	6	92
staff		40	4	86	-	582	205	6	92
stage	NoC	58	4	88	-	384	196	6	87
stage		55	4	88	-	319	175	6	86
stages		3	3	64	-	74	21	6	86
stand	Verb	247	4	94	+	5	224	6	93
stand		117	4	88	+	0	112	6	92
standing		68	4	89	+	2	60	6	85
stands		15	4	90	-	10	24	6	91
stood		47	4	87	+	23	28	6	91
start	Verb	660	4	98	-	67	800	6	90
start		320	4	98	-	40	396	6	92
started		234	4	99	-	20	280	6	83
starting		46	4	88	-	16	65	6	92
starts		61	4	89	+	0	60	6	91
state	NoC	38	4	96	-	520	189	6	78

Word	PoS	FrC	R	DD		LL	FrT	R	DG
state		37	4	94	−	387	157	6	83
states		2	4	50	−	152	32	6	53
statement	NoC	12	4	87	−	652	148	6	76
statement		8	4	74	−	539	118	6	76
statements		4	4	77	−	116	31	6	76
station	NoC	63	4	92	−	143	139	6	88
station		56	4	90	−	82	109	6	88
stations		6	4	81	−	82	30	6	82
stay	Verb	308	4	94	+	231	163	6	88
stay		204	4	94	+	162	106	6	90
stayed		29	4	83	−	0	30	6	70
staying		59	4	94	+	124	17	6	88
stays		16	4	93	+	6	10	6	84
stick	Verb	197	4	91	+	226	87	6	92
stick		93	4	90	+	65	50	6	90
sticking		24	4	89	+	27	10	6	93
sticks		10	4	80	+	11	4	5	72
stuck		70	4	85	+	142	21	6	85
still	Adv	801	4	96	+	36	697	6	96
stop	Verb	443	4	95	+	248	259	6	93
stop		307	4	94	+	206	169	6	95
stopped		88	4	90	+	29	59	6	85
stopping		29	4	91	+	16	17	6	87
stops		19	4	84	+	3	14	6	89
story	NoC	101	4	80	−	43	148	6	88
stories		22	4	80	−	31	42	6	84
story		79	4	78	−	18	106	6	89
straight	Adv	136	4	87	+	120	67	6	89
street	NoC	121	4	89	−	71	187	6	83
street		105	4	88	−	56	160	6	82
streets		16	4	71	−	16	28	6	79
structure	NoC	4	4	57	−	809	147	6	74
structure		4	4	60	−	721	131	6	73
structures		0	1	00	−	88	15	6	82
stuff	NoC	390	4	92	+	334	196	6	79
stuff		389	4	92	+	334	196	6	79
stupid	Adj	172	4	76	+	713	21	6	86
subject	NoC	24	4	93	−	373	128	6	86
subject		18	4	94	−	293	99	6	90
subjects		6	4	82	−	79	29	6	67
such	DetP	183	4	83	−	55	253	6	91
suggest	Verb	30	4	84	−	902	244	6	87
suggest		19	4	89	−	374	117	6	87

Word	PoS	FrC	R	DD		LL	FrT	R	DG
suggested		8	4	69	−	246	66	6	85
suggesting		2	3	62	−	209	43	6	85
suggests		1	3	50	−	88	19	6	85
Sunday	NoP	236	4	91	+	325	94	6	77
Sunday		224	4	91	+	314	88	6	78
Sundays		12	4	81	+	12	5	6	61
support	NoC	22	4	46	−	575	163	6	79
support		22	4	44	−	566	161	6	79
supports		0	1	00	−	10	2	4	55
support	Verb	16	4	83	−	981	219	6	77
support		11	4	71	−	673	149	6	75
supported		1	2	42	−	207	37	6	79
supporting		4	4	75	−	72	22	6	86
supports		1	2	29	−	41	10	6	58
suppose	Verb	387	4	98	+	275	209	6	90
suppose		380	4	98	+	278	203	6	89
supposed		7	4	82	+	6	3	6	79
supposing		0	1	00	−	10	2	5	66
supposed	Adj	215	4	89	+	348	77	6	87
sure	Adj	442	4	94	−	19	504	6	93
system	NoC	65	4	81	−	1008	347	6	84
system		57	4	83	−	764	279	6	88
systems		8	4	62	−	252	67	6	62
T / t	Lett	199	4	84	−	91	294	6	91
t		191	4	84	−	85	281	6	91
t.		8	4	78	−	5	13	6	82
table	NoC	189	4	91	+	7	167	6	86
table		168	4	90	+	17	135	6	85
tables		21	4	78	−	10	32	6	91
take	Verb	2006	4	97	−	0	2026	6	97
take		1215	4	96	+	27	1104	6	95
taken		138	4	92	−	285	295	6	92
takes		125	4	94	−	0	127	6	96
taking		198	4	98	−	21	241	6	93
took		330	4	90	+	44	258	6	85
talk	Verb	684	4	85	−	78	839	6	95
talk		240	4	80	−	18	284	6	94
talked		32	4	89	−	151	92	6	94
talking		398	4	87	−	15	449	6	95
talks		14	4	85	+	0	13	6	84
tape	NoC	353	4	85	+	1134	66	6	83
tape		261	4	85	+	769	55	6	86
tapes		92	4	82	+	380	11	6	51
tax	NoC	76	4	82	−	112	146	6	90
tax		70	4	85	−	99	133	6	89
taxes		6	4	51	−	13	13	6	79
tea	NoC	328	4	95	+	925	72	6	79
tea		322	4	95	+	918	70	6	79
teas		6	4	61	+	9	2	6	71
teacher	NoC	99	4	84	−	67	158	6	64
teacher		62	4	83	−	3	71	6	74
teachers		37	4	86	−	99	87	6	54
team	NoC	58	4	77	−	224	155	6	86
team		47	4	79	−	176	124	6	87
teams		11	4	68	−	48	31	6	78
tell	Verb	1601	4	97	+	1038	893	6	95
tell		894	4	95	+	530	514	6	93
telling		148	4	91	+	102	81	6	93
tells		40	4	90	−	0	43	6	88
told		518	4	98	+	467	255	6	95
ten	Num	614	4	94	−	1	636	6	91
ten		604	4	94	−	1	624	6	91
tens		10	4	75	−	0	12	6	71
tend	Verb	46	4	90	−	286	152	6	93
tend		38	4	89	−	141	100	6	95
tended		1	4	81	−	66	16	6	80

Two common swearwords

The spoken component of the BNC confirms the common-sense intuition that people swear much more in everyday interaction than in more formal speech.

If we look at the frequencies for the two most common swearwords, we can see that *bloody* is far more common than *fucking* in spoken British English (frequencies are shown in words per million):

	Demographic	Context-governed
bloody (adjective)	559	35
bloody (adverb)	212	10
fucking (adjective)	278	2
fucking (adverb)	226	0

Interestingly, however, when used as a modifying adverb (e.g. *fucking unbelievable, bloody marvellous*), *fucking* is slightly more frequent than *bloody*.

Word	PoS	FrC R DD	LL	FrT R DG	Word	PoS	FrC R DD	LL	FrT R DG
tending		0 2 42 −	14	4 6 83	to	Inf	14353 4 99 −	2223	18162 6 98
tends		6 4 71 −	90	32 6 86	~na*		2372 4 92 +	5035	695 6 82
term	NoC	66 4 92 −	570	255 6 83	~ta*		628 4 94 +	1979	120 6 83
term		55 4 89 −	169	134 6 83	*to*		11353 4 98 −	6231	17347 6 98
terms		12 4 96 −	494	120 6 82	to	Prep	5575 4 98 −	1980	7890 6 97
terrible	Adj	125 4 89 +	131	57 6 86	today	Adv	575 4 95 +	72	454 6 92
than	Conj	593 4 97 −	85	744 6 96	together	Adv	181 4 94 −	186	317 6 97
thank	Verb	424 4 88 −	377	719 6 79	tomorrow	Adv	407 4 93 +	900	115 6 85
thank		421 4 88 −	375	714 6 79	tonight	Adv	275 4 93 +	372	111 6 70
thanked		2 4 57 −	0	2 4 53	too	Adv	764 4 96 +	201	537 6 95
thanking		1 4 80 −	2	3 6 79	top	NoC	268 4 97 +	143	159 6 86
thanks	NoC	175 4 88 +	7	153 6 88	*top*		258 4 97 +	134	154 6 87
that	Adv	225 4 95 +	261	98 6 93	*tops*		10 4 77 +	9	5 6 79
that	Conj	3410 4 99 −	15927	9870 6 93	towards	Prep	58 4 91 −	272	168 6 90
that	DetP	16329 4 98 +	2121	12831 6 95	town	NoC	130 4 90 −	75	200 6 79
the	Det	27351 4 98 −	28176	47987 6 97	*town*		127 4 90 −	47	181 6 77
their	Det	649 4 97 −	2440	1719 6 91	*towns*		3 4 64 −	66	19 6 78
themselves	Pron	48 4 88 −	407	183 6 88	trade	NoC	19 4 85 −	872	208 6 75
theirselves		4 4 86 +	0	3 5 66	*trade*		18 4 85 −	793	192 6 74
themselves		44 4 86 −	424	179 6 88	*trades*		0 2 42 −	83	15 6 52
then	Adv	4173 4 97 +	980	2997 6 89	traffic	NoC	54 4 81 −	245	155 6 68
there	Adv	4012 4 95 +	2990	2130 6 90	*traffic*		54 4 81 −	245	155 6 68
there		4011 4 95 +	2989	2130 6 90	training	NoC	27 4 89 −	942	244 6 83
there	Ex	3390 4 91 −	816	4530 6 98	*training*		27 4 90 −	949	244 6 83
therefore	Adv	25 4 73 −	955	240 6 84	trouble	NoC	178 4 93 +	63	118 6 88
these	DetP	1071 4 96 −	222	1404 6 97	*trouble*		176 4 94 +	72	112 6 88
they	Pron	14235 4 96 +	1654	11341 6 94	*troubles*		3 2 42 −	5	6 6 79
'em		65 4 88 +	5	53 6 68	true	Adj	173 4 96 −	0	180 6 91
them		3737 4 93 +	834	2707 6 94	*true*		173 4 96 −	0	180 6 91
they		10434 4 96 +	911	8581 6 93	try	Verb	782 4 98 −	15	852 6 96
thing	NoC	2053 4 99 −	111	2368 6 94	*tried*		117 4 97 +	7	99 6 94
thing		1248 4 96 +	76	1060 6 94	*tries*		8 4 75 −	3	12 6 84
things		805 4 97 −	594	1308 6 94	*try*		378 4 98 −	5	408 6 95
think	Verb	5377 4 98 +	137	4848 6 97	*trying*		279 4 93 −	23	332 6 93
think		3732 4 98 −	108	4145 6 96	Tuesday	NoP	127 4 93 +	131	59 6 84
thinking		202 4 96 +	22	162 6 91	*Tuesday*		122 4 93 +	123	57 6 84
thinks		81 4 86 +	42	49 6 85	*Tuesdays*		5 4 82 +	8	2 5 66
thought		1361 4 97 +	2191	492 6 94	turn	Verb	445 4 96 +	150	298 6 95
third	Ord	71 4 92 −	218	174 6 88	*turn*		264 4 94 +	156	152 6 92
thirty	Num	448 4 93 −	99	593 6 91	*turned*		121 4 94 +	33	85 6 91
thirties		5 4 84 −	56	21 6 81	*turning*		33 4 92 −	0	34 6 90
thirty		444 4 93 −	80	572 6 90	*turns*		26 4 92 −	0	27 6 90
this	DetP	4734 4 96 −	1025	6237 6 96	twelve	Num	275 4 91 −	0	283 6 89
those	DetP	848 4 96 −	485	1307 6 92	*twelve*		275 4 91 −	0	281 6 89
though	Adv	709 4 96 +	1526	205 6 92	*twelves*		1 2 36 −	2	2 5 55
thousand	NoC	318 4 78 −	759	713 6 84	twenty	Num	888 4 96 −	18	971 6 87
thousand		302 4 78 −	678	663 6 82	*twenties*		10 4 84 −	3	14 6 75
thousands		17 4 72 −	87	51 6 81	*twenty*		878 4 96 −	17	957 6 86
three	Num	1516 4 94 −	200	1885 6 95	two	Num	2478 4 96 −	158	2892 6 95
three		1499 4 94 −	206	1873 6 95	*two*		2465 4 95 −	159	2878 6 95
threes		17 4 41 +	3	13 5 48	*twos*		14 4 73 −	0	14 6 56
through	Adv	124 4 91 −	46	177 6 93	type	NoC	88 4 94 −	219	200 6 92
through	Prep	433 4 98 −	399	739 6 98	*type*		74 4 92 −	119	147 6 94
throw	Verb	155 4 90 +	115	82 6 90	*types*		14 4 75 −	119	53 6 82
threw		22 4 87 +	26	10 6 78	U / u	Lett	58 4 75 −	359	191 6 90
throw		84 4 91 +	100	36 6 86	*u*		56 4 73 −	359	186 6 90
throwing		18 4 89 +	2	14 6 77	*u.*		3 4 73 −	3	5 5 39
thrown		25 4 82 +	3	19 6 93	under	Prep	169 4 91 −	133	279 6 92
throws		6 4 75 +	3	4 6 81	understand	Verb	134 4 93 −	335	305 6 91
Thursday	NoP	150 4 94 +	253	52 6 89	*understand*		124 4 92 −	231	256 6 92
Thursday		142 4 93 +	228	52 6 89	*understanding*		1 4 80 −	43	11 6 78
Thursdays		7 4 65 +	35	1 3 50	*understands*		3 4 81 −	0	4 6 68
till	Prep	183 4 91 +	209	81 6 75	*understood*		6 4 92 −	102	34 6 86
time	NoC	1950 4 99 −	79	2207 6 93	union	NoC	18 4 68 −	1284	275 6 72
time		1712 4 99 −	44	1892 6 94	*union*		15 4 67 −	984	216 6 72
times		238 4 94 −	54	316 6 88	*unions*		3 3 66 −	301	59 6 74

Word	PoS	FrC	R	DD		LL	FrT	R	DG
university	NoC	30	4	91	–	302	126	6	34
universities		2	3	54	–	79	19	6	33
university		28	4	93	–	231	106	6	35
unless	Conj	126	4	93	+	1	119	6	94
until	Conj	116	4	97	–	22	151	6	96
up	Adv	3765	4	99	+	1836	2293	6	93
up	Prep	214	4	94	+	184	108	6	89
up to	Prep	271	4	94	+	56	199	6	93
upon	Prep	17	4	85	–	438	124	6	81
upstairs	Adv	129	4	92	+	499	18	6	78
use	NoC	43	4	91	–	303	150	6	91
use		41	4	92	–	270	138	6	92
uses		2	3	54	–	36	12	6	74
use	Verb	622	4	96	–	482	1021	6	91
use		393	4	96	–	61	498	6	89
used		126	4	93	–	329	292	6	91
uses		21	4	84	–	0	23	6	83
using		82	4	87	–	277	208	6	89
used (to)	VMod	607	4	95	–	178	835	6	61
usually	Adv	166	4	95	+	21	130	6	84
value	NoC	26	4	87	–	347	126	6	91
value		25	4	84	–	240	101	6	92
values		1	2	40	–	126	25	6	82
various	Adj	18	4	81	–	611	158	6	91
very	Adv	1533	4	95	–	2227	2947	6	93
view	NoC	29	4	91	–	1451	338	6	81
view		24	4	96	–	1126	269	6	81
views		4	3	59	–	327	69	6	80
wait	Verb	388	4	99	+	511	158	6	98
wait		272	4	98	+	468	94	6	98
waited		9	4	74	+	0	7	6	86
waiting		105	4	97	+	75	56	6	93
waits		3	4	53	+	3	1	3	40
walk	Verb	406	4	92	+	552	163	6	84
walk		184	4	91	+	219	80	6	80
walked		93	4	88	+	177	30	6	86
walking		109	4	90	+	117	50	6	84
walks		20	4	78	+	59	4	6	90
wall	NoC	147	4	89	+	166	65	6	93
wall		121	4	89	+	149	51	6	88
walls		26	4	88	+	19	14	6	85
want	Verb	3574	4	96	+	2864	1846	6	96
wan~		473	4	88	+	1846	65	6	75
want		2420	4	93	+	1623	1335	6	95
wanted		360	4	96	+	46	283	6	95
wanting		31	4	87	+	0	31	6	93
wants		291	4	98	+	309	133	6	88
war	NoC	49	4	89	–	815	271	6	79
war		45	4	89	–	781	256	6	79
wars		4	3	51	–	34	15	6	67
wash	Verb	145	4	86	+	445	29	6	70
wash		78	4	85	+	251	14	6	66
washed		37	4	81	+	103	8	6	74
washes		3	4	57	+	5	1	3	52
washing		28	4	91	+	87	5	5	63
watch	Verb	438	4	93	+	1101	109	6	88
watch		275	4	90	+	770	61	6	85
watched		56	4	89	+	148	13	6	85
watches		4	4	73	+	9	1	5	74
watching		103	4	92	+	188	34	6	89
water	NoC	272	4	91	–	4	294	6	73
water		271	4	91	–	1	283	6	73
waters		1	3	59	–	50	12	6	65
way	NoC	1122	4	98	–	297	1519	6	96
way		1081	4	98	–	166	1368	6	97
ways		41	4	86	–	328	151	6	83
we	Pron	8667	4	96	–	5148	13449	6	96
us		798	4	99	–	472	1237	6	95
we		7869	4	95	–	4675	12212	6	96
wear	Verb	255	4	93	+	534	75	6	85
wear		144	4	92	+	399	33	6	82
wearing		59	4	85	+	93	22	6	88
wears		18	4	89	+	80	2	4	66
wore		16	4	86	+	5	10	6	71
worn		17	4	85	+	13	9	6	80
Wednesday	NoP	149	4	93	+	182	63	6	82
Wednesday		143	4	93	+	173	61	6	82
Wednesdays		6	4	75	+	8	2	5	72
week	NoC	993	4	95	+	225	717	6	93
week		774	4	94	+	227	533	6	93
weeks		219	4	98	+	14	184	6	91
weekend	NoC	166	4	93	+	251	62	6	92
weekend		149	4	92	+	250	53	6	91
weekends		16	4	84	+	8	10	6	84
well	Adv	7713	4	96	+	7540	3665	6	96
what	DetP	9138	4	97	+	3170	6065	6	94
whatever	DetP	286	4	98	–	0	291	6	94
when	Adv	656	4	97	+	205	445	6	91
when	Conj	2574	4	95	+	315	2037	6	92
where	Adv	1649	4	97	+	367	1196	6	97
where	Conj	163	4	96	+	0	159	6	93
whether	Conj	281	4	95	–	314	503	6	96
which	DetP	818	4	98	–	7093	3159	6	93
while	Conj	158	4	90	+	0	154	6	96
white	Adj	195	4	90	+	212	88	6	87
white		194	4	90	+	211	88	6	87
who	Pron	1534	4	95	–	244	1948	6	93
whole	Adj	181	4	94	–	133	294	6	95
why	Adv	1551	4	94	+	1195	813	6	94
wife	NoC	81	4	92	–	82	141	6	91
wife		78	4	93	–	58	127	6	90
wives		3	3	47	–	40	14	6	76
will	VMod	6726	4	97	+	1880	4674	6	96
'll		4559	4	97	+	5040	2044	6	92
will		1244	4	96	–	1652	2332	6	90
wo~		923	4	96	+	1741	298	6	98
win	Verb	193	4	86	+	62	130	6	72
win		85	4	85	+	27	58	6	69
winning		12	4	90	–	0	13	6	72
wins		6	4	58	–	1	8	6	58
won		89	4	86	+	53	51	6	72
window	NoC	204	4	93	+	174	102	6	74
window		136	4	96	+	150	61	6	84
windows		68	4	84	+	32	41	6	57
wish	Verb	105	4	91	–	51	157	6	79
wish		88	4	92	–	40	130	6	79
wished		14	4	80	+	4	9	6	74
wishes		1	4	80	–	43	11	6	80
wishing		2	3	58	–	12	7	5	75
with	Prep	3932	4	99	–	428	4798	6	98
within	Prep	49	4	82	–	1442	392	6	85
without	Prep	171	4	90	–	100	265	6	95
woman	NoC	255	4	88	–	271	450	6	76
woman		173	4	86	–	62	114	6	79
women		81	4	88	–	804	336	6	74
wonder	Verb	249	4	96	+	132	148	6	92
wonder		174	4	95	+	137	90	6	86
wondered		38	4	98	+	9	27	6	84
wondering		35	4	92	+	5	27	6	92
wonders		2	4	80	–	1	3	6	85
word	NoC	309	4	86	–	213	495	6	90
word		167	4	86	–	76	246	6	87

Word	PoS	FrC	R	DD		LL	FrT	R	DG	Word	PoS	FrC	R	DD		LL	FrT	R	DG
words		142	4	85	–	144	248	6	90	*wrote*		55	4	92	–	3	65	6	89
work	NoC	457	4	97	–	255	700	6	92	wrong	Adj	290	4	95	+	19	245	6	92
work	Verb	705	4	96	–	403	1086	6	91	X / x	Lett	24	4	56	–	900	226	6	76
work		323	4	96	–	148	478	6	92	*x*		21	4	57	–	764	194	6	77
worked		94	4	92	–	167	192	6	84	*x.*		3	3	42	–	136	32	6	66
working		212	4	93	–	129	330	6	89	yeah	Int	13955	4	96	+	32679	3741	6	78
works		77	4	87	–	2	86	6	95	year	NoC	1014	4	96	–	1200	1844	6	95
worker	NoC	15	4	79	–	480	126	6	84	*year*		562	4	97	–	534	967	6	90
worker		7	4	74	–	55	25	6	90	*years*		452	4	91	–	676	877	6	94
workers		8	4	61	–	443	101	6	79	yep	Int	176	4	98	+	209	76	6	68
world	NoC	115	4	90	–	576	343	6	84	yes	Int	4247	4	88	+	303	3562	6	91
world		112	4	90	–	586	341	6	84	yesterday	Adv	277	4	95	+	391	109	6	87
worlds		3	4	64	+	0	2	5	63	yet	Adv	403	4	93	+	209	241	6	96
worry	Verb	153	4	95	+	136	75	6	95	yo	Uncl	175	4	94	+	358	53	6	70
worried		1	4	81	–	3	3	6	83	York	NoP	18	4	89	–	1110	246	6	47
worries		4	4	71	–	4	7	6	77	you	Pron	32334	4	99	+	10464	21796	6	92
worry		142	4	94	+	171	61	6	93	*ya*		246	4	81	+	1035	29	6	58
worrying		5	4	92	+	0	4	6	79	*ye*		3	2	42	–	0	3	4	57
worth	Prep	122	4	95	+	3	109	6	94	*you*		32085	4	99	+	10086	21764	6	92
would	VMod	3737	4	99	–	875	4975	6	94	young	Adj	184	4	93	–	72	265	6	87
'd		1360	4	97	+	161	1081	6	85	*young*		135	4	92	–	84	211	6	87
would		2378	4	99	–	1826	3894	6	94	*younger*		38	4	94	–	4	47	6	85
write	Verb	335	4	90	–	162	499	6	90	*youngest*		11	4	86	+	4	7	6	79
write		178	4	90	–	28	226	6	84	your	Det	3436	4	97	+	810	2465	6	90
writes		6	4	80	–	4	10	6	60	*your*		3435	4	97	+	809	2465	6	90
writing		40	4	84	–	62	78	6	90	yours	Pron	176	4	95	+	449	43	6	87
written		55	4	91	–	119	120	6	95	yourself	Pron	182	4	96	+	0	182	6	91

3.1

List 3.2. Distinctiveness list contrasting conversational v. task-oriented speech (not lemmatized)

Based on the spoken demographically sampled and context governed parts of the BNC. Ordered by Log Likelihood; not lemmatized; minimum log likelihood of 300.

PoS = Part of speech

FrC = Rounded frequency (per million word tokens) in demographically sampled (conversational) speech

LL = Log Likelihood, indicating the distinctiveness (or significance of the difference) between the frequencies in conversational and task-oriented speech

FrT = Rounded frequency (per million word tokens) in context-governed (task-oriented) speech

\+ = Higher frequency in conversational speech

\− = Higher frequency in task-oriented speech

Word	PoS	FrC		LL	FrT	Word	PoS	FrC		LL	FrT
oh	Int	9884	+	33062	1746	nice	Adj	1101	+	2901	262
yeah	Int	13955	+	32679	3741	in~*	Verb	452	+	2859	13
the	Det	27351	−	28176	47987	one	Pron	3542	+	2795	1841
she	Pron	8010	+	25899	1485	mummy	NoC	388	+	2790	2
I	Pron	39817	+	25333	22356	council	NoC	65	−	2746	670
of*	Prep	7989	−	22702	19038	ha	Int	499	+	2728	29
~n't	Neg	18418	+	21862	7967	ai~*	Verb	500	+	2697	30
no	Int	7830	+	18948	2034	like	Adv	1332	+	2666	410
he	Pron	11465	+	16728	4412	from	Prep	1315	−	2593	2769
that	Conj	3410	−	15927	9870	ca~	VMod	1919	+	2503	789
's	Verb	24009	+	15738	13345	Mr	NoC	156	−	2498	845
er	Uncl	5075	+	10677	10913	as	Conj	851	−	2457	2040
you	Pron	32085	+	10086	21764	their	Det	649	−	2440	1719
it	Pron	30417	+	9928	20465	also	Adv	160	−	2370	827
said	Verb	4617	+	9714	1363	is	Verb	8343	−	2368	11409
mm	Int	5202	+	9146	1768	alright*	Adj	714	+	2355	129
got	Verb	7435	+	8005	3377	government	NoC	28	−	2292	478
do	Verb	12854	+	7687	7365	county	NoC	14	−	2269	425
well	Adv	7713	+	7540	3665	very	Adv	1533	−	2227	2947
which	DetP	818	−	7093	3159	on	Adv	2618	−	2214	1323
cos*	Conj	2705	+	6251	734	eh	Int	461	+	2202	41
to	Inf	11353	−	6231	17347	thought	Verb	1361	+	2191	492
in	Prep	8506	−	6113	13731	that	DetP	16329	+	2121	12831
mum	NoC	951	+	5615	39	our	Det	666	−	2117	1655
erm	Uncl	3946	−	5387	7454	policy	NoC	9	−	2064	369
'll	VMod	4559	+	5040	2044	local	Adj	41	−	2053	479
~na*	Inf	2372	+	5035	695	fucking	Adj	278	+	1998	2
know	Verb	7527	+	4883	4198	an	Det	1149	−	1985	2323
her	Pron	1531	−	4740	301	to	Prep	5575	−	1980	7890
we	Pron	7869	+	4675	12212	~ta*	Inf	628	+	1979	120
ah	Int	1394	+	4663	246	members	NoC	14	−	1931	368
~n~*	Neg	836	+	4617	46	be	Verb	4558	−	1914	6633
ooh	Int	917	+	4268	87	may	VMod	151	−	1866	705
did	Verb	4805	+	4247	2386	'm	Verb	3334	+	1865	1950
go	Verb	4192	+	4105	1990	wan~	Verb	473	+	1846	65
and	Conj	21569	−	3800	27701	up	Adv	3765	+	1836	2293
by	Prep	783	−	3652	2265	would	VMod	2378	−	1826	3894
gon~	Verb	1918	+	3526	631	point	NoC	258	−	1800	896
as	Prep	298	−	3439	1339	her*	Det	1052	+	1793	365
me	Pron	3536	+	3378	1698	daddy	NoC	256	+	1782	3
people	NoC	1114	−	3358	2712	wo~	VMod	923	+	1741	298
what	DetP	9138	+	3170	6065	important	Adj	48	−	1718	439
get	Verb	4712	+	3118	2611	report	NoC	19	−	1707	350
dad	NoC	598	+	3082	42	fucking	Adv	226	+	1677	0
bloody	Adj	559	+	3002	34	du~*	Verb	357	+	1669	33
him	Pron	2111	+	2996	826	will	VMod	1244	−	1652	2332
there	Adv	4011	+	2989	2130	fact	NoC	177	−	1633	707

Word	PoS	FrC		LL	FrT	Word	PoS	FrC		LL	FrT
want	Verb	2420	+	1623	1335	training	NoC	27	−	949	244
like	Prep	2400	+	1604	1325	meeting	NoC	39	−	947	273
~no*	Verb	332	+	1601	29	hello	Int	392	+	939	103
though	Adv	709	+	1526	205	bed	NoC	330	+	931	73
nineteen	Num	111	−	1515	548	've	Verb	5528	+	930	4192
alright*	Adv	703	+	1493	206	community	NoC	14	−	929	202
of*	Verb	343	+	1487	38	areas	NoC	21	−	928	225
within	Prep	49	−	1442	392	clearly	Adv	6	−	926	176
off	Adv	1243	+	1419	549	case	NoC	78	−	925	356
chairman	NoC	5	−	1418	251	land	NoC	34	−	921	257
area	NoC	112	−	1393	524	of course	Adv	288	−	920	717
eat	Verb	347	+	1337	49	tea	NoC	322	+	918	70
lovely	Adj	437	+	1306	90	national	Adj	34	−	915	255
dear	Int	324	+	1297	42	city	NoC	23	−	911	226
particular	Adj	35	−	1294	328	they	Pron	10434	+	911	8581
look	Verb	1581	+	1293	810	see	Verb	3079	+	909	2116
come	Verb	2303	+	1282	1349	tomorrow	Adv	407	+	900	115
committee	NoC	25	−	1276	297	general	Adj	33	−	898	250
in terms of	Prep	7	−	1262	235	settlement	NoC	2	−	895	150
information	NoC	35	−	1259	323	part	NoC	156	−	885	491
question	NoC	94	−	1259	459	for	Prep	5366	−	883	6837
at	Prep	3274	−	1253	4691	girl	NoC	295	+	881	61
car	NoC	639	+	1245	201	okay*	Adv	618	−	871	1177
development	NoC	8	−	1241	233	district	NoC	13	−	865	189
mind	Verb	454	+	1239	104	shut	Verb	220	+	861	30
goes	Verb	802	+	1227	299	quid	NoC	212	+	854	28
actually	Adv	790	−	1221	1546	management	NoC	7	−	854	166
bloody	Adv	212	+	1207	10	bought	Verb	348	+	850	89
night	NoC	749	+	1207	270	darling	NoC	130	+	849	3
why	Adv	1551	+	1195	813	out	Adv	2846	+	844	1954
put	Verb	2168	+	1181	1278	are	Verb	3929	−	837	5166
just	Adv	4621	+	1171	3273	them	Pron	3737	+	834	2707
has	Verb	1098	−	1160	1940	being	Verb	370	−	834	814
mhm	Int	392	−	1158	947	hell	NoC	234	+	829	38
funny	Adj	321	+	1133	52	says	Verb	1038	+	828	537
mine	Pron	344	+	1127	63	Christmas	NoC	345	+	824	91
view	NoC	24	−	1126	269	C / c	Lett	217	−	824	577
went	Verb	1302	+	1118	654	region	NoC	4	−	822	150
into	Prep	670	−	1116	1339	there	Ex	3390	−	816	4530
York	NoP	18	−	1110	246	level	NoC	39	−	814	249
motion	NoC	4	−	1108	197	budget	NoC	12	−	811	177
plan	NoC	19	−	1103	248	your	Det	3435	+	809	2465
between	Prep	125	−	1096	485	really	Adv	2175	+	808	1420
anyway	Adv	785	+	1094	311	dinner	NoC	198	+	808	25
group	NoC	70	−	1078	372	percent	NoC	81	−	805	337
certainly	Adv	102	−	1071	434	women	NoC	81	−	804	336
because*	Conj	1494	−	1071	2411	trade	NoC	18	−	793	192
councillor	NoC	2	−	1040	174	da	Uncl	145	+	790	8
ya	Pron	246	+	1035	29	hair	NoC	222	+	787	36
shit	NoC	160	+	1032	4	lord	NoC	26	−	784	212
authority	NoC	7	−	1030	194	war	NoC	45	−	781	256
issue	NoC	5	−	1029	186	number	NoC	299	−	773	690
against	Prep	79	−	1028	379	kind	NoC	109	−	771	381
my	Det	2857	+	1025	1882	watch	Verb	275	+	770	61
this	DetP	4734	+	1025	6237	tape	NoC	261	+	769	55
down	Adv	1934	+	1009	1155	particularly	Adv	36	−	768	234
services	NoC	16	−	1003	222	home	Adv	436	+	766	148
bet	Verb	211	+	1002	19	system	NoC	57	−	764	279
union	NoC	15	−	984	216	X / x	Lett	21	−	764	194
then	Adv	4173	+	980	2997	never	Adv	978	+	762	510
more	Adv	342	−	979	818	for example	Adv	13	−	762	171
problems	NoC	61	−	965	329	health	NoC	37	−	761	234
a	Det	17055	−	962	19719	int	Uncl	135	+	760	7
therefore	Adv	25	−	955	240	planning	NoC	8	−	759	155
pounds	NoC	306	−	954	754	public	Adj	11	−	759	164
situation	NoC	37	−	954	271	boy	NoC	291	+	759	70

Word	PoS	FrC		LL	FrT
service	NoC	68	–	753	298
officers	NoC	5	–	752	143
sense	NoC	41	–	743	240
little	Adj	974	+	743	513
fuck	Verb	100	+	737	0
problem	NoC	167	–	735	471
position	NoC	26	–	728	201
structure	NoC	4	–	721	131
million	NoC	42	–	719	236
colleagues	NoC	1	–	717	120
stupid	Adj	172	+	713	21
dog	NoC	241	+	706	51
love	Verb	246	+	702	54
hundred	NoC	712	–	701	1235
god	NoC	203	+	697	34
looks	Verb	377	+	697	123
concerned	Adj	30	–	689	204
gone	Verb	622	+	688	279
door	NoC	414	+	688	146
cor	Int	116	+	687	5
major	Adj	15	–	683	165
indeed	Adv	49	–	682	245
issues	NoC	5	–	681	131
thousand	NoC	302	–	678	663
years	NoC	452	–	676	877
support	Verb	11	–	673	149
basis	NoC	11	–	672	151
or	Conj	2800	–	670	3738
perhaps	Adv	247	–	668	579
figures	NoC	17	–	666	167
social	Adj	22	–	665	179
congress	NoC	0	–	659	105
bag	NoC	191	+	655	32
president	NoC	5	–	655	125
urgh	Int	104	+	650	3
schools	NoC	24	–	649	182
me	Det	362	+	648	122
a bit	Adv	711	+	647	349
available	Adj	18	–	640	163
authorities	NoC	4	–	634	118
simply	Adv	15	–	631	154
bye	Int	264	+	629	69
buy	Verb	415	+	626	156
client	NoC	2	–	624	110
big	Adj	772	+	623	397
M / m	Lett	104	–	621	336
hey	Int	151	+	620	19

Word	PoS	FrC		LL	FrT
figure	NoC	15	–	618	152
reckon	Verb	178	+	616	30
period	NoC	23	–	616	171
various	Adj	18	–	611	158
Greater	NoP-	1	–	610	104
Oxford	NoP	14	–	608	146
doo	Uncl	96	+	608	3
provide	Verb	12	–	600	140
sort	NoC	473	–	599	875
things	NoC	805	–	594	1308
education	NoC	27	–	589	176
world	NoC	112	–	586	341
political	Adj	5	–	586	116
decision	NoC	17	–	585	152
agreed	Verb	11	–	585	135
sit	Verb	342	+	584	119
staff	NoC	40	–	582	205
one	Num	2540	–	581	3372
department	NoC	14	–	581	144
process	NoC	8	–	578	125
European	Adj	5	–	577	114
future	NoC	19	–	576	154
d'	Verb	145	+	575	19
cost	NoC	27	–	575	175
secretary	NoC	17	–	574	150
clear	Adj	42	–	573	207
labour*	Adj	29	–	572	178
business	NoC	98	–	570	312
bloke	NoC	140	+	570	18
pound	NoC	490	+	568	215
support	NoC	22	–	566	161
forward	Adv	50	–	561	221
here	Adv	2003	+	561	1391
mean	Verb	2675	+	560	1960
da	NoC	81	+	558	1
about	Prep	2274	–	552	3042
item	NoC	5	–	547	110
A / a	Lett	235	–	541	521
housing	NoC	10	–	540	124
children	NoC	206	–	539	477
statement	NoC	8	–	539	118
provision	NoC	1	–	539	90
however	Adv	16	–	538	140
needs	NoC	7	–	538	114
product	NoC	2	–	536	97
scheme	NoC	10	–	536	124
agree	Verb	47	–	534	210
year	NoC	562	–	534	967
G / g	Lett	72	–	532	257
tell	Verb	894	+	530	514
financial	Adj	11	–	529	125
employment	NoC	5	–	529	106
aware	Adj	14	–	527	134
industry	NoC	10	–	527	123
greenbelt	NoC	0	–	526	86
during	Prep	53	–	526	220
effect	NoC	16	–	521	136
evidence	NoC	13	–	518	129
debate	NoC	2	–	513	93
power	NoC	40	–	511	191
certain	Adj	66	–	509	240
police	NoC	77	–	507	260
country	NoC	90	–	507	283
like	Verb	1349	+	506	879
chicken	NoC	99	+	506	7
birthday	NoC	150	+	504	26

3.2

Interjections, discourse markers and fillers
Their use in conversation and in more public or formal speech

Most interjections (e.g. *oh, ah, hello*) are much more characteristic of everyday conversation than of more formal/public 'task-oriented' speech. However, the voiced hesitation fillers *er* and *erm* and the discourse markers *mhm* and *um* prove to be more characteristic of formal/public speech. We recognize *er, erm* and *um* as common thought pauses in careful public speech. *Mhm* is likely to be a type of feedback in formal dialogues both indicating understanding and inviting continuation. In conversation, people use *yeah* and *yes* much more, and overwhelmingly prefer the informal pronunciation *yeah* to *yes*. In formal speech, on the other hand, *yes* is slightly preferred to *yeah*.

Word	PoS	FrC		LL	FrT	Word	PoS	FrC		LL	FrT
member	NoC	15	–	502	132	need	NoC	28	–	436	150
upstairs	Adv	129	+	499	18	in order	ClO	5	–	435	88
coat	NoC	108	+	498	10	officer	NoC	16	–	433	121
possible	Adj	52	–	496	212	involved	Adj	17	–	432	124
based	Verb	13	–	494	124	conditions	NoC	5	–	432	90
British	Adj	48	–	494	204	sites	NoC	6	–	431	92
terms	NoC	12	–	494	120	oi	Int	67	+	431	2
policies	NoC	4	–	493	94	with	Prep	3932	–	428	4798
cold	Adj	197	+	493	50	past	Prep	270	+	428	98
proposals	NoC	0	–	492	80	Britain	NoP	16	–	428	119
other	Adj	1016	–	491	1517	most	DetP	140	–	427	343
men	NoC	105	–	491	304	themselves	Pron	44	–	424	179
Jean	NoP	106	+	491	10	project	NoC	19	–	424	128
become	Verb	29	–	491	163	current	Adj	6	–	423	93
reasons	NoC	11	–	491	118	fairly	Adv	37	–	423	166
action	NoC	18	–	489	136	Charlotte	NoP	82	+	422	6
further*	Adj	6	–	487	102	as to	Prep	9	–	422	101
given	Verb	106	–	485	305	increase	NoC	6	–	421	92
those	DetP	848	–	485	1307	horrible	Adj	113	+	420	17
role	NoC	7	–	485	106	bad	Adj	431	+	420	205
result	NoC	11	–	484	117	changes	NoC	12	–	420	108
environment	NoC	9	–	484	112	cheese	NoC	88	+	418	8
obviously	Adv	160	–	482	389	additional	Adj	0	–	416	68
public	NoC	8	–	482	106	course	NoC	57	–	415	202
safety	NoC	8	–	479	108	does	Verb	1852	+	414	1342
hm	Int	91	+	477	6	environmental	Adj	3	–	413	80
interest	NoC	45	–	474	193	B / b	Lett	201	–	413	429
so that	Conj	113	–	473	312	itself	Pron	33	–	412	154
us	Pron	798	–	472	1237	Ann	NoP	107	+	410	15
costs	NoC	7	–	471	104	only	Adv	1331	+	408	907
conference	NoC	9	–	469	109	accept	Verb	26	–	407	140
wait	Verb	272	+	468	94	mate	NoC	94	+	406	11
amendment	NoC	2	–	468	85	nature	NoC	10	–	404	100
resources	NoC	5	–	468	96	function	NoC	4	–	403	82
told	Verb	518	+	467	255	present	Adj	11	–	402	101
produce	Verb	6	–	467	98	society	NoC	24	–	402	134
appropriate	Adj	7	–	467	103	Freud	NoP	1	–	401	71
morning	NoC	634	+	465	339	Europe	NoP	9	–	401	98
economic	Adj	3	–	465	87	chocolate	NoC	93	+	400	10
hate	Verb	130	+	463	21	through	Prep	433	–	399	739
points	NoC	32	–	462	164	wear	Verb	144	+	399	33
existing	Adj	2	–	460	84	groups	NoC	22	–	398	128
drink	NoC	137	+	460	24	deal	Verb	19	–	397	122
continue	Verb	9	–	458	106	councils	NoC	3	–	395	76
most	Adv	92	–	456	273	yesterday	Adv	277	+	391	109
and so on	Adv	18	–	455	130	referred	Verb	1	–	391	66
application	NoC	6	–	454	96	centre	NoC	53	–	389	188
opportunity	NoC	13	–	454	118	ee	Int	80	+	388	7
eighty	Num	164	–	452	387	example	NoC	17	–	388	116
first	Ord	715	–	452	1123	in	Adv	1576	+	387	1122
yours	Pron	176	+	449	43	chairman	NoP	0	–	387	60
sector	NoC	7	–	448	98	state	NoC	37	–	387	157
companies	NoC	13	–	447	115	transport	NoC	10	–	387	97
good	Adj	1883	+	447	1349	cat	NoC	111	+	387	18
specific	Adj	5	–	445	93	grandma	NoC	65	+	386	3
round	Adv	578	+	445	304	North	NoP-	3	–	385	74
quality	NoC	27	–	444	148	made	Verb	372	–	385	653
questions	NoC	61	–	443	216	Tim	NoP	95	+	384	12
workers	NoC	8	–	443	101	concern	NoC	3	–	384	76
difficult	Adj	95	–	443	275	greater	Adj	5	–	384	81
although	Conj	66	–	442	224	P / p	Lett	224	–	383	452
w	Uncl	47	–	440	190	fund	NoC	6	–	382	83
positive	Adj	8	–	439	100	ones	NoC	451	+	382	228
many	DetP	457	–	438	788	document	NoC	4	–	382	77
upon	Prep	17	–	438	124	company	NoC	71	–	381	218
telly	NoC	92	+	438	8	section	NoC	25	–	381	132

Word	PoS	FrC		LL	FrT		Word	PoS	FrC		LL	FrT
tapes	NoC	92	+	380	11		form	NoC	58	–	334	185
play	Verb	298	+	378	124		stuff	NoC	389	+	334	196
necessary	Adj	15	–	377	109		love	NoC	188	+	333	64
over there	Adv	169	+	376	48		any	DetP	1223	–	332	1662
thank	Verb	421	+	375	714		approach	NoC	6	–	331	76
cake	NoC	104	+	374	17		huh	Int	62	+	330	4
suggest	Verb	19	–	374	117		used	Verb	126	–	329	292
extent	NoC	8	–	374	90		cases	NoC	18	–	329	106
law	NoC	26	–	373	131		ways	NoC	41	–	328	151
tonight	Adv	275	+	372	111		views	NoC	4	–	327	69
Emma	NoP	72	+	370	5		consider	Verb	15	–	327	99
mentioned	Verb	40	–	369	159		produced	Verb	4	–	326	69
bath	NoC	91	+	367	12		throughout	Prep	7	–	325	76
summat	Pron	65	+	367	3		bit*	NoC	807	+	324	517
where	Adv	1649	+	367	1196		act	NoC	11	–	324	87
site	NoC	20	–	364	118		red	Adj	201	+	322	73
large	Adj	44	–	361	165		paragraph	NoC	11	–	322	87
production	NoC	6	–	361	80		association	NoC	3	–	322	64
sales	NoC	13	–	361	101		benefits	NoC	6	–	322	74
peasants	NoC	0	–	360	59		amount	NoC	63	–	321	190
Christopher	NoP	72	+	359	6		consultation	NoC	0	–	321	53
U / u	Lett	56	–	359	186		meetings	NoC	9	–	320	83
discussion	NoC	9	–	359	89		stage	NoC	55	–	319	175
silly	Adj	124	+	358	26		its	Det	218	–	318	420
yo	Uncl	175	+	358	53		fridge	NoC	60	+	317	4
strategy	NoC	1	–	357	63		bathroom	NoC	71	+	317	7
care	NoC	31	–	357	139		when	Conj	2574	+	315	2037
kitchen	NoC	136	+	356	33		in relation to	Prep	2	–	315	59
reason	NoC	89	–	355	242		flats	NoC	16	–	314	98
advice	NoC	13	–	355	99		whether	Conj	281	–	314	503
been	Verb	1762	–	355	2300		Sunday	NoP	224	+	314	88
half	DetP	590	+	354	337		Harlow	NoP	1	–	314	55
shoes	NoC	104	+	352	18		products	NoC	3	–	313	64
ow	Int	54	+	351	1		leave	Verb	403	+	311	211
much	Adv	289	–	350	529		previous	Adj	9	–	310	82
honourable	Adj	0	–	350	55		Oxfordshire	NoP	0	–	309	51
response	NoC	3	–	350	70		for instance	Adv	10	–	309	83
supposed	Adj	215	+	348	77		rather than	Prep	38	–	309	143
strategic	Adj	0	–	346	56		set	Verb	91	–	309	232
Saturday	NoP	232	+	346	88		press	NoC	14	–	309	93
individual	Adj	10	–	346	89		wants	Verb	291	+	309	133
pardon	NoC	189	+	346	62		different	Adj	356	–	308	599
investment	NoC	8	–	345	85		review	NoC	3	–	308	63
data	NoC	7	–	345	81		comments	NoC	15	–	307	94
better	Adv	297	+	344	130		human	Adj	9	–	306	79
have*	Verb	8093	+	343	7074		regional	Adj	9	–	303	78
please	Adv	495	+	343	269		yes	Int	4247	+	303	3562
Harrogate	NoP	0	–	343	55		raised	Verb	5	–	302	67
experience	NoC	37	–	342	148		likes	Verb	89	+	302	15
drink	Verb	98	+	341	16		procedure	NoC	3	–	302	62
chips	NoC	80	+	341	9		unions	NoC	3	–	301	59
party	NoC	126	–	340	296		future	Adj	4	–	301	63
criteria	NoC	1	–	339	59		homes	NoC	9	–	301	77
happen	Verb	74	–	338	212		ideas	NoC	20	–	301	104
minute	NoC	322	+	338	148		movement	NoC	8	–	301	75
Ben	NoP	71	+	335	6		're	Verb	4681	+	300	3963

List 4.1. Alphabetical frequency list: imaginative v. informative writing (lemmatized)

FrIm = Rounded frequency (per million word tokens) in imaginative writing
R = Range (0–19 for imaginative writing; 0–71 for informative writing)
D1 = Dispersion (Juilland's D) in imaginative writing
LL = Log Likelihood, indicating the distinctiveness (or significance of the difference) between imaginative writing and informative writing
FrIn = Rounded frequency (per million word tokens) in informative writing
D2 = Dispersion (Juilland's D) in informative writing
+ = Higher frequency in imaginative writing
– = Higher frequency in informative writing

Word	PoS	FrIm	R	D1	LL	FrIn	R	D2
&	Conj	13	19	75 –	4461	187	71	93
'	Gen	225	19	94 –	4628	594	71	97
's	Gen	4694	19	98 –	300	5010	71	97
1	Num	37	19	70 –	12695	530	71	92
1		37	19	70 –	12680	529	71	92
1s		0	2	22 –	17	1	26	65
2	Num	27	19	65 –	11992	477	71	93
2		27	19	65 –	11964	476	71	93
2s		0	1	00 –	27	1	25	65
3	Num	23	19	73 –	8363	345	71	94
3		23	19	73 –	8353	345	71	94
3s		0	1	00 –	10	1	19	70
4	Num	20	19	76 –	6618	277	71	94
4		20	19	76 –	6598	277	71	94
4s		0	0	00 –	21	1	24	76
5	Num	19	19	74 –	5592	242	71	94
5		19	19	74 –	5566	241	71	94
5s		0	0	00 –	28	1	23	68
10	Num	12	19	85 –	6786	259	71	93
10		12	19	85 –	6739	257	71	93
10s		0	1	00 –	46	2	34	71
1989	Num	1	9	70 –	5871	187	71	71
1990	Num	2	13	75 –	6995	223	71	74
1990		1	10	72 –	6614	209	71	72
1990s		0	6	62 –	393	14	71	90
a	Det	21722	19	99 –	66	22037	71	99
A / a	Lett	73	19	91 –	3764	296	71	94
a		73	19	91 –	3760	296	71	94
a.		0	0	00 –	4	0	8	64
a bit	Adv	185	19	93 +	3011	46	70	92
a little	Adv	263	19	94 +	4090	69	71	94
able	Adj	259	19	97 –	133	310	71	97
about	Adv	469	19	97 +	163	400	71	97
about	Prep	2170	19	97 +	9242	1181	71	97
above	Prep	199	19	97 +	399	134	71	97
accept	Verb	135	19	95 –	682	228	71	96
accept		66	19	94 –	270	107	71	94
accepted		56	19	95 –	237	91	71	96
accepting		11	19	90 –	66	20	71	95
accepts		1	11	75 –	207	11	70	93
according to	Prep	40	19	94 –	3140	205	71	94
account	NoC	64	19	94 –	3054	249	71	93
account		45	19	93 –	1981	167	71	94
accounts		19	19	92 –	1077	81	71	88
achieve	Verb	33	19	95 –	3904	218	71	97
achieve		13	19	93 –	1514	86	71	96
achieved		17	19	92 –	1764	103	71	96
achieves		0	2	27 –	126	5	66	92
achieving		2	18	85 –	519	24	71	95
across	Prep	434	19	97 +	3969	167	71	97
act	NoC	75	19	81 –	4240	319	71	88
act		68	19	79 –	3563	277	71	87
acts		7	19	87 –	690	42	71	93
action	NoC	76	19	95 –	4783	344	71	96
action		62	19	95 –	3935	281	71	95
actions		14	19	89 –	848	63	71	94
activity	NoC	37	19	95 –	6030	305	71	94
activities		16	19	93 –	3223	154	71	95
activity		21	19	94 –	2818	151	71	91
add	Verb	245	19	93 –	158	300	71	95
add		34	19	94 –	722	91	71	93
added		185	19	92 +	163	143	71	93
adding		23	19	92 –	91	36	71	94
adds		3	16	79 –	622	29	71	92
afraid	Adj	195	19	94 +	5389	25	71	92
after	Conj	231	19	98 –	19	249	71	95
after	Prep	983	19	98 +	2	969	71	95
again	Adv	1193	19	97 +	15754	357	71	97
against	Prep	579	19	97 –	12	602	71	96
age	NoC	156	19	95 –	1101	288	71	94
age		129	19	95 –	1105	251	71	93
ages		27	19	91 –	40	37	70	93
ago	Adv	217	19	97 +	79	184	71	91
agree	Verb	213	19	96 –	52	241	71	91
agree		64	19	95 –	37	77	71	84
agreed		139	19	94 –	1	143	71	89
agreeing		6	19	88 –	13	9	71	93
agrees		3	18	86 –	133	12	70	88
agreement	NoC	25	19	92 –	4216	211	71	85
agreement		24	19	92 –	3246	174	71	84
agreements		1	9	72 –	1058	36	71	86
air	NoC	305	19	97 +	1066	177	71	93
air		302	19	97 +	1051	175	71	93
airs		2	16	82 +	16	1	31	73
all	Adv	339	19	97 +	2397	150	71	96
all	DetP	2807	19	98 +	2502	2165	71	98
all right*	Adv	266	19	96 +	11203	11	68	90
allow	Verb	203	19	96 –	1824	401	71	95
allow		61	19	94 –	812	137	71	97
allowed		115	19	96 –	177	156	71	88
allowing		24	19	93 –	307	53	71	96
allows		3	19	88 –	1400	55	71	92
almost	Adv	506	19	97 +	1731	295	71	97
along	Prep	214	19	96 +	1147	107	71	95
already	Adv	379	19	97 +	47	345	71	98
also	Adv	352	19	96 –	21968	1581	71	98
although	Conj	251	19	95 –	2709	524	71	97
always	Adv	678	19	97 +	2511	386	71	96
American	Adj	59	19	90 –	2070	197	71	92
among	Prep	132	19	95 –	1539	283	71	97

Word	PoS	FrIm	R D1	LL	FrIn	R D2	Word	PoS	FrIm	R D1	LL	FrIn	R D2
amount	NoC	40 19 95 –		3217	208 71	87	*asks*		27 19 71 +		42	19 71	94
amount		37 19 95 –		2535	176 71	85	at	Prep	5572 19 99 +		2286	4685 71	97
amounts		3 19 85 –		732	32 71	94	at all	Adv	256 19 95 +		2200	102 71	96
an	Det	2516 19 98 –		8424	3897 71	99	at least	Adv	252 19 97 –		22	272 71	98
analysis	NoC	9 19 88 –		5139	195 71	91	authority	NoC	46 19 91 –		8142	400 71	93
analyses		0 9 75 –		404	15 66	88	*authorities*		11 19 84 –		4067	169 71	92
analysis		8 19 88 –		4736	180 71	91	*authority*		34 19 91 –		4179	231 71	92
and	Conj	26345 19 99 –		374	27173 71	99	available	Adj	32 19 92 –		7947	358 71	95
another	DetP	649 19 98 +		219	555 71	98	award	NoC	4 18 81 –		7035	235 71	36
answer	Verb	225 19 95 +		2704	73 71	93	*award*		3 18 82 –		6192	205 71	27
answer		94 19 94 +		682	41 71	90	*awards*		1 8 64 –		851	31 70	84
answered		116 19 93 +		2570	20 71	94	away	Adv	915 19 98 +		15449	221 71	94
answering		13 19 93 +		69	6 71	94	away from	Prep	246 19 95 +		2325	93 71	96
answers		3 16 83 –		12	5 66	92	B / b	Lett	18 19 73 –		4298	195 71	91
any	DetP	1080 19 98 –		236	1217 71	95	back	Adv	1824 19 98 +		29081	465 71	94
anyone	Pron	266 19 97 +		1677	124 71	94	back	NoC	447 19 97 +		5503	141 71	93
anything	Pron	585 19 96 +		8591	161 71	96	*back*		429 19 97 +		5544	131 71	93
anyway	Adv	236 19 96 +		5692	37 71	93	*backs*		18 19 93 +		59	11 69	91
appear	Verb	248 19 97 –		543	356 71	98	bad	Adj	384 19 98 +		1543	213 71	95
appear		55 19 96 –		948	135 71	96	*bad*		228 19 97 +		1250	113 71	95
appeared		166 19 96 +		434	104 71	96	*worse*		104 19 97 +		497	54 71	92
appearing		12 19 94 –		22	16 71	95	*worst*		52 19 96 +		11	46 71	94
appears		16 19 92 –		1733	100 71	96	bank	NoC	120 19 91 –		1827	282 71	89
application	NoC	29 19 31 –		3904	209 71	85	*bank*		96 19 90 –		1006	198 71	90
application		24 19 31 –		1946	126 71	88	*banks*		24 19 89 –		912	84 71	86
applications		5 12 30 –		2098	83 71	77	base	Verb	16 19 93 –		6291	256 71	96
apply	Verb	41 19 81 –		4197	248 71	92	*base*		1 1 79 –		91	6 70	94
applied		16 19 91 –		1337	86 71	95	*based*		14 19 93 –		6157	246 71	96
applies		4 16 49 –		762	36 71	87	*bases*		0 2 31 –		19	1 44	87
apply		16 19 74 –		1747	101 71	90	*basing*		0 2 22 –		45	2 61	91
applying		5 19 88 –		375	25 71	94	basis	NoC	14 19 90 –		4362	188 71	95
approach	NoC	29 19 95 –		4343	225 71	94	*basis*		14 19 90 –		4362	186 7l	95
approach		27 19 95 –		3483	190 71	94	*bases*		0 10 75 –		8	2 69	87
approaches		2 16 78 –		897	36 71	91	be*	Verb	41719 19 99 +		748	40274 71	99
April	NoP	21 19 84 –		4084	195 71	84	*'m*		1526 19 96 +		46376	163 71	90
April		21 19 84 –		4084	195 71	84	*'re*		1303 19 96 +		30433	215 71	87
area	NoC	113 19 94 –		12582	719 71	94	*'s*		4413 19 97 +		76773	1034 71	88
area		98 19 93 –		5515	416 71	92	*am*		468 19 94 +		3746	194 71	87
areas		15 19 94 –		7873	303 71	94	*are*		2062 19 98 +		41680	5398 71	97
argue	Verb	59 19 95 –		1821	185 71	94	*be*		4944 19 99 –		12000	7208 71	98
argue		24 19 94 –		255	50 70	94	*been*		2977 19 98 +		402	2699 71	98
argued		16 19 93 –		1321	85 71	93	*being*		669 19 98 –		1342	945 71	98
argues		1 9 72 –		938	32 70	90	*is*		4078 19 97 +		98451	11484 71	97
arguing		18 19 92 +		0	18 71	94	*was*		15782 19 99 +		89362	7707 71	97
arm	NoC	575 19 95 +		10771	125 71	92	*were*		3498 19 97 +		322	3226 71	97
arm		278 19 96 +		6001	51 71	86	because*	Conj	783 19 97 +		147	697 71	97
arms		297 19 94 +		4878	74 71	92	because of	Prep	96 19 96 –		1087	204 71	98
around	Adv	318 19 96 +		972	192 71	95	become	Verb	422 19 97 –		3400	807 71	97
around	Prep	382 19 96 +		1475	215 71	96	*became*		177 19 97 –		463	261 71	93
arrive	Verb	227 19 97 +		761	133 71	96	*become*		181 19 96 –		1723	364 71	97
arrive		34 19 95 +		6	30 71	95	*becomes*		15 19 93 –		1761	99 71	95
arrived		166 19 94 +		1034	78 71	95	*becoming*		49 19 95 –		250	84 71	97
arrives		7 19 86 –		15	10 71	94	bed	NoC	500 19 96 +		10477	95 71	91
arriving		20 19 94 +		19	16 71	95	*bed*		476 19 96 +		11643	74 71	90
art	NoC	67 19 92 –		3290	264 71	85	*beds*		24 19 92 +		3	21 69	91
art		55 19 90 –		2223	195 71	82	before	Adv	294 19 98 +		3709	91 71	96
arts		12 19 89 –		1104	68 71	88	before	Conj	534 19 97 +		3513	244 71	97
as	Adv	715 19 98 +		765	537 71	98	before	Prep	460 19 97 +		0	459 71	97
as	Conj	3587 19 97 +		1213	3067 71	98	begin	Verb	721 19 97 +		2541	417 71	94
as	Prep	791 19 98 –		17621	2154 71	98	*began*		482 19 97 –		3682	205 71	88
as if	Conj	555 19 96 +		15781	67 71	94	*begin*		69 19 95 –		37	83 71	96
as well as	Prep	63 19 93 –		2480	222 71	97	*beginning*		97 19 95 +		599	46 71	97
ask	Verb	1352 19 98 +		18182	399 71	95	*begins*		15 19 90 –		310	40 71	95
ask		322 19 98 +		2686	131 71	90	*begun*		58 19 95 +		58	44 71	95
asked		908 19 97 +		16581	202 71	96	behind	Prep	480 19 97 +		6449	142 71	96
asking		94 19 95 +		500	47 71	96	believe	Verb	439 19 97 +		449	332 71	96

Word	PoS	Frlm R D1	LL	Frln R D2
believe		329 19 96 +	1488	175 71 94
believed		85 19 96 –	6	91 71 96
believes		10 19 90 –	797	51 71 92
believing		16 19 94 +	1	15 71 94
benefit	NoC	20 19 92 –	3991	191 71 93
benefit		16 19 92 –	1584	95 71 91
benefits		4 18 82 –	2551	96 71 94
beside	Prep	220 19 97 +	6936	22 71 93
better	Adv	244 19 96 +	1668	109 71 96
between	Prep	458 19 98 –	7413	1101 71 96
big	Adj	390 19 94 +	583	277 71 92
big		341 19 94 +	1334	191 71 93
bigger		33 19 93 +	3	31 71 93
biggest		16 19 92 –	608	56 70 89
bit*	NoC	215 19 93 +	2260	76 71 92
bit		172 19 94 +	2041	56 71 92
bits		43 19 90 +	271	20 70 89
black	Adj	376 19 98 +	1741	199 71 94
black		374 19 98 +	1709	198 71 93
blacker		2 16 83 +	35	0 19 79
blackest		1 12 78 +	14	0 23 79
blue	Adj	209 19 96 +	2778	62 71 94
board	NoC	91 19 62 –	948	188 71 93
board		76 19 57 –	735	154 71 93
boards		14 19 84 –	218	34 71 88
body	NoC	443 19 96 +	577	322 71 96
bodies		57 19 92 –	114	80 71 95
body		387 19 95 +	1021	243 71 95
book	NoC	280 19 92 –	690	409 71 94
book		170 19 93 –	597	266 71 94
books		110 19 92 –	126	143 71 93
both	Adv	185 19 97 –	3384	466 71 97
both	DetP	281 19 97 –	138	335 71 98
boy	NoC	452 19 93 +	5318	148 71 93
boy		340 19 92 +	6272	75 71 92
boys		112 19 91 +	254	73 71 92
break	Verb	282 19 98 +	748	177 71 96
break		73 19 96 +	89	54 71 96
breaking		38 19 96 +	36	29 71 95
breaks		7 19 89 –	46	12 70 94
broke		102 19 95 +	841	42 71 92
broken		62 19 97 +	147	40 71 94
breath	NoC	207 19 92 +	6818	18 70 88
breath		199 19 91 +	6599	18 70 88
breaths		8 19 92 +	221	1 29 78
bring	Verb	532 19 98 +	425	416 71 98
bring		174 19 97 +	106	140 71 97
bringing		47 19 96 –	2	50 71 97
brings		18 19 91 –	179	37 71 96
brought		293 19 97 +	689	189 71 97
Britain	NoP	25 19 84 –	7845	334 71 93
British	Adj	75 19 88 –	7902	461 71 94
brother	NoC	224 19 93 +	1577	99 71 93
brethren		1 9 66 –	2	2 50 87
brother		179 19 93 +	1921	63 71 92
brothers		44 19 89 +	29	35 71 93
build	Verb	114 19 96 –	1779	270 71 96
build		27 19 91 –	752	80 71 96
building		15 19 94 –	179	32 71 96
builds		1 10 71 –	138	7 68 91
built		71 19 96 –	788	150 71 94
building	NoC	141 19 93 –	1048	264 71 94
building		102 19 92 –	656	184 71 95
buildings		39 19 92 –	401	80 71 91
business	NoC	263 19 95 –	1387	450 71 93
business		259 19 95 –	883	402 71 92

Word	PoS	Frlm R D1	LL	Frln R D2
businesses		4 18 87 –	1095	47 71 91
but	Conj	5962 19 98 +	12442	3958 71 97
buy	Verb	216 19 96 –	24	235 71 95
bought		94 19 94 +	63	75 71 95
buy		97 19 97 –	28	111 71 95
buying		22 19 94 –	188	43 71 95
buys		3 17 83 –	29	6 67 89
by	Prep	2568 19 98 –	42966	6250 71 98
call	Verb	671 19 97 +	920	484 71 97
call		200 19 97 +	1201	95 71 96
called		394 19 96 +	259	316 71 97
calling		59 19 96 +	143	38 71 92
calls		18 19 91 –	156	36 71 94
can	VMod	2015 19 97 –	1654	2526 71 97
ca~		598 19 97 +	12906	110 71 91
can		1417 19 97 –	7354	2417 71 96
car	NoC	503 19 95 –	1622	299 71 90
car		441 19 95 +	2318	222 71 90
cars		63 19 92 –	44	78 71 87
care	NoC	86 19 95 –	2075	242 71 89
care		85 19 95 –	2093	242 71 89
cares		1 11 70 +	1	1 33 85
carry	Verb	278 19 97 –	147	334 71 97
carried		120 19 97 –	108	152 71 97
carries		7 19 93 –	203	22 71 95
carry		76 19 96 –	137	105 71 96
carrying		75 19 95 +	98	54 71 96
case	NoC	248 19 93 –	7079	752 71 92
case		220 19 94 –	3270	513 71 92
cases		28 19 90 –	4793	239 71 92
catch	Verb	353 19 97 +	4998	100 71 94
catch		90 19 96 +	1026	30 71 94
catches		6 17 82 +	4	5 65 91
catching		28 19 95 +	275	10 69 93
caught		230 19 96 +	3890	55 71 94
cause	Verb	102 19 93 –	1736	250 71 97
cause		22 19 94 –	751	72 71 95
caused		57 19 92 –	544	115 71 96
causes		3 19 87 –	475	25 70 94
causing		20 19 89 –	160	38 71 95
central	Adj	37 19 92 –	4516	251 71 94
centre	NoC	102 19 96 –	3781	348 71 94
centre		98 19 96 –	2431	279 71 93
centres		4 18 83 –	1756	69 71 91
century	NoC	50 19 91 –	5258	307 71 93
centuries		17 19 89 –	338	45 71 92
century		33 19 90 –	5141	262 71 93
certain	Adj	152 19 96 –	618	245 71 95
certainly	Adv	191 19 94 +	40	169 71 96
chair	NoC	268 19 96 +	5618	51 71 90
chair		223 19 96 +	5087	38 71 87
chairs		45 19 95 +	624	13 71 91
chance	NoC	189 19 97 +	81	158 71 93
chance		168 19 96 +	205	124 71 93
chances		21 19 93 –	97	34 71 92
change	NoC	97 19 96 –	7412	488 71 95
change		79 19 96 –	2405	246 71 94
changes		18 19 93 –	5724	242 71 94
change	Verb	269 19 97 +	0	266 71 97
change		95 19 96 –	80	119 71 97
changed		144 19 96 +	253	99 71 96
changes		4 17 85 –	51	9 69 94
changing		26 19 96 –	72	39 71 96
chapter	NoC	77 19 87 –	1760	212 71 91
chapter		75 19 86 –	1312	185 71 91
chapters		2 15 77 –	598	27 69 91

4.1

Word	PoS	FrIm R D1	LL	FrIn R D2	Word	PoS	FrIm R D1	LL	FrIn R D2
child	NoC	583 19 92 –	764	774 71 93	condition	NoC	57 19 91 –	4846	307 71 96
child		*286 19 92 +*	*73*	*249 71 89*	*condition*		*37 19 92 –*	*900*	*104 71 93*
children		*297 19 92 –*	*1760*	*524 71 94*	*conditions*		*20 19 89 –*	*4331*	*203 71 95*
choose	Verb	129 19 96 –	340	190 71 97	consider	Verb	130 19 93 –	2927	355 71 95
choose		*41 19 96 –*	*330*	*78 71 95*	*consider*		*44 19 93 –*	*1465*	*144 71 94*
chooses		*3 18 89 –*	*41*	*7 71 92*	*considered*		*72 19 92 –*	*983*	*163 71 95*
choosing		*8 19 89 –*	*138*	*20 71 94*	*considering*		*11 19 88 –*	*298*	*32 71 94*
chose		*38 19 94 +*	*43*	*28 71 96*	*considers*		*2 15 78 –*	*292*	*16 71 94*
chosen		*38 19 93 –*	*100*	*57 71 97*	contain	Verb	68 19 94 –	2510	232 71 94
church	NoC	155 19 89 –	956	276 71 90	*contain*		*13 19 92 –*	*817*	*59 71 94*
church		*147 19 89 –*	*539*	*231 71 90*	*contained*		*32 19 93 –*	*219*	*59 71 93*
churches		*8 18 74 –*	*699*	*44 71 86*	*containing*		*17 19 90 –*	*505*	*52 71 90*
city	NoC	178 19 94 –	1106	317 71 95	*contains*		*6 19 87 –*	*1366*	*62 71 94*
cities		*14 19 84 –*	*699*	*56 71 92*	continue	Verb	221 19 95 –	577	327 71 97
city		*164 19 94 –*	*635*	*261 71 94*	*continue*		*47 19 93 –*	*1376*	*144 71 96*
claim	Verb	54 19 94 –	3420	244 71 93	*continued*		*158 19 94 +*	*298*	*107 71 94*
claim		*18 19 93 –*	*568*	*58 71 95*	*continues*		*6 19 81 –*	*1071*	*53 71 95*
claimed		*23 19 91 –*	*1534*	*108 71 89*	*continuing*		*11 19 89 –*	*132*	*23 71 95*
claiming		*7 19 90 –*	*367*	*28 71 92*	contract	NoC	25 19 87 –	4003	204 71 82
claims		*5 18 85 –*	*1062*	*50 71 85*	*contract*		*20 19 87 –*	*2771*	*146 71 81*
class	NoC	69 19 90 –	4063	301 71 92	*contracts*		*6 18 81 –*	*1239*	*58 71 83*
class		*55 19 90 –*	*2848*	*224 71 92*	control	NoC	91 19 95 –	4072	343 71 95
classes		*14 19 88 –*	*1234*	*77 71 91*	*control*		*85 19 95 –*	*3392*	*301 71 95*
clear	Adj	175 19 97 –	567	269 71 96	*controls*		*7 19 82 –*	*718*	*42 71 87*
clear		*167 19 97 –*	*526*	*255 71 96*	corner	NoC	195 19 97 +	2323	63 71 94
clearer		*7 19 90 –*	*20*	*10 71 94*	*corner*		*166 19 96 +*	*2185*	*50 71 93*
clearest		*1 10 73 –*	*32*	*3 66 93*	*corners*		*29 19 96 +*	*190*	*13 69 92*
close	Adj	190 19 96 +	101	156 71 98	cost	NoC	24 19 89 –	8293	345 71 94
close		*162 19 96 +*	*143*	*125 71 98*	*cost*		*17 19 86 –*	*4148*	*188 71 94*
closer		*23 19 91 +*	*1*	*22 71 96*	*costs*		*7 19 88 –*	*4203*	*157 71 93*
closest		*5 19 87 –*	*35*	*9 71 94*	could	VMod	3159 19 99 +	27055	1263 71 98
close	Verb	270 19 97 +	2478	104 71 92	council	NoC	39 19 86 –	8927	410 71 90
close		*44 19 95 +*	*58*	*32 71 93*	*council*		*38 19 86 –*	*7792*	*368 71 89*
closed		*190 19 96 +*	*2539*	*56 71 89*	*councils*		*1 13 80 –*	*1193*	*42 71 89*
closes		*3 16 77 –*	*11*	*5 70 93*	country	NoC	172 19 93 –	6660	601 71 93
closing		*33 19 94 +*	*417*	*10 71 95*	*countries*		*13 19 88 –*	*5595*	*224 71 90*
club	NoC	96 19 84 –	1770	243 71 87	*country*		*159 19 93 –*	*2482*	*377 71 94*
club		*83 19 84 –*	*1280*	*196 71 86*	couple	NoC	202 19 95 +	890	109 71 93
clubs		*13 19 80 –*	*525*	*47 71 89*	*couple*		*192 19 95 +*	*1190*	*90 71 92*
coffee	NoC	188 19 93 +	4224	33 71 91	*couples*		*10 19 91 –*	*70*	*18 71 89*
coffee		*186 19 93 +*	*4189*	*32 71 92*	course	NoC	84 19 94 –	4043	328 71 91
coffees		*2 14 79 +*	*37*	*1 13 58*	*course*		*77 19 93 –*	*1957*	*222 71 93*
cold	Adj	231 19 97 +	3097	68 71 92	*courses*		*7 18 89 –*	*2572*	*106 71 84*
cold		*224 19 96 +*	*3076*	*65 71 92*	court	NoC	82 19 88 –	7134	447 71 86
colder		*6 19 88 +*	*53*	*2 57 88*	*court*		*74 19 88 –*	*5526*	*368 71 84*
coldest		*1 13 78 +*	*0*	*1 45 87*	*courts*		*8 19 86 –*	*1675*	*79 71 88*
come	Verb	2643 19 98 +	25137	994 71 97	cover	Verb	159 19 97 –	188	208 71 96
came		*996 19 98 +*	*11254*	*335 71 96*	*cover*		*35 19 95 –*	*359*	*72 71 96*
come		*1203 19 98 +*	*13278*	*412 71 96*	*covered*		*99 19 96 +*	*79*	*77 71 95*
comes		*119 19 95 –*	*73*	*145 71 95*	*covering*		*20 19 94 –*	*98*	*34 71 95*
cometh		*0 4 51 +*	*0*	*0 14 75*	*covers*		*4 19 91 –*	*392*	*24 71 94*
comin'		*4 16 80 +*	*151*	*0 13 66*	create	Verb	48 19 94 –	4704	281 71 96
coming		*319 19 97 +*	*3917*	*101 71 95*	*create*		*14 19 91 –*	*2009*	*106 71 96*
committee	NoC	26 19 84 –	5796	268 71 93	*created*		*22 19 93 –*	*1654*	*110 71 96*
committee		*24 19 84 –*	*4902*	*233 71 93*	*creates*		*2 16 83 –*	*411*	*19 70 93*
committees		*2 14 80 –*	*919*	*35 71 91*	*creating*		*9 19 92 –*	*673*	*46 71 96*
common	Adj	56 19 95 –	3025	232 71 95	cry	Verb	232 19 92 +	7183	24 70 89
community	NoC	23 19 90 –	8704	356 71 93	*cried*		*133 19 89 +*	*5355*	*7 62 89*
communities		*1 10 67 –*	*1592*	*56 71 91*	*cries*		*5 19 60 +*	*38*	*2 51 88*
community		*21 19 90 –*	*7146*	*300 71 93*	*cry*		*52 19 95 +*	*1186*	*9 68 86*
company	NoC	159 19 95 –	10548	739 71 92	*crying*		*43 19 92 +*	*1071*	*6 64 87*
companies		*12 19 86 –*	*6106*	*237 71 92*	cut	Verb	191 19 98 +	9	180 71 95
company		*147 19 95 –*	*5429*	*502 71 91*	*cut*		*162 19 98 +*	*63*	*137 71 95*
computer	NoC	37 19 85 –	3709	219 71 84	*cuts*		*6 19 85 –*	*91*	*13 71 91*
computer		*31 19 83 –*	*2843*	*174 71 84*	*cutting*		*23 19 94 –*	*22*	*29 71 95*
computers		*6 19 87 –*	*874*	*45 71 81*	dark	Adj	363 19 96 +	8629	58 71 93

4.1

Word	PoS	FrIm R D1	LL	FrIn R D2	Word	PoS	FrIm R D1	LL	FrIn R D2
dark		345 19 96 +	8729	51 71 93	director	NoC	34 19 85 –	3751	215 71 93
darker		14 19 94 +	102	6 66 87	*director*		27 19 83 –	2662	158 71 93
darkest		4 19 85 +	28	2 53 90	*directors*		7 17 76 –	1096	57 71 89
data/datum*	NoC	8 17 74 –	6832	247 71 87	do	Verb	8745 19 98 +	88201	3172 71 97
data		8 17 74 –	6812	246 71 87	*d'*		46 19 87 +	2297	1 31 80
datum		0 1 00 –	19	1 30 82	*did*		3011 19 97 +	49688	743 71 97
date	NoC	45 19 93 –	3335	223 71 75	*do*		4312 19 98 +	50145	1422 71 96
date		36 19 91 –	3251	201 71 73	*does*		573 19 97 +	8	591 71 95
dates		9 19 92 –	153	22 71 93	*doing*		342 19 97 +	1961	166 71 96
day	NoC	1186 19 97 +	1593	859 71 96	*done*		446 19 98 +	1813	247 71 97
day		803 19 97 +	1576	540 71 96	*doth*		1 15 83 –	0	1 37 84
days		383 19 97 +	178	319 71 96	*du~***		13 19 51 +	524	1 14 62
dead	Adj	276 19 94 +	3816	80 71 93	doctor	NoC	275 19 90 +	2039	119 71 92
dead		276 19 94 +	3814	80 71 93	*doctor*		255 19 89 +	4005	66 71 90
deal	Verb	76 19 95 –	1377	191 71 95	*doctors*		21 19 88 –	397	53 71 90
deal		37 19 94 –	318	72 71 94	door	NoC	1007 19 97 +	28874	120 71 93
dealing		21 19 92 –	571	62 71 93	*door*		903 19 97 +	29059	85 71 93
deals		2 16 83 –	315	16 71 92	*doors*		104 19 95 +	1198	35 71 92
dealt		16 19 92 –	289	41 71 93	down	Adv	1688 19 99 +	20723	535 71 95
death	NoC	262 19 94 +	14	246 71 95	down	Prep	217 19 96 +	3344	57 71 91
death		247 19 94 +	62	216 71 95	draw	Verb	293 19 96 +	328	219 71 97
deaths		14 19 85 –	149	30 71 89	*draw*		43 19 95 –	104	62 71 96
decide	Verb	285 19 97 +	84	246 71 97	*drawing*		40 19 93 +	31	31 71 95
decide		43 19 94 –	206	73 71 96	*drawn*		74 19 96 –	12	82 71 97
decided		224 19 97 +	600	140 71 97	*draws*		4 17 85 –	170	14 69 94
decides		5 19 85 –	66	10 71 94	*drew*		133 19 93 +	2490	29 71 96
deciding		12 19 91 –	83	23 71 93	drive	Verb	284 19 95 +	2026	125 71 94
decision	NoC	67 19 91 –	4287	305 71 93	*drive*		74 19 95 +	461	34 71 94
decision		54 19 91 –	2528	208 71 92	*driven*		43 19 94 +	82	29 71 95
decisions		13 19 89 –	1853	97 71 94	*drives*		6 18 86 –	4	7 68 92
deep	Adj	188 19 96 +	1389	81 71 96	*driving*		57 19 95 +	226	32 71 89
deep		168 19 95 +	1624	63 71 95	*drove*		104 19 92 +	1980	22 70 91
deeper		13 19 93 –	0	14 71 94	drop	Verb	206 19 97 +	1755	82 71 95
deepest		7 19 85 +	12	5 70 93	*drop*		50 19 95 +	299	24 71 94
department	NoC	40 19 91 –	5182	282 71 87	*dropped*		127 19 97 +	1463	42 71 94
department		37 19 92 –	3858	226 71 84	*dropping*		24 19 94 +	192	10 70 94
departments		3 17 81 –	1398	56 71 90	*drops*		5 17 86 –	6	7 68 93
describe	Verb	60 19 93 –	4733	307 71 96	during	Prep	161 19 94 –	6065	554 71 96
describe		21 19 92 –	368	52 71 94	each	DetP	252 19 95 –	4209	613 71 96
described		30 19 94 –	3457	196 71 94	each other	Pron	194 19 97 +	1178	92 71 95
describes		2 13 76 –	958	36 71 95	early	Adj	146 19 97 –	4068	438 71 97
describing		7 19 83 –	256	24 71 95	*earlier*		29 19 94 –	806	87 71 95
design	NoC	32 19 89 –	3270	193 71 92	*earliest*		4 18 86 –	384	24 71 93
design		21 19 90 –	2959	157 71 92	*early*		113 19 97 –	2914	327 71 97
designs		11 19 79 –	381	36 71 90	easy	Adj	179 19 97 –	32	200 71 95
detail	NoC	80 19 96 –	1751	217 71 95	*easier*		34 19 94 –	61	48 71 95
detail		27 19 95 –	557	72 71 95	*easiest*		5 18 87 –	19	8 70 92
details		53 19 96 –	1194	145 71 93	*easy*		140 19 97 –	1	144 71 95
develop	Verb	31 19 92 –	6679	313 71 95	eat	Verb	264 19 96 +	2600	97 71 91
develop		10 19 89 –	2556	113 71 95	*ate*		55 19 95 +	1354	8 69 90
developed		16 19 90 –	2989	145 71 94	*eat*		124 19 95 +	1072	49 71 90
developing		5 19 91 –	824	41 71 94	*eaten*		33 19 96 +	296	13 68 90
develops	•	1 8 69 –	321	13 71 93	*eating*		48 19 96 +	266	24 69 90
development	NoC	18 19 90 –	13677	500 71 93	*eats*		4 19 85 +	6	3 60 90
development		14 19 90 –	11999	431 71 93	economic	Adj	7 18 79 –	9389	321 71 89
developments		4 19 84 –	1700	69 71 93	education	NoC	23 19 88 –	8245	342 71 92
die	Verb	316 19 96 +	699	207 71 91	*education*		23 19 88 –	8261	342 71 92
die		105 19 93 +	913	42 71 93	effect	NoC	87 19 94 –	6470	431 71 95
died		166 19 97 +	60	142 71 87	*effect*		73 19 93 –	3594	289 71 94
dies		10 19 90 –	1	11 69 91	*effects*		14 19 91 –	3115	143 71 93
dying		35 19 93 +	336	13 71 92	either	Adv	166 19 97 –	355	237 71 96
difference	NoC	64 19 96 –	2606	229 71 94	election	NoC	13 19 71 –	5142	208 71 78
difference		58 19 96 –	671	124 71 94	*election*		11 19 68 –	2865	128 71 83
differences		6 19 88 –	2649	105 71 92	*elections*		1 13 75 –	2368	79 71 66
different	Adj	239 19 98 –	3337	544 71 95	else	Adv	402 19 97 +	5314	121 71 96
difficult	Adj	134 19 97 –	908	245 71 97	end	NoC	414 19 98 –	94	468 71 98

Word	PoS	Frlm	R D1	LL	Frln	R D2
end		394	19 98 –	57	434	71 98
ends		20	19 93 –	92	33	71 93
England	NoP	102	19 92 –	2533	290	71 93
England		102	19 92 –	2530	290	71 93
enough	Adv	451	19 98 +	3483	191	71 96
ensure	Verb	24	19 90 –	3612	186	71 94
ensure		15	19 90 –	2764	135	71 93
ensured		4	18 83 –	124	13	71 95
ensures		0	5 54 –	334	12	71 93
ensuring		4	18 88 –	467	26	71 94
environment	NoC	11	19 86 –	4735	190	71 89
environment		10	19 88 –	4239	170	71 90
environments		1	6 35 –	495	20	68 78
especially	Adv	92	19 96 –	1338	212	71 96
establish	Verb	27	19 94 –	4761	235	71 95
establish		10	19 92 –	1303	69	71 95
established		15	19 91 –	2700	133	71 95
establishes		0	2 31 –	135	5	68 90
establishing		2	17 85 –	643	28	71 94
Europe	NoP	33	19 89 –	4443	237	71 92
Europe		33	19 89 –	4440	237	71 92
European	Adj	18	19 67 –	6262	260	71 92
even	Adv	971	19 98 +	1473	688	71 96
evening	NoC	319	19 96 +	3225	115	71 93
evening		293	19 96 +	3114	103	71 92
evenings		26	19 89 +	144	13	70 92
event	NoC	71	19 94 –	3197	267	71 96
event		28	19 92 –	1963	134	71 94
events		43	19 94 –	1289	132	71 95
ever	Adv	486	19 98 +	4045	197	71 96
every	Det	482	19 97 +	423	372	71 97
everyone	Pron	211	19 95 +	892	115	71 95
everything	Pron	361	19 97 +	4340	116	71 95
evidence	NoC	68	19 90 –	3442	273	71 94
evidence		68	19 90 –	3440	272	71 94
evidences		0	3 42 –	2	0	17 70
example	NoC	20	19 92 –	5899	255	71 93
example		16	19 92 –	3414	160	71 93
examples		4	17 80 –	2541	95	71 92
expect	Verb	329	19 97 +	62	293	71 95
expect		144	19 94 +	321	94	71 96
expected		130	19 97 –	134	167	71 94
expecting		51	19 95 +	751	14	71 93
expects		5	18 87 –	213	18	69 77
experience	NoC	83	19 96 –	2860	275	71 95
experience		75	19 96 –	2190	230	71 95
experiences		8	19 93 –	725	44	71 92
explain	Verb	225	19 98 +	54	197	71 97
explain		93	19 97 +	41	78	71 95
explained		109	19 96 +	308	67	71 96
explaining		16	19 93 –	10	20	71 95
explains		6	18 81 –	495	32	70 95
eye	NoC	1420	19 94 +	41246	165	71 94
eye		187	19 97 +	1515	77	71 95
eyes		1233	19 93 +	44487	88	71 93
face	NoC	1098	19 97 +	30027	142	71 95
face		1014	19 97 +	29261	119	71 95
faces		84	19 93 +	1249	23	71 93
fact	NoC	317	19 95 –	583	442	71 96
fact		286	19 95 –	373	379	71 96
facts		31	19 92 –	296	63	71 90
factor	NoC	11	19 85 –	5041	199	71 93
factor		8	19 86 –	1747	82	71 91
factors		3	15 74 –	3392	117	71 93
fail	Verb	90	19 97 –	1096	196	71 97
fail		18	19 95 –	219	39	71 96
failed		56	19 96 –	441	107	71 95
failing		11	19 93 –	173	26	71 95
fails		5	19 82 –	345	24	71 94
fall	Verb	427	19 97 +	1406	252	71 96
fall		84	19 96 +	43	69	71 96
fallen		62	19 96 +	292	32	71 95
falling		69	19 96 +	231	40	71 96
falls		10	19 88 –	205	26	71 95
fell		202	19 96 +	1614	84	71 93
family	NoC	317	19 95 –	1031	488	71 95
families		28	19 92 –	1205	103	71 93
family		289	19 95 –	390	385	71 95
far	Adj	180	19 97 –	1279	333	71 97
far		107	19 95 +	599	52	71 96
farther		3	19 85 +	35	1	28 81
farthest		2	12 77 +	19	0	25 80
*further**		66	19 96 –	3641	278	71 96
furthest		3	16 84 +	10	2	46 88
far	Adv	348	19 97 +	58	312	71 97
father	NoC	627	19 94 +	9389	169	71 93
father		618	19 94 +	9966	156	71 92
fathers		10	19 86 –	20	14	70 90
feel	Verb	1491	19 96 +	21714	412	71 95
feel		451	19 95 +	3529	189	71 94
feeling		165	19 92 +	3320	33	71 93
feels		33	19 88 +	0	33	71 94
felt		841	19 97 +	17906	157	71 95
feeling	NoC	214	19 94 +	1052	111	71 94
feeling		139	19 95 +	1086	58	71 95
feelings		76	19 91 +	126	53	71 91
few	DetP	584	19 98 +	705	431	71 97
field	NoC	136	19 92 –	749	235	71 93
field		82	19 90 –	867	171	71 93
fields		53	19 92 –	27	64	71 92
figure	NoC	160	19 96 –	1574	325	71 94
figure		119	19 96 –	509	194	71 92
figures		41	19 93 –	1312	131	71 94
financial	Adj	21	19 92 –	4643	215	71 93
find	Verb	1277	19 98 +	1494	946	71 97
find		555	19 97 +	1144	369	71 96
finding		69	19 95 +	57	54	71 97
finds		17	19 89 –	161	34	71 94
found		636	19 98 +	583	489	71 97
finger	NoC	312	19 95 +	9055	36	70 92
finger		97	19 95 +	2298	16	70 92
fingers		215	19 93 +	6872	21	69 91
finish	Verb	199	19 98 +	1659	81	71 93
finish		38	19 95 +	192	20	71 93
finished		150	19 97 +	1751	50	71 93
finishes		2	16 85 –	4	3	58 89
finishing		9	19 92 –	0	9	67 90
fire	NoC	238	19 95 +	1250	120	71 91
fire		220	19 95 +	1221	109	71 91
fires		18	19 89 +	44	12	71 90
firm	NoC	36	19 91 –	3492	211	71 88
firm		32	19 92 –	1173	110	71 86
firms		4	17 78 –	2727	101	71 88
first	Ord	862	19 97 –	2651	1312	71 98
five	Num	218	19 94 –	616	326	71 95
five		217	19 94 –	611	325	71 95
fives		1	6 56 –	5	1	31 72
floor	NoC	300	19 96 +	4170	86	71 94
floor		286	19 96 +	4468	74	71 94
floors		15	19 91 +	6	12	68 90
follow	Verb	355	19 97 –	1017	534	71 92
follow		84	19 95 –	48	102	71 96

4.1

Word	PoS	FrIm	R	D1	LL	FrIn	R	D2	Word	PoS	FrIm	R	D1	LL	FrIn	R	D2
followed		202	19	97 +	208	153	71	97	give		465	19	97 +	194	390	71	97
following		61	19	96 −	914	143	71	93	given		225	19	97 −	1894	436	71	97
follows		8	18	88 −	3403	137	71	70	gives		36	19	93 −	1323	123	71	96
food	NoC	159	19	95 −	442	237	71	93	giving		123	19	96 −	1	127	71	97
food		156	19	95 −	217	209	71	94	glance	Verb	203	19	93 +	9827	4	61	90
foods		2	16	83 −	651	28	70	81	glance		14	19	87 +	480	1	50	90
foot	NoC	482	19	97 +	5979	151	71	93	glanced		154	19	94 +	8058	2	44	84
feet		352	19	97 +	5309	94	70	93	glances		3	16	76 +	78	0	22	81
foot		130	19	96 +	925	57	71	92	glancing		32	19	91 +	1431	1	38	84
for	Conj	203	19	91 +	391	137	71	94	glass	NoC	323	19	95 +	5825	73	70	92
for	Prep	6477	19	99 −	13744	9230	71	99	glass		254	19	94 +	4302	61	70	92
for example	Adv	17	19	91 −	7977	315	71	94	glasses		69	19	94 +	1571	12	69	91
force	NoC	95	19	92 −	3333	316	71	90	go	Verb	3499	19	97 +	41355	1141	71	95
force		75	19	93 −	938	164	71	95	go		1404	19	97 +	16798	454	71	95
forces		20	19	82 −	2906	152	71	84	goes		97	19	95 −	20	110	71	95
foreign	Adj	41	19	88 −	3252	212	71	83	goin'*		18	15	66 +	759	1	19	69
forget	Verb	285	19	97 +	4734	70	71	95	going*		525	19	96 +	5129	194	71	94
forget		127	19	95 +	1783	36	71	94	gone		435	19	98 +	7632	101	71	95
forgets		3	14	73 −	16	1	47	88	went		1020	19	96 +	14909	281	71	95
forgetting		18	19	92 +	261	5	69	92	God	NoP	310	19	95 +	1558	159	71	84
forgot		41	19	95 +	1121	5	69	92	going	Verb	610	19	96 +	11910	127	71	94
forgotten		96	19	96 +	1711	22	71	95	going*		593	19	96 +	11559	123	71	94
form	NoC	74	19	95 −	8139	468	71	95	gon~		17	17	78 +	351	3	41	78
form		62	19	94 −	5385	338	71	95	good	Adj	1417	19	98 +	1045	1120	71	96
forms		12	19	92 −	2854	129	71	93	best		234	19	96 --	130	282	71	96
form	Verb	63	19	95 −	2773	235	71	96	better		243	19	97 +	176	193	71	97
form		18	19	92 −	1656	102	71	96	good		940	19	98 +	1676	646	71	96
formed		32	19	94 −	727	88	71	94	government	NoC	51	19	86 −	22080	882	71	88
forming		11	19	90 −	97	22	71	95	government		48	19	87 −	20464	819	71	88
forms		2	15	80 −	535	23	71	95	governments		3	15	72 −	1616	63	71	91
former	DetP	25	19	91 −	4732	229	71	89	great	Adj	504	19	95 −	895	699	71	97
forward	Adv	232	19	96 +	1397	110	71	95	great		447	19	95 −	1	453	71	96
four	Num	233	19	95 −	1457	416	71	96	greater		30	19	92 −	3134	183	71	95
four		230	19	95 −	1469	413	71	96	greatest		27	19	90 −	387	63	71	96
fours		3	18	83 −	0	3	51	82	ground	NoC	212	19	95 −	27	233	71	96
free	Adj	157	19	96 −	334	224	71	96	ground		186	19	95 +	76	156	71	95
free		156	19	96 −	318	221	71	96	grounds		26	19	89 −	685	77	71	94
freer		1	11	63 −	25	3	57	88	group	NoC	115	19	96 −	13956	775	71	96
freest		0	1	00 −	1	0	9	67	group		94	19	95 −	8388	521	71	96
friend	NoC	472	19	96 +	1358	290	71	83	groups		21	19	93 −	5784	254	71	94
friend		250	19	96 +	767	150	71	69	grow	Verb	241	19	97 +	180	190	71	95
friends		222	19	96 +	592	139	71	94	grew		84	19	95 +	494	41	71	95
from	Prep	3452	19	98 −	4643	4595	71	99	grow		49	19	96 −	17	58	71	93
full	Adj	288	19	98 −	8	301	71	98	growing		45	19	94 +	44	34	71	95
full		285	19	98 −	1	291	71	98	grown		55	19	94 +	48	42	71	94
fuller		2	17	81 −	82	7	70	93	grows		7	19	89 −	83	15	70	92
fullest		1	11	78 −	43	3	63	90	hair	NoC	453	19	97 +	10401	77	71	81
game	NoC	130	19	95 −	961	242	71	88	hair		441	19	97 +	10347	72	71	81
game		96	19	94 −	567	169	71	88	hairs		12	19	91 +	128	4	53	78
games		34	19	93 −	413	73	71	88	half	DetP	236	19	97 +	344	168	71	96
garden	NoC	201	19	94 +	395	136	71	90	hand	NoC	1397	19	97 +	23368	340	71	97
garden		166	19	93 −	607	95	71	90	hand		857	19	97 +	12980	229	71	97
gardens		35	19	93 −	10	40	71	89	hands		540	19	97 +	10581	111	71	95
general	Adj	49	19	92 −	7489	386	71	95	hang	Verb	221	19	96 +	3796	52	71	93
get	Verb	2945	19	96 +	32969	997	71	94	hang		47	19	93 +	517	16	71	93
get		1388	19	97 +	12732	533	71	95	hanged		8	19	80 +	34	4	62	85
gets		77	19	95 +	61	60	70	93	hanging		59	19	95 +	1010	14	69	92
gettin'		5	14	69 +	170	0	11	67	hangs		6	19	84 +	4	5	64	91
getting		283	19	96 +	1732	134	71	95	hung		102	19	95 +	2724	14	70	92
got		1192	19	95 +	21494	269	71	92	happen	Verb	534	19	98 +	3829	234	71	95
gotten		1	15	83 +	2	1	28	80	happen		127	19	97 +	585	67	71	95
girl	NoC	627	19	96 +	10202	157	71	92	happened		296	19	97 +	3811	90	71	94
girl		470	19	95 +	11049	77	71	91	happening		60	19	94 +	364	28	71	94
girls		157	19	93 +	803	80	71	91	happens		51	19	95 +	2	48	71	95
give	Verb	1314	19	98 +	39	1256	71	98	happy	Adj	215	19	96 +	1409	99	71	94
gave		465	19	96 +	4206	180	71	97	happier		18	19	92 +	159	7	69	93

Word	PoS	Frlm R D1	LL	Frln R D2
happiest		4 18 89 +	10	3 57 90
happy		193 19 96 +	1251	89 71 94
hard	Adj	229 19 95 +	334	163 71 95
hard		213 19 95 +	419	143 71 95
harder		11 19 92 –	16	15 71 92
hardest		4 18 88 –	0	4 63 91
have*	Verb	18005 19 99 +	42028	11650 71 99
'ave		8 11 59 +	303	0 6 16
'd		1085 19 94 +	39202	77 70 87
's		339 19 95 +	7359	62 69 78
've		1309 19 97 +	29872	223 71 89
had		9558 19 98 +	100954	3366 71 95
has		863 19 96 –	37335	3186 71 96
have		4508 19 98 +	43	4393 71 98
having		335 19 97 –	2	343 71 98
of*		1 7 43 +	12	0 11 70
he	Pron	21446 19 98 +	368739	5086 71 95
'e		29 14 50 +	1356	1 12 53
'im		15 12 61 +	701	0 9 55
he		16475 19 98 +	260201	4240 71 95
him		4927 19 98 +	111990	845 71 95
head	NoC	1025 19 97 +	15621	272 71 96
head		953 19 97 +	16717	221 71 95
heads		72 19 94 +	109	51 71 94
health	NoC	38 19 94 –	6251	314 71 92
health		38 19 94 –	6249	314 71 92
hear	Verb	875 19 98 +	14457	216 71 94
hear		314 19 97 +	5373	75 71 94
heard		517 19 97 +	9377	116 71 93
hearing		37 19 96 +	150	20 71 93
hears		7 19 88 +	16	4 66 92
heart	NoC	311 19 91 +	2674	124 71 95
heart		292 19 90 +	2796	109 71 95
hearts		20 19 92 +	17	15 69 90
help	Verb	441 19 97 +	12	422 71 96
help		316 19 97 +	126	266 71 96
helped		84 19 97 +	2	80 71 95
helping		32 19 94 –	38	42 71 95
helps		9 19 92 –	387	33 70 94
her*	Det	7893 19 94 +	227730	930 71 93
here	Adv	1272 19 97 +	15090	414 71 96
herself	Pron	707 19 93 +	25103	53 71 92
high	Adj	282 19 95 –	4869	694 71 97
high		239 19 95 –	1545	431 71 98
higher		31 19 95 –	3584	202 71 94
highest		11 19 87 –	954	61 71 97
himself	Pron	714 19 96 +	8148	239 71 95
his	Det	9471 19 98 +	98224	3375 71 95
'is		8 12 60 +	394	0 7 55
his		9463 19 98 +	98011	3375 71 95
history	NoC	65 19 92 –	3174	255 71 93
histories		1 13 74 –	202	10 66 87
history		63 19 92 –	2986	245 71 93
hold	Verb	618 19 97 +	484	485 71 95
held		328 19 97 +	52	295 71 92
hold		124 19 96 +	67	101 71 96
holding		151 19 97 +	1400	57 71 95
holds		16 19 83 –	146	32 71 96
home	Adv	369 19 95 +	3544	138 71 92
home	NoC	265 19 95 –	1193	438 71 94
home		251 19 95 –	585	363 71 94
homes		14 19 88 –	1143	74 71 92
hope	Verb	307 19 97 +	843	191 71 92
hope		156 19 97 +	526	91 71 89
hoped		92 19 95 +	478	46 71 95
hopes		4 17 79 –	424	24 69 85
hoping		56 19 95 +	264	29 70 87
horse	NoC	202 19 85 +	872	109 70 80
horse		120 19 86 +	439	69 70 79
horses		82 19 83 +	445	40 70 81
hospital	NoC	111 19 92 –	829	208 71 89
hospital		106 19 92 –	432	171 71 89
hospitals		5 18 85 –	689	37 70 88
hour	NoC	402 19 97 +	882	264 71 95
hour		191 19 97 +	1462	81 71 94
hours		211 19 96 +	60	183 71 95
house	NoC	835 19 95 +	1921	542 71 94
house		753 19 95 +	2533	442 71 93
houses		82 19 94 –	52	100 71 94
how	Adv	1480 19 98 +	7172	769 71 97
however	Adv	187 19 96 –	10427	788 71 96
human	Adj	101 19 91 –	1297	224 71 94
husband	NoC	209 19 94 +	1081	106 71 92
husband		198 19 94 +	1175	95 71 91
husbands		11 19 91 –	0	11 70 88
I	Pron	20929 19 97 +	409704	4320 71 93
I		17216 19 97 +	323569	3719 71 93
me		3703 19 97 +	87658	601 71 92
idea	NoC	311 19 97 –	20	333 71 95
idea		264 19 97 +	275	199 71 96
ideas		47 19 93 –	1156	133 71 94
if	Conj	2488 19 98 +	1440	2022 71 96
imagine	Verb	191 19 95 +	2780	53 71 94
imagine		122 19 94 +	1423	40 71 94
imagined		55 19 93 +	1290	9 70 92
imagines		2 14 77 +	5	1 50 88
imagining		12 19 92 +	244	2 64 90
important	Adj	146 19 95 –	4822	473 71 96
in	Adv	887 19 97 +	6488	385 71 96
in	Prep	12667 19 99 +	53631	20612 71 99
include	Verb	37 19 91 –	11022	474 71 96
include		13 19 87 –	5060	205 71 95
included		19 19 90 –	3296	163 71 94
includes		3 16 77 –	2511	91 71 92
including		2 16 87 –	273	14 71 95
including	Prep	34 19 92 –	6340	308 71 95
increase	Verb	27 19 92 –	5175	249 71 95
increase		7 19 89 –	2244	94 71 95
increased		15 19 89 –	1650	96 71 93
increases		1 8 70 –	766	26 71 93
increasing		5 19 88 –	628	33 71 96
indeed	Adv	150 19 93 –	218	202 71 95
industry	NoC	16 19 86 –	8275	322 71 93
industries		2 12 73 –	1649	58 71 91
industry		15 19 85 –	6640	263 71 92
information	NoC	88 19 94 –	7920	490 71 93
information		88 19 94 –	7916	490 71 93
informations		0 0 00 –	5	0 10 69
interest	NoC	141 19 96 –	4911	468 71 95
interest		120 19 96 –	2774	332 71 95
interests		21 19 95 –	2407	136 71 93
international	Adj	17 19 90 –	7512	300 71 91
into	Prep	2494 19 99 +	7827	1494 71 98
involve	Verb	56 19 93 –	4562	293 71 96
involve		8 19 89 –	995	54 71 95
involved		40 19 92 –	1241	126 71 97
involves		2 16 81 –	1487	56 71 94
involving		5 19 91 –	1234	57 71 95
issue	NoC	22 19 93 –	8373	344 71 95
issue		18 19 91 –	4055	187 71 95
issues		4 18 87 –	4442	157 71 95
it	Pron	13762 19 99 +	44994	8146 71 98

Word	PoS	FrIm	R D1	LL	FrIn	R D2	Word	PoS	FrIm	R D1	LL	FrIn	R D2
't		11	14 57 +	334	1	22 66	lead		43	19 96 –	836	111	71 98
it		13751	19 99 +	44861	8145	71 98	leading		49	19 97 –	22	58	71 97
its	Det	874	19 97 –	12640	2017	71 96	leads		10	19 92 –	679	47	71 95
itself	Pron	150	19 96 –	1081	279	71 96	led		149	19 97 –	61	175	71 95
job	NoC	270	19 96 –	104	315	71 94	leader	NoC	38	19 84 –	3480	214	71 86
job		244	19 96 +	119	202	71 94	leader		30	19 81 –	1458	117	71 86
jobs		25	19 89 –	1579	113	71 91	leaders		9	19 87 –	2178	97	71 86
John	NoP	231	19 87 –	836	363	71 92	lean	Verb	209	19 96 +	7716	14	69 89
join	Verb	164	19 97 –	41	186	71 96	lean		14	19 91 +	168	4	59 86
join		76	19 96 +	0	76	71 95	leaned		113	19 94 +	5381	3	53 84
joined		71	19 96 –	9	78	71 94	leaning		55	19 95 +	1795	5	63 86
joining		14	19 93 –	77	25	71 95	leans		5	16 65 +	74	1	38 84
joins		2	16 84 –	102	8	69 91	leant		23	19 89 +	972	1	34 83
June	NoP	20	19 88 –	4022	191	71 83	learn	Verb	179	19 97 –	40	202	71 95
just	Adv	1843	19 97 +	14934	759	71 95	learn		72	19 96 –	36	86	71 95
keep	Verb	782	19 98 +	3678	411	71 96	learned		63	19 95 +	78	46	71 92
keep		409	19 97 +	1882	217	71 95	learning		19	19 95 –	289	45	70 92
keeping		82	19 96 +	148	56	71 95	learns		2	18 84 –	32	6	65 90
keeps		27	19 91 +	18	22	71 94	learnt		23	19 92 +	6	20	71 94
kept		263	19 97 +	1874	116	71 96	leave	Verb	1146	19 98 +	7644	520	71 97
kill	Verb	266	19 93 +	1278	138	71 90	leave		340	19 97 +	3135	130	71 96
kill		110	19 92 +	1590	31	71 92	leaves		21	19 93 –	68	32	70 95
killed		128	19 93 +	321	82	71 88	leaving		158	19 97 +	625	88	71 97
killing		23	19 91 +	4	21	71 90	left		627	19 98 +	4675	270	71 96
kills		4	18 84 –	4	6	66 89	leg	NoC	257	19 95 +	2954	85	71 89
kind	NoC	298	19 96 +	74	261	71 95	leg		79	19 90 +	250	47	71 86
kind		284	19 96 +	412	203	71 95	legs		178	19 96 +	3360	38	70 90
kinds		14	19 92 –	745	58	71 93	less	Adv	141	19 96 –	1414	288	71 96
kitchen	NoC	258	19 93 +	5676	46	71 90	let	Verb	666	19 97 +	10951	165	71 96
kitchen		248	19 94 +	5844	41	69 89	let		604	19 97 +	10466	142	71 96
kitchens		10	19 88 +	35	6	63 87	lets		9	19 88 +	0	9	67 87
know	Verb	3417	19 98 +	54701	868	71 97	letting		53	19 95 +	802	14	71 94
knew		897	19 98 +	25343	110	71 93	letter	NoC	237	19 94 +	37	213	71 95
know		2021	19 98 +	40946	401	71 95	letter		155	19 94 +	58	132	71 94
knowing		109	19 95 +	1412	33	70 95	letters		82	19 91 +	0	81	71 95
known		224	19 96 –	89	263	71 97	level	NoC	62	19 95 –	8623	458	71 95
knows		153	19 96 +	1318	61	71 92	level		52	19 95 –	4896	298	71 95
~no*		13	19 51 +	521	1	14 62	levels		10	19 86 –	3915	160	71 93
lady	NoC	305	19 89 +	4499	83	71 92	lie (/lay)	Verb	404	19 97 +	4323	142	71 96
ladies		60	19 91 +	506	24	69 89	lain		10	19 92 +	214	2	51 88
lady		244	19 88 +	4134	59	71 92	lay		197	19 96 +	4115	38	71 94
land	NoC	113	19 94 –	1245	238	71 94	lie		69	19 95 +	328	36	71 95
land		99	19 94 –	1165	214	71 93	lies		20	19 90 –	214	42	71 95
lands		14	19 83 –	86	25	70 89	lying		108	19 97 +	1997	24	71 93
language	NoC	51	19 93 –	4592	285	71 88	life	NoC	729	19 97 +	77	669	71 96
language		44	19 92 –	3855	241	71 87	life		668	19 97 +	189	579	71 96
languages		7	19 88 –	737	44	71 86	lifes		0	0 00 –	31	1	20 63
large	Adj	262	19 96 –	3237	572	71 96	lives		61	19 96 –	146	88	71 95
large		226	19 96 –	1337	398	71 96	light	NoC	424	19 95 +	5035	138	71 96
larger		26	19 93 –	1128	97	71 95	light		317	19 95 +	3459	109	71 93
largest		9	19 87 –	1538	77	71 94	lights		107	19 92 +	1626	29	69 92
last	Ord	585	19 97 –	319	705	71 91	like	Prep	2041	19 97 +	22010	709	71 95
late	Adj	215	19 97 –	860	346	71 97	like	Verb	788	19 97 +	11283	221	71 94
late		160	19 97 –	5	168	71 96	like		579	19 97 +	7450	177	71 94
later		27	19 95 –	1114	97	71 93	liked		164	19 95 +	3655	29	70 92
latest		29	19 95 –	704	81	71 92	likes		36	19 94 +	349	13	70 92
later	Adv	344	19 96 +	8	330	71 96	liking		9	19 91 +	181	2	50 88
laugh	Verb	382	19 96 +	13492	29	68 91	likely	Adj	79	19 95 –	3300	287	71 96
laugh		60	19 96 +	1439	10	67 90	likelier		0	2 31 –	0	0	9 62
laughed		228	19 95 +	10114	8	64 87	likeliest		1	9 70 +	0	0	19 73
laughing		85	19 95 +	2746	8	62 89	likely		78	19 95 –	3315	286	71 96
laughs		9	18 75 +	76	4	52 87	line	NoC	264	19 97 –	355	351	71 96
law	NoC	62	19 93 –	7471	415	71 91	line		185	19 96 –	177	237	71 96
law		51	19 93 –	6424	353	71 90	lines		79	19 93 –	193	115	71 95
laws		10	19 91 –	1048	62	71 94	lip	NoC	286	19 90 +	10879	17	70 91
lead	Verb	251	19 98 –	870	391	71 97	lip		57	19 91 +	1588	7	69 91

Word	PoS	FrIm	R D1	LL	FrIn	R D2	Word	PoS	FrIm	R D1	LL	FrIn	R D2
lips		229 19 89 +	9499		10 68	90	*manage*		57 19 96 +	164		35 71	96
listen	Verb	284 19 96 +	5267		62 71	93	*managed*		125 19 96 +	589		66 71	96
listen		126 19 96 +	2181		30 71	93	*manages*		3 16 84 −	69		8 70	93
listened		77 19 95 +	1968		11 68	88	*managing*		9 19 88 −	12		12 71	95
listening		78 19 95 +	1283		19 70	92	management	NoC	17 19 83 −	7242		289 71	91
listens		3 16 82 +	4		2 53	88	*management*		16 19 83 −	7244		287 71	91
little	Adj	682 19 97 +	12482		152 71	94	*managements*		1 7 60 −	17		2 45	81
little	DetP	162 19 97 −	173		209 71	97	manager	NoC	46 19 85 −	4015		251 71	91
live	Verb	437 19 96 +	807		297 71	95	*manager*		41 19 85 −	2339		174 71	89
live		195 19 96 +	479		125 71	95	*managers*		5 18 79 −	1837		77 71	92
lived		132 19 96 +	620		70 71	94	many	DetP	413 19 96 −	8034		1065 71	97
lives		27 19 93 +	2		25 69	91	March	NoP	17 19 91 −	4345		193 71	83
living		82 19 94 +	2		78 71	96	market	NoC	52 19 95 −	9125		451 71	93
local	Adj	99 19 95 −	9021		555 71	95	*market*		49 19 95 −	7099		371 71	93
London	NoP	254 19 95 −	1016		409 71	94	*markets*		3 17 84 −	2128		80 71	90
London		254 19 95 −	1014		408 71	94	material	NoC	44 19 95 −	4307		259 71	94
Londons		0 0 00 −	6		0 2	07	*material*		37 19 94 −	2360		168 71	94
long	Adj	556 19 98 +	1501		347 71	93	*materials*		8 18 86 −	2074		91 71	93
long		529 19 98 +	2118		294 71	97	matter	NoC	216 19 97 −	140		264 71	93
longer		22 19 95 −	196		44 71	96	*matter*		172 19 97 +	0		171 71	93
longest		5 19 80 −	38		10 71	94	*matters*		44 19 94 −	504		94 71	92
long	Adv	313 19 98 +	1850		150 71	97	May	NoP	29 19 87 −	3553		196 71	84
look	NoC	288 19 96 +	5142		66 71	92	*May*		29 19 87 −	3541		195 71	84
look		258 19 95 +	4868		55 71	93	*Mays*		0 0 00 −	14		0 14	69
looks		30 19 92 +	332		10 67	89	may	VMod	326 19 95 −	19751		1440 71	95
look	Verb	2736 19 98 +	49281		618 71	96	maybe	Adv	232 19 95 +	4955		43 70	92
look		745 19 98 +	8385		251 71	96	mean	Verb	717 19 91 +	2895		397 71	97
looked		1335 19 98 +	44322		118 71	94	*mean*		446 19 97 +	5857		134 71	97
looking		540 19 97 +	6737		169 71	95	*meaning*		14 19 95 −	9		17 71	94
looks		116 19 92 +	194		80 71	94	*means*		67 19 96 −	910		152 71	96
lose	Verb	311 19 97 +	79		271 71	95	*meant*		190 19 97 +	1030		94 71	97
lose		74 19 95 +	30		62 71	95	meet	Verb	455 19 96 +	629		328 71	96
loses		4 17 85 −	89		10 70	94	*meet*		175 19 96 +	134		138 71	96
losing		35 19 95 −	0		36 71	94	*meeting*		42 19 93 −	16		49 71	93
lost		199 19 97 +	105		163 71	95	*meets*		5 19 87 −	183		17 71	94
loss	NoC	46 19 96 −	2667		199 71	93	*met*		233 19 96 +	1062		124 71	95
loss		43 19 95 −	1617		147 71	94	meeting	NoC	108 19 90 −	1406		240 71	90
losses		4 19 91 −	1215		52 71	85	*meeting*		89 19 90 −	833		178 71	89
lot*	NoC	247 19 95 +	983		137 71	94	*meetings*		19 19 88 −	642		62 71	93
lot		247 19 95 +	985		137 71	94	member	NoC	90 19 90 −	10605		594 71	90
lots		0 1 00 −	1		0 8	64	*member*		42 19 90 −	3482		222 71	84
love	NoC	338 19 93 +	4201		106 70	91	*members*		48 19 88 −	7179		372 71	92
love		336 19 93 +	4218		105 70	91	method	NoC	23 19 90 −	5218		241 71	93
loves		2 18 84 +	3		1 45	84	*method*		12 19 89 −	2545		120 71	94
love	Verb	375 19 95 +	6536		88 70	91	*methods*		11 19 87 −	2674		121 71	93
love		202 19 95 +	3389		49 70	90	might	VMod	878 19 98 +	2901		518 71	97
loved		138 19 94 +	2876		26 70	92	million	NoC	44 19 92 −	6670		345 71	89
loves		21 19 91 +	154		9 66	89	*million*		33 19 91 −	6619		313 71	88
loving		14 19 88 +	254		3 57	87	*millions*		12 19 89 −	251		32 71	93
low	Adj	185 19 98 −	1191		334 71	95	mind	NoC	468 19 96 +	3859		191 71	94
low		134 19 97 −	143		174 71	96	*mind*		444 19 96 +	4500		160 71	94
lower		46 19 95 −	1265		138 71	94	*minds*		24 19 92 −	21		31 71	94
lowest		4 18 91 −	328		22 71	95	minister	NoC	48 19 78 −	8099		405 71	76
main	Adj	99 19 96 −	2819		299 71	97	*minister*		43 19 78 −	5891		313 71	75
major	Adj	27 19 91 −	7034		312 71	96	*ministers*		6 16 75 −	2280		92 71	80
make	Verb	2305 19 99 +	125		2167 71	98	minute	NoC	379 19 96 +	1624		206 71	92
made		1090 19 99 +	225		965 71	98	*minute*		136 19 95 +	1407		48 71	89
make		828 19 98 +	102		754 71	97	*minutes*		244 19 95 +	568		158 71	92
makes		109 19 95 −	506		182 71	96	miss*	NoC	314 19 86 +	8453		42 70	90
maketh		0 2 31 −	0		0 8	62	*miss*		312 19 86 +	8520		41 70	89
making		278 19 97 +	6		266 71	98	*misses*		2 10 65 +	2		1 42	83
man	NoC	1997 19 97 +	17009		801 71	95	model	NoC	35 19 90 −	4411		241 71	92
man		1433 19 97 +	18739		433 71	94	*model*		26 19 90 −	3039		170 71	92
mans		0 1 00 −	8		0 13	68	*models*		9 19 83 −	1376		71 71	92
men		564 19 94 +	1277		367 71	95	moment	NoC	671 19 96 +	13060		139 71	95
manage	Verb	194 19 96 +	531		121 71	97	*moment*		601 19 96 +	12626		114 71	96

4.1

Word	PoS	Frlm	R D1	LL	Frln	R D2
moments		71 19 94 +	713	26 70	92
money	NoC	353 19 95 +	4	343 71	94
money .		353 19 95 +	6	341 71	94
moneys		0 0 00 –	64	2 21	47
month	NoC	206 19 95 –	2615	454 71	95
month		61 19 95 –	1491	173 71	93
months		144 19 95 –	1227	280 71	95
more	Adv	954 19 99 –	2940	1453 71	97
more	DetP	714 19 98 +	63	659 71	97
more than*	Adv	52 19 94 –	2139	187 71	94
morning	NoC	475 19 97 +	7890	117 71	93
morning		460 19 97 +	7763	111 71	93
mornings		16 19 91 +	154	6 64	90
most	Adv	286 19 95 –	4689	690 71	97
most	DetP	235 19 97 –	2591	494 71	97
mother	NoC	699 19 93 +	9506	205 71	93
mother		678 19 93 +	11294	166 71	93
mothers		21 19 90 –	148	39 71	88
mouth	NoC	363 19 93 +	11136	38 69	93
mouth		349 19 93 +	11081	34 69	93
mouths		15 19 89 +	206	4 64	91
move	Verb	604 19 97 +	2656	325 71	97
move		156 19 96 +	185	115 71	96
moved		308 19 96 +	3226	109 71	96
moves		12 19 84 –	99	23 71	95
moving		128 19 96 +	383	78 71	96
movement	NoC	110 19 95 –	947	215 71	94
movement		80 19 94 –	784	162 71	93
movements		30 19 94 –	170	53 71	91
Mr	NoC	585 19 91 –	351	711 71	79
Mr		553 19 91 +	50	510 71	82
Mr.		32 18 69 –	3392	198 67	37
Mrs	NoC	512 19 90 +	6611	156 71	90
Mrs		485 19 90 +	7256	131 71	89
Mrs.		27 14 76 +	1	25 56	68
much	Adv	398 19 98 +	10	382 71	97
much	DetP	617 19 97 +	561	474 71	97
must	VMod	945 19 98 +	1262	685 71	95
my	Det	3288 19 97 +	44840	961 71	91
me		3 2 02 +	158	0 0	00
mine		1 8 65 +	8	0 13	74
my		3284 19 97 +	44749	960 71	91
myself	Pron	300 19 96 +	4884	75 71	92
name	NoC	438 19 97 +	905	291 71	94
name		371 19 97 +	1378	211 71	94
names		67 19 95 –	34	80 71	94
national	Adj	26 19 92 –	12717	498 71	92
nature	NoC	76 19 94 –	2082	227 71	95
nature		76 19 94 –	2068	225 71	95
natures		1 6 61 –	14	2 39	73
necessary	Adj	70 19 95 –	2310	226 71	95
need	NoC	135 19 93 –	2179	324 71	96
need		117 19 94 –	504	192 71	96
needs		17 19 91 –	2528	132 71	93
need	Verb	568 19 97 –	22	598 71	97
need		316 19 97 +	2	309 71	96
needed		190 19 97 +	28	171 71	97
needing		12 19 91 +	7	10 71	94
needs		50 19 96 –	599	108 71	96
never	Adv	1158 19 98 +	13409	383 71	95
new	Adj	467 19 96 –	13261	1411 71	97
new		463 19 96 –	13187	1400 71	97
newer		2 15 72 –	60	6 69	93
newest		2 16 82 –	19	4 66	90
next	Ord	397 19 97 –	14	416 71	94
nice	Adj	211 19 94 +	4035	45 71	92
nice		202 19 94 +	3972	41 71	92
nicer		6 19 88 +	88	2 44	84
nicest		3 18 86 +	11	1 36	78
night	NoC	733 19 97 +	6376	290 71	90
night		685 19 97 +	6119	268 71	89
nights		47 19 94 +	279	23 70	91
no	Det	1775 19 99 +	2584	1267 71	98
no	Int	864 19 97 +	30342	66 71	95
no		864 19 97 +	30344	66 71	95
no one*	Pron	196 19 96 +	2741	56 71	94
nod	Verb	299 19 96 +	14388	7 61	89
nod		8 19 87 +	231	1 36	83
nodded		265 19 95 +	13559	3 53	86
nodding		22 19 94 +	797	1 44	83
nods		4 13 70 +	127	1 21	79
north	NoC	81 19 94 –	1301	194 71	95
not	Neg	12309 19 98 +	84161	5527 71	98
*~n~**		15 19 56 +	564	1 21	68
~n't		7183 19 97 +	184002	1036 71	92
not		5111 19 98 +	1190	4490 71	97
nothing	Pron	825 19 98 +	13444	206 71	96
notice	Verb	234 19 97 +	3735	60 71	94
notice		61 19 96 +	415	28 71	93
noticed		154 19 97 +	3412	27 70	94
notices		3 16 67 +	5	2 61	90
noticing		16 19 91 +	362	3 58	90
now	Adv	1998 19 98 +	10471	1007 71	96
number	NoC	185 19 96 –	8601	710 71	96
number		156 19 96 –	6717	574 71	97
numbers		30 19 92 –	1904	135 71	95
occur	Verb	64 19 95 –	1922	198 71	93
occur		12 19 92 –	1249	73 71	93
occurred		46 19 94 –	69	63 71	92
occurring		1 12 73 –	387	17 69	92
occurs		4 17 82 –	1024	45 70	93
of*	Prep	18997 19 98 –	122912	34244 71	98
of course	Adv	562 19 96 +	5349	211 71	96
of		562 19 96 +	5347	211 71	96
off	Adv	850 19 97 +	7200	342 71	94
off	Prep	323 19 97 +	1593	167 71	94
offer	Verb	180 19 97 –	1507	348 71	96
offer		51 19 96 –	772	119 71	95
offered		98 19 96 –	46	116 71	97
offering		27 19 93 –	187	50 71	94
offers		4 17 82 –	1532	62 71	93
office	NoC	268 19 96 –	155	325 71	95
office		249 19 93 –	29	272 71	95
offices		19 19 90 –	433	53 71	94
officer	NoC	114 19 88 –	660	200 71	94
officer		76 19 88 –	86	98 71	94
officers		39 19 85 –	787	102 71	92
often	Adv	187 19 94 –	3131	455 71	95
oh	Int	730 19 96 +	29725	36 70	91
old	Adj	982 19 96 +	3468	568 71	94
old		879 19 96 +	4199	459 71	93
older		91 19 96 –	0	93 71	89
oldest		12 19 86 –	17	16 71	94
on	Adv	1192 19 97 +	9927	484 71	96
on	Prep	5802 19 99 +	2140	6768 71	96
once	Adv	285 19 97 +	951	167 71	96
one	Num	1838 19 99 –	0	1839 71	98
one	Pron	916 19 98 +	617	732 71	97
only	Adj	263 19 98 +	109	220 71	98
only	Adv	1294 19 98 –	15	1331 71	98
open	Adj	301 19 97 +	531	207 71	93
open	Verb	450 19 97 +	3438	191 71	96

4.1

Word	PoS	FrIm R D1	LL	FrIm R D2	Word	PoS	FrIm R D1	LL	FrIm R D2
open		115 19 97 +	420	66 71 96	performances		4 19 84 –	358	21 71 87
opened		285 19 96 +	3966	82 71 95	perhaps	Adv	561 19 96 +	2963	282 71 96
opening		41 19 96 +	129	24 71 95	period	NoC	40 19 90 –	7677	369 71 95
opens		10 19 81 –	87	20 71 92	period		34 19 89 –	6604	316 71 95
operation	NoC	42 19 90 –	3069	206 71 94	periods		6 19 91 –	1073	53 71 93
operation		30 19 90 –	1662	126 71 94	person	NoC	179 19 94 –	1156	323 71 91
operations		12 19 81 –	1442	80 71 92	person		169 19 95 –	683	272 71 92
opportunity	NoC	60 19 95 –	1983	195 71 95	persons		11 19 68 –	743	52 71 87
opportunities		7 19 90 –	1643	76 71 94	personal	Adj	79 19 93 –	1817	218 71 94
opportunity		53 19 94 –	711	119 71 95	pick	Verb	296 19 97 +	3719	92 71 94
or	Conj	2246 19 97 +	15730	4135 71 96	pick		80 19 96 +	489	38 71 94
order	NoC	129 19 94 –	1856	297 71 90	picked		171 19 96 +	3428	35 71 93
order		82 19 92 –	2168	240 71 89	picking		39 19 96 +	394	14 70 94
orders		47 19 92 –	27	57 71 93	picks		5 18 82 –	0	6 67 91
other	Adj	838 19 98 –	4850	1468 71 98	place	NoC	639 19 97 +	368	520 71 98
other	NoC	319 19 96 –	297	406 71 97	place		564 19 97 +	599	424 71 98
other		108 19 96 +	106	82 71 96	places		75 19 96 –	71	96 71 96
others		211 19 95 –	672	324 71 97	plan	NoC	112 19 94 –	1493	251 71 93
our	Det	669 19 96 –	1651	978 71 95	plan		62 19 90 –	746	134 71 92
out	Adv	2374 19 98 +	11998	1214 71 97	plans		49 19 94 –	749	116 71 93
out of	Prep	931 19 98 +	7834	376 71 96	plant	NoC	39 19 82 –	2766	188 71 91
over	Adv	715 19 98 +	488	570 71 85	plant		18 19 80 –	1479	95 71 91
over	Prep	864 19 99 +	343	729 71 98	plants		21 19 82 –	1290	93 71 89
own	DetP	845 19 97 +	446	693 71 97	play	Verb	309 19 97 –	371	405 71 93
p	NoC	2 11 71 –	6560	206 68 82	play		110 19 96 –	195	152 71 93
p		2 8 68 –	20	3 44 83	played		82 19 96 –	261	126 71 93
p.		1 3 28 –	6528	203 64 66	playing		108 19 97 +	13	98 71 91
ps		0 1 00 –	4	0 5 43	plays		9 19 91 –	291	29 70 93
paper	NoC	240 19 95 +	6	229 71 95	please	Adv	218 19 95 +	2270	78 70 89
paper		163 19 94 –	2	167 71 95	point	NoC	260 19 97 –	2194	504 71 97
papers		77 19 94 +	49	62 71 90	point		231 19 97 –	870	366 71 96
parent	NoC	133 19 92 –	686	227 71 92	points		29 19 80 –	2000	138 71 95
parent		9 19 89 –	723	46 71 91	police	NoC	210 19 89 –	529	309 71 86
parents		125 19 92 –	293	181 71 91	police		210 19 89 –	529	309 71 86
part	NoC	319 19 97 –	4268	716 71 98	policy	NoC	17 19 89 –	12015	443 71 92
part		281 19 96 –	2795	572 71 98	policies		3 16 80 –	3245	115 71 92
parts		38 19 95 –	1719	144 71 96	policy		14 19 89 –	8777	329 71 92
particular	Adj	58 19 94 –	3804	268 71 94	political	Adj	31 19 90 –	9649	411 71 92
particularly	Adv	81 19 94 –	2745	266 71 97	poor	Adj	212 19 96 +	204	162 71 95
party	NoC	196 19 92 –	6935	655 71 87	poor		209 19 96 +	373	144 71 95
parties		28 19 90 –	2790	166 71 86	poorer		2 15 80 –	171	11 69 92
party		168 19 91 –	4391	489 71 87	poorest		1 13 78 –	133	7 69 89
pass	Verb	296 19 97 +	700	191 71 97	population	NoC	11 19 87 –	4948	196 71 92
pass		67 19 94 –	41	54 71 96	population		11 19 87 –	4372	176 71 92
passed		182 19 96 +	870	95 71 96	populations		0 6 58 –	587	20 68 89
passes		8 19 89 –	70	16 71 93	position	NoC	109 19 95 –	3053	328 71 96
passing		38 19 94 +	78	25 71 95	position		100 19 96 –	2293	276 71 96
patient	NoC	55 19 80 –	5233	318 71 71	positions		9 19 88 –	853	52 71 93
patient		33 19 77 –	636	85 71 79	possible	Adj	176 19 97 –	2665	413 71 96
patients		22 19 81 –	5067	232 71 65	power	NoC	147 19 93 –	4958	481 71 95
pattern	NoC	48 19 93 –	2363	190 71 91	power		129 19 93 –	3768	394 71 95
pattern		34 19 93 –	1206	114 71 91	powers		19 19 89 –	1244	87 71 93
patterns		14 19 90 –	1197	76 70 90	practice	NoC	40 19 87 –	5191	282 71 93
pay	Verb	235 19 97 –	1070	389 71 95	practice		36 19 88 –	3780	222 71 93
paid		91 19 96 –	470	155 71 94	practices		4 19 71 –	1484	61 71 90
pay		106 19 97 –	464	174 71 94	president	NoC	30 19 78 –	4156	219 71 76
payed		0 1 00 –	1	0 10 69	president		28 18 77 –	4013	212 71 76
paying		32 19 93 –	45	43 71 94	presidents		1 13 79 –	142	8 63 78
pays		6 19 91 –	141	17 70 94	price	NoC	51 19 94 –	6180	342 71 92
people	NoC	828 19 94 –	2420	1248 71 96	price		40 19 94 –	3320	211 71 92
people		825 19 94 –	2259	1229 71 96	prices		11 19 88 –	2976	131 71 92
peoples		3 17 85 –	351	19 70 88	private	Adj	97 19 96 –	1121	208 71 95
per cent	NoC	23 19 86 –	13841	523 71 89	probably	Adv	268 19 96 +	94	229 71 96
per cent		23 19 86 –	13757	521 71 89	problem	NoC	182 19 95 –	7658	663 71 97
performance	NoC	35 19 91 –	3049	191 71 94	problem		118 19 96 –	2707	326 71 97
performance		31 19 91 –	2694	169 71 94	problems		64 19 94 –	5268	337 71 97

4.1

Word	PoS	FrIm	R	D1	LL	FrIn	R	D2
process	NoC	29	19	90 –	8208	357	71	94
process		26	19	90 –	6289	285	71	95
processes		3	16	83 –	1959	73	71	90
produce	Verb	68	19	93 –	6415	390	71	96
produce		20	19	92 –	2601	140	71	96
produced		38	19	91 –	2253	165	71	96
produces		3	16	78 –	769	33	71	94
producing		8	19	92 –	893	51	71	95
product	NoC	16	19	86 –	7244	287	71	90
product		9	19	89 –	3541	145	71	90
products		7	19	78 –	3711	142	71	90
production	NoC	20	19	77 –	4704	214	71	94
production		17	19	79 –	4754	207	71	94
productions		3	10	57 –	42	7	69	89
programme	NoC	29	19	90 –	7258	327	71	93
programme		23	19	91 –	5230	242	71	92
programmes		6	19	84 –	2038	85	71	94
project	NoC	26	19	82 –	5417	254	71	89
project		21	19	80 –	3656	181	71	87
projects		5	19	78 –	1790	73	71	92
property	NoC	36	19	93 –	3613	215	71	91
properties		4	18	83 –	1252	54	71	93
property		32	19	93 –	2433	161	71	88
provide	Verb	68	19	90 –	14195	667	71	96
provide		27	19	94 –	6435	293	71	96
provided		28	19	88 –	2844	169	71	96
provides		4	16	64 –	3142	114	71	94
providing		8	19	86 –	2012	90	71	96
public	Adj	62	19	91 –	6203	369	71	96
pull	Verb	375	19	98 +	7193	79	71	93
pull		66	19	95 +	470	29	70	91
pulled		238	19	97 +	6499	31	70	92
pulling		63	19	96 +	1111	14	71	92
pulls		8	18	77 +	30	5	62	91
purpose	NoC	59	19	92 –	1899	188	71	92
purpose		48	19	94 –	721	112	71	93
purposes		11	19	82 –	1403	76	71	90
push	Verb	256	19	97 +	3790	70	71	95
push		39	19	94 +	78	26	71	93
pushed		162	19	97 +	3859	26	71	95
pushes		3	15	79 +	3	2	60	91
pushing		53	19	96 +	695	16	71	94
put (/ putt)	Verb	932	19	98 +	4711	476	71	96
put		820	19	98 +	5068	385	71	96
puts		19	19	85 –	70	31	70	95
putted		0	2	14 +	0	0	10	65
putting		92	19	96 +	212	60	71	96
quality	NoC	42	19	93 –	3892	238	71	94
qualities		10	19	90 –	302	32	71	94
quality		32	19	91 –	3656	206	71	94
question	NoC	307	19	96 –	357	401	71	94
question		195	19	96 –	211	252	71	94
questions		112	19	93 –	146	149	71	94
quickly	Adv	243	19	95 +	2048	98	71	96
quite	Adv	556	19	95 +	2897	281	71	96
raise	Verb	194	19	97 +	19	211	71	97
raise		28	19	94 –	568	73	71	95
raised		140	19	97 +	310	92	71	96
raises		3	15	78 –	304	18	70	93
raising		23	19	94 –	10	28	71	96
range	NoC	33	19	91 –	5271	268	71	94
range		32	19	90 –	5045	258	71	94
ranges		1	8	67 –	230	10	70	91
rate	NoC	35	19	94 –	8885	397	71	92
rate		29	19	94 –	4920	244	71	91
rates		6	19	85 –	4094	152	71	92

Word	PoS	FrIm	R	D1	LL	FrIn	R	D2
rather	Adv	315	19	95 +	1037	186	71	96
rather than	Prep	45	19	95 –	3022	211	71	96
reach	Verb	371	19	97 +	1128	224	71	98
reach		65	19	96 –	23	75	71	97
reached		258	19	96 +	2159	105	71	96
reaches		7	18	82 –	83	15	71	93
reaching		41	19	93 +	57	30	71	96
read	Verb	310	19	96 +	70	273	71	80
read		238	19	96 +	31	216	71	75
reading		65	19	96 +	102	46	71	93
reads		7	19	84 –	26	11	70	94
real	Adj	226	19	94 –	13	241	71	96
real		226	19	94 –	13	241	71	96
realise	Verb	199	19	86 +	1666	80	71	95
realise		50	19	85 +	53	37	70	93
realised		131	19	86 +	2058	34	71	95
realises		1	12	76 –	22	3	62	89
realising		17	19	83 +	174	6	68	92
really	Adv	660	19	97 +	6084	253	71	94
reason	NoC	234	19	96 –	294	308	71	96
reason		188	19	96 –	6	179	71	96
reasons		46	19	93 –	1124	129	71	95
receive	Verb	91	19	96 –	3339	309	71	96
receive		21	19	95 –	1285	94	71	95
received		57	19	95 –	1402	162	71	96
receives		2	14	79 –	375	17	71	94
receiving		11	19	89 –	386	36	71	94
recent	Adj	29	19	93 –	3898	210	71	96
record	NoC	60	19	94 –	3182	247	71	93
record		37	19	94 –	2106	157	71	93
records		24	19	91 –	1080	90	71	89
red	Adj	217	19	97 +	1322	103	71	95
red		216	19	97 +	1302	102	71	95
redder		1	13	74 +	20	0	19	76
reduce	Verb	20	19	92 –	5242	234	71	96
reduce		5	19	89 –	2451	94	71	95
reduced		13	19	90 –	1493	85	71	96
reduces		0	3	46 –	476	16	71	92
reducing		2	17	84 –	963	39	71	94
relation	NoC	24	19	91 –	3627	187	71	89
relation		6	19	87 –	638	37	71	87
relations		18	19	91 –	2995	150	71	87
relationship	NoC	66	19	90 –	2717	238	71	96
relationship		58	19	90 –	1310	159	71	95
relationships		9	19	87 –	1664	80	71	92
remain	Verb	154	19	95 –	1797	330	71	97
remain		40	19	93 –	956	113	71	98
remained		92	19	94 –	17	103	71	93
remaining		7	19	88 –	70	14	71	96
remains		14	19	90 –	1841	100	71	96
remember	Verb	536	19	97 +	7154	159	70	94
remember		318	19	97 +	3376	112	70	94
remembered		166	19	96 +	3632	30	70	94
remembering		46	19	94 +	1031	8	70	93
remembers		6	18	80 –	28	10	70	92
reply	Verb	237	19	92 +	5315	42	71	94
replied		200	19	91 +	5377	27	71	92
replies		2	9	66 –	28	4	60	88
reply		30	19	95 +	424	9	71	90
replying		5	19	88 +	44	2	53	88
report	NoC	63	19	90 –	7039	401	71	87
report		43	19	90 –	5630	305	71	85
reports		19	19	90 –	1437	96	71	93
report	Verb	50	19	94 –	3580	243	71	89
report		20	19	92 –	77	32	71	94
reported		24	19	93 –	2595	150	71	85

4.1

Word	PoS	Frlm R D1	LL	Frln R D2
reporting		4 18 87 –	153	15 71 94
reports		2 16 78 –	1245	47 71 67
represent	Verb	22 19 91 –	4178	203 71 95
represent		7 19 87 –	1165	59 71 95
represented		11 19 88 –	1229	70 71 94
representing		2 18 83 –	687	30 71 93
represents		2 16 79 –	1162	44 71 95
require	Verb	49 19 88 –	7226	377 71 94
require		14 19 87 –	1572	90 71 94
required		29 19 89 –	3367	191 71 94
requires		3 17 77 –	1872	72 71 93
requiring		2 16 75 –	532	24 71 93
research	NoC	22 19 88 –	8513	348 71 83
research		21 19 88 –	8587	346 71 83
researches		2 12 71 –	7	3 56 87
rest	NoC	204 19 98 +	533	128 71 97
rest		203 19 98 +	552	127 71 97
rests		1 11 75 –	11	2 52 86
result	NoC	55 19 94 –	8583	438 71 96
result		34 19 94 –	4484	243 71 97
results		20 19 89 –	4122	195 71 92
return	Verb	327 19 95 +	565	226 71 97
return		86 19 95 +	0	84 71 96
returned		191 19 95 +	1065	94 71 95
returning		46 19 95 +	54	34 71 95
returns		5 18 83 –	130	15 71 93
right	Adj	438 19 97 +	1929	235 71 83
right		438 19 97 +	1931	235 71 83
right	Adv	264 19 96 +	2696	95 71 93
right	NoC	148 19 97 +	2553	364 71 93
right		128 19 97 –	386	194 71 94
rights		20 19 93 –	3416	170 71 91
rise	Verb	217 19 97 +	299	156 71 92
rise		31 19 94 –	25	38 71 92
risen		13 19 93 –	38	20 71 93
rises		3 14 75 –	117	11 71 93
rising		49 19 96 +	53	36 71 95
rose		122 19 96 +	956	51 71 84
road	NoC	323 19 96 +	22	301 71 91
road		295 19 95 +	70	259 71 90
roads		28 19 92 –	83	42 71 91
role	NoC	33 19 92 –	5514	275 71 95
role		28 19 92 –	4830	239 71 95
roles		5 19 87 –	686	36 71 93
room	NoC	916 19 97 +	14451	236 71 92
room		843 19 97 +	15858	182 71 93
rooms		74 19 93 +	87	54 71 88
round	Adv	296 19 95 +	6174	57 71 94
round	Prep	270 19 95 +	5261	56 71 95
royal	Adj	49 19 91 –	2289	189 71 92
rule	NoC	51 19 93 –	3402	237 71 91
rule		23 19 92 –	1438	103 71 90
rules		28 19 91 –	1965	134 71 91
run	Verb	590 19 97 +	1639	365 71 94
ran		239 19 95 +	4207	55 71 94
run		187 19 96 +	23	170 71 94
runnin'		1 8 59 +	32	0 4 51
running		144 19 96 +	345	93 71 93
runs		19 19 92 –	328	47 70 93
same	DetP	471 19 98 –	783	647 71 97
say	Verb	6829 19 97 +	90759	2038 71 91
said		5387 19 96 +	102711	1145 71 88
say		937 19 98 +	7018	402 71 91
sayin'		2 11 61 +	101	0 4 50
saying		248 19 95 +	1896	105 71 95
says		255 19 82 –	738	384 71 85

Word	PoS	Frlm R D1	LL	Frln R D2
scheme	NoC	19 19 90 –	4905	218 71 93
scheme		15 19 89 –	3283	152 71 93
schemes		4 19 80 –	1639	65 71 93
school	NoC	253 19 90 –	3902	598 71 92
school		241 19 90 –	1135	401 71 93
schools		13 19 87 –	4812	196 71 90
second	Ord	169 19 95 –	3089	426 71 97
secretary	NoC	56 19 92 –	2221	198 71 85
secretaries		5 18 85 –	46	9 69 91
secretary		52 19 91 –	2194	189 71 85
section	NoC	46 19 68 –	5256	299 71 87
section		39 19 64 –	4036	238 71 85
sections		7 19 85 –	1236	61 71 93
security	NoC	53 19 90 –	2417	200 71 88
securities		0 6 59 –	788	27 58 82
security		52 19 90 –	1829	174 71 88
see	Verb	2927 19 98 +	15265	1478 71 94
saw		683 19 97 +	11896	160 71 96
see		1628 19 98 +	7083	879 71 90
seeing		126 19 96 +	1316	45 71 96
seen		465 19 97 +	460	354 71 97
sees		25 19 90 –	105	41 71 94
seek	Verb	73 19 94 –	1834	210 71 95
seek		24 19 90 –	579	67 71 94
seeking		20 19 91 –	477	57 71 96
seeks		2 13 76 –	408	20 71 91
sought		27 19 93 –	456	66 71 92
seem	Verb	1069 19 97 +	5502	543 71 96
seem		185 19 97 +	19	169 70 96
seemed		736 19 97 +	15858	135 71 94
seeming		14 19 88 +	364	2 63 91
seems		134 19 95 –	784	236 71 96
sell	Verb	112 19 94 –	1245	237 71 94
sell		47 19 93 –	219	78 71 93
selling		22 19 92 –	278	48 71 94
sells		3 16 86 –	130	11 70 89
sold		40 19 93 –	693	99 71 94
send	Verb	313 19 97 +	384	230 71 96
send		94 19 96 +	115	69 71 95
sending		37 19 95 +	88	23 71 94
sends		7 19 91 +	0	6 69 91
sent		176 19 96 +	198	131 71 96
sense	NoC	215 19 96 –	44	242 71 94
sense		188 19 96 –	105	227 71 94
senses		27 19 88 +	122	15 70 86
series	NoC	33 19 93 –	3101	188 71 95
serve	Verb	95 19 95 –	882	190 71 96
serve		29 19 93 –	357	64 71 95
served		48 19 95 –	166	75 71 93
serves		4 19 86 –	321	21 71 93
serving		14 19 92 –	170	30 71 94
service	NoC	101 19 92 –	12677	695 71 94
service		79 19 92 –	5344	372 71 95
services		22 19 90 –	7821	324 71 93
set	Verb	305 19 97 –	796	450 71 98
set		271 19 97 –	442	370 71 98
sets		6 19 87 –	419	28 71 95
setting		28 19 94 –	192	52 71 97
several	DetP	176 19 95 –	698	282 71 97
shake	Verb	389 19 96 +	14029	28 71 93
shake		34 19 94 +	613	8 69 92
shaken		21 19 91 +	341	5 68 93
shakes		6 19 76 +	81	2 46 88
shaking		72 19 95 +	2456	6 66 92
shook		256 19 95 +	11796	7 64 89
shall	VMod	300 19 94 +	1063	173 71 87

4.1

Word	PoS	FrIm	R	D1	LL	FrIn	R	D2
sha~		18	19	93 +	747	1	28	78
shall		282	19	94 +	821	173	71	87
share	NoC	27	19	88 –	4122	212	71	87
share		20	19	92 –	1670	106	71	87
shares		7	18	69 –	2559	106	71	84
she	Pron	18233	19	94 +	635930	1426	71	92
'er		8	11	63 +	297	1	6	20
her		4334	19	94 +	160981	286	71	92
she		13891	19	95 +	475282	1140	71	92
short	Adj	194	19	98 –	12	207	71	97
short		181	19	98 –	0	183	71	97
shorter		11	19	93 –	82	21	71	94
shortest		2	14	79 –	16	4	65	91
should	VMod	855	19	98 –	1392	1170	71	96
shoulder	NoC.	319	19	96 +	9231	37	69	91
shoulder		160	19	96 +	4425	20	68	90
shoulders		159	19	96 +	4820	17	68	89
shout	Verb	195	19	92 +	5362	25	71	92
shout		23	19	93 +	413	5	67	90
shouted		119	19	91 +	4131	9	70	89
shouting		48	19	91 +	1008	9	69	91
shouts		5	17	78 +	84	1	41	84
show	Verb	366	19	98 –	2894	697	71	95
show		147	19	97 –	152	190	71	97
showed		110	19	96 –	6	117	71	93
showing		52	19	97 –	55	67	71	96
shown		43	19	95 –	2708	194	71	91
shows		14	19	93 –	2686	129	71	95
side	NoC	568	19	98 +	1593	351	71	96
side		518	19	97 +	2216	282	71	96
sides		50	19	96 –	90	69	71	95
silence	NoC	222	19	96 +	7036	22	71	94
silence		220	19	96 +	7006	21	71	94
silences		3	17	81 +	47	1	30	81
similar	Adj	36	19	95 –	4255	239	71	96
simple	Adj	97	19	97 –	784	186	71	95
simple		88	19	97 –	612	162	71	95
simpler		5	19	88 –	70	11	69	93
simplest		4	17	86 –	129	12	70	91
simply	Adv	156	19	95 –	118	195	71	96
since	Conj	272	19	97 –	147	328	71	97
since	Prep	90	19	95 –	1448	216	71	93
single	Adj	88	19	96 –	1441	212	71	96
sir	NoC	369	19	88 +	3095	149	71	90
sir		368	19	88 +	3088	149	71	90
sirs		1	6	44 +	6	1	16	57
sister	NoC	229	19	93 +	3384	63	71	93
sister		198	19	92 +	3577	45	71	93
sisters		31	19	89 +	110	18	70	93
sit	Verb	870	19	97 +	21088	136	71	94
sat		471	19	96 +	16517	36	71	91
sit		172	19	96 +	2566	46	71	94
sits		16	19	82 +	38	11	71	93
sitting		211	19	96 +	4233	42	71	93
site	NoC	25	19	89 –	3711	192	71	92
site		21	19	89 –	1972	120	71	93
sites		4	18	84 –	1845	72	71	88
situation	NoC	85	19	96 –	1837	228	71	96
situation		78	19	96 –	1095	178	71	96
situations		6	19	90 –	954	50	71	92
six	Num	166	19	96 –	581	259	71	95
six		165	19	96 –	572	258	71	95
sixes		0	6	65 –	14	1	29	77
sleep	Verb	194	19	96 +	4295	35	70	90
sleep		100	19	96 +	2125	19	69	89
sleeping		28	19	93 +	477	7	68	91
sleeps		5	18	84 +	47	2	42	84
slept		61	19	95 +	1758	7	66	91
slowly	Adv	257	19	97 +	6113	41	71	93
small	Adj	583	19	97 +	50	539	71	96
small		535	19	97 +	278	440	71	96
smaller		39	19	93 –	510	86	71	96
smallest		8	19	89 –	17	12	71	94
smile	NoC	310	19	91 +	12356	16	70	91
smile		291	19	91 +	12170	13	70	91
smiles		18	19	91 +	401	3	60	89
smile	Verb	535	19	95 +	23967	17	67	89
smile		41	19	93 +	1309	4	59	89
smiled		385	19	94 +	19076	7	63	86
smiles		8	17	77 +	129	2	52	86
smiling		101	19	93 +	4165	5	59	89
so	Adv	2498	19	98 +	12682	1275	71	97
so	Conj	437	19	95 +	3193	190	71	95
so that	Conj	197	19	96 +	1	193	71	95
social	Adj	49	19	92 –	12701	564	71	92
society	NoC	48	19	88 –	7082	369	71	94
societies		2	17	82 –	1575	59	71	90
society		46	19	87 –	5609	310	71	95
some	DetP	1534	19	99 –	305	1719	71	97
someone	Pron	411	19	97 +	5079	130	71	94
something	Pron	1013	19	97 +	14273	288	71	96
sometimes	Adv	224	19	95 +	35	201	71	95
son	NoC	213	19	92 +	184	165	71	87
son		184	19	92 +	344	125	71	89
sons		29	19	89 –	49	40	71	79
soon	Adv	264	19	96 +	1064	146	71	96
sorry	Adj	288	19	97 +	9875	24	71	91
sorrier		1	9	73 +	22	0	5	57
sorry		287	19	97 +	9858	23	71	91
sort	NoC	275	19	95 +	1573	134	71	96
sort		252	19	95 +	1800	111	71	96
sorts		23	19	93 +	0	23	71	95
sound	NoC	259	19	96 +	2134	106	71	88
sound		212	19	96 +	1900	83	71	88
sounds		47	19	93 +	260	23	69	86
sound	Verb	248	19	96 +	4352	58	71	91
sound		63	19	95 +	751	21	70	90
sounded		119	19	96 +	4079	10	69	92
sounding		17	19	93 +	324	4	59	87
sounds		48	19	94 +	270	23	70	89
source	NoC	34	19	93 –	3555	208	71	95
source		27	19	93 –	1574	118	71	95
sources		6	19	90 –	2140	90	71	94
south	NoC	76	19	89 –	1492	197	71	95
south		76	19	89 –	1491	197	71	95
speak	Verb	547	19	97 +	6126	185	71	96
speak		195	19	97 +	2326	63	71	95
speaking		75	19	96 +	199	47	71	96
speaks		12	19	84 –	13	16	71	94
spoke		202	19	96 +	4169	39	71	94
spoken		62	19	97 +	759	20	71	94
special	Adj	95	19	95 –	2284	267	71	97
spend	Verb	233	19	97 +	2	227	71	96
spend		70	19	95 –	0	71	71	95
spending		20	19	92 –	87	32	71	93
spends		5	19	88 –	15	8	70	93
spent		138	19	97 +	57	116	71	96
staff	NoC	73	19	91 –	3450	282	71	93
staff		71	19	91 –	3470	279	71	93
staffs		1	9	73 –	16	2	49	85
staves		0	11	66 +	3	0	22	73
stage	NoC	94	19	93 –	1807	241	71	96

Word	PoS	Frlm R D1	LL	Frln R D2	Word	PoS	Frlm R D1	LL	Frln R D2
stage		88 19 93 –	994	187 71 96	*suggests*		6 19 87 –	2189	91 70 94
stages		6 19 93 –	1134	54 71 94	support	NoC	33 19 93 –	5108	262 71 94
stand	Verb	853 19 98 +	14561	204 71 96	*support*		32 19 93 –	5096	258 71 94
stand		146 19 96 +	739	74 71 96	*supports*		1 11 77 –	30	4 65 90
standing		198 19 98 +	3767	42 71 95	support	Verb	42 19 94 –	3774	233 71 94
stands		20 19 87 –	89	33 71 95	*support*		19 19 92 –	2029	118 71 93
stood		489 19 97 +	14558	54 71 94	*supported*		14 19 91 –	1108	72 71 95
standard	NoC	26 19 91 –	3747	197 71 95	*supporting*		7 19 94 –	238	24 71 94
standard		12 19 87 –	1184	70 71 94	*supports*		1 10 75 –	478	19 71 80
standards		14 19 94 –	2580	126 71 94	suppose	Verb	280 19 95 +	5672	56 70 93
stare	Verb	406 19 96 +	18602	12 67 89	*suppose*		246 19 95 +	5199	47 70 93
stare		31 19 92 +	1091	2 54 88	*supposed*		32 19 94 +	648	6 67 90
stared		237 19 94 +	12024	3 52 85	*supposes*		0 6 63 –	8	1 40 85
stares		4 16 75 +	113	1 29 83	*supposing*		1 10 67 –	1	2 45 84
staring		133 19 96 +	5710	5 67 90	sure	Adj	519 19 97 +	8181	134 71 94
start	Verb	482 19 96 +	652	348 71 96	*sure*		518 19 97 +	8232	133 71 94
start		145 19 97 +	52	123 71 95	*surer*		1 6 62 –	0	1 26 82
started		276 19 95 +	1540	136 71 95	*surest*		0 5 58 –	3	1 30 83
starting		39 19 93 –	25	48 71 95	system	NoC	71 19 88 –	18406	818 71 89
starts		21 19 92 –	182	41 70 92	*system*		60 19 89 –	12407	584 71 93
state	NoC	99 19 94 –	9477	574 71 91	*systems*		11 19 79 –	6122	233 71 81
state		95 19 94 –	7034	470 71 90	table	NoC	428 19 98 +	3077	188 71 93
states		4 19 86 –	2741	103 71 88	*table*		390 19 98 +	3183	160 71 93
stay	Verb	378 19 97 +	4244	128 71 94	*tables*		38 19 94 +	51	27 71 94
stay		243 19 96 +	3044	76 71 94	take	Verb	2239 19 99 +	2701	1650 71 98
stayed		73 19 95 +	849	24 70 94	*take*		822 19 98 +	810	625 71 98
staying		54 19 92 +	515	20 71 91	*taken*		333 19 98 –	83	378 71 98
stays		7 19 87 +	0	7 70 92	*takes*		60 19 92 –	737	131 71 97
still	Adv	1064 19 98 +	3572	625 71 97	*taking*		247 19 97 +	96	209 71 98
stone	NoC	188 19 95 +	843	101 71 89	*took*		777 19 98 +	6786	307 71 96
stone		139 19 95 +	737	69 71 90	talk	Verb	599 19 97 +	8784	165 71 95
stones		50 19 93 +	130	31 70 86	*talk*		270 19 95 +	4071	72 71 94
stop	Verb	577 19 97 +	8356	160 71 95	*talked*		100 19 94 +	1557	26 71 94
stop		247 19 97 +	2596	87 71 94	*talkin'*		3 11 63 +	96	0 10 62
stopped		290 19 96 +	6616	49 71 94	*talking*		219 19 97 +	3198	60 71 94
stopping		26 19 94 +	153	12 71 94	*talks*		7 19 87 +	5	6 65 92
stops		14 19 88 +	9	11 70 93	tax	NoC	12 19 90 –	6104	238 71 88
story	NoC	207 19 93 +	30	187 71 94	*tax*		9 19 89 –	5289	201 71 88
stories		48 19 92 –	0	49 71 93	*taxes*		3 17 85 –	831	37 71 89
story		159 19 92 +	46	137 71 94	tea	NoC	208 19 94 +	3950	45 71 93
street	NoC	345 19 94 +	721	229 71 93	*tea*		206 19 94 +	4061	42 71 93
street		268 19 94 +	491	183 71 92	*teas*		2 16 86 –	0	2 43 79
streets		77 19 92 +	243	46 71 93	teacher	NoC	51 19 86 –	3756	252 71 89
strong	Adj	183 19 96 –	76	215 71 97	*teacher*		35 19 85 –	953	104 71 89
strong		150 19 96 –	56	175 71 97	*teachers*		16 19 77 –	3072	148 71 88
stronger		28 19 95 +	0	28 71 96	team	NoC	59 19 87 –	4192	285 71 91
strongest		5 19 86 –	89	13 71 94	*team*		53 19 87 –	3242	235 71 91
structure	NoC	17 19 89 –	5634	236 71 93	*teams*		6 17 79 –	990	50 71 91
structure		13 19 90 –	4141	177 71 93	tell	Verb	1802 19 97 +	29430	450 71 94
structures		3 18 80 –	1495	60 71 92	*tell*		806 19 97 +	19651	125 71 94
student	NoC	46 19 89 –	5024	290 71 88	*tellin'*		2 8 63 +	82	0 4 48
student		21 19 89 –	1396	98 71 89	*telling*		130 19 96 +	2098	33 71 94
students		25 19 88 –	3679	192 71 87	*tells*		34 19 90 –	3	37 70 93
study	NoC	48 19 92 +	9127	439 71 87	*told*		830 19 97 +	10647	255 71 92
studies		9 19 84 –	4812	186 71 84	ten	Num	210 19 96 +	316	149 71 95
study		39 19 91 –	4520	254 71 88	*ten*		207 19 96 +	386	141 71 95
subject	NoC	85 19 94 –	3931	325 71 88	*tens*		2 13 73 –	77	8 70 91
subject		77 19 94 –	1986	222 71 85	term	NoC	69 19 94 –	5586	361 71 91
subjects		9 19 86 –	2327	103 71 87	*term*		26 19 88 –	2500	151 71 93
such	DetP	511 19 96 –	3105	906 71 95	*terms*		43 19 94 –	3095	210 71 90
such as	Prep	36 19 92 –	9928	436 71 96	test	NoC	29 19 92 –	3756	204 71 93
suddenly	Adv	414 19 94 +	11583	52 71 94	*test*		19 19 91 –	2625	139 71 92
suggest	Verb	165 19 96 –	1676	339 71 95	*tests*		10 19 88 –	1133	65 71 93
suggest		43 19 92 –	669	103 71 94	than	Conj	991 19 98 –	150	1095 71 97
suggested		97 19 96 –	59	118 71 95	thank	Verb	226 19 95 +	5094	39 71 90
suggesting		18 19 92 –	46	27 71 93	*thank*		202 19 95 +	4836	32 71 89

Word	PoS	Frlm	R	D1	LL	Frln	R	D2
thanked		19	19	93 +	314	5	65	89
thanking		4	19	88 +	31	2	48	86
thanks		0	5	57 +	0	0	19	79
that	Conj	5891	19	98 −	6778	7684	71	97
that	DetP	4821	19	98 +	38534	2001	71	95
the	Det	51846	19	98 −	60053	67675	71	99
their	Det	1910	19	96 −	6654	2982	71	98
themselves	Pron	160	19	96 −	837	273	71	96
themselves		159	19	96 −	839	273	71	96
then	Adv	2661	19	98 +	23481	1046	71	97
theory	NoC	29	19	93 −	4269	222	71	90
theories		6	19	90 −	960	49	70	88
theory		23	19	91 −	3309	173	71	90
there	Adv	1195	19	98 +	18278	317	71	96
there	Ex	2667	19	98 +	932	2273	71	98
therefore	Adv	37	19	92 −	5781	294	71	94
these	DetP	520	19	95 −	12112	1442	71	96
they	Pron	7298	19	97 +	15469	4829	71	97
'em		31	19	81 +	669	6	56	84
them		2477	19	97 +	10775	1338	71	97
they		4791	19	97 +	6253	3485	71	97
thing	NoC	1213	19	97 +	11791	450	71	95
thing		594	19	96 +	8010	175	71	94
things		619	19	96 +	4325	275	71	95
think	Verb	2877	19	98 +	51666	653	71	96
think		1384	19	97 +	22358	349	71	95
thinking		204	19	97 +	3392	50	71	95
thinks		58	19	93 +	276	31	70	93
thought		1231	19	98 +	26802	223	71	96
third	Ord	83	19	95 −	2476	256	71	96
this	DetP	3264	19	98 −	8593	4828	71	97
those	DetP	567	19	96 −	2578	938	71	96
though	Conj	315	19	95 +	145	262	71	95
thought	NoC	338	19	95 +	4311	104	71	94
thought		212	19	95 +	2282	74	71	94
thoughts		126	19	95 +	2130	30	70	92
three	Num	489	19	96 −	1496	744	71	97
three		487	19	96 −	1505	743	71	97
threes		1	14	74 +	4	1	38	86
through	Prep	986	19	98 +	1496	699	71	98
throw	Verb	246	19	98 +	2824	82	71	95
threw		99	19	96 +	2421	15	70	92
throw		52	19	96 +	402	22	71	95
throwing		36	19	95 +	344	13	70	93
thrown		54	19	97 +	320	26	71	94
throws		5	19	81 −	0	5	69	92
thus	Adv	36	19	87 −	5330	277	71	93
time	NoC	2062	19	99 +	840	1735	71	98
time		1841	19	99 +	1608	1424	71	98
times		221	19	97 −	436	311	71	96
to	Inf	16506	19	99 +	3	16440	71	99
*~na**		22	18	80 +	373	5	48	76
*~ta**		7	18	83 +	174	1	31	82
to		16477	19	99 +	1	16434	71	99
to	Prep	8875	19	99 −	1364	9813	71	99
today	Adv	161	19	97 −	597	255	71	91
together	Adv	368	19	97 +	209	299	71	97
too	Adv	1290	19	97 +	9466	559	71	96
touch	Verb	199	19	95 +	4188	37	71	94
touch		65	19	95 +	1206	14	70	92
touched		102	19	95 +	2744	14	70	95
touches		4	19	84 +	0	3	64	90
touching		28	19	92 +	501	6	64	90
towards	Prep	502	19	97 +	2619	254	71	97
town	NoC	148	19	95 −	697	247	71	92
town		139	19	95 −	257	194	71	90

Word	PoS	Frlm	R	D1	LL	Frln	R	D2
towns		9	19	89 −	871	53	71	90
trade	NoC	35	19	89 −	4805	257	71	92
trade		34	19	89 −	4495	242	71	92
trades		1	14	82 −	313	15	71	92
training	NoC	30	19	90 −	4775	242	71	92
tree	NoC	273	19	94 +	1887	122	71	93
tree		103	19	91 +	459	55	71	93
trees		169	19	94 +	1504	66	71	92
true	Adj	201	19	97 +	37	179	71	96
true		200	19	97 +	40	177	71	96
truer		1	12	79 −	0	1	46	87
truest		0	5	61 −	4	1	25	78
try	Verb	941	19	98 +	6780	412	71	96
tried		352	19	97 +	4745	104	71	95
tries		11	19	86 −	35	16	70	94
try		242	19	97 +	457	164	71	95
trying		336	19	98 +	3154	128	71	95
turn	Verb	1099	19	98 +	15313	316	71	96
turn		169	19	97 +	416	108	71	95
turned		764	19	98 +	17169	133	71	95
turning		132	19	96 +	1604	42	71	95
turns		34	19	85 +	0	32	70	94
two	Num	1177	19	97 −	1084	1494	71	98
two		1175	19	97 −	1091	1493	71	98
twos		2	14	74 +	8	1	42	87
type	NoC	48	19	94 −	5993	329	71	90
type		39	19	94 −	3408	212	71	87
types		9	19	83 −	2690	117	71	94
UK	NoP	6	19	48 −	7078	247	71	91
U.K.		0	3	36 −	133	5	55	79
UK		6	17	46 −	6935	241	71	91
UK.		0	0	00 −	6	0	11	70
under	Prep	470	19	97 −	600	621	71	94
understand	Verb	362	19	97 +	1350	206	71	96
understand		264	19	97 +	1769	120	71	94
understanding		11	19	91 −	108	23	71	93
understands		7	19	90 −	0	7	70	93
understood		80	19	95 +	122	56	71	96
union	NoC	25	19	88 −	5781	265	71	88
union		22	19	89 −	4378	208	71	87
unions		3	14	76 −	1421	57	71	90
unit	NoC	30	19	85 −	4447	232	71	94
unit		24	19	83 −	2340	140	71	94
units		7	19	80 −	2186	92	71	93
university	NoC	46	19	87 −	3813	244	71	88
universities		2	17	70 −	839	35	71	88
university		44	19	88 −	3042	209	71	86
until	Conj	396	19	97 +	1638	218	71	97
until	Prep	101	19	96 −	858	197	71	95
up	Adv	2989	19	98 +	20931	1327	71	96
up to	Prep	240	19	97 +	1333	118	71	97
upon	Prep	177	19	90 −	556	271	71	94
US	NoP	10	18	86 −	5911	225	71	85
U.S.		0	4	51 −	163	6	49	82
US		10	18	86 −	5743	219	71	85
use	NoC	71	19	96 −	7193	426	71	95
use		68	19	96 −	6769	403	71	95
uses		3	17	85 −	425	23	71	91
use	Verb	376	19	97 −	13827	1281	71	96
use		137	19	97 −	2517	346	71	95
used		165	19	96 −	6530	583	71	96
uses		7	19	91 −	794	46	71	93
using		66	19	95 −	4358	306	71	94
usually	Adv	105	19	96 −	1156	221	71	94
value	NoC	34	19	92 −	7034	330	71	94
value		28	19	92 −	4532	229	71	94

Word	PoS	Frlm	R	D1	LL	Frln	R	D2
values		6	19	87 –	2561	102	71	91
various	Adj	51	19	94 –	2229	190	71	96
very	Adv	1267	19	97 +	1255	962	71	97
view	NoC	125	19	96 –	2827	342	71	95
view		106	19	95 –	1608	249	71	95
views		19	19	95 –	1398	93	71	95
voice	NoC	729	19	97 +	20689	89	71	93
voice		671	19	96 +	20529	71	71	92
voices		58	19	93 +	734	18	70	92
wait	Verb	591	19	98 +	12668	109	71	95
wait		192	19	97 +	3451	43	71	95
waited		156	19	96 +	5127	14	71	92
waiting		238	19	98 +	4676	49	71	94
waits		5	18	83 +	17	3	56	90
walk	Verb	593	19	97 +	12674	110	71	92
walk		128	19	95 –	1547	41	71	91
walked		348	19	96 +	10924	35	71	91
walking		106	19	96 +	1544	29	71	91
walks		11	19	86 +	72	5	68	92
wall	NoC	379	19	96 +	4037	133	71	92
wall		256	19	95 +	3058	83	71	92
walls		123	19	95 +	1026	50	71	92
want	Verb	1691	19	97 +	21716	518	71	95
wan~		5	18	77 +	45	2	33	69
want		969	19	97 +	12635	293	71	94
wanted		565	19	96 +	9475	137	71	95
wantin'		1	5	54 +	28	0	1	00
wanting		51	19	94 +	629	16	71	94
wants		101	19	96 +	175	70	71	91
war	NoC	176	19	89 –	1548	346	71	94
war		166	19	89 –	1428	324	71	94
wars		10	19	88 –	121	22	71	93
watch	Verb	544	19	98 +	11115	107	71	93
watch		111	19	95 +	998	43	71	93
watched		238	19	97 +	6919	28	71	92
watches		6	17	83 +	61	2	53	87
watching		189	19	96 +	4153	34	71	93
water	NoC	397	19	95 +	13	378	71	92
water		375	19	94 +	18	353	71	92
waters		22	19	92 –	3	25	71	90
way	NoC	1362	19	98 +	1633	1005	71	97
way		1293	19	98 +	3131	829	71	97
ways		70	19	97 –	1292	176	71	95
we	Pron	3958	19	97 +	2406	3200	71	95
us		773	19	96 +	1502	521	71	95
we		3186	19	97 +	1304	2679	71	95
wear	Verb	328	19	97 +	4092	103	71	92
wear		67	19	95 +	401	32	71	90
wearing		120	19	96 +	1735	33	71	91
wears		10	19	80 +	21	6	63	87
wore		97	19	95 +	2347	15	68	91
worn		34	19	96 +	220	15	71	92
week	NoC	345	19	96 –	455	458	71	93
week		212	19	96 –	483	306	71	92
weeks		133	19	95 –	38	153	71	94
well	Adv	1187	19	97 +	9567	490	71	97
what	DetP	3840	19	98 +	36613	1443	71	96
when	Adv	467	19	98 +	122	407	71	97
when	Conj	2224	19	99 +	4313	1500	71	97
where	Adv	823	19	97 +	3078	468	71	97
where	Conj	407	19	98 –	359	514	71	96
whether	Conj	189	19	94 –	1460	357	71	95
which	DetP	1689	19	96 –	34975	4464	71	98
while	Conj	486	19	97 –	141	557	71	98
white	Adj	378	19	97 +	2486	173	71	95
white		377	19	97 +	2475	172	71	95
whiter		1	15	83 +	5	1	22	70
who	Pron	2004	19	98 –	75	2108	71	97
whole	Adj	245	19	97 +	113	204	71	97
whose	DetP	136	19	95 –	768	237	71	98
why	Adv	1025	19	97 +	14721	287	71	95
wide	Adj	110	19	96 +	638	193	71	96
wide		97	19	95 –	105	126	71	96
wider		12	19	93 –	998	63	71	95
widest		1	10	74 –	49	4	67	93
wife	NoC	311	19	94 +	1304	170	71	90
wife		288	19	94 +	1385	150	71	90
wives		23	19	93 +	5	20	71	88
will	VMod	3083	19	97 –	4	3114	71	95
'll		1568	19	96 +	47727	167	71	88
will		1185	19	97 –	19879	2887	71	95
wo~		330	19	97 +	7112	61	70	88
win	Verb	86	19	93 –	3179	294	71	90
win		34	19	91 –	852	98	71	89
winning		10	19	91 –	498	40	71	89
wins		3	16	79 –	148	11	69	89
won		39	19	92 –	1710	145	71	90
window	NoC	425	19	96 +	4906	141	71	84
window		302	19	96 +	6344	57	71	93
windows		124	19	95 +	234	84	71	75
wish	Verb	268	19	97 +	1059	149	71	95
wish		144	19	96 +	372	91	71	93
wished		91	19	96 +	1245	27	71	94
wishes		9	19	88 –	87	18	71	91
wishing		24	19	91 +	82	14	71	95
with	Prep	7136	19	99 +	333	6740	71	99
within	Prep	155	19	94 –	6306	554	71	96
without	Prep	537	19	98 +	136	469	71	98
woman	NoC	853	19	97 +	1217	611	71	93
woman		578	19	97 +	8649	156	71	93
women		275	19	95 –	1249	455	71	92
wonder	Verb	375	19	97 +	10211	49	71	94
wonder		88	19	96 +	1310	24	71	94
wondered		202	19	97 +	7933	11	69	92
wondering		82	19	95 +	2373	10	69	93
wonders		3	17	78 –	3	4	67	91
word	NoC	602	19	97 +	1280	398	71	93
word		265	19	98 +	609	172	71	92
words		337	19	96 +	672	226	71	93
work	NoC	340	19	95 –	4168	742	71	96
work		340	19	96 –	4168	742	71	96
work	Verb	527	19	97 –	285	635	71	97
work		203	19	98 –	154	252	71	96
worked		144	19	97 +	69	119	71	96
working		150	19	95 –	149	192	71	96
works		28	19	94 –	470	69	71	96
wrought		2	17	84 +	0	2	58	90
worker	NoC	31	19	91 +	4578	238	71	91
worker		11	19	93 –	581	46	71	90
workers		20	19	87 –	4086	192	71	91
world	NoC	404	19	96 –	2246	701	71	96
world		393	19	96 –	2307	690	71	96
worlds		12	19	80 +	1	11	67	92
would	VMod	4464	19	98 +	22818	2271	71	97
'd		859	19	97 +	25050	99	70	90
would		3604	19	98 +	11068	2172	71	97
write	Verb	328	19	86 –	288	414	71	96
write		91	19	92 –	10	99	71	94
writes		7	18	87 –	520	34	71	89
writing		40	19	92 –	215	69	71	95
written		71	19	95 –	281	113	71	96
wrote		120	19	60 +	58	99	71	94

Word	PoS	Frlm	R	D1	LL	Frln	R	D2
wrong	Adj	249	19	98 +	1874	107	71	95
wrong		249	19	97 +	1873	107	71	95
year	NoC	751	19	96 –	13694	1889	71	96
year		212	19	95 –	11089	864	71	94
years		539	19	96 –	4234	1025	71	97
yes	Int	873	19	96 +	31021	65	71	94
yesterday	Adv	77	19	93 –	2096	228	69	76
yet	Adv	456	19	97 +	846	311	71	96
you	Pron	12855	19	97 +	249236	2683	71	92
y'		0	2	12 +	0	0	7	55
ya		5	15	76 +	94	1	32	81
ye		55	19	50 +	1531	7	62	78
you		12794	19	97 +	247719	2674	71	92
young	Adj	560	19	96 +	1445	354	71	96
young		482	19	96 +	1463	291	71	95
younger		65	19	95 +	53	51	71	94
youngest		14	19	87 +	3	12	70	85
your	Det	2048	19	96 +	11409	1007	71	91
yer		29	19	72 +	750	4	29	49
your		2019	19	96 +	10972	1003	71	91
yourself	Pron	202	19	96 +	2103	72	70	89

4.1

List 4.2. Distinctiveness list contrasting imaginative v. informative writing (not lemmatized)

FrIm = Rounded frequency (per million word tokens) in imaginative writing
LL = Log Likelihood, indicating the distinctiveness (or significance of the difference) between the frequencies in imaginative and informative writing, down to a minimum log likelihood of 2811.
FrIn = Rounded frequency (per million word tokens) in informative writing
+   = Higher frequency in imaginative writing
−   = Higher frequency in informative writing

Word	PoS	FrIm		LL	FrIn	Word	PoS	FrIm		LL	FrIn
she	Pron	13891	+	475282	1140	up	Adv	2989	+	20931	1327
I	Pron	17216	+	323569	3719	down	Adv	1688	+	20723	535
he	Pron	16475	+	260201	4240	voice	NoC	671	+	20529	71
you	Pron	12794	+	247719	2674	government	NoC	48	−	20464	819
her*	Det	7893	+	227730	930	will	VMod	1185	−	19879	2887
~n't	Neg	7183	+	184002	1036	may	VMod	326	−	19751	1440
her	Pron	4334	+	160981	286	tell	Verb	806	+	19651	125
of*	Prep	18997	−	122912	34244	smiled	Verb	385	+	19076	7
him	Pron	4927	+	111990	845	man	NoC	1433	+	18739	433
said	Verb	5387	+	102711	1145	there	Adv	1195	+	18278	317
had	Verb	9558	+	100954	3366	felt	Verb	841	+	17906	157
is	Verb	4078	−	98451	11484	as	Prep	791	−	17621	2154
his	Det	9463	+	98011	3375	turned	Verb	764	+	17169	133
was	Verb	15782	+	89362	7707	go	Verb	1404	+	16798	454
me	Pron	3703	+	87658	601	head	NoC	953	+	16717	221
's	Verb	4754	+	84044	1096	asked	Verb	908	+	16581	202
the	Det	51846	−	60053	67675	sat	Verb	471	+	16517	36
in	Prep	12667	−	53631	20612	room	NoC	843	+	15858	182
do	Verb	4312	+	50145	1422	seemed	Verb	736	+	15858	135
did	Verb	3011	+	49688	743	going*	Verb	1119	+	15802	318
'll	VMod	1568	+	47727	167	as if	Conj	555	+	15781	67
'm	Verb	1526	+	46376	163	again	Adv	1193	+	15754	357
it	Pron	13751	+	44861	8145	or	Conj	2246	−	15730	4135
my	Det	3284	+	44749	960	away	Adv	915	+	15449	221
eyes	NoC	1233	+	44487	88	here	Adv	1272	+	15090	414
looked	Verb	1335	+	44322	118	just	Adv	1843	+	14934	759
by	Prep	2568	−	42966	6250	went	Verb	1020	+	14909	281
are	Verb	2062	−	41686	5399	why	Adv	1025	+	14721	287
know	Verb	2021	+	40946	401	stood	Verb	489	+	14558	54
'd (=had)	Verb	1085	+	39177	78	something	Pron	1013	+	14273	288
that	DetP	4821	+	38534	2001	per cent	NoC	23	−	13757	521
has	Verb	863	−	37335	3186	for	Prep	6477	−	13744	9230
what	DetP	3840	+	36613	1443	nodded	Verb	265	+	13559	3
which	DetP	1689	−	34975	4464	nothing	Pron	825	+	13444	206
yes	Int	873	+	31021	65	never	Adv	1158	+	13409	383
're	Verb	1303	+	30433	215	come	Verb	1203	+	13278	412
no	Int	864	+	30344	66	new	Adj	463	−	13187	1400
've	Verb	1309	+	29872	223	hand	NoC	857	+	12980	229
oh	Int	730	+	29725	36	ca~	VMod	598	+	12906	110
face	NoC	1014	+	29261	119	get	Verb	1388	+	12732	533
back	Adv	1824	+	29081	465	national	Adj	26	−	12717	498
door	NoC	903	+	29059	85	social	Adj	49	−	12701	564
could	VMod	3159	+	27055	1263	so	Adv	2498	+	12682	1275
thought	Verb	1231	+	26802	223	1	Num	37	−	12680	529
knew	Verb	897	+	25343	110	its	Det	874	−	12640	2017
herself	Pron	707	+	25103	53	want	Verb	969	+	12635	293
'd (=would)	VMod	859	+	25050	99	moment	NoC	601	+	12626	114
then	Adv	2661	+	23481	1046	little	Adj	682	+	12482	152
think	Verb	1384	+	22358	349	but	Conj	5962	+	12442	3958
like	Prep	2041	+	22010	709	system	NoC	60	−	12407	584
also	Adv	352	−	21968	1581	smile	NoC	291	+	12170	13
got	Verb	1192	+	21495	269	these	DetP	520	−	12112	1442

Word	PoS	Frlm		LL	Frln	Word	PoS	Frlm		LL	Frln
stared	Verb	237	+	12024	3	council	NoC	38	–	7792	368
be	Verb	4944	–	12000	7208	morning	NoC	460	+	7763	111
development	NoC	14	–	11999	431	gone	Verb	435	+	7632	101
out	Adv	2374	+	11998	1214	international	Adj	17	–	7512	300
2	Num	27	–	11964	476	general	Adj	49	–	7489	386
saw	Verb	684	+	11908	160	like	Verb	579	+	7450	177
shook	Verb	256	+	11796	7	between	Prep	458	–	7413	1101
bed	NoC	476	+	11643	74	can	VMod	1417	–	7354	2417
suddenly	Adv	414	+	11583	52	Mrs	NoC	485	+	7256	131
mother	NoC	678	+	11294	166	management	NoC	16	–	7244	287
came	Verb	996	+	11254	335	off	Adv	850	+	7200	342
all right*	Adv	266	+	11203	11	members	NoC	48	–	7179	372
year	NoC	212	–	11089	864	how	Adv	1480	+	7172	769
mouth	NoC	349	+	11081	34	community	NoC	21	–	7146	300
would	VMod	3604	+	11068	2172	wo~	VMod	330	+	7112	61
girl	NoC	470	+	11049	77	market	NoC	49	–	7099	371
your	Det	2019	+	10972	1003	see	Verb	1628	+	7083	879
walked	Verb	348	+	10924	35	major	Adj	27	–	7034	312
them	Pron	2477	+	10775	1338	state	NoC	95	–	7034	470
told	Verb	830	+	10647	255	say	Verb	937	+	7018	402
hands	NoC	540	+	10581	111	silence	NoC	220	+	7006	21
now	Adv	1998	+	10471	1007	beside	Prep	220	+	6936	22
let	Verb	604	+	10466	142	UK	NoP	6	–	6935	241
however	Adv	187	–	10427	788	watched	Verb	238	+	6919	28
hair	NoC	441	+	10347	72	fingers	NoC	215	+	6872	21
laughed	Verb	228	+	10114	8	data	NoC	8	–	6812	246
father	NoC	618	+	9966	156	took	Verb	777	+	6786	307
such as	Prep	36	–	9928	436	that	Conj	5891	–	6778	7684
on	Adv	1192	+	9927	484	use	NoC	68	–	6769	403
sorry	Adj	287	+	9858	23	10	Num	12	–	6739	257
political	Adj	31	–	9649	411	looking	Verb	540	+	6737	169
well	Adv	1187	+	9567	490	number	NoC	156	–	6717	574
lips	NoC	229	+	9499	10	their	Det	1910	–	6654	2982
wanted	Verb	565	+	9475	137	industry	NoC	15	–	6640	263
too	Adv	1290	+	9466	559	million	NoC	33	–	6619	313
economic	Adj	7	–	9389	321	stopped	Verb	290	+	6616	49
heard	Verb	517	+	9377	116	1990	Num	1	–	6614	209
about	Prep	2170	+	9242	1181	period	NoC	34	–	6604	316
local	Adj	99	–	9021	555	breath	NoC	199	+	6599	18
policy	NoC	14	–	8777	329	4	Num	20	–	6598	277
dark	Adj	345	+	8729	51	used	Verb	165	–	6530	583
woman	NoC	578	+	8649	156	p.	NoC	1	–	6528	203
this	DetP	3264	–	8593	4828	pulled	Verb	238	+	6499	31
anything	Pron	585	+	8591	161	in	Adv	887	+	6488	385
research	NoC	21	–	8587	346	behind	Prep	480	+	6449	142
miss*	NoC	312	+	8520	41	provide	Verb	27	–	6435	293
an	Det	2516	–	8424	3897	law	NoC	51	–	6424	353
group	NoC	94	–	8388	521	window	NoC	302	+	6344	57
look	Verb	745	+	8385	251	including	Prep	34	–	6340	308
3	Num	23	–	8353	345	within	Prep	155	–	6306	554
education	NoC	23	–	8261	342	process	NoC	26	–	6289	285
sure	Adj	518	+	8232	133	boy	NoC	340	+	6272	75
himself	Pron	714	+	8148	239	European	Adj	18	–	6262	260
glanced	Verb	154	+	8058	2	they	Pron	4791	+	6253	3485
many	DetP	413	–	8034	1065	health	NoC	38	–	6249	314
thing	NoC	594	+	8010	175	whispered	Verb	127	+	6244	2
for example	Adv	17	–	7977	315	public	Adj	62	–	6203	369
available	Adj	32	–	7947	358	award	NoC	3	–	6192	205
wondered	Verb	202	+	7933	11	round	Adv	296	+	6174	57
information	NoC	88	–	7916	490	based	Verb	14	–	6157	246
British	Adj	75	–	7902	461	systems	NoC	11	–	6122	233
areas	NoC	15	–	7873	303	night	NoC	685	+	6119	268
Britain	NoP	25	–	7845	334	slowly	Adv	257	+	6113	41
out of	Prep	931	+	7834	376	companies	NoC	12	–	6106	237
into	Prep	2494	+	7827	1494	really	Adv	660	+	6084	253
services	NoC	22	–	7821	324	during	Prep	161	–	6065	554

4.2

Word	PoS	Frlm		LL	Frln		Word	PoS	Frlm		LL	Frln
arm	NoC	278	+	6001	51		shoulders	NoC	159	+	4820	17
minister	NoC	43	−	5891	313		studies	NoC	9	−	4812	186
paused	Verb	123	+	5875	3		schools	NoC	13	−	4812	196
1989	Num	1	−	5871	187		cases	NoC	28	−	4793	239
mean	Verb	446	+	5857	134		aunt	NoC	128	+	4779	8
shrugged	Verb	120	+	5855	2		training	NoC	30	−	4775	242
kitchen	NoC	248	+	5844	41		production	NoC	17	−	4754	207
groups	NoC	21	−	5784	254		tried	Verb	352	+	4745	104
therefore	Adv	37	−	5781	294		analysis	NoC	8	−	4736	180
1991	Num	0	−	5781	179		former	DetP	25	−	4732	229
US	NoP	10	−	5743	219		desk	NoC	159	+	4723	18
changes	NoC	18	−	5724	242		most	Adv	286	−	4689	690
staring	Verb	133	+	5710	5		waiting	Verb	238	+	4676	49
anyway	Adv	236	+	5692	37		left	Verb	627	+	4675	270
report	NoC	43	−	5630	305		30	Num	3	−	4657	159
sighed	Verb	108	+	5625	1		hon.	Adj	1	−	4649	148
society	NoC	46	−	5609	310		from	Prep	3452	−	4643	4595
countries	NoC	13	−	5595	224		financial	Adj	21	−	4643	215
5	Num	19	−	5566	241		'	Gen	225	−	4628	594
back	NoC	429	+	5544	131		mind	Verb	167	+	4573	22
court	NoC	74	−	5526	368		hers	Pron	109	+	4560	5
area	NoC	98	−	5515	416		1992	Num	1	−	4550	144
softly	Adv	120	+	5442	4		grinned	Verb	90	+	4540	1
company	NoC	147	−	5429	502		value	NoC	28	−	4532	229
murmured	Verb	101	+	5421	1		Luke	NoP	139	+	4528	13
afraid	Adj	195	+	5389	25		study	NoC	39	−	4520	254
form	NoC	62	−	5385	338		central	Adj	37	−	4516	251
leaned	Verb	113	+	5381	3		mind	NoC	444	+	4500	160
replied	Verb	200	+	5377	27		trade	NoC	34	−	4495	242
hear	Verb	314	+	5373	75		per	Prep	9	−	4494	176
cried	Verb	133	+	5355	7		stairs	NoC	134	+	4490	11
of course	Adv	562	+	5347	211		result	NoC	34	−	4484	243
service	NoC	79	−	5344	372		floor	NoC	286	+	4468	74
thus	Adv	36	−	5330	277		&	Conj	13	−	4461	187
else	Adv	402	+	5314	121		issues	NoC	4	−	4442	157
feet	NoC	352	+	5309	94		Europe	NoP	33	−	4440	237
tax	NoC	9	−	5289	201		1988	Num	2	−	4432	145
Maggie	NoP	120	+	5269	4		Lucy	NoP	112	+	4431	6
problems	NoC	64	−	5268	337		shoulder	NoC	160	+	4425	20
round	Prep	270	+	5261	56		12	Num	8	−	4394	168
programme	NoC	23	−	5230	242		growth	NoC	10	−	4394	174
suppose	Verb	246	+	5199	47		party	NoC	168	−	4391	489
Ruth	NoP	129	+	5150	7		union	NoC	22	−	4378	208
20	Num	5	−	5143	183		population	NoC	11	−	4372	176
century	NoC	33	−	5141	262		basis	NoC	14	−	4362	186
waited	Verb	156	+	5127	14		using	Verb	66	−	4358	306
support	NoC	32	−	5096	258		March	NoP	17	−	4345	193
chair	NoC	223	+	5087	38		everything	Pron	361	+	4340	116
someone	Pron	411	+	5079	130		conditions	NoC	20	−	4331	203
as though	Conj	183	+	5071	23		things	NoC	619	+	4325	275
put	Verb	820	+	5068	385		when	Conj	2224	+	4313	1500
patients	NoC	22	−	5067	232		glass	NoC	254	+	4302	61
include	Verb	13	−	5060	205		B / b	Lett	18	−	4298	195
range	NoC	32	−	5045	258		6	Num	14	−	4290	184
maybe	Adv	232	+	4955	43		individual	Adj	13	−	4285	179
rate	NoC	29	−	4920	244		ah	Int	111	+	4263	7
committee	NoC	24	−	4902	233		similar	Adj	36	−	4255	239
level	NoC	52	−	4896	298		labour*	Adj	8	−	4244	165
quietly	Adv	157	+	4894	16		environment	NoC	10	−	4239	170
myself	Pron	300	+	4884	75		years	NoC	539	−	4234	1025
arms	NoC	297	+	4878	74		sitting	Verb	211	+	4233	42
look	NoC	258	+	4868	55		love	NoC	336	+	4218	105
other	Adj	838	−	4850	1468		each	DetP	252	−	4209	613
thank	Verb	202	+	4836	32		ran	Verb	239	+	4207	55
role	NoC	28	−	4830	239		gave	Verb	465	+	4206	180
important	Adj	146	−	4822	473		costs	NoC	7	−	4203	157

Word	PoS	Frlm		LL	Frln		Word	PoS	Frlm		LL	Frln
old	Adj	879	+	4199	459		Adam	NoP	126	+	3657	15
coffee	NoC	186	+	4189	32		project	NoC	21	−	3656	181
authority	NoC	34	−	4179	231		quality	NoC	32	−	3656	206
spoke	Verb	202	+	4169	39		liked	Verb	164	+	3655	29
work	NoC	340	−	4168	742		somewhere	Adv	167	+	3644	30
smiling	Verb	101	+	4165	5		further*	Adj	66	−	3641	278
watching	Verb	189	+	4153	34		economy	NoC	7	−	3635	139
cost	NoC	17	−	4148	188		remembered	Verb	166	+	3632	30
structure	NoC	13	−	4141	177		increase	NoC	3	−	3611	126
am	Verb	487	+	4137	195		effect	NoC	73	−	3594	289
lady	NoC	244	+	4134	59		income	NoC	12	−	3593	154
shouted	Verb	119	+	4131	9		higher	Adj	31	−	3584	202
results	NoC	20	−	4122	195		sister	NoC	198	+	3577	45
rates	NoC	6	−	4094	152		still	Adv	1064	+	3572	625
15	Num	6	−	4094	152		act	NoC	68	−	3563	277
a little	Adv	263	+	4090	69		dad	NoC	151	+	3559	25
workers	NoC	20	−	4086	192		July	NoP	14	−	3551	158
April	NoP	21	−	4084	195		home	Adv	369	+	3544	138
sounded	Verb	119	+	4079	10		industrial	Adj	12	−	3543	154
talk	Verb	270	+	4071	72		product	NoC	9	−	3541	145
labour*	NoC	15	−	4070	180		May	NoP	29	−	3541	195
technology	NoC	8	−	4069	158		specific	Adj	10	−	3537	148
authorities	NoC	11	−	4067	169		feel	Verb	451	+	3529	189
tea	NoC	206	+	4061	42		before	Conj	534	+	3513	244
issue	NoC	18	−	4055	187		existing	Adj	4	−	3494	124
ever	Adv	486	+	4045	197		enough	Adv	451	+	3483	191
section	NoC	39	−	4036	238		approach	NoC	27	−	3483	190
June	NoP	20	−	4022	191		member	NoC	42	−	3482	222
president	NoC	28	−	4013	212		1987	Num	2	−	3475	119
doctor	NoC	255	+	4005	66		hesitated	Verb	73	+	3474	2
nice	Adj	202	+	3972	41		staff	NoC	71	−	3470	279
across	Prep	434	+	3969	167		light	NoC	317	+	3459	109
opened	Verb	285	+	3966	82		described	Verb	30	−	3457	196
throat	NoC	122	+	3946	11		wait	Verb	192	+	3451	43
action	NoC	62	−	3935	281		evidence	NoC	68	−	3440	272
tears	NoC	148	+	3928	20		Rose	NoP	108	+	3436	10
kissed	Verb	86	+	3924	2		picked	Verb	171	+	3428	35
coming	Verb	319	+	3917	101		7	Num	11	−	3425	147
levels	NoC	10	−	3915	160		rights	NoC	20	−	3416	170
software	NoC	2	−	3904	129		example	NoC	16	−	3414	160
muttered	Verb	79	+	3899	1		noticed	Verb	154	+	3412	27
recent	Adj	29	−	3898	210		type	NoC	39	−	3408	212
caught	Verb	230	+	3890	55		resources	NoC	8	−	3408	137
current	Adj	16	−	3885	175		follows	Verb	8	−	3403	137
lay	Verb	244	+	3867	62		thinking	Verb	204	+	3392	50
pushed	Verb	162	+	3859	26		control	NoC	85	−	3392	301
department	NoC	37	−	3858	226		Mr.	NoC	32	−	3392	198
language	NoC	44	−	3855	241		factors	NoC	3	−	3392	117
hell	NoC	146	+	3818	21		love	Verb	202	+	3389	49
dead	Adj	276	+	3814	80		Soviet	Adj	12	−	3385	147
association	NoC	9	−	3813	153		both	Adv	185	−	3384	466
happened	Verb	296	+	3811	90		1986	Num	1	−	3381	111
significant	Adj	12	−	3808	161		remember	Verb	318	+	3376	112
gaze	NoC	96	+	3807	5		required	Verb	29	−	3367	191
particular	Adj	58	−	3804	268		silent	Adj	131	+	3363	19
let's	Verb	148	+	3788	22		legs	NoC	178	+	3360	38
practice	NoC	36	−	3780	222		Corbett	NoP	74	+	3356	2
legal	Adj	17	−	3770	174		darkness	NoC	122	+	3345	16
power	NoC	129	−	3768	394		down	Prep	217	+	3344	57
standing	Verb	198	+	3767	42		capital	NoC	22	−	3340	172
A / a	Lett	73	−	3760	296		different	Adj	239	−	3337	544
products	NoC	7	−	3711	142		investment	NoC	11	−	3325	142
before	Adv	294	+	3710	91		price	NoC	40	−	3320	211
began	Verb	482	+	3682	205		feeling	Verb	165	+	3320	33
students	NoC	25	−	3679	192		likely	Adj	78	−	3315	286
United	NoP-	11	−	3663	153		theory	NoC	23	−	3309	173

Word	PoS	Frlm		LL	Frln		Word	PoS	Frlm		LL	Frln
included	Verb	19	–	3296	163		model	NoC	26	–	3039	170
environmental	Adj	2	–	3295	111		snapped	Verb	81	+	3027	5
at last	Adv	142	+	3288	24		common	Adj	56	–	3025	232
scheme	NoC	15	–	3283	152		rather than	Prep	45	–	3022	211
Robyn	NoP	63	+	3281	1		treatment	NoC	22	–	3011	161
employment	NoC	10	–	3275	138		a bit	Adv	185	+	3011	46
case	NoC	220	–	3270	513		effective	Adj	11	–	3006	132
while	NoC	164	+	3256	33		in terms of	Prep	7	–	3003	120
pale	Adj	122	+	3256	16		relations	NoC	18	–	2995	150
Lily	NoP	69	+	3253	2		beneath	Prep	147	+	2993	29
foreign	Adj	41	–	3252	212		grey	Adj	142	+	2992	27
date	NoC	36	–	3251	201		developed	Verb	16	–	2989	145
agreement	NoC	24	–	3246	174		history	NoC	63	–	2986	245
policies	NoC	3	–	3245	115		Rachel	NoP	88	+	2984	7
team	NoC	53	–	3242	235		provision	NoC	5	–	2977	114
shut	Verb	125	+	3228	18		lifted	Verb	125	+	2976	20
moved	Verb	308	+	3226	109		prices	NoC	11	–	2976	131
activities	NoC	16	–	3223	154		context	NoC	5	–	2966	114
darling	NoC	78	+	3222	4		C / c	Lett	10	–	2966	129
gently	Adv	134	+	3216	21		perhaps	Adv	561	+	2963	282
commission	NoC	10	–	3206	136		basic	Adj	15	–	2963	142
talking	Verb	219	+	3198	60		region	NoC	9	–	2960	124
so	Conj	437	+	3193	190		empty	Adj	152	+	2959	32
table	NoC	390	+	3183	160		design	NoC	21	–	2959	157
published	Verb	9	–	3173	133		majority	NoC	11	–	2956	130
Carrie	NoP	62	+	3157	1		stepped	Verb	105	+	2952	13
trying	Verb	336	+	3154	128		EC	NoP	1	–	2944	94
in front of	Prep	172	+	3143	38		past	Prep	149	+	2943	30
provides	Verb	4	–	3142	114		more	Adv	954	–	2940	1453
according to	Prep	40	–	3140	205		25	Num	4	–	2921	107
leave	Verb	340	+	3135	130		Athelstan	NoP	51	+	2916	0
greater	Adj	30	–	3134	183		early	Adjᶜ	113	–	2914	327
often	Adv	187	+	3131	21		October	NoP	15	–	2912	140
sector	NoC	4	–	3131	113		forces	NoC	20	–	2906	152
way	NoC	1293	+	3131	829		glad	Adj	120	+	2905	19
uncle	NoC	117	+	3119	16		Alice	NoP	93	+	2904	9
effects	NoC	14	–	3115	143		might	VMod	878	+	2901	518
evening	NoC	293	+	3114	103		quite	Adv	556	+	2897	281
11	Num	8	–	3111	127		January	NoP	13	–	2896	133
such	DetP	511	–	3105	906		parliament	NoC	11	–	2896	128
series	NoC	33	–	3101	188		slid	Verb	71	+	2893	3
terms	NoC	43	–	3095	210		species	NoC	12	–	2886	130
primary	Adj	5	–	3092	115		loved	Verb	138	+	2876	26
second	Ord	169	–	3089	426		December	NoP	10	–	2870	124
sir	NoC	368	+	3088	149		election	NoC	11	–	2865	128
16	Num	4	–	3087	112		Kate	NoP	89	+	2862	8
cheeks	NoC	74	+	3079	3		cheek	NoC	78	+	2862	5
where	Adv	823	+	3078	468		forms	NoC	12	–	2854	129
1985	Num	2	–	3077	103		class	NoC	55	–	2848	224
cold	Adj	224	+	3076	65		provided	Verb	28	–	2844	169
teachers	NoC	16	–	3072	148		computer	NoC	31	–	2843	174
Isabel	NoP	64	+	3070	1		frowned	Verb	63	+	2836	2
wall	NoC	256	+	3058	83		opposition	NoC	10	–	2823	123
sales	NoC	11	–	3057	134		13	Num	4	–	2819	105
8	Num	11	–	3055	133		main	Adj	99	–	2819	299
18	Num	4	–	3052	112		clothes	NoC	181	+	2818	47
Anna	NoP	102	+	3050	11		activity	NoC	21	–	2818	151
stay	Verb	243	+	3044	76		14	Num	6	–	2817	110
Emily	NoP	82	+	3043	5		voice	Verb	4	–	2811	103
university	NoC	44	–	3042	209		Harry	NoP	137	+	2811	27

List 5.1. Frequency list of common nouns in the whole corpus (by lemma)

(minimum frequency: 10 per million words)

word	freq	word	freq	word	freq	word	freq
time	1833	court	344	lot*	246	care	198
year	1639	effect	336	decision	243	record	197
people	1256	result	334	street	243	manager	197
way	1108	idea	328	patient	242	project	197
man	1003	use	328	industry	242	example	196
day	940	study	327	mind	241	training	194
thing	776	name	326	class	241	window	194
child	710	job	326	church	238	light	191
Mr	673	body	325	condition	237	difference	191
government	670	report	325	paper	237	university	191
work	653	line	323	bank	234	air	191
life	645	law	318	century	233	wife	190
woman	631	face	315	section	232	sir	189
system	619	friend	315	hundred	231	relationship	189
case	613	authority	313	activity	231	quality	188
part	612	road	313	table	231	rule	187
group	607	minister	305	death	230	tax	184
number	606	rate	303	building	229	story	184
world	600	hour	302	sort	229	pound	184
house	598	door	302	sense	229	worker	184
area	585	office	300	staff	227	model	183
company	579	right	299	team	226	data/datum*	183
problem	565	war	297	experience	223	nature	182
service	549	mother	295	student	222	officer	181
place	534	person	290	Mrs	221	structure	181
hand	532	reason	289	language	221	method	180
party	529	view	289	town	221	hospital	180
school	529	term	288	plan	220	bed	180
country	486	period	283	department	219	unit	180
point	484	centre	282	morning	219	movement	179
week	476	society	282	management	219	detail	178
member	471	figure	282	product	217	date	177
end	458	police	278	committee	217	wall	175
state	440	city	275	practice	216	computer	174
word	438	need	273	ground	215	approach	171
family	428	million	272	meeting	215	bit*	171
fact	426	community	272	evidence	215	amount	171
head	402	kind	271	letter	215	award	170
month	398	price	271	foot	214	scheme	170
side	398	control	270	boy	213	president	170
business	394	process	269	game	212	chapter	169
night	393	action	269	back	212	theory	168
eye	392	issue	269	union	211	property	167
home	390	cost	269	food	211	son	166
question	390	position	268	role	210	director	165
information	387	course	267	event	208	leader	165
power	385	minute	266	land	208	south	165
change	384	education	260	art	206	firm	163
per cent	384	type	259	support	204	application	163
interest	376	research	258	voice	203	north	163
development	375	subject	256	stage	203	king	162
money	375	programme	255	teacher	203	secretary	162
book	374	girl	254	range	203	board	162
water	372	moment	254	trade	203	production	162
other	367	father	252	club	202	operation	161
form	365	age	252	arm	202	share	161
room	364	value	250	field	201	chance	161
level	360	force	250	history	201	opportunity	161
car	353	order	250	parent	201	lord	160
council	348	matter	248	account	200	agreement	160
policy	348	act	248	material	199	picture	159
market	346	health	246	situation	198	test	159

contract	159	analysis	143	task	129	help	110
thousand	158	thought	142	function	129	sector	110
security	158	region	141	provision	129	oil	110
source	157	relation	140	county	129	circumstance	110
election	157	set	140	sound	129	client	110
future	156	statement	140	behaviour	128	direction	109
colour	156	space	140	east	128	seat	109
site	155	list	140	defence	128	attack	109
shop	154	attention	140	resource	128	attitude	108
loss	154	labour*	139	floor	127	disease	107
animal	153	demand	139	west	127	employment	107
evening	153	step	139	science	127	goal	107
heart	152	principle	139	style	127	sign	106
standard	152	sea	139	college	126	appeal	106
purpose	152	player	138	horse	126	affair	106
benefit	152	couple	138	response	126	technique	105
page	151	hotel	138	skill	126	show	105
music	150	choice	138	hall	126	campaign	105
hair	150	capital	138	feeling	126	item	105
doctor	150	station	137	user	125	medium	105
love	150	village	137	character	125	holiday	105
factor	150	film	136	army	124	version	105
pattern	149	association	135	dog	124	ability	105
charge	149	attempt	135	investment	124	fish	105
basis	148	income	135	Dr	124	pupil	105
p	148	individual	135	look	124	advice	104
piece	148	feature	135	answer	124	press	104
design	148	cup	134	economy	124	sales	104
tree	147	organisation	134	brother	123	library	104
population	147	effort	134	husband	123	drug	104
plant	146	technology	133	argument	122	visit	104
performance	146	machine	132	responsibility	122	surface	103
pressure	146	difficulty	132	season	122	advantage	103
knowledge	146	cell	131	concern	121	memory	102
news	145	energy	131	bill	121	variety	102
fire	145	treatment	131	glass	120	return	102
environment	144	degree	131	element	120	culture	102
garden	144	growth	131	duty	119	island	102
size	144	lady	130	increase	119	blood	102
series	144	mile	130	claim	118	television	102
success	143	top	129	leg	118	majority	101
rest	143	risk	129	title	118	speaker	101
				park	118	goods	101
				fund	118	competition	101
				one	118	talk	101
				note	117	parliament	101
				discussion	116	bar	101
				chairman	116	extent	101
				aspect	116	no	100
				summer	116	access	100
				sun	115	star	100
				daughter	115	text	100
				baby	115	deal	100
				institution	114	mouth	99
				box	114	trouble	99
				customer	114	payment	99
				river	114	cause	99
				profit	113	base	98
				conference	112	reference	98
				stone	112	context	98
				division	112	second	98
				measure	112	survey	98
				procedure	111	facility	98
				post	111	object	97
				proposal	111	chair	97
				commission	111	importance	97
				image	110	article	97

Sports

Frequency of mention in the BNC confirms that football is Britain's favourite sport: often called the 'national sport' in spite of disappointing international performances. The most frequent sporting nouns are:

football	67	*fishing*	32
cricket	34	*hunting*	32
golf	34	*swimming*	18
rugby	29	*boxing*	12
tennis	28	*shooting*	12
soccer	13	*sailing*	9

Note that many of these terms are somewhat ambiguous, and do not have 100% sporting reference. This is especially true of the *-ing* terms on the right, which often have other uses. To limit this distorting factor, however, the frequencies are given for the use of each term as a **noun** only.

earth	97	partner	88	adult	79	visitor	70
card	96	Christmas	88	consequence	79	drink	70
collection	96	tea	88	proportion	78	commitment	70
planning	96	failure	88	speed	78	legislation	70
public	96	shoulder	88	assessment	78	volume	70
species	96	hill	88	consideration	78	smile	69
communication	96	band	88	fig*	78	entry	69
agency	96	reader	88	beginning	78	yard	69
means	96	expression	88	route	78	stuff	69
possibility	96	sale	88	understanding	77	introduction	69
sister	95	status	88	impact	77	background	69
document	95	owner	87	credit	77	cabinet	69
supply	95	trust	87	track	76	engine	69
budget	94	truth	87	danger	76	administration	69
solution	94	turn	87	progress	76	victim	69
influence	94	marriage	87	reaction	76	author	69
software	94	farm	86	path	76	manner	69
weight	94	sentence	86	half	76	bus	68
career	94	past	86	video	76	song	68
organization	93	start	86	flower	76	investigation	68
fear	93	safety	86	distance	75	relief	68
opinion	93	file	86	skin	75	wage	68
damage	93	trial	86	belief	75	row	68
rock	93	newspaper	86	comment	75	regulation	68
requirement	93	league	85	content	75	mountain	68
district	93	balance	85	bag	75	coffee	68
bird	93	copy	85	conclusion	75	tradition	67
quarter	92	wind	85	aim	75	tour	67
stock	92	nation	85	link	75	football	67
exchange	92	branch	85	justice	75	interview	67
opposition	92	length	85	gold	75	wood	67
miss*	92	front	84	politics	75	exhibition	67
edge	92	doubt	84	dad	74	category	67
option	92	train	84	estate	74	traffic	67
whole	92	move	84	sight	74	dinner	67
call	92	pain	84	winter	74	consumer	67
network	91	studio	84	boat	74	meal	67
railway	91	accident	84	prison	74	construction	66
occasion	91	spirit	84	wine	74	bridge	66
aid	91	official	83	reality	74	gentleman	66
match	91	contact	83	weekend	73	description	66
executive	91	strength	83	writer	73	TV	66
concept	91	transport	82	clothes	73	lip	66
radio	91	works	82	vehicle	73	housing	66
target	91	gas	82	debt	73	improvement	66
arrangement	91	contribution	82	objective	73	existence	66
lack	90	museum	82	offer	73	appearance	66
corner	90	cash	82	employer	73	flat	66
race	90	reform	82	colleague	72	discipline	66
forest	90	shape	82	battle	72	sheet	66
sex	90	debate	82	hole	72	session	66
mum	90	pair	81	expert	72	contrast	66
finger	90	protection	81	farmer	72	distribution	66
equipment	89	English	81	package	72	loan	65
ball	89	artist	81	injury	72	representative	65
crime	89	presence	81	telephone	72	conversation	65
message	89	agent	81	sample	71	prince	65
afternoon	89	rise	81	key	71	audience	65
employee	89	meaning	80	painting	71	crisis	65
review	89	master	80	insurance	71	theatre	65
scale	89	hope	80	confidence	71	code	65
strategy	89	driver	80	phone	71	respect	64
scene	89	candidate	80	generation	71	unemployment	64
peace	89	vote	80	threat	70	freedom	64
kitchen	89	queen	80	judge	70	plate	64
sport	89	play	79	conflict	70	magazine	64
speech	89	exercise	79	ship	70	explanation	64

5.1–10

Word	Freq	Word	Freq	Word	Freq	Word	Freq
flight	64	fee	58	troop	54	defendant	49
rain	64	republic	58	faith	54	mass	49
pension	64	waste	58	soldier	54	fashion	49
asset	64	solicitor	58	spot	54	championship	49
writing	64	desire	58	lane	53	distinction	49
limit	64	weather	58	crown	53	enemy	49
youth	63	component	58	coal	53	leadership	49
dream	63	lunch	58	castle	53	desk	49
challenge	63	institute	58	membership	53	panel	49
while	63	photograph	58	revenue	53	tear	49
spring	63	expenditure	57	flow	53	dress	48
capacity	63	silence	57	mistake	53	negotiation	48
factory	63	household	57	total	53	establishment	48
victory	63	block	57	breath	53	liability	48
selection	63	brain	57	release	53	iron	48
finance	63	publication	57	motion	53	roof	48
intention	62	program	57	Corp	53	welfare	48
examination	62	guest	57	variation	53	fan	48
egg	62	treaty	57	literature	53	advance	48
thanks	62	nurse	57	wing	53	milk	48
aircraft	62	screen	57	alternative	53	drawing	48
decade	62	guide	57	criterion	52	ticket	48
output	62	experiment	57	ring	52	motor	48
mark	62	map	56	incident	52	soil	48
notice	62	sequence	56	index	52	shoe	48
definition	62	crowd	56	suggestion	52	engineer	48
reduction	61	captain	56	winner	52	beach	48
will	61	metal	56	border	52	nose	48
offence	61	trip	56	pocket	52	tank	48
tape	60	pool	56	valley	52	servant	48
run	60	phase	56	passage	52	potential	48
address	60	sky	56	religion	51	origin	48
neck	60	cover	56	leaf	51	vision	47
murder	60	connection	56	square	51	palace	47
bottom	60	violence	56	pub	51	height	47
appointment	60	scientist	56	surprise	51	expense	47
concentration	60	sum	56	characteristic	51	trend	47
pp	60	search	56	lake	51	editor	47
kid	60	noise	56	fruit	51	general	47
bedroom	60	assumption	56	request	51	warning	47
enterprise	60	curriculum	56	restaurant	51	chief	47
middle	60	congress	56	foundation	51	significance	47
weapon	60	initiative	56	tone	51	cancer	47
error	59	journey	56	engineering	51	citizen	47
absence	59	ministry	55	device	51	convention	47
birth	59	cat	55	billion	51	bone	47
bottle	59	heat	55	walk	51	fuel	47
criticism	59	instrument	55	specialist	51	round	47
acid	59	location	55	deputy	51	champion	47
transfer	59	display	55	representation	51	gift	47
module	59	gate	55	observation	50	prisoner	47
assembly	59	theme	55	shot	50	cross	46
ear	59	gun	55	circle	50	living	46
instruction	59	gallery	55	present	50	achievement	46
teaching	59	reading	55	fall	50	signal	46
settlement	59	professor	55	strike	50	outcome	46
store	59	emphasis	55	creation	50	knee	46
wave	59	learning	54	chain	50	rail	46
MP	58	opening	54	marketing	49	comparison	46
pleasure	58	interpretation	54	god	49	notion	46
implication	58	combination	54	mechanism	49	expectation	46
channel	58	tooth	54	impression	49	lawyer	46
lead*	58	hell	54	clause	49	lesson	46
grant	58	prospect	54	coast	49	democracy	46
temperature	58	priority	54	atmosphere	49	working	46
cut	58	tool	54	neighbour	49	CO / Co	46
recognition	58	drive	54	revolution	49	diet	46

being	46	stress	42	green	39	tendency	36
parish	46	spokesman	42	bomb	39	final	36
passenger	45	coat	42	recession	39	estimate	36
root	45	premise	42	recovery	39	shirt	36
manufacturer	45	prize	42	plaintiff	39	chip	36
complaint	45	manufacturing	42	layer	39	deposit	36
shadow	45	extension	42	trading	39	chamber	36
territory	45	constitution	42	agriculture	39	cigarette	36
touch	45	partnership	42	purchase	39	researcher	36
tenant	45	pollution	42	average	39	intervention	36
plastic	45	gene	42	empire	39	qualification	36
councillor	45	mill	42	shareholder	39	reply	36
m	45	wheel	41	camera	39	guy	36
inflation	45	string	41	silver	39	core	36
gap	45	depth	41	inspector	39	frequency	36
plane	45	delivery	41	critic	39	gain	36
corporation	45	obligation	41	judgment	38	rent	36
breakfast	45	regime	41	wealth	38	honour	36
shock	45	decline	41	presentation	38	dozen	36
pay	45	framework	41	muscle	38	relative	36
score	45	protein	41	soul	38	jacket	36
grass	45	frame	41	arrival	38	awareness	36
independence	45	command	41	penalty	38	secret	36
charity	45	inch	41	electricity	38	festival	36
column	45	female	41	illness	38	phenomenon	36
finding	45	holder	41	self	38	furniture	35
beauty	44	German	41	bread	38	intelligence	35
boundary	44	advertising	41	resistance	38	recording	35
database	44	saving	41	cake	38	investor	35
ref	44	poem	41	perspective	38	dealer	35
formation	44	ice	41	meat	38	mixture	35
supporter	44	port	41	beer	38	co-operation	35
accommodation	44	rose	41	peak	38	cheek	35
transaction	44	boot	41	efficiency	38	equation	35
politician	44	approval	40	sugar	38	substance	35
male	44	boss	40	steel	38	duke	35
exception	44	load	40	uncle	38	discovery	35
struggle	44	setting	40	drama	38	dance	35
resident	44	bishop	40	laboratory	38	throat	35
identity	44	cottage	40	promotion	37	routine	35
inquiry	44	cycle	40	chancellor	37	apple	35
licence	44	governor	40	lifespan	37	tourist	35
topic	44	stairs	40	certificate	37	landlord	35
resolution	44	crew	40	possession	37	instance	35
buyer	44	maintenance	40	custom	37	retirement	35
dispute	44	chest	40	coach	37	lad	35
assistance	43	travel	40	philosophy	37	American	35
novel	43	protest	40	zone	37	French	35
preparation	43	restriction	40	cloud	37	breach	35
proceeding	43	hat	40	angle	37	emotion	35
metre	43	profession	40	symptom	37	pipe	35
phrase	43	mode	40	alliance	37	promise	35
mirror	43	export	40	dollar	37	scope	35
camp	43	funding	40	mood	37	birthday	34
emergency	43	recommendation	40	abuse	37	left	34
currency	43	input	39	variable	37	pace	34
break	43	habit	39	PC	37	golf	34
thinking	43	sleep	39	bay	37	sand	34
tension	43	guard	39	ratio	37	enquiry	34
quantity	43	reputation	39	spending	37	infection	34
taste	43	countryside	39	personality	37	fun	34
fault	43	creature	39	bid	37	mortgage	34
minority	43	suit	39	expansion	37	consent	34
pilot	43	autumn	39	producer	37	guitar	34
Unix	42	poll	39	actor	36	entrance	34
tower	42	focus	39	wedding	36	hero	34
involvement	42	landscape	39	bond	36	curtain	34

darkness	34	luck	32	vessel	29	composition	27
allowance	34	occupation	32	breast	29	acceptance	27
hearing	34	percentage	32	lover	29	limitation	27
disk	34	consultant	32	tunnel	29	pride	27
medicine	34	lecture	32	poetry	29	storm	27
paragraph	34	watch	32	replacement	29	discourse	27
rank	34	anxiety	32	turnover	29	participation	27
shift	34	remark	32	salary	29	ceiling	27
judgement	34	supplier	32	percent	29	weakness	27
journal	34	poet	32	wire	29	architect	27
permission	34	net	31	proof	29	universe	27
DNA	34	preference	31	pot	29	detective	27
anger	34	stomach	31	drop	29	departure	27
interaction	34	ownership	31	consultation	29	cathedral	27
fight	34	indication	31	win	29	excitement	27
tale	34	tip	31	import	29	red	27
witness	34	prayer	31	admission	29	summit	27
stream	34	poverty	31	determination	29	transition	27
cricket	34	mine	31	strain	29	check	27
platform	34	observer	31	tissue	29	deficit	27
policeman	34	dark	31	label	29	venture	27
disaster	34	fortune	31	leisure	29	constituency	27
carpet	34	opponent	31	economics	29	register	27
knife	34	crop	31	cheque	29	assistant	27
print	34	practitioner	31	merchant	29	joy	27
mail	34	symbol	31	squad	29	local	27
curve	34	hold	31	stake	29	black	27
reserve	34	moon	31	smoke	29	pit	27
delay	33	alcohol	31	unity	29	belt	27
province	33	snow	31	designer	29	gesture	27
peasant	33	climate	31	shopping	29	treasury	27
perception	33	measurement	31	fabric	29	stick	26
cream	33	heaven	31	steam	29	concert	26
airport	33	operating	31	rugby	29	cap	26
personnel	33	conservative*	31	childhood	29	mummy	26
defeat	33	barrier	31	comfort	28	expertise	26
bath	33	smell	31	magistrate	28	canal	26
acquisition	33	pitch	31	bathroom	28	margin	26
salt	33	catalogue	30	movie	28	psychology	26
clock	33	princess	30	participant	28	leather	26
demonstration	33	sheep	30	corridor	28	album	26
sake	33	enthusiasm	30	profile	28	repair	26
aunt	33	operator	30	complex	28	uncertainty	26
chemical	33	summary	30	lift	28	chart	26
human	33	interval	30	surgery	28	dust	26
host	33	implementation	30	conviction	28	tin	26
adviser	33	wish	30	tongue	28	shelf	26
joke	33	evaluation	30	addition	28	glance	26
edition	33	architecture	30	tennis	28	passion	26
priest	33	processing	30	reward	28	bench	26
circuit	33	burden	30	standing	28	pole/Pole	26
consumption	33	confusion	30	draft	28	stand	26
pack	32	publisher	30	brick	28	consciousness	26
formula	32	professional	30	amendment	28	coin	26
count	32	democrat	30	mouse	28	ban	26
journalist	32	historian	30	vegetable	28	ward	26
guidance	32	schedule	30	sergeant	28	opera	26
workshop	32	cheese	30	mystery	28	cow	26
tail	32	dimension	30	imagination	28	coalition	26
compensation	32	talent	30	favour	28	trousers	26
seed	32	tube	30	bell	28	constraint	26
statistics	32	storage	30	classroom	28	objection	26
earnings	32	bowl	30	grade	28	guideline	26
fishing	32	satisfaction	30	announcement	28	prosecution	26
mission	32	dish	30	headquarters	28	assault	26
survival	32	shell	30	refugee	28	timber	26
tie	32	conduct	29	twin	27	virtue	26

clerk	26	junction	24	stranger	23	rope	22
folk	26	terrace	24	mortality	23	miner	22
cattle	26	earl	24	invitation	23	angel	22
fellow	26	commander	24	calculation	23	stability	22
horror	26	slope	24	withdrawal	23	publishing	22
paint	26	friendship	24	roll	23	lamp	22
guardian	26	blow	24	mayor	23	illustration	21
infant	26	lock	24	chapel	23	gaze	21
button	26	ally	24	mineral	23	anniversary	21
reception	26	stop	24	youngster	23	go	21
grammar	26	carriage	24	trick	23	shortage	21
diary	26	purchaser	24	humour	23	clothing	21
flesh	25	resignation	24	rubbish	23	delight	21
lease	25	conversion	24	interface	23	monopoly	21
privilege	25	chocolate	24	federation	23	Tory	21
conservation	25	essay	24	bike	23	worth	21
charter	25	sympathy	24	collapse	23	wound	21
publicity	25	maker	24	cotton	23	tribunal	21
specimen	25	discount	24	crash	23	lion	21
format	25	attraction	24	cry	23	allegation	21
nerve	25	silk	24	suspicion	23	merger	21
completion	25	seller	24	entertainment	23	jurisdiction	21
potato	25	audit	24	voter	23	controversy	21
craft	25	vendor	24	molecule	23	desert	21
reflection	25	garage	24	dictionary	22	fat	21
closure	25	borough	24	complexity	22	insect	21
punishment	25	petrol	24	fence	22	episode	21
agenda	25	emperor	24	fragment	22	Christian	21
chicken	25	disc	24	Jew	22	fleet	21
portrait	25	registration	24	constable	22	adjustment	21
printer	25	strip	24	coverage	22	colony	21
taxation	25	wonder	24	competitor	22	gear	21
companion	25	depression	24	laughter	22	minimum	21
evolution	25	destruction	24	equity	22	raid	21
carbon	25	commissioner	24	clinic	22	nursery	21
traveller	25	assurance	24	kit	22	butter	21
patch	25	plot	24	equivalent	22	celebration	21
accounting	25	organ	24	daddy	22	piano	21
volunteer	25	particle	24	interior	22	fiction	21
jury	25	favourite	24	guarantee	22	white	21
blue	25	remedy	24	cinema	22	escape	21
ocean	25	conception	23	isle	22	specification	21
pig	25	ambition	23	pond	22	banking	21
rabbit	25	stimulus	23	accountant	22	bible	21
pen	25	grain	23	insight	22	tournament	21
ideology	25	harm	23	disability	22	rhythm	21
VAT/vat	25	pop	23	era	22	therapy	21
van	25	needle	23	lie	22	brand	21
kingdom	25	logic	23	arrest	22	photo	21
disorder	25	fibre	23	statute	22	emission	21
cold	25	resort	23	advertisement	22	hardware	21
good	25	darling	23	ceremony	22	navy	21
alarm	25	incentive	23	tonne	22	effectiveness	21
funeral	25	inspection	23	farming	22	temple	21
rival	25	excuse	23	domain	22	invasion	21
dividend	25	fate	23	removal	22	crystal	21
cousin	25	disposal	23	processor	22	motive	21
cable	25	declaration	23	taxi	22	transformation	21
mate	25	allocation	23	explosion	22	fighting	21
innovation	24	dose	23	leave	22	villa	21
applicant	24	flame	23	acre	22	trustee	21
machinery	24	pile	23	tide	22	grip	21
integration	24	correspondent	23	running	22	toy	21
planet	24	identification	23	server	22	myth	21
rat	24	directive	23	cm	22	battery	21
exposure	24	shade	23	cloth	22	mess	21
pass	24	hypothesis	23	satellite	22	necessity	21

switch	21	productivity	20	sculpture	19	riot	18		
rebel	21	pensioner	20	midnight	19	liberation	18		
bulk	21	mud	20	pet	19	nest	18		
menu	20	businessman	20	grave	19	tutor	18		
warmth	20	refusal	20	shower	19	trainer	18		
adventure	20	essence	20	speculation	19	pause	18		
gang	20	indicator	20	isolation	19	lung	18		
discrimination	20	verse	20	residence	19	instinct	18		
skirt	20	triumph	20	fantasy	19	teenager	18		
toilet	20	counter	20	bureau	19	trader	18		
graphics	20	apartment	19	recipe	19	radiation	18		
lorry	20	probability	19	modification	19	spell	18		
chemistry	20	separation	19	stance	19	sphere	18		
disadvantage	20	capitalism	19	norm	19	swimming	18		
flag	20	portfolio	19	installation	19	eagle	18		
proposition	20	juice	19	rod	19	plc	18		
singer	20	stroke	19	heading	19	guilt	18		
ghost	20	cupboard	19	crack	19	panic	18		
uniform	20	seminar	19	truck	19	tune	18		
pope	20	developer	19	hip	19	divorce	18		
gender	20	continent	19	polytechnic	19	bean	18		
doctrine	20	availability	19	physics	19	bonus	18		
compound	20	whisky	19	dialogue	19	coup	18		
widow	20	computing	19	diagnosis	19	incidence	18		
restoration	20	trace	19	laugh	19	spread	18		
clue	20	bastard	19	accent	19	subsidiary	18		
loyalty	20	premium	19	sin	19	nightmare	18		
cliff	20	forum	19	musician	19	packet	18		
landing	20	justification	19	directory	19	scandal	18		
ride	20	kiss	19	offender	19	Easter	18		
shore	20	lifetime	19	breed	19	motivation	18		
heating	20	reporter	19	sandwich	19	Christianity	18		
colonel	20	graduate	19	defender	19	redundancy	18		
rumour	20	carrier	19	killer	19	assignment	18		
chap	20	breeding	19	collector	19	auditor	18		
tragedy	20	oak	19	envelope	19	commonwealth	18		
leaflet	20	palm	19	subsidy	18	mm	18		
launch	20	builder	19	inn	18	pity	18		
dock	20	discretion	19	ambulance	18	correlation	18		
virus	20	oxygen	19	timing	18	photographer	17		
harbour	20	shame	19	pavement	18	brush	17		
ease	20	classification	19	tactic	18	engagement	17		
wildlife	20	worry	19	ingredient	18	pint	17		
rape	20	fluid	19	scholar	18	translation	17		
airline	20	duration	19	holding	18	rider	17		
testing	20	courage	19	reign	18	GP	17		
nail	20	suicide	19	glory	18	jaw	17		
heel	20	missile	19	finish	18	lighting	17		
devil	20	fool	19	tray	18	flavour	17		
outline	20	analyst	19	thesis	18	striker	17		
theft	20	delegate	19	delegation	18	casualty	17		
flexibility	20	avenue	19	autonomy	18	intensity	17		
hierarchy	20	succession	19	basket	18	remainder	17		
heritage	20	fraud	19	bear	18	constituent	17		
abbey	20	copper	19	Ms	18	liver	17		
champagne	20	density	19	hunting	18	trap	17		
filter	20	receipt	19	entity	18	parameter	17		
successor	20	merit	19	consensus	18	limb	17		
painter	20	sensation	19	horizon	18	fighter	17		
attendance	20	compromise	19	jet	18	carer	17		
receiver	20	doorway	19	clash	18	contest	17		
mathematics	20	duck	19	pregnancy	18	organiser	17		
sociology	20	shit	19	organism	18	rating	17		
hint	20	appendix	19	concession	18	disappointment	17		
fraction	20	sword	19	wool	18	accuracy	17		
spectrum	20	liberty	19	diagram	18	regard	17		
creditor	20	AIDS	19	capability	18	thief	17		

counterpart	17	nonsense	16	flood	16	charm	15
venue	17	pursuit	16	grandfather	16	wisdom	15
rescue	17	reservation	16	rice	16	bureaucracy	15
supervision	17	yield	16	container	16	handling	15
boom	17	dear	16	founder	16	grandmother	15
happiness	17	plain	16	saint	16	vol	15
monster	17	sauce	16	adoption	16	log	15
beam	17	dining	16	correspondence	16	lounge	15
bush	17	giant	16	ruler	16	pan	15
walking	17	bloke	16	Greek	16	segment	15
sensitivity	17	elite*	16	hedge	16	moor	15
ideal	17	chaos	16	undertaking	16	seal	15
orchestra	17	inhabitant	16	barn	16	abortion	15
diamond	17	criminal	16	exam	16	commodity	15
hostility	17	handle	16	stretch	16	beef	15
pardon	17	dot	16	utility	16	distress	15
tribute	17	sterling	16	lap	16	wrist	15
relevance	17	fly	16	rally	16	disturbance	15
questionnaire	17	arrow	16	Scot	16	ad	15
kick	17	collar	16	prey	16	regiment	15
similarity	17	sleeve	16	shelter	16	runner	15
blanket	17	mention	16	fitness	16	plea	15
archbishop	17	competence	16	oven	16	encouragement	15
terminal	17	respondent	16	electron	16	hook	15
matrix	17	reach	16	tent	16	lump	15
hit	17	coffin	16	prejudice	16	destination	15
neighbourhood	17	biscuit	16	prediction	16	pulse	15
republican	17	keeper	16	comedy	16	goodness	15
starting	17	elbow	16	ac	16	tobacco	15
execution	17	predecessor	16	ladder	16	Italian	15
toe	17	supermarket	16	antibody	16	catholic	15
cab	17	breakdown	16	submission	16	custody	15
north-east	17	grace	16	helicopter	16	km	15
try	17	transmission	16	marble	16	extract	15
socialism	17	sanction	16	pH	16	composer	15
ridge	17	cave	16	washing	16	drinking	15
forecast	17	affection	16	equality	16	voting	15
bronze	17	hut	16	cutting	16	supplement	15
clay	17	virgin	16	drum	16	rejection	15
monitoring	17	commerce	16	workstation	16	basin	15
memorial	17	stitch	16	tile	15	encounter	15
slave	17	broadcasting	16	referendum	15	soap	15
deck	17	tumour	16	mask	15	imprisonment	15
surgeon	17	verdict	16	Roman	15	integrity	15
frustration	17	dolphin	16	circulation	15	magic	15
maximum	17	miracle	16	thigh	15	contradiction	15
stamp	17	Russian	16	nut	15	swing	15
faculty	17	atom	16	embassy	15	tomato	15
equilibrium	17	mix	16	draw	15	electronics	15
legend	17	tap	16	vein	15	handful	15
orange	17	pie	16	terrorist	15	Gen	15
geography	17	evil	16	prevention	15	straw	15
exploration	17	script	16	suite	15	slide	15
poster	17	drawer	16	portion	15	banker	15
ton	17	trophy	16	hazard	15	administrator	15
dismissal	17	economist	16	suspension	15	ankle	15
blade	17	fist	16	signature	15	manual	15
exclusion	17	contractor	16	petition	15	dawn	15
chin	16	workforce	16	European	15	restraint	15
killing	16	cooking	16	liquid	15	penny	15
horn	16	classic	16	St	15	ulcer	15
owl	16	recruitment	16	alteration	15	soup	15
debut	16	lamb	16	defect	15	quid	15
terror	16	candle	16	certainty	15	handicap	15
current	16	shield	16	pump	15	cluster	15
medal	16	supper	16	odds	15	trail	15
echo	16	brass	16	desktop	15	mining	15

ballet	15	pin	14	popularity	14	caravan	13
expedition	15	thumb	14	monument	13	feedback	13
mobility	15	quota	14	inside	13	intent	13
elephant	15	obstacle	14	viewer	13	jeans	13
auction	15	dioxide	14	Indian	13	reproduction	13
academy	15	headline	14	behalf	13	salmon	13
waist	15	ambassador	14	steward	13	activist	13
manor	15	glove	14	make-up	13	grid	13
conscience	15	parallel	14	enforcement	13	praise	13
powder	15	beat	14	temper	13	mist	13
spine	15	collaboration	14	offering	13	gravel	13
bowel	15	bacterium	14	gospel	13	garment	13
inequality	15	bucket	14	double	13	exemption	13
parking	15	outlet	14	donation	13	towel	13
slice	15	protocol	14	whale	13	cabin	13
remains	15	psychologist	14	10%	13	rage	13
can	15	manufacture	14	harmony	13	sink	13
takeover	15	meantime	14	privatisation	13	textile	13
tourism	15	stem	14	predator	13	south-east	13
fortnight	15	tyre	14	cage	13	fitting	13
corruption	15	librarian	14	appreciation	13	ozone	13
squadron	15	substitute	14	gardener	13	printing	13
single	15	covenant	14	telecommunication	13	lace	13
grief	15	dilemma	14	sufferer	13	reactor	13
loch	15	injection	14	counselling	13	dependence	13
breeze	15	canvas	14	configuration	13	ft	13
maturity	15	girlfriend	14	contrary	13	trainee	13
strand	14	verb	14	patent	13	deed	13
valuation	14	bunch	14	archive	13	contempt	13
referee	14	kilometre	14	misery	13	vocabulary	13
ritual	14	bias	14	fox	13	membrane	13
faction	14	layout	14	learner	13	shooting	13
fare	14	forehead	14	ash	13	arch	13
stall	14	warehouse	14	pence	13	negligence	13
well	14	dealing	14	caution	13	erosion	13
interference	14	ranger	14	probe	13	ruling	13
salad	14	march	14	brochure	13	promoter	13
rush	14	skull	14	serum	13	down	13
diesel	14	bow	14	peer	13	lab	13
barrel	14	manuscript	14	tiger	13	mistress	13
treasure	14	continuity	14	soccer	13	surplus	13
revelation	14	embarrassment	14	despair	13	tablet	13
yacht	14	IT	14	borrowing	13	throne	13
taxpayer	14	decoration	14	stay	13	brigade	13
making	14	CD	14	lordship	13	ace	13
migration	14	frontier	14	outsider	13	quarry	13
fossil	14	eyebrow	14	dignity	13	aspiration	13
statue	14	revision	14	£100	13	inheritance	13
suffering	14	retailer	14	woodland	13	laser	13
ferry	14	timetable	14	calendar	13	aggression	13
booking	14	diameter	14	loop	13	feather	13
lecturer	14	lid	14	realm	13	eating	13
motorway	14	validity	14	invention	13	testament	13
dancer	14	lifestyle	14	sunshine	13	relaxation	13
habitat	14	driving	14	senate	13	bullet	13
joint	14	occurrence	14	usage	13	guerrilla	13
£1	14	tribe	14	width	13	shaft	13
pencil	14	worship	14	boyfriend	13	array	13
discharge	14	clergy	14	nursing	13	jewellery	13
graph	14	beast	14	node	13	attribute	13
rug	14	dwelling	14	vitamin	13	dragon	13
inspiration	14	commentator	14	exploitation	13	sunlight	13
highway	14	shed	14	utterance	13	cylinder	13
diversity	14	wicket	14	actress	13	motif	13
decision-making	14	heir	14	syndrome	13	reminder	13
sexuality	14	lemon	14	compliance	13	tel	13
lawn	14	excess	14	communist	13	calcium	13

monk	13	sovereignty	12	costume	12	pylorus	11
ancestor	13	bargain	12	pact	12	sacrifice	11
bat	13	backing	12	provider	12	placement	11
temptation	13	hydrogen	12	yarn	12	pepper	11
morality	13	mammal	12	sofa	12	hunger	11
philosopher	13	queue	12	sailor	12	ballot	11
illusion	13	cart	12	surveyor	12	assertion	11
fringe	13	apology	12	disagreement	12	R / rev	11
bee	13	curiosity	12	rear	12	£10	11
headmaster	13	mosaic	12	mercy	12	warrior	11
foreigner	12	documentation	12	valve	12	preservation	11
knot	12	gathering	12	headache	12	solidarity	11
revival	12	smoking	12	polymer	12	alpha	11
surroundings	12	boxing	12	viewpoint	12	outfit	11
marker	12	snake	12	hammer	12	luxury	11
cooperation	12	planner	12	doll	12	cast	11
emergence	12	complication	12	abolition	12	punch	11
thread	12	fame	12	conspiracy	12	apparatus	11
wit	12	orientation	12	vice-president	12	listener	11
sponsorship	12	sponsor	12	genius	12	courtesy	11
bolt	12	patience	12	rib	12	scholarship	11
major	12	slip	12	exit	12	deadline	11
herb	12	cleaning	12	accusation	12	inability	11
intake	12	bride	12	baron	12	majesty	11
min	12	texture	12	propaganda	12	query	11
worm	12	reconstruction	12	reporting	12	close	11
follower	12	patron	12	sweat	12	50%	11
scrutiny	12	likelihood	12	solo	12	dominance	11
controller	12	jail	12	theology	12	supervisor	11
selling	12	corpse	12	fury	12	survivor	11
booklet	12	dancing	12	threshold	12	analogy	11
parcel	12	grin	12	trunk	12	pier	11
outlook	12	precision	12	murderer	12	dressing	11
tariff	12	telegraph	12	spur	12	lobby	11
referral	12	brow	12	fever	11	bomber	11
debtor	12	ch	12	flash	11	ending	11
humanity	12	goat	12	opposite	11	formulation	11
chemist	12	census	12	subscription	11	sentiment	11
broadcast	12	willingness	12	impulse	11	romance	11
knight	12	outbreak	12	recipient	11	descent	11
exile	12	pine	12	bicycle	11	performer	11
confrontation	12	mechanic	12	locality	11	cure	11
sickness	12	fur	12	amnesty	11	Englishman	11
onion	12	spectator	12	keyboard	11	pudding	11
narrative	12	confirmation	12	ignorance	11	folly	11
bargaining	12	sigh	12	quotation	11	lodge	11
choir	12	locomotive	12	stool	11	hunt	11
synthesis	12	sack	12	unionist	11	racism	11
metaphor	12	appraisal	12	ml	11	decree	11
enzyme	12	bull	12	adaptation	11	bankruptcy	11
gravity	12	halt	12	renaissance	11	reservoir	11
suspect	12	associate	12	balcony	11	monkey	11
spectacle	12	grouping	12	suburb	11	mainframe	11
fusion	12	cleaner	12	butterfly	11	cassette	11
sock	12	presidency	12	repayment	11	liberal*	11
recorder	12	precedent	12	glimpse	11	fisherman	11
congregation	12	sketch	12	pillow	11	harvest	11
mount	12	maid	12	scent	11	clarity	11
legacy	12	intellectual	12	pad	11	sediment	11
disclosure	12	wolf	12	electorate	11	liaison	11
crossing	12	sail	12	salvation	11	honey	11
accountability	12	torch	12	landowner	11	resentment	11
wake	12	pill	12	patrol	11	projection	11
bile	12	principal	12	wardrobe	11	chorus	11
fertility	12	parade	12	photography	11	passport	11
corn	12	feminist	12	hostage	11	staircase	11
inclusion	12	corps	12	prosperity	11	investigator	11

5.1–10

immigration	11	catch	11	jazz	10	dairy	10
retreat	11	bladder	11	Soviet	10	shilling	10
notebook	11	daylight	11	vegetation	10	north-west	10
broker	11	variant	11	knitting	10	ram	10
ruin	11	mucosa	11	hemisphere	10	herd	10
renewal	11	drill	11	commentary	10	T-shirt	10
bombing	11	flock	11	balloon	10	magnitude	10
calf	11	rifle	11	bracket	10	rehearsal	10
biology	11	newcomer	11	toast	10	coral	10
bin	11	Japanese	11	enthusiast	10	primary	10
express	11	amusement	11	para	10	stadium	10
privacy	11	copyright	11	bass	10	reasoning	10
greenhouse	11	repetition	11	heap	10	brewery	10
deficiency	11	mainland	11	monarchy	10	lb	10
brake	11	burial	11	injunction	10	nationality	10
warrant	11	fog	11	spider	10	mould	10
revenge	11	cult	11	gown	10	blast	10
rebellion	11	refuge	11	lieutenant	10	ed	10
jungle	11	fridge	11	extreme	10	scrap	10
memorandum	11	bearing	11	bulb	10	adjective	10
hatred	11	boost	10	residue	10	elder	10
insider	11	default	10	jam	10	contemporary	10
superintendent	11	mug	10	waiting	10	waiter	10
pony	11	ego	10	fine	10	listing	10
ambiguity	11	enjoyment	10	hire	10	dirt	10
methodology	11	wartime	10	nationalism	10	housewife	10
monitor	11	velocity	10	semi-final	10	fax	10
proceed	11	fork	10	irony	10	ribbon	10
20%	11	aluminium	10	asylum	10	£1,000	10
fit	11	prescription	10	poison	10	ant	10
appetite	11	jar	10	guild	10	colitis	10
nuisance	11	agony	10	infrastructure	10	wheat	10
donor	11	axis	10	biography	10	spelling	10
flour	11	rainbow	10	pillar	10	holly	10
programming	11	bowler	10	chord	10	monarch	10
welcome	11	reluctance	10	nationalist	10	voltage	10
triangle	11	gall	10	cargo	10	morale	10

List 5.2. Frequency list of verbs in the whole corpus (by lemma)

(minimum frequency: 10 per million words)

be	42277	tell	775	going	417	offer	293
have	13655	must	723	help	416	consider	289
do	5594	put (/ putt)	700	start	414	suggest	288
will	3357	mean	677	run	406	expect	288
say	3344	become	675	write	400	read	284
would	2904	leave	647	set	398	let	284
can	2672	work	646	move	391	require	284
get	2210	need	627	play	386	continue	283
make	2165	feel	624	pay	381	lose	277
go	2078	seem	624	hear	367	add	275
see	1920	might	614	include	353	fall	273
know	1882	ask	610	believe	347	change	273
take	1797	show	598	allow	342	remember	268
could	1683	try	552	meet	339	remain	268
think	1520	call	535	lead	334	buy	262
come	1512	provide	505	live	329	speak	261
give	1284	keep	505	stand	326	stop	255
look	1151	hold	481	happen	325	send	250
may	1135	turn	465	carry	313	receive	247
should	1112	follow	460	talk	308	decide	245
use	1071	begin	440	appear	307	win	241
find	990	bring	439	produce	304	understand	238
want	945	like	424	sit	300	develop	237

describe	237	present	143	record	101	concentrate	71
agree	236	point	142	depend	101	lift	71
open	235	arrive	142	enable	101	cross	70
reach	234	ensure	142	complete	100	approach	70
build	230	plan	141	cost	100	test	70
involve	229	pull	140	sound	100	experience	69
spend	227	refer	138	check	100	touch	69
return	225	act	137	laugh	98	charge	69
draw	224	relate	134	realise	98	sleep	68
die	220	affect	133	extend	97	grant	68
hope	219	close	133	arise	96	prefer	68
create	217	manage	133	notice	96	commit	68
walk	215	identify	133	define	95	threaten	68
sell	213	thank	131	fit	95	acquire	68
wait	213	compare	130	examine	95	repeat	68
shall	208	obtain	127	study	94	demonstrate	68
cause	206	announce	127	recognise	93	feed	67
pass	204	note	126	bear	93	insist	67
accept	202	forget	124	shake	93	launch	67
watch	202	indicate	124	hang	93	promote	66
raise	196	wonder	124	sign	93	limit	66
base	194	maintain	123	attend	91	measure	65
apply	193	suffer	123	fly	90	deliver	65
break	193	publish	123	gain	89	retain	65
learn	193	express	121	perform	88	own	65
explain	193	avoid	121	result	88	consist	64
increase	192	suppose	121	travel	88	attract	64
cover	191	finish	120	protect	87	promise	64
grow	191	determine	119	adopt	87	assess	64
report	189	tend	118	confirm	87	hide	64
claim	189	save	118	let's	84	reject	64
support	188	listen	118	stare	84	belong	64
lie (/lay)	187	design	118	demand	84	contribute	64
cut	184	treat	117	imagine	83	invite	63
form	184	share	116	beat	82	vary	63
stay	183	control	116	attempt	82	cry	63
contain	181	remove	115	born	82	impose	63
reduce	178	visit	115	associate	81	sing	63
establish	176	throw	115	marry	81	warn	63
join	174	exist	114	care	81	declare	62
wish	170	encourage	113	voice	80	destroy	62
seek	169	force	113	collect	80	worry	62
achieve	169	reflect	113	employ	79	address	62
choose	168	smile	112	issue	79	name	61
deal	168	admit	112	release	79	head	61
face	164	assume	112	mind	78	ought	61
fail	161	replace	111	emerge	78	stick	61
serve	159	prepare	111	mark	77	divide	61
end	158	improve	110	deny	77	nod	60
occur	157	fill	110	aim	77	train	60
kill	157	mention	110	shoot	77	recognize	60
used	156	fight	108	appoint	76	clear	59
drive	156	miss	108	supply	76	undertake	59
represent	155	intend	108	order	76	combine	59
rise	155	drop	107	observe	75	spread	59
discuss	150	push	107	reply	75	attack	59
place	150	hit	107	drink	75	recommend	59
love	150	discover	107	strike	74	handle	59
pick	150	refuse	106	settle	74	shout	59
prove	149	prevent	106	ring	74	realize	59
wear	149	regard	105	propose	74	influence	59
argue	149	teach	104	ignore	74	select	58
catch	147	lay	104	link	74	account	58
enjoy	146	reveal	104	press	73	step	57
introduce	144	state	103	respond	73	welcome	57
eat	144	operate	103	survive	72	recall	57
enter	143	answer	103	arrange	72	secure	57

climb	57	switch	46	predict	38	tackle	31
transfer	57	justify	46	struggle	38	assure	31
contact	57	knock	46	locate	38	borrow	31
conclude	56	permit	45	preserve	38	exceed	30
organise	56	occupy	45	owe	37	emphasise	30
imply	56	surround	45	cook	37	slide	30
display	56	lack	45	pour	37	transform	30
disappear	56	list	45	shift	37	qualify	30
illustrate	56	benefit	45	cast	37	cease	30
dress	56	appreciate	45	lock	37	concern	30
investigate	55	paint	44	dance	37	advance	30
direct	55	connect	44	invest	37	strengthen	30
generate	55	abandon	44	ai~*	36	perceive	29
escape	55	engage	44	kick	36	favour	29
remind	55	construct	44	race	36	practise	29
rely	54	complain	44	kiss	36	tear	29
succeed	54	quote	44	light	36	scream	29
advise	54	dominate	44	purchase	36	sustain	29
hand	54	view	44	retire	36	participate	29
inform	54	blame	44	monitor	35	pose	29
afford	54	separate	43	breathe	35	lend	29
earn	54	proceed	43	bend	35	satisfy	29
fear	53	dismiss	43	register	35	grab	29
approve	53	incorporate	43	celebrate	35	smoke	29
vote	53	stress	43	resist	35	consult	28
burn	53	acknowledge	43	print	35	outline	28
matter	52	search	43	date	35	dry	28
last	52	interpret	43	fire	35	adapt	28
ride	52	defend	42	organize	34	reinforce	28
jump	52	alter	42	comprise	34	adjust	28
match	52	arrest	42	swing	34	shrug	28
gather	52	expand	42	finance	34	dig	28
derive	52	suit	42	detect	34	snap	28
conduct	52	tie	42	range	34	ban	28
shut	52	analyse	42	overcome	34	highlight	28
elect	52	possess	42	decline	34	encounter	27
cope	52	bother	42	behave	34	pretend	27
persuade	52	implement	42	differ	33	wave	27
recover	51	review	42	need* (modal)	33	request	27
blow	51	mix	41	guarantee	33	trade	27
estimate	51	calculate	41	relax	33	sail	27
score	51	resolve	41	store	33	rid	27
slip	51	assist	41	oppose	33	amount	27
hate	50	suspect	41	resign	33	confine	27
count	50	wake	41	rush	33	trace	27
lean	49	question	41	waste	33	absorb	27
exercise	49	glance	41	drag	33	block	27
roll	49	rule	41	pause	33	entitle	27
attach	49	reckon	40	pack	33	delay	27
house	49	appeal	40	install	32	plant	27
wash	49	specify	40	compete	32	react	26
explore	48	guess	40	sink	32	dream	26
rest	48	damage	40	expose	32	fulfil	26
accompany	48	restore	40	whisper	32	flow	26
accuse	48	challenge	40	split	32	cite	26
judge	48	clean	40	negotiate	32	lower	26
bind	48	restrict	40	mount	32	seize	26
steal	48	distinguish	39	found	32	process	26
stretch	47	urge	39	sweep	31	swim	25
comment	47	trust	39	distribute	31	allocate	25
withdraw	47	constitute	39	capture	31	communicate	25
exclude	47	convert	39	enhance	31	govern	25
focus	47	submit	39	doubt	31	defeat	25
hurt	47	feature	38	deserve	31	injure	25
pursue	46	land	38	award	31	fund	25
fix	46	solve	38	phone	31	protest	25
back	46	sort	38	bury	31	stir	25

5.1–10

hurry	25	interrupt	21	repair	18	ship	16
smell	25	chase	21	exhibit	18	dump	16
wander	25	copy	21	instruct	18	market	16
burst	25	leap	21	resume	18	vanish	16
exploit	25	devote	21	plead	18	scatter	16
pray	25	overlook	21	insert	18	shop	16
sigh	25	witness	21	export	18	sue	16
double	25	mutter	21	update	18	stage	16
undergo	25	risk	21	assign	18	tempt	16
ease	24	accommodate	21	cater	18	import	16
wipe	24	brush	21	concede	18	formulate	16
evaluate	24	assert	21	opt	18	classify	16
compose	24	book	21	persist	18	aid	16
eliminate	24	age	21	isolate	18	advertise	16
wrap	24	await	21	spin	18	impress	16
grin	24	criticise	21	disclose	18	crack	16
confront	24	spell	21	spring	18	suck	16
remark	24	trap	21	conceive	18	dispose	16
interview	24	comply	21	interfere	18	dissolve	16
collapse	24	forgive	21	regulate	18	lie (/lied)	15
anticipate	24	initiate	21	peer	18	warm	15
weigh	24	undermine	21	fancy	18	omit	15
suspend	24	squeeze	21	inherit	18	praise	15
slow	23	evolve	21	speed	18	subject	15
attribute	23	stimulate	20	regret	18	tremble	15
condemn	23	enforce	20	extract	18	signal	15
bound	23	provoke	20	label	20	enclose	17
murder	23	drift	20	descend	20	commence	15
spot	23	in~*	20	boost	20	taste	15
dare	23	situate	20	incur	17	halt	15
cancel	23	sense	20	facilitate	17	tighten	15
gaze	23	emphasize	20	fold	17	discharge	15
wind	23	research	20	please	17	top	15
swear	23	freeze	20	excuse	17	draft	15
telephone	23	exchange	20	intervene	17	enquire	15
balance	23	hire	20	criticize	17	erect	15
free	23	pop	20	conceal	17	hunt	15
reverse	23	object	20	tip	17	access	15
inspire	23	recruit	20	flash	17	smash	15
modify	23	beg	20	advocate	17	depict	15
bet	23	float	20	breed	17	inspect	15
devise	23	echo	20	grasp	17	spoil	15
correspond	23	fade	20	explode	17	target	15
prompt	23	consume	19	assemble	17	reward	15
convince	23	value	19	upset	17	file	15
rub	23	equip	19	commission	17	relieve	15
guide	23	progress	19	embrace	17	contrast	15
shine	22	reserve	19	decorate	17	seal	15
bite	22	execute	19	drain	17	round	15
crash	22	convey	19	edit	17	precede	15
hesitate	22	park	19	contemplate	17	originate	15
swallow	22	unite	19	strip	17	tuck	15
integrate	22	twist	19	function	17	clarify	14
induce	22	respect	19	rescue	17	bid	14
greet	22	administer	19	cling	17	melt	14
tap	22	command	19	deem	16	thrust	14
murmur	22	educate	19	centre	16	widen	14
load	22	invent	19	sponsor	16	summon	14
translate	22	abolish	19	reproduce	16	amend	14
knit	22	correct	19	confess	16	desire	14
yield	22	allege	19	contract	16	compensate	14
admire	22	frown	19	decrease	16	couple	14
line	22	march	19	endorse	16	plunge	14
render	22	fetch	19	coincide	16	depart	14
disturb	22	envisage	18	spare	16	circulate	14
shape	21	resemble	18	creep	16	characterise	14
flee	21	price	18	schedule	16	surprise	14

sum	14	disagree	13	wound	12	empty	11
guard	14	dictate	13	alert	12	flush	11
stem	14	stroke	13	divert	12	plot	11
weaken	14	confuse	13	gasp	12	drill	11
shed	14	underline	13	fine	12	host	11
manufacture	14	confer	13	surrender	12	frame	11
drown	14	position	13	picture	12	prosecute	11
activate	14	clutch	13	scan	12	type	11
diminish	14	bounce	13	revise	12	pile	11
rain	14	pin	13	fuck	12	chair	11
bang	14	counter	13	summarise	12	spit	11
arouse	14	grip	13	crawl	12	glare	11
suppress	14	prescribe	13	tolerate	12	furnish	11
slam	14	long	13	differentiate	12	screw	11
transmit	14	merge	13	pronounce	12	dive	11
rent	14	proclaim	13	survey	12	accelerate	11
neglect	14	conform	13	accumulate	12	fish	11
tour	14	term	13	curl	12	inflict	11
entertain	14	sack	13	specialise	12	kneel	11
fling	14	heat	13	trouble	12	stab	11
spill	14	crush	12	honour	12	postpone	11
figure	14	attain	12	stride	12	pledge	10
tax	14	trigger	12	dare	12	co-ordinate	10
cool	14	renew	12	steer	12	obscure	10
compile	14	cheer	12	obey	12	rock	10
transport	14	rip	12	narrow	12	comfort	10
entail	14	frighten	12	mistake	11	roar	10
reassure	14	shiver	12	quit	11	straighten	10
embark	14	arm	12	discourage	11	flourish	10
bow	14	total	12	repay	11	swell	10
deprive	14	dislike	12	joke	11	donate	10
revive	14	boast	12	trail	11	offset	10
sentence	14	embody	12	cure	11	level	10
campaign	14	stamp	12	model	11	prohibit	10
supplement	14	weep	12	terminate	11	accord	10
project	14	penetrate	12	divorce	11	demolish	10
part	13	multiply	12	apologise	11	strive	10
forbid	13	stuff	12	designate	11	venture	10
effect	13	exert	12	seat	11	harm	10
calm	13	abuse	12	service	11	indulge	10
manipulate	13	compel	12	stumble	11	invoke	10
debate	13	presume	12	bless	11	nominate	10
chat	13	scratch	12	document	11	evoke	10
time	13	boil	12	haul	11	invade	10
punish	13	exhaust	12	exclaim	11	credit	10
supervise	13	snatch	12	flick	11	chop	10
substitute	13	motivate	12	endure	11	diagnose	10
convict	13	inhibit	12	screen	11	smooth	10
strain	13	prevail	12	lodge	11	root	10
flood	13	colour	12	sniff	11	equal	10
dedicate	13	rate	12	insure	11	rob	10
rebuild	13	yell	12	preach	11	foster	10
toss	13	carve	12	weave	11	inject	10
regain	13	deposit	12	desert	11	chew	10
characterize	13	dip	12				

List 5.3. Frequency list of adjectives in the whole corpus (by lemma)

(minimum frequency: 10 per million words)

other	1336	small	518	long	392	possible	342
good	1276	different	484	young	379	big	338
new	1154	large	471	national	376	little	306
old	648	local	445	British	357	political	306
great	635	social	422	right	354	able	304
high	574	important	392	early	353	late	302

general	301	serious	124	practical	77
full	289	previous	123	official	77
far	288	total	122	separate	77
low	286	prime	121	key	76
public	285	significant	121	chief	75
available	272	industrial	116	regular	75
bad	264	sorry	115	due	75
main	245	dead	114	additional	74
sure	241	specific	113	active	73
clear	239	appropriate	113	powerful	72
major	238	top	112	complex	72
economic	236	Soviet	109	standard	72
only	231	basic	109	impossible	71
likely	228	military	108	light	71
real	227	original	108	warm	70
black	226	successful	108	middle	70
particular	223	aware	108	fresh	69
international	221	hon	107	sexual	69
special	220	popular	106	front	69
difficult	220	heavy	105	domestic	69
certain	220	professional	105	actual	68
open	219	direct	104	united	68
whole	216	dark	104	technical	68
white	207	cold	103	ordinary	68
free	200	ready	102	cheap	68
short	198	green	101	strange	68
easy	198	useful	101	internal	67
strong	197	effective	99	excellent	67
European	195	western	99	quiet	66
central	193	traditional	99	soft	66
similar	184	Scottish	98	potential	66
human	183	German	98	northern	66
true	183	independent	98	religious	66
common	182	deep	97	quick	66
necessary	181	interesting	96	very	65
single	177	considerable	96	famous	65
personal	176	involved	96	cultural	65
hard	176	physical	95	proper	65
private	173	left	95	broad	65
poor	166	hot	94	joint	64
financial	165	existing	94	formal	64
wide	165	responsible	94	limited	64
foreign	161	complete	94	conservative*	64
simple	159	medical	93	lovely	64
recent	158	blue	92	usual	64
concerned	158	extra	92	Ltd	64
American	157	past	89	unable	64
various	155	male	89	rural	63
close	154	interested	88	initial	62
fine	150	fair	87	substantial	62
English	150	essential	87	Christian	62
wrong	149	beautiful	87	bright	62
present	148	civil	87	average	62
royal	147	primary	86	leading	61
natural	142	obvious	85	reasonable	61
individual	136	future	85	immediate	61
nice	134	environmental	84	suitable	61
French	134	positive	83	equal	61
following	134	senior	82	detailed	60
current	133	nuclear	81	working	60
modern	131	annual	81	overall	60
labour*	131	relevant	79	female	60
legal	131	huge	79	afraid	60
happy	129	rich	79	democratic	59
final	129	commercial	79	growing	59
red	126	safe	78	sufficient	59
normal	124	regional	78	scientific	59

Adjectives for regions and nations

This list makes the obvious, if unpalatable, point that a British corpus reflects the assumption that Britain stands at the centre of the known universe, and that the importance of a region or nation diminishes roughly in proportion to its 'remoteness' from Britain (frequencies per million).

British	357
European	195
American	157
English	150
French	134
Soviet	109
Scottish	98
German	98
Irish	59
Russian	52
Japanese	51
African	43
Italian	40
Chinese	40
Indian	38
Welsh	37
Spanish	34
Greek	29
Australian	24
Dutch	23
Arab	22
Asian	19
Iraqi	17
Polish	15
Israeli	15
Swiss	14
Canadian	14
Turkish	14
Korean	12
Palestinian	10

eastern	59
correct	59
Inc	59
Irish	59
expensive	59
educational	59
mental	58
dangerous	58
critical	58
increased	57

familiar	57	used	45	outside	37	strategic	30
unlikely	57	criminal	44	acceptable	36	holy	30
double	57	contemporary	44	sensitive	36	smooth	30
perfect	56	sharp	44	false	36	dominant	30
slow	56	sick	44	living	36	remote	30
tiny	56	near	44	pure	36	theoretical	30
dry	56	Roman	44	global	36	outstanding	30
historical	56	massive	44	emotional	36	pink	30
thin	56	unique	43	sad	36	pretty	30
daily	55	secondary	43	secret	36	clinical	30
southern	55	parliamentary	43	rapid	36	minimum	30
increasing	55	African	43	adequate	36	honest	30
wild	55	unknown	43	fixed	36	impressive	30
alone	54	subsequent	43	sweet	36	related	30
urban	54	angry	43	administrative	35	residential	29
empty	54	alive	43	wooden	35	extraordinary	29
married	54	guilty	42	remarkable	35	plain	29
narrow	54	lucky	42	comprehensive	35	visible	29
liberal*	54	enormous	42	surprising	35	accurate	29
supposed	54	well	42	solid	35	distant	29
upper	54	communist	42	rough	35	still	29
apparent	53	yellow	41	mere	35	Greek	29
tall	53	unusual	41	mass	35	complicated	29
busy	53	net	41	brilliant	35	musical	29
bloody	53	long-term	41	maximum	35	precise	29
prepared	53	tough	41	absolute	35	gentle	29
Russian	52	dear	41	Tory	34	broken	29
moral	52	extensive	41	electronic	34	live	29
careful	52	glad	41	visual	34	silly	29
clean	52	remaining	41	electric	34	fat	28
attractive	52	agricultural	41	cool	34	tight	28
Japanese	51	alright	40	Spanish	34	monetary	28
vital	51	healthy	40	literary	34	round	28
thick	51	Italian	40	continuing	34	psychological	28
alternative	51	principal	40	supreme	33	violent	28
fast	50	tired	40	chemical	33	unemployed	28
ancient	50	efficient	40	genuine	33	inevitable	28
elderly	50	comfortable	40	exciting	33	junior	28
rare	50	Chinese	40	written	33	sensible	28
external	49	relative	39	stupid	33	grateful	27
capable	49	friendly	39	advanced	33	pleasant	27
brief	49	conventional	39	extreme	33	dirty	27
wonderful	49	willing	39	classical	33	structural	27
grand	49	sudden	39	fit	33	welcome	27
typical	49	proposed	39	favourite	33	so-called	27
entire	48	voluntary	39	socialist	33	deaf	27
grey	48	slight	39	widespread	32	above	27
constant	47	valuable	39	confident	32	continuous	26
vast	47	dramatic	39	straight	32	blind	26
surprised	47	golden	39	catholic	32	overseas	26
ideal	47	temporary	38	proud	32	mean	26
terrible	47	federal	38	numerous	32	entitled	26
academic	47	keen	38	opposite	32	delighted	26
funny	47	flat	38	distinct	32	loose	26
minor	47	silent	38	mad	32	occasional	26
pleased	47	Indian	38	helpful	32	evident	26
severe	47	video-taped	38	given	31	desperate	26
ill	46	worried	38	disabled	31	fellow	26
corporate	46	pale	38	consistent	31	universal	26
negative	45	statutory	37	anxious	31	square	26
permanent	45	Welsh	37	nervous	31	steady	26
weak	45	dependent	37	awful	31	classic	26
brown	45	firm	37	stable	31	equivalent	25
fundamental	45	wet	37	constitutional	31	intellectual	25
odd	45	competitive	37	satisfied	31	Victorian	25
crucial	45	armed	37	conscious	31	level	25
inner	45	radical	37	developing	31	ultimate	25

creative	25	frequent	24	multiple	22	confused	19
lost	25	experimental	24	ruling	22	unfair	19
medieval	25	spiritual	23	curious	22	aggressive	19
clever	25	intense	23	Arab	22	spare	19
linguistic	25	rational	23	sole	22	painful	19
convinced	25	ethnic	23	Jewish	22	abstract	19
judicial	25	generous	23	managing	22	Asian	19
raw	25	inadequate	23	pregnant	22	associated	19
sophisticated	25	prominent	23	Latin	22	legislative	19
asleep	25	logical	23	nearby	22	monthly	19
vulnerable	25	bare	23	exact	22	intelligent	19
illegal	24	historic	23	underlying	22	hungry	19
outer	24	modest	23	identical	22	explicit	19
revolutionary	24	Dutch	23	satisfactory	22	nasty	19
bitter	24	acute	23	marginal	22	just	19
changing	24	electrical	23	distinctive	22	faint	19
Australian	24	valid	23	electoral	22	coloured	19
native	24	weekly	23	urgent	22	ridiculous	19
imperial	24	gross	23	presidential	21	amazing	19
strict	24	automatic	23	controversial	21	comparable	19
wise	24	loud	23	oral	21	successive	19
informal	24	reliable	22	everyday	21	working-class	19
flexible	24	mutual	22	encouraging	21	realistic	19
collective	24	liable	22	organic	21	back	19
				continued	21	decent	19
				expected	21	unnecessary	19
				statistical	21	flying	19
				desirable	21	fucking	18
				innocent	21	random	18
				improved	21	influential	18
				exclusive	21	dull	18
				marked	21	genetic	18
				experienced	21	neat	18
				unexpected	21	marvellous	18
				superb	21	crazy	18
				sheer	21	damp	18
				disappointed	21	giant	18
				frightened	21	secure	18
				full-time	21	bottom	18
				gastric	21	skilled	18
				capitalist	21	subtle	18
				romantic	21	elegant	18
				naked	20	brave	18
				reluctant	20	lesser	18
				magnificent	20	parallel	18
				convenient	20	steep	18
				established	20	intensive	18
				closed	20	casual	18
				uncertain	20	tropical	18
				artificial	20	lonely	18
				diplomatic	20	partial	18
				tremendous	20	preliminary	18
				marine	20	concrete	18
				mechanical	20	alleged	18
				retail	20	assistant	18
				institutional	20	vertical	18
				mixed	20	upset	18
				required	20	delicate	18
				biological	20	mild	18
				known	20	occupational	17
				functional	20	excessive	17
				straightforward	20	progressive	17
				superior	20	Iraqi	17
				digital	20	exceptional	17
				part-time	20	integrated	17
				spectacular	19	striking	17
				unhappy	19	continental	17

Colours

Berlin and Kay (1969) studied the colour terms that exist in a sample of the world's languages. From such data they extracted a natural hierarchy of colour terms which would enable one to predict what other colour terms are or are not present in a given language. For example, a language that contains a term for *red* must also contain *black* and *white*. A language that contains *green* must also contain *red*. Some terms (such as *white* and *black*) do not have any obvious precedence between them, and so are listed at the same point in the hierarchy.

Berlin and Kay's hierarchy of eleven basic colour terms was as follows:

$$
\begin{matrix} white \\ black \end{matrix} < red < \begin{matrix} green \\ yellow \end{matrix} < blue < brown < \begin{matrix} purple \\ pink \\ orange \\ grey \end{matrix}
$$

The frequency with which colour terms (adjectives) are used in present-day British English, as shown in the BNC, in fact exhibits a very similar rank ordering:

black	226
white	207
red	126
green	101
blue	92
grey	48
brown	45
yellow	41
pink	30
orange	14
purple	11

The main differences with the hierarchy are the demotion of *yellow* to a relatively low frequency, and the promotion of *blue* and (especially) *grey* to a higher position.

okay	17	sympathetic	15	calm	14	incredible	12
harsh	17	well-known	15	irrelevant	14	devoted	12
combined	17	empirical	15	patient	14	prior	12
fierce	17	head	15	compact	14	tragic	12
handsome	17	shallow	15	profitable	14	respectable	12
characteristic	17	vague	15	rival	14	optimistic	12
chronic	17	naval	15	loyal	14	convincing	12
compulsory	17	depressed	15	moderate	14	unacceptable	12
interim	17	shared	15	distinguished	13	decisive	12
objective	17	added	15	interior	13	competent	12
splendid	17	shocked	15	noble	13	spatial	12
magic	17	mid	15	insufficient	13	respective	12
short-term	17	worthwhile	15	eligible	13	binding	12
systematic	17	qualified	15	mysterious	13	relieved	12
obliged	17	missing	15	varying	13	nursing	12
payable	17	blank	15	middle-class	13	toxic	12
fun	17	absent	15	managerial	13	select	12
horrible	17	favourable	15	molecular	13	redundant	12
primitive	17	Polish	15	Olympic	13	integral	12
fascinating	17	Israeli	15	linear	13	then	12
ideological	17	developed	15	prospective	13	probable	12
metropolitan	17	profound	15	printed	13	amateur	12
surrounding	17	representative	15	parental	13	fond	12
estimated	17	enthusiastic	14	diverse	13	passing	12
peaceful	17	dreadful	14	elaborate	13	specified	12
premier	17	rigid	14	furious	13	territorial	12
operational	17	reduced	14	fiscal	13	horizontal	12
technological	16	cruel	14	burning	13	old-fashioned	12
kind	16	coastal	14	useless	13	inland	12
advisory	16	peculiar	14	semantic	13	cognitive	12
hostile	16	racial	14	embarrassed	13	regulatory	12
precious	16	ugly	14	inherent	13	miserable	12
gay	16	Swiss	14	philosophical	13	resident	12
accessible	16	crude	14	deliberate	13	polite	12
determined	16	extended	14	awake	13	scared	12
excited	16	selected	14	variable	13	Marxist	12
impressed	16	eager	14	promising	13	gothic	12
provincial	16	feminist	14	unpleasant	13	civilian	12
smart	16	Canadian	14	varied	13	instant	12
endless	16	bold	14	sacred	13	lengthy	12
isolated	16	relaxed	14	selective	13	adverse	12
post-war	16	corresponding	14	inclined	13	Korean	12
drunk	16	running	14	tender	13	unconscious	12
geographical	16	planned	14	hidden	13	anonymous	12
like	16	applicable	14	worthy	13	aesthetic	12
dynamic	16	immense	14	intermediate	13	orthodox	12
boring	16	allied	14	sound	13	static	12
forthcoming	16	comparative	14	protective	13	unaware	12
unfortunate	16	uncomfortable	14	fortunate	13	costly	12
definite	16	conservation	14	slim	13	fantastic	12
super	16	productive	14	Islamic	13	foolish	12
notable	16	beneficial	14	defensive	13	fashionable	12
indirect	16	bored	14	divine	13	causal	12
stiff	16	charming	14	stuck	13	compatible	12
wealthy	16	minimal	14	driving	13	wee	12
awkward	16	mobile	14	invisible	13	implicit	12
lively	16	Turkish	14	misleading	13	dual	12
neutral	16	orange	14	circular	13	OK	12
artistic	16	rear	14	mathematical	13	cheerful	12
content	16	passive	14	inappropriate	13	subjective	12
mature	16	suspicious	14	liquid	13	forward	12
colonial	15	overwhelming	14	persistent	13	surviving	12
ambitious	15	fatal	14	solar	13	exotic	11
evil	15	resulting	14	doubtful	13	purple	11
magnetic	15	symbolic	14	manual	12	cautious	11
verbal	15	registered	14	architectural	12	visiting	11
legitimate	15	neighbouring	14	intact	12	aggregate	11

5.1-10

ethical	11	rising	11	homeless	11	puzzled	10
protestant	11	shy	11	supporting	11	worldwide	10
teenage	11	novel	11	coming	11	handicapped	10
large-scale	11	balanced	11	renewed	11	organisational	10
dying	11	delightful	11	excess	11	sunny	10
disastrous	11	arbitrary	11	retired	11	eldest	10
delicious	11	adjacent	11	rubber	11	eventual	10
confidential	11	psychiatric	11	chosen	11	spontaneous	10
underground	11	worrying	11	outdoor	11	vivid	10
thorough	11	weird	11	embarrassing	11	rude	10
grim	11	unchanged	11	preferred	11	nineteenth-century	10
autonomous	11	rolling	11	bizarre	11	faithful	10
atomic	11	evolutionary	11	appalling	11	ministerial	10
frozen	11	intimate	11	agreed	10	innovative	10
colourful	11	sporting	11	imaginative	10	controlled	10
injured	11	disciplinary	11	governing	10	conceptual	10
uniform	11	formidable	11	accepted	10	unwilling	10
ashamed	11	lexical	11	vocational	10	civic	10
glorious	11	noisy	11	Palestinian	10	meaningful	10
wicked	11	gradual	11	mighty	10	disturbing	10
coherent	11	accused	11				

List 5.4. Frequency list of adverbs in the whole corpus (not lemmatized)

(minimum frequency: 10 per million words)

so	1893	away	371	clearly	153	otherwise	88
up	1795	perhaps	350	at all	148	directly	88
then	1595	right	346	more than	148	like	88
out	1542	already	343	further	144	completely	86
now	1382	yet	337	better	143	normally	83
only	1298	later	317	before	143	best	81
just	1277	almost	316	round	138	slowly	79
more	1275	of course	310	forward	137	relatively	79
also	1248	far	310	please	133	apparently	78
very	1165	together	308	finally	130	early	76
well	1119	probably	273	quickly	124	merely	76
how	1016	today	263	recently	123	instead	75
down	845	actually	260	anyway	122	alone	74
back	793	ever	259	a bit	119	for instance	74
on	756	at least	257	suddenly	118	largely	73
there	746	enough	244	generally	116	possibly	73
still	718	less	243	nearly	115	nevertheless	72
even	716	for example	239	as well	113	carefully	72
too	701	therefore	232	obviously	110	hard	71
here	699	particularly	220	exactly	107	mainly	71
where	628	either	220	okay*	105	currently	70
however	605	around	215	maybe	105	somewhere	70
over	584	rather	213	a little	104	along	70
in	573	else	209	immediately	102	entirely	69
as	567	sometimes	205	easily	99	previously	69
most	565	thus	205	though	99	tonight	69
again	561	ago	198	earlier	97	extremely	68
never	559	yesterday	195	through	95	fairly	67
why	509	home	194	up to	94	in particular	67
off	486	all	193	above	94	increasingly	66
really	481	usually	191	tomorrow	93	equally	66
always	462	indeed	188	highly	91	all right*	64
about	447	certainly	186	eventually	91	surely	63
when	431	once	183	fully	89	ahead	63
quite	412	long	181	slightly	89	twice	63
much	390	simply	177	hardly	88	straight	59
both	378	especially	177	no longer	88	sort of	59
often	376	soon	161	below	88	absolutely	58

totally	58	moreover	43	everywhere	32	forever	18
frequently	58	naturally	43	truly	32	eg	18
partly	57	rarely	42	whenever	32	sooner	18
seriously	57	significantly	42	definitely	32	locally	18
elsewhere	57	close	42	by	32	backwards	18
necessarily	57	in general	42	primarily	31	OK*	18
properly	57	quietly	41	basically	31	officially	18
widely	56	at first	41	inevitably	31	over there	18
under	56	late	41	constantly	31	happily	18
closely	55	anywhere	41	reasonably	31	besides	18
neither	54	heavily	41	et al	30	simultaneously	18
outside	53	gently	40	furthermore	29	separately	18
that	52	a lot	40	considerably	29	severely	18
pretty	52	firmly	40	at present	29	faster	17
effectively	51	occasionally	40	ultimately	29	safely	17
etc	50	less than	40	since	29	downstairs	17
inside	50	mostly	39	secondly	29	alternatively	17
and so on	49	abroad	39	approximately	28	firstly	17
e.g.	49	regularly	39	readily	28	substantially	17
meanwhile	48	shortly	38	deliberately	28	from time to time	17
hence	48	initially	38	automatically	28	exclusively	17
o'clock	47	specifically	38	newly	27	politically	17
unfortunately	47	deeply	37	deep	27	tightly	17
somewhat	46	once again	37	thereby	27	no	17
strongly	46	no doubt	37	personally	27	steadily	17
afterwards	46	subsequently	37	surprisingly	26	scarcely	17
i.e.	46	gradually	37	closer	26	solely	17
that is	46	essentially	36	purely	26	fortunately	16
rapidly	46	at once	36	commonly	26	near	16
similarly	45	aside	36	sufficiently	26	consistently	16
originally	45	apart	35	upstairs	25	by no means	16
somehow	45	precisely	35	consequently	25	half	16
in addition	45	across	35	sharply	25	instantly	16
least	45	behind	34	softly	25	nowadays	16
little	45	successfully	34	potentially	24	freely	16
perfectly	44	greatly	33	etc.	24	broadly	16
at last	44	longer	33	undoubtedly	24	publicly	16
virtually	44	presumably	33	notably	24	upwards	16
fast	44	briefly	33	once more	24	hitherto	16
badly	43	respectively	32	nowhere	24	invariably	16
alright*	43	altogether	32	roughly	23	differently	15
				accordingly	23	regardless	15
				barely	23	dramatically	15
				wherever	23	socially	15
				wholly	22	actively	15
				formally	22	seldom	15
				by now	22	rightly	15
				namely	22	remarkably	15
				typically	21	ie	15
				thoroughly	21	evidently	15
				past	21	even so	15
				in part	21	reportedly	15
				traditionally	21	thereafter	14
				any	20	just about	14
				bloody	20	honestly	14
				physically	20	as yet	14
				literally	20	accurately	14
				formerly	20	onwards	14
				strictly	20	genuinely	14
				mentally	20	practically	14
				specially	20	a great deal	14
				desperately	20	daily	14
				whereby	20	independently	14
				lightly	20	on board	14
				sadly	19	nearby	14
				correctly	19	forwards	13
				hopefully	19	positively	13

Top twenty frequency adverbs

English has a considerable range of adverbs for saying 'how often' something happens. The first two positions in the list below are taken by adverbs showing the two extremes of the frequency scale, 'zero times' and 'all (possible) times'.

never	559	*normally*	83
always	462	*increasingly*	66
often	376	*twice*	63
ever	259	*frequently*	58
sometimes	205	*rarely*	42
usually	191	*in general*	42
once	183	*occasionally*	40
generally	116	*mostly*	39
hardly	88	*regularly*	39
no longer	88	*constantly*	31

5.1–10

neatly	13	predominantly	12	comparatively	12	high	11
importantly	13	fucking	12	overnight	12	far from	11
continually	13	beyond	12	alike	12	pm	11
for ever	13	beautifully	12	ideally	12	incidentally	11
utterly	13	abruptly	12	worldwide	12	loudly	11
partially	13	et al.	12	legally	12	am	10
nonetheless	13	openly	12	adequately	11	indirectly	10
within	13	swiftly	12	sincerely	11	allegedly	10
forth	13	easier	12	jointly	11	no matter how	10
explicitly	13	seemingly	12	angrily	11	as it were	10
repeatedly	13	permanently	12	individually	11	strangely	10
temporarily	13	privately	12	efficiently	11	sexually	10
in short	13	silently	12	bitterly	11	technically	10
overall	13	likewise	12	annually	11	economically	10
terribly	13	overseas	12	tight	11	unusually	10
as usual	13						

List 5.5. Frequency list of pronouns in the whole corpus (not lemmatized)

(minimum frequency: 10 per million words)

it	10875	us	623	myself	125	lots	45
I	8875	something	526	each other	108	ourselves	45
you	6954	nothing	341	yourself	107	yours	42
he	6810	himself	311	none	84	one another	28
they	4332	anything	288	no one*	81	hers	25
she	3801	itself	237	somebody	73	no-one*	21
we	3578	themselves	237	nobody	62	ours	17
who	2055	someone	187	everybody	61	'em	16
them	1733	everything	187	anybody	50	ye	15
him	1649	herself	172	his*	49	whoever	15
me	1364	anyone	150	plenty	46	ya	14
her	1085	everyone	133	mine	46	theirs	10
one	953	whom	129				

List 5.6. Frequency list of determiners in the whole corpus

(minimum frequency: 10 per million words)
NOTE: Consider this list together with List 5.7.

the	61847	their	2608	my	1525	our	950
a	21626	her*	2183	your	1383	every	401
his	4285	its	1632	no	1343	me (=my)	23
an	3430						

List 5.7. Frequency list of determiner/pronouns in the whole corpus

(minimum frequency: 10 per million words)
NOTE: These words function both as determiners and as pronouns in the noun phrase: e.g. **This** *book is mine* (determiner function); **This** *is my book* (pronoun function).

this	4623	many	902	each	508	former	170
that	3792	those	888	few	450	whatever	132
which	3719	such	763	most	422	less	101
what	2493	more	699	both	310	enough	82
all	2436	own	695	several	240	latter	78
some	1712	same	615	half	209	either	58
these	1254	another	581	whose	198	fewer	31
any	1220	much	531	little	183	neither	28

List 5.8. Frequency list of prepositions in the whole corpus

(Minimum frequency: 10 per million words)

of*	29391	off	214	apart from	65	but	22
in	18214	behind	202	onto	62	regarding	20
to	9343	since	178	beside	58	in accordance with	20
for	8412	because of	178	below	55	except for	20
with	6575	as well as	176	v.	54	in response to	20
on	6475	rather than	169	subject to	51	in the light of	18
by	5096	until	167	along with	51	as opposed to	17
at	4790	according to	157	beneath	48	in charge of	17
from	4134	up to	152	in relation to	46	with regard to	17
as	1774	despite	146	amongst	45	x	16
into	1634	near	138	via	45	by means of	16
about	1524	above	137	other than	43	in connection with	16
like	1064	per	135	unlike	40	on the part of	15
after	927	along	123	in favour of	36	in view of	15
between	903	away from	120	in addition to	34	by way of	14
through	743	throughout	116	v	32	contrary to	13
over	735	outside	116	prior to	31	with respect to	13
against	562	round	115	concerning	31	let alone	13
under	553	beyond	105	next to	30	in touch with	13
out of	491	worth	102	except	30	minus	13
without	456	in terms of	102	alongside	29	toward	13
within	449	down	98	in respect of	29	in conjunction with	13
during	440	on to	92	in spite of	28	in line with	12
before	434	up	83	till	28	opposite	12
such as	321	due to	78	on behalf of	27	following	12
towards	286	inside	74	aged	27	amid	11
around	237	as to	73	ahead of	26	in support of	11
upon	234	instead of	72	on top of	26	in search of	10
including	230	plus	70	as for	25	underneath	10
among	229	past	67	depending on	23	relative to	10
across	217	in front of	66				

List 5.9 Frequency list of conjunctions in the whole corpus

(Minimum frequency: 10 per million words; Note: this list includes both subordinating and coordinating conjunctions.)

and	26817	before	305	once	90	whether or not	29
that	7308	since	295	even if	87	like	25
but	4577	so	258	whereas	62	till	24
or	3707	though	245	even though	59	even when	24
as	3006	until	242	whilst	58	in case	22
if	2369	after	233	as though	54	and/or	19
when	1712	so that	197	rather than	46	in that	18
than	1033	cos*	163	as soon as	45	albeit	14
because*	852	as if	157	except	41	except that	14
while	503	for	139	now that	30	so long as	13
where	458	&	136	provided	30	given that	12
although	436	nor	124	as long as	29	provided that	11
whether	332	unless	110				

List 5.10. Frequency list of interjections and discourse markers in the whole corpus

(Minimum frequency: 10 per million words)

yeah	834	ah	99	dear	37	bye	17
oh	684	mhm	75	eh	35	yep	13
no	662	aye	52	ha	30	goodbye	10
yes	606	ooh	46	aha	26		
mm	330	hello	38	hey	18		

List 6.1.1. Alphabetical list of grammatical word classes: the whole corpus

(Spoken and written English)

Freq = frequency per million tags
Ra = range (maximum = 100)
Di = dispersion (Juilland's D)

For the meanings of the tags, see pp. 20–3.

Tag	Freq	Ra	Di	Tag	Freq	Ra	Di	Tag	Freq	Ra	Di	Tag	Freq	Ra	Di
APPGE	12759	100	95	JJT	751	100	94	PNX1	3	5	54	VBDZ	8102	100	95
AT	53690	100	96	JK	276	96	93	PPGE	318	78	88	VBG	700	99	95
AT1	22274	100	98	MC	15146	100	90	PPH1	17059	100	94	VBI	6298	100	95
BCL	94	49	83	MC1	2897	100	95	PPHO1	2132	97	90	VBM	1846	90	91
CC	30572	100	98	MC2	286	80	86	PPHO2	2430	100	94	VBN	2212	100	95
CCB	5258	100	97	MCMC	356	41	72	PPHS1	9885	100	91	VBR	7342	100	96
CS	10323	100	97	MD	3501	100	95	PPHS2	6549	100	94	VBZ	18781	100	95
CSA	2081	100	95	MF	178	39	44	PPIO1	1984	92	91	VD0	4297	100	91
CSN	812	100	94	ND1	356	70	83	PPIO2	846	95	91	VDD	2383	98	91
CST	6424	100	95	NN	2896	100	93	PPIS1	18977	98	92	VDG	582	89	90
CSW	542	97	94	NN1	121078	100	97	PPIS2	7059	99	91	VDI	1484	99	92
DA	1772	100	95	NN2	41320	100	95	PPX1	720	100	90	VDN	618	97	92
DA1	632	99	96	NNA	15	15	69	PPX2	335	98	92	VDZ	1032	97	93
DA2	1061	100	94	NNB	2192	95	83	PPY	15538	98	92	VH0	6046	100	94
DAR	904	100	95	NNL1	1155	96	85	RA	496	100	93	VHD	3189	100	92
DAT	382	97	93	NNL2	63	26	63	REX	309	73	84	VHG	410	100	94
DB	3420	100	96	NNO	851	95	88	RG	5026	100	96	VHI	2693	100	95
DB2	293	96	93	NNO2	111	61	85	RGQ	501	93	90	VHN	457	98	92
DD	3255	100	95	NNT1	6301	100	96	RGQV	22	31	81	VHZ	3161	100	96
DD1	14340	100	95	NNT2	2163	100	96	RGR	695	98	91	VM	17464	100	97
DD2	2472	100	95	NNU	2247	93	77	RGT	362	90	90	VMK	366	84	87
DDQ	7392	100	96	NNU1	428	78	75	RL	4802	100	94	VV0	19876	100	94
DDQGE	127	74	89	NNU2	311	82	86	RP	10545	100	94	VVD	17978	100	93
DDQV	217	89	91	NP	23	18	62	RPK	34	44	87	VVG	13252	100	98
EX	2924	100	96	NP1	31867	100	92	RR	35332	100	97	VVGK	1190	89	90
FU	11573	76	88	NP2	155	68	87	RRQ	3212	100	95	VVI	29047	100	98
FW	665	59	78	NPD1	685	84	89	RRQV	67	65	89	VVN	20753	100	97
GE	3788	100	92	NPD2	30	28	76	RRR	1000	100	96	VVNK	24	36	85
IF	7664	100	97	NPM1	958	95	88	RRT	83	75	91	VVZ	6897	100	95
II	58283	100	97	PN	321	93	92	RT	6821	100	95	XX	12071	100	93
IO	22267	100	94	PN1	4522	100	93	TO	15687	100	98	ZZ1	3442	93	85
IW	5900	100	96	PNQO	72	49	82	UH	16380	87	88	ZZ2	65	31	73
JJ	56336	100	96	PNQS	1916	100	94	VB0	103	68	86				
JJR	1674	100	95	PNQV	14	21	79	VBDR	3020	100	93				

List 6.1.2. Rank frequency list of grammatical word classes: the whole corpus

Tag	Freq	Tag	Freq	Tag	Freq	Tag	Freq	Tag	Freq	Tag	Freq
NN1	121078	VVG	13252	PN1	4522	CSA	2081	DA1	632	MF	178
II	58283	APPGE	12759	VD0	4297	PPIO1	1984	VDN	618	NP2	155
JJ	56336	XX	12071	GE	3788	PNQS	1916	VDG	582	DDQGE	127
AT	53690	FU	11573	MD	3501	VBM	1846	CSW	542	NNO2	111
NN2	41320	RP	10545	ZZ1	3442	DA	1772	RGQ	501	VB0	103
RR	35332	CS	10323	DB	3420	JJR	1674	RA	496	BCL	94
NP1	31867	PPHS1	9885	DD	3255	VDI	1484	VHN	457	RRT	83
CC	30572	VBDZ	8102	RRQ	3212	VVGK	1190	NNU1	428	PNQO	72
VVI	29047	IF	7664	VHD	3189	NNL1	1155	VHG	410	RRQV	67
AT1	22274	DDQ	7392	VHZ	3161	DA2	1061	DAT	382	ZZ2	65
IO	22267	VBR	7342	VBDR	3020	VDZ	1032	VMK	366	NNL2	63
VVN	20753	PPIS2	7059	EX	2924	RRR	1000	RGT	362	RPK	34
VV0	19876	VVZ	6897	MC1	2897	NPM1	958	ND1	356	NPD2	30
PPIS1	18977	RT	6821	NN	2896	DAR	904	MCMC	356	VVNK	24
VBZ	18781	PPHS2	6549	VHI	2693	NNO	851	PPX2	335	NP	23
VVD	17978	CST	6424	DD2	2472	PPIO2	846	PN	321	RGQV	22
VM	17464	NNT1	6301	PPHO2	2430	CSN	812	PPGE	318	NNA	15
PPH1	17059	VBI	6298	VDD	2383	JJT	751	NNU2	311	PNQV	14
UH	16380	VH0	6046	NNU	2247	PPX1	720	REX	309	PNX1	3
TO	15687	IW	5900	VBN	2212	VBG	700	DB2	293		
PPY	15538	CCB	5258	NNB	2192	RGR	695	MC2	286		
MC	15146	RG	5026	NNT2	2163	NPD1	685	JK	276		
DD1	14340	RL	4802	PPHO1	2132	FW	665	DDQV	217		

List 6.2.1. Alphabetical list of grammatical word classes: spoken v. written English

FrS = frequency in spoken English (per million tags)
Ra = range (maximum = 50 for both speech and writing)
FrW = frequency in written English (per million tags)

+ = Higher frequency in speech
– = Higher frequency in writing

Tag	FrS	Ra	Di		LL	FrW	Ra	Di	Tag	FrS	Ra	Di		LL	FrW	Ra	Di
APPGE	10393	50	96	–	870	15101	50	92	NNU2	283	41	80	–	5	339	41	80
AT	39031	50	95	–	7997	68200	50	98	NP	33	10	50	+	9	13	8	62
AT1	20015	50	98	–	452	24510	50	98	NP1	14469	50	94	–	19819	49089	50	92
BCL	31	14	69	–	90	156	35	83	NP2	77	27	77	–	81	232	41	86
CC	28484	50	97	–	281	32638	50	97	NPD1	891	49	87	+	123	482	35	82
CCB	6289	50	97	+	400	4238	50	95	NPD2	35	18	78	+	1	25	10	52
CS	12630	50	97	+	1023	8040	50	96	NPM1	468	49	85	–	518	1443	46	86
CSA	1383	50	92	–	471	2772	50	95	PN	419	50	93	+	59	225	43	85
CSN	644	50	93	–	69	979	50	92	PN1	6802	50	96	+	2369	2264	50	87
CST	6482	50	91	+	1	6366	50	95	PNQO	16	11	70	–	98	128	38	81
CSW	740	49	94	+	145	347	48	90	PNQS	1768	50	94	–	22	2061	50	90
DA	1292	50	94	–	259	2247	50	94	PNQV	23	18	79	+	15	4	3	40
DA1	694	50	94	+	12	570	49	94	PNX1	0	0	00	–	8	6	5	55
DA2	836	50	89	–	95	1285	50	93	PPGE	500	49	87	+	215	139	29	80
DAR	912	50	94	+	0	895	50	91	PPH1	25899	50	96	+	9462	8308	50	94
DAT	266	47	90	–	69	496	50	91	PPHO1	2374	50	88	+	54	1892	47	82
DB	4091	50	96	+	260	2757	50	95	PPHO2	3350	50	94	+	702	1520	50	88
DB2	209	46	88	–	48	376	50	93	PPHS1	12139	50	89	+	1020	7655	50	85
DD	3722	50	92	+	132	2793	50	95	PPHS2	9468	50	96	+	2651	3660	50	92
DD1	20945	50	98	+	6215	7802	50	96	PPIO1	2617	50	93	+	405	1357	42	79
DD2	2567	50	95	+	7	2378	50	92	PPIO2	984	49	92	+	44	708	46	82
DDQ	9476	50	96	+	1172	5329	50	95	PPIS1	31379	50	95	+	17304	6701	48	82
DDQGE	46	30	85	–	108	206	44	89	PPIS2	10880	50	93	+	4292	3277	49	84
DDQV	325	49	91	+	110	110	40	87	PPX1	518	50	92	–	113	919	50	86
EX	3642	50	95	+	350	2213	50	94	PPX2	277	48	89	–	20	394	50	90
FU	23010	50	93	+	29404	252	26	67	PPY	26531	50	96	+	16894	4656	48	81
FW	89	16	63	–	1176	1235	43	78	RA	490	50	93	–	0	502	50	89
GE	1813	50	95	–	2137	5743	50	92	REX	164	31	81	–	141	454	42	81
IF	6284	50	96	–	492	9030	50	96	RG	6186	50	96	+	531	3878	50	94
II	44809	50	97	–	6200	71619	50	98	RGQ	776	50	90	+	314	229	43	86
IO	13406	50	93	–	7156	31039	50	95	RGQV	16	12	73	–	3	28	19	75
IW	4580	50	97	–	588	7208	50	96	RGR	356	48	87	–	340	1031	50	91
JJ	36979	50	97	–	13395	75496	50	97	RGT	133	40	84	–	308	589	50	91
JJR	1280	50	95	–	184	2063	50	94	RL	6519	50	95	+	1234	3103	50	91
JJT	485	50	91	–	190	1014	50	94	RP	14260	50	95	+	2632	6867	50	91
JK	289	48	89	+	1	263	48	91	RPK	27	22	82	–	2	40	22	81
MC	15575	50	83	+	24	14721	50	91	RR	42555	50	98	+	2928	28183	50	97
MC1	3124	50	93	+	35	2673	50	94	RRQ	4380	50	96	+	854	2056	50	92
MC2	221	40	77	–	29	351	40	84	RRQV	65	32	86	–	0	70	33	84
MCMC	0	0	00	–	974	707	41	73	RRR	892	50	95	–	22	1106	50	95
MD	2939	50	94	–	178	4057	50	92	RRT	58	35	87	–	16	109	40	88
MF	234	9	16	+	35	122	30	74	RT	9034	50	96	+	1439	4631	50	93
ND1	119	27	66	–	339	590	43	82	TO	16144	50	97	+	26	15234	50	97
NN	2693	50	91	–	28	3097	50	89	UH	31705	50	92	+	35177	1210	37	74
NN1	89193	50	96	–	16762	152639	50	98	VB0	84	35	87	–	7	122	33	78
NN2	25432	50	94	–	12373	57048	50	96	VBDR	2736	50	90	–	52	3301	50	90
NNA	0	0	00	–	41	30	15	71	VBDZ	7920	50	93	–	8	8282	50	91
NNB	993	48	77	–	1367	3378	47	81	VBG	558	50	92	–	57	840	49	94
NNL1	381	48	88	–	1120	1921	48	84	VBI	5554	50	95	–	173	7034	50	92
NNL2	4	1	00	–	136	121	25	63	VBM	3060	50	94	+	1706	644	40	79
NNO	1232	50	87	+	348	474	45	83	VBN	1883	50	95	–	97	2538	50	93
NNO2	79	25	75	–	19	144	36	82	VBR	9316	50	97	+	1057	5388	50	94
NNT1	6507	50	96	+	13	6097	50	93	VBZ	26524	50	97	+	6472	11117	50	95
NNT2	1920	50	95	–	53	2403	50	94	VD0	7395	50	94	+	4875	1230	50	83
NNU	553	48	83	–	2841	3924	45	76	VDD	3702	50	92	+	1520	1077	48	85
NNU1	669	43	69	+	282	190	35	77	VDG	1011	50	93	+	693	158	39	84

VDI	2474	50	95 +	1414	505	49	87	VV0	28729	50	97 +	8037	11113	50	91
VDN	1012	50	94 +	534	228	47	91	VVD	13558	50	94 −	2165	22352	50	90
VDZ	1588	49	94 +	621	482	48	89	VVG	12950	50	98 −	13	13551	50	96
VH0	9180	50	97 +	3356	2944	50	94	VVGK	2214	50	94 +	2051	176	39	81
VHD	2824	50	92 −	82	3550	50	87	VVI	33705	50	98 +	1477	24437	50	96
VHG	486	50	93 +	27	336	50	91	VVN	16641	50	98 −	1618	24824	50	96
VHI	3651	50	96 +	685	1745	50	93	VVNK	26	21	82 +	0	21	15	74
VHN	701	50	92 +	269	216	48	88	VVZ	6289	50	95 −	106	7500	50	92
VHZ	3436	50	95 +	47	2889	50	92	XX	18067	50	95 +	6127	6135	50	91
VM	20781	50	98 +	1248	14181	50	95	ZZ1	5212	50	84 +	1878	1690	43	68
VMK	644	48	89 +	467	91	36	84	ZZ2	91	18	64 +	20	40	13	64

List 6.2.2. Rank frequency list of grammatical word classes: spoken (compared with written) English

FrS = frequency in spoken English (per million tags)
FrW = frequency in written English (per million tags)

+ = Higher frequency in speech
− = Higher frequency in writing

Tag	FrS	LL	FrW	Tag	FrS	LL	FrW	Tag	FrS	LL	FrW
NN1	89193	− 16762	152639	RG	6186	+ 531	3878	VMK	644	+ 467	91
II	44809	− 6200	71619	VBI	5554	− 173	7034	CSN	644	− 69	979
RR	42555	+ 2928	28183	ZZ1	5212	+ 1878	1690	VBG	558	− 57	840
AT	39031	− 7997	68200	IW	4580	− 588	7208	NNU	553	− 2841	3924
JJ	36979	− 13395	75496	RRQ	4380	+ 854	2056	PPX1	518	− 113	919
VVI	33705	+ 1477	24437	DB	4091	+ 260	2757	PPGE	500	+ 215	139
UH	31705	+ 35177	1210	DD	3722	+ 132	2793	RA	490	− 0	502
PPIS1	31379	+ 17304	6701	VDD	3702	+ 1520	1077	VHG	486	+ 27	336
VV0	28729	+ 8037	11113	VHI	3651	+ 685	1745	JJT	485	− 190	1014
CC	28484	− 281	32638	EX	3642	+ 350	2213	NPM1	468	− 518	1443
PPY	26531	+ 16894	4656	VHZ	3436	+ 47	2889	PN	419	+ 59	225
VBZ	26524	+ 6472	11117	PPHO2	3350	+ 702	1520	NNL1	381	− 1120	1921
PPH1	25899	+ 9462	8308	MC1	3124	+ 35	2673	RGR	356	− 340	1031
NN2	25432	− 12373	57048	VBM	3060	+ 1706	644	DDQV	325	+ 110	110
FU	23010	+ 29404	252	MD	2939	− 178	4057	JK	289	+ 1	263
DD1	20945	+ 6215	7802	VHD	2824	− 82	3550	NNU2	283	− 5	339
VM	20781	+ 1248	14181	VBDR	2736	− 52	3301	PPX2	277	− 20	394
AT1	20015	− 452	24510	NN	2693	− 28	3097	DAT	266	− 69	496
XX	18067	+ 6127	6135	PPIO1	2617	+ 405	1357	MF	234	+ 35	122
VVN	16641	− 1618	24824	DD2	2567	+ 7	2378	MC2	221	− 29	351
TO	16144	+ 26	15234	VDI	2474	+ 1414	505	DB2	209	− 48	376
MC	15575	+ 24	14721	PPHO1	2374	+ 54	1892	REX	164	− 141	454
NP1	14469	+ 19819	49089	VVGK	2214	+ 2051	176	RGT	133	− 308	589
RP	14260	+ 2632	6867	NNT2	1920	− 53	2403	ND1	119	− 339	590
VVD	13558	− 2165	22352	VBN	1883	− 97	2538	ZZ2	91	+ 20	40
IO	13406	− 7156	31039	GE	1813	− 2137	5743	FW	89	− 1176	1235
VVG	12950	− 13	13551	PNQS	1768	− 22	2061	VB0	84	− 7	122
CS	12630	+ 1023	8040	VDZ	1588	+ 621	482	NNO2	79	− 19	144
PPHS1	12139	+ 1020	7655	CSA	1383	− 471	2772	NP2	77	− 81	232
PPIS2	10880	+ 4292	3277	DA	1292	− 259	2247	RRQV	65	− 0	70
APPGE	10393	− 870	15101	JJR	1280	− 184	2063	RRT	58	− 16	109
DDQ	9476	+ 1172	5329	NNO	1232	+ 348	474	DDQGE	46	− 108	206
PPHS2	9468	+ 2651	3660	VDN	1012	+ 534	228	NPD2	35	+ 1	25
VBR	9316	+ 1057	5388	VDG	1011	+ 693	158	NP	33	+ 9	13
VH0	9180	+ 3356	2944	NNB	993	− 1367	3378	BCL	31	− 90	156
RT	9034	+ 1439	4631	PPIO2	984	+ 44	708	RPK	27	− 2	40
VBDZ	7920	− 8	8282	DAR	912	+ 0	895	VVNK	26	+ 0	21
VD0	7395	+ 4875	1230	RRR	892	− 22	1106	PNQV	23	+ 15	4
PN1	6802	+ 2369	2264	NPD1	891	+ 123	482	PNQO	16	− 98	128
RL	6519	+ 1234	3103	DA2	836	− 95	1285	RGQV	16	− 3	28
NNT1	6507	+ 13	6097	RGQ	776	+ 314	229	NNL2	4	− 136	121
CST	6482	+ 1	6366	CSW	740	+ 145	347	PNX1	0	− 8	6
CCB	6289	+ 400	4238	VHN	701	+ 269	216	MCMC	0	− 974	707
VVZ	6289	− 106	7500	DA1	694	+ 12	570	NNA	0	− 41	30
IF	6284	− 492	9030	NNU1	669	+ 282	190				

List 6.2.3. Rank frequency list of grammatical word classes: written (compared with spoken) English

FrS = frequency in spoken English (per million tags)
FrW = frequency in written English (per million tags)

+ = Higher frequency in speech
− = Higher frequency in writing

Tag	FrS	+/−	LL	FrW	Tag	FrS	+/−	LL	FrW	Tag	FrS	+/−	LL	FrW
NN1	89193	−	16762	152639	NNB	993	−	1367	3378	VDI	2474	+	1414	505
JJ	36979	−	13395	75496	VBDR	2736	−	52	3301	RA	490	−	0	502
II	44809	−	6200	71619	PPIS2	10880	+	4292	3277	DAT	266	−	69	496
AT	39031	−	7997	68200	RL	6519	+	1234	3103	NPD1	891	+	123	482
NN2	25432	−	12373	57048	NN	2693	−	28	3097	VDZ	1588	+	621	482
NP1	14469	−	19819	49089	VH0	9180	+	3356	2944	NNO	1232	+	348	474
CC	28484	−	281	32638	VHZ	3436	−	47	2889	REX	164	−	141	454
IO	13406	−	7156	31039	DD	3722	+	132	2793	PPX2	277	−	20	394
RR	42555	+	2928	28183	CSA	1383	−	471	2772	DB2	209	−	48	376
VVN	16641	−	1618	24824	DB	4091	−	260	2757	MC2	221	−	29	351
AT1	20015	−	452	24510	MC1	3124	+	35	2673	CSW	740	+	145	347
VVI	33705	+	1477	24437	VBN	1883	−	97	2538	NNU2	283	−	5	339
VVD	13558	−	2165	22352	NNT2	1920	−	53	2403	VHG	486	+	27	336
TO	16144	+	26	15234	DD2	2567	+	7	2378	JK	289	+	1	263
APPGE	10393	−	870	15101	PN1	6802	+	2369	2264	FU	23010	+	29404	252
MC	15575	+	24	14721	DA	1292	−	259	2247	NP2	77	−	81	232
VM	20781	+	1248	14181	EX	3642	+	350	2213	RGQ	776	−	314	229
VVG	12950	−	13	13551	JJR	1280	−	184	2063	VDN	1012	+	534	228
VBZ	26524	+	6472	11117	PNQS	1768	−	22	2061	PN	419	+	59	225
VV0	28729	+	8037	11113	RRQ	4380	+	854	2056	VHN	701	+	269	216
IF	6284	−	492	9030	NNL1	381	−	1120	1921	DDQGE	46	−	108	206
PPH1	25899	+	9462	8308	PPHO1	2374	+	54	1892	NNU1	669	+	282	190
VBDZ	7920	−	8	8282	VHI	3651	+	685	1745	VVGK	2214	+	2051	176
CS	12630	+	1023	8040	ZZ1	5212	+	1878	1690	VDG	1011	+	693	158
DD1	20945	+	6215	7802	PPHO2	3350	+	702	1520	BCL	31	−	90	156
PPHS1	12139	+	1020	7655	NPM1	468	−	518	1443	NNO2	79	−	19	144
VVZ	6289	−	106	7500	PPIO1	2617	+	405	1357	PPGE	500	+	215	139
IW	4580	−	588	7208	DA2	836	−	95	1285	PNQO	16	−	98	128
VBI	5554	−	173	7034	FW	89	−	1176	1235	VB0	84	−	7	122
RP	14260	+	2632	6867	VD0	7395	+	4875	1230	MF	234	+	35	122
PPIS1	31379	+	17304	6701	UH	31705	+	35177	1210	NNL2	4	−	136	121
CST	6482	+	1	6366	RRR	892	−	22	1106	DDQV	325	+	110	110
XX	18067	+	6127	6135	VDD	3702	+	1520	1077	RRT	58	−	16	109
NNT1	6507	+	13	6097	RGR	356	−	340	1031	VMK	644	+	467	91
GE	1813	−	2137	5743	JJT	485	−	190	1014	RRQV	65	−	0	70
VBR	9316	+	1057	5388	CSN	644	−	69	979	ZZ2	91	−	20	40
DDQ	9476	+	1172	5329	PPX1	518	−	113	919	RPK	27	−	2	40
PPY	26531	+	16894	4656	DAR	912	+	0	895	NNA	0	−	41	30
RT	9034	+	1439	4631	VBG	558	−	57	840	RGQV	16	−	3	28
CCB	6289	+	400	4238	PPIO2	984	+	44	708	NPD2	35	+	1	25
MD	2939	−	178	4057	MCMC	0	−	974	707	VVNK	26	+	0	21
NNU	553	−	2841	3924	VBM	3060	+	1706	644	NP	33	+	9	13
RG	6186	+	531	3878	ND1	119	−	339	590	PNX1	0	−	8	6
PPHS2	9468	+	2651	3660	RGT	133	−	308	589	PNQV	23	+	15	4
VHD	2824	−	82	3550	DA1	694	+	12	570					

List 6.2.4. Distinctiveness list of grammatical word classes: spoken v. written English

FrS = frequency in spoken English (per million tags)   + = higher frequency in speech
FrW = frequency in written English (per million tags)   − = higher frequency in writing

Tag	FrS	LL	FrW	Tag	FrS	LL	FrW	Tag	FrS	LL	FrW
UH	31705	+ 35177	1210	RRQ	4380	+ 854	2056	NP2	77	− 81	232
FU	23010	+ 29404	252	PPHO2	3350	+ 702	1520	DAT	266	− 69	496
NP1	14469	− 19819	49089	VDG	1011	+ 693	158	CSN	644	− 69	979
PPIS1	31379	+ 17304	6701	VHI	3651	+ 685	1745	PN	419	+ 59	225
PPY	26531	+ 16894	4656	VDZ	1588	+ 621	482	VBG	558	− 57	840
NN1	89193	− 16762	152639	IW	4580	− 588	7208	PPHO1	2374	+ 54	1892
JJ	36979	− 13395	75496	VDN	1012	+ 534	228	NNT2	1920	− 53	2403
NN2	25432	− 12373	57048	RG	6186	+ 531	3878	VBDR	2736	− 52	3301
PPH1	25899	+ 9462	8308	NPM1	468	− 518	1443	DB2	209	− 48	376
VV0	28729	+ 8037	11113	IF	6284	− 492	9030	VHZ	3436	+ 47	2889
AT	39031	− 7997	68200	CSA	1383	− 471	2772	PPIO2	984	+ 44	708
IO	13406	− 7156	31039	VMK	644	+ 467	91	NNA	0	− 41	30
VBZ	26524	+ 6472	11117	AT1	20015	− 452	24510	MF	234	+ 35	122
DD1	20945	+ 6215	7802	PPIO1	2617	+ 405	1357	MC1	3124	+ 35	2673
II	44809	− 6200	71619	CCB	6289	+ 400	4238	MC2	221	− 29	351
XX	18067	+ 6127	6135	EX	3642	+ 350	2213	NN	2693	− 28	3097
VD0	7395	+ 4875	1230	NNO	1232	+ 348	474	VHG	486	+ 27	336
PPIS2	10880	+ 4292	3277	RGR	356	− 340	1031	TO	16144	+ 26	15234
VH0	9180	+ 3356	2944	ND1	119	− 339	590	MC	15575	+ 24	14721
RR	42555	+ 2928	28183	RGQ	776	+ 314	229	RRR	892	− 22	1106
NNU	553	− 2841	3924	RGT	133	− 308	589	PNQS	1768	− 22	2061
PPHS2	9468	+ 2651	3660	NNU1	669	+ 282	190	PPX2	277	− 20	394
RP	14260	+ 2632	6867	CC	28484	− 281	32638	ZZ2	91	+ 20	40
PN1	6802	+ 2369	2264	VHN	701	+ 269	216	NNO2	79	− 19	144
VVD	13558	− 2165	22352	DB	4091	+ 260	2757	RRT	58	− 16	109
GE	1813	− 2137	5743	DA	1292	− 259	2247	PNQV	23	+ 15	4
VVGK	2214	+ 2051	176	PPGE	500	+ 215	139	VVG	12950	− 13	13551
ZZ1	5212	+ 1878	1690	JJT	485	− 190	1014	NNT1	6507	+ 13	6097
VBM	3060	+ 1706	644	JJR	1280	− 184	2063	DA1	694	+ 12	570
VVN	16641	− 1618	24824	MD	2939	− 178	4057	NP	33	+ 9	13
VDD	3702	+ 1520	1077	VBI	5554	− 173	7034	PNX1	8	− 8	6
VVI	33705	+ 1477	24437	CSW	740	+ 145	347	VBDZ	7920	− 8	8282
RT	9034	+ 1439	4631	REX	164	− 141	454	DD2	2567	+ 7	2378
VDI	2474	+ 1414	505	NNL2	4	− 136	121	VB0	84	− 7	122
NNB	993	− 1367	3378	DD	3722	+ 132	2793	NNU2	283	− 5	339
VM	20781	+ 1248	14181	NPD1	891	+ 123	482	RGQV	16	− 3	28
RL	6519	+ 1234	3103	PPX1	518	− 113	919	RPK	27	− 2	40
FW	89	− 1176	1235	DDQV	325	+ 110	110	NPD2	35	+ 1	25
DDQ	9476	+ 1172	5329	DDQGE	46	− 108	206	JK	289	+ 1	263
NNL1	381	− 1120	1921	VVZ	6289	− 106	7500	CST	6482	+ 1	6366
VBR	9316	+ 1057	5388	PNQO	16	− 98	128	VVNK	26	+ 0	21
CS	12630	+ 1023	8040	VBN	1883	− 97	2538	RRQV	65	− 0	70
PPHS1	12139	+ 1020	7655	DA2	836	− 95	1285	DAR	912	+ 0	895
MCMC	0	− 974	707	BCL	31	− 90	156	RA	490	− 0	502
APPGE	10393	− 870	15101	VHD	2824	− 82	3550				

List 6.3.1. Alphabetical list of grammatical word classes: conversation v. task-oriented speech

Note: The maximum range, for both conversational and task-oriented speech, is 25.

+ = higher frequency in conversational speech

− = higher frequency in task-oriented speech

Tag	FrCo	Ra	DiCo		LL	FrTO	Ra	DiTO	Tag	FrCo	Ra	DiCo		LL	FrTO	Ra	DiTO
APPGE	10670	25	95	+	7	10117	25	95	NP1	18270	25	96	+	994	10691	25	89
AT	27949	25	96	−	3142	50046	25	96	NP2	83	14	64	+	0	70	13	72
AT1	17885	25	96	−	223	22133	25	98	NPD1	1320	25	87	+	211	465	24	77
BCL	0	0	00	−	42	62	14	73	NPD2	45	11	72	+	2	26	7	65
CC	25392	25	96	−	331	31558	25	97	NPM1	393	25	81	−	12	543	24	79
CCB	6766	25	96	+	35	5814	25	95	PN	419	25	91	+	0	419	25	89
CS	12988	25	97	+	10	12273	25	94	PN1	7792	25	97	+	142	5818	25	93
CSA	812	25	90	−	239	1950	25	93	PNQO	6	3	45	−	6	26	8	66
CSN	547	25	92	−	14	741	25	91	PNQS	1557	25	91	−	24	1978	25	92
CST	3278	25	90	−	1631	9667	25	94	PNQV	28	10	73	+	1	18	8	68
CSW	626	24	93	−	17	853	25	91	PPGE	848	25	90	+	263	153	24	87
DA	1049	25	95	−	45	1534	25	91	PPH1	31325	25	97	+	1127	20507	25	95
DA1	743	25	92	+	3	646	25	91	PPHO1	4022	25	93	+	1236	737	25	82
DA2	502	25	90	−	134	1167	25	87	PPHO2	4084	25	94	+	159	2620	25	92
DAR	826	25	91	−	8	998	25	93	PPHS1	20333	25	94	+	5946	3995	25	86
DAT	164	23	86	−	39	368	24	90	PPHS2	10886	25	95	+	209	8059	25	94
DB	4512	25	94	+	42	3673	25	95	PPIO1	3607	25	95	+	377	1634	25	92
DB2	200	23	85	−	0	217	23	82	PPIO2	695	25	92	−	85	1272	24	91
DD	2948	25	95	−	159	4490	25	89	PPIS1	40640	25	97	+	2729	22175	25	93
DD1	22212	25	98	+	75	19685	25	96	PPIS2	7788	25	94	−	877	13953	25	91
DD2	2035	25	93	−	109	3095	25	94	PPX1	514	25	92	−	0	521	25	86
DDQ	9754	25	96	+	8	9200	25	94	PPX2	150	23	88	−	59	403	25	89
DDQGE	57	16	80	+	2	36	14	80	PPY	31165	25	97	+	800	21925	25	93
DDQV	328	25	87	+	0	322	24	87	RA	462	25	89	−	1	517	25	91
EX	3007	25	94	−	109	4273	25	94	REX	34	10	65	−	115	292	21	83
FU	17087	25	93	−	1519	28897	25	91	RG	6004	25	95	−	5	6366	25	95
FW	49	8	62	−	18	129	8	51	RGQ	765	25	93	−	0	787	25	83
GE	1978	25	94	+	14	1648	25	91	RGQV	4	1	00	−	10	28	11	75
IF	5524	25	96	−	90	7040	25	95	RGR	144	23	83	−	133	568	25	89
II	36784	25	98	−	1423	52785	25	98	RGT	57	16	80	−	46	209	24	83
IO	7723	25	95	−	2450	19053	25	95	RL	7928	25	95	+	302	5118	25	92
IW	4036	25	97	−	63	5120	25	95	RP	17784	25	97	+	865	10757	25	94
JJ	33182	25	97	−	384	40753	25	96	RPK	16	7	65	−	4	38	15	81
JJR	1191	25	94	−	6	1369	25	94	RR	44356	25	98	+	75	40766	25	96
JJT	391	25	89	−	18	578	25	88	RRQ	4866	25	96	+	53	3896	25	94
JK	170	23	87	−	49	407	25	88	RRQV	55	13	77	−	1	74	19	83
MC	10893	25	94	−	1408	20229	25	75	RRR	786	25	93	−	12	998	25	93
MC1	2643	25	93	−	73	3603	25	90	RRT	34	13	74	−	9	81	22	87
MC2	136	17	77	−	33	306	23	69	RT	9714	25	97	+	50	8358	25	91
MD	2509	25	94	−	62	3367	25	92	TO	14181	25	98	+	235	18095	25	97
MF	4	2	31	−	297	463	7	15	UH	48244	25	97	+	8915	15268	25	88
ND1	53	10	50	−	38	185	17	59	VB0	103	20	86	+	4	64	15	74
NN	1711	25	89	−	361	3669	25	90	VBDR	2513	25	88	−	18	2959	25	84
NN1	72212	25	98	−	3204	106071	25	97	VBDZ	8369	25	94	+	25	7473	25	87
NN2	16512	25	96	−	3148	34297	25	96	VBG	405	25	89	−	42	710	25	92
NNB	448	25	87	−	312	1536	23	72	VBI	4402	25	94	−	236	6698	25	95
NNL1	324	24	82	−	8	437	24	84	VBM	3724	25	94	+	142	2401	25	89
NNL2	0	0	00	−	5	8	1	00	VBN	1693	25	94	−	18	2071	25	92
NNO	788	25	86	−	161	1674	25	83	VBR	9167	25	97	−	2	9463	25	95
NNO2	30	9	67	−	31	127	16	72	VBZ	30857	25	98	+	699	22217	25	95
NNT1	7193	25	96	+	71	5825	25	93	VD0	9815	25	97	+	793	4989	25	92
NNT2	1746	25	94	−	15	2093	25	94	VDD	4690	25	95	+	262	2721	25	84
NNU	506	25	83	−	3	600	23	71	VDG	1201	25	92	+	35	823	25	87
NNU1	593	23	82	−	8	745	20	46	VDI	2764	25	94	+	33	2186	25	91
NNU2	275	22	79	−	0	290	19	67	VDN	1177	25	93	+	26	849	25	92
NP	28	7	64	−	0	38	3	16	VDZ	1879	25	95	+	52	1298	24	90

VH0	9837	25	98	+ 46	8527	25	94	VVG	13090	25	97 + 1	12810 25 96
VHD	2971	25	94	+ 7	2679	25	85	VVGK	2582	25	93 + 60	1848 25 91
VHG	486	25	91	+ 0	485	25	89	VVI	34089	25	98 + 4	33323 25 97
VHI	4111	25	96	+ 57	3194	25	95	VVN	15584	25	98 − 66	17691 25 97
VHN	840	25	89	+ 27	562	25	90	VVNK	47	18	85 + 17	6 3 45
VHZ	3963	25	95	+ 79	2912	25	92	VVZ	7292	25	93 + 158	5291 25 94
VM	21141	25	98	+ 6	20424	25	96	XX	23767	25	97 + 1800	12402 25 94
VMK	747	24	88	+ 16	541	24	79	ZZ1	2624	25	83 − 1323	7783 25 81
VV0	33417	25	98	+ 756	24071	25	95	ZZ2	43	9	67 − 26	139 9 55
VVD	17237	25	96	+ 994	9902	25	91					

List 6.3.2. Distinctiveness list of grammatical word classes: conversation v. task-oriented speech

+ = higher frequency in conversational speech
− = higher frequency in task-oriented speech

Tag	FrCo	LL	FrTO	Tag	FrCo	LL	FrTO	Tag	FrCo	LL	FrTO
UH	48244	+ 8915	15268	DA2	502	− 134	1167	VVNK	47	+ 17	6
PPHS1	20333	+ 5946	3995	RGR	144	− 133	568	CSW	626	− 17	853
NN1	72212	− 3204	106071	REX	34	− 115	292	VMK	747	+ 16	541
NN2	16512	− 3148	34297	EX	3007	− 109	4273	NNT2	1746	− 15	2093
AT	27949	− 3142	50046	DD2	2035	− 109	3095	GE	1978	+ 14	1648
PPIS1	40640	+ 2729	22175	IF	5524	− 90	7040	CSN	547	− 14	741
IO	7723	− 2450	19053	PPIO2	695	− 85	1272	RRR	786	− 12	998
XX	23767	+ 1800	12402	VHZ	3963	+ 79	2912	NPM1	393	− 12	543
CST	3278	− 1631	9667	DD1	22212	+ 75	19685	RGQV	4	− 10	28
FU	17087	− 1519	28897	RR	44356	+ 75	40766	CS	12988	+ 10	12273
II	36784	− 1423	52785	MC1	2643	− 73	3603	RRT	34	− 9	81
MC	10893	− 1408	20229	NNT1	7193	+ 71	5825	NNU1	593	− 8	745
ZZ1	2624	− 1323	7783	VVN	15584	− 66	17691	NNL1	324	− 8	437
PPHO1	4022	+ 1236	737	IW	4036	− 63	5120	DAR	826	− 8	998
PPH1	31325	+ 1127	20507	MD	2509	− 62	3367	DDQ	9754	+ 8	9200
VVD	17237	+ 994	9902	VVGK	2582	+ 60	1848	VHD	2971	− 7	2679
NP1	18270	+ 994	10691	PPX2	150	− 59	403	APPGE	10670	+ 7	10117
PPIS2	7788	− 877	13953	VHI	4111	+ 57	3194	PNQO	6	− 6	26
RP	17784	+ 865	10757	RRQ	4866	+ 53	3896	JJR	1191	− 6	1369
PPY	31165	+ 800	21925	VDZ	1879	+ 52	1298	VM	21141	+ 6	20424
VD0	9815	+ 793	4989	RT	9714	+ 50	8358	NNL2	0	− 5	8
VV0	33417	+ 756	24071	JK	170	− 49	407	RG	6004	− 5	6366
VBZ	30857	+ 699	22217	VH0	9837	+ 46	8527	RPK	16	− 4	38
JJ	33182	− 384	40753	RGT	57	− 46	209	VB0	103	+ 4	64
PPIO1	3607	+ 377	1634	DA	1049	− 45	1534	VVI	34089	+ 4	33323
NN	1711	− 361	3669	BCL	0	− 42	62	NNU	506	− 3	600
CC	25392	− 331	31558	DB	4512	+ 42	3673	DA1	743	+ 3	646
NNB	448	− 312	1536	VBG	405	− 42	710	NPD2	45	+ 2	26
RL	7928	+ 302	5118	DAT	164	− 39	368	VBR	9167	− 2	9463
MF	4	− 297	463	ND1	53	− 38	185	DDQGE	57	+ 2	36
PPGE	848	+ 263	153	CCB	6766	+ 35	5814	RA	462	− 1	517
VDD	4690	+ 262	2721	VDG	1201	+ 35	823	RRQV	55	− 1	74
CSA	812	− 239	1950	VDI	2764	+ 33	2186	VVG	13090	+ 1	12810
VBI	4402	− 236	6698	MC2	136	− 33	306	PNQV	28	+ 1	18
TO	14181	− 235	18095	NNO2	30	− 31	127	NP	28	− 0	38
AT1	17885	− 223	22133	VHN	840	+ 27	562	NP2	83	+ 0	70
NPD1	1320	+ 211	465	ZZ2	43	− 26	139	DB2	200	− 0	217
PPHS2	10886	+ 209	8059	VDN	1177	+ 26	849	NNU2	275	− 0	290
NNO	788	− 161	1674	VBDZ	8369	+ 25	7473	RGQ	765	− 0	787
PPHO2	4084	+ 159	2620	PNQS	1557	− 24	1978	DDQV	328	+ 0	322
DD	2948	− 159	4490	VBN	1693	− 18	2071	PPX1	514	− 0	521
VVZ	7292	+ 158	5291	FW	49	− 18	129	VHG	486	+ 0	485
VBM	3724	+ 142	2401	VBDR	2513	− 18	2959	PN	419	+ 0	419
PN1	7792	+ 142	5818	JJT	391	− 18	578				

List 6.4.1. Alphabetical list of grammatical word classes: imaginative v. informative writing

Note: The maximum range is 11 for imaginative writing and 39 for informative writing.

+ = higher frequency in imaginative writing
− = higher frequency in informative writing

Tag	FrIm	Ra	DiIm		LL	FrIn	Ra	DiIn	Tag	FrIm	Ra	DiIm		LL	FrIn	Ra	DiIn
APPGE	26889	11	92	+	2310	11707	39	95	NNU2	179	10	78	−	25	385	31	78
AT	56039	11	96	−	654	71702	39	98	NP	0	0	00	−	6	17	8	63
AT1	22407	11	97	−	53	25116	39	98	NP1	42123	11	91	−	295	51095	39	90
BCL	9	2	33	−	62	198	33	84	NP2	188	7	70	−	2	245	34	84
CC	30402	11	96	−	44	33282	39	97	NPD1	241	9	65	−	40	551	26	81
CCB	5885	11	91	+	170	3764	39	95	NPD2	18	3	44	−	0	27	7	44
CS	9349	11	94	+	59	7663	39	95	NPM1	286	9	67	−	366	1776	37	87
CSA	3043	11	90	+	7	2693	39	94	PN	469	11	83	+	64	154	32	83
CSN	965	11	90	−	0	983	39	90	PN1	5622	11	92	+	1165	1297	39	94
CST	5269	11	86	−	56	6681	39	94	PNQO	170	8	57	+	3	116	30	81
CSW	366	11	84	+	0	341	37	88	PNQS	2319	11	78	+	9	1987	39	89
DA	1801	11	84	−	26	2376	39	94	PNQV	13	2	29	+	5	1	1	00
DA1	635	11	91	+	2	551	38	92	PNX1	0	0	00	+	3	8	5	55
DA2	724	11	83	−	80	1446	39	94	PPGE	456	11	89	+	163	48	18	78
DAR	840	11	92	−	1	911	39	89	PPH1	13755	11	93	+	912	6739	39	96
DAT	223	11	86	−	51	574	39	91	PPHO1	5823	11	92	+	1851	761	36	86
DB	3539	11	94	+	60	2531	39	94	PPHO2	2878	11	81	+	300	1129	39	92
DB2	411	11	84	+	0	365	39	92	PPHS1	19944	11	92	+	4579	4115	39	85
DD	2744	11	89	+	0	2807	39	94	PPHS2	5693	11	87	+	292	3074	39	93
DD1	9662	11	96	+	121	7267	39	95	PPIO1	4598	11	87	+	1745	423	31	78
DD2	1662	11	90	−	67	2584	39	91	PPIO2	1247	11	81	+	103	553	35	75
DDQ	5760	11	91	+	9	5205	39	94	PPIS1	20829	11	92	+	6748	2633	37	79
DDQGE	125	8	74	−	10	229	36	89	PPIS2	5023	11	79	+	241	2775	38	79
DDQV	170	10	80	+	8	93	30	85	PPX1	1998	11	80	+	303	609	39	93
EX	2735	11	87	+	33	2063	39	93	PPX2	505	11	82	+	8	362	39	88
FU	854	9	64	+	324	78	17	70	PPY	15315	11	91	+	5506	1587	37	83
FW	684	8	28	−	81	1394	35	78	RA	438	11	84	−	2	520	39	87
GE	4791	11	87	−	47	6017	39	91	REX	107	8	65	−	101	553	34	81
IF	6627	11	94	−	198	9722	39	96	RG	5086	11	92	+	101	3530	39	94
II	58430	11	97	−	734	75417	39	99	RGQ	474	11	84	+	63	158	32	83
IO	17589	11	90	−	1909	34912	39	96	RGQV	22	5	65	−	0	30	14	71
IW	6627	11	95	−	13	7375	39	95	RGR	550	11	84	−	74	1170	39	91
JJ	53729	11	96	−	1956	81764	39	98	RGT	250	11	80	−	67	686	39	92
JJR	1417	11	92	−	63	2249	39	93	RL	6154	11	92	+	734	2225	39	95
JJT	608	11	92	−	52	1131	39	93	RP	12508	11	87	+	1157	5243	39	92
JK	170	10	74	−	10	290	38	91	RPK	76	8	76	+	8	30	14	75
MC	4849	11	82	−	2409	17563	39	93	RR	33561	11	95	+	283	26634	39	96
MC1	2284	11	88	−	16	2785	39	94	RRQ	3781	11	93	+	360	1560	39	93
MC2	27	4	55	−	131	444	36	85	RRQV	40	6	68	−	4	78	27	82
MCMC	40	5	54	−	284	900	36	74	RRR	1390	11	89	+	19	1024	39	94
MD	2431	11	89	−	210	4525	39	92	RRT	58	8	75	−	7	124	32	88
MF	0	0	00	−	61	157	30	75	RT	7414	11	90	+	430	3830	39	93
ND1	259	9	75	−	64	686	34	81	TO	13840	11	96	−	37	15636	39	96
NN	2024	11	83	−	118	3406	39	87	UH	4540	11	83	+	2073	251	26	70
NN1	127590	11	97	−	1235	159852	39	98	VB0	313	10	73	+	69	67	23	78
NN2	33275	11	94	−	3225	63893	39	97	VBDR	3597	11	92	+	7	3216	39	88
NNA	4	1	00	−	8	37	14	71	VBDZ	12397	11	91	+	534	7097	39	89
NNB	3316	11	75	−	0	3396	36	76	VBG	764	10	79	−	2	862	39	94
NNL1	862	10	74	−	200	2226	38	83	VBI	4505	11	88	−	290	7762	39	92
NNL2	13	1	00	−	40	152	24	63	VBM	2208	11	87	+	854	194	29	82
NNO	223	10	80	−	44	546	35	82	VBN	2181	11	82	−	15	2641	39	93
NNO2	134	8	74	−	0	147	28	78	VBR	4893	11	87	−	13	5531	39	94
NNT1	6399	11	91	+	4	6010	39	91	VBZ	11239	11	89	+	0	11081	39	94
NNT2	2163	11	85	−	7	2472	39	93	VD0	3504	11	87	+	962	575	39	93
NNU	63	6	62	−	1836	5036	39	77	VDD	2806	11	89	+	644	579	37	85
NNU1	130	8	72	−	6	207	27	73	VDG	358	9	79	+	60	100	30	86

VDI	1095	11	87	+	166	335	38	88	VV0	16892	11	88	+ 783	9448 39 89
VDN	349	11	90	+	16	193	36	90	VVD	44514	11	93	+ 5379	15970 39 90
VDZ	782	11	85	+	48	395	37	87	VVG	17406	11	91	+ 297	12440 39 97
VH0	3200	11	90	+	6	2870	39	92	VVGK	501	11	81	+ 137	82 28 85
VHD	6480	11	81	+	603	2706	39	86	VVI	32641	11	96	+ 740	22075 39 96
VHG	447	11	80	+	9	304	39	90	VVN	16253	11	88	- 939	27292 39 97
VHI	2069	11	93	+	16	1651	39	91	VVNK	22	3	38	+ 0	21 12 72
VHN	264	11	80	+	2	202	37	86	VVZ	7820	11	72	+ 3	7407 39 93
VHZ	1721	11	84	-	153	3225	39	92	XX	12160	11	93	+ 1450	4400 39 95
VM	16986	11	95	+	153	13373	39	93	ZZ1	165	7	69	- 592	2128 36 67
VMK	192	11	79	+	27	62	25	84	ZZ2	27	4	55	- 1	44 9 59

List 6.4.2. Distinctiveness list of grammatical word classes: imaginative v. informative writing

+ = higher frequency in imaginative writing
– = higher frequency in informative writing

Tag	Frim		LL	Frin	Tag	Frim		LL	Frin	Tag	Frim		LL	Frin
PPIS1	20829	+	6748	2633	IF	6627	-	198	9722	VHI	2069	+	16	1651
PPY	15315	+	5506	1587	CCB	5885	-	170	3764	VDN	349	+	16	193
VVD	44514	+	5379	15970	VDI	1095	+	166	335	VBN	2181	-	15	2641
PPHS1	19944	+	4579	4115	PPGE	456	+	163	48	IW	6627	-	13	7375
NN2	33275	-	3225	63893	VM	16986	+	153	13373	VBR	4893	-	13	5531
MC	4849	-	2409	17563	VHZ	1721	-	153	3225	JK	170	-	10	290
APPGE	26889	+	2310	11707	VVGK	501	+	137	82	DDQGE	125	-	10	229
UH	4540	+	2073	251	MC2	27	-	131	444	VHG	447	+	9	304
JJ	53729	-	1956	81764	DD1	9662	+	121	7267	DDQ	5760	+	9	5205
IO	17589	-	1909	34912	NN	2024	-	118	3406	PNQS	2319	+	9	1987
PPHO1	5823	+	1851	761	PPIO2	1247	+	103	553	NNA	4	-	8	37
NNU	63	-	1836	5036	REX	107	-	101	553	PPX2	505	+	8	362
PPIO1	4598	+	1745	423	RG	5086	+	101	3530	DDQV	170		8	93
XX	12160	+	1450	4400	FW	684	-	81	1394	RPK	76	+	8	30
NN1	127590	-	1235	159852	DA2	724	-	80	1446	RRT	58	-	7	124
PN1	5622	+	1165	1297	RGR	550	-	74	1170	VBDR	3597	+	7	3216
RP	12508	+	1157	5243	VB0	313	+	69	67	CSA	3043	+	7	2693
VD0	3504	+	962	575	RGT	250	-	67	686	NNT2	2163	-	7	2472
VVN	16253	-	939	27292	DD2	1662	-	67	2584	NP	0	-	6	17
PPH1	13755	+	912	6739	PN	469	+	64	154	VH0	3200	+	6	2870
VBM	2208	+	854	194	ND1	259	-	64	686	NNU1	130	-	6	207
VV0	16892	+	783	9448	JJR	1417	-	63	2249	PNQV	13	+	5	1
VVI	32641	+	740	22075	RGQ	474	+	63	158	NNT1	6399	+	4	6010
RL	6154	+	734	2225	BCL	9	-	62	198	RRQV	40	+	4	78
II	58430	-	734	75417	MF	0	-	61	157	VVZ	7820	+	3	7407
AT	56039	-	654	71702	DB	3539	+	60	2531	PNQO	170	+	3	116
VDD	2806	+	644	579	VDG	358	+	60	100	PNX1	0	-	3	8
VHD	6480	+	603	2706	CS	9349	-	59	7663	VHN	264	+	2	202
ZZ1	165	-	592	2128	CST	5269	-	56	6681	NP2	188	-	2	245
VBDZ	12397	+	534	7097	AT1	22407	-	53	25116	RA	438	-	2	520
RT	7414	+	430	3830	JJT	608	-	52	1131	DA1	635	+	2	551
NPM1	286	-	366	1776	DAT	223	-	51	574	VBG	764	+	2	862
RRQ	3781	+	360	1560	VDZ	782	+	48	395	ZZ2	27	-	1	44
FU	854	+	324	78	GE	4791	-	47	6017	DAR	840	-	1	911
PPX1	1998	+	303	609	NNO	223	+	44	546	DB2	411	+	0	365
PPHO2	2878	+	300	1129	CC	30402	-	44	33282	NPD2	18	-	0	27
VVG	17406	+	297	12440	NNL2	13	-	40	152	VBZ	11239	+	0	11081
NP1	42123	-	295	51095	NPD1	241	-	40	551	RGQV	22	-	0	30
PPHS2	5693	+	292	3074	TO	13840	-	37	15636	NNB	3316	-	0	3396
VBI	4505	-	290	7762	EX	2735	+	33	2063	CSW	366	+	0	341
MCMC	40	-	284	900	VMK	192	+	27	62	DD	2744	-	0	2807
RR	33561	+	283	26634	DA	1801	-	26	2376	NNO2	134	-	0	147
PPIS2	5023	+	241	2775	NNU2	179	-	25	385	CSN	965	-	0	983
MD	2431	-	210	4525	RRR	1390	+	19	1024	VVNK	22	+	0	21
NNL1	862	-	200	2226	MC1	2284	-	16	2785					